Fax, Modem, and Text for IP Telephony

David Hanes, CCIE No. 3491
Gonzalo Salgueiro, CCIE No. 4541

Cisco Press

Cisco Press
800 East 96th Street
Indianapolis, IN 46240 USA

Fax, Modem, and Text for IP Telephony

David Hanes, Gonzalo Salgueiro

Copyright © 2008 Cisco Systems, Inc.

Published by:
Cisco Press
800 East 96th Street
Indianapolis, IN 46240 USA

Printed in the United States of America

First Printing June 2008

Library of Congress Cataloging-in-Publication data is on file.

ISBN-13: 978-1-58705-269-9

ISBN-10: 1-58705-269-5

Warning and Disclaimer

This book is designed to provide information about fax, modem, and text technologies for IP Telephony. Every effort has been made to make this book as complete and as accurate as possible, but no warranty or fitness is implied.

The information is provided on an "as is" basis. The authors, Cisco Press, and Cisco Systems, Inc. shall have neither liability nor responsibility to any person or entity with respect to any loss or damages arising from the information contained in this book or from the use of the discs or programs that may accompany it.

The opinions expressed in this book belong to the authors and are not necessarily those of Cisco Systems, Inc.

Trademark Acknowledgments

All terms mentioned in this book that are known to be trademarks or service marks have been appropriately capitalized. Cisco Press or Cisco Systems, Inc., cannot attest to the accuracy of this information. Use of a term in this book should not be regarded as affecting the validity of any trademark or service mark.

Corporate and Government Sales

The publisher offers excellent discounts on this book when ordered in quantity for bulk purchases or special sales, which may include electronic versions and/or custom covers and content particular to your business, training goals, marketing focus, and branding interests. For more information, please contact: **U.S. Corporate and Government Sales** 1-800-382-3419 corpsales@pearsontechgroup.com

For sales outside the United States please contact: **International Sales** international@pearsoned.com

Feedback Information

At Cisco Press, our goal is to create in-depth technical books of the highest quality and value. Each book is crafted with care and precision, undergoing rigorous development that involves the unique expertise of members from the professional technical community.

Readers' feedback is a natural continuation of this process. If you have any comments regarding how we could improve the quality of this book, or otherwise alter it to better suit your needs, you can contact us through e-mail at feedback@ciscopress.com. Please make sure to include the book title and ISBN in your message.

We greatly appreciate your assistance.

Publisher	Paul Boger
Associate Publisher	Dave Dusthimer
Cisco Representative	Anthony Wolfenden
Cisco Press Program Manager	Jeff Brady
Executive Editor	Chuck Toporek
Managing Editor	Patrick Kanouse
Senior Development Editor	Christopher Cleveland
Project Editor	Mandie Frank
Copy Editor	Keith Cline
Technical Editors	Richard Collette, John Combs, Bryan Deaver, Steve Ganem, Paul Giralt, Dr. Judy Harkins, Paul E. Jones, Aaron Leonard, Matthew Miller, Robert Moran, Thomas Runyan, Anne Smith, Michael Whitley, Brett Wiggins
Editorial Assistant	Vanessa Evans
Book Designer	Louisa Adair
Cover Designer	Louisa Adair
Composition	Octal Publishing, Inc.
Indexer	Tim Wright
Proofreader	Williams Woods Publishing Services, LLC

Americas Headquarters
Cisco Systems, Inc.
170 West Tasman Drive
San Jose, CA 95134-1706
USA
www.cisco.com
Tel: 408 526-4000
800 553-NETS (6387)
Fax: 408 527-0883

Asia Pacific Headquarters
Cisco Systems, Inc.
168 Robinson Road
#28-01 Capital Tower
Singapore 068912
www.cisco.com
Tel: +65 6317 7777
Fax: +65 6317 7799

Europe Headquarters
Cisco Systems International BV
Haarlerbergpark
Haarlerbergweg 13-19
1101 CH Amsterdam
The Netherlands
www-europe.cisco.com
Tel: +31 0 800 020 0791
Fax: +31 0 20 357 1100

Cisco has more than 200 offices worldwide. Addresses, phone numbers, and fax numbers are listed on the Cisco Website at **www.cisco.com/go/offices.**

About the Authors

David Hanes, CCIE No. 3491, currently works as an engineer for the Cisco Customer Assurance Engineering (CAE) group based out of Research Triangle Park, North Carolina supporting various emerging technologies through product testing and field trials. In addition, David is a technical expert for Cisco in the area of fax over IP technologies and assists with network design and troubleshooting for critical fax over IP deployments. Since joining Cisco in 1997, he has worked as a Technical Assistance Center (TAC) engineer for the WAN, WAN Switching, and Multiservice Voice teams, a team lead for the Multiservice Voice team, and an Escalation Engineer covering a variety of voice and fax technologies. David has troubleshot escalated issues in Cisco customer networks worldwide and remains a technical resource for other Cisco employees and customers. Before working at Cisco, David was a Systems Engineer for Sprint, where he gained his first computer networking experience working on the Frame Relay and X.25 protocols. He holds a bachelor of science degree in electrical engineering from North Carolina State University.

Gonzalo Salgueiro, CCIE No. 4541, is a senior engineer for the Unified Communications Infrastructure Escalation team of the Technical Assistance Center (TAC) in Research Triangle Park, North Carolina. In his current role, he is a technical leader for fax and voice over IP technologies working directly with Cisco development engineering, TAC support teams, and product serviceability organization, providing support for various Unified Communications products and technologies. Over the past 12 years at Cisco, he has specialized in troubleshooting complex issues for some of the largest VoIP networks and has provided technical leadership for some of the most critical worldwide voice and fax deployments. Before joining the Escalation team in 1999, Gonzalo had roles as a TAC engineer for both the Access/Dial and Multiservice Voice teams and as a team lead for the Access/Dial team. Gonzalo has developed and delivered all levels of training and documentation on these technologies both internally to Cisco technical teams and externally to Cisco customers worldwide. He holds a bachelor of science degree in physics from Jacksonville University and a master of science degree in physics from the University of Miami.

About the Technical Reviewers

Richard Collette is a senior project manager for Sagem-Interstar, where his primary focus is the development and troubleshooting of Voice over IP applications. He holds a bachelor's degree in electrical engineering from l'École Polytechnique de Montréal. Richard has been involved in the design and development of fax applications for more than 15 years.

John Combs is manager of Accessibility/Safety/Telecom for the Cisco Compliance & Certification department. He is responsible for ensuring that Cisco products meet all applicable accessibility, safety, and telecom government regulatory requirements in all the countries where Cisco products are sold. He started the first Cisco accessibility program and test lab in 1999, and is a technical expert on analog and digital telephony, and Telephone Devices for the Deaf (TDD/TTY). John has been at Cisco for 10 years and has worked in the field of regulatory compliance testing for 25 years.

Bryan Deaver is an escalation engineer in the Technical Assistance Center in San Jose, California. He has worked in various technologies and positions in the TAC since joining Cisco in 1993. He primarily focuses on Cisco VoIP products and also has experience in WAN and access technologies. He is a double CCIE in Routing and Voice and works on some of the most complex field issues.

Steve Ganem is the former vice president of World Wide Customer Service for Brooktrout Technology where he was responsible for providing support and training worldwide to customers developing, installing, and maintaining Brooktrout based applications. Steve spent 18 years with Brooktrout (later Cantata and Dialogic) and was heavily involved with Brooktrout's fax products since their introduction in 1990. Steve previously worked in product development at Motorola where he developed telephony circuit boards and embedded software for Motorola communications devices. Steve holds a bachelor's degree in electrical and computer engineering from Northeastern University. Steve currently provides consulting services to technology companies in the Boston area who are looking to improve their customer support and sustaining engineering teams.

Paul Giralt, CCIE Voice, CCIE Routing and Switching No. 4973, is a customer support engineer in the Cisco Voice Technology Group (VTG) and has been with Cisco for 10 years. He assists in designs, troubleshoots problems, and does testing for VTG's most strategic customers. Paul provides feedback to the development teams on feature requirements and participates in feature design meetings to help ensure features are designed to work in real-world customer environments. He also assists in alpha and early field trials of VTG products with the goal of finding and resolving issues in a real-world environment before the products get into customer hands.

Dr. Judy Harkins is a professor in Gallaudet University's Department of Communication Studies. She is the founding director of the Technology Access Program, and has directed approximately 15 sponsored projects on access to communications and educational applications of technology. She is a principal investigator on two Rehabilitation Engineering Research Centers (RERC)—one on Telecommunications Access in cooperation with the Trace Center, University of Wisconsin, and one on Hearing Enhancement, in cooperation with the Department of Audiology and Speech-Language Pathology at Gallaudet. These centers are funded by the National Institute on Disability and Rehabilitation Research. Dr. Harkins also teaches coursework on communication accessibility to Gallaudet undergraduates.

Paul E. Jones has been involved in research and development of protocols and system architectures in the area of multimedia communications, including voice, video, and data conferencing over IP networks, since 1996. In addition to architecture and software development activities within the Cisco Voice Technology Group, he has actively participated in a number of standards and industry organizations, including the ITU, TIA, IETF, ETSI, and the IMTC. Most notably, he served as editor of ITU-T Recommendation H.323 and more recently as Rapporteur for the H.323 experts group. He is also an active participant in accessibility-related work in the ITU and TIA, with a particular emphasis on technology needed for the deaf and hard of hearing. He is presently engaged in the study of an advanced multimedia system within the ITU-T, which is envisaged to enable users to use a multiplicity of devices and networks in parallel to realize richer multimedia communication capabilities.

Aaron Leonard is a customer support engineer in Cisco TAC's Core Infrastructure escalation team. He's been with Cisco for 12 years, providing last-line technical support for TCP/IP stacks, modems, and now 802.11. In his 20+ years in the networking field, Aaron has done everything from vampire-tapping a transceiver into a 10BASE5 cable to chasing down audio glitches heard on WiFi phones in a pet supplies store.

Matthew Miller, product manager at Sagem-Interstar, is responsible for the entire XMediusFAX product line life cycle, from strategic planning to tactical activities. He also manages the Technology Partner Program, building and maintaining relationships with key technology vendors and their associated partnership programs. Matthew has worked for Sagem-Interstar for the past six years, held positions in both the Support and Sales Engineering groups, and has extensive knowledge of IP and fax over IP technology.

Robert Moran is the fax product line director at Dialogic Corporation. Rob is responsible for the profitability of Dialogic's fax products, including the Dialogic Brooktrout TR1034, SR140, and TruFax product lines. Rob defines the product requirements for engineering, supports the Dialogic sales team, and manages other aspects of his portfolio such as pricing and forecasts to ensure the success of his products. Rob has been a product manager in the telecommunications industry for more than 11 years. Before Dialogic, Rob held several positions with Lucent Technologies.

Thomas Runyan is a customer support engineer for Cisco Customer Assurance Engineering. He is part of a team that evaluates and supports Cisco emerging technologies through field trials, internal lab testing, and critical accounts support. Tom was introduced to facsimile and teletype when he started working at 3M in the 1970s. At that time, 3M was a leader in the facsimile and telecommunications field. Since then, he has spent the majority of his career in the telecommunications field. Over the past 10 years, Tom has held various positions within Cisco, working on emerging technologies, voice, and telecommunications projects.

Anne Smith is a technical writer in the CallManager support group at Cisco. Her expertise lies in comprehending and distilling complex technical information into comprehensive, accurate, and readable documentation.

Michael Whitley, CCIE R&S and Voice No. 3645, recently transitioned into a sales engineering role in Cisco Federal Area, specializing in Unified Communications. In his previous eight years at Cisco, Michael supported Cisco UC products and technologies on the TAC Escalation team. Responsibilities included finding, re-creating, and documenting problems while working escalated customer cases. Michael has been at Cisco for nearly 12 years.

Brett Wiggins, CCIE No. 4998, is a technical marketing engineer for the Cisco Voice Solutions Engineering team in Research Triangle Park, North Carolina. This team's main charter is to publish the Unified Communications *Solution Reference Network Design* (SRND) guides on Cisco.com. He has been focused on Cisco voice solutions in a variety of roles for the majority of his 10 year career at Cisco. He graduated from North Carolina State University with a bachelor of science degree in 1996.

Dedications

David Hanes: I dedicate this book to my three girls—my loving wife, Holly, and our beautiful daughters, Haley and Hannah. You all are true blessings and the joys of my life.

Gonzalo Salgueiro: I dedicate this book to my loving family. To my wife, Rebecca, the love of my life, who has unconditionally supported and encouraged me throughout this long endeavor. To my amazing son, Alejandro, who has given me a new perspective on life.

I also dedicate this book to my parents, Alberto and Elena, whose love, support, and example have served as life-long inspiration.

Acknowledgments

David Hanes: First, I would like to thank Gonzalo Salgueiro for co-authoring this book with me. I can honestly say that this book would never have happened without him. Gonzalo's diligence in ensuring that this book achieved the highest level of excellence and accuracy was unparalleled. His meticulous attention to detail and long hours late at night working in the lab and reviewing chapters required many sacrifices and time away from his family. In addition to being my co-author in the writing of this book, Gonzalo is also a great friend. For his tireless dedication and countless hours spent on this book, I will always be appreciative.

Thanks to Anne Smith for being my guide and mentor throughout this book writing process. What started out as a simple e-mail asking how to get started writing a technical book has resulted in this. From the proposal submission to chapter reviews to helping me deal with all the different twists and turns of being an author, Anne was always there to help out. She never failed to take the time out of her own busy schedule to answer questions, edit chapters, and provide wisdom, insight, and perspective based on her own extensive publishing experience.

Thanks to Paul Giralt for providing the inspiration and motivation to write this book. While writing a book was always a goal of mine, it was not until Paul and company wrote *Troubleshooting Cisco IP Telephony* that I really decided to make this goal a reality. I can only hope that this book receives half the acclaim and notoriety of Paul's book, a tour de force in the technical book world that I still refer to quite regularly. Also, I want to thank Paul for always taking the time to provide assistance with anything related to Unified Communications and for being a technical reviewer of this book.

Thanks to my manager Jim Hofmann and to Robert Santiago, John Selden, Mike Quinn, and the rest of the CAE organization for their support of this book. I have always felt very fortunate for the opportunity to work with such a wonderful group of professionals in an organization where I can truly make a difference. A special personal thanks goes to Jim, who has been especially understanding and patient with the numerous deadlines and delays that come along with authoring a book. It is an honor and a privilege to work for someone like Jim while being a part of such a great organization like CAE.

Thanks to all the technical reviewers—Richard Collette, John Combs, Bryan Deaver, Steve Ganem, Paul Giralt, Dr. Judy Harkins, Paul E. Jones, Aaron Leonard, Matthew Miller, Rob Moran, Tom Runyan, Anne Smith, Mike Whitley, and Brett Wiggins—for their dedication and long hours in proofreading chapters within this book. Additional thanks goes to Bryan Deaver and Mike Whitley, two top engineers at Cisco whom I deeply respect and admire who served as full-book reviewers and technically reviewed every chapter. Mike and Bryan possess a combination of incomparable technical depth and breadth of IP telephony along with a punctilious attention to detail that helped ensure the technical integrity of this book.

Thanks to Tomas DeLeon, Paul Giralt, Dave Goodwin, Marty Hussey, Jose Martinez, Peng Mok, Rafael Muller, Steve Penna, Joe Pinkus, Gonzalo Salgueiro, Markus Schneider, Mike Whitley, and all the people whom I served with in the old RTP VNT team. I learned something new practically every day I worked with all of you, and I will always be proud to have been a part of such an amazing group of engineers.

Thanks to Steve Penna for teaching me so much about faxes and modems over the years and for always being there to help out no matter what the problem is. From complex fax and modem corruption issues to lending a hand with customer proof-of-concept testing, Steve is a wealth of knowledge and expertise, and he never ceases to amaze me. Even more important, Steve is a loyal friend whose admirable qualities of honesty, integrity, and generosity are unsurpassed.

Thanks to Gordon Earl, Wei Wang, Ron Rappel, Hanh Luong, and the rest of the folks in the Santa Barbara DSP team for always taking the time to answer questions and provide detailed explanations. You guys are always a pleasure to work with, and your assistance with understanding the complex operation of the DSPs in Cisco voice gateways was crucial to this book.

Thanks to my teammates Mike O'Brien and Jim Frauenthal for lending their expertise and experience and taking the time to review and edit the loss planning section.

Thanks to Stacy Shepherd for her assistance with helping me understand the various IOS processes and how they relate to the DSP and for always being willing to give me a hand with IOS- and DSP-related issues.

Thanks to Sébastien Biore-Lavigne, Marco Brugge, Richard Collette, Nick Diciaccio, Steve Ganem, Bob Green, Matthew Miller, Rob Moran, and Jennifer Van Lent for educating me on fax server technology. I have enjoyed working with each and every one of you, and thanks for always being there to answer my questions.

Thanks to Chris Cleveland, Mandie Frank, and Kristin Weinberger at Cisco Press for all their hard work in getting this book published. Your professionalism and dedication made working on this project together a pleasure.

I also want to thank the following individuals and groups for their contributions to the book: Arun Arunachalam for answering all of my SIP questions; Adam Gensler for assisting with all of those lab re-creates; Christina Hattingh for always finding an answer to any VoIP-related question; Wenqing Jin for answering our questions on T.37; Jeff Johnson for his help with secure modem relay; John Kane for developing my idea into a proposal that ultimately led to this book; James Rafferty for assisting with the fax history section; Chester Rieman for answering SP-related fax questions; Brent Rindal and Matt Portoni for their assistance with the Cisco fax server; Andrea Saks for answering questions on text telephony; Avery Till for answering our VG248 questions; Steven White for his white papers and vision into the FoIP world; all the worldwide TAC engineers whom I have worked with over the years, especially the RTP engineers for being the best support engineers in the business; all the DEs and technical people within Cisco who have taken time to answer questions and write documents explaining how fax, modem, and text works with Cisco voice gateways; and of course, all the customers who I have worked with over the years for teaching me and helping me grow as an engineer.

Gonzalo Salgueiro: First and foremost, I want to extend my deepest gratitude to my friend and co-author David Hanes for presenting me with the once-in-a-lifetime opportunity to be a part of this project. Despite the endless hours, grueling work, and stressful deadlines, this experience was both fulfilling and enjoyable because of his involvement. His single-minded dedication and willingness to persevere through all obstacles have made this book possible.

Heartfelt thanks to Michael Whitley for his steadfast commitment to the success of this book. His guidance and counsel on so many aspects of this project were vital, especially taking on the colossal task of reviewing the entire manuscript. Mike's unmatched technical expertise and willingness to help are surpassed only by his character and integrity.

I'd like to give special recognition to Bryan Deaver for providing his expertise in voice and fax to this project and investing countless hours in carefully reviewing the entire book and in the process making it superior.

Sincere thanks to Aaron Leonard for all his technical material on modems that he made freely available to me and his willingness to answer my many questions.

I'd like to thank Carla Kochmann for all that she has taught me over the years about modems and her assistance on many difficult customer issues. I'm also grateful to Brooks Read for his help on better understanding the operation of modem relay for this book.

Thanks to Budd Carle and his team for years of valuable development support. Special thanks goes to Stacy Shepherd for her assistance on this project and for years of tireless help and countless discussions.

Thanks to Gordon Earl for his endless help and support over the past decade of working on myriad fax and voice DSP issues. Also, thanks to Dan Lai and Gordon for always making their development teams available to me for assistance, especially Hanh Luong, who has been instrumental on many fax-related issues.

Thanks to Steven White for his help and support of this book and the chance to support and lend design assistance to some of the biggest fax customers of Cisco. I appreciate the opportunity to contribute to the development of some of the new fax and text over IP features that Cisco has released over the years.

Thanks to all the technical reviewers: Richard Collette, John Combs, Bryan Deaver, Steve Ganem, Paul Giralt, Dr. Judy Harkins, Paul E. Jones, Aaron Leonard, Matthew Miller, Rob Moran, Tom Runyan, Anne Smith, Mike Whitley, and Brett Wiggins. This book wouldn't be the same without your dedication, hard work, and technical expertise.

Wholehearted thanks to Steve Penna for the countless hours he has spent imparting his amazing knowledge and immeasurable talents in teaching me about voice and dial technologies over the past dozen years. He remains the gold standard, and I owe much of the success in my career at Cisco to him.

Thanks to Paul Giralt for his help with this book and for always having the good will to share his mastery of Unified Communications with me.

Thanks to Michael Whitley, Steve Penna, Paul Giralt, David Hanes, Jose Martinez, Rafael Muller, Joe Pinkus, Markus Schneider, and Tomas DeLeon of the RTP Voice Network Team (VNT), whom I have had the pleasure to work with for many years and from whom I have learned a tremendous amount about voice and fax.

A big "thank you" goes out to the production team for this book, especially Christopher Cleveland, Mandie Frank, and Kristin Weinberger, who have been incredibly professional, responsive, and a true pleasure to work with. In addition, I want to thank John Kane for all of his initial work in taking this idea off the ground and turning this book into a reality.

Thanks to my teammates Peng Mok, Arun Arunachalam, and Wes Sisk for answering my questions and providing superb and skillful help during this project.

Thanks to my managers Michael Stallings and Scott Lawrence for their constant support and encouragement during the course of this two year endeavor. This thanks extends to Joe Novak, Marty Martinez, and the rest of the Customer Advocacy (CA) leadership team who have allowed me to pursue this unique opportunity.

Many thanks to Bob Green from Dialogic, and Jennifer Van Lent and Marco Brugge from Captaris, for their cooperation and assistance and for the opportunity to communicate our knowledge of FoIP to the fax server community.

Thanks to the engineers of the worldwide Voice and Access support teams whom I have worked with over my years in technical support. A special thanks goes to Adam Gensler and George Matroni for providing lab gear and assisting with portions of the testing done for this book.

A hearty thanks to all the customers, developers, engineers, and technical writers with whom I have worked during my years at Cisco. I am appreciative of the constant help and the knowledge that they have imparted to me throughout my very enjoyable career in networking. Special thanks to Christina Hattingh, Wenqing Jin, Jeff Johnson, Nandita Shenoy, and Avery Till for their direct assistance with various technical issues in this book.

This Book Is Safari Enabled

The Safari® Enabled icon on the cover of your favorite technology book means the book is available through Safari Bookshelf. When you buy this book, you get free access to the online edition for 45 days.

Safari Bookshelf is an electronic reference library that lets you easily search thousands of technical books, find code samples, download chapters, and access technical information whenever and wherever you need it.

To gain 45-day Safari Enabled access to this book:

- Go to http://www.informit.com/onlineedition

- Complete the brief registration form

- Enter the coupon code 44J1-F9SK-9Y71-5DKG-K6QX

If you have difficulty registering on Safari Bookshelf or accessing the online edition, please e-mail customer-service@safaribooksonline.com.

Contents at a Glance

Contents

Icons Used in This Book

 Voice-Enabled Access Server

 Server

 Cisco Unity Server

 Fax Server

 Voice-Enabled Router

 Voice Gateway

 IP Telephony Router

 Cisco Unified CallManager

 Cisco CallManager

 Text Telephone

 Analog Phone

 Modem

 IP Phone

 Fax Machine

 Printer

 PBX Switch

 PC

 Laptop

 Web Browser

 Network Cloud

Ethernet Connection

Serial Line Connection

Command Syntax Conventions

The conventions used to present command syntax in this book are the same conventions used in the IOS Command Reference. The Command Reference describes these conventions as follows:

- **Boldface** indicates commands and keywords that are entered literally as shown. In actual configuration examples and output (not general command syntax), boldface indicates commands that are manually input by the user (such as a **show** command).

- *Italic* indicates arguments for which you supply actual values.

- Vertical bars (|) separate alternative, mutually exclusive elements.

- Square brackets ([ ]) indicate an optional element.

- Braces ({ }) indicate a required choice.

- Braces within brackets ([{ }]) indicate a required choice within an optional element.

Introduction

The advent of VoIP has led to revolutionary changes in the world of telecommunications. Information that was transported on traditional telephony infrastructures such as voice, video, and modulated data is transitioning to IP backbones. However, in this transition process, modulated data such as fax, modem, and text is often overlooked. Fax, modem, and text are treated like regular voice communications in many cases when in fact they have different transport requirements and usually need unique transport protocols for communication to be reliable.

We, the authors of this book, have about 25 years of combined networking experience with the majority of it focusing on faxes, modems, and VoIP. We have seen and experienced firsthand as Cisco TAC engineers the problems that are encountered with fax and modem communications. While one of the most common problems we encounter is the failure to take into account the unique transport requirements of fax, modem, and text, we also have seen problems with the configuration of the multitude of fax-, modem-, and text-related commands in Cisco voice gateways. In addition, we have realized that many times there is just a lack in understanding of basic passthrough and relay fundamentals as they are implemented on Cisco voice products. Addressing these problems and how to troubleshoot them were our main focus while writing this book.

Therefore, you will notice that this book includes a comprehensive design guide for getting fax, modem, and text deployments working successfully from the start, a commonsense configuration section, and a thorough troubleshooting guide. Equally as important, we devoted a whole section to the fundamentals of passthrough and relay and how they are implemented on Cisco voice products. In this book, we address all the main difficulties that we have seen with the implementation of fax and modems in IP environments.

We have written this book to be the definitive resource for understanding, designing, configuring, and troubleshooting fax, modem, and text in today's IP networks. Whether you are a network designer, voice engineer, or simply someone who must support fax, modem, and text communications over IP networks, this book is practically a necessity. If you understand basic VoIP, this book will just build upon that core knowledge.

Many books and other resources are available that discuss VoIP, and some even have a casual mention of transporting fax or modem communications. However, this book is the only one that provides a comprehensive, one-stop reference for addressing all aspects of fax, modem, and text communication.

Target Release: Cisco IOS Software Version 12.4(9)T1

The examples and features explained throughout this book for Cisco IOS voice gateways target Cisco IOS Software Release 12.4(9)T1. However, other IOS versions should be applicable to the majority of this book, too. Be aware, however, that features and implementations might differ somewhat in other IOS versions. Other software versions for devices such as Cisco Unified Communications Manager, 6608, and the VG248 are noted in the text when applicable.

Goals and Methods

This book is designed to be the only resource you will ever need for handling fax, modem, and text communications in IP telephony environments. From basic theory to design solutions to configuration to troubleshooting, all aspects are covered in a clear, concise manner.

Who Should Read This Book?

Just about every IP telephony (IPT) installation has at least one fax machine, and larger installations often include modems and text telephony devices, too. If you work with IPT, your job has already required or more than likely will require in the future that you handle fax, modem, and text communications in your network. For this reason, this book is an indispensable resource that should reside beside your other books dealing with IPT.

In some areas, this book expects you to have basic IPT knowledge. You should be familiar with the Internet Protocol, possess a good grasp of voice fundamentals, and be familiar with at least one of the various call control protocols. If you work with IPT on a consistent basis, you probably already have this knowledge.

Because of this book's comprehensive coverage of fax, modem, and text, it contains relevant information for a wide variety of readers who work with IPT. For anyone who works in IPT network design, such as design engineers, network architects, or systems engineers, this book features a comprehensive design and planning section. If you deploy and install IPT networks, an easy-to-understand configuration section provides the pertinent commands and sample configurations necessary for successfully transporting fax, modem, and text communications. Lastly, for those who support IPT networks, such as customer support engineers, field engineers, network administrators, and escalation engineers, a detailed troubleshooting section equips you with the knowledge and techniques to handle any issue that arises.

If you work with IPT, you will encounter fax, modem, and text devices if you have not already. These devices have special requirements and protocols that must be addressed for successful IP integration and deployment. When it comes time to handle fax, modem, and text communications as part of your job in IPT, this is the one resource that you want by your side.

How This Book Is Organized

This book is logically laid out with critical, fundamental concepts defined at the beginning in Chapters 1 to 6. Later chapters build upon these concepts to assist you with network design, configuration, and troubleshooting. Once the initial fundamental chapters are covered in the first two sections, the remaining chapters do not have to be read in any particular order even though the listed chapter sequence is what we believe to be the most beneficial for learning the subject matter.

The chapters in this book are divided into the following sections and cover the following topics:

- **Part I   Laying the Groundwork**

  Provides the fundamentals of how faxes, modems, and text telephony devices work.

  - **Chapter 1, "How Modems Work"**—Discusses modem architecture, different modem types, and the methods and modulations used by modems for communication. In addition, a basic modem call is analyzed, including the negotiation phases and data mode.

  - **Chapter 2, "How Fax Works"**—Covers the core elements of fax technology, including the common group classifications and standards, an in-depth section on fax messaging, and page encoding.

  - **Chapter 3, "How Text Telephony Works"**—Provides an introductory look at text telephony and its fundamantals. Basic text telephony operation and concepts are covered along with a technical discussion of the Baudot text telephone protocol.

- **Part II   IP Solutions and Design**

  Describes the various switchover methods and transport options that are used to handle fax, modem, and text communications. Design chapters then help you determine the best solution for transporting your fax, modem, and text traffic.

  - **Chapter 4, "Passthrough"**—Shows you the fundamental methods and principles necessary for using a voice codec for transporting fax, modem, and text. The different passthrough methods on Cisco voice gateways and their various switchovers are also discussed.

  - **Chapter 5, "Relay"**—Details the intricacies of relay operation and its various transport methods and switchover types for fax, modem, and text.

  - **Chapter 6, "T.37 Store-and-Forward Fax"**—Demonstrates the workings and fundamentals of fax and e-mail integration using onramp and offramp faxing.

  - **Chapter 7, "Design Guide for Fax, Modem, and Text"**—Provides pertinent design information and best practices for integrating fax, modem, and text telephony into your IP network.

  - **Chapter 8, "Fax Servers"**—Concentrates on the design and planning aspects of integrating fax servers into your network. In addition to fax server benefits and integration models, fax server–specific configuration and troubleshooting information is also provided.

- **Part III   Configuration**

  Details the configuration tasks for a variety of Cisco products that are essential for transporting fax, modem, and text successfully.

  — **Chapter 9, "Configuring Passthrough"**—Provides the configuration commands for enabling passthrough and its various features on Cisco products.

  — **Chapter 10, "Configuring Relay"**—Illustrates the numerous commands for successfully configuring the different relay transport methods and features on Cisco products. Also included are IOS voice gateways sample configurations of common deployment scenarios.

  — **Chapter 11, "Configuring T.37 Store-and-Forward Fax"**—Breaks down the somewhat confusing T.37 store-and-forward fax configuration process for onramp and offramp into simplified steps. Within each configuration step, the applicable commands are shown.

- **Part IV   Troubleshooting**

  Discusses the troubleshooting techniques and procedures used by Cisco TAC engineers for resolving fax, modem, and text issues.

  — **Chapter 12, "Troubleshooting Passthrough and Relay"**—Details a fax, modem, and text troubleshooting methodology that efficiently resolves passthrough and relay problems. Each step of this troubleshooting methodology correlates directly to a section within the chapter that shows you the key commands, debugs, and troubleshooting steps to execute for rapidly resolving issues from the most basic to the complex.

  — **Chapter 13, "Troubleshooting T.37 Store-and-Forward Fax"**—Highlights graphical troubleshooting models for onramp and offramp faxing that allow you to zero in on problems quickly. In-depth debugging techniques and procedures for the different processes within the graphical model are also provided.

Comments for the Authors

The authors are interested in your comments and suggestions about this book. Please send feedback to the following e-mail address:

faxmodemtextbook@external.cisco.com

Further Reading

The authors recommend the following resources for more information.

Cisco.com

The Cisco website is one of the best resources for additional documents related to fax, modem, and text technologies and IP telephony in general. Usually the easiest way to find a document is to use the web page's search feature. Other useful links on Cisco.com include the following:

- For design related documents, see http://www.cisco.com/go/srnd.
- For Unified Communications product information, refer to http://www.cisco.com/go/unified.
- For a listing of support information links, including command references, design and troubleshooting documents, and configuration guides, go to http://www.cisco.com/go/support.

The following technical books are also recommended for supplementing the information in this book and for increasing your overall IP telephony knowledge. These books can be examined at a local technical bookseller or by entering the title in the search box at http://www.ciscopress.com.

Voice over IP Fundamentals, Second Edition

The book *Voice over IP Fundamentals* (ISBN 1-58705-257-1) is a good place to start for those making a move into the IP telephony world, and it is also a handy reference for those already familiar with VoIP.

Troubleshooting Cisco IP Telephony

You can find comprehensive troubleshooting information for all the major components of a Unified Communications network in the book *Troubleshooting Cisco IP Telephony* (ISBN 1-58705-075-7).

Laying the Groundwork

CHAPTER 1

How Modems Work

Although analog modem technology stood on its own for many years in public switched telephone network (PSTN) environments, the rapid evolution of IP telephony (IPT) is now requiring that modem communications work successfully over IP networks. However, before discussing this complicated convergence of modems and IP, it is important to first attain a solid foundation in basic analog modem operation and communication.

This chapter addresses the basics of analog modem technology and prepares you for working with modems in IP networks. Specifically, this chapter covers the following topics:

- **A Brief History of Modems**: Highlights important developments and achievements since the modem's inception
- **Architecture of a Modem**: Details important modem components
- **Modem Types**: Covers different modem classifications and highlights important differences
- **Terminal-to-Modem Communication**: Discusses DTE/DCE interaction, RS-232, asynchronous framing, and the modem user interface
- **Modem-to-Modem Communication**: Illustrates the concepts of modulation and the various schemes that are used
- **Modem Call Analysis**: Provides a detailed analysis of all phases of a modem call

This chapter aims to be as comprehensive as possible, but because of the complicated nature of the topic in conjunction with the large number of specifications addressing modem operation, only the most important aspects of modem technology as it relates to IPT are covered.

A Brief History of Modems

Like several other core Internet and computer technologies, the modem was first developed in the 1950s for the Semi-Automatic Ground Environment (SAGE) air defense system. The modems were used to transmit military data over dedicated telephone lines between terminals at the various participating sites.

As commercial computer use increased, so did the need for communications between them. AT&T manufactured the first commercial modem, known as the Bell 103, in 1962. The Bell 103 allowed full-duplex transmission and employed Frequency Shift Keying (FSK) modulation with a data rate of up to 300 bits per second.

NOTE   The section "Modulation," later in this chapter, covers FSK and the other modulation schemes in detail.

Early modems by law were not allowed to connect directly to the telephone network. Usually they had an integrated acoustic coupler that allowed for a standard telephone handset to rest on the microphone/speaker cradle to convert between audio signals and digital data. Figure 1-1 illustrates an acoustic coupler connection. A major drawback is that the remote telephone number must be manually dialed before the handset is placed into the acoustic coupler for the modem training and connect sequence.

Figure 1-1   *Acoustically Coupled Modem*

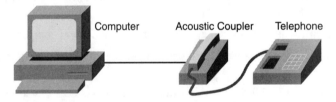

A landmark event in modem development was the introduction of the Hayes command set in 1977. Developed by Hayes Microcomputer Products for their Smartmodem product, this set of machine instructions allows the computer to control the modem's functions. Due to its popularity, the Hayes command set became the de facto standard, and most manufacturers still support it or one of its variants today. This development, along with changes in the telecommunication laws that allowed direct connection and dialing to the PSTN, spurred enormous growth in the modem industry.

Throughout the 1970s and 1980s, there were continuous improvements in the data rates of modems. These advancements were largely due to more sophisticated modulation techniques, improvements in telephony infrastructure, introduction of echo canceling methods, and the integration of error correction and data compression algorithms. A culmination of these advances was the release of the V.34 specification in 1994 by the international standards body known as the International Telecommunications Union Standardization Sector (ITU-T). You can find all the pertinent ITU-T Recommendations that are mentioned throughout this book at http://www.itu.int/ITU-T/.

The maximum speed of a V.34 connection is 33.6 Kbps. Unlike older specifications, V.34 employs multiple modulation schemes and multiple impairment compensation techniques to robustly adapt to poor line quality.

Despite the fact that it was thought that V.34 rates achieved the maximum throughput possible for a telephone line, it was only a few years later that 56-Kbps-capable modems became available. By taking advantage of pulse code modulation (PCM) and reducing the number of analog-to-digital (A/D) conversions from two to one, a data rate of 56 Kbps was achieved. Figure 1-2 shows how the typical modem topology has changed with the advent of 56K modem technology. Only a single A/D conversion is necessary because the central/ISP (Internet service provider) side modem is digitally terminated, typically with a digital T1 or E1 connected to an access server with onboard modems.

Figure 1-2 *Analog and Digital Modem Topologies*

Before: Typical modem topology prior to V.90/V.92 Digital modems.

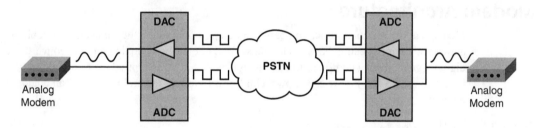

After: Typical modem topology with V.90/V.92 Digital modems.

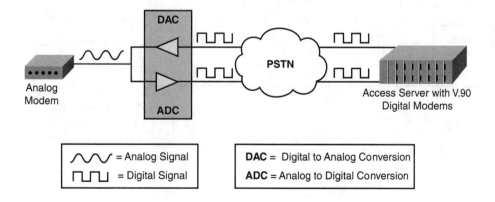

K56Flex, developed by Lucent and Rockwell, and X2, created by US Robotics (now known as 3Com), were the two early releases of the 56K protocol. These two protocols did not interoperate and this caused many problems and added unnecessary overhead. Consequently, V.90 was released as the international 56K modem standard for interoperability between different vendors. V.90 allows for data signaling rates of 56 Kbps downstream speed and 33.6 Kbps (V.34) upstream

The most recent widespread improvement to modem performance was the release of the V.92 standard. The ITU-T Recommendation V.92 made several minor incremental improvements over V.90. These included a drastic decrease in the amount of time it takes a modem to train and slight throughput upgrades by using an improved data compression scheme (V.44). In addition, V.92 provided advanced new features such as modem-on-hold (MoH). This feature allows an Internet user to suspend his data connection and accept an incoming voice call. Upon completion of the voice call, the data connection can be resumed.

Modem Architecture

Modems allow for communication between computers in much the same way a telephone allows for communication between humans. Fundamentally, an analog modem converts the digital signals from a computer to analog signals that are transmitted over voice-grade access to the PSTN. Figure 1-3 shows a high-level view of the architecture of an analog modem.

Figure 1-3   *Analog Modem Architecture*

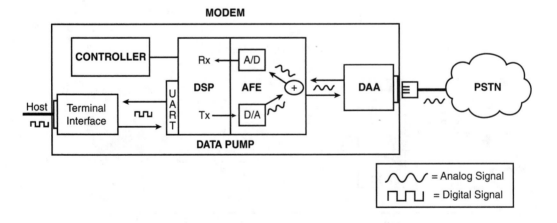

Modem architecture can generally be broken down into four main functional units:

1 **Data pump**: Responsible for carrying out the two primary functions of a modem (that is, the ones that give it its name):

   • **mo**dulation: Conversion of the digital bit stream received from the terminal into an analog signal that is sent over the telephone line.

   • **dem**odulation: Conversion of the analog waveform received over the telephone line into binary data that is sent to the terminal.

   Therefore, the data pump is commonly viewed as the engine of the modem. A typical data pump is comprised of two main functional subunits:

   — **Analog front end (AFE)**: Comprised principally of analog-to-digital (A/D) converters and digital-to-analog (D/A) converters. The A/D converters convert the voltages on the phone line to discrete binary values for the digital signal processor to process. Likewise, the D/A converters convert the binary data from the DSP and smoothes the output to form an analog signal.

   — **Digital signal processor (DSP)**: A specialized processor that is optimized for various signal-processing functions. Most important, it executes in real time the mathematically intensive operations involved in executing the different modulation/demodulation algorithms for the various modem protocols. It also handles echo cancellation, tone generation, and other specialized functions.

2 **Controller**: Handles the command interface to the terminal, AT command interpretation and execution, performs error correction and data compression algorithms, handles flow control between terminal and the data pump, and various other supervisory and miscellaneous functions. In this context, the controller is often referred to as the CPU of the modem.

3 **Data access arrangement (DAA)**: Contains the analog circuitry that electrically isolates the modem from the telephone network and also provides the physical interface (that is, line impedance, hybrid circuitry, and so on) to connect to a plain old telephone system (POTS) line.

4 **Terminal interface**: The asynchronous serial interface between the modem and the terminal. The section "Terminal to Modem Communication," later in this chapter, covers the transmission protocol (RS232) and asynchronous character framing that occurs on this connection in greater detail.

This is obviously a broad and simplified overview, and many modems exist that have variations on this general architecture, depending on the amount of integration and the type of modem that they are. For example, some modems have no controller at all, whereas others can have more than one processor. Primary function, modem type, and particular manufacturer largely dictate these various hybrid schemes.

Modem Types

Several methods of classifying modems exist based on the way they are connected to a computer, their general architecture, and their capabilities. The sections that follow address the most common classifications along with their pros and cons.

External Versus Internal Modems

An external modem physically resides outside the computer and has its own chassis, power supply, front-panel indicator LEDs, and so on. Also, it is connected to the computer with a cable that generally connects to the serial interface on a COM port. Internal modems reside in the computer, typically in a PCI or ISA slot, and usually create a virtual COM port. Table 1-1 provides a quick comparison of external versus internal modems.

Table 1-1   *External and Internal Modem Comparison*

Modem Type	Advantages
External	Easier to troubleshoot
	Viewable modem status LEDs
	Ease of installation
	Richer feature set
Internal	Less expensive
	Integrated with computer system for added mobility and convenience

Hardware Versus Software Modems

The architecture of a modem, discussed earlier, determines whether a modem is classified as a hardware modem or a software modem. A hardware modem is one that has hardware that handles all the data pump and controller functions on its own. On the other hand, a software modem is one that offloads one or both of those responsibilities to the host computer.

NOTE   Although "WinModem" is a USR brand of modem, it has become a popular term used to refer to software modems.

The two major types of software modems are as follows:

- **Controllerless modems**: A controllerless modem does not have its own on-board controller hardware. Rather, it offloads the controller's function to the computer's processor. The controllerless modem does have its own DSP hardware carrying out the data pump functions, which are generally the most processor intensive.

- **Host signal processor (HSP) modems**: HSP modems have neither controller nor data pump hardware of their own. Instead, they run software that offloads both of those functions to the host computer's CPU. From a hardware standpoint, an HSP modem is not much more than a DAA, because all of its other functions are carried out entirely in software. This is why it is commonly referred to as a softmodem. Handling these processor-intensive tasks takes away from the computer's processor and memory resources and could potentially cause a noticeable degradation in performance, especially on slower computers.

NOTE   External modems are always hardware modems. However, internal modems can be either hardware or software, although recently, most internal modems are software based.

Table 1-2 lists some of the advantages and disadvantages of hardware modems versus software modems.

Table 1-2   *Hardware and Software Modem Comparison*

Modem Type	Advantages
Hardware	Contains own processing resources, so host computer's performance is not degraded
	Typically more robust connections and better performance
	Generally better compatibility with different operating systems
Software	Less expensive
	Easier to upgrade firmware
	Smaller and easier to integrate into laptop computers

Fax Modems

Another type of modem relevant to the discussions in this book is the fax modem. This type of modem is nothing more than a modem that runs software that enables it to transmit documents to a fax machine or another fax modem. Most modems sold since the early 1990s contain fax modem functionality. Fax modems, like regular modems, can be either internal or external.

Fax modems have become popular because of certain advantages they offer over regular fax machines. One advantage is that fax modems are less expensive and require less maintenance.

Another is the convenience of directly sending documents in electronic format without the need to print them out. In addition, maintaining the document in electronic form ensures consistent image quality and efficient storage of the fax pages.

A series of standards, known as fax classes, were developed to differentiate and define the responsibilities of the computer versus those of the fax modem. Figure 1-4 shows how those responsibilities vary with class designation.

Figure 1-4   *Modem Versus Host Responsibilities for Different Fax Classes*

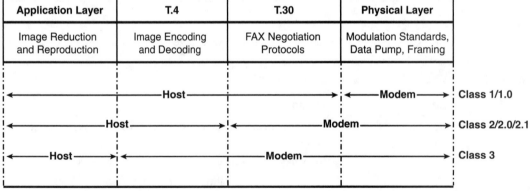

Application Layer	T.4	T.30	Physical Layer
Image Reduction and Reproduction	Image Encoding and Decoding	FAX Negotiation Protocols	Modulation Standards, Data Pump, Framing

◄———————Host———————► ◄——Modem——►	Class 1/1.0
◄————————Host————————► ◄———————Modem———————►	Class 2/2.0/2.1
◄——Host——► ◄———————Modem———————►	Class 3

NOTE   The class of a modem only defines the way in which the computer's fax software controls/ interfaces with the fax modem. It has nothing to do with negotiation between two fax modems or a fax modem and a fax machine.

Table 1-3 defines the classes for determining a modem's ability to conduct a fax session.

Table 1-3   *Fax Class Designations for Modems*

Fax Modem Type	Standard	Description
Class 0	N/A	The modem has no fax capabilities and functions only in data mode.
Class 1	EIA/TIA-578 and ITU-T T.31	The computer fax software manages virtually the entire fax session. It is responsible for the fax negotiation (T.30 protocol), and the image encoding/decoding (T.4 protocol). The modem, on the other hand, provides the minimum services for a fax session. It is responsible for modulation/demodulation, fax command/response interface, and the conversion from the asynchronous data from the computer to the synchronous High-Level Data Link Control (HDLC) packets required for fax communication.
Class 1.0	ITU-T T.31 Annex B	Much like Class 1, but with V.34-fax (Super G3) capability added.
Class 2	EIA/TIA SP-2388A (now obsolete)	The modem has more intelligence regarding the fax session than Class 1. In this case, the modem handles much of the fax negotiation (T.30 protocol), whereas the computer fax application deals with the image generation and page data (T.4 protocol). The Class 2 standard was in draft status for a long time. Therefore, modem manufacturers made modems that adhered to this draft rather than the final ratified standard. Thus, the Class 2 standard is now obsolete, but is still supported by various vendors.
Class 2.0	EIA/TIA-592 and ITU-T T.32	Modems adhering to the first Class 2 draft are said to be Class 2 compliant, and those adhering to the final approved standard are said to be Class 2.0 compliant. There were improvements between Class 2 and Class 2.0, such as implementing Error Correction Mode (ECM) support on the modem, resolving flow-control problems, and fixing data underrun/overrun issues.

continues

Table 1-3 *Fax Class Designations for Modems (Continued)*

Fax Modem Type	Standard	Description
Class 2.1	ITU-T T.32	Similar to Class 2.0, but with V.34-fax (Super G3) capability added. This is defined in Annex C of specification T.32
Class 3	N/A	The computer fax software offloads even more of the faxing responsibilities to the modem. For this class, the modem handles the bulk of both the fax negotiation (that is, T.30 protocol) and the image data conversion (that is, T.4 protocol) responsibilities. Class 3 is not an official standard yet, so it is not commonly seen in practice.

NOTE   T.30 and T.4 fax protocols are discussed in great detail when fax is covered in Chapter 2, "How Fax Works."

Table 1-4 highlights some of the advantages of Class 1 and Class 2 fax modems.

Table 1-4 *Class 1 and Class 2 Fax Modem Comparison*

Fax Modem Type	Advantage
Class 1/1.0	Provides greater flexibility because there is no need to upgrade the modem firmware or wait for modem manufacturer to support a new feature because faxing is done almost wholly by the computer software.
Class 2/2.0/2.1	Because the modem does most of the T.30 fax negotiation, this relieves the host computer of processing resources that can be used for something else. This could be beneficial for slow or overtaxed systems.

Although many vendors support all these variants of Class 2, there is no guarantee of compatibility. Also, Class 2 is a closed standard, so any changes to T.30 would require a modem firmware upgrade.

Terminal-to-Modem Communication

This section deals with the protocols typically used on the asynchronous serial link between the host and the modem. First, you are introduced to the concept of data terminal equipment (DTE) and data circuit-terminating equipment (DCE). Then, the communications link between terminal and modem is divided into three layers. From the bottom up, they are as follows:

- **RS-232 physical layer**: This defines the mechanical, electrical, and hardware signaling used on the terminal-to-modem cable.

- **Async framing layer**: This specifies the format used to frame characters on an asynchronous serial link.

- **AT command layer**: This is a command language used by the host to configure and control the modem.

DTE and DCE

Various international standards bodies agreed on specifications that detail how to facilitate the connection of data communications equipment. These standards discuss the interface between DTE and DCE. The specifications describe the physical and electrical interface between a DTE and a particular type of DCE. As an example, the ITU-T V-series recommendations deal with the connection of a DTE to a modem (the DCE).

DTE is equipment that acts as a data source/sink from the point of view that it converts user information into signals to be transmitted by the DCE. The most frequently used example of a DTE is a computer. Correspondingly, DCE is the equipment that establishes and provides access to a communications link over a channel connecting the source and destination DTEs. Therefore, a DCE provides a data link service for DTEs to communicate over. In this chapter, the DCE will always be a modem. Figure 1-5 shows the logical location and function of both DTE and DCE. The practical significance in distinguishing between these two types of equipment is that they are pinned and cabled differently.

Figure 1-5   *DTE and DCE Topology*

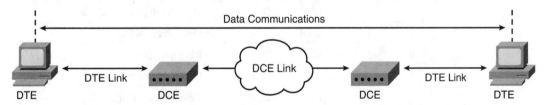

RS-232 Signaling

RS-232 is a serial transmission system designed to support communications for short distances between a DTE and a low-speed DCE. It has evolved through several generations of standards (EIA-232C, EIA-232D, EIA-232E, and a variant has separately been standardized by the ITU as V.24). RS-232 supports a variety of applications, including synchronous and asynchronous transmission. This discussion focuses on full-duplex async DTE links to contemporary modems and uses the term RS-232 in its generic sense; for more precise details, consult the standards.

A standard RS-232 link will use the DB-25 connector. Normally (but not necessarily), the DTE port is male, and the DCE port is female. PC DTE ports often use a DB-9 connector, whereas Cisco normally uses a nonstandard 8-pin modular (RJ-45) connector for its async ports. Table 1-5 summarizes the pinouts for all three of these interface types. (Pinouts are from the plug side. Jack side pinouts are rolled.)

NOTE   Technically PC DTE ports use a DE-9 connector. The misnomer "DB-9" is not a connector that exists in practice, but it is mistakenly used so frequently that it has become the de facto term for a PC DTE interface. Consequently, this book will henceforth use the commonly used DB-9 nomenclature when referring to the connector of a PC DTE port.

Table 1-5   *Pinouts for Different RS-232 Interfaces*

DB-25	DB-9	RJ-45	Name	From	Description
1			GND	gnd	Protective (shield) Ground
7	5	4, 5	SG	gnd	Signal Ground
2	3	6	TxD	DTE	Transmitted Data
3	2	3	RxD	DCE	Received Data
4	7	8	RTS	DTE	Request to Send (hw flow control)
5	8	1	CTS	DCE	Clear to Send (hw flow control)
6	6	2	DSR	DCE	Data Set Ready (DCE ready)
20	4	7	DTR	DTE	Data Terminal Ready
22	9		RI	DCE	Ring Indicator
8	1	(2)	CD	DCE	Data Carrier Detect
21			RL	DCE	Remote Loop / sig quality
23			CH/CI	DTE/DCE	Signal Rate Selector
24			DA	DTE	DTE Tx Timing
15			DB	DCE	DCE Tx Timing
17			DD	DCE	Rx Timing
14			SBA	DTE	Secondary TxD
16			SBB	DCE	Secondary RxD

Table 1-5   *Pinouts for Different RS-232 Interfaces (Continued)*

DB-25	DB-9	RJ-45	Name	From	Description
19			SCA	DTE	Secondary RTS
13			SCB	DCE	Secondary CTS
12			SCF	DCE	Secondary DCD

Not all 25 conductors are used; for async applications, typically from 3 to 9 conductors will be used, depending on whether hardware (hw) flow control or modem control signaling is required.

RS-232 does not specify bit rates per se. However, for async transmission, the following rates have been typically seen: 50, 75, 110, 134.5, 150, 300, 600, 1200, 2400, 4800, 9600, 19200, 38400, 57600, 76800, 115200, 230400 bps. As specified in the standards, RS-232 is officially considered to be suitable only for data rates of up to 20 Kbps and distances of up to 50 feet. In practice, RS-232 is often run at 115200 bps for distances of up to 20 feet, and at 9600 bps for distances of as much as 500 feet.

The RS-232 protocol defines nine electrical circuits to handle all the handshaking between a DTE and DCE. These electrical circuits (also referred to as leads, pins, or signals) are grouped into three categories: data interchange circuits, control interchange circuits, and the ground circuit.

Data leads are used to signal the exchange of data. Control leads govern the call signaling states between a DTE and a DCE and manage the flow control between them. As its name suggests, the ground lead is the reference ground for the DTE and the DCE. Table 1-6 details each of the nine RS-232 pins and their individual function.

NOTE   Terminology, such as "raise" or "assert," with regard to the RS-232 pins implies putting a particular voltage on it. Likewise, the terms "lower" and "drop" imply changing the polarity of that voltage.

Table 1-6   *RS-232 Circuits and Their Function*

Circuit Type	Circuit Name	Circuit Function
Ground	**SG** Signal Ground	Reference Ground.
Data	**TxD** Transmit Data	Data transmitted by the DTE to the DCE.

continues

Table 1-6   *RS-232 Circuits and Their Function (Continued)*

Circuit Type	Circuit Name	Circuit Function
Data	**RxD** Receive Data	Data received by the DTE from the DCE.
Control - Modem Control	**DTR** Data Terminal Ready	Raised by the DTE when it is ready to get access to the DCE link. The modem will not dial unless it sees DTR asserted by the host.
Control - Modem Control	**DSR** Data Set Ready	Raised by the DCE when it is powered up and in such a state where the communications channel is available for transmission/reception. The DTE will not request the modem to dial unless it sees DSR high from the modem.
Control - Modem Control	**CD** Carrier Detect	Raised by the local DCE when it detects a carrier signal from the remote DCE.
Control - Modem Control	**RI** Ring Indicator	Raised by the DCE to signal to the DTE that there is an incoming call. RI is asserted in accordance with the incoming ring cadence on the phone line.
Control - Flow Control	**CTS** Clear To Send	Raised by the DCE to signal it is ready to receive data from the DTE. If the modem temporarily lowers CTS, it backpressures the DTE link.
Control - Flow Control	**RTS** Request To Send	Raised by the DTE to signal it has data to transmit to the DCE. If the host temporarily lowers RTS, it backpressures the DCE link.

Electrically, the RS-232 data interchange circuit's (for example, TxD and RxD) "mark" state (logical 1) is signaled as a voltage level less than –3V, and a "space" state (logical 0) is signaled as a voltage level greater than +3V. For control interchange circuits, an OFF state is signaled as a voltage level less than –3V, and an ON state is signaled as a voltage level greater than +3V. The signal ground lead must be connected to the equipment on each side of the link to provide a voltage reference.

Now that you know the definitions of all the RS-232 circuits, Figure 1-6 puts them into practice by tracing through all the RS-232 signaling involved in placing a modem call from one host to another. This example illustrates the transitions of the various control pins. Note that when the call is up, the actual data transmission and reception will be signaled by the data pins (TxD, RxD).

Figure 1-6   *RS-232 Signaling for a Modem Call Setup*

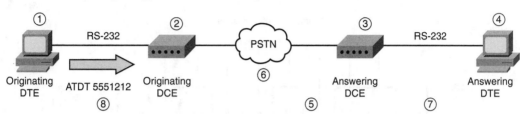

1. Originating DTE raises DTR and transmits AT dial string (DSR is high at this point)
2. Originating DCE places a call to the Answering DCE
3. Answering DCE raises RI to signal to the Answering DTE that there is an incoming call
4. Answering DTE raises DTR
5. Answering DCE goes off-hook
6. Answering DCE sends answer back tone and modems train
7. Answering DCE signals CONNECT and raises DCD
8. Originating DCE signals CONNECT and raises DCD

Asynchronous Framing

All data transmission requires that the receiver somehow synchronize with the transmitter to know when to detect symbol state changes. In synchronous framing, the receiver maintains a clock that is kept in sync with the transmitter's clock. This synchronization can be maintained either by some external hardware signal (for example, a timing circuit in sync RS-232) or by some recurring framing pattern in the received signal (for example, the framing bits in a T1 frame). In asynchronous framing, the receiver synchronizes anew with some pattern seen at the front of each frame. Examples are Ethernet (where the receiver syncs to the frame's preamble) and async character framing.

Async character framing is used on both async RS-232 links and in modem links where an error control framing protocol isn't used. In this scheme, each character (of 5, 6, 7 or 8 databits) is encapsulated in a separate frame, which is composed of a start bit (a space bit), the payload containing the databits and an optional parity bit, and 1, 1.5, or 2 stop bits (mark bits). While the async link is idle, the transmitter sends mark bits. The receiver, which must be preconfigured knowing the payload length, will synchronize on the start bit for each frame. Figure 1-7 shows an async frame and all its components.

Figure 1-7   *Asynchronous Framing*

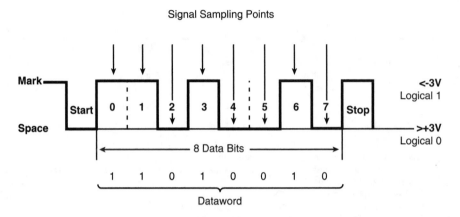

Very old equipment might have required more than 1 stop bit, but such equipment is rarely seen now. However, a transmitter being configured for excess stop bits won't cause communications problems, only reduced payload transfer rate, as the extra stop bits are interpreted by the receiver as idle bits.

By far the most prevalent async character frame formats encountered now are these:

- 7 databits, 1 parity bit (usually even), 1 stop bit (7E1)
- 8 databits, no parity, 1 stop bit (8N1)

In both of these cases, the payload size is 8 bits, which meshes nicely with the standard byte size used on contemporary computers and in octet-oriented transmissions protocols.

With 1 start bit, 8 payload bits, and 1 stop bit, async framing has 20 percent overhead. Thus, an 115200 bps 8N1 async framed link will have a payload throughput rate of 92160 bps. Relative to sync transmission, this is rather high overhead. For RS-232 DTE links, where the DTE speed is significantly higher than the DCE rate (for example, when using an 115200 bps DTE link for a 28800 bps V.34 link), this overhead is not especially costly. However, for the relatively precious bandwidth on the DCE link, this overhead can be considered to be excessive, which is one of the motivations for using error control (EC) framing on the DCE link instead (discussed later in this chapter).

User Interface

The standard method used for an async DTE to control its DCE (for example, modem) is through a command-line interface (CLI) protocol called the AT interface. AT stands for ATtention; each command line sent by the DTE is prefixed with AT, which serves to get the CLI's attention.

As discussed earlier in the history section, the AT interface was introduced by Hayes Microcomputer Products (now a brand of Zoom Telephonics) in 1981. It has existed as an evolving de facto standard, with many vendor-specific oddities and extensions, since then. The ITU attempted to codify the standard in 1995 with V.25ter, although by then it was probably too late to impose order on the menagerie of existing command sets. Still, there is a core set of AT commands, honored by almost all modem manufacturers, that have been standardized by the V.25ter syntax.

The AT command interface is a simple CLI implemented in the DCE's controller. Figure 1-8 depicts how the CLI reads AT commands from the async DTE link, executes them as needed, and returns responses to the DTE. These responses are sent by the DCE, in the form of result codes, in reply to AT commands from the DTE and activity on the line.

Figure 1-8   *Asynchronous DTE Link Communication*

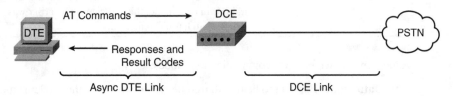

One of the main uses of the AT interface is to provide a method for supervisory and address signaling between the DTE and DCE. This includes allowing the DTE to control call setup, training, and teardown, and to allow the DCE to communicate status to the DTE. Table 1-7 shows some sample AT commands the DTE sends the DCE to establish a call. This table also highlights some typical result codes from the DCE to the DTE in response to such AT commands.

Table 1-7   *Sample AT Commands and Result Codes*

AT Command	Description
ATD*number*	Dial *number* then start training in originate mode.
ATD*number;*	Dial *number* then return to AT command mode without training.
ATDT*number*	Dial *number* using DTMF address signaling.
ATDP*number*	Dial *number* using pulse signaling.
ATDL	Redial the last number dialed.
ATA	Go offhook and begin training in answer mode.

continues

Table 1-7   *Sample AT Commands and Result Codes (Continued)*

Result Code	Description
CONNECT	Modems have trained and have gone into data mode.
CONNECT 2400	Modems have trained at 2400 bps.
CONNECT 26400/REL – MNP	Modems have trained at 26400 bps and have negotiated a reliable link with MNP error control.
RING	An incoming call is arriving from the circuit network (sent by the answer modem).
NO DIALTONE	The originate modem went offhook but did not hear dial tone.
BUSY	A busy signal was detected.
NO CARRIER	If in call setup mode, this indicates that the modems failed to train. If in data mode, this indicates that carrier was lost and that the call has disconnected.

A modem has two primary communication modes:

- **Data mode**: For data to be transferred between two hosts, the modems must be in data mode.

- **Command mode**: All the call control functions (dialing, hang up, auto answer, and so on) are handled in command mode.

Before a call is established, the DTE link is used for the AT interface; as soon as the modem sends the DTE a "CONNECT" result code with the connection speed baud rate displayed, the modem switches from command mode to data mode, and user data can begin to be transmitted between DTEs. The AT interface is inoperative in data mode.

On traditional modems, the AT interface operates in-band on the transmit/receive data path in the DTE link. This is the same path used to transmit data while in data mode. There is a significant problem associated with using in-band control: when the DTE links are in data mode, there is no guaranteed method to distinguish in-band signals from user data. Thus, if available, an out-of-band signaling path such as the RS-232 DTR, DCD and RI leads are preferable. However, in-band controls have the advantage of being cheap and easy to use. Therefore, in-band signals are what are commonly used in practice.

Because the AT interface uses the data path between the DTE and the DCE for both application data and for commands, it would be useful to have a method whereby, while the AT interface is in data mode, the DTE can tell the DCE to enter command mode, while remaining connected to the peer DTE. The standard method of escaping data mode uses this key sequence: <pause>+++<pause>.

The mode that is entered from data mode after the escape sequence has been entered is commonly referred to as online command mode. In this mode, the communication link remains established, but data transmission is suspended. The modem does accept commands like it does in regular command mode, when there is no call up.

Table 1-8 illustrates a sample modem session that will serve to highlight some aspects of how this works. The originate modem session is on the left, the answer modem session on the right. AT commands entered by the DTE are in **bold** text, and the result codes from the DCE are in *italics*. Application data is in normal text and is shown on the transmitter's side.

Table 1-8   *Sample User Interface Session*

Originate-Side Session	Answer-Side Session
AT	
OK	
! The **OK** response signals the originate DCE's AT parser's ability to accept command input.	
ATD1234	
! Modem goes offhook, hears dial tone, transmits DTMF, and waits to hear answerback tone	
! (ABT). The modem gets a fast busy.	
NO CARRIER	
ATD5703933	
! This time the call goes through and the PSTN presents ring voltage to the answer modem.	
	RING
! The answer DCE transmits this on the AT interface; it also toggles the RS-232 RI signal.	
	ATA
! Normally an answer modem will automatically answer upon incoming ring, but in this case	
! the answering application sends an explicit **ATA** command due to the *RING* or *RI*, which	
! causes the answer modem to go offhook, then starts transmitting ABT. The modems train	
! successfully.	
CONNECT 26400/REL – LAPM	*CONNECT 26400 /V.42/V.42bis*
! The modems output their *CONNECT* strings; note the differing but equivalent formats. Then	
! the modems raise DCD. At this point the DTE links are in data mode and are out of AT	
! command mode.	

continues

Table 1-8 *Sample User Interface Session (Continued)*

Originate-Side Session	Answer-Side Session
	Welcome! Please login with username CISCO, password cisco.
	User Access Verification
	Username:
CISCO	
	CISCO
! This text is echoed by the answer DTE.	
	Password:
cisco	
! This text is not echoed.	
	access-3>
+++	
	+++
! The originate DTE transmits **+++**, which causes the client DTE link to switch out of data ! mode and into AT command mode (while leaving the DCE link intact).	
OK	
AT@e1	
CONNECTION STATUS	
Modulation Type: V.34	
TX/RX Speed: 26400 26400 BPS	
TX/RX Symbol Rate: 3200 3200 Hz	
TX/RX Carrier Frequency: 1920 1829 Hz	
OK	
! The user enters a (nonstandard) AT command to display some technical information on the ! modem connection (output edited for brevity).	
ATO	
CONNECT 26400/REL – LAPM	
! The **ATO** command tells the DCE to put the DTE link back into data mode (that is, go back ! "online").	

Generally, AT commands can be divided into two groups: control commands and configuration commands. Control commands cause the modem to perform call control functions, such as call setup, dialing, and teardown. Table 1-8 contains a sample of AT control commands and explains how they work. In addition to control commands, AT commands can be used to configure various modem settings. Except for the small subset of AT commands specified in V.25ter, there are enormous variations in the AT command set used by the different modem manufacturers.

Another way to configure a modem is through the status registers, usually referred to as S-registers. Register is a term used to describe a specific physical location in memory. In the case of modems, the S-registers are memory locations containing configuration information that can have their stored values read or (in most cases) altered via ATS commands. Some S-registers cannot be changed; these are known as read-only registers. Those registers that can be written to (that is, altered) are used to configure/change many of the modem's functions.

S-registers can have all the bits in that memory location represent a single configuration option, or they can be bitmapped registers with a single value representing multiple configuration options. Figure 1-9 shows both types of registers. The purpose of using bitmapped registers is to pack lots of configuration information into a small space.

Figure 1-9   *Standard and Bitmapped S-Register Comparison*

Standard S-Register	Bit-Mapped S-Register
Register Name: S1 Register Function: Ring Counter Default: 0 Range: 0-255 rings	Register Name: S51 Register Function: Multifunction Default: 0 Bit Value Result 0 1 MNP/V.42 disabled in V.22. 1 2 MNP/V.42 disabled in V.22bis. 2 4 MNP/V.42 disabled in V.32bis. 3-7 - Reserved.

NOTE   A typical modem has dozens of S-registers. The first few are standard across most modem manufacturers, but the rest are all different depending on modem manufacturer and model.

An S-register is configured according to ATS$n = x$, where n is the register number and x is the new value assigned to the register. So ATS0 = 3 sets register 0 to a value of 3 (that is, auto-answer in 3 rings). Writing to an S-register changes the total value of the register. Therefore, if altering a bitmapped register, you must ensure that cumulative total is such that it properly configures the group of bit values for each configuration option.

Modem-to-Modem Communication

Modulation is the most fundamental aspect of modem communications. It the means by which the binary digital data from the DTE link is encoded onto an analog signal that is sent over the PSTN. Different protocols describe the different types of modulations, and one of these protocols must be successfully negotiated between each modem on a point-to-point link for any communication to be possible. In this section, the various modulation schemes and how they correlate with the various ITU-T V-series modulation standards are discussed.

Modulation

The analog signals used in the transmission of modulated data are simply sinusoidal waveforms, and the primary components of any waveform are the amplitude, the frequency, and the phase. Figure 1-10 helps explain these concepts visually.

Figure 1-10 *Components of a Wave*

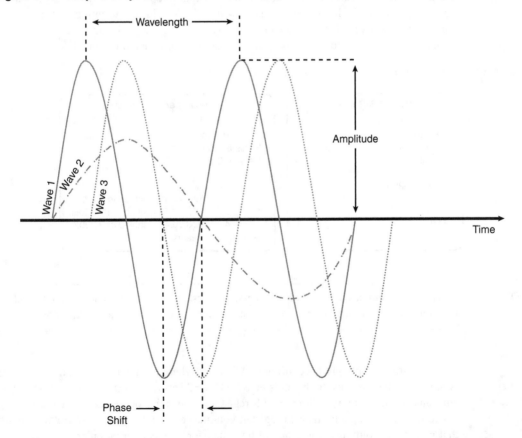

The amplitude is the magnitude of the wave. In the diagram, Wave 1 has twice the amplitude of Wave 2. The frequency is the inverse of the wavelength and thus is the number of oscillations occurring in a period. Note that in Figure 1-10 Wave 1 has half the wavelength of Wave 2, and hence it has twice the frequency. The phase is the position of the wave in its cycle period. Figure 1-10 shows Wave 3 to be 90 degrees out of phase with Wave 1.

There is a continuous analog signal between two modems during a call that is always present, known as the carrier signal. A pure sinusoidal carrier with no change in amplitude, frequency, phase, or some combination of these is unable to convey any information. To remedy this, modems change (or modulate) one or more of the components of the carrier wave to encode information onto it. The method in which the modem modifies one or more of these three wave characteristics is known as the modulation scheme.

The exact method of encoding the binary user data from the RS-232 DTE link onto the carrier is laid out in the specific modulation scheme that is negotiated. Each modulation scheme uses varying means of manipulating different combinations of the wave characteristics of the carrier signal. These differences produce diverse efficiencies in the amount of data per second that each modulation scheme can transmit over the data channel.

When talking about transmission rates for modems, two terms are commonly used. One is the familiar data rate in units of bits per second. The other is the more cryptic symbol rate in units of symbols per second. Sometimes you will hear the term baud rate, which is essentially equivalent to the symbol rate, but is no longer used in newer modulation standards because it as an antiquated term that is often misused.

A symbol represents a unique value assigned to each distinct state on a channel. In the context of modulation schemes, a symbol represents the possible states for encoding binary data. For example, assume a modulation scheme that varies the amplitude of the carrier at two distinct values. This is two unique states, which is the information carried by 1 bit of information in a binary system. If the example is extended by using a different modulation technique, whereby both the amplitude and phase of the carrier are changed, it will produce four distinct values. In this case, there are four unique states, which is the information carried by 2 bits in a binary system. Therefore, the more sophisticated a modulation scheme is, the more bits that are sent per symbol. Based on this explanation, you can clearly see that the symbol rate is equal to the data rate only when a symbol represents 1 bit of information (two states).

There are some practical applications of this concept of symbols. For example, when analyzing a modulation scheme that changes the phase or that changes both the phase and amplitude, a useful diagram, called a constellation, is used. A constellation diagram maps out points representing the various symbol states possible for a given modulation scheme. Effectively, each point in the constellation defines a sequence of bits to be transferred. Constellation diagrams are used in subsequent sections when discussing different modulation schemes.

Many different modulation schemes covering various aspects of data communications exist, but for the discussion on modems in this section coverage is limited to the following:

- Frequency Shift Keying (FSK)

- Phase Shift Keying (PSK)

- Amplitude Modulation (AM)

- Quadrature Amplitude Modulation (QAM)

- Trellis Coded Modulation (TCM)

Frequency Shift Keying (FSK)

FSK simply uses one frequency tone to represent a 1 and another different frequency tone to represent a 0. Thus, it is able to produce an analog representation of the two logical states of binary digital data. For example, the digital base signal in Figure 1-11 is represented as a modulated carrier signal made up of two distinct frequencies. These two distinct frequencies are shown as f0 and f1, where f0 represents a space (or binary 0), and f1 represents a mark (or binary 1). The amplitude of the carrier is constant.

Figure 1-11   *FSK Modulation*

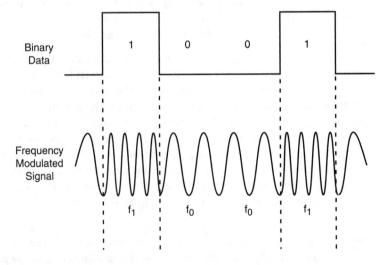

Because two states can be represented with binary FSK, there is only 1 bit per symbol. There is a single frequency per symbol and direction. Therefore, for full-duplex transmission, a set of four distinct frequencies is needed. The two most common standards that use FSK are Bell 103 and V.21 (used in fax transmissions).

Phase Shift Keying (PSK)

PSK uses a different phase to represent a binary state. For example, in binary PSK (BPSK), the phase of a constant amplitude and constant frequency carrier signal moves between 0 and 180 degrees to represent a logical 0 and a logical 1. Figure 1-12 illustrates the symbol states of binary PSK in a constellation diagram.

Figure 1-12 *Symbol States for BPSK Modulation*

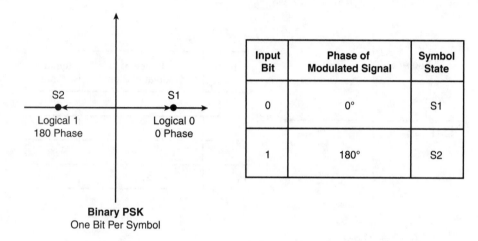

Input Bit	Phase of Modulated Signal	Symbol State
0	0°	S1
1	180°	S2

In Figure 1-13, the BPSK modulated carrier varies its phase between 0 and 180 degrees based on whether it receives a 0 or a 1 from the digital binary signal.

Figure 1-13 *BPSK Modulation*

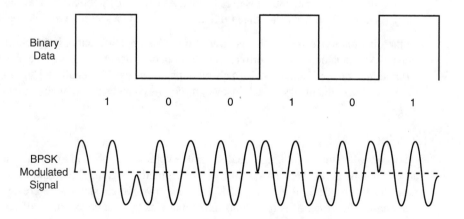

One way to increase the transmission rate without changing the bandwidth requirements is to increase the number of bits represented by each phase change (that is, symbol). If the phase of the carrier is now varied between 0, 90, 180, and 270 degrees, you now have the ability to represent four different states (or 2 bits worth of information). This higher order of PSK is known as Quadrature PSK (QPSK) or 4-PSK and is shown graphically in Figure 1-14.

Figure 1-14   *Symbol States for QPSK Modulation*

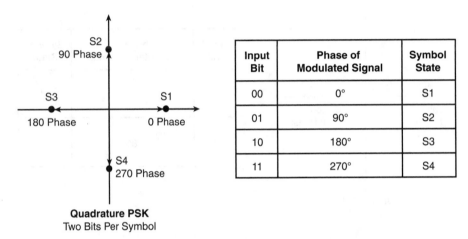

Input Bit	Phase of Modulated Signal	Symbol State
00	0°	S1
01	90°	S2
10	180°	S3
11	270°	S4

Clearly, the symbol rate in QPSK is double that of binary PSK and, consequently, so is the transmission rate. Higher orders of PSK are used, such as 8-PSK, which has eight states and is thus able to encode 3 bits per symbol.

Fax modulation V.27ter at 4800 bps uses 8-PSK. As expected, 8-PSK is 3 times faster than binary PSK and 1.5 times faster than QPSK, but it is more susceptible to link degradation.

Another modulation technique that is a variation of PSK is Differential Phase Shift Keying (DPSK). As the name suggests, differential PSK encodes using changes in the phase of the carrier signal, rather than the carrier's absolute phase (as used in regular PSK). So, DPSK doesn't represent the binary signal; instead, it records changes in the binary stream.

Amplitude Modulation (AM)

AM occurs when the originating signal's variable voltage is applied to a carrier, causing the carrier's amplitude to change according to the originating signal. The digital form of AM, known as Amplitude Shift Keying (ASK), has only two logical states to re-create in the binary case. Therefore, ASK represents the digital data by using two amplitude levels, one of which is typically 0.

For example, a binary signal such as the one shown in Figure 1-15 would have an ASK modulated signal that appears as a burst of sinusoidal waves when there is a mark to transmit.

Figure 1-15 *Amplitude Modulation*

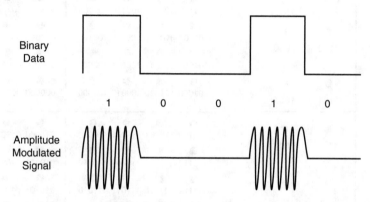

As with other schemes, ASK can have more sophisticated encoding schemes with additional amplitude levels (that is, four levels to represent 2 bits, eight levels to represent 3 bits, and so on). ASK is the simplest of the modulation techniques, but it has the drawback of being more susceptible to error, because amplitude is affected more by noise than frequency or phase.

Quadrature Amplitude Modulation (QAM)

The concepts of ASK and PSK can be combined to form QAM, where both phase and amplitude deviations can be used to encode the digital data. The dual nature of QAM allows for an increased number of unique states since many different phase shifts and amplitude level combinations can be used. Figure 1-16 illustrates how this increase in the number of symbols in the constellation pattern allows for more bits per symbol and therefore a greater data rate.

Figure 1-16 *Constellation Patterns for 16-QAM Versus 64-QAM*

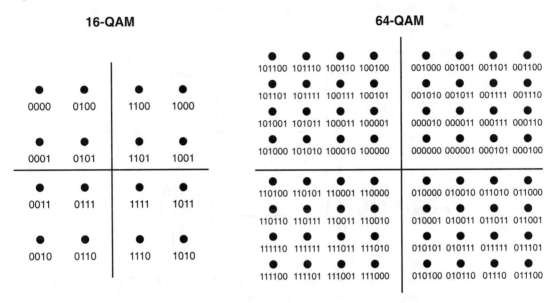

There are limitations on bandwidth and signal-to-noise ratio (SNR) on an analog circuit that put an upper bound on the amount of data that can be transmitted per second. With regard to the constellation pattern of higher-order QAM, the problem manifests itself when the constellation points are close enough together that the receiving end is unable to distinguish one symbol from the next. This is due to the quantization and other noise that will invariably exist on the channel, limiting the overall throughput. Therefore, higher-order QAM is clearly more bandwidth efficient, but is much more susceptible to noise and distortion.

Trellis Coded Modulation (TCM)

TCM should be thought of as QAM with Trellis coding applied to it. Trellis coding is a mathematical algorithm that on the encoding side takes a certain number of bits (n-bits) as an input and produces a larger number of bits (m-bits) as an output. On the decoding side, an algorithm is used to find out the most likely n-bit sequence that would have produced the larger m-bit sequence, even if some of the bits were altered due to noise on the line.

For example, if a symbol is shifted by noise and falls close to a boundary, the modem uses the algorithm to examine the extra data (that is, the m-bit sequence) from the previous symbol to check the accuracy of the current symbol. Essentially, Trellis coding adds a form of error correction (known as Forward Error Correction [FEC]) to help the decoder deal with the effects of line noise.

NOTE	The error correction done by Trellis coding is used at the modulation layer, so it can be done in addition to standard error correction protocols done at the data layer (that is, MNP4 and LAP-M, which are discussed in detail later in this chapter).

Therefore, TCM adds redundancy to the data and in return allows that data to be decoded with a lower error rate than plain QAM. V.32 and V.34 standards use TCM as their modulation scheme.

Modulation Standards

The preceding discussion focused on the theoretical nature of the different methods of modulation. Over time, public and proprietary standards have been defined based upon the different modulation schemes. These modulation standards can generically be broken down into two categories: analog modem modulation and digital modem modulation. The primary difference between the two is the carrier used. Analog modulation uses an analog carrier, whereas digital modulation uses a digital carrier.

Table 1-9 summarizes the primary modem modulation standards by order of chronology, which also correlates to increasing carrier rates. Also noted is the range of speeds that the protocol is usable over, and the speed increments that dictate how the protocol steps through the range of available speeds to find the most optimum bandwidth.

Table 1-9   *Modulation Standards Comparison*

Protocol	Carrier Rate (bps)	Carrier Increment	Carrier Type	Modulation Scheme
Bell103	300	N/A	Analog	FSK
V.21	300	N/A	Analog	FSK
Bell212A	1200	N/A	Analog	DPSK
V.22	1200	N/A	Analog	DPSK
V.22bis	1200 or 2400	N/A	Analog	QAM
V.23	600 or 1200 with optional 75 bps back channel	N/A	Analog	FSK
V.32	2400 to 9600	2400	Analog	QAM/TCM
V.32bis	4800 to 14400	2400	Analog	QAM/TCM

continues

Table 1-9   *Modulation Standards Comparison (Continued)*

Protocol	Carrier Rate (bps)	Carrier Increment	Carrier Type	Modulation Scheme
V.32Terbo	4800 to 19200	2400	Analog	QAM/TCM
V.FC	24000, 26400, 28800	N/A	Analog	TCM
V.34	2400 to 28800	2400	Analog	TCM
V.34+	2400 to 33600	2400	Analog	TCM
X2	28000 to 56000	1333	Digital	PCM/TCM
K56Flex	28000 to 56000	1333	Digital	PCM/TCM
V.90	28000 to 56000	1333	Digital	PCM/TCM

Modem Call Analysis

This section analyzes a call in its entirety. For the purpose of this discussion, the modem call is broken down into three component parts:

- The first part deals with the call setup and training sequence between modems.
- The second part covers the protocols and procedures associated with data transmission, including speedshifts, retrains, error control, and data compression.
- The third, and final part, discusses the call disconnect sequence.

Keep in mind that this subdivision of a modem call into three parts, as shown in Figure 1-17, is not based on any specification; instead, it is a logical division for this particular call analysis.

There are certain features and aspects common to all modulations, but for an in-depth analysis, these broad generalities become limiting. For a detailed treatment such as this, there are simply too many modulations to discuss individually, and there are too many differences between them to group them effectively. Thus, for this discussion, only one has been selected, V.34, as the backbone of the analysis. Wherever possible, the discussion tries to illustrate how the newer modulations, such as V.90, differ from the V.34 behavior being explained.

Figure 1-17 *Breakdown of a Modem Call*

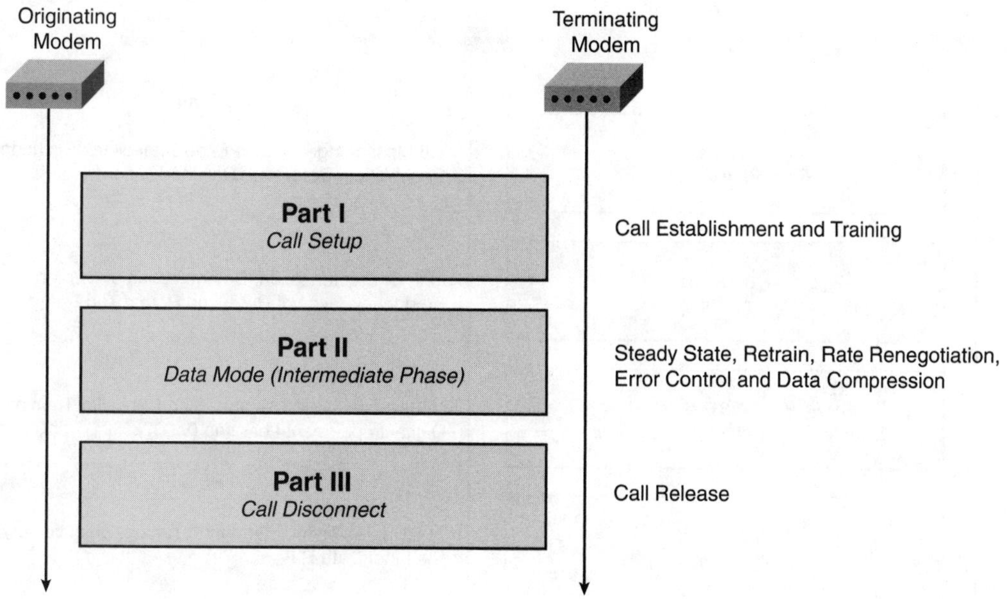

There are three principal reasons for using V.34:

- V.34 was a major and groundbreaking specification that introduced new concepts that were the foundation for subsequent modulations (that is, V.90 and V.92).
- V.34 is used for Super G3 faxes, so it ties in nicely with future topics of discussion.
- V.34 is still considered relatively modern and is still in common use today.

Call Setup

The V.34 initial handshaking procedure between an originating modem and a terminating modem can be broken down into the four primary phases shown in Figure 1-18.

Figure 1-18 *V.34 Modem Call Setup Procedure*

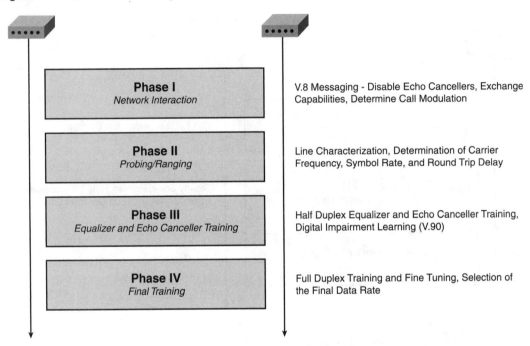

Phase I — Network Interaction	V.8 Messaging - Disable Echo Cancellers, Exchange Capabilities, Determine Call Modulation
Phase II — Probing/Ranging	Line Characterization, Determination of Carrier Frequency, Symbol Rate, and Round Trip Delay
Phase III — Equalizer and Echo Canceller Training	Half Duplex Equalizer and Echo Canceller Training, Digital Impairment Learning (V.90)
Phase IV — Final Training	Full Duplex Training and Fine Tuning, Selection of the Final Data Rate

Each of these phases has its own separate message exchange to fulfill its precise role in setting up a successful modem call. This section discusses each of these phases in detail and elaborates on the state of the call as it progresses through its handshake sequence.

Phase I: Network Interaction

The V.8 recommendation defines the first messages that are communicated between V.34 modems. This specification is used by a number of ITU-T V series modulations to establish communication and preliminary negotiations before the actual modulation begins. The V.8 negotiation identifies the capabilities of each device and determines the best modulation to use and some other parameters. Figure 1-19 illustrates the V.8 message exchange that occurs at the beginning of a V.34 modem call.

When the call is first answered by the terminating modem, it plays an answer tone called ANSam. Consisting of a 2100 Hz tone that is phase reversed approximately every 450 ms and amplitude modulated by a sine wave at 15 Hz, the ANSam lasts for a duration of three to four seconds and is used to disable network echo cancellers in the call path.

Figure 1-19 *V.34 Phase I Startup Procedure (V.8)*

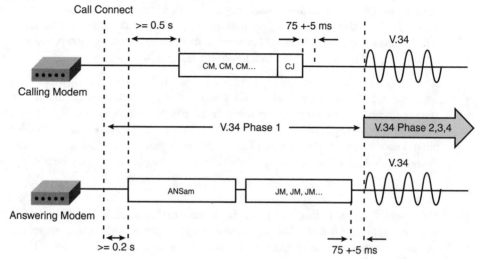

When the calling modem detects the ANSam, it sends a sequence of continuous CM (Calling Menu) messages. The CM message contains a detailed capabilities list (including modulation) of the calling modem. After detecting at least two identical CM messages, the answering modem responds with a continuous sequence of JM (Joint Menu) messages that contain the capabilities common to both calling and answering modems. If the answering modem for some reason does not support one of the capabilities advertised by the calling modem in the CM message, it may offer an alternative in its JM message sequence.

After detecting at least two identical JM messages, the calling device then transmits a CM terminator message (known as CJ) to acknowledge the JM message. After sending the CJ message, the calling modem pauses for about 75 ms and then begins operating in the selected mode. The CJ message just indicates the termination of the V.8 session, and it does not contain any additional information. When the answering modem receives the CJ message, it stops transmitting the JM sequence and pauses for approximately 75 ms before beginning to operate with the capabilities selected by the CM/JM exchange.

NOTE   V.8 messages are transferred by V.21 at 300 bps.

V.8 was released along with V.34 as a means of speeding up the initial answering sequence of modems. Older modulations used a large range of answer tones exchanged between the calling and called modems until they found one that matched as a means to determine an initial modulation. The V.8 CM/JM automatic modulation determination procedure (automode) did away with this and allowed for faster initial training.

It is worth noting that V.90 optionally uses a revised version of V.8 known as V.8bis. Both are procedures for exchanging capabilities and setting the mode of operation, but there are some differences between the two. One difference is that V.8bis has a more detailed list of modes that it can negotiate. It doesn't support some of the older modulations that V.8 does, but it does add newer ones. Another key difference is that V.8bis can negotiate a change in operating mode in the middle of a call, whereas V.8 can only do it at the beginning.

TIP   V.8bis was designed to facilitate switching a voice call into data mode, but this was never widely used, so the use of V.8bis is optional (unless using K56Flex), and in fact it can be useful to turn it off, because disabling it saves two or so seconds at the start of the training.

Phase II: Probing/Ranging

After a modulation has been selected via the V.8 procedure, the call progresses to Phase II. In this phase, the modems collect and exchange information about the characteristics of the line. The two primary methods of obtaining this detailed view of the channel are line probing and ranging. Line probing determines the SNR and the bandwidth of the channel, whereas ranging determines the network round-trip delay. This line analysis allows V.34/V.90 modem to choose the optimum operating parameters for the fastest and most robust connection for a particular line condition.

An elementary way of describing the message exchanges in Phase II is that it is an initial information exchange (INFO_0), followed by the ranging sequence, then the line probing sequence, and ending with a final information exchange (INFO_1). Figure 1-20 illustrates this simplified view of Phase II.

NOTE   Both INFO_0 and INFO_1 signals are designated by an *a* if sent by the answering modem or *c* if sent by the calling modem.

The initial information exchange in Phase II is via the INFO_0 message to convey the available capabilities and modulation parameters of both the calling and answering modems. An example of a parameter exchanged via INFO_0 is the supported symbol rates for the call.

Figure 1-20 *V.34 Phase II Startup Procedure*

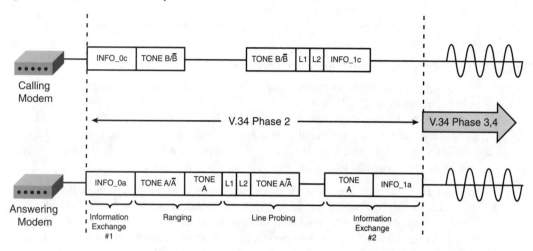

The next step of Phase II is ranging, which is the determination of the round-trip delay of the connection. This round-trip delay is used to set the modem's far-end echo canceller. The modems obtain this information by sending tones and transitioning to a phase reversal of that tone.

NOTE   Tone A is 2400 Hz, and Tone A̅ is the tone obtained by a 180 degree phase reversal of Tone A. Likewise, Tone B is 1200 Hz and Tone B̅ is its phase reversed counterpart.

When ranging has completed, the line probing process begins. This process yields the characteristics of the line, such as the bandwidth and SNR of the channel. The modems analyze the channel by sending the L1 and L2 signals, which are known as line-probing signals. L1 and L2 are made up of a list of tones with frequencies from 150 Hz to 3750 Hz in increments of 150 Hz (with 900 Hz, 1200 Hz, 1800 Hz, and 2400 Hz missing). The modems transmit these multitone signals to sweep the band and thus analyze the resultant distortion, SNR, and bandwidth of the channel.

The last thing to occur in Phase II is the information exchange between the two modems via the INFO_1 messages. The principal information carried by the INFO_1 messages is the results of the line probing that were collected. These results are provided as projected maximum data rates at the various symbol rates.

NOTE	Phase II in V.90 uses virtually an identical structure as V.34.

Phase III: Equalizer and Echo Canceller Training

The next step in setting up the physical connection is the equalizer and echo canceller training phase. An equalizer is an adaptive device in the modem that needs to be trained to compensate for distortion introduced by the PSTN transmission facilities. Likewise, the echo canceller in a modem requires training to eliminate signal reflections caused by hybrids in the call path. A hybrid is a tunable, impedance-matching device that converts between two-wire and four-wire circuits in telephony networks.

Phase III trains both these devices with a half-duplex training procedure as Figure 1-21 illustrates. The half-duplex nature of this phase is evident in Figure 1-21, which shows the originating modem is quiet while the terminating modem sends a sequence of signals to train its echo canceller. Correspondingly, the answering modem is quiet while the calling modem transmits a similar sequence to train its echo canceller.

Figure 1-21 *V.34 Phase III Startup Procedure*

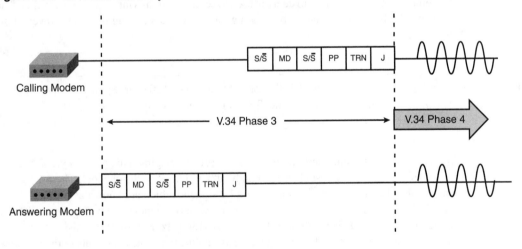

This training sequence is composed of an optional manufacturer-specific echo canceller training signal (MD) whose duration is determined by the round-trip delay that was obtained in Phase II. This proprietary MD signal is present in case the mandatory train signal (TRN) is unable to train the modem echo canceller. In addition to training the echo canceller of the transmitting modem, the TRN signal assists in training the remote modem's equalizer. The PP signal is a sliding frequency signal used for initially training the equalizer of the remote modem. Lastly, the J sequence is a repetition of a 16-bit sequence that determines the constellation size to be used in phase IV.

One big difference between V.34 and V.90 occurs in Phase III. V.90 adds a digital impairment learning (DIL) capability, which is used to identify digital impairments, such as robbed bit signaling (RBS) trunks, digital padding, and so on. This process occurs by the analog modem (client side) sending manufacturer-specific parameters, known as the DIL descriptor, to the digital modem (server side). The digital modem uses this description of the DIL sequence and then generates the DIL tone. This proprietary DIL tone is specific to each modem manufacturer. The analog modem receives this DIL sequence and analyzes it for possible digital impairments. Although it is theoretically possible to negotiate V.90 without the DIL sequence, it is extremely unlikely.

Phase IV: Final Training

As a result of the work in Phase III, the echo characteristics for the connection have now been learned, and the echo cancellers have been trained. Therefore, in Phase IV, both modems can transmit simultaneously and use the full bandwidth of the channel for the first time. Phase IV is a short phase that includes a fine-tuning while determining the final data rate to be used. Figure 1-22 shows this full-duplex training and its associated messaging.

Figure 1-22 *V.34 Phase IV Startup Procedure*

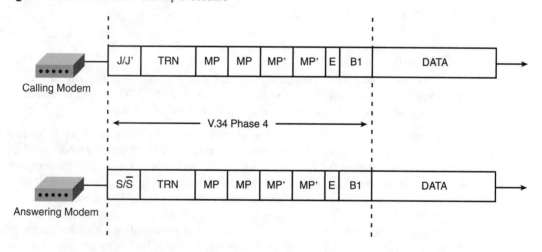

The TRN signal is a training sequence used to fine-tune the echo canceller and equalizer. This is followed by a sequence of exchanged modulation parameters, known as the MP signals. The modulation parameters sent between the modems are to be used for data mode transmission and include such things as maximum call modem–to–answer modem data signaling rate, maximum answer modem–to–call modem data signaling rate, and the trellis coder selection. The MP' signals are merely MP signals with the acknowledge bit set.

The E signal is a 20-bit sequence that marks the end of modulation parameter exchange. The last signal sent is B1, which is one data frame made up of scrambled 1s as its payload. Because this is the first time the modem is sending information using all the selected modulation parameters that will be used in data mode, this serves as a final test of the connection. After this, regular user data transmission begins.

V.90 has a similar Phase IV negotiation as V.34. One main difference is that in V.90 there are constellation parameters (CP) sent from the analog modem to the digital modem rather than MP signals. These constellation parameters contain information such as the downstream data signaling rate and the set of constellations.

Data Mode

The part of the call analyzed in this section is data mode. This is where Phase IV negotiations have completed and the procedures and protocols to begin data transmission occur. At this point of the call, several things can happen. Among them are the possible occurrences of speedshifts/retrains as an adaptive tool that the modulation protocol uses as a means of coping with the varying line conditions after the initial training. This is also the part of the call that will involve negotiation of higher-layer protocols, such as error control and data compression.

Retrains and Speedshifts

After the modems determine a final data rate, there is no guarantee that this will not change. The connection can, and likely will, undergo a speedshift/retrain. The newer modulation standards have made it mandatory for modems to support both of these.

A speedshift, also known as a rate renegotiation, is a relatively minor and quick procedure used to change the data rate in either direction. It can be invoked by either modem and at anytime after data transmission mode has begun. The shift in speed can be to a higher speed (fall forward) for improved throughput when line conditions improve, or to a slower one (fallback) when encountering impairments such as data errors and line noise. When a speedshift is initiated, it essentially goes back through Phase IV negotiation again. It just picks up at the TRN sequence, and then goes through the modulation parameter exchange (MP), the terminating E signal, and the B1 test data frame. Figure 1-23 illustrates the occurrence of a speedshift during a modem call. Note that just like in initial training, this sequence will yield a new negotiated data rate.

Figure 1-23 *Speedshift During a V.34 Modem Call*

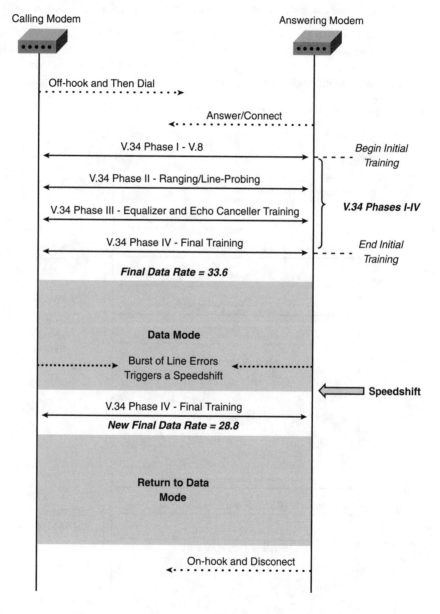

A retrain is a drastic measure that is a much longer and more involved process than a speedshift. Just like a speedshift, a retrain can be requested by either modem at any time and must be allowed by the other modem. Retrains occur for a variety of reasons, including serious line impairments, drastic changes in line conditions, or when multiple, successive speedshifts are ineffective. If retrains occur at precise, regular intervals, this is usually indicative of clock slips on a digital circuit in the modem transmission path.

Retrains require the modems to go all the way back to the beginning of Phase II (ranging and line probing) and undergo the remainder of the startup procedure. Clearly, the amount of time that data transfer is suppressed is much longer for a retrain than a speedshift. Figure 1-24 highlights how a retrain is negotiated within a modem call.

Figure 1-24 *Retrain During a V.34 Modem Call*

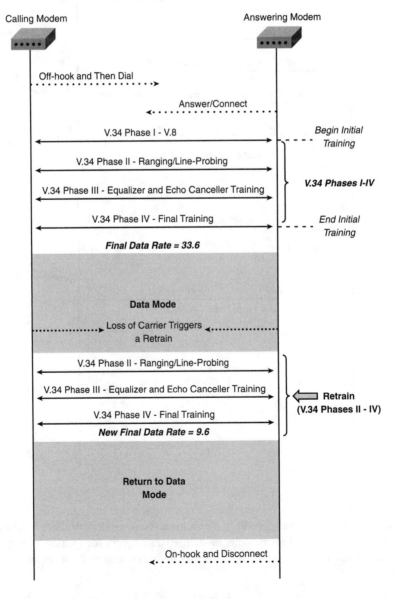

In the vast majority of cases, the initial connect speed reported for a call is not indicative of the actual throughput for the call. Because the speaker on most modems is off after initial training has completed, the potentially negative effects of retrains and speedshifts are usually hidden from the user. Excessive retrains are especially pernicious and are commonly a symptom of bad lines or serious problems in the transmission path.

Error Control

The modulation section discussed that Trellis coded modulation (TCM) added redundancy to the data, so line noise produced lower error rates. This form of error control, known as Forward Error Correction, is done during the modulation scheme and it is a part of the training sequence. Virtually all protocols since V.32 (that is, V.34, V.90, and so on) have such a form of error control embedded in the modulation itself.

The error control offered by TCM may reduce bit errors, but does not eliminate them entirely. In addition to the error correction in the modulation protocol, modems may optionally negotiate an error control (EC) protocol after modem training has completed. This EC protocol running in an upper layer is necessary to guarantee reliable data transport over a modem link.

Without EC, data is transmitted over the DCE link as it comes in on the DTE link. That is, it will use asynchronous framing to send the data over the PSTN link. Remember that async framing sends data as a 10-bit character at a time (that is, 8 data bits, 1 start bit, and 1 stop bit). This overhead yields only an 80 percent channel efficiency.

If an EC protocol is used, the data between the modems is transported using synchronous framing. This data is placed into link layer frames, as shown in Figure 1-25. Consequently, EC allows for a much more efficient use of the bandwidth (that is, around 95 percent channel efficiency). In addition, EC is required for data compression, which can yield even greater throughput benefits.

Figure 1-25 *V.42 Synchronous Framing*

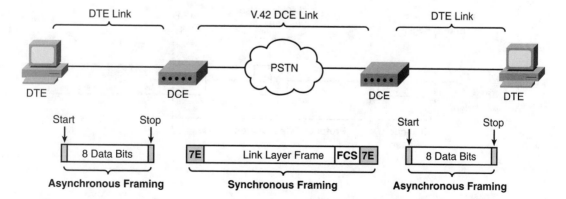

The two major EC protocols are Link Access Procedure for Modems (LAPM) and Microcom Network Protocol Class 4 (MNP4). The standard used by most modems to negotiate an error correcting procedure is ITU-T V.42. This standard designates LAPM as the primary EC protocol, but optionally allows fallback to MNP4 if LAPM is not negotiated. If neither EC protocol is negotiated, then async framing will be used.

NOTE   LAPM is an HDLC variant and has the same basic HDLC frame format and frame types used in Link Access Procedure on the B channel (LAPB), Link Access Procedure on the D channel (LAPD), and other HDLC-based protocols. The section "Message Format Overview" in the next chapter goes into more detail about HDLC.

After modems have completed training to their appropriate modulation, the V.42 LAPM EC protocol may be subsequently established. This establishment process is divided into two different phases: the detection phase and the protocol establishment phase. Figure 1-26 shows how the modems progress through these phases to set up a synchronously framed, error corrected connection.

Figure 1-26   *V.42 LAPM Protocol Negotiation*

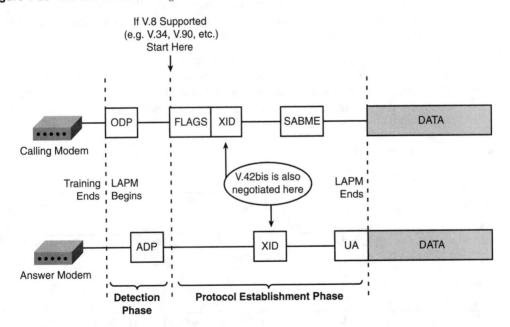

The purpose of the V.42 detection phase is to determine whether the remote side supports LAPM error correcting. This phase is undergone by modems that trained to an older modulation that does not support V.8. There is a well-defined bit pattern, known as the Originator Detection Pattern (ODP), that the LAPM originating modem sends to announce that it can do LAPM. If the answering modem is V.42 capable, it responds with another bit pattern known as the Answer Detection Pattern (ADP) indicating that LAPM EC protocol will be used, or that no EC is desired. If the ADP is not detected within a prescribed amount of time (T400 timer), the modem tries an alternate EC protocol (such as MNP4), if available, or falls back to non-EC mode. The newer modulations that support V.8 skip the detection phase altogether. The reason they do this is because they indicate the ability to do V.42 EC in the CM/JM exchange of V.8.

When both modems have agreed that they support LAPM, they continue on to the protocol establishment phase of V.42. The purpose of the protocol establishment phase is to negotiate the operating parameters of the EC session and establish the EC session between the modems. Figure 1-26 illustrated the message exchange in this phase. The central part of the negotiation is the interchange of Exchange Identification frames (XID). The XID exchange is used to negotiate the parameters of the V.42 EC session. Parameters such as frame length (128 bytes by default), various timers, maximum retransmission counters, and so forth are set here. Finally, the phase ends in the usual HDLC-like SABME/UA exchange to put the EC session into a connected state.

When doing V.42, if LAPM is not negotiated or fails, there is the provision to allow the modems to alternately negotiate MNP4 as the EC protocol. As Figure 1-27 shows, the frame formats of MNP4 and LAPM differ, so they are not compatible with each other. Despite this, they both share several basic things in common that make them EC protocols.

Figure 1-27 *LAPM and MNP Frame Formats*

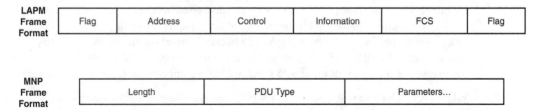

Both LAPM and MNP4 use a cyclic redundancy check (CRC) algorithm to detect bit errors. In the case of LAPM, the sending modem adds the result of a 16-bit or 32-bit CRC calculation as a 2- or 4-byte Frame Check Sequence (FCS) field to the end of the data frame. When the receiving modem gets the data frame, it performs the same calculation. If the results of the CRC calculation are not the same, this indicates a line error. Therefore, the CRC algorithm is the error detection portion of the EC protocol.

When errors are detected, both LAPM and MNP4 are able to retransmit the corrupted data frames. This adds the error correction element to V.42. In the case of LAPM, when the receiving modem has determined that there is a transmission error, due to the CRC result comparison, it sends a reject frame (REJ) to the sending modem. This REJ allows the receiving modem to request a retransmission of a range of corrupted frames. Optionally, LAPM can also negotiate the ability to send a Selective Reject (SREJ) frame to request the retransmission of the single frame that contained the error.

One benefit of having the EC protocol perform the error detection and correction is that it doesn't need to be delegated to higher-layer protocols. If no EC were negotiated, and async framing were done on the DCE link, the next-layer protocol, such as PPP, would have to do the error detection. Also, in that case, the error correction would come in the form of a TCP retransmission. A TCP retransmission of an IP packet may be much more data than a single HDLC frame. This means that recovering from a line error is typically much quicker if an EC protocol is negotiated. Therefore, this is yet another reason why the effective throughput is better for a connection with EC enabled on it.

Data Compression

Data compression is a means by which modems can increase their effective throughput for a particular modulation. If EC is negotiated on a link, the modems may then optionally negotiate a data compression method. Three data compression methods are widely implemented by modems: V.42bis, V.44, and MNP5. Of the three, V.44 is normally preferred because it usually yields better compression than the other two. The actual amount of compression achieved always depends on the type and amount of data and the quality of the link.

MNP5 uses two types of compression: Adaptive Huffman Encoding and Run Length Encoding. These two compression types are not discussed here because they are covered in detail in the section "Modified Huffman" in the next chapter. Sending already compressed data is counterproductive when using MNP5 because, based on the nature of the two compression forms it uses, it will actually increase the size of the data if the data is already compressed or highly random. MNP5 typically has a compression ratio of less than 2:1.

V.42bis is much more widespread than MNP5 and is optionally negotiated as part of V.42 LAPM EC protocol. The V.42bis compression session and its parameters are set in the XID exchange of LAPM. Some of the parameters negotiated are number of codewords and maximum string length.

V.42bis is based on a variant of the Lempel-Ziv compression algorithm that detects string repetition on-the-fly. The algorithm allows the modem to dynamically analyze the incoming data for repeated character strings and build a tree structure dictionary for these strings. Indices to the repeated strings in the self-building tree dictionary are called codewords. When the data is being transmitted, these much shorter codewords are substituted for the repeated strings. This method allows for compression ratios of around 4:1.

In addition to superior compression ratios, V.42bis has another significant advantage over MNP5. V.42bis has two operating modes: compressed mode and transparent mode. The controller doing the compression can gauge whether data compression is yielding an improved throughput. If it determines that it is not, it switches from compressed mode to transparent mode and sends out raw, uncompressed data. The controller continually switches from compressed mode to transparent mode and back again as many times as needed throughout the length of a call. Therefore, unlike with MNP5 when sending already compressed data, V.42bis never yields less throughput than that of the original data stream.

V.44 is the latest modem compression standard released, and it is used in conjunction with the V.92 modulation. Like V.42bis, it is also negotiated during the XID exchange of V.42 LAPM. It is based on another variation of the Lempel-Ziv compression algorithm. It has slightly better compression ratios than V.42bis and is optimized for carrying HTML data.

In many cases, the DTE itself performs data compression (ZIP, RAR, JPG, and so on), and this might appear to be a better alternative to modem compression. The question of whether to use modem compression or the compression available with the DTE devices will depend on the specific circumstances. DTE-based compression might appear to offer better compression ratios because the speed between the DTE and modem will often only exceed the carrier speed of the modem by a factor of two, thus limiting the usefulness of modem-based compression. However, DTE compression might be limited by CPU issues that will not scale as the number of modem connections increase per DTE device.

Call Disconnect

A modem can commence a graceful disconnect at any time after data mode is entered. It can be done from the AT command interface (typically ATH), or a drop in DTR, or any other reason that makes the modem go on-hook in an orderly manner. Such a disconnect can be initiated by either the calling or the answering modem.

A normal modem disconnect is typically done by sending a disconnect frame. The type of disconnect frame depends on the EC protocol that was negotiated. For V.42, a LAPM disconnect frame (DISC) is used, whereas for MNP4 a Link Disconnect (LD) frame is used.

For calls with no EC or where the disconnect frame doesn't arrive, is corrupted by noise, or is incompatible, the modulation protocol itself can disconnect the call. Newer modulations (that is, V.32bis, V.34, V.90, and so on) all support their own graceful disconnect procedure. This procedure, known as cleardown, works much like a speedshift. As in rate renegotiation, the disconnect initiating modem essentially goes back through Phase IV negotiations. The difference being that in cleardown the MP signals have the "maximum call modem–to–answer modem data signaling rate" and the "maximum answer modem–to–call modem data signaling rate" fields set to 0. Therefore, as Figure 1-28 illustrates, a cleardown is merely a speedshift to a 0 speed.

Figure 1-28 *V.34 Cleardown Sequence*

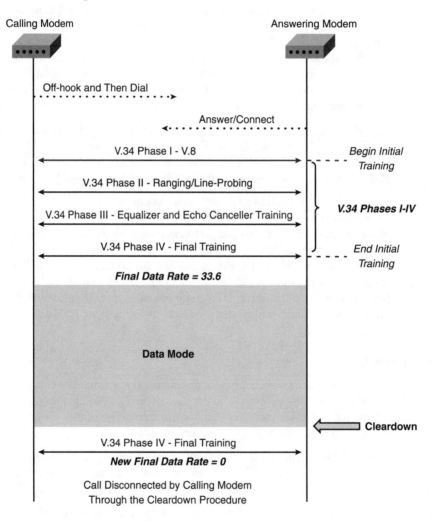

Summary

This chapter provides a meaningful look at core modem technology that will be applicable when the discussion turns to modem calls going over an IP network. The beginning sections are meant to clarify modem architecture and classifications. The middle of the chapter delves deeper into the various protocols and standards that govern the communication and negotiation between the modem and the host, and between two modems. The remainder of the chapter takes a more practical approach and breaks down and details the component parts of a modem call. This chapter is intended to give you a good working knowledge of modem operation and serve as a building block to future discussions that reference this material.

CHAPTER 2

How Fax Works

With the advent of IP telephony (IPT), fax technology became meshed with a transport path quite different from a traditional public switched telephone network (PSTN) environment. However, the basic rules and specifications of standard fax technology still apply to fax over an IP network. This merging of an old and new technology makes it imperative for anyone working with fax technology in today's IPT world to have a fundamental grasp of basic fax principles.

The focus of this chapter revolves around Group 3 (G3) fax technology and messaging. The G3 fax standard ensures worldwide interoperability among fax devices from different vendors. This chapter covers the following topics:

- **A Brief History of Fax**: Provides a historical context to the evolution of fax technology.

- **Fax Components**: Explains the architecture of basic fax devices.

- **Group Classifications**: Details the different fax group classifications.

- **Specifications and Standards**: Discusses the industry standards that define fax technology.

- **Fax Modulations**: Specifies the modulation standards used in G3 fax calls.

- **Fax Messaging**: Explains the phases and messages associated with a fax call. This section also includes a complete fax call analysis, explanation of call timers, and detailed coverage of the optional Error Correction Mode (ECM) and Super G3 features.

- **Page Encoding**: Details the creation of a fax page image using scan lines and discusses the three primary image encoding algorithms: Modified Huffman (MH), Modified READ (MR), and Modified Modified READ (MMR).

Rarely seen features and options such as Group 4 (G4) faxing, color faxes, and nontraditional G3 messaging scenarios are beyond the scope of this book. Only the pertinent areas essential to understanding faxes in the complex world of IPT are given full coverage.

A Brief History of Fax

Fax machines can trace their roots back to a patent issued in 1843 to the Scottish clockmaker Alexander Bain (1811–1877). Bain discovered a way to transmit a two-dimensional image as a series of electrical pulses across two wires.

The genius of Bain's patent was the stylus mechanism used to scan the image. Building on his knowledge as a clockmaker, Bain invented a stylus that was an electrically conductive swinging pendulum. As the pendulum swung back and forth across a raised image on a copper plate, electrical pulses were generated. In addition, each swing of the pendulum moved the copper image up a small amount so that the pendulum was able to scan the entire plate surface.

These electrical pulses were then sent across two wires to a receiving device that also contained a pendulum. The receiving device's pendulum was synchronized with the sending device's pendulum, which allowed the receiving side to generate an exact replica of the original image using electrically sensitive paper. Figure 2-1 shows Bain's original drawing submitted as part of British patent 9745.

Although Bain's facsimile apparatus patent was never realized as a working fax device during his lifetime, the concepts and principles discovered by Bain are still found in fax machines today. Bain's stylus has been replaced by sophisticated electronic scanners, and pendulums are no longer required for synchronization. However, images are still scanned progressively, line by line, and sent across wires as electrical pulses. Bain was truly a man ahead of his time, and even ahead of telephony pioneer, Alexander Graham Bell, who would not patent his telephone until more than 30 years later.

In 1852, English physicist Frederick Bakewell demonstrated the first fax transmission at the World's Fair in London. Bakewell's device was somewhat different from Bain's in that it used tinfoil-covered revolving drums for image transmission and reception. On the transmitting side, the image was written on tinfoil with a nonconductive "ink" and wrapped around the cylinder. On the receiving side, the image was drawn using an electrified stylus that contacted chemically treated paper encircling the turning cylinder.

In 1862, L'Abbé Caselli legitimized Bain's genius by successfully testing a fax apparatus, the pantelegraph, that bore a remarkable similarity to Bain's design. The pantelegraph was a large device made of cast iron that stood more than 6 feet tall. In 1865, it started operating between Paris and Lyon and sent nearly 5000 facsimile transmissions in its first year. Unfortunately, the pantelegraph was not commercially successful and subsequently fell into disuse by about 1870.

Figure 2-1 *Alexander Bain's Facsimile Apparatus, British Patent 9745[1]*

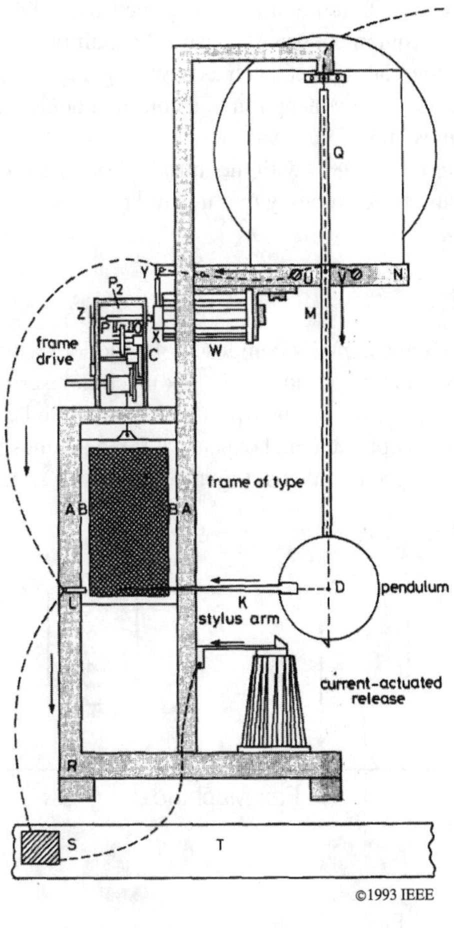

©1993 IEEE

Notable improvements to fax technology by Elisha Gray and Dr. Arthur Korn moved fax technology closer to what we know today. Elisha Gray patented a handwriting transmission system named the telautograph that was first demonstrated in 1893. What made Gray's telautograph so special was its ability to write on normal stationery paper. In 1902, Dr. Arthur Korn demonstrated a photoelectric scanning system. Previously, all other fax systems relied on some sort of stylus directly contacting the image, as first patented by Bain. Korn's invention allowed for an electronic eye to scan an image and create electrical pulses based on the dark and light areas present on the image itself.

---

1. Figure 2-1 appears courtesy of "Alexander Bain, a most ingenious and meritorious inventor" by Professor R. W. Burns, Engineering Science and Education Journal.

From that point forward, fax technology started to take hold commercially and become a viable method for the transmission of information such as pictures. Fax networks started operating in the United States and Europe in the early 1900s, but access was somewhat limited because the equipment was expensive. In addition, these first fax networks addressed only a niche commercial market, such as news organizations. The progression of fax technology from its initial conception to a common device that tens of millions of people have in their homes and offices was slow considering that its invention preceded the telephone. Not until the 1980s with the introduction of the G3 standard would faxing become the ubiquitous technology that it is today.

Fax Components

A fax machine is fundamentally composed of a modem with an image scanner and printer attached to it. The modem portion of the fax machine uses standard modulations to send and receive images, and the scanner/printer function handles the input and output of fax documents. More complicated and expensive fax machines provide better scanners and printers and higher-speed modems. Figure 2-2 shows a simple overview of a fax machine.

Figure 2-2 *Simple View of a Fax Machine*

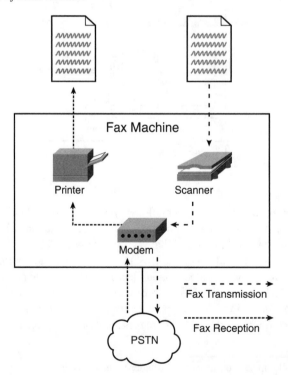

Present trends are showing a decline in standalone fax machines. Fax functionality today is being packaged in "all-in-one" devices that also include a scanner, printer, and copier. As illustrated in Figure 2-2, combining a fax capability with these other functions is a natural fit.

Group Classifications

In the beginning, facsimile communication was achieved through proprietary solutions with a dedicated use, such as sending and receiving pictures for newspapers. With the evolution of fax groupings pertaining to varying standards, fax messaging has grown rapidly, and interoperability is no longer a major issue.

An international standards body called the International Telecommunications Union Standardization Sector (ITU-T) recognized the need for establishing transmission standards that could be applied industry-wide for use by all fax devices. The results are (to date) four different categories ranging from Group 1 to Group 4. These group designations are a quick identifier for fax particulars such as the speed of the fax machine in question and basic information about the device's capabilities. Table 2-1 summarizes the official ITU-T fax group classifications.

Table 2-1   *ITU-T Fax Group Classifications*

Group Designation	Relevant Specifications	Transmission Time (8.5" x 11" page)
G1 (Group 1)	ITU-T Recommendation T.2	6 minutes
G2 (Group 2)	ITU-T Recommendation T.3	3 minutes
G3 (Group 3)	ITU-T Recommendation T.30, T.4, and T.6	1 minute or less
G4 (Group 4)	ITU-T Recommendation T.6, T.503, T.521, T.563, T.72, T.62, T.62 bis, T.70, and F.161	Less than a minute

Group 1 and Group 2 fax machines are older and not really used anymore. The main problem with Group 1 fax devices was the absence of worldwide compatibility. The T.2 recommendation used for Group 1 fax defined a frequency of 1300 Hz for white areas on the page and 2300 Hz for black. However, in North America, 1500 Hz was used for white and 2300 or 2400 Hz for black. The different frequency usage by Group 1 faxes prevented the interoperability of fax machines between different parts of the world.

Group 2 faxes resolved the Group 1 interoperability problem while increasing the speed at which pages could be sent and received. Group 2 faxes were based off the ITU-T Recommendation T.3 which specified a more efficient modulation scheme. This allowed Group 2 faxes to send and receive pages about twice as fast as Group 1. Because of the demands for even faster transmission speeds and a higher resolution, however, Group 2 fax was eventually replaced by the current Group 3 standard.

Group 3 or G3 is the most common fax machine type today and supports page transmission speeds up to 14400 bps. Basically, any fax machine that is in use today on the PSTN is Group 3 compliant. G3 faxes make use of ITU-T Recommendations T.30, T.4, and T.6 to ensure proper communication between all G3 fax devices. Note that the ITU-T T.30 specification that G3 is based on has evolved over the years. Enhancements such as color faxing, higher resolutions, and faster modulation speeds have been added. These added features should not affect G3 compatibility between different fax machines, but newer features included as part of Group 3 faxing might not be available on older G3 fax devices.

Super G3 is an extension of the Group 3 classification, and it specifies transmission at V.34 speeds up to 33600 bps. Although Super G3 is not given its own official Group designation, more and more fax machines are offering support for Super G3. Be aware that some fax machine manufacturers may refer to Super G3 as SG3, high-speed faxing, or V.34 fax. Super G3 is backward compatible with G3 so in a PSTN environment there should not be any incompatibilities between Super G3 and G3 fax devices. The section "Super G3 Faxing," later in this chapter, discusses Super G3 in more depth.

The last fax classification is Group 4, and this is used with fax devices that connect via ISDN. Group 4 faxes are the fastest in terms of transmission speed, but they are also the most expensive and not as common as G3 and Super G3. Group 4 fax devices are not compatible with Group 3 devices.

Specifications and Standards

Because all modern mainstream fax devices adhere to the G3 classification, the standards that make up G3 are the most relevant for discussion in this book. The three main ITU-T recommendations that commonly define G3 are ITU-T T.30, ITU-T T.4, and ITU-T T.6. The T.30 specification describes how fax devices communicate with one another, and T.4 and T.6 define how page information is encoded for transmission. Figure 2-3 illustrates the use of the T.30, T.4, and T.6 protocols during a fax transmission.

The T.30 specification defines the exact protocol that fax devices use to communicate with one another over a telephony network, and it is responsible for all the signaling and nego-tiation that needs to occur before pages can be transmitted. With each fax call, both fax devices must agree to myriad options before a page can be sent or received. Recommendation T.30 handles all of this negotiation and continues to be involved as pages are acknowledged. At the conclusion of the fax call, T.30 makes sure that a graceful disconnect occurs between the fax devices.

The T.4 and T.6 specifications specify how the page information is encoded in a fax transaction. When a fax page is scanned, it contains a large amount of information, especially at the higher-resolution settings. This information needs to be transmitted as efficiently as possible without any loss of page information.

Figure 2-3   *Recommendation T.30, T.4, and T.6 Protocols During a Fax Transmission*

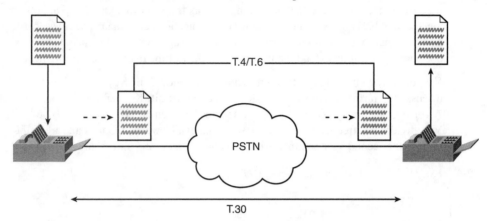

Encoding schemes are compression algorithms that define how fax page information will be communicated between fax devices. The three encoding schemes seen in G3 faxes are Modified Huffman (MH), Modified READ (MR), and Modified Modified READ (MMR). All of these encoding methods divide the page into horizontal lines, or scan lines, but MH encoding is the simplest. MH counts the continuous groupings of black and white pixels in each line, and then these are encoded. MR is a more complicated two-dimensional encoding algorithm that defines a reference line and then encodes changes between the reference line and the next line. Compared to MH, MR encoding can improve page compression by up to 50 percent.

MMR is defined in ITU-T Recommendation T.6 for G4 faxing (MH and MR are defined in T.4), but it is also seen with G3 fax pages transmitted using Error Correction Mode (ECM). ECM is an optional G3 fax feature that ensures the integrity of the fax page data through the use of an error correction procedure. Other than a few notable differences, the MMR encoding scheme is actually very similar to MR while offering further compression of the fax page. The encoding schemes of MH, MR, and MMR are covered in more detail at the end of this chapter.

Fax Modulations

Fax devices use multiple modulation schemes for communication. Many of these modulation schemes may seem familiar because they are used by modems. You can learn more about the concept of modulation, and read a discussion about common modem modulation types in the section "Modulation" in Chapter 1, "How Modems Work."

The ITU-T Recommendation V.21 is one of the first modulation standards created, and it is used for all the messaging that occurs in a G3 fax transmission. Operating at 300 bps, the low speed of V.21 ensures a more reliable communication between fax machines, particularly over low-quality phone lines. Because the fax messages are small in size, the lower speed does not significantly extend the transmission time of the overall fax communication.

V.21 employs a modulation type known as Frequency Shift Keying (FSK), which is discussed in further detail in the section "Frequency Shift Keying (FSK)" in Chapter 1. A voice-grade line typically allows frequencies between 300 Hz and 3400 Hz to pass, and V.21 divides this frequency range into two channels. However, G3 fax calls are half duplex, so only the second V.21 channel is implemented. Figure 2-4 shows an example.

Figure 2-4   *FSK Modulation Used by Half-Duplex V.21*

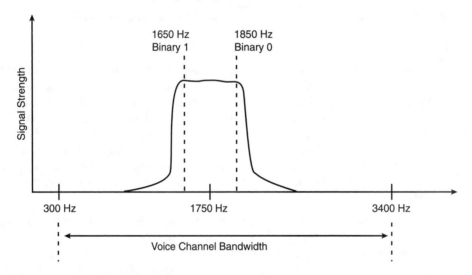

The second channel of V.21 defines the nominal mean frequency as 1750 Hz. From this base, V.21 then specifies the frequency values representing a binary 0 and 1. A binary 1 occurs at 1650 Hz (100 Hz below the nominal mean frequency) and a binary 0 occurs at 1850 Hz (100 Hz above the nominal mean frequency).

When the actual fax page is transmitted, a higher-speed modulation is used rather than V.21. The V.21 speed of 300 bps is much too slow for the large amount of data that makes up a fax page, so a faster speed is needed.

Fax machines may be capable of a few different modulations, and within each of these modulations there are different speeds. Table 2-2 summarizes the common modulations that are used in G3 fax calls.

Table 2-2   *Common Modulations Used in G3 Fax Calls*

ITU Standard	Speeds (bps)	Modulation Type
V.21	300	FSK (Frequency Shift Keying)
V.27 ter	2400, 4800	DPSK (Differential Phase Shift Keying)
V.29	4800, 7200, 9600	QAM (Quadrature Amplitude Modulation)
V.17	7200, 9600, 12200, 14400	TCM (Trellis Coded Modulation)

Fax machines always attempt to transmit their pages at the highest possible speeds, and the V.17 standard, with a top speed of 14400 bps, provides the fastest page-transmission speed for a G3 fax call. If both fax machines support V.17, this is the modulation that will be attempted. If the faxes fail to train using V.17 at 14.4 Kbps, the fax devices try the next fastest speed within that same modulation. Training is a process that occurs when fax machines attempt to agree on the modulation that will be used for page transmission.

If V.17 is not supported by one of the fax devices, the sending device tries the next modulation with highest possible speed. Similarly, if all the modulation speeds within V.17 failed to train, the sending device tries another slower modulation type, such as V.29.

Fax Messaging

If you've spent any time at all around fax machines, you've probably heard the tones and chirping sounds that a fax machine makes when it starts talking to another fax device. Or you may have heard the short beeping tone that plays when a fax machine mistakenly dials a nonfax number. Sometimes this fax beeping tone is even left in voice mail as a message. These sounds that are heard emanating from fax machines all have specific purposes and they need to be understood, especially for anyone working with fax transmissions in IPT environments.

Before diving into specific messages, it is important to take a broad look at what happens when a document is passed between two fax machines. From a telephony perspective, a fax call begins just like a voice call, with the fax device going off-hook and digits being passed to route the call to the proper destination. On the receiving end, the call is answered by the terminating fax machine. At this point, a negotiation occurs between the two machines. Both machines have to agree on a number of parameters before the fax document can be sent. These parameters include the enabling of error correction, the page resolution, the modulation used for page transmission, and more. After the parameters are set in both machines, the document can then be sent and received successfully. After the successful page transmissions and confirmation messages, the fax call gracefully disconnects, and both fax machines return to their on-hook, idle states.

Phases of a Fax Call

To simplify the fax messaging process further, T.30 breaks down a fax call into five distinct phases. Recognizing these phases assists you in further understanding the messaging that occurs between two fax devices. Figure 2-5 summarizes these fax messaging phases.

Figure 2-5   *Phases of a T.30 Fax Call*

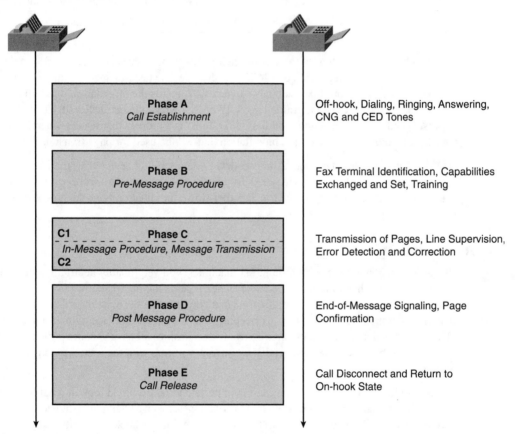

Phase A is the call establishment phase. This includes the calling fax machine going off-hook, dialing the answering fax machine, and playing the calling tone (CNG). More information on the CNG tone is found in the section "CNG Tone" later in this chapter. The answering fax machine rings and then answers the call with an initial answer tone known as the called terminal identification (CED) tone. After the answer tone, fax negotiation begins and the call enters Phase B. The CED tone is covered in detail in a later section titled "CED Tone."

Phase B is known as the pre-message procedure. At this point, the fax negotiation occurs before the page is sent. In reality, this negotiation is more of a capabilities exchange followed by the calling fax determining the parameters that will be used for the page transmission to the terminating fax. Along with the identification of capabilities, Phase B also includes modulation training and optional activities such as polling and terminal identification. As soon as the fax page starts to be transmitted, Phase C begins.

Phase C is divided into two subphases, C1 and C2, and deals with the actual transmission of the fax page information. Phase C1 is the in-message procedure and occurs at the same time as the page transmission. This phase controls message signaling such as synchronization, error detection and correction, and line supervision. Phase C2 is the actual message transmission and this is typically covered by ITU-T Recommendation T.4. When fax pages are being actively sent and received, the fax devices are in Phase C.

Phase D, the post-message procedure, includes information pertaining to end-of-message, confirmation, multipage, and end-of-facsimile procedure signaling. After each page is sent, the calling fax machine notifies the answering machine that the sending of page information is complete and waits for a confirmation. The machines enter Phase D each time there is a break or cessation of the fax page information. When there is no more page information to be sent, the fax machines move to Phase E, the last phase in a fax transaction.

Phase E manages call release and the return of both fax machines to an on-hook, idle state. A specific T.30 disconnect message (DCN) indicates the initialization of Phase E. After Phase E is completed and the call is released, the fax machines are able to repeat these phases for subsequent fax calls.

Message Format Overview

With the exception of certain signals that are nothing but single frequency tones, the T.30 messages used in communication between two fax devices consist of binary coded data. From a high-level overview, this can simply be viewed as a preamble followed by the binary data itself in the form of High-Level Data Link Control (HDLC) frame(s) as shown in Figure 2-6.

Figure 2-6   *Primary Components of a T.30 Fax Message*

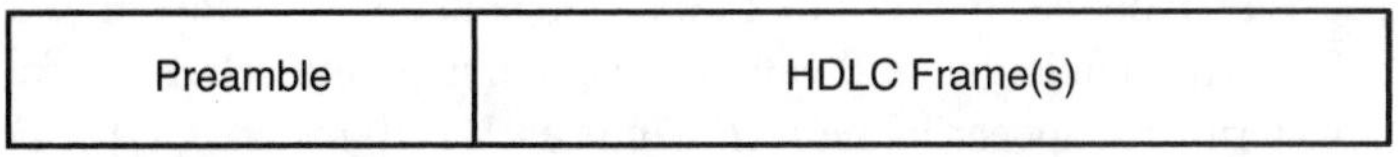

Preamble	HDLC Frame(s)

A G3 fax preamble occurs every time new information is sent in either direction. The preamble consists of repeated flag sequences that last for about one second. These flags help condition the line so that the ensuing real data can pass without problems. If you're listening during a fax transmission, the preamble sounds like warbling tones through the fax machine speaker. These preamble tones occur quite often because they precede any HDLC frame or group of frames from either the sending or receiving side, usually following short silence periods.

At least one mandatory message contained in an HDLC frame will follow every preamble, and in many cases optional messages in additional HDLC frames will also be present. When optional T.30 messages are present, they precede the mandatory message and come right after the preamble. All of this binary information (preamble and HDLC frames) is then modulated using V.21 at a speed of 300 bps. An illustration of this concept is shown later in Figures 2-12 and 2-16 when the specific fax negotiation messages are discussed in more detail.

In addition to T.30 fax messaging, HDLC is the basis of many other data protocols, and its frame format is straightforward. As illustrated in Figure 2-7, HDLC uses flags at each end of the frame with an address, control, information, and Frame Check Sequence (FCS) field in the middle.

Figure 2-7   *HDLC Frame Format Overview*

Flag	Address	Control	Information	FCS	Flag

ITU-T T.30 defines fixed values for the flag, address, and control fields of the HDLC frame. These three fields are all 1 byte in length. The flag value is the common 7E or 0111 1110, whereas the address field is always set to all 1s or 1111 1111. The control field uses a value of 1100 X000, where X is always set to 0 unless it is the final HDLC frame in a sequence, in which case it is set to 1.

The 2-byte FCS field will vary for each HDLC frame. Often referred to as a cyclic redundancy check (CRC), the FCS is a binary calculation using the bits that comprise the HDLC frame minus the flags. Like a fancier version of the asynchronous parity bit, the FCS is an error detection mechanism that helps to ensure that the HDLC frame is received error free.

With most of the HDLC frame fields set to fixed or calculated values, the information field becomes the location where all the actual fax messaging occurs. As Figure 2-8 shows, the information field in an HDLC fax frame is divided into two parts: the facsimile control field (FCF) and the facsimile information field (FIF).

The FCF defines the type of T.30 message that is contained in the HDLC frame. This is an 8- or 16-bit field that is always at the beginning of the HDLC information field. Specific bit patterns that appear in the FCF define each T.30 message type. For example, a digital identification signal (DIS) message is represented by a pattern of 0000 0001 in the FCF field. You can find a complete listing of the bit patterns used by each message in Section 5.3.6.1 of ITU-T Recommendation T.30. You can find ITU-T Recommendations at http://www.itu.int/ITU-T/.

The FIF follows the FCF within the information field of the fax HDLC frame. The parameters and capabilities defined for the FIF depend on what T.30 message type is defined in the FCF. For example, if a DIS message is defined in the FCF, the parameters that follow in the FIF are specific to that DIS message.

Figure 2-8   *FCF and FIF Fields Within a Fax HDLC Frame*

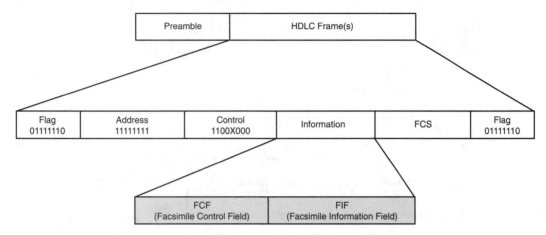

Analyzing a Basic Fax Call

Although the phases of a fax call provide a general overview of how fax calls work, the next step is to look into the actual T.30 messages and tones that make up these phases. Analyzing a basic call is the easiest way to get acquainted with fax signals. Figure 2-9 illustrates an example of a typical, two-page G3 fax transaction.

In Figure 2-9, the fax machine on the left is originating a call to the fax machine on the right. The CNG and CED signals are simple tones that occur in the very beginning of the call. These tones are followed by the T.30 messages that set up the parameters that will be used for the message transmission. Other than the CNG and CED signals (which are just single-frequency tones), all the other T.30 signals are modulated using V.21 at 300 bps; these are shown as low-speed messages in Figure 2-9. Fortunately, the message contents are relatively small, so the 300 bps speed used in the T.30 messages is adequate. The actual message or fax page information is sent using a modulation of a much higher speed. The exact modulation and speed is determined during exchange of the T.30 DIS and digital command signal (DCS) messages. Using a V.17 modulation, normal G3 faxes can transmit pages at 14400 bps.

The T.30 messages illustrated in Figure 2-9 are critical to every basic G3 fax transaction. Now we'll take an in-depth look at these signals along with some other important ones that are not included in the figure.

Figure 2-9 *Two-Page G3 Fax Transaction*

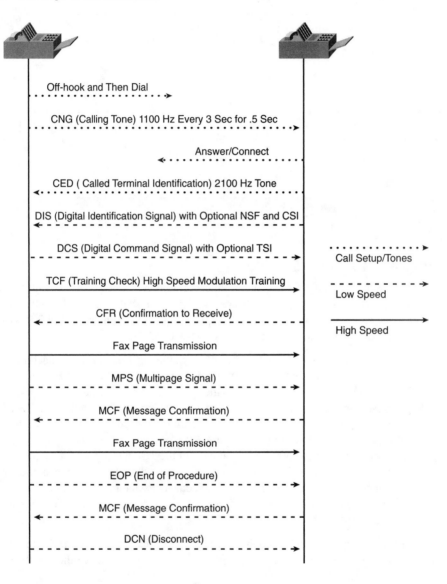

CNG Tone

As the call is connecting, the originating fax machine starts playing a CNG or calling tone. The CNG signal is simply an 1100 Hz tone that plays for half a second, and then repeats every three seconds. As defined in the T.30 specification, it is permissible for the timing of the CNG tone to vary by ± 15 percent, and for the frequency to be within 38 Hz of the 1100 Hz value.

The purpose of this tone is to notify the answering device or person that a fax machine is originating the call on the other end. People who have had the unpleasant experience of a fax machine mistakenly trying to continuously fax something to their house or office phone are probably familiar with this tone.

The CNG tone has other functions, too. The tone lets the answering fax machine know that the originating fax machine has a document to send and is awaiting a DIS to begin fax negotiation. The CNG is also used by some multifunction devices to determine whether an incoming call is fax or voice so that the call can be handled appropriately. Figure 2-10 illustrates the T.30 fax CNG tone.

Figure 2-10 *T.30 Fax CNG Tone*

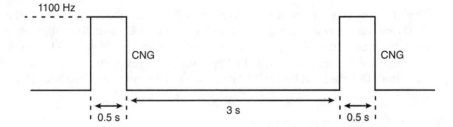

CED Tone

When the terminating fax machine answers the call, it sends a called terminal identification or CED signal. The CED signal is just a 2100 Hz tone that typically plays for about 3 seconds. As defined in T.30, the CED tone is "a continuous 2100 Hz ± 15 Hz tone for a duration of not less than 2.6 s and not more than 4.0 s." Figure 2-11 illustrates a T.30 fax CED tone.

Figure 2-11 *T.30 Fax CED Tone*

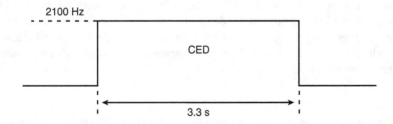

The purpose of the CED tone is to disable any echo suppressors that are in the call path. The 2100 Hz CED tone defined in ITU-T T.30 is identical to the 2100 Hz tone defined in ITU-T Recommendation G.164. The G.164 specification covers echo suppressors and their operation and details a 2100 Hz tone as the signal to disable echo suppressors on a line. A G3 fax transmission requires that all echo suppressors in the fax path be disabled to prevent distortion in the modulation.

This tone can easily be heard by calling a fax from any phone. The CED should be the first tone that is heard, and it identifies the end device as a fax or a low-speed modem.

DIS, NSF, and CSI Messages

Unlike the preceding CNG and CED signals, the digital identification signal (DIS), nonstandard facilities (NSF), and called subscriber identification (CSI) messages actually contain data and are transmitted using the V.21 modulation.

These three messages occur after the receiving side answers the incoming call and plays the CED tone. Each message is encapsulated in its own HDLC frame. The DIS message is the most important of these messages, and the ITU-T T.30 specification considers it mandatory. The NSF and CSI are optional, and all optional messages are transmitted before the mandatory DIS message. Figure 2-12 illustrates the arrangement of the NSF, CSI, and DIS frames.

Figure 2-12 *NSF, CSI, and DIS Frame Arrangement*

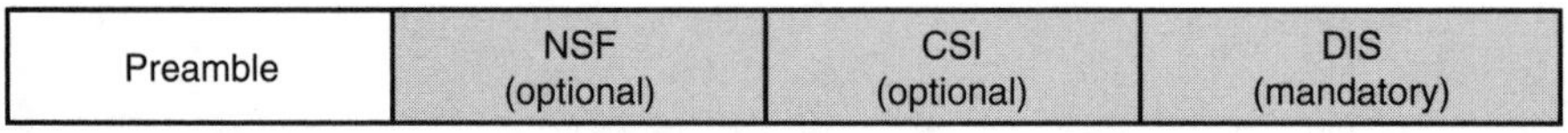

Preamble	NSF (optional)	CSI (optional)	DIS (mandatory)

The DIS message contains the capabilities of the terminating fax device. Parameters such as page modulation speed, image resolution, support of ECM, and page size are contained within the FIF of the DIS message.

Figure 2-13 diagrams the basic DIS frame and highlights some of the important DIS FIF bits. A comprehensive list of all the DIS FIF bits can be found in Table 2 of ITU-T Recommendation T.30. The FIF bits just define the capabilities of the terminating fax device. They let the originating fax device know what the terminating device can and cannot support. The originating fax device then analyzes these capabilities and decides what parameters to use for the fax transmission.

NOTE   You can download ITU-T Recommendation T.30 from http://www.itu.int/rec/ T-REC-T.30-200509-I/.

Figure 2-13 *T.30 DIS Frame*

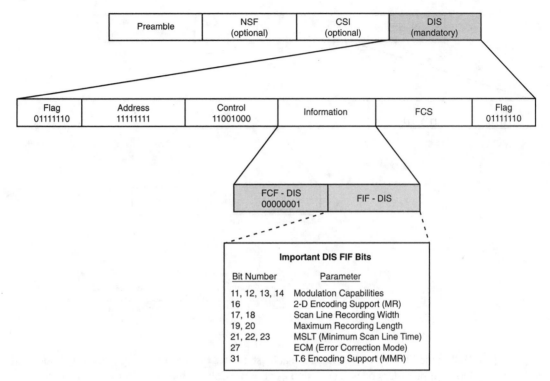

The NSF or nonstandard facilities message allows fax capabilities to extend beyond what is defined in ITU-T Recommendation T.30. By using a specific country and vendor or terminal provider coding in the FIF field, a terminating fax device can signal that it is capable of vendor proprietary messaging and features. Assuming that the originating fax device is also enabled with this same capability, it will respond with a nonstandard facilities setup (NSS), and the two machines will proceed into a proprietary mode of operation that may deviate from the T.30 specification. Figure 2-14 illustrates the T.30 optional NSF frame.

Figure 2-14 *T.30 NSF Frame*

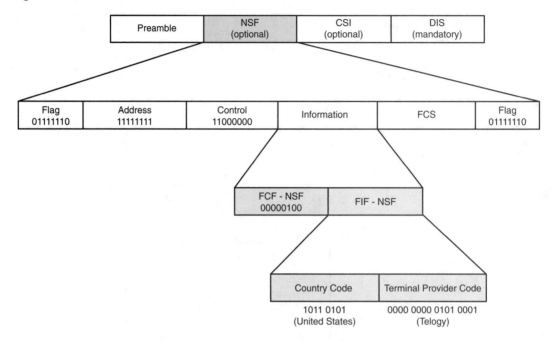

Within the FIF of the NSF, there are at least 2 bytes of data consisting of country codes and terminal provider codes. The country codes are defined in ITU-T Recommendation T.35, and the terminal provider codes are defined by national organizations outside of the ITU. The sample NSF frame detailed in Figure 2-14 shows the country and provider codes set to United States and Telogy, respectively. These are the default settings seen when the NSF value is set by Cisco gateways.

Like the NSF, the CSI field is also optional. The purpose of the CSI is to identify the device that is being called. Some fax machines display this value when it is received so that the user can confirm their fax destination.

The CSI consists of 20 digits, and it should contain the full international phone number of the device, which includes the + character, the telephone country code, area code, and subscriber number. The exact binary encoding of these FIF values is defined in Table 3 of ITU-T Recommendation T.30. However, it is common to see ASCII text in this field as an alternative. Many fax devices support ASCII values in the CSI FIF, and this usually does not cause a problem even though ASCII text is not defined in T.30. Figure 2-15 diagrams the CSI frame format.

Figure 2-15 *T.30 CSI Frame*

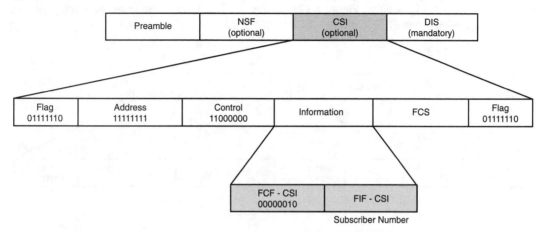

DCS and TSI Messages

The digital command signal (DCS) and transmitting subscriber identification (TSI) messages are typically seen as a response to the DIS message. Like the DIS message, the DCS message is the important mandatory message, whereas TSI is similar to CSI and is optional. Figure 2-16 shows the arrangement of the TSI and DCS messages following the fax preamble.

Figure 2-16 *TSI and DCS Frame Arrangement*

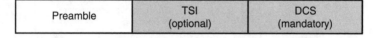

The DCS message is transmitted by the originating fax device after it has analyzed the capabilities specified in the DIS message. Because the originating fax machine already knows its own capabilities, it can easily compare these settings with the settings received in the DIS. The DCS message then commands the terminating fax to use specific parameters for the fax transmission. The originating fax machine has the responsibility of commanding the terminating fax to only use a setting or parameter that was listed as an option in the DIS message.

The DCS FIF uses the same bits as the DIS FIF and these bit settings are defined in Table 2 of ITU-T Recommendation T.30. However, even with the same bits being used, the settings might be somewhat different. For example, when looking at the modulation bits (11, 12, 13, 14), the DIS bit settings specify a modulation like V.17 or V.29. Meanwhile, the DCS can use the same bits to define a specific speed within that modulation, such as V.17 14400 bps or V.17 9600 bps. Figure 2-17 diagrams the T.30 DCS message and highlights some of the important FIF bit settings.

Figure 2-17 *T.30 DCS Frame*

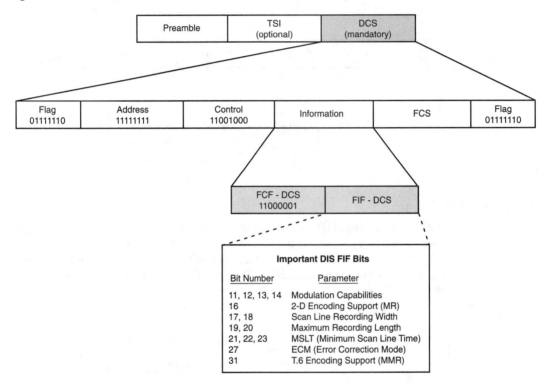

The optional TSI message carries the subscriber number of the originating fax device. Like the CSI, this value is programmed into the fax device by the user, or in some cases there is a default value already assigned. The terminating fax device may display the TSI information for the user so that the identification of the device that is sending the fax can be confirmed. Figure 2-18 illustrates the T.30 TSI message.

The T.30 specification defines other optional HDLC frames that can be sent along with DCS other than TSI. This includes such frames as NSS, subaddress (SUB), and sender identification (SID), among a few others. These optional frames are rarely seen; for additional information on these frames, refer to Table 2-3 or Section 5.3.6.1.3 of ITU-T Recommendation T.30.

Figure 2-18 *T.30 TSI Frame*

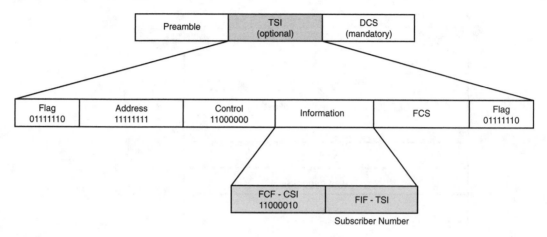

TCF, CFR, and FTT Messages

The training check frame (TCF) and confirmation (CFR) are the last transactions that occur before the fax page transmission begins. Within the DCS message, a modulation and speed has been sent to the receiving fax device. Both fax devices are now prepared for a test sequence pattern of all 0s sent for 1.5 seconds using the modulation and speed specified in the DCS message. This test pattern of all 0s is known as the TCF and is sent by the originating fax machine. Unlike most other T.30 messages, it does not use an HDLC frame.

If the test pattern is received with little or no errors, the receiving fax machine sends a CFR response. Otherwise, a failure to train (FTT) message is sent. Upon receipt of a FTT, the originating device resends the DCS to retry the same training speed again, fall back to a slower speed within the same modulation, or even try a different modulation. The originating device then sends the TCF again using any new modulations or speeds dictated by the DCS. This process repeats itself until the receiving fax device gets a clean TCF and responds with a CFR. Figure 2-19 demonstrates a retraining and fallback scenario between two fax machines. In this scenario, notice that the originating fax machine even repeated trainings at 4800 bps and 2400 bps in an effort to get a successful TCF through.

Figure 2-19 *Fax Retraining and Fallback Scenario*

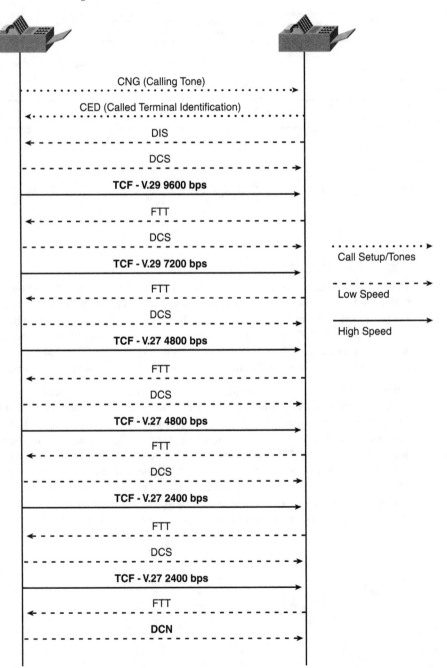

The TCFs make sure that the transmission path can handle the modulation and speed before actual page data is sent. If the TCF can be sent across the transmission path cleanly, then usually the fax page data transmits clean, too, with little or no errors.

Both the CFR and FTT messages use HDLC frames, but they contain no FIF. Only the FCF identifying the message as a CFR or FTT is present. This occurs because these messages are used only to validate the TCF, and no additional information is necessary. Figure 2-20 diagrams a T.30 CFR frame.

Figure 2-20 *T.30 CFR Frame*

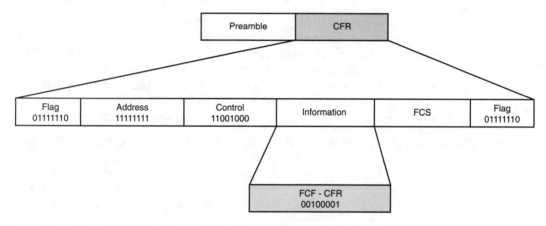

MPS, EOP, EOM, MCF, RTP, RTN, and DCN Messages

After the first page has been sent using the modulation specified in the DCS, the page information is followed by a multipage signal (MPS) message. Like the rest of the T.30 messages, MPS is sent using the 300 bps V.21 modulation even though it immediately follows the higher-speed page data. MPS informs the receiving device that the page is completed and that the sender is waiting for a confirmation message before transmitting the next page.

Instead of the MPS, there could be an end of procedure (EOP) message following a fax page. This message lets the receiving fax device know that the preceding page is complete and that there are no further pages or other documents to be sent. The originating side is ready to disconnect the call after this page has been confirmed.

A less-used signal called end of message (EOM) can also be used in place of an MPS or EOP to indicate that a renegotiation of settings is required. This message is most commonly seen when the next page is of a different page resolution than the preceding page.

After receiving a fax page and an MPS or EOP message, the terminating fax device has a few common messages with which to reply. Usually the response is a message confirmation (MCF). MCF indicates that the previous page was received satisfactorily and that the receiving device is ready for additional pages.

If the page is received with some errors, usually a retrain positive (RTP) or retrain negative (RTN) message is sent rather than the MCF. RTP does indicate that the page was received satisfactorily but that there were probably some issues or small errors not severe enough to warrant a resending of the entire page. Instead, perhaps, retraining to possibly a different modulation will remedy any problems or errors for subsequent fax pages.

An RTN response means that the page was not received satisfactorily and a retrain must take place before further page information can be sent. Ideally, the page that was not received satisfactorily should be re-sent. However, this does not always happen because not all fax machines buffer the faulty page, making it impossible for this page to be retransmitted. In addition, even if the faulty page is re-sent, a mechanism does not exist for the receiving side to know whether the page following an RTN is a retransmission. Therefore, you might find inconsistencies in the ways that different fax machine vendors handle RTN messages.

Fax devices typically have predefined error thresholds for determining when an RTP or RTN message needs to be sent. The main type of error that is tracked is the number of invalid scan lines. When the number of bad scan lines for a page reaches the RTP or RTN threshold, one of these messages is triggered. These thresholds may be configurable on some fax devices, but they are usually preset to vendor-specific values and are not changeable.

The disconnect, or DCN message, is the last message seen in a fax transaction and indicates the initiation of Phase E, call disconnect. A response or acknowledgment is not needed for this message. This message signifies a graceful disconnect to the fax call, and both sides prepare for a new fax transaction by returning to an on-hook state.

Like the FTT and CFR messages, the MPS, EOP, MCF, RTP, RTN, and DCN message frames do not contain an FIF. Varying FCF values are the main criteria that distinguish these messages from one another. Figure 2-21 illustrates the common frame format shared among the MPS, EOP, MCF, RTP, RTN, and DCN messages.

Figure 2-21 *T.30 MPS, EOP, EOM, MCF, RTP, RTN, and DCN Frames*

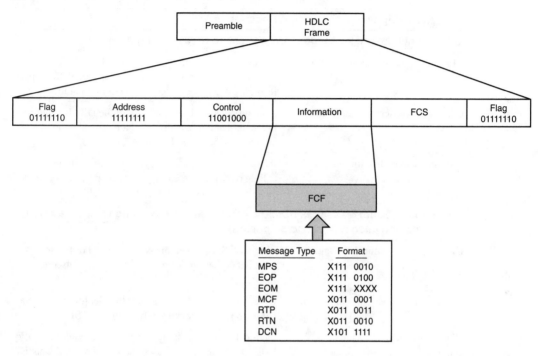

Other T.30 Messages

Table 2-3 provides a comprehensive list of the G3 fax messages defined in the T.30 Recommendation dated September 2005. Although many of the messages in Table 2-3 have already been discussed earlier in this chapter, many more have not been specifically addressed because they are rarely used. All are mentioned here for completeness and as a reference in case you ever encounter them.

Table 2-3 *Comprehensive Listing of Fax T.30 Messages*

Message or Signal	Description
CNG (calling tone)	An 1100 Hz tone for 0.5 second duration occurring every 3 seconds. Indicates a calling nonspeech terminal.
CED (called terminal identification)	A 2100 Hz tone lasting between 2.6 seconds and 4.0 seconds that occurs when a called fax device answers. Disables echo suppressors in the transmission path.

continues

Table 2-3 *Comprehensive Listing of Fax T.30 Messages (Continued)*

Message or Signal	Description
Initial Identification: Messages from the called to the calling terminal	
DIS (digital identification signal)	Contains the capabilities of the called fax device. Includes important parameters such as modulations, page resolutions, page compressions, and ECM ability.
CSI (called subscriber identification)	An optional signal sent along with the DIS that indicates the identification (usually the international phone number) of the called fax terminal.
NSF (nonstandard facilities)	An optional signal sent with the DIS that notifies the calling device of the ability to handle proprietary vendor encodings beyond what is defined in T.30.
Command to Send: Messages from the calling terminal wanting to be a receiver of fax information (also referred to as polling)	
DTC (digital transmit command)	Like a DCS message, this is a command response to a DIS that defines the parameters that will be used for the fax transaction.
CIG (calling subscriber identification)	Optional message that indicates the identification of the calling terminal. Functionally similar to TSI.
NSC (nonstandard facilities command)	Optional message response to an NSF. Signals the ability to handle proprietary vendor encodings beyond what is specified in T.30.
PWD (password)	Optional message used as a password for the polling mode.
SEP (selective polling)	Optional message that defines a subaddress for the polling mode or identifies a specific document number.
PSA (polled subaddress)	Optional message that defines a subaddress for polling.
CIA (calling subscriber Internet address)	Optional message that defines an Internet address for the calling fax device.
ISP (Internet selective polling address)	Optional message that defines an Internet address for the calling device in polling mode.
Command to Receive: Messages from the transmitter to the receiver	
DCS (digital command signal)	Mandatory message that defines the parameters for the fax transaction.
TSI (transmitting subscriber identification)	Optional message that identifies the calling terminal. It is usually the subscriber number of the calling device.

Table 2-3 *Comprehensive Listing of Fax T.30 Messages (Continued)*

Message or Signal	Description
NSS (nonstandard facilities setup)	Optional message sent as a response to an NSC or NSF signal. Used in setting up proprietary encodings beyond what is defined in the T.30 specification.
SUB (subaddress)	Optional message that specifies additional addressing or routing information for the terminating destination.
SID (sender identification)	Optional message that allows for the specification of a user-configured sender identity.
TCF (training check)	A modulated series of all 0s sent as a test to verify the transmission path before transmitting the actual page information.
CTC (continue to correct)	Only used with ECM. A response message sent after the fourth PPR message indicating that the transmitter will continue to correct the previous message.
TSA (transmitting subscriber Internet address)	Optional message that details the Internet address of the transmitting device. Used only when Internet capabilities were previously set in the DIS.
IRA (Internet routing address)	Optional message specifies an Internet address that can be used to provide additional routing information for gateways. Only sent if bit 102 in DIS/DTC is set.
Premessage Response Signals: Messages from the receiver to the transmitter	
CFR (confirmation to receive)	Message that confirms the premessage procedure and the TCF. Page data can now be sent.
FTT (failure to train)	Message that rejects the TCF and requests a retrain.
CTR (response for continue to correct)	An ECM message that is the response to a CTC that indicates that the receiving device accepts the contents included with the CTC message.
CSA (called subscriber Internet address)	Optional message sent along with CFR that specifies the called device's Internet address. Only sent when Internet capabilities in DCS are enabled.
Post-Message Commands: Phase D messages from the transmitter to the receiver	
EOM (end of message)	Indicates the end of a fax page and a return to Phase B.
MPS (multipage signal)	Indicates the end of a fax page and a return to Phase C.

continues

Table 2-3   *Comprehensive Listing of Fax T.30 Messages (Continued)*

Message or Signal	Description
EOP (end of procedure)	Indicates the end of the fax page and that there is no further information to be sent. Proceed to Phase E.
PRI-EOM (procedure interrupt-end of message)	Same as an EOM message along with the additional request of operator intervention.
PRI-MPS (procedure interrupt-multipage signal)	Same as the MPS message along with the additional request of operator intervention.
PRI-EOP (procedure interrupt-end of procedure)	Same as the EOP message along with the additional request of operator intervention.
EOS (end of selection)	Optional message used in conjunction with SEP to indicate the end of the selected document.
PPS (partial page signal)	Indicates the end of a page or partial page of information during ECM.
EOR (end of retransmission)	Indicates the end of retransmission of error frames for the previous partial page during ECM.
RR (receive ready)	Indicates receiver status and flow control during ECM.
Post-Message Responses: Phase D messages from the receiver to the transmitter	
MCF (message confirmation)	Indicates satisfactory message reception and that additional information may follow.
RTP (retrain positive)	Indicates satisfactory message reception and that additional information may follow but only after a retraining.
RTN (retrain negative)	Indicates that the preceding message has not been received satisfactorily. A retraining is needed before further information can be sent.
PIP (procedure interrupt positive)	Indicates that the previous message has been received and that operator intervention is needed before further transmissions are possible.
PIN (procedure interrupt negative)	Indicates that the previous or in-process message was not received satisfactorily and operator intervention is needed before further transmissions are possible.
PPR (partial page request)	Indicates that there are errors in the previous partial page during ECM. The frames specified must be re-sent.
RNR (receive not ready)	Indicates that the receiver is not ready for more data during ECM.
ERR (response for end of retransmission)	Response for the EOR message.

Table 2-3   *Comprehensive Listing of Fax T.30 Messages (Continued)*

Message or Signal	Description
FDM (file diagnostics message)	Optional message that can be used in place of MCF when binary file transfers are being sent.
Other Line Control Signals: Messages for handling errors and maintaining control of the connection	
DCN (disconnect)	Indicates call release and the beginning of Phase E. No response is required.
CRP (command repeat)	Optional message indicates that the previous command was received in error and it needs to be retransmitted.
FNV (field not valid)	Optional message indicates that one of the following messages is not accepted or is invalid: PWD, SEP, SUB, SID, TSI, PSA, or secure fax signal.
TNR (transmit not ready)	Optional message available in flow control mode that indicates the transmitter is not ready.
TR (transmit ready)	Optional message available in flow control mode that requests the transmitter status.

Understanding Error Correction Mode

Initially found on more expensive fax machines, ECM is a feature that is found increasingly more often on today's fax devices. Defined by ITU-T Recommendation T.30 Annex A, ECM ensures a much higher level of fax page data integrity than what is consistently achieved on non-ECM G3 fax transactions. Whereas normal G3 fax transactions typically present a fax with acceptable quality, ECM usually guarantees near perfect quality.

The ECM feature is negotiated at the beginning of a fax call during the DIS/DCS message exchange. If both the sending and receiving fax devices support ECM, it is typically used during the fax call. If either device does not support or agree to ECM, the fax transaction will proceed as a normal G3, non-ECM call. This allows fax devices that support ECM to be compatible with other fax devices that do not support the feature.

During a non-ECM fax transaction, the error checking and error correction ability is limited, which allows for errors to corrupt the fax page data. The errors can come from a number of sources but are usually caused by impairments in the transmission path. If the number of errors is too great, an RTN message is usually sent by the receiving fax device. However, this RTN message does not guarantee that the corrupted page will be re-sent. Page errors during a non-ECM fax call are not usually corrected, as evidenced by received fax pages that suffer from poor quality.

When a non-ECM fax page suffers from poor quality and contains errors, you will see portions of the text on the page that are unreadable and distorted because bad scan lines cannot be resolved into meaningful information. The text on the page may also appear condensed or bunched up, or white horizontal streaks might be seen correlating with the bad scan lines.

ECM fax calls, on the other hand, have a method for accurately detecting and correcting errors in the fax page data. Each fax page is divided into one or more blocks of data. Within each of these blocks are HDLC frames that contain an FCS value to help ensure the integrity of the data. When the answering fax machine receives the block, it uses the FCS value to checksum each frame so that it can request a retransmission of any frames that contain errors. This retransmission process usually continues until all pages are correct or until the fax machines give up. Because of ECMs tenacity at getting pages sent correctly, faxes may take longer and sometimes not even complete. Most fax machines automatically redial if a fax transmission does not make it through. ECM relies on this automatic redial to try again at another time when there will be an opportunity for a better-quality connection.

Compared to a non-ECM fax call, ECM has the advantage of ensuring that page information is received error free. This is obviously important for transmissions such as legal documents containing small fonts. However, ECM faxes might take a long time or never complete in conditions where there are a lot of errors in the transmission path. You can see these kinds of conditions with poor-quality PSTN connections. If it is important to get the fax through quickly and having occasional page errors is acceptable, a non-ECM fax call might be advantageous. For these types of situations, most fax machines that support the ECM feature also include a means for disabling it.

ECM Call Analysis

Conceptually, an ECM fax call is almost identical to a non-ECM call. The important principle regarding ECM is that a fax page is broken into partial pages or blocks of a fixed size; it may take multiple partial pages or blocks to send a single fax page.

Figure 2-22 shows a two-page fax transaction using ECM. The first page is broken into two blocks while the second page fits into one block. Each block or partial page is followed by a partial page signal (PPS) message. A PPS-NULL message follows any partial page that is not the last block for a page. The last page block is followed by a PPS-MPS. For the final block of the last page, a PPS-EOP message signals that there are no further pages to be sent.

Figure 2-22 *Two-Page Fax Transaction Using ECM*

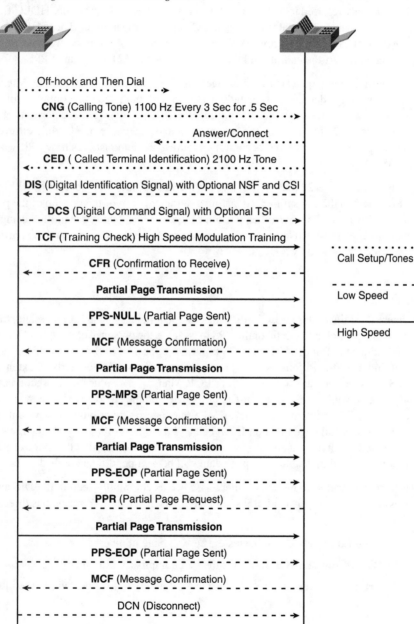

The partial page transmissions shown in Figure 2-22 contain the actual fax page data, which is commonly referred to as fax coded data (FCD). The FCD is simply HDLC frames of a 64-or 256-byte size that also contain an FCF and a frame number. These HDLC frames are streamed at the negotiated high-speed modulation until the entire partial page or page block has been sent. At the end of the block, the low-speed, V.21-modulated PPS is found.

The partial page request (PPR) message is also occasionally seen in an ECM call flow. A PPR message details the specific portions of a partial page that contain errors. Upon receiving a PPR message, the transmitting device learns what errored portions of the partial page to resend. This prevents the retransmission of the entire block while ensuring that all the fax page data is received accurately. Figure 2-22 demonstrates how PPR works in an ECM call flow.

Notice in Figure 2-22 that the last page of the fax transaction is received with some errors. PPR is sent to the transmitter requesting a retransmission of the portion of the partial page that is corrupted. This corrupted portion of the block is then retransmitted using another partial page message. No errors are detected in the retransmission, and the partial page is confirmed, followed by a DCN.

PPS and PPR

Figure 2-23 illustrates an ECM PPS message. Unlike a typical T.30 message, the main distinguishing characteristic of the PPS message is the presence of a second FCF. You might have noticed in Figure 2-22 that PPS messages appear as PPS-MPS or PPS-EOP. The first FCF indicates the PPS message type, whereas the second FCF details an extension to the PPS message such as NULL, MPS, or EOP. Many of the values in the secondary FCF are identical to what is seen in a non-ECM fax call, and they also have the same meaning. For example, a PPS-MPS message and an MPS message are functionally equivalent, except that one follows a full page in a non-ECM call and the other follows a partial page when ECM is enabled. Both of these messages inform the receiving side that this page or partial page is complete and that additional page data will be sent pending a confirmation.

Like many other T.30 messages, there's no FIF as commonly seen in the DIS and DCS messages. However, instead of just an FCF by itself, the PPS message has three additional fields

- **Page Counter(PC)**: Indicates the current page number
- **Block Counter(BC)**: Indicates the block number within that page
- **Frame Counter (FC)**: Specifies the total number of frames within the block

Figure 2-23 *T.30 PPS Frame*

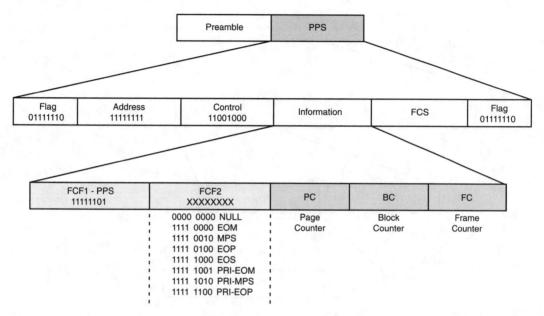

The frames that the FC refers to are HDLC frames full of page data. Each HDLC frame is either 64 or 256 bytes depending on what is specified in the DCS message. Up to a maximum of 256 of these HDLC frames form a block with FC noting the exact number. If the page data requires more than 256 HDLC frames or 1 block, multiple blocks or partial pages are sent. By dividing the page data into blocks made up of HDLC frames, ECM takes advantage of HDLC's CRC function to verify small segments of page information. This provides more detailed error detection while preventing a full-page retransmission when error correction is necessary.

A PPR message occurs during an ECM fax transaction when there are errors in a partial page. The receiving device uses the PPR message to notify the transmitting device of the HDLC frames that have errors. The transmitting device then retransmits the HDLC frames specified by the PPR message. Figure 2-24 illustrates the PPR message format.

Figure 2-24 *T.30 PPR Frame*

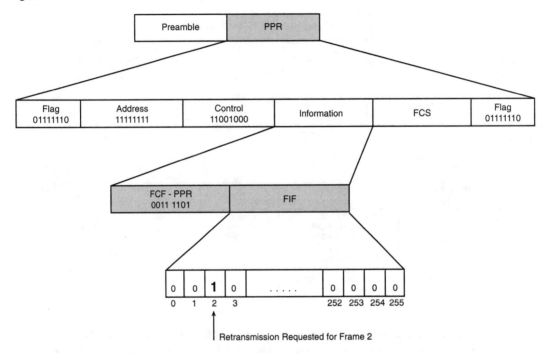

The PPR frame format contains the standard 1-byte FCF followed by a 256-bit FIF. The 256 bits in the FIF correspond to the 256 HDLC frames that were just received in the preceding partial page. Any frames that were received with errors are flagged by setting the corresponding PPR FIF bit to 1. HDLC frames that were received correctly have a bit setting of 0. Implementing this error correction methodology allows ECM to easily notify the sender of corrupted frames. These frames are then re-sent by the originating fax device before proceeding to the next partial page.

Important G3 Timers

Table 2-4 defines the basic T.30 message timers for G3 faxing. These timers are used in error recovery and to make sure that the fax transaction never gets stuck in a hung state. In calling scenarios involving international connections or satellite hops, fax calls may experience a delay that is high enough to cause certain timers to expire.

Table 2-4   *T.30 Protocol Timers*

Timer	Value	Description
T0	60 ± 5 sec	Amount of time a calling fax machine waits for an answer from the terminating side. Usually a CED or DIS stops this timer.
T1	35 ± 5 sec	Amount of time a fax device attempts to identify the other fax device. This timer is active during the DIS/DCS negotiation.
T2	6 ± 1 sec	Amount of time a fax device waits to receive a command. This timer also detects the loss of command/response synchronization.
T3	10 ± 5 sec	Amount of time a fax device alerts an operator after a procedural interrupt.
T4	3 sec ± 15%	Amount of time a fax device waits for a response to a sent message.
T5	60 ± 5 sec	Amount of time a transmitting fax device waits for a busy condition on the receiving fax device to clear. This timer is only used during ECM.

All the timers are important, but the T4 timer with its low three-second value is more susceptible to network delay than the other timers. When this timer expires, message retransmissions and possible call failures can occur. Therefore, understanding the function of this timer is important.

Figure 2-25 demonstrates a scenario where the T4 timer expires. In this example, the terminating fax answers the fax call by sending a DIS signal. When a response to this DIS message is not received before the T4 timer expires, the DIS message is repeated. Typically, a fax device repeats a message three times before disconnecting the call.

Figure 2-25 *T4 Timer Expiration*

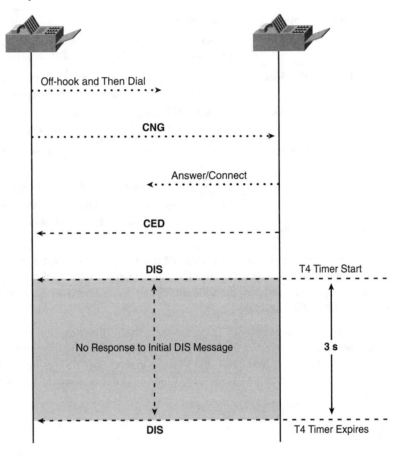

Super G3 Faxing

Defined in ITU-T Recommendation T.30 Annex F, the Super G3 fax classification is a high-speed alternative to a G3 fax call. Whereas G3 has a maximum page transmission speed of 14.4 Kbps, Super G3 can transmit at speeds up to 33.6 Kbps using the V.34 modulation. Consequently, Super G3 faxing is also called V.34 faxing. The V.34 modulation is covered in detail in the section "Modem Call Analysis" in Chapter 1.

Comparison of SG3 and G3

Table 2-5 shows the key differences between SG3 and G3. Many of these differences occur right at the start of the call. First, the answer tone by the receiving fax device is an ANSam tone, not a CED. Second, the initial setup message sent during an SG3 call startup is a V.8 Calling Menu (CM), whereas a G3 fax call issues a DIS along with optional NSF and CSI messages. And finally, the Super G3 call using V.34 initializes a low-speed control channel for the fax messaging and a high-speed primary channel for transmitting page information; a G3 fax call uses the same channel for fax messaging and page transmission.

Table 2-5   *Key Differences Between G3 and Super G3*

Difference	G3	Super G3
Answer tone	CED (2100 Hz)	ANSam (2100 Hz amplitude modulated with phase reversals)
Initial setup message	DIS with optional NSF and CSI	Calling Menu (CM)
Communications channels	1 channel (used for T.30 messaging and page transmission)	2 channels (a low-speed control channel for T.30 messaging and a high-speed primary channel for page transmission)
ECM	Optional	Mandatory
TCF training signal	Required	Not applicable

Additional differences between Super G3 and G3 involve the ECM feature and the TCF signal. Whereas ECM is an optionally negotiated feature for a G3 fax call, Super G3 mandates that ECM be enabled. The TCF message in G3 is a training signal that verifies the transmission path before the fax page is sent. However, during a Super G3 call, the TCF message is not necessary because V.34 initializes and verifies the primary channel used for page data along with the control channel when the call is first set up. For additional information on V.8, CM, and V.34 modulation, refer to the section "Phase I: Network Interaction" in Chapter 1.

Super G3 Call Analysis

Figure 2-26 shows a Super G3 fax call from beginning to end. As soon as the call connects, the V.8 message procedure begins, including the ANSam and the calling menu/joint menu or CM/JM exchange. The JM message is simply a response to the CM that contains the terminating fax machine's capabilities. This first phase of the V.34 initialization along with the other V.34 phases were discussed previously in the section "Modem Call Analysis" in Chapter 1.

Figure 2-26 *Super G3 Fax Call*

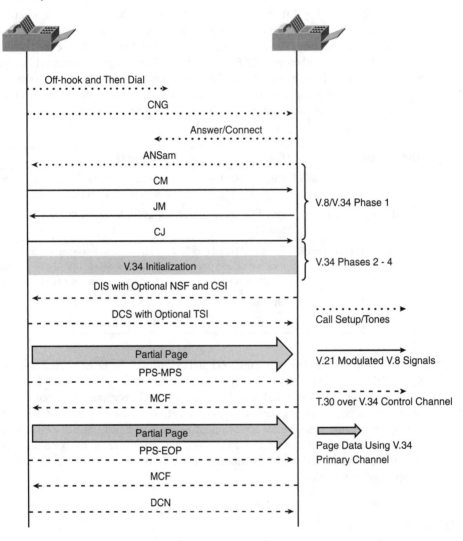

Upon the completion of the V.8 procedure, Phases 2 through 4 of V.34 occur. Included in these V.34 phases are procedures such as line probing, equalizer training, and modem parameter exchange. The most important event that occurs here is the setup of the control channel and the primary channel. The control channel handles the T.30 fax messaging, and the primary channel handles the high-speed transmission of the fax page data.

With V.34 initialized, the rest of the fax messaging matches a regular ECM fax call as discussed in Figure 2-23. The only difference is the absence of the TCF, which is not needed because the primary channel synchronization is handled by V.34 outside of the data channel messaging.

Page Encoding

G3 faxing is a digital process. Therefore, before transmission, the page information is digitized by the fax device's scanner. First, the page is divided into horizontal lines known as scan lines. The scanner then moves across each line and based on the brightness level creates black and white picture elements (pixels). The typical scan line has 1728 pixels.

The terms *pixels per inch* (ppi) and *dots per inch* (dpi) are often used interchangeably when discussing fax pages. Technically, however, dpi refers to the output of an image by a printer, whereas pixels correspond to scanned images.

Fax devices can usually send and receive at multiple resolutions. The two most common are normal or standard resolution, which is 200 x 100 dots per inch (dpi), and fine resolution, which is 200 x 200 dpi. At the fine resolution setting, a scanned 8.5 x 11 inch page has 1728 x 2200 pixels. Figure 2-27 illustrates the scan line concept and how each scan line is constructed of black and white pixels. Scan lines are created traveling from left to right and top to bottom.

Figure 2-27 *Fax Page Scan Lines*

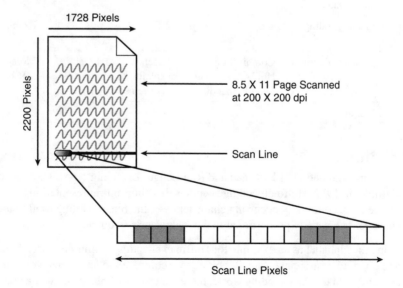

Continuing with the 200 x 200 dpi example shown in Figure 2-27, the number of pixels that will constitute a full page is 3,801,600. With each pixel represented by 1 bit, this equates to more than 475 KB. Even when sending all of this information at the fastest G3 fax speed of 14.4 Kbps, it will take well over four minutes to transmit this size page. If even more detailed resolutions are used, the amount of transmission time increases greatly.

Fortunately, every exact bit that makes up a page is not transmitted. There are a few options available for compressing the binary page information. The first and most commonly supported option is Modified Huffman (MH). All G3-compatible fax devices must support MH encoding.

Another option is Modified READ (MR). MR offers a more advanced compression than MH and is more efficient even though it employs MH principles. The third compression option is Modified Modified READ (MMR). MMR requires error-free communication, but it typically offers the best compression. Table 2-6 gives a quick comparison between the three different encoding types and subsequent sections discuss each type in more detail.

Table 2-6   *Comparison of MH, MR, and MMR Page Encodings*

Encoding Characteristics	MH	MR	MMR
Compression Efficiency (for an 8.5 x 11 page of text)	Good	Better	Best
Specification (ITU-T Recommendation)	T.4	T.4	T.6
Dimensional coding type	1-D	2-D	Extended 2-D
Compression algorithm	Combination of Huffman and Run Length Encoding	Superset of MH that exploits the similarities between successive lines	More efficient MR-based encoding
ECM required	No	No	Yes

Modified Huffman

MH is a combination of Huffman and Run Length Encoding types. Developed by David Huffman in 1952, Huffman coding specifies that short bit representations should be used for the most commonly occurring characters. So, the binary coding used to identify a character is inversely proportional to that character's frequency.

Using the alphabet as an example for Huffman encoding, commonly used letters such as *T* and *E* would be assigned a smaller bit pattern compared to letters that are rarely used such as *X* and *Z*. In the fax encoding world, there are groups of black and white pixels that make up a scan line. Applying Huffman encoding, commonly repeated black and white pixel groupings are given smaller bit representations.

Run Length Encoding (RLE), one of the simplest of all compression algorithms, takes advantage of repetitive data. These consecutive data values are broken into groupings known as runs and replaced with a count number and a value. Fax page images contain many runs of alternating black and white pixels that are a perfect fit for RLE. A simple but efficient encoding algorithm is achieved when RLE is combined with Huffman coding principles.

MH encoding uses special coding tables to compress the bits that compose a scan line. Detailed in ITU-T T.4, these tables are divided into two groupings, terminating codes and make-up codes.

NOTE   You can download ITU-T Recommendation T.4 from http://www.itu.int/rec/T-REC-T.4/.

Terminating codes address white and black run lengths from 0 to 63 bits with each scan line always beginning with a white run. If the scan line happens to start with a black pixel, a white run length of 0 is coded at the start of the scan line. Figure 2-28 provides an example of how a scan line is coded using MH.

Figure 2-28 *MH Coding Example*

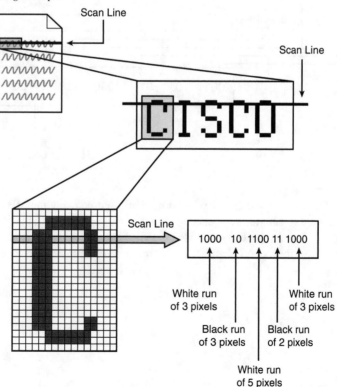

Because the terminating code tables only cover run lengths of less than 64 bits, make-up codes address longer run lengths. Make-up codes are defined for black and white runs in multiples of 64 bits, and they always precede the terminating codes.

For long run lengths, a scan line is first represented by the make-up code that is equal to or less than the required pixel run. The terminating code then follows the make-up code, addressing the difference in pixels between the required run length and the run covered by the make-up code. Figure 2-29 illustrates the coding of a pixel run that requires a make-up code.

Figure 2-29 *MH Scan Line Encoding Using a Make-Up Code*

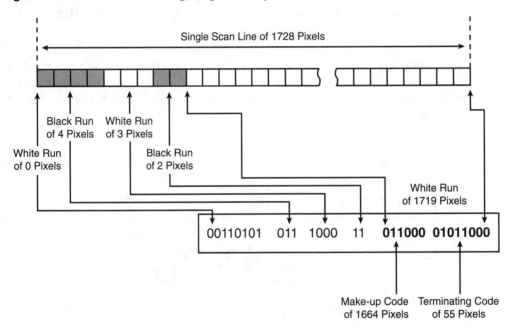

In addition to the scan line pixel information captured using the MH encoding method, additional bit patterns are needed to form a complete, transmittable scan line. One of these patterns is the unique end of line (EOL) bit sequence; the other is an optional fill pattern. Figure 2-30 shows how scan lines are composed of data, fill, and EOL bit segments.

Figure 2-30 *Scan Line Data, Fill, and EOL Segments*

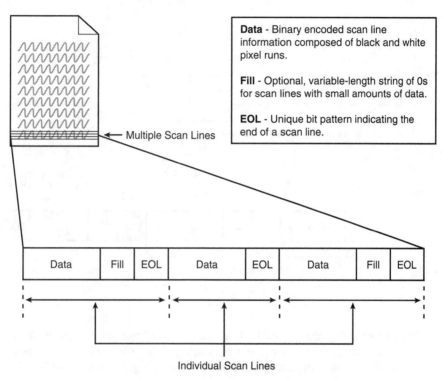

The EOL pattern designates the end of a scan line. Consisting of eleven 0s followed by a 1 (000000000001), the EOL is a unique sequence that is never found within the actual scan line data. When a receiver encounters an EOL, the current line is ended and the next one below it starts. In addition, because EOL also allows for the decoding of each line independently, errors affecting a single line are not propagated to other scan lines.

At the end of the fax page, a series of six consecutive EOL patterns occur. Known as a return to control (RTC) signal, these EOLs serve as notification that the fax page has ended and that post-page messaging will now be sent using the V.21 modulation as specified in T.30.

The EOL is also the required pattern that serves as the beginning of the fax page. Figure 2-31 illustrates how EOLs designate the beginning and end of fax pages in addition to terminating each scan line.

Figure 2-31 *EOL Bit Patterns Designating the Beginning and End of a Fax Page*

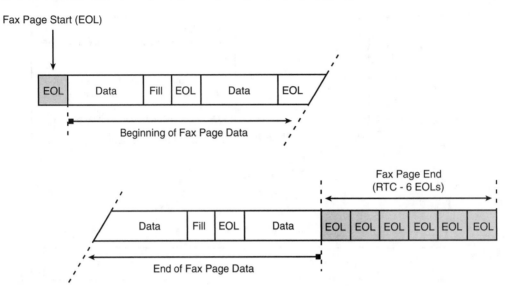

In addition to MH data bits and EOL bit sequences, fill patterns can also be found in a scan line. A fill pattern is just a variable length string of 0s. To prevent overrunning a receiving fax device's printer, fill patterns are inserted to bring highly compressed scan lines up to a predefined minimum scan line time (MSLT).

The MSLT parameter is set during the DIS/DCS message exchange at the beginning of a fax call. This MSLT value is a length of time in milliseconds that represents the minimum threshold for the reception of a full scan line.

For example, if the DIS/DCS message exchange specifies an MSLT value of 10 ms and the fax page transmission speed is 4800 bps, each scan line must be at least 48 bits. If the scan line is less than 48 bits, fill bits must be inserted between the actual pixel data and the EOL. Figure 2-32 illustrates an example of how the fill pattern works.

Figure 2-32 *Fill Bit Pattern Insertion*

MSLT = 10 ms
Transmission rate = 4800 bps

Minimum bits per scan line:
4800 Bits/s X 10 ms = 48 Bits

1728-pixel scan line is compressed to a
size of 43 bits (31 data bits + 12 bit EOL).
To obtain a scan line minimum of 48 bits,
the sending fax device inserts **5 Fill bits.**

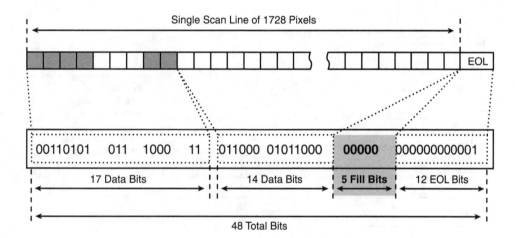

Modified READ

Defined in ITU-T Recommendation T.4, Modified Relative Element Address Designate
(READ) or simply MR encoding, exploits the correlation between successive scan lines.
Research has shown that a high percentage of consecutive scan lines only contain single
pixel transitions to the right or left. Instead of compressing each line independently like MH
does, MR establishes reference lines and then encodes any changes that occur between the
reference line and the scan lines that follow.

MR encoding builds on the encoding algorithms already established by MH. In fact,
reference lines found in MR are actually encoded using the MH algorithm. However,
subsequent lines use MR encoding until the next MH encoded reference line is encountered.
The parameter that defines how many MR encoded scan lines are present for each MH
encoded reference line is known as K.

For normal resolution faxes, K is set to a value of 2 and K-1 is always defined as the number
of lines that use 2-Dimensional (2-D), MR coding. The reference lines use 1-Dimenional
(1-D) or MH encoding. With a K value of 2, reference lines are encoded every other scan
line. Figure 2-33 illustrates the K parameter and how MR encoding appears for the values
of K=2 and K=4. Note that K settings of 2 and 4 would never appear on the same page.

Figure 2-33 *K Parameter for MR Encoding*

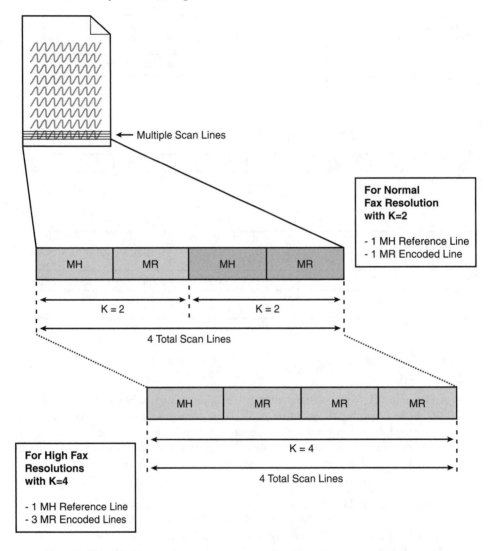

Low K values prevent any errors in the reference line from propagating too far into subsequent scan lines. In much higher resolutions using MR encoding, the K value can be as high as 24.

As pixel elements change between a reference line and the subsequent scan line, MR defines parameters for determining how the pixel element changes are encoded. Figure 2-34 illustrates and defines these parameters.

Figure 2-34 *MR Changing Pixel Element Parameters*

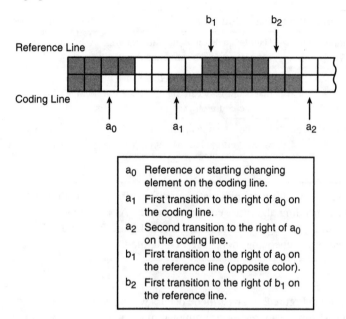

In Figure 2-34, the top scan line is the MH-encoded reference line. The line below is referred to as the coding line, and you can see that there are minor changes between this line and the reference line. MR takes advantage of these minor changes that typically occur between scan lines and uses an algorithm to encode only the line changes rather than the whole scan line.

The parameters defined in Figure 2-34 are designed to address any conceivable pixel pattern changes that can occur between a reference line and a coding line. Therefore, the position of these parameters might end up being quite different from what is shown in Figure 2-34.

Depending on how the MR parameters in Figure 2-34 match the changing pixel elements between scan lines, one of three functional encoding modes may be utilized under MR: pass mode, vertical mode, or horizontal mode. Each of these modes handles a different pixel element changing scenario and defines its encoding scheme. Table 2-7 summarizes these three MR encoding modes.

Table 2-7 *MR Encoding Modes*

Encoding Mode	Pixel Scenario	Parameter Positions
Pass mode	Handles pixels in code line that are not present in the reference line	b_1 and b_2 reside between a_0 and a_1.
Vertical mode	Addresses the minor pixel changes that occur between the reference line and the coding line	b_1 occurs within 3 pixels to either side of a_1.
Horizontal mode	Handles the remaining situations where vertical mode cannot be used	Distance between a_1 and b_1 is greater than 3 pixels.

TIP

Because of the additional parameters and the different encoding modes, MR is a more complex encoding algorithm compared to MH. As the encoding modes are discussed in more detail, you might need to refer back to Figure 2-34 and Table 2-7 where these parameters and encoding modes are first defined.

Illustrated in Figure 2-35, pass mode occurs when parameters b_1 and b_2 fall between a_0 and a_1. This MR mode addresses groupings of pixels in the code line that do not contain a pixel grouping that is present in the reference line.

Figure 2-35 *MR Pass Mode*

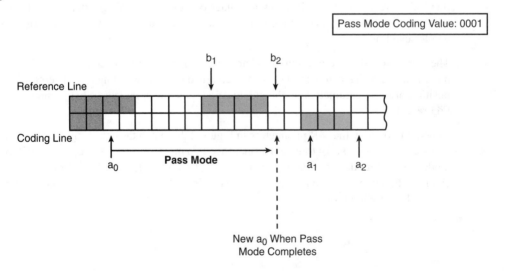

Pass mode is represented by a bit pattern of 0001 when the scan line is binary encoded. Because the value of b_1 is known by the encoder, pass mode does not need to include a value such as a run length. This makes pass mode quite efficient and allows for varying numbers of pixels to be encoded with just 4 bits.

In preparation for the next encoding, pass mode resets the a_0 parameter to the position of b_2. Parameters b_1 and b_2 must then be recalculated. Also, b_2 cannot be just above a_1. Pass mode occurs only when b_2 is to the left of a_1.

Vertical mode occurs when b_1 is within 3 pixels of a_1. Vertical mode efficiently handles the slight changes that can occur between scan lines. Figure 2-36 shows an example of MR vertical mode.

Figure 2-36 *MR Vertical Mode*

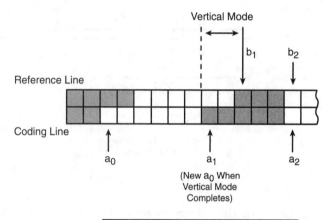

Figure 2-36 shows how vertical mode is designed to handle the subtle changes of a text character as it is scanned line by line. As long as there is not a variation of more than three pixels to either side, vertical mode can effectively encode the changes.

Vertical mode is represented by seven different bit patterns. Each pattern designates the position of a_1 in relation to b_1. After a group of pixels is encoded using vertical mode, pixel position a_1 is now regarded as a_0 for the next encoding.

Horizontal mode occurs in the situations where vertical mode cannot be used, basically, in the instances where the separation between a_1 and b_1 is greater than 3 pixels. Figure 2-37 illustrates a horizontal mode encoding example.

Figure 2-37 *MR Horizontal Mode*

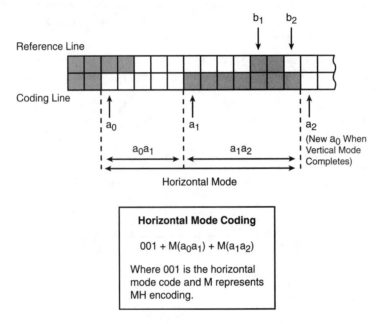

MH encoding is used in horizontal mode to represent the pixel groupings between a_0a_1 and a_1a_2. This makes horizontal mode the least efficient MR encoding mode. However, when encoding text, vertical and pass mode should be used the majority of the time. Upon completion of horizontal mode, a_0 is set to the a_2 position.

When an MR scan line is constructed it will be composed of multiple pass mode, vertical mode, and horizontal mode bit patterns. These bit patterns address every possible pixel-changing scenario based on the positions of the MR parameters in the reference and coding lines.

Although MR encoding can handle any type of image, it is optimized for text characters with the highly efficient pass and vertical modes. Pass mode provides the ability to encode variable-length pixel groups with only 4 bits. Vertical mode handles slight pixel changes (3 pixels or fewer) between the reference and coding line that tend to occur with text characters. Ideally, the use of the inefficient horizontal mode that addresses larger variations (more than 3 pixels) between the reference and coding lines should be minimal for the encoding of text characters.

Just as in MH encoding, fill bits can be added for scan lines whose length falls below the MSLT and there are EOL bit sequences at the end of a scan line. However, the EOL sequence for MH encoding will also contain an additional bit denoting the coding of the next line. The EOL+1 sequence signifies that the next line is a 1-D encoded or MH reference line, whereas EOL+0 indicates that the next line uses 2-D or MR encoding. Figure 2-38 illustrates EOL and fills for MR encoding.

Figure 2-38 *EOLs and Fills for an MR Fax Page*

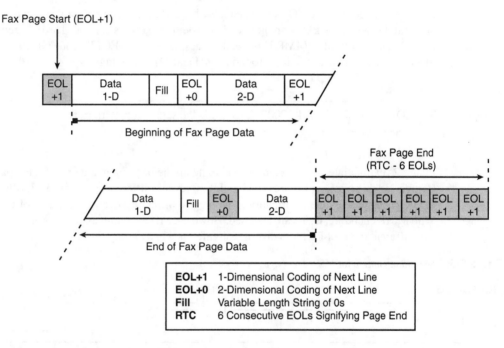

In Figure 2-38, notice that the K parameter is set to a value of 2 as evidenced by the alternating 1-D and 2-D encoded scan lines. This is a common setting for fax devices using MR encoding because any errors in the reference line are only propagated down to one line before another reference line is encoded using MH.

Modified Modified READ

Modified Modified READ or MMR encoding is defined in ITU-T Recommendation T.6. Other than a few minor variations, this encoding is fundamentally the same as MR. Pass mode, vertical mode, and horizontal mode are implemented and coded exactly the same.

The main difference between MMR and MR is that MMR does not use a K parameter and recurring reference lines. An imaginary scan line of all white pixels is used as the first line on the page, and 2-D encoded lines follow until the full page is covered. This imaginary scan line of all white pixels serves as the reference line for the entire fax page.

Because an error in this case could conceivably be propagated down the page, MMR requires that ECM be used. With ECM enabled, MMR is guaranteed to receive error-free scan lines so that 2-D encoding can be used for all lines of the fax page.

Also, MMR does not use EOL characters. With ECM mode required and a known horizontal page width, EOLs are not needed to delineate each scan line. The only required control character used in MMR is the end of facsimile block (EOFB) code which is functionally the same as the RTC found in MH and MR encodings.

TIP   The EOFB (000000000001 000000000001) is the same bit pattern as two EOLs.

Figure 2-39 illustrates MMR scan lines making up the beginning and end of a fax page. Comparing this figure to Figures 2-38 and 2-30 reveals differences in how MH, MR, and MMR organize scan line information. The biggest difference occurs in the use of EOLs. With MMR encoding, EOLs are not used. However, MH encoding uses EOLs and MR uses two different types of EOLs to distinguish reference and coding lines.

Figure 2-39 *Scan Line Data in an MMR Fax Page*

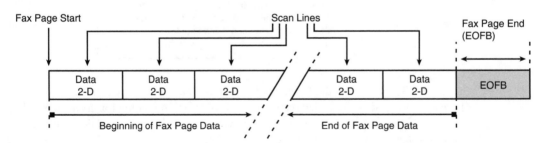

Summary

Over the past 150 years, the evolution of fax technology has culminated in the G3 fax classification. Practically all fax devices today adhere to this standard.

Detailed in ITU-T Recommendations T.30 and T.4, G3 contains specific phases, messages, and page encodings that govern the communication between fax devices in a normal PSTN environment. Optional features such as ECM and Super G3 can enhance the speed and quality of G3 faxes.

This chapter provided core information concerning the operation of fax devices in a PSTN environment. Furthermore, understanding this basic fax knowledge allows for an easier progression into working with fax transmissions in the complex world of IP telephony.

CHAPTER 3

How Text Telephony Works

Text telephony provides a way for those with hearing and speech disabilities to interface with others using the public switched telephone network (PSTN). Users can type their conversations to one another instead of depending on hearing and speaking for communication. This makes text telephony an integral part of the growing trend of providing accessibility in IP telephony (IPT) environments to all users.

Accessibility in many cases is federally mandated here in the United States by legislation such as the Americans with Disabilities Act, Section 255 of the Telecommunications Act, and Section 508 of the Rehabilitation Act. This legislation helps to ensure that users who are hearing or speech disabled are afforded the same communications resources as everyone else. As traditional voice networks continue their migration to VoIP, text telephony remains the primary method for providing equal access to telephony-based communications for users with hearing and speech disabilities.

For most people outside of the hearing- and speech-disabled communities, PSTN text telephone technology is rarely seen and pretty much unknown. However, millions of people depend on this technology, and it must work in today's IPT networks.

This chapter takes an introductory look at how text telephony works from a user perspective while also digging into the underlying technical aspects. Basic text phone operation, conversation etiquette, and text technology fundamental concepts are discussed in the beginning. These topics are then followed by technical coverage of Baudot, the main text communication protocol for the United States and a few other countries.

A Brief History of Text Telephony

Teletypewriters or TTYs were originally used by businesses such as telephone and media companies to relay printed text. On the receiving end, electrical pulses over a line were converted to typed letters on a page. Many TTYs featured a keyboard and a printer and this allowed two-way typed communication between units.

Early TTYs were massive machines weighing several hundred pounds, and some were even fittingly painted battleship gray. Composed of gears, clutches, levers, and other moving parts, these metallic monsters could shake the floor and walls when operating. However, by the early 1960s, many of these TTYs, which implemented the older Baudot signaling protocol, had reached the end of their useful lives. Companies were standardizing on the next generation of data communications based on ASCII signaling and discarding the older Baudot TTYs. One of these older TTYs, a Model 28 by Teletype Corporation, is illustrated in Figure 3-1.

Figure 3-1   *1950 Era Model 28 TTY by Teletype Corporation*

Fortunately, these discarded, mechanized telegraphs were a solution for those with disabilities that did not allow them to use a traditional telephone. The ability to type and read over the phone system as opposed to speaking and hearing meant that these Baudot TTYs were destined for a new life as text telephones for deaf and hard of hearing people.

The technical challenge that prevented the immediate attachment of the TTYs to the telephone network was that the phone company did not allow direct connections. All connections into the telephone network had to occur through an approved device, namely a telephone provided by the phone company itself.

In 1964, Robert H. Weitbrecht, a deaf physicist, solved the connection problem between TTYs and the PSTN. He invented an acoustic coupler that was inserted between the TTY machine and the telephone handset. His invention was called the Phonetype and is often referred to in technical circles as the Weitbrecht modem. Figure 3-2 shows Weitbrecht's first modem, which dates back to 1964.

Figure 3-2   *Robert Weitbrecht's First Modem, Courtesy of Jim Haynes*

Two other people also played prominent roles and assisted Weitbrecht with the development of his acoustic coupler: James C. Marsters, a deaf orthodontist; and Andrew Saks, a deaf businessman. Both Marsters and Saks provided moral, financial, and engineering support to Weitbrecht. They were also keen visionaries. Marsters first proposed a national TTY network for the deaf and Saks envisioned a TTY relay service to bridge the gap between deaf and hearing telephone users.

Even though it took 90 years after the invention of the telephone to make the first TTY call over the PSTN, today a nationwide TTY network exists for the hearing and speech impaired. Without the work of Weitbrecht, Marsters, and Saks, those with hearing and speech disabilities would not have the equal access to the telephone network that the majority of us take for granted.

Text Telephone Terminology

In the beginning TTY just referred to a mechanical teletypewriter, as mentioned previously. Today, however, a TTY also means any device that can replicate the function of a teletypewriter and provide a disabled person access to the telephone network. The use of the term TTY to represent a modern-day text telephone is widely used in North America and Australia. The term TDD (telecommunication device for the deaf) can also refer to a text telephone. TDD was initially used to differentiate the newer portable TTY units from the original mechanical teletypewriters. However, the TDD term is becoming less used because it implies that only deaf people use these devices when in fact hearing people use them, too.

Internationally, the terms text telephone and text phone have gained broad acceptance, and this notation is used in international documentation and standards, such as ITU-T V.18. For the purposes of this book, we adhere to this terminology and use "text telephone" or "text phone" for all references to devices designed for those with hearing and speech disabilities.

Standards and Specifications

There are a number of different text telephone protocols in the world today because each country defines text telephone standards for use on their own telephony networks. Unfortunately, this has led to many incompatibilities and interoperability issues on international text telephone calls. Table 3-1 shows the common text phone protocols in use by some countries today.

Table 3-1   *Common Text Phone Protocols*

Text Phone Protocol	Countries Used By	Carrier Type
Baudot at 45.45 bps	United States, Canada, Ireland, Iceland, South Africa, and some usage in the United Kingdom	Carrierless
Baudot at 50 bps	Australia and New Zealand	Carrierless
Bell 103	United States	Carrier based
DTMF	Holland and Denmark	Carrierless
EDT (European Deaf Telephone) utilizing V.21 at 110 bps	Germany, Switzerland, Italy, Austria, Spain	Carrierless
ITU-T V.23	France and Belgium	Carrier based
ITU-T V.21 encoded per ITU-T T.50	United Kingdom, Norway, Sweden, and Finland	Carrier based

To complicate things even further, there can even be a number of different protocols within a single country. For example, within the United States, there are three text telephone protocols that are commonly seen: Baudot, Bell 103, and Turbo Code by UltraTec. Although Baudot is considered the default standard, the added features and speed make ASCII based Bell 103 and the proprietary Turbo Code more enticing options for many users.

Carrier Based Versus Carrierless Protocols

The text phone protocols listed in Table 3-1 can be broken down into carrier based and carrierless groupings. Carrier-based protocols implement a constant carrier signal even when text data is not being sent or received. Carrierless protocols either do not use a carrier or only have a carrier present when information is being communicated.

The presence of a carrier signal is common with data modem protocols, as detailed in the "Modulation" section of Chapter 1, "How Modems Work." Because many text protocols use a data modem modulation standard, these implementations must be carrier based. Other text phone protocols, with roots going back to the original teletype devices that predate modems, use a carrierless design. Figure 3-3 exemplifies a carrier based and a carrierless text protocol.

Figure 3-3   *Carrier Based and Carrierless Modulation*

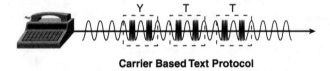

Carrier Based Text Protocol

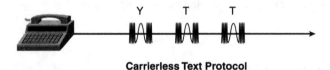

Carrierless Text Protocol

There is an inherent benefit to the carrierless text phone protocols. Because a carrier is not always present, mixing speech and text signaling on the same line is simple. When text telephone data is not being sent then the user can speak if necessary while possibly still receiving responses on the text telephone. This type of scenario is common with deaf people who sometimes like to speak instead of type.

In order to mix both text and speech with carrier-based text protocols, the carrier must be interrupted. This is usually done through picking up the handset or hitting a key on the text device. At this point, voice communication can occur but if the text conversation is resumed then the carrier must be re-connected. Compared to a carrierless design, carrier-based text protocols have an additional step when transitioning between text and voice.

ITU-T Recommendation V.18

The V.18 specification issued by the ITU is a dual standard designed to address some of the issues with text telephone communication. While defining interoperability processes among the major text telephone protocols, V.18 also details a completely new text protocol.

As illustrated by the disparate text protocols in Table 3-1, interoperability is a major issue among text phone users, especially on international calls. V.18 addresses these interoperability issues by detailing how multiple text phone protocols can be consolidated into a single device.

Specifically, V.18 addresses the interoperability between the following widely used text protocols: Baudot at 45.45 baud, Baudot at 50 baud, V.21, DTMF, and EDT. Coverage of these protocols allows a V.18 text device to easily interoperate with most of the international text telephones.

The new text telephone protocol defined in V.18 is often referred to as V.18 native mode. This protocol is composed of a V.21 modulation at 300 bps with the character set defined by ITU-T T.140. V.18 native mode is a part of the ITU-T V.151 specification that details the transport of text telephony information over IP.

In spite of the benefits offered by V.18 to text telephone interoperability, V.18 has never caught on and enjoyed mainstream support. One reason is that to interoperate with the different text protocols, V.18 must probe the text device on the other side to determine what protocol it is running. This probing may take upward of 55 seconds, and this is too long for many users.

Text Telephone Operation

Because of the unfamiliarity with text telephones for most people, the basic operation and function of a text phone needs to be discussed. The terminology, conversation conventions, and even the connection options are much different from a typical phone. Figure 3-4 illustrates a modern-day text telephone.

Figure 3-4   *A Text Telephone from Ultratec*

For example, because words are being typed rather than spoken, some shortcuts and syntax conventions are applicable only to a text telephone conversation. In addition, some text protocols mandate a half-duplex conversation. So, users must signal each other when they have finished talking so that the other user can then type.

There might even be a difference in how text telephony devices connect to the phone network compared to a regular telephone. Many text telephones still use acoustic couplers, which can be an awkward process for those unfamiliar with connecting a phone in this manner.

Acoustic Coupling Versus Direct Connections

Because of telephone company restrictions, the very first text telephones used an acoustic coupler to connect to the PSTN. Until the laws were changed many years later, direct connections were not allowed into the telephone company network.

Today's text telephones offer either acoustic coupling or direct connections or both. Figure 3-5 illustrates a text telephone with an acoustic coupler that is connected to a Cisco IP Phone.

Figure 3-5 *Text Telephone with an Acoustic Coupler Connected to a Cisco IP Phone*

A text telephone with an acoustic coupler as shown in Figure 3-5 provides the users with access to any phone that uses a basic handset. This type of text phone is better for some users because handsets are usually easier to access than wall jacks. In addition, acoustically coupled text devices can be used at public telephones where a direct connection is not available.

The main drawback of acoustically coupled text telephones is the leaking in of outside noise into the connection. Handsets come in a variety of shapes and sizes, and it can be difficult to get a good fit between the phone handset and the couplers. In louder environments, the ambient noise can have an even more negative effect on text telephone performance. This is the reason that most text telephone vendors recommend a direct connection to an analog line as opposed to acoustic coupling.

Direct connection text telephones also offer the simplicity of plugging the text phone into a wall jack just as you would a normal phone. More recent text telephones may even support a direct connection to a cell phone for text users who require additional mobility.

Originating and Receiving Text Telephone Calls

Call initiation and termination procedures for a text telephone are different than for a normal phone. The main difference is the reliance on visual cues compared to the typical auditory ones.

The following steps illustrate the placement of a typical text telephone call:

Step 1   Power on the text device.

Step 2   For text phones with an acoustic coupler, place the handset on the coupler. For phones with a direct connection, make sure that the text phone is properly connected.

Step 3   Dial the telephone number. Most numbers can be dialed from the text device itself, but actual procedures will vary based on device model and vendor.

Step 4   Observe the ring indicator. This might also be called "signal" on the text telephone display, and it is simply a notification that sound is present on the line.

   — A long flashing, intermittent light indicates ringing.

   — A short steady blinking light indicates a busy signal.

   — Irregular flickering means that the destination has been answered by voice. Pressing any key should let the person know that this is a text call. They may need to move their handset over to an acoustic coupler if they have a text telephone.

When making a text call, it is appropriate to allow the phone to ring 10 times or more. Without the audible ringing of a normal phone, text users might need more time to notice the visual cues that alert them to an incoming call.

The following steps detail how a text telephone call is received:

Step 1   Observe the flashing of the light that indicates "ring" or an incoming call. This light may reside on the text unit itself or be an accessory to a normal telephone.

Step 2   If using an acoustically coupled text device, make sure that the handset is placed on the coupler.

Step 3   Make sure the text device is powered on. Text telephones may use ring voltage to light the lamp, but then must be powered on to work.

Step 4   Answer the call by just typing or hit an "online" or "answer" key.

Step 5   After pressing the spacebar a few times, a typical answer greeting would be "HELLO JOE HERE GA."

Conversation Conventions

Over the years, text users have adopted certain conversation conventions and other shortcuts to make text telephone communication more efficient. Some of these conventions were brought about by the half-duplex nature of the Baudot protocol itself, whereas others have been created to save time and speed up the pace of a typed conversation.

The two most notable conventions or initialisms are GA (go ahead) and SK (stop keying). GA is used when a user has finished typing to notify the other party that it is his turn to type. Because the Baudot protocol is half duplex, GA is used to prevent two parties from talking simultaneously. During a Baudot text conversation, interrupting someone and typing while he is typing should not be done because this can garble the transmissions of both parties.

NOTE   Some text telephone protocols are not half duplex like Baudot, and the GA and SK conventions are not necessary. However, users will still exercise explicit turn-taking to avoid typing over each during a conversation.

SK is typically seen at the termination of a text telephone call. This message signals the other party that you are done with the call and ready to disconnect. Because of the heavy usage of GA and SK in text telephone conversations, some text devices provide dedicated GA and SK buttons. Table 3-2 highlights some common text telephone conversation acronyms and abbreviations.

Table 3-2   *Common Text Telephone Acronyms and Abbreviations*

Abbreviation/Acronym	Definition
ABT	About
ANS	Answer
BEC, CUZ	Because
CD, CU	Could
CN	Can
GA	Go ahead
GA to SK	Go ahead if you have more to say but I am finished
HD, HLD	Hold
LV	Leave
MIN	Minute
MSG	Message
MTG	Meeting

Table 3-2   *Common Text Telephone Acronyms and Abbreviations (Continued)*

Abbreviation/Acronym	Definition
NBR, NU	Number
OIC	Oh, I see
OPR	Operator
PLS	Please
Q, QQ	Question
R	Are
SHD	Should
SK	Stop keying, goodbye, end of call
SKSK	Hanging up
TY	Thank you
U	You
UR	Your
XX	Error, mistake

Many of the abbreviations and acronyms listed in Table 3-2 are familiar to most people. The proliferation of IM (instant messaging) and e-mail in today's world make many of these shortcuts quite common, whereas others are more text telephone specific.

There are a couple of additional conventions to be aware of when operating a text telephone:

- Text telephone conversations are usually displayed in all capital letters. As discussed later in the "Baudot Character Set" section of this chapter, the Baudot character set does not define any lowercase letters. With e-mail and IM, many consider typing in all capital letters as yelling or shouting, and it can be difficult to read. However, this is how many text telephone conversations appear.

- A common way to correct typing mistakes is the XX or XXX notation. For example, "I WD LUKE XX LIKE TO MEET U LATER." Notice how the XX corrects LUKE to LIKE.

Text Telephone Relay Services

While text telephones provide access to the telephone network for the hearing and speech impaired, both parties must have a text device for a conversation to take place. So, what happens when a text user needs to make a doctor's appointment, call the plumber, or even contact a friend or relative who does not have a text telephone? These situations require the use of a TRS (telecommunications relay service).

Many countries provide a nationwide TRS system for text telephone users. In the United States, there is a national TRS operated by states and long-distance carriers that was mandated by the Americans with Disabilities Act. Text telephone users in the United States and Canada can access their TRS service by dialing 711.

Contacting a TRS connects the text user to a CA (communications assistant) who serves as a translator between the text telephone user and the voice user. The CA has a text telephone that connects to one party and then the CA talks and listens in a traditional phone conversation with the other party. Figure 3-6 demonstrates a call between a text user and a voice user using a TRS CA.

Figure 3-6   *Text Telephone Call Involving a TRS*

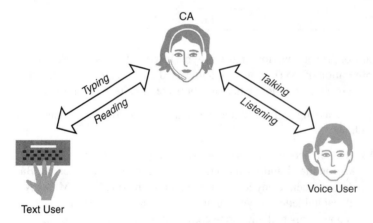

A TRS also provides access for voice users so that they can originate calls to text users. One common example is a teacher's need to contact the deaf parents of a student. A TRS enables this communication to take place without the need for the teacher to own a text device.

In addition to TRS, other relay services are available, too. Most of these are similar to a traditional TRS with minor modifications or enhancements. Table 3-3 provides an overview of other types of relay services for text telephones.

Table 3-3   *Overview of Relay Services for Text Telephones*

TRS Type	Definition
Text telephone TRS	This is the traditional TRS associated with text devices. CAs serve as the bridge between text users and voice users.
VCO (voice carry over)	A variation of text telephone TRS that allows the text user to speak to the voice user directly while reading the voice user's response.
HCO (hearing carry over)	A variation of text telephone TRS that allows the text user to listen to the voice user directly while typing responses.
STS (speech-to-speech) relay	A form of TRS where a CA who is specially trained in understanding a variety of speech disorders repeats the caller's words in a more understandable format.
CapTel by Ultratec	Similar to VCO, CapTel allows a user to speak normally. However, a CA repeats all incoming responses to this user into an automatic speech recognition system which transcribes them. The other party's voice can then be listened to and his speech is also captioned, appearing as text on the user's specialized phone. Imagine closed captioning (CC) or subtitles for the hearing impaired that are used in the TV world applied to a telephone conversation.
VRS (video relay service)	An Internet-based form of TRS for those whose primary language is ASL (American Sign Language). Using videoconferencing equipment, CA translates between ASL and a traditional voice phone call.
IP relay	A text-based form of TRS that uses the Internet rather than phone lines to bridge the connection between the disabled user and the CA.

A number of TRS choices are available today for the text telephone user, but a growing number are choosing the newer relay technologies such as IP relay. As broadband Internet access continues to become more accessible, the use of traditional TRS services is declining.

HCO (Hearing Carry Over)

During a normal text telephone conversation, both parties read and type as their means of communication. HCO offers those who can hear but maybe not speak the option to listen to the other party but type responses instead of speaking them. HCO is usually implemented with a TRS, but it also works between two text telephones. Figure 3-7 illustrates a text call with HCO involving a TRS.

Figure 3-7   *Text Telephone Call Using HCO*

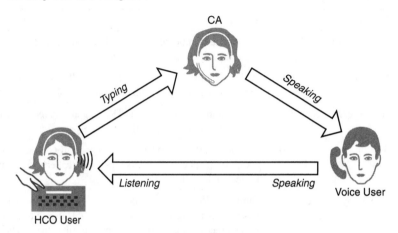

HCO is beneficial to all parties because it generally speeds up the conversation. The CA serves as the "mouth" of the disabled person by speaking whatever is typed.

VCO (Voice Carry Over)

As its name implies, VCO is a text telephone option that allows a party to speak his responses while reading information that is directed to him. The CA in a VCO scenario acts as the "ears" for the disabled person and translates the voice directed to that person into text. Figure 3-8 demonstrates VCO with a CA.

Figure 3-8   *Text Telephone Call Using VCO*

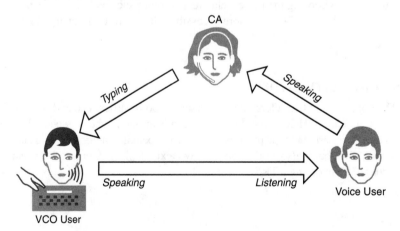

Some text devices have built-in VCO features that allow the user to pick up the handset to speak while still being able to read messages. Other text devices may not even include a keyboard and be dedicated VCO devices. There is only a screen for reading and a handset for speaking.

Text devices without VCO support must use a more complicated procedure for implementing VCO functionality. The text user must return the handset to the acoustic coupler to type responses and then pick it up again to listen to the other party.

As with HCO, VCO can also be implemented between two text telephones without a TRS. Although built-in HCO/VCO features are nice, the only requirements for HCO/VCO functionality are acoustically coupled text devices or those with attached handsets.

Baudot Protocol

The Baudot text protocol is the de facto standard for text telephone communication in North America and the protocol that will be focused on in this section. Other text protocol options such as ASCII and Turbo Code are available in North America, but they are optional features on some text telephones, and Turbo Code is a proprietary implementation.

Additional text telephone protocols may be used in other countries (see Table 3-1). The best resource for technical details on these other text protocols is the ITU-T V.18 specification at http://www.itu.int/rec/T-REC-V.18.

Baudot Character Set

The original Baudot code was invented by Emile Baudot around 1870. Subsequent modifications adapted the code for teletypewriter use and altered it into its present-day form. The Baudot code used in today's text telephone protocols implements a character set that is defined by TIA/EIA-825-A. This specification categorizes each character as a letter or a figure accessible by a shift function. Table 3-4 details the TIA/EIA-825-A Baudot character set.

Table 3-4   *Baudot Character Set as Defined by TIA/EIA-825-A*

Binary	Hex	Letters	Figures
00000	00	backspace	backspace
00001	01	E	3
00010	02	LF	LF
00011	03	A	-
00100	04	Space	Space

continues

Table 3-4   *Baudot Character Set as Defined by TIA/EIA-825-A (Continued)*

Binary	Hex	Letters	Figures
00101	05	S	BELL
00110	06	I	8
00111	07	U	7
01000	08	CR	CR
01001	09	D	$
01010	A	R	4
01011	B	J	'
01100	C	N	,
01101	D	F	!
01110	E	C	:
01111	F	K	(
10000	10	T	5
10001	11	Z	"
10010	12	L	)
10011	13	W	2
10100	14	H	=
10101	15	Y	6
10110	16	P	0
10111	17	Q	1
11000	18	O	9
11001	19	B	?
11010	1A	G	+
11011	1B	FIGURES SHIFT	FIGURES SHIFT
11100	1C	M	.
11101	1D	X	/
11110	1E	V	;
11111	1F	LETTERS SHIFT	LETTERS SHIFT

Baudot code is composed of 5 bits, which allows for a representation of just 32 characters (2^5). However, with 26 letters and 10 number symbols in the English language and punctuation marks, more characters are needed. So, the Baudot code implements a nifty shift function to extend the number of characters that can be represented by 5 bits.

This shift function is typically transparent to the user. If you type B4, this will require a shift between the B and the 4 because the B is a letter and the 4 is a figure. Baudot would send B4 as B, FIGURES SHIFT, 4. As you can see, three Baudot characters are transmitted to represent these two characters. Today's text equipment handles this transition seamlessly for the user so that only the characters B and 4 need to be typed.

Occasionally, text users might experience a scenario in which the text devices lose their shift synchronization. This issue can be caused by users typing at the same time or by line errors that result in the shift being lost. Often referred to as "going out of sync," words will appear garbled as one side sends bits representing letters while the other side is interpreting the bits as figures.

Pressing the spacebar a few times is the accepted method to resynchronize or "resync" the text devices. More advanced text devices may even offer the capability of reversing any garbled characters caused by a shift problem.

As mentioned earlier in this chapter, another limitation imposed by the Baudot code is that there are not enough bits to represent both uppercase and lowercase letters. This is the reason that every Baudot text conversation is displayed in all capital letters.

Baudot Modulation Details

In addition to standardizing the Baudot character set, EIA-TIA-825-A also details how these bits are modulated asynchronously across a PSTN network using character oriented FSK (Frequency Shift Keying). A binary 1 is represented by a 1400 Hz tone, and a 0 is encoded with a 1800 Hz tone. Each of these bits is transmitted for a duration of 22 ms for a signaling rate of 45.45 bps. For more detailed information on FSK modulation, see the section "Frequency Shift Keying (FSK)" in Chapter 1.

NOTE   Be aware that another version of Baudot exists where the bit duration is 20 ms. This equates to a speed of 50 bps, but it is not used in North America.

Each 5-bit character is preceded by a binary 0, which is used as a start bit, and a binary 1 is used as a stop bit. The duration of the stop should be 1.5 times the normal bit duration of 22 ms. Figure 3-9 illustrates a how a single Baudot character is formatted.

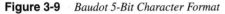

Figure 3-9 *Baudot 5-Bit Character Format*

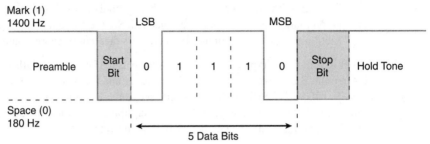

Before the Baudot character, there is a preamble, which is just a mark or binary 1 that is transmitted for 150 ms. After the character, a hold tone follows for a period of 150 ms to 300 ms and prevents echo reflections from being perceived as valid characters. The preamble and hold tones are not needed for Baudot characters transmitted consecutively.

Following the start bit, the Least Significant Bit (LSB) is transmitted first. So, for the letter A, which is coded as a binary 00011 in Baudot, the transmission order would be Start Bit, 1,1,0,0,0, and then the Stop Bit.

Summary

Text telephony is a technology area that is unfamiliar to most people. Used by the hearing and speech impaired to communicate over the PSTN, this technology is becoming more prominent in today's IP world.

This chapter covered many aspects of text telephony. A brief history described the Weitbrecht modem, which allowed large discarded TTY machines to be used over the PSTN. Then, text telephone functions such as sending and receiving calls, conversation conventions, and TRS were covered.

Last of all, there was an in-depth look at the Baudot text protocol, the text telephony communication method for the United States and a few other countries. All the information in this chapter provides a firm foundation in the workings of text telephony before diving deeper in subsequent chapters and integrating text with IP.

CHAPTER 4

Passthrough

When the public switched telephone network (PSTN) was initially constructed, voice communication was the primary goal. However, as data communications such as fax, modem, and text became more important, they also were made to work over the PSTN using special protocols and transport methods. Today, with VoIP taking the place of the PSTN, voice communication is still the primary objective, and specific protocols and procedures are again needed to transport fax, modem, and text communications.

One such feature that voice gateways can implement to transport modem, fax, or text telephony traffic is passthrough. This transport mechanism is the easiest and simplest way for a voice gateway to pass modulated data.

For the most part, passthrough works just like a normal voice call. The voice gateway receives an analog waveform from the modem, fax, or text device and encodes it using an appropriate coder/decoder (codec). These encoded samples are then encapsulated and transported over the packet network using the Real-Time Protocol (RTP).

You will also commonly hear passthrough referred to as voice-band data (VBD) by more recent literature and many of the specifications. These two terms are used interchangeably for the remainder of this book.

This chapter provides an in-depth look at how passthrough operates and the different ways that it is implemented to transport modem, fax, and text data. Specifically, this chapter discusses the following topics:

- Passthrough Fundamentals
- NSE-Based Passthrough
- Protocol-Based Pass-Through for Fax
- Text over G.711
- A Future Look at ITU-T V.152

Passthrough Fundamentals

With only a few minor variations that are discussed at the end of this section, a passthrough call is treated the same as a VoIP call from a voice gateway perspective. The human voice sample that is processed by the gateway on a VoIP call is simply replaced with the modulated data used by faxes and modems.

For both voice and passthrough calls, a process known as pulse code modulation (PCM) converts an analog signal to an equivalent digital representation. This digital signal is what is packetized and transported over the IP network. Figure 4-1 illustrates how PCM works.

Figure 4-1 *Pulse Code Modulation*

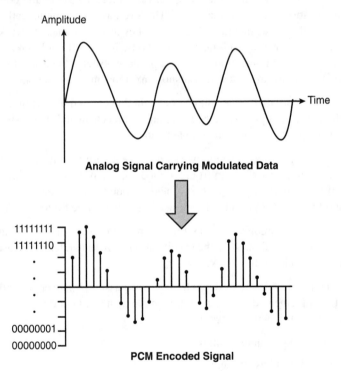

PCM first filters out all frequencies greater than 4000 Hz because the majority of human speech occurs in the 300 Hz to 3200 Hz range. Nyquist's theorem specifies that to accurately reconstruct a signal, it must be sampled at twice the highest frequency of that signal. Because a band-limited 4000 Hz filter is used, the original analog signal must therefore be sampled at 8000 times a second.

Sampling is merely taking an amplitude reading of the original signal. This process is known as pulse amplitude modulation (PAM). PCM takes it one step further than PAM and quantizes the signal.

Quantization is the process of breaking up the continuous amplitude spectrum into discrete intervals. Each quantization level is assigned an 8-bit codeword. Therefore, there are 256 distinct amplitude levels with a unique 8-bit codeword assigned to each one. Figure 4-1 illustrates an analog signal encoded as digital PCM through the process detailed in the preceding paragraphs.

For a VoIP call, there are a number of codecs to choose from. A codec integrates with PCM and defines a particular encoding scheme to be used in the conversion of an analog signal into its digitally encoded version. Codecs vary in bandwidth requirements, voice quality, and computational requirements.

For example, voice is commonly transported over the WAN using high compression codecs, such as G.729 (8 Kbps) or G.723 (5.3 Kbps/6.3 Kbps). Because these codecs are optimized for human speech, they do a great job in preserving speech quality while at the same time offering a high compression rate that saves bandwidth.

However, the tones used for modem and fax negotiation are very different in nature from human speech and in many instances not even in the same frequency range. This makes it difficult to optimize a high-compression codec for both voice and fax/modem tones. These high-compression, speech-optimized codecs distort modulated data signals to the point where modems and fax machines are unable to communicate successfully.

Although codecs such as clear-channel codec or 32 Kbps compressed G.726 may transport modem or fax tones in-band, this discussion will be limited to using G.711 as the VBD codec. This is because it is overwhelmingly the most frequently used and the only one officially supported for Cisco passthrough features. G.711 is a 64 Kbps uncompressed voice codec that implements a PCM scheme that is compatible with modulated data.

Rather than the uniform quantization seen in Figure 4-1, the G.711 codec uses a nonuniform quantization scheme, known as companding. This has the effect of a greater concentration of quantization levels at the lower amplitudes, and conversely the higher-amplitude values have quantization levels assigned more sparsely. Figure 4-2 shows this uneven distribution of quantization levels for the amplitude.

Figure 4-2   *G.711 Companding of a PCM Signal*

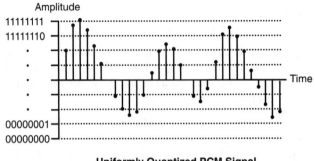

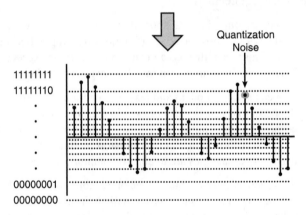

Companding is appropriate for voice because the majority of human speech occurs at the lower end of the amplitude spectrum. This allows for greater fidelity and improved voice quality for the lower-amplitude signal, which is the bulk of human speech.

Two types of companding are used in G.711: μ-law and a-law. They are similar in many ways, but μ-law has a bit less distortion for lower-amplitude signals, whereas a-law has a greater dynamic range than μ-law. The biggest difference is that μ-law is used by North America and Japan, whereas a-law is used by the rest of the world. It is important to note that these two companding schemes are not compatible, and any calls between countries that use different companding types have to convert between the two.

The major impairment that results from analog-to-digital conversions, such as PCM, is the introduction of noise. Any difference between the actual amplitude value of the original signal and its assigned value of the closest discrete quantization level will introduce quantization noise.

As Figure 4-2 highlights, the nonlinear distribution of quantization levels used in companding will produce less quantization noise at the lower-amplitude signals and more quantization noise at the higher-amplitude signals. This keeps the signal-to-noise ratio (SNR) relatively constant over the entire signal amplitude range.

Now that the process of digitally encoding an analog signal has been discussed, it is important to understand how these PCM samples of modem, fax, and text data are packetized for transport over the IP network. Like in any data communication, the payload is independently encapsulated by the corresponding protocol of each of the OSI layers. For example, Figure 4-3 is an illustration of how PCM modulated data samples would be encapsulated for transmission over an IP configured Ethernet interface.

Figure 4-3   *Encapsulation of an RTP Packet over Ethernet*

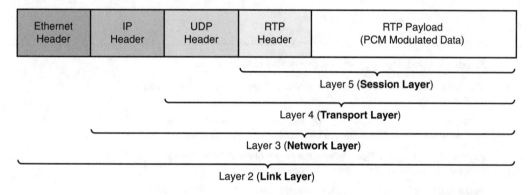

Because of the real-time nature of the transport of the PCM-encoded modulated data, it is important to take a closer look at the RTP header. From Figure 4-3, you can see that the G.711 encoded samples of voice-band modulated data become the payload of an RTP encapsulated packet. Figure 4-4 illustrates the RTP header, which is defined in RFC 3550.

All real-time traffic that is encapsulated in RTP maintains the timing characteristics of the original analog signal via the Timestamp field in the RTP header. Likewise, the PCM encoded samples can be played out in the same order as they were received because of the Sequence Number field. For this discussion, the most important field is the Payload Type.

Figure 4-4 *RTP Packet Header*

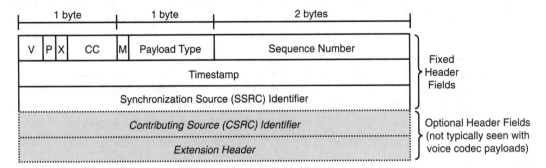

V: Version, identifies the version of RTP.

P: Padding, if set the packet contains one or more additional padding octets.

X: Extension, indicates the presence of a header extension field.

CC: CSRC Count, specifies the number of CSRC fields that follow the fixed header.

M: Marker, defined by a profile with the intention of allowing significant events such as frame boundaries to be marked in the packet stream.

Payload Type: Payload Type, defines the format of the RTP payload and determines its interpretation by the application.

Sequence Number: A counter that increments by one for each RTP packet sent while the receiver uses it to detect packet loss and out of sequence packets.

Timestamp: Reflects the sampling instant of the first octet in the RTP packet.

Synchronization Source (SSRC) Identifier: Identifies the source with a unique, random identifier.

Contributing Source (CSRC) Identifier: Identifies up to 15 contributing sources for the payload contained in the RTP packet.

Extension Header: A variable length extension to the RTP header that allows individual implementations to experiment with new payload-format-independent functions.

The Payload Type field identifies the type of data being carried in the RTP packet. This defines how the packet will be interpreted and dealt with by the remote side. Table 4-1 shows the Payload Type values that are defined in RFC 3551.

Table 4-1   *Payload Type Values*

Payload Type	Payload Encoding	Payload Type	Payload Encoding
0	PCM μ-law	25	CelB
1	reserved	26	JPEG
2	reserved	27	Unassigned
3	GSM	28	nv
4	G.723	29	Unassigned
5	DVI4	30	Unassigned
6	DVI4	31	H.261
7	LPC	32	MPV
8	PCM a-law	33	MP2T
9	G.722	34	H.263
10	L16	35–71	Unassigned
11	L16	72–76	Reserved
12	QCELP	77–95	Unassigned
13	CN	96–127	Dynamic
14	MPA	dyn	G.726 (40 kbps)
15	G.728	dyn	G.726 (32 kbps)
16	DVI4	dyn	G.726 (24 kbps)
17	DVI4	dyn	G.726 (16 kbps)
18	G.729	dyn	G.729D
19	Reserved	dyn	G.729E
20	Unassigned	dyn	GSM-EFR
21	Unassigned	dyn	L8
22	Unassigned	dyn	RED
23	Unassigned	dyn	VDVI
24	Unassigned	dyn	H.263-1998

Table 4-1 shows a number of dynamic and unassigned payload types. The dynamically assigned portion of this range is what is primarily discussed in this chapter. Unless explicitly configured on the gateway, Cisco uses the dynamic and unassigned payload type values shown in Table 4-2 by default.

Table 4-2   *Dynamic and Unassigned Payload Types Commonly Used by Cisco*

Default Dynamic and Unassigned Payload Type	Payload Encoding
90	RFC 2198 Passthrough Redundancy
96	Cisco Fax Relay Switchover
97	Cisco Fax Relay Switchover ACK
100	Named Signaling Event
101	Named Telephony Event
119	Cisco Text Relay
121	Cisco RTP DTMF Relay
122	Cisco Fax Relay
123	Cisco CAS Payload
125	Cisco Clear-Channel

When using passthrough, a voice gateway identifies the contents it is transmitting as simply PCM (PT=0 for G.711 -law or PT=8 for G.711 a-law). Thus, it makes no distinction within the RTP packet between a voice call and a modem/fax/text call.

As Figure 4-5 highlights, the fax/modem modulated data is transparently carried over the IP network, and the data is never demodulated within the IP infrastructure. This is the principal difference between passthrough and relay, which is covered in Chapter 5, "Relay."

Figure 4-5   *Fax and Modem Passthrough*

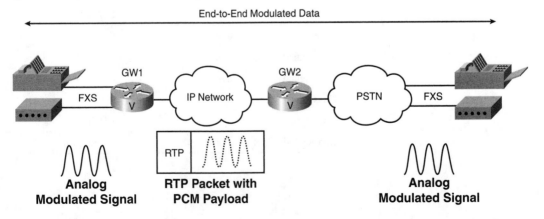

When the passthrough feature is initiated on a Cisco voice gateway, additional events take place to ensure that the modulated data is successfully transported across IP. The most important event is known as codec upspeed.

Codec upspeed makes sure that the passthrough call uses a low-compression codec such as G.711 μ-law or G.711 a-law. Passthrough calls start out in the beginning as regular voice calls. This means that the call could be using a high-compression codec such as G.729. However, when the passthrough feature is initiated, this codec is changed to G.711 in what is termed codec upspeed.

In addition to codec upspeed, another change also takes place in the Cisco voice gateway when it switches into VBD mode and prepares for a passthrough call. To make the IP path as transparent as possible, the DSP disables Voice Activity Detection (VAD). VAD is a bandwidth-saving feature that sends packets only when there is voice detected during the call. If VAD were to remain enabled for the passthrough calls, signals could be clipped, negatively affecting the data being transported.

Slight changes are also made to the DSP's jitter or playout buffer. While in voice mode, the playout buffer is adaptive and constantly adjusts to changing network conditions. However, during passthrough mode, the playout buffer becomes fixed to an optimum value for the call. For a more comprehensive discussion of what a jitter buffer is and the specifics of how it behaves during a passthrough call, see the "IP Troubleshooting" section of Chapter 12, "Troubleshooting Passthrough and Relay."

After the detection of certain tones by the DSP, the switchover to passthrough is signaled in one of two ways. One is NSE-based passthrough signaling, which involves the exchange of Named Signaling Events (NSE) packets between the gateways. The other is protocol-based passthrough signaling, in which a direct negotiation occurs in the protocol stack of the call signaling protocol.

NSE-Based Passthrough

When passthrough is configured on a voice gateway, it takes the modulated data from a fax, modem, or text device and transparently transports it in the media stream as PCM samples encapsulated in RTP.

The terminating gateway (TGW) always switches to NSE-based passthrough mode first by detecting the appropriate tone from the answering modem or fax machine. This tone is the 2100 Hz CED from a standard fax machine or the 2100 Hz ANSam tone from a modem or SG3 fax machine.

When the TGW detects this tone, it undergoes a passthrough switchover, including a codec upspeed to the VBD codec (G.711). In conjunction with this switchover to NSE-based passthrough, the TGW also transmits an in-band signal in the media stream to the originating gateway (OGW). In this message, the TGW signals to the OGW to switch into passthrough mode. This signal is communicated using NSE packets.

NSEs are a Cisco proprietary message that are sent as part of the RTP stream and are identified using a payload type of 100 in the RTP header by default. Despite being a proprietary message, the NSE packet format is the same as for standards-based Named Telephony Events (NTE), described in RFC 2833. Figure 4-6 shows the NSE/NTE packet format.

Figure 4-6   *NSE Packet Format*

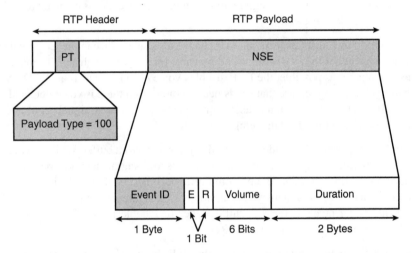

Event ID: Identifier that specifies the purpose of the NSE message.

E: End bit, specifies the end of the event when set.

R: Reserved, set to 0 and reserved for future use.

Volume: Indicates the signal power level for DTMF digits and other events representable as tones.

Duration: Typically used for events like DTMF to express the duration of the tone in timestamp units.

NOTE   The NSE payload type is configurable on a Cisco IOS voice gateway to be any value between 98 and 119. The default value is 100.

The Event ID field uses Cisco-defined events to signal in-band the coordination of a variety of tasks. Table 4-3 shows the NSE event numbers used for passthrough. Notice that NSE-192 is used by the TGW to signal to the OGW to go into VBD mode.

NOTE	The Volume and Duration fields in the NSE packet will always be set to 0s for the discussions in this chapter. Only the event ID is pertinent.

Table 4-3   *Cisco NSE Event IDs Used for Passthrough*

NSE Event Number	Description of Operation
192	Triggered by the detection of 2100 Hz tone, which is typically a fax CED or modem ANSam tone. This message instructs the remote gateway to switch over to passthrough (VBD) mode (upspeed codec to G.711, disable VAD, set the jitter buffer to a fixed value, and so on).
193	Triggered by a modem ANSam tone (or phase reversals in any 2100 Hz tone). This message instructs the other gateway to disable echo cancellers.
194	Triggered by a local detection of 4 seconds of silence or carrier loss detection. This message instructs the remote gateway to return to voice mode. Basically, all the changes made by NSE-192 and NSE-193 are undone.

When VoIP calls are transitioned to fax and modem passthrough calls using NSEs, the NSE signaling occurs within the RTP media stream. The signaling protocol is generally unaware that this out-of-band messaging is even occurring. So, NSE-based passthrough is supported in just about all Cisco voice gateways implementing the common signaling protocols of H.323, Session Initiation Protocol (SIP), Media Gateway Control Protocol (MGCP), and Skinny Client Control Protocol (SCCP).

The procedures that a fax call and a modem call use to set up NSE-based passthrough are slightly different. Therefore, the cases of fax passthrough and modem passthrough are analyzed independently and in more detail.

Fax Passthrough with NSE

In this section, the information exchange and negotiations between a TGW and an OGW for an NSE-signaled fax passthrough call are covered. Figure 4-7 illustrates this message flow for a typical fax call.

Figure 4-7 *Fax Passthrough Call with NSE Signaling*

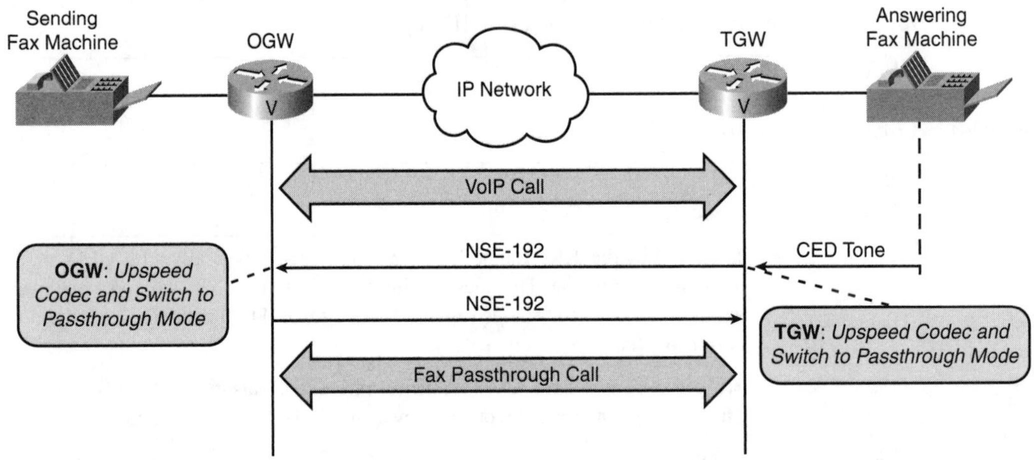

NOTE   The NSE signaling flow shown in Figure 4-7 does not indicate a specific voice signaling protocol. NSE-based fax passthrough is compatible with H.323, SIP, MGCP, and SCCP, and the call flow from an NSE perspective is identical.

When the calling fax machine places a call to the answering fax machine, the call is initially set up as a simple voice call between the voice gateways. At this point, with both gateways having been configured for NSE-based passthrough, the DSP on the TGW is listening for a 2100 Hz answer tone.

When the terminating fax machine answers the call, it transmits its 2100 Hz CED tone. The DSP on the TGW detects and recognizes this tone. This triggers a codec upspeed and a switch to passthrough or VBD mode on the TGW.

In addition, detection of the fax CED by the TGW triggers a notification by the DSP to IOS that a fax call has been detected. In response, IOS sends an instruction to the DSP to send an in-band RTP signal with payload type 100 to the OGW instructing it to upspeed its codec and switch to VBD mode, too. This signal is an NSE with event ID 192 (for example, NSE-192) and is shown in Figure 4-7. The OGW replies by sending an NSE-192 back to the TGW.

TIP   In reality, more than one NSE message is passed between the gateways to protect against packet loss or other network problems. Typically, the NSE message is repeated three times. For the NSE-192 messages in Figure 4-7, three NSE messages are sent from the TGW to the OGW, and then three messages are sent in the reverse direction as a response. This is true of practically all NSE signaling messages, but for simplicity this is just shown as one NSE message in the NSE call-flow diagrams.

At this point, both gateways have completely transitioned from voice mode to VBD mode. The fax negotiation will proceed normally as PCM packets over the IP network. The modulated data is end to end between the two fax machines.

Although not shown in Figure 4-7 because it is rarely seen, an NSE-194 may occur at the completion of the fax call if the fax machines do not hang up. An NSE-194 will occur after 4 seconds of silence and will switch the passthrough call back to voice mode. However, because fax machines usually immediately disconnect upon call completion, it is not necessary for the voice gateways to transmit NSE-194 messages.

Modem Passthrough with NSE

The basic difference between the fax passthrough feature and the modem passthrough feature is whether the 2100 Hz answer tone from the answering fax/modem contains phase reversals. If the answer tone contains phase reversals, the modem passthrough feature is engaged but an additional NSE message will be triggered. Devices with transmission rates faster than a typical fax machine, such as high-speed modems (using V.34 modulation speeds and higher) and Super G3 (SG3) faxes, send an ANSam tone that contains phase reversals.

Figure 4-8 shows the message exchange for NSE-signaled modem passthrough. Just like in the fax passthrough case, a normal VoIP call is first established, and then an NSE-192 is sent upon the TGW detecting a 2100 Hz answer tone. In the case of a modem, however, this 2100 Hz answer tone is typically an ANSam.

Figure 4-8 *Modem Passthrough Call with NSE Signaling*

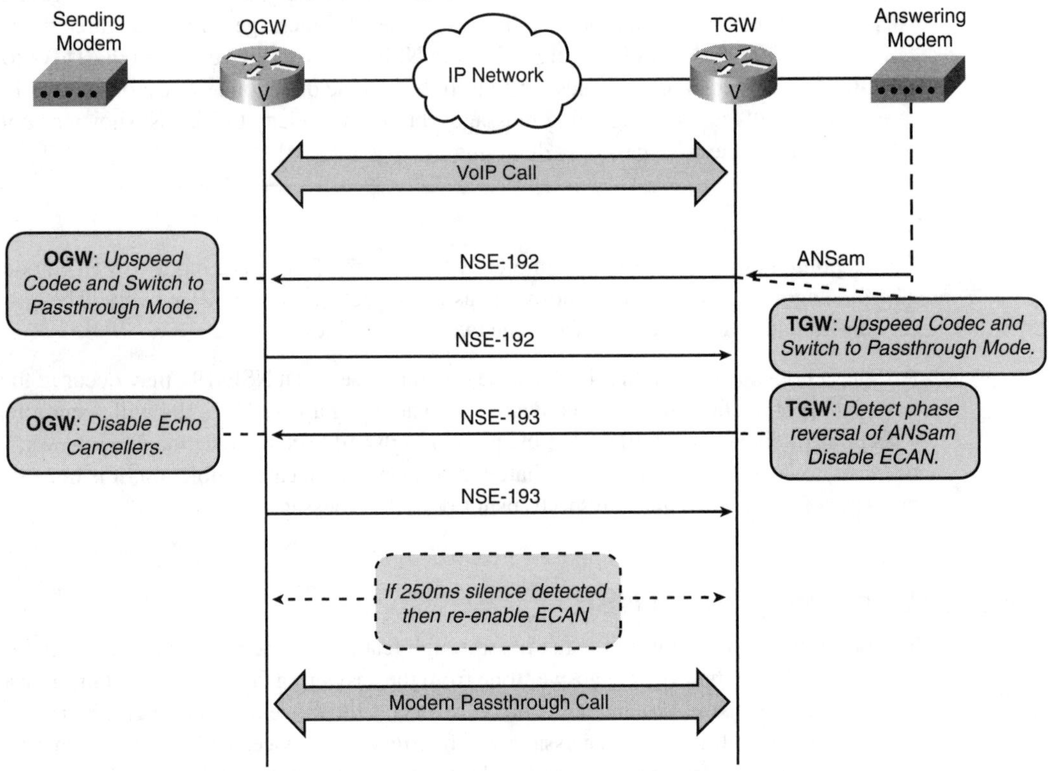

NOTE   As with NSE-based fax passthrough, the NSE call flow above remains the same no matter if the voice signaling protocol is H.323, SIP, MGCP, or SCCP.

The in-band signal detection by the TGW's DSP of the answer tone from the terminating modem will trigger the exact same codec upspeed and switchover to VBD mode seen in the fax passthrough case. The only difference is that in this case there is the additional detection of phase reversals in the answer tone. This phase-reversal detection instructs the DSP in the TGW to disable the echo canceller.

Also, this detection of an answer tone with phase reversals triggers a notification by the DSP to IOS that an answer tone with phase reversals was received. IOS responds with a command to the DSP to send an in-band RTP message to the OGW's DSP to also disable its echo canceller. The message is an NSE packet with event ID 193 (NSE-193). As illustrated in Figure 4-8, the TGW sends an NSE-193 and that is replied to by the OGW with the transmission of another NSE-193 message.

If low-speed modems are used that do not implement an ANSam tone, the NSE call flow will resemble fax passthrough in Figure 4-7 rather than modem passthrough in Figure 4-8. Low-speed modems are typically defined as 14.4 Kbps, and below and like the modulations used for fax, any 2100 Hz tones that are used do not contain phase reversals. So, an NSE-193 would never be triggered in the absence of phase reversals, and the call would proceed with just an NSE-192 as in Figure 4-7.

Protocol-Based Pass-Through for Fax

The other method used to trigger a transition from voice mode to passthrough mode is in the messaging of the VoIP call signaling protocol. Although the call signaling protocol's primary responsibility is to set up and tear down the VoIP call, it can also be used to transition to passthrough mode.

At this point, a distinction needs to be made between the term *passthrough* and *pass-through*. The term *passthrough* is what has been used until now when referring to the VBD feature in general and the mode where the passthrough switchover is signaled by NSE packets. This terminology will not change. However, to indicate a transition to VBD mode via messages in the voice call control protocol, the term *pass-through* is used going forward.

This terminology difference arises from a command-line interface (CLI) configuration convention used on Cisco IOS voice gateways. The **modem passthrough nse** command enables the VBD feature for fax and modem calls using NSE signaling. Thus when handling a fax call using NSE signaled VBD, this is commonly referred to as "fax passthrough" or "NSE-based passthrough."

The command **fax protocol pass-through** indicates that a fax call is being handled by the signaling protocol. Therefore, if the VBD mode is signaled via protocol signaling messages, this is commonly referred to as "fax pass-through" or "protocol-based pass-through."

NOTE   The two configuration methods for passthrough are covered in detail in Chapter 9, "Configuring Passthrough."

There is no protocol-based pass-through for modems. Only fax calls can take advantage of pass-through using the call signaling protocol. Unlike NSE-based passthrough, which is triggered by a 2100 Hz tone, protocol-based pass-through can be triggered only by a fax V.21 preamble.

The principal reason to use the protocol-based signaling rather than the Cisco proprietary NSE-based signaling for a fax passthrough call is that it allows for interoperability with third-party voice gateways. NSE-based signaling is proprietary, so protocol-based signaling is the only solution for Cisco voice gateways to interoperate with voice gateways from other vendors.

The two fax pass-through implementations that are discussed involve the H.323 and SIP protocol stacks. H.323 and SIP are the only supported call signaling protocols for pass-through signaling on Cisco voice gateways.

TIP   There is not a protocol-based pass-through solution for the MGCP protocol stack on Cisco voice gateways due to protocol conflicts and reliability concerns. NSE-based passthrough should be used instead.

Fax Pass-Through with H.323 Signaling

H.323 fax pass-through occurs when a VoIP call is set up using the H.323 protocol stack, and then H.323 messages are used to transition the call to pass-through mode. Figure 4-9 illustrates pass-through using the H.323 call signaling protocol.

Initially, the VoIP call is established using the H.323 signaling protocol. When the terminating fax machine answers the call it plays a 2100 Hz CED tone. However, unlike NSE-based passthrough, this tone does not trigger a pass-through switchover.

Following the CED tone, the terminating fax machine begins the transmission of the DIS and optional NSF and CSI fax messages. These messages are flagged with a V.21 preamble. The V.21 preamble is the signal that triggers the transition to pass-through.

Upon detection of the V.21 preamble by the TGW, a passthrough switchover is initiated with the H.323 protocol stack. H.245 request mode messages signal the switchover to the G.711 codec while H.245 logical channel messages are responsible for closing the previous voice mode logical channels (typically using a high-compression codec such as G.729), opening the new logical channels for the G.711 codec, and acknowledging the same.

Upon completion of the H.245 message exchange, the fax pass-through session is established. The fax call should now be able to complete successfully.

Figure 4-9 *Fax Pass-Through Call with H.323 Signaling Protocol*

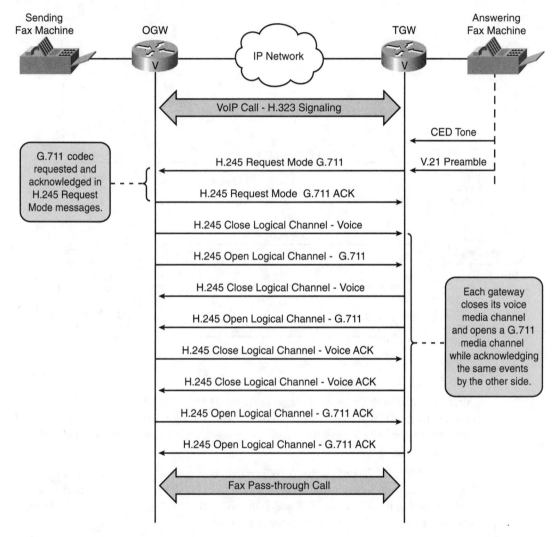

Fax Pass-Through with SIP Signaling

With SIP as the call signaling protocol, fax pass-through is very similar to H.323. SIP sets up a normal VoIP call, and then when the V.21 preamble is detected, SIP handles the transition to pass-through mode. Figure 4-10 illustrates fax pass-through with SIP as the call signaling protocol.

Figure 4-10 *Fax Pass-Through Call with SIP Signaling Protocol*

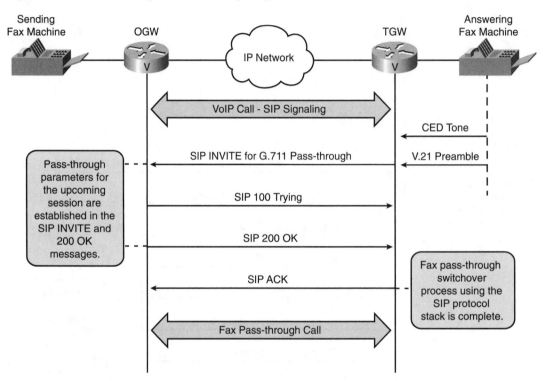

After the initial VoIP call is established using the SIP signaling protocol, a V.21 preamble detected by the TGW triggers the switchover to pass through. However, unlike NSE-based passthrough, the SIP protocol will handle the pass-through transition rather than NSE messages.

A SIP re-INVITE is issued by the TGW to transition to pass-through mode. The most important occurrence here is the codec upspeed to G.711. The pass-through parameters enclosed within the SIP re-INVITE are confirmed in the SIP 200 OK message. A SIP ACK from the TGW completes the pass-through switchover.

Text over G.711

Text telephony poses a major challenge to both NSE-based and protocol-based passthrough mechanisms. There is not a common tone implemented by the different text telephony protocols that can be focused on to trigger a passthrough switchover. So, to pass text telephone protocols in a passthrough mode, a manual version of passthrough must be configured. This is referred to as text over G.711.

With text over G.711, dedicated voice connections (using dial-peers on IOS gateways) are configured specifically for the use of text telephone protocols. These text-specific configurations on the voice gateways force all calls across this connection to use the G.711 codec while disabling silence suppression or VAD.

From a call-flow perspective, there is no need for any switchovers using NSEs or the call signaling protocol because the call is set up from the beginning to handle text telephone traffic. Figure 4-11 illustrates text over G.711.

Figure 4-11   *Text over G.711 Call*

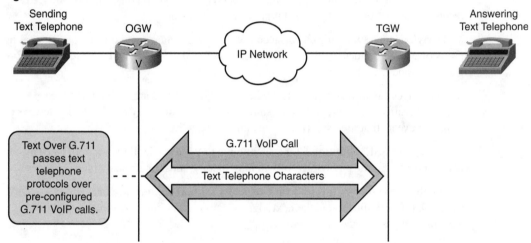

Text over G.711 is signaling protocol independent. So, voice signaling protocols such as H.323, SIP, MGCP, and SCCP are compatible with G.711 over text because these protocols can be configured on voice gateways to set up simple G.711 VoIP calls with silence suppression/VAD disabled.

A Future Look at ITU-T V.152

Both NSE-based passthrough and protocol-based pass-through have their positives and negatives. NSE-based passthrough works for modem and faxes, but this solution is Cisco proprietary and excludes Cisco voice gateways from interoperating with other vendors. On the other hand, protocol-based pass-through offers third-party interoperability, but this is only an option for fax calls. Modem calls do not work with protocol-based pass-through.

The ITU-T has a specification titled V.152 that details a standards-based form of passthrough or VBD for faxes and modems over an IP infrastructure. Although relatively new, V.152 presents a passthrough solution that possesses the relative strengths of NSE-based passthrough and protocol-based pass-through without any of the previously mentioned drawbacks. Furthermore, V.152 supports text telephone protocols, too.

V.152 specifies two methods for transitioning to VBD mode from normal voice mode: payload type switching and SSE (State Signaling Event) messages. Payload type switching is similar to protocol-based pass-through. VBD parameters are negotiated in the call signaling protocol stack and a predefined VBD RTP payload type is established. V.152 recommends that the VBD payload type be a dynamic one.

VBD payload type switching can be accomplished with a number of different call signaling protocols. V.152 defines specific VBD parameters for SDP (used by SIP, MGCP, and H.248 gateways) and H.323.

SSE messages can also signal a V.152 VBD switchover. SSEs are defined in Annexes C, E, and F of V.150.1. These messages are similar to NSEs in that they notify other gateways of signaling events that are usually modem and fax related.

V.152 declares SSEs as optional for transitioning to VBD mode. If one or both gateways do not support SSEs, the payload type switching method must be implemented.

Although Cisco voice gateways do not currently support the recently ratified ITU-T V.152 standard, this specification is the next logical step for handling fax, modem, and text telephony in passthrough scenarios.

Summary

Passthrough or VBD is a transport method for passing modulated data such as fax, modem, and text telephone protocols over an IP network. Transitioning to passthrough mode involves additional changes beyond a normal voice call. In Cisco voice gateways, this passthrough switchover can be signaled in one of two ways: NSE-based passthrough or protocol-based pass-through.

NSE-based passthrough uses Cisco proprietary NSE messages between the originating and terminating voice gateways to transition to passthrough. This signaling method is compatible with the common call signaling protocols of H.323, SIP, MGCP, and SCCP, but interoperating with third-party gateways is not possible.

Protocol-based pass-through is available only for fax calls because it is triggered by a V.21 preamble that is not present for modems. Unlike NSEs that communicate over the RTP media stream, protocol-based pass-through uses the voice signaling protocol to handle the pass-through transition. Only the call signaling protocols of H.323 and SIP support this signaling method, but interoperability with third-party gateways is possible.

For handling text telephone protocols, a manually configured version of passthrough must be used that is referred to as text over G.711. Text over G.711 can be used with any call signaling protocol or third-party gateway that supports the G.711 codec.

The ITU-T V.152 specification is a standards-based form of passthrough or VBD. Although this is a relatively new specification that is not widely implemented, it offers the benefits of both NSE-based passthrough and protocol-based pass-through without the current drawbacks.

Relay

Relay is the other transport method for passing modulated data over IP networks. However, relay uses a much different process than passthrough for establishing communication between fax, modem, and text devices.

Although passthrough digitizes the modulated waveform using pulse code modulation (PCM), relay decodes the modulated waveform and then passes the decoded frame over IP using a relay protocol. Because the modulated waveform sent by a fax or modem is simply carrying digital information, relay strips off this modulation and passes just the original binary information. On the other side, this binary information is remodulated into an analog waveform. Figure 5-1 provides an overview of a relay call.

Figure 5-1 *Relay Call Overview*

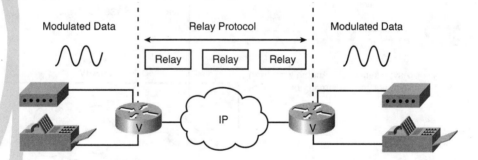

To accommodate fax, modem, and text devices, a different relay protocol must be implemented for each. The following sections address in detail the different relay types supported by Cisco gateways in addition to the fundamental concepts behind the relay transport method.

Relay Fundamentals

Compared to passthrough, the IP transport mechanism of relay is more complicated. During a relay call, the gateway plays a more active role in the communication occurring between the data devices. The voice gateway configured for relay must be able to "understand" and "speak" the protocols that are being used by the fax, modem, or text devices themselves.

For example, when a fax relay call takes place, the voice gateways understand the T.30 and T.4 messaging that occurs between the fax machines. This understanding of the fax protocols allows the voice gateways to efficiently package the pertinent information for transport across the IP network using a designated fax relay protocol.

The best way to illustrate the concept of relay is through a graphical comparison of passthrough and relay. Figure 5-2 details a modem passthrough call and a modem relay call from a gateway perspective.

Figure 5-2 *Passthrough and Relay Call Comparison*

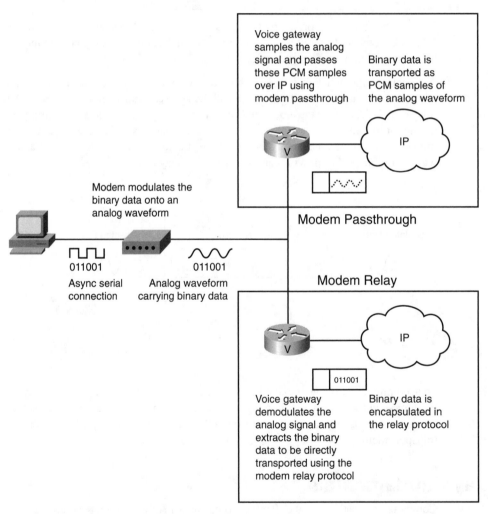

The gateways in Figure 5-2 have completely different behaviors when they implement relay as opposed to passthrough. The input of modulated data is the same in each case, but the treatment of this modulated information by the gateway differs.

Passthrough samples the analog waveform hoping that the samples taken can accurately reproduce the analog waveform on the other side. Relay demodulates and extracts the binary information from the analog signal with the expectation that the gateway on the other side can modulate this binary stream back into the correct analog signal.

Although Figure 5-2 details a modem specific passthrough and relay call scenario, the diagram is also applicable to fax and text calls, too. With fax and text relay however, the relay protocol will differ.

Cisco voice gateways define three relay implementations: fax relay, modem relay, and text relay. These relay implementations correlate with the type of modulated traffic that needs to be transported across the IP network. To decide which method to use for transportation, the Cisco voice gateway depends on certain triggers to transition back and forth between voice mode, passthrough, and the different relay modes. Figure 5-3 demonstrates how Cisco voice gateways transition between voice mode, passthrough, fax relay, modem relay, and text relay from a state machine perspective.

A digital signal processor (DSP) residing in the voice gateway is the catalyst for detecting and triggering the transitions detailed in Figure 5-3. Although all calls start and end as a voice call, any transitions to passthrough or relay must be processed by the DSP.

For example, if the DSP detects a 2100 Hz tone, a switchover to modem passthrough occurs. Once in passthrough mode, the DSP can transition the call to fax relay (T.38 or Cisco fax relay) if a V.21 preamble of High-Level Data Link Control (HDLC) flags is detected, transition the call to modem relay if a Calling Menu (CM) message is seen, or take the call back to voice mode if there is four seconds of silence.

In Figure 5-3, note that fax pass-through is shown with fax relay because both of these transport methods are initiated by the detection of the V.21 fax preamble. However, unlike fax relay, fax pass-through cannot coexist with modem passthrough. If both modem passthrough and fax pass-through are configured, fax pass-through has precedence, and modem passthrough is disabled by the IOS.

Cisco text relay operates a bit differently from passthrough and both fax and modem relay. Instead of exiting voice mode and negotiating a complete switchover, Cisco text relay activates itself only when Baudot tones are detected.

The available relay protocols for fax, modem, and text will now be examined more closely. Be aware that some relay protocols are proprietary implementations and detailed technical information about them is not freely available. Coverage of these proprietary relay protocols might not be as deep as those protocols that are standards-based.

Fax relay, including ITU-T T.38 and Cisco fax relay, is discussed first. Following this is a discussion of Cisco modem relay and, finally, Cisco text relay.

Figure 5-3 *IOS Voice Gateway State Machine for Voice, Passthrough, and Relay*

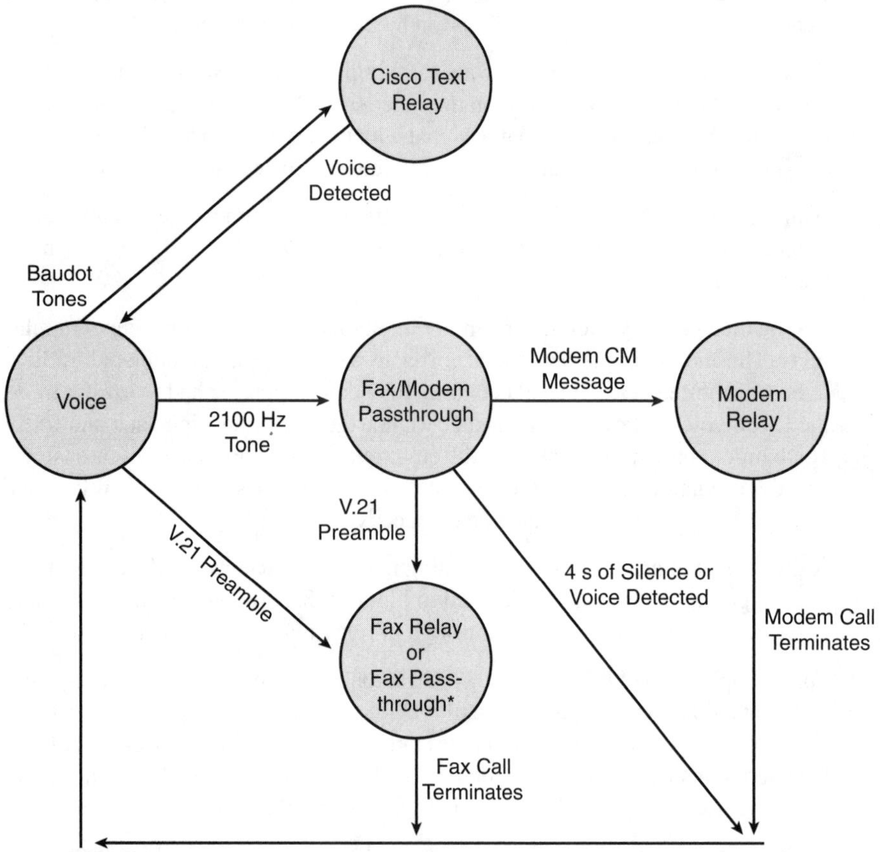

*Transitioning through modem passthrough first to get to fax pass-through is not possible since the configuration of fax pass-through causes modem passthrough to be disabled.

Fax Relay

Cisco voice gateways are capable of two different fax relay implementations: T.38 and Cisco fax relay. Both of these fax relay protocols accomplish the same thing from a functional perspective: relaying a fax call across an IP network.

TIP	Cisco gateways only support G3 fax calls with either T.38 or Cisco fax relay. To properly handle the higher speeds of SG3 calls, modem passthrough must be used. Further discussion of this topic is in the section "Super G3" in Chapter 7, "Design Guide for Fax, Modem, and Text."

When a voice gateway implements T.38 or Cisco fax relay, analog fax signals are demodulated and broken into their basic HDLC frames. Because the voice gateways understand the T.30 and T.4 fax protocols, the HDLC frames can now be properly transported across IP using either fax relay protocol. The differences between T.38 and Cisco fax relay occur in the actual packet transport formats and the switchover method. Because every fax call starts out as a voice call from the gateway's perspective, a switchover must occur to transition the gateway's DSP from voice mode to the configured fax relay protocol.

T.38 can transition from voice to fax relay using one of two methods: a Named Signaling Event (NSE)-based switchover or a protocol-based switchover. Cisco fax relay, which is a Cisco proprietary protocol, handles its switchover only through an exchange of certain RTP dynamic payload types.

Because of the proprietary nature of Cisco fax relay, T.38 is the more widely chosen option. Therefore, the workings and switchover methods of T.38 are discussed first, followed by Cisco fax relay.

T.38 Fax Relay

T.38 is a fax relay standard defined by the ITU-T. Because it is a standard, T.38 is now the predominant choice for fax relay scenarios, especially in networks where multivendor interoperability is necessary.

Cisco voice gateways fully support the original 1998 version of the T.38 specification. Although later versions of T.38 introduce such features as Real-Time Protocol (RTP) encapsulation and support for SG3/V.34 faxing, these are not discussed in this chapter. Only the aspects of T.38 related to the Cisco-supported 1998 version are covered.

T.38 defines three transport methods: UDP, TCP, and RTP. Currently, Cisco voice gateways only use UDP encapsulation as diagrammed in Figure 5-4. The TCP encapsulation method is optional, and RTP encapsulation is introduced in a later version of the T.38 specification.

Figure 5-4   *UDP Encapsulated T.38*

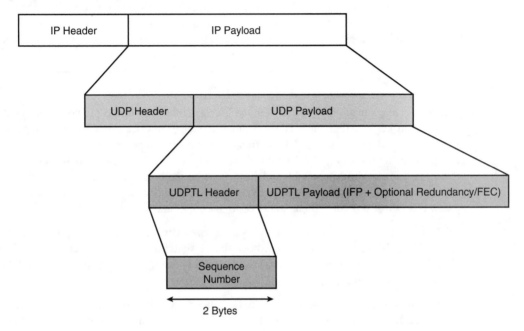

For T.38 to provide additional error control when using UDP, a UDP transport layer (UDPTL) header is included. This header is simply a 2-byte sequence number to assist in internet fax packet (IFP) reordering at the receiving gateway. Also, the T.38 UDPTL encapsulation does not use an assigned UDP port number. In the case of Cisco voice gateways, the existing RTP port numbers set up during the initial voice call are reused by T.38 fax relay.

Inside the UDPTL payload, IFPs transport the T.30 and T.4 fax information. Optional redundancy or forward error checking (FEC) packets may also reside in the UDPTL payload.

There are two types of IFPs: T30_INDICATOR packets and T30_DATA packets. Indicator packets signal T.30 messages such as calling tone (CNG), called terminal identification (CED), and the various trainings for different modulations, while T30_DATA handles the HDLC message framing and the transmission of fax page data.

Both of these IFP types include a sequence number. Upon transmission of a T30_INDICATOR or T30_DATA IFP, this sequence number becomes the UDPTL header. When this occurs, the IFP packet immediately following the UDPTL header in the UDPTL payload is referred to as the primary. Additional IFPs can be included after the primary, and these are referred to as secondaries. Secondary IFP packets are mostly seen when an error correction method such as redundancy is used. Redundancy for T.38 fax relay along with primary and secondary IFPs are discussed later in this section. The IFP format for a T30_INDICATOR packet is illustrated in Figure 5-5.

Figure 5-5   *T.38 T30_INDICATOR IFP Frame Format*

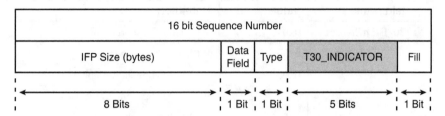

The T30_INDICATOR packet is only 2 bytes, not including the sequence number. The most important field is the T30_INDICATOR field itself, and the value here specifies the exact T.30 message that is being signaled. Table 5-1 defines the T30_INDICATOR field and the other fields that make up this IFP.

Table 5-1   *T.38 T30_INDICATOR IFP Frame Field Definitions*

Field Name	Value	Definition
Sequence Number	0x00–0x1111	16-bit sequence number to uniquely identify the IFP
IFP Size (in bytes)	1	1-byte for T30_INDICATOR packets (does not include sequence number or IFP Size fields)
Data Field	0	Only set when optional data field is present
Type	0	T30_INDICATOR message
T30_INDICATOR	0x00	No Signal
	0x01	CNG
	0x02	CED
	0x03	V.21 Preamble (HDLC flags)
	0x04	V.27 2400 bps training
	0x05	V.27 4800 bps training
	0x06	V.29 7200 bps training
	0x07	V.29 9600 bps training
	0x08	V.17 7200 bps short training
	0x09	V.17 7200 bps long training

continues

Table 5-1 *T.38 T30_INDICATOR IFP Frame Field Definitions (Continued)*

Field Name	Value	Definition
T30_INDICATOR *(Continued)*	0x0a	V.17 9600 bps short training
	0x0b	V.17 9600 bps long training
	0x0c	V.17 12000 bps short training
	0x0d	V.17 12000 bps long training
	0x0e	V.17 14400 bps short training
	0x0f	V.17 14400 bps long training
Fill	0	Last bit set to 0

The T30_INDICATOR IFP provides an efficient method for transporting fax signals across VoIP. Instead of CNG and CED tones and training signals being captured and played out on the far side, T.38 uses a simple T30_INDICATOR IFP message. This saves bandwidth and processing time on the voice gateways.

NOTE   As Figure 5-3 illustrates, Cisco voice gateways do not switch over to T.38 fax relay until the V.21 preamble or fax flags are detected. Because the CNG and CED signals are transmitted before the V.21 preamble and the subsequent switchover to T.38 fax relay, the CNG and CED signals are passed using the original voice codec in the RTP media stream. Therefore, the CNG and CED T30_INDICATOR messages are not typically seen with Cisco gateways. However, other vendors do use these messages frequently, and they can be seen when Cisco voice gateways interoperate with third-party T.38 devices.

An interesting T30_INDICATOR message to note is No Signal. This message specifies that there is currently not a TDM fax signal present on the voice gateway. When fax signals are not being received on the telephony interface, Cisco gateways tend to send this message quite regularly, whereas other brands of voice gateways might send this message more sparingly.

The other IFP packet type found in T.38 is T30_DATA. These packets handle the T.30 HDLC control information and the Phase C image data. The frame format for a T30_DATA IFP is diagrammed in Figure 5-6.

Figure 5-6   *T.38 T30_DATA IFP Frame Format*

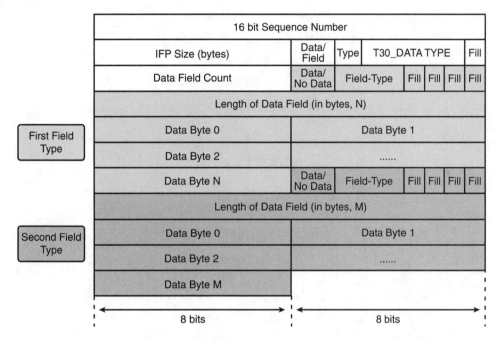

The T30_DATA packet contains some fields that are the same as those found in the T30_ INDICATOR message. However, there are also a number of new fields that may contain a range of values. Table 5-2 details each of the IFP frame fields and their values for a T.38 T30_DATA packet.

Table 5-2   *T.38 T30_DATA IFP Frame Field Definitions*

Field Name	Value	Definition
Sequence Number	0x00–0x1111	16-bit sequence number to uniquely identify IFP frames.
IFP Size (in bytes)	0x00–0x11	Length measured from first Data Field to last Data Byte N, not including IFP Size field.
Data Field	1	Data Field is present.
Type	1	T30_DATA message.

continues

Table 5-2   *T.38 T30_DATA IFP Frame Field Definitions (Continued)*

Field Name	Value	Definition
T30_DATA TYPE	0x00	V.21 300 bps.
	0x01	V.27 2400 bps.
	0x02	V.27 4800 bps.
	0x03	V.29 7200 bps.
	0x04	V.29 9600 bps.
	0x05	V.17 7200 bps.
	0x06	V.17 9600 bps.
	0x07	V.17 12000 bps.
	0x08	V.17 14400 bps.
Data Field Count	Variable	Number of data fields in IFP packet. Each data field consists of Data/No Data Indicator, Field-Type, Length of Data Field (optional), and Data Bytes (optional).
Data/No Data Indicator	1	Current Data Field has data.
	0	Current Data Field does not have data.
Field-Type	0x0	HDLC data. (Data bytes that follow contain some or all of a fax HDLC frame.)
	0x1	HDLC-Sig-end. (HDLC signaling has ended; no data bytes with this Field-Type.)
	0x2	HDLC-FCS-OK. (Indicates the end of an HDLC frame and correct FCS has been received; no data bytes with this Field-Type.)
	0x3	HDLC-FCS-BAD. (Indicates the end of an HDLC frame and the FCS is incorrect; no data bytes with this Field-Type.)
	0x4	HDLC-FCS-OK-Sig-End. (Indicates the end of an HDLC frame and a correct FCS has been received; no additional HDLC frames follow this one; no data bytes with this Field-Type.)

Table 5-2   *T.38 T30_DATA IFP Frame Field Definitions (Continued)*

Field Name	Value	Definition
Field-Type *(Continued)*	0x5	HDLC-FCS-BAD-Sig-End. (Indicates the end of an HDLC frame and an incorrect FCS has been received; no additional HDLC frames follow this one; no data bytes with this Field-Type.)
	0x6	T.4-Non-ECM. (T.4 image data that is not sent using Error Correction Mode [ECM] or Training Check Function [TCF] data; additional data will follow.)
	0x7	T.4-Non-ECM-Sig-End. (T.4 image data that is not sent using ECM or TCF data; end of data.)
Length of Data Field	0x00 – 0x1111	(Number of data bytes) – 1.
	N/A	If Data/No Data is 0.
Fill	0	Last bit filled with a 0.

The shaded fields in Figure 5-6 illustrate how multiple Field-Types can be transported in the same T30_DATA IFP. The lighter shading indicates the first Field-Type and its information, and the darker shading highlights an additional Field-Type within the same IFP. One common example of multiple Field-Types in a single IFP may occur at the end of a T.30 message. The last portion of data for the T.30 message and the HDLC frame's FCS status can occupy the same IFP and a Field-Type of HDLC Data and HDLC-FCS-OK will be present.

On the other hand, when there are large HDLC frames present, such as during the transfer of fax image data, it might be necessary to separate an HDLC frame into multiple packets. Although sending large T.38 packets is possible, the T.38 standard recommends that smaller packets be sent. Figure 5-7 illustrates this concept by showing how a T.30 digital identification signal (DIS) message is broken into IFP packets by a Cisco voice gateway. Note that the data transport headers are not shown, and only the basic IFP fields of T30_DATA TYPE and Field-Type are shown for simplicity.

Figure 5-7   *Segmenting of a T.30 Message into T.38 IFPs*

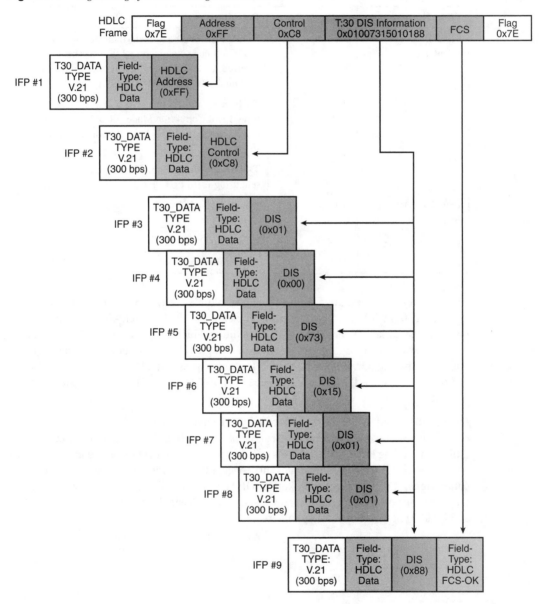

At the top of Figure 5-7, an HDLC frame carrying a T.30 DIS message is shown. The DIS message and its HDLC frame format was covered in detail in the section "DIS, NSF, and CSI Messages" in Chapter 2, "How Fax Works." When packaging the information from this

DIS HDLC frame into T.38 IFPs, the flags are stripped off, and only the shaded portion of the HDLC frame is transported.

Under the HDLC frame in Figure 5-7, nine IFPs are shown. Each of these IFPs is encapsulated in UDPTL and sent across an IP network as a separate packet. The Cisco voice gateway stuffs only 1 byte from this DIS HDLC frame into each IFP. Consequently, nine IFP packets are needed for transporting this HDLC frame via T.38 fax relay. Be aware that other vendor's implementations may not use numerous, small IFPs for the transport of this same frame. A vendor might opt for a single, larger IFP instead.

Two important fields highlighted in the IFPs in Figure 5-7 are T30_DATA TYPE and Field-Type. Because a DIS HDLC frame is V.21 modulated at 300 bps, the T30_DATA TYPE is set to V.21. The Field-Type is set to HDLC Data for each IFP where a data byte from the DIS HDLC frame is present.

Notice that the last IFP contains two Field-Types. The first Field-Type is set to HDLC Data, and it contains the last data byte from the DIS frame, 0x88. Following this data byte is the second Field-Type, HDLC-FCS-OK. This Field-Type indicates that the FCS for the DIS HDLC frame was received correctly. Also, it is important to note that the HDLC-FCS-OK Field-Type always has its Data/No Data Indicator field set to zero, so no data follows this Field-Type.

Now that the T.38 packet formats have been explained, it is important to visualize how these various T.38 packets form a typical T.38 call flow using Cisco voice gateways. Figure 5-8 illustrates how T.38 fax relay transports a fax call across an IP network.

As shown in Figure 5-8, the analog fax signals are received by each voice gateway and converted into T.38 T30_INDICATOR and T30_DATA IFPs for transportation across the IP network. The T30_INDICATOR IFPs are lightly shaded in the diagram, and the darker shading represents T30_DATA IFPs. The T30_DATA IFPs also specify the T30_Data Type and Field-Type parameters for each message.

If the T.38 IFPs are removed from the center of Figure 5-8, this diagram illustrates most of the same concepts and messaging as Figure 2-9. However, Figure 5-8 integrates Cisco voice gateways into the path and shows how a basic fax transaction functions when it is transported by T.38 fax relay. From a fax machine perspective, the T.38 transport is not visible.

The CNG and CED tones are not present in Figure 5-8 because this diagram aims to show what the T.38 messaging looks like for a call between Cisco voice gateways. With Cisco voice gateways, the CNG and CED tones are carried by the voice codec and not seen in the T.38 messaging. In the case of other vendors, the CNG and CED tones may be passed via the appropriate T30_INDICATOR messages.

Figure 5-8 *Fax Call Flow Using T.38 Fax Relay*

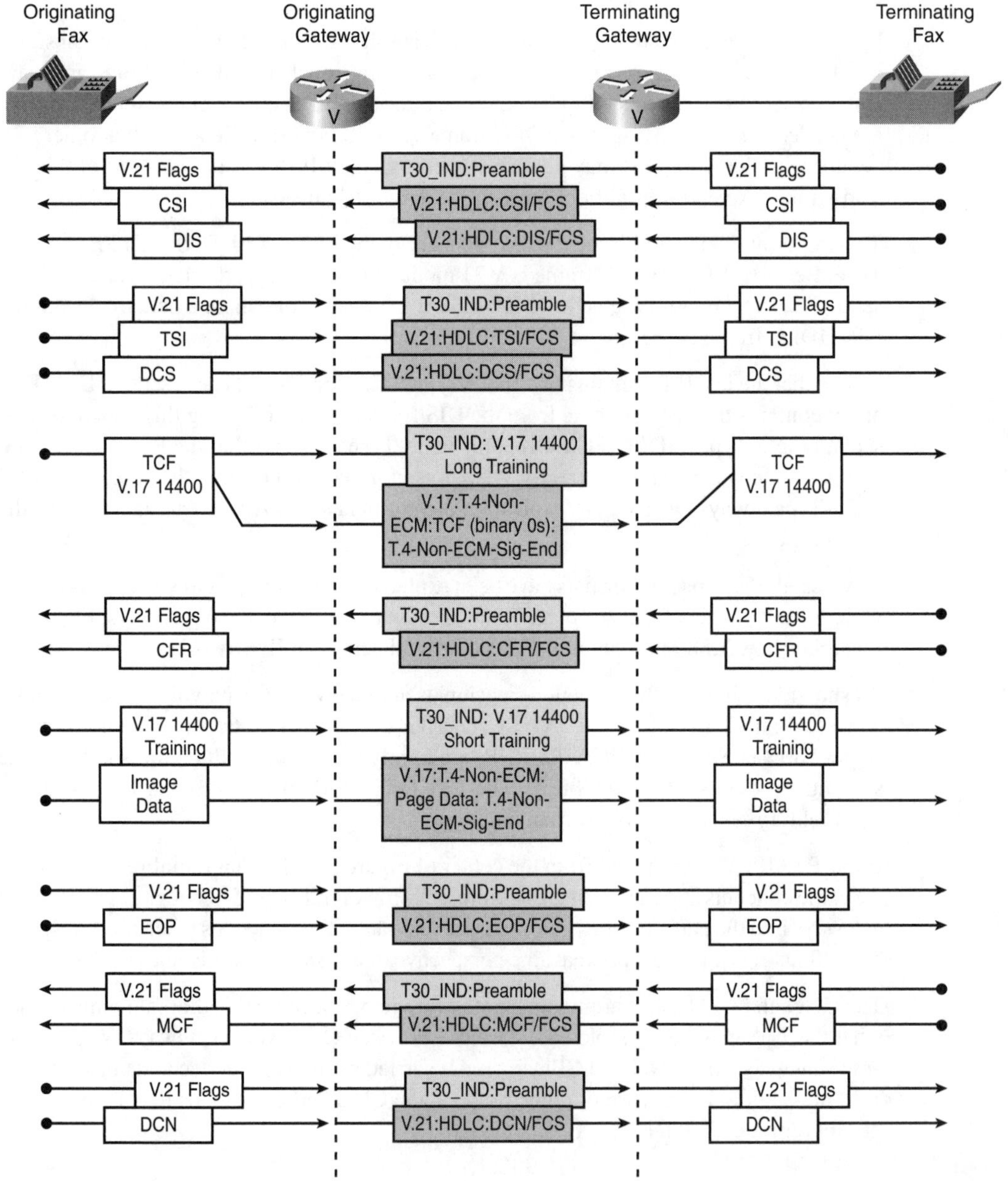

Figure 5-8 begins with the terminating fax machine transmitting a T.30 called subscriber identification (CSI) and DIS message. These messages are preceded by a T30_INDICATOR message where the Type field is set to V.21 Preamble, which indicates the presence of V.21

modulated HDLC flags. T30_DATA IFPs with the T30_DATA TYPE set to V.21 and the Field-Type set to HDLC Data actually carry the CSI and DIS frames. An equivalent process is used to transport the T.30 transmitting subscriber identification (TSI) and digital command signal (DCS) messages from the originating fax machine.

The training or TCF occurs next in Figure 5-8. The T.38 specification defines two methods for handling the TCF training signal. These two methods are formally known as data rate management method 1 and data rate management method 2.

Data rate management 1 requires that the TCF is regenerated locally by the terminating gateway. The actual TCF data stream is not propagated across the T.38 session. This method is used with TCP encapsulated T.38, and it is optional for the UDP encapsulation.

Data rate management 2 passes the TCF bits within the T.38 session. This method of data rate management is used by Cisco voice gateways and is shown in Figure 5-8. A 14400 bps TCF is transported across T.38 using a T30_INDICATOR packet that signals a V.17 14400 bps long training, and then a T30_DATA T.4-Non-ECM packet carries the binary 0s of the actual training pattern. For more information on the TCF message, see the section "TCF, CFR, and FTT Messages" in Chapter 2.

After the training has been confirmed with a T.30 CFR message, the fax page data is transmitted. A T30_INDICATOR message signals a short training before the page data is sent using T30_DATA messages. The first message, T.4-Non-ECM, is transmitted for each IFP containing actual page data. After all the page data has been transmitted the T30_DATA message, T.4-Non-ECM-Sig-End is sent to signal the end of the page transmission.

The fax call is torn down after one page is sent using the T.30 end of procedure (EOP), message confirmation (MCF), and disconnect (DCN) messages. The transport of these messages follows the procedures for the CSI, DIS, TSI, and DCS messages from the beginning of the call.

T.38 is capable of different error correction features like FEC and redundancy. Although these features are optional, Cisco voice gateways support redundancy rather than FEC. This is a configurable option for both the low-speed V.21 messages and the high-speed training and data-transfer messages. Figure 5-9 illustrates how two redundant T.38 IFPs are transported along with a primary IFP in a UDTPL packet.

In Figure 5-9, the first data field at the top of the frame is the UDPTL header. As mentioned previously, the UDPTL header is just the sequence number that references the primary T.38 IFP. The primary T.38 IFP is composed of the lightly shaded fields following the sequence number.

When T.38 redundancy is enabled, a 2-byte field specifying the number of redundant IFPs is present. In the case of Figure 5-9, this field would be set to a value of 0x0002, which indicates that two redundant IFPs follow.

Notice in Figure 5-9 that sequence numbers are not present for the redundant IFP messages. Instead, the redundant IFPs always are an offset of the primary IFP's sequence number that is defined in the UDPTL header. The first redundant IFP's sequence number is one less than the sequence number of the primary IFP, and the second redundant IFP's sequence number is two less. Because the sequence numbers for the redundant IFP messages always follow this format, only the sequence number for the primary IFP in the UDPTL header is necessary. Therefore, with a redundancy level of two as shown in Figure 5-9, every T.38 packet will be composed of the current primary IFP and redundant copies of the two previous primary IFP messages.

Figure 5-9   *T.38 Redundancy Frame Format*

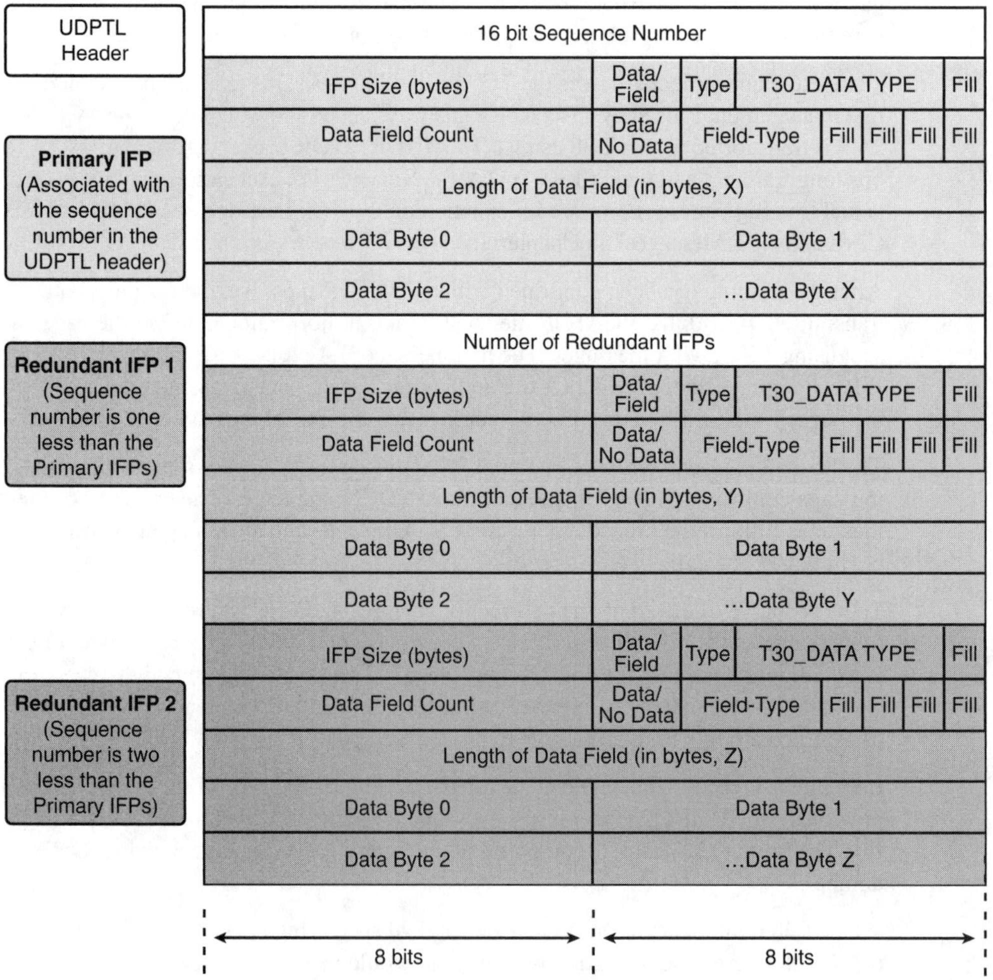

Both the primary and redundant IFP messages in Figure 5-9 can have a varying number of data bytes. For the low-speed T.30 messages, Cisco voice gateways typically only have 1 byte of data, as illustrated previously in Figure 5-7. However, during the high-speed transmission of the page data, many data bytes are present. Therefore, Figure 5-9 uses the field names of Data Byte X, Data Byte Y, and Data Byte Z to represent the varying amounts of data bytes that may exist in each IFP message.

In addition to understanding how the T.38 fax relay protocol works, you must understand how a Cisco voice gateway transitions to this fax transport protocol. Cisco voice gateways can transition from voice mode to T.38 fax relay using one of two signaling methods. One method is based on NSE packets, and the other takes advantage of the voice signaling protocol to effect the T.38 switchover.

NSE-Based Switchover for T.38

The proprietary NSE switchover method for T.38 fax relay is similar to the use of NSE messages during modem passthrough. The main difference is that unique NSE event IDs for T.38 fax switchover are used that are different from the event IDs used for modem passthrough. Table 5-3 lists the NSE event IDs found in an NSE-based T.38 fax relay switchover. For more information on NSE messages and their exact format within RTP, see the section "NSE-Based Passthrough" in Chapter 4, "Passthrough."

Table 5-3 *NSE Event IDs for T.38 Fax Relay Switchover*

NSE Event ID	Explanation
200	Instructs the peer gateway to switch over to T.38.
201	An ACK to an NSE-200 confirming that the peer gateway has initiated a switchover to T.38 and is ready to accept T.38 packets.
202	This is a NACK to an NSE-200 message signifying that the peer gateway cannot process T.38 packets for the call. The call will remain in voice mode and not switch over to T.38.

When a Cisco voice gateway is configured to use Cisco Named Signaling Events (NSE) for switching over to T.38, the signaling protocol in use (H.323, Session Initiation Protocol [SIP], Media Gateway Control Protocol [MGCP], or Skinny Client Control Protocol [SCCP]) is not involved or even aware that this switchover is taking place. The voice gateways themselves control the switchover within the RTP media stream that has already been set up by the signaling protocol. Figure 5-10 details a T.38 fax switchover using Cisco proprietary NSE packets.

Figure 5-10 *T.38 Fax Relay Switchover Using NSE Packets*

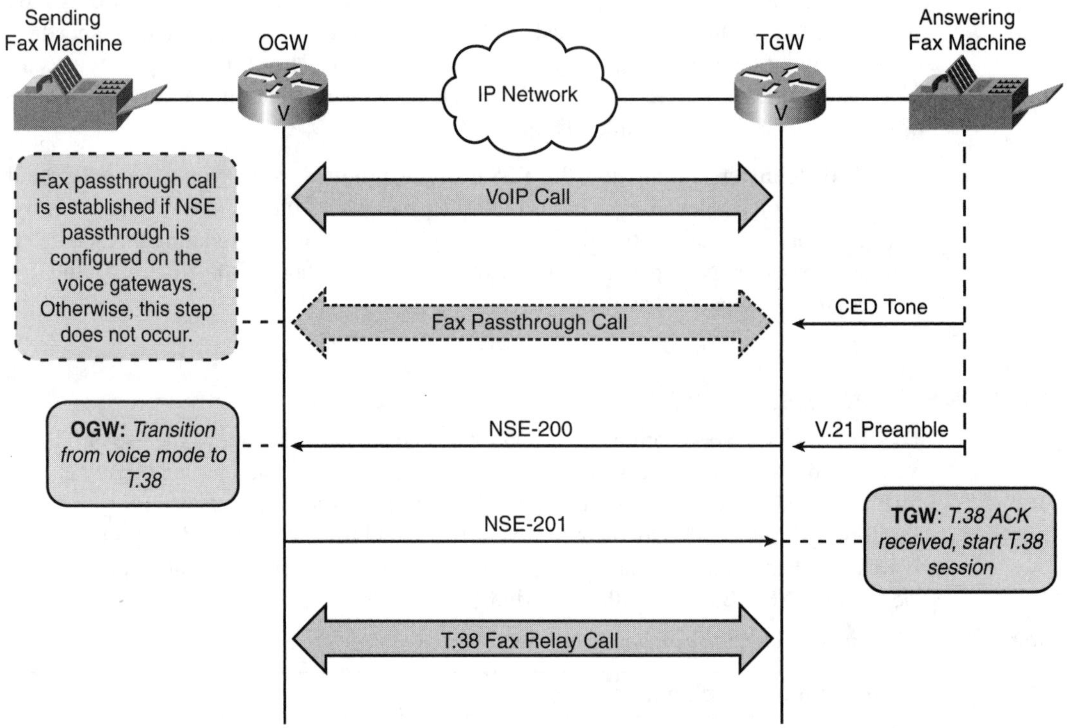

Notice in Figure 5-10 that the fax call will actually transition to passthrough first if NSE-based passthrough has been configured. As discussed in the preceding chapter, NSE-based passthrough is triggered by the 2100 Hz fax CED tone, whereas T.38 will not be activated until later in the call when the fax V.21 preamble is detected. If NSE-based passthrough is not configured on the Cisco voice gateway, the 2100 Hz fax CED tone is ignored, and the call transitions straight to T.38 fax relay from voice mode upon detection of the V.21 preamble.

Even though the NSE switchover occurs independently of the voice signaling protocol, a Cisco voice gateway will still announce its support of an NSE-based switchover. This announcement is listed as a nonstandard capability in the H.245 terminal capability set (TCS) message for H.323, and it is present as an X-NSE line in the Session Description Protocol (SDP) portion of both SIP and MGCP messages. The purpose of this announcement is to validate ahead of time that both voice gateways will support an NSE-based switchover should one be necessary at any point during the VoIP call. The NSE values for both passthrough and T.38 are communicated using these methods. You can find more detailed information concerning this announcement of NSE switchover support in the section "Troubleshooting NSE-Based Switchovers" in Chapter 12, "Troubleshooting Passthrough and Relay."

Protocol-Based Switchover for T.38

The handling of the T.38 switchover by the call signaling protocol is another method for handling the gateway transition from voice mode to T.38 fax relay. This method must be used for Cisco voice gateways to interoperate with other vendor's equipment.

The three call signaling protocols supported by Cisco voice gateways for a T.38 switchover are H.323, SIP, and MGCP. As opposed to a T.38 switchover using NSEs, a protocol-based T.38 switchover uses the call control protocol for complete control of the transition from voice mode to T.38 fax relay.

For the H.323 call signaling protocol, the initial voice call is established using the underlying H.225 and H.245 protocols. When the fax V.21 preamble is detected by the terminating gateway (TGW), the voice gateways exchange H.245 request mode messages that establish the T.38 parameters for the fax relay session. Then, new media channels are created while the initial voice channels are closed. Figure 5-11 illustrates the T.38 fax relay switchover procedure for the H.323 protocol stack.

When SIP is the call signaling protocol, a mid-call INVITE message triggers the T.38 fax relay switchover process. This mid-call INVITE or re-INVITE message contains the request from the TGW to change the media stream from voice to T.38. Specific T.38 capabilities and parameter settings are included, too, in this re-INVITE, along with the socket information for the upcoming T.38 session.

The originating gateway (OGW) accepts this media change from voice mode to T.38 with a SIP 200 OK message. The SIP 200 OK message confirms the T.38 session parameters while providing the IP socket information for the OGW. Figure 5-12 illustrates the SIP messaging that occurs for a T.38 fax relay switchover.

Figure 5-11 *T.38 Fax Relay Switchover for H.323*

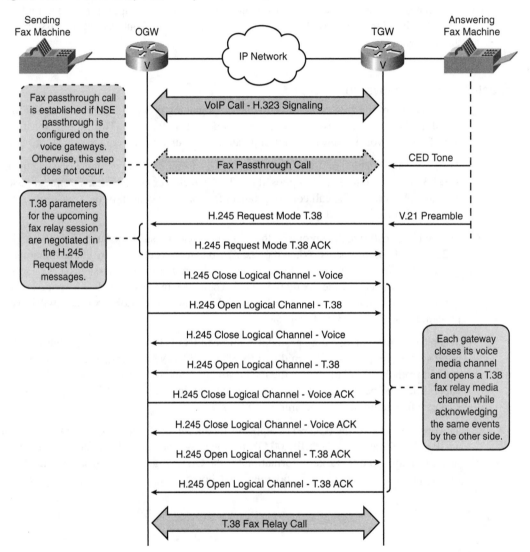

Figure 5-12 *T.38 Fax Relay Switchover for SIP*

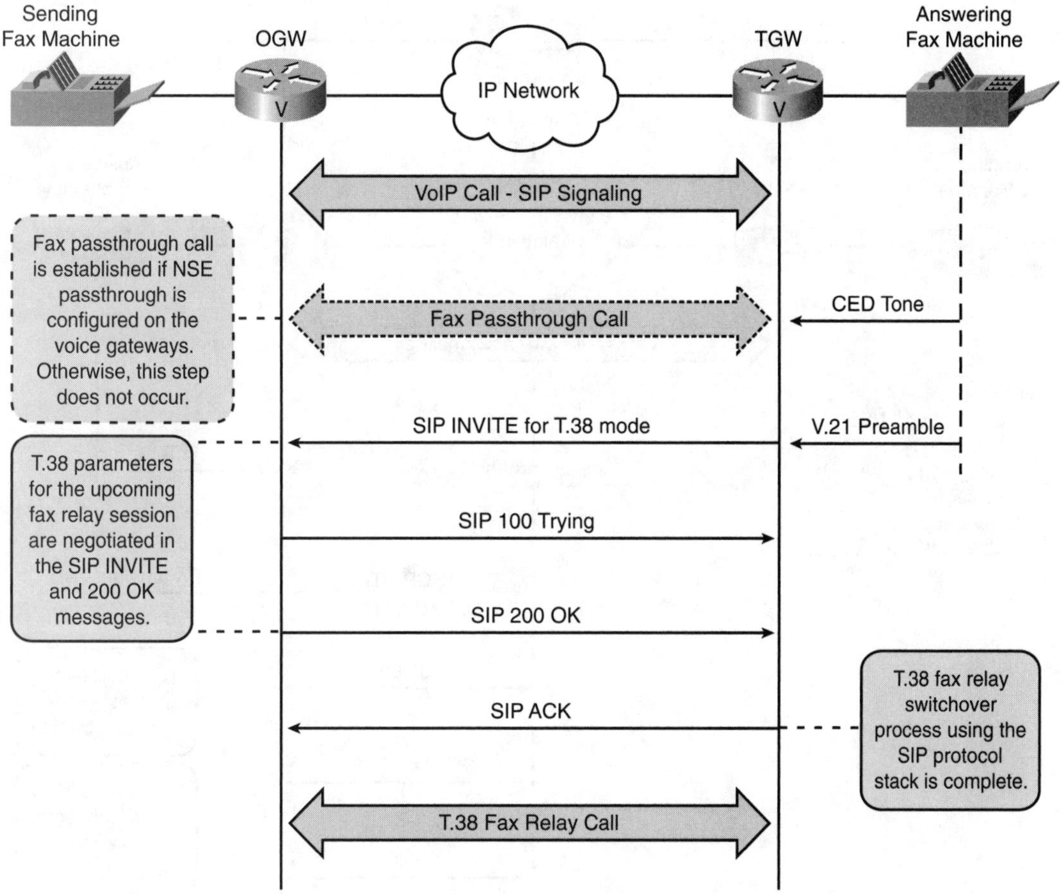

A transition from a voice call to a T.38 fax relay call can also occur using the MGCP protocol stack. Although both H.323 and SIP can handle their switchovers with messages directly between the gateways, MGCP gateways must communicate through a call agent (CA). Figure 5-13 illustrates a T.38 switchover using the MGCP protocol stack.

Figure 5-13 *T.38 Fax Relay Switchover for MGCP*

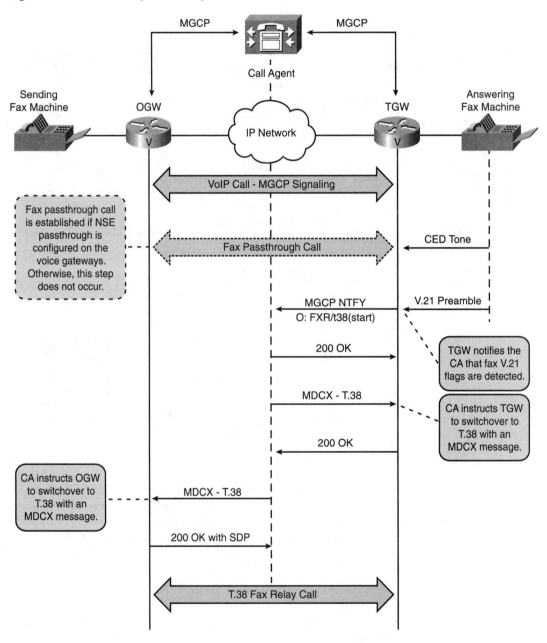

TIP	A T.38 fax relay switchover within the MGCP protocol stack as shown in Figure 5-13 is referred to as CA-controlled mode. Using NSEs for the T.38 fax relay switchover with MGCP as illustrated previously in Figure 5-10 is known as gateway-controlled mode.

Upon detection of the V.21 fax preamble, the MGCP TGW signals the CA using a notify (NTFY) message. This message contains the important observed event of FXR/t38(start). With confirmation that a fax call is now present, the CA can now begin the switchover process to T.38 fax relay.

A modify connection (MDCX) message is sent to the TGW from the CA instructing a switchover from voice mode to T.38 mode. Within this MDCX message is T.38 parameter information and the media connection information for the OGW, including the IP address and port. Generally, the same IP address and port that were used for the initial voice call are reused for the T.38 call. When this is not the case, the call flow in Figure 5-13 will vary.

Another MDCX message is sent to the OGW instructing it to transition to T.38. Again, any T.38 parameter information along with the other gateway's connection information is included in this message.

Once both MDCX messages have been sent and acknowledged by MGCP 200 OK messages, the OGW and TGW have all the information necessary to start communicating using the T.38 protocol. The switchover to T.38 fax relay at this point is complete.

NOTE	Although this section provides a general overview of the call flow for protocol-based T.38 switchovers involving the H.323, SIP, and MGCP protocols, more detailed analysis of the key, specific messages for each of these protocols is provided in the section "Troubleshooting Protocol-Based Switchovers" in Chapter 12.

Cisco Fax Relay

Cisco fax relay is a proprietary fax relay implementation on Cisco voice gateways. Developed before the T.38 fax relay standard, Cisco fax relay provides the same basic functionality as T.38, but there are differences with regard to packet formats and the mechanisms used for switching into fax relay mode.

Just like T.38, Cisco fax relay demodulates all incoming fax signals and passes the fax tones and HDLC frames across the IP network using data packets. At the far end, these data packets are modulated back into analog signals and transmitted to the attached fax devices.

Being a Cisco proprietary protocol, a detailed look at the packet formats and other operational intricacies is not possible with Cisco fax relay. However, a simple high-level overview can be provided. Figure 5-14 illustrates the basic Cisco fax relay packet structure.

Figure 5-14   *Cisco Fax Relay Packet Structure*

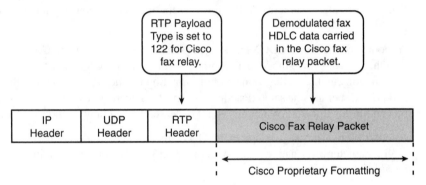

Cisco fax relay frames are transported using RTP. What distinguishes Cisco fax relay packets from other real-time traffic is the unique RTP payload type of 122. Looking back to Table 4-1, you will see that this payload type is a dynamic one and suited for proprietary implementations such as Cisco fax relay.

To switch over to Cisco fax relay, Cisco voice gateways use special signaling packets in the RTP stream. However, unlike the previous RTP stream signaling packets that have been discussed, these packets are not NSEs. Instead, specific RTP dynamic payload types are used for the signaling. The switchover is not NSE or protocol-based but rather based on the RTP payload type (PT). Figure 5-15 details the Cisco fax relay switchover process.

The detection of fax flags (V.21 preamble) at the terminating gateway triggers the transition to Cisco fax relay. The TGW notifies the OGW of the impending switchover with a special RTP message using a PT value of 96 (PT-96). Note that this RTP message is different from NSE messages, which use a payload type of 100 followed by a specific event ID.

The PT-96 Cisco fax relay switchover packet from the TGW to the OGW is ACK'd (acknowledged) with a PT-97 message from the OGW back to the TGW. This switchover message and ACK process is then repeated in the direction from the OGW to the TGW before the Cisco fax relay call is established.

You should realize that the PT-96 and PT-97 packets are only seen during the switchover to coordinate the gateway's transition from voice mode to Cisco fax relay. After the switchover has completed, Cisco fax relay packets use a PT of 122.

Figure 5-15 *Cisco Fax Relay Switchover*

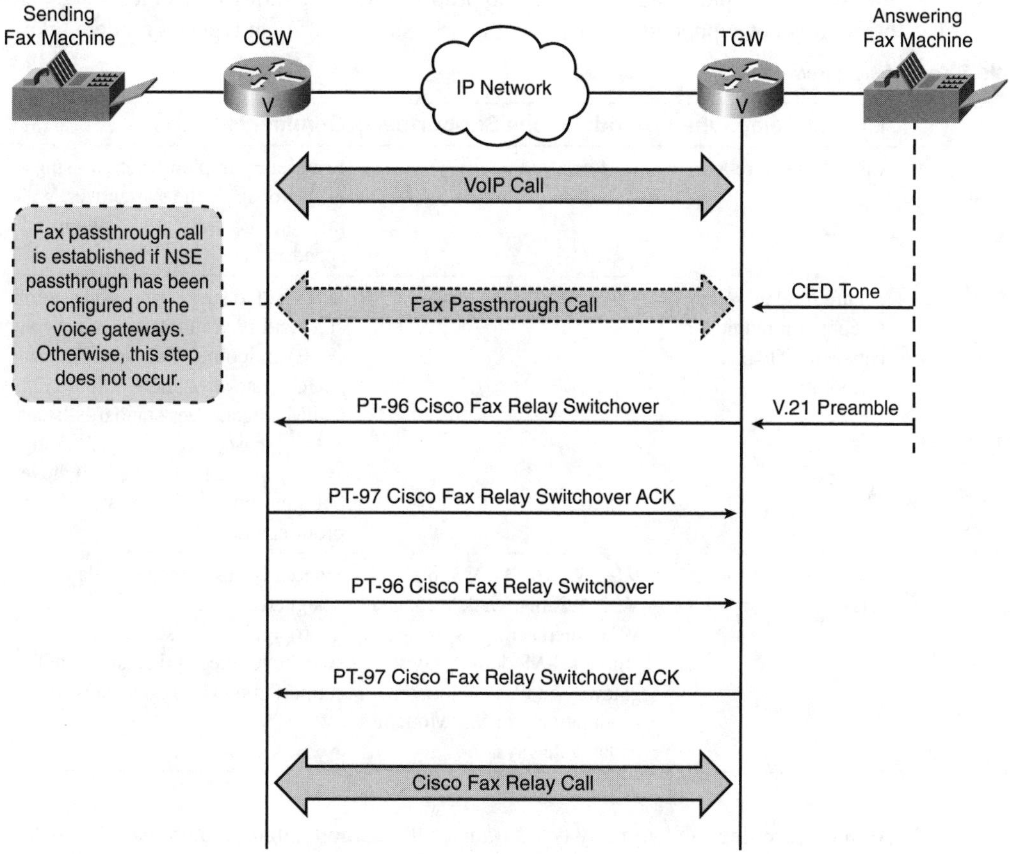

NOTE   Because of the use of the RTP voice stream for communicating the Cisco fax relay switchover, the call signaling protocol stack is not directly involved with the switchover process. No special provisions are needed within the call signaling protocol itself, so Cisco fax relay can work with H.323, SIP, MGCP, and SCCP gateways.

Modem Relay

Modem relay is functionally equivalent to fax relay except that modems are the end devices rather than fax machines. Voice gateways demodulate and modulate the modem signals as they enter and exit the IP network while the actual modem data is "relayed" across IP using special modem relay protocols.

From a Cisco voice gateway perspective, there are multiple modem relay implementations. Two of these implementations are Cisco proprietary, and although the other is standards based, it is not supported. Table 5-4 summarizes these different types of modem relay.

Table 5-4 *Modem Relay Types*

Modem Relay Type	Modulations Supported	Comments
Cisco modem relay	V.34 and V.90	Proprietary implementation using NSEs to signal the switchover. V.90 modulations are forced down to V.34 speeds.
Secure modem relay (secure communication between STE endpoints)	V.32 and V.34	Designed to support line-side, trunk-side, and IP secure terminal equipment (STE) endpoints. Requires SCCP/MGCP gateways and Unified CallManager. Uses standards-based V.150.1-based SSE (state signaling events) messages for the switchover, but other protocol aspects are Cisco proprietary.
ITU-T V.150.1 modem relay	V.92, V.90, V.34, V.32bis, V.32, V.22bis, V.22, V.23, and V.21 when acting as Universal-Modem Relay gateway and V.8 negotiated modulations for V.8-Modem Relay gateways	Standards-based modem relay designed for multivendor interoperability. Uses an SSE switchover mechanism and is not supported on Cisco gateways.

All the preceding modem relay types transfer the demodulated modem data across the IP network using some form of SPRT (Simple Packet Relay Transport). Formally defined in Annex B of the ITU-T V.150.1 specification, SPRT is a low-overhead, reliable protocol running over UDP/IP. Figure 5-16 highlights the basic SPRT frame format as defined by ITU-T V.150.1.

NOTE The Cisco proprietary modem relay methods might not implement this exact SPRT packet format, but it is still shown for reference to provide a glimpse of the underlying modem relay transport protocol.

Figure 5-16 *ITU-T V.150.1 SPRT Packet Format*

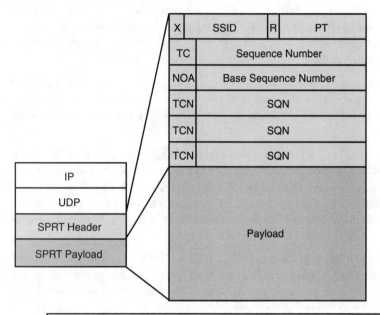

X: Header Extension Bit - set to 0, reserved for ITU-T.

SSID: SubSession ID - identifies a SPRT transmitter subsession.

R: Reserved - set to 0.

PT: Payload Type - value assigned by external call signaling upon call setup.

TC: Transport Channel ID - indicates sequencing and reliability parameters as defined in Table B.1 of ITU-T V.150.1.

Sequence Number: Used by SPRT transmitter for packet sequencing when required.

NOA: Number of Acknowledgments - specifies number of ACK fields in SPRT header.

Base Sequence Number: Identifies the sequence number of the next packet that will be received for the specified TC.

TCN, SQN: ACK indication fields, up to 3 as specified by NOA, TCN identifies the Transport Channel ID for the proceeding SQN (Sequence Number) value.

Because standards-based modem relay is not currently supported on Cisco voice gateways, a detailed, technical discussion of V.150.1 is not pertinent to this section. Therefore, the remainder of this section focuses on Cisco modem relay, the most popular modem relay implementation for Cisco voice gateways. Additional information about secure modem relay is provided in the section "Secure Modem Relay" in Chapter 7.

Most modem connections today negotiate the use of an error correction (EC) protocol. These EC protocols typically introduce some sort of synchronous framing for the modem call so that asynchronous frames are no longer needed on the connection between the modems.

For modem relay, a synchronous frame structure is mandatory for efficiently transporting the modem data. Although other modem relay implementations may support multiple EC protocols, Cisco modem relay takes advantage of the Link Access Procedure for Modems (LAPM) framing specified by the V.42 EC protocol. For more information on the V.42 EC protocol and LAPM framing, see the section "Error Control" in Chapter 1, "How Modems Work."

In a traditional modem-to-modem V.42 connection, the connection parameter negotiation, which includes items such as window and frame size, is handled by the modems themselves through XID (Exchange Identification) frames. However, with Cisco modem relay, the V.42 negotiation is handled independently by the voice gateways. Figure 5-17 depicts the interaction of the V.42 protocol with Cisco modem relay.

Figure 5-17   *ITU-T V.42/V.42bis Negotiation Within Cisco Modem Relay*

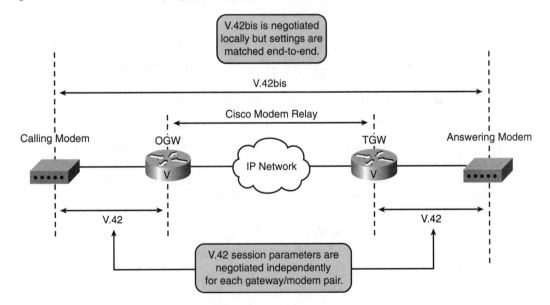

The V.42 negotiation sets up the synchronous, link layer connection. Parameters such as window size and frame size are specified. These parameters might not necessarily match between each voice gateway and modem because of the independent negotiation that occurs between each modem and gateway pair.

V.42bis details the data compression procedures used in conjunction with V.42. Cisco modem relay supports compression in only a single direction, both directions, or compression can be disabled altogether.

When V.42bis compression is present, the modems themselves handle the compression and decompression functions. V.42bis is not terminated locally by the gateways like V.42 is. The Cisco voice gateways just ensure that the V.42bis parameters between the modems are synchronized. See the section "Data Compression" in Chapter 1 if you need more detailed information about V.42bis.

The only switchover mechanism available for Cisco modem relay uses NSE packets. Like the other NSE switchover methods, this procedure is call signaling protocol independent and works the same for H.323, SIP, MGCP, and SCCP. Figure 5-18 details the NSE switchover for Cisco modem relay.

Two specific NSE messages are associated with Cisco modem relay. The first is an NSE-199, which allows the gateways to inform each other that they support Cisco modem relay. This NSE message is sent out by the terminating gateway as soon as the ANSam tone has been detected and the NSE-192 has been sent to trigger modem passthrough.

Until the gateways are sure that this VoIP call is a modem call that can be supported by Cisco modem relay, there cannot be a formal switchover to modem relay. For example, after only the ANSam tone has been heard, the call could end up being an SG3 fax call. An SG3 fax call is not compatible with Cisco modem relay, but it looks the same at this stage of the call.

The second NSE message used in Cisco modem relay is the NSE-203. This NSE message forces the Cisco modem relay switchover assuming that the NSE-199 messages have been properly exchanged. The NSE-203 message is only triggered by the detection of a valid V.8 CM (Calling Menu) by the OGW. After the appropriate V.8 CM has been detected, the gateways are sure that this is a supportable modem call, and the modem relay feature can be invoked.

Figure 5-18 *Cisco Modem Relay Switchover Using NSE Packets*

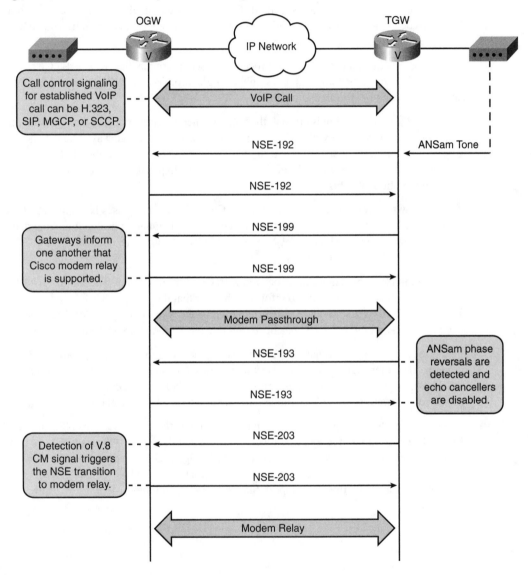

TIP	The switchover implementation of Cisco modem relay discussed above is referred to as gateway controlled or gw-controlled in the Cisco IOS gateway CLI. Introduced in Cisco IOS Release 12.4(4)T, this implementation requires no work on the part of the call signaling protocol with regard to the switchover process.
	In earlier codes, a method known as signaling-assisted modem relay was used. Instead of exchanging NSE-199 messages, this switchover method depended on information exchanged within the voice signaling protocol to confirm that both sides were capable of Cisco modem relay. However, NSE-203 messages were still used to trigger the actual switchover.

Cisco Text Relay

Cisco text relay provides the functional equivalent of fax and modem relay for text telephones. The Baudot tones used by text devices are decoded and passed as characters across the IP network before being played back as Baudot signals once again on the far side.

Cisco text relay is a proprietary solution that leverages portions of different specifications to implement a viable method for transporting text over IP. Table 5-5 details the multiple specifications that Cisco text relay uses.

Table 5-5   *Specifications Used by Cisco Text Relay*

Specification	Description
ITU-T V.151	Procedure for the end-to-end connection of public switched telephone network (PSTN) text telephones using text relay over IP.
ITU-T T.140	Specifies a simple text protocol for conversing between text devices.
IETF RFC 4351	Describes how to transport real-time text session contents based on ITU-T T.140 in RTP packets.
IETF RFC 2198	Specifies an RTP payload format for encoding redundant audio data. RFC 4351 details how RFC 2198 can also be used with redundant text data.

From an implementation perspective, Cisco text relay is much closer to a feature such as Dual Tone Multi Frequency (DTMF) relay than modem or fax relay. DTMF relay does not have a switchover procedure but instead only relays DTMF digits when they are detected in the voice media stream. Cisco text relay operates in the same fashion, only activating when a Baudot text character is detected in the voice media stream.

With modem and fax relay, the original voice media stream is replaced by a special relay protocol after the triggering of a switchover using NSEs or the signaling protocol stack. This does not happen with Cisco text relay because an explicit switchover does not occur and the voice media stream remains intact for the call duration.

Because Cisco text relay does not create a new media session, it must use the existing voice media stream, including the same UDP ports. So, how does Cisco text relay distinguish itself from the actual voice packets already using these established IP sockets?

Cisco text relay implements a unique RTP payload type (PT) to coexist within the same media stream as the RTP voice packets. The voice packets will always use a standard RTP PT indicating the voice codec negotiated for that connection. Cisco text relay implements a dynamic RTP PT, which is set to 119 by default. Figure 5-19 illustrates voice and text relay packets within the same RTP media stream.

Figure 5-19 *Cisco Text Relay over an Existing RTP Voice Stream*

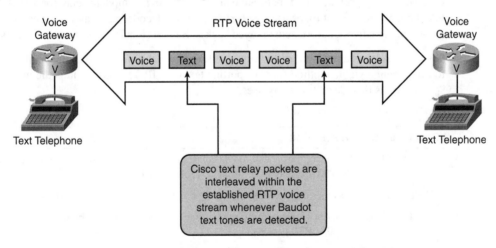

Of course, for many text telephone conversations, there will not be any voice exchanged over the connection unless Hearing Carry Over (HCO) or Voice Carry Over (VCO) is being used. In these situations, even though the call is initially created as a voice call, practically all the packets across the media stream will be Cisco text relay. The concepts of HCO and VCO were discussed previously in the sections "HCO (Hearing Carry Over)" and "VCO (Voice Carry Over)" in Chapter 3, "How Text Telephony Works."

The packet format implemented by Cisco text relay is derived from RFC 4351. This specification mandates an RTP encapsulation with ITU-T T.140 encoding for the text characters in the RTP payload. However, because Cisco text relay forces redundancy to be enabled, the RTP payload must be able to handle redundancy. Figure 5-20 illustrates the RTP portion of a Cisco text relay packet when redundancy is set to a value of 1.

Figure 5-20 *Cisco Text Relay Packet Format with a Single Level of Redundancy*

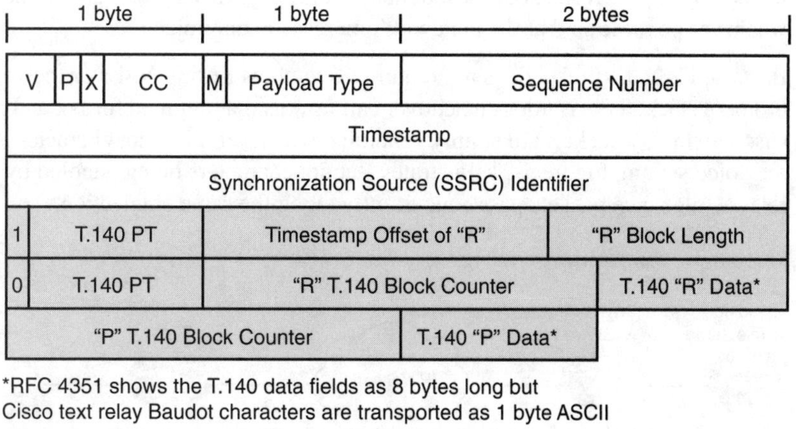

*RFC 4351 shows the T.140 data fields as 8 bytes long but
Cisco text relay Baudot characters are transported as 1 byte ASCII

NOTE   You can find additional information concerning the RTP header and its contents in the section "Passthrough Fundamentals" in Chapter 4.

The shaded portion of Figure 5-20 highlights the RTP payload, and the unshaded portion indicates the RTP header. The RTP payload supporting redundant text characters is defined in RFC 4351. Elements of RFC 2198 are used by RFC 4351 to address the actual packet formatting of these redundant characters. Table 5-6 defines the RTP payload fields used in transporting text characters with redundancy.

Table 5-6   *Cisco Text Relay Redundancy Frame Field Definitions*

Cisco Text Relay Redundancy Field	Definition
T.140 PT	T.140 payload type, set to 119 for Cisco text relay.
Timestamp Offset	Offset of redundant block relative to the timestamp given in the RTP header.
Block Length	Length of data block not including the header.
T.140 Block Counter	16-bit counter used to detect lost blocks and to avoid duplication of blocks. Separate block counters are used for R (redundant) characters and P (primary) characters.
T.140 "R" Data	R or Redundant Data field repeats a previously transmitted primary character in 1-byte ASCII format.
T.140 "P" Data	P or Primary Data field is a new character being transmitted for the first time as 1-byte ASCII.

Cisco text relay defaults to a redundancy value of 2. Adding redundancy to the RTP payload increases the packet size, but the redundant data "piggybacks" along with the primary data whenever possible so that the bandwidth increase is minimized.

Because Cisco text relay does not require a switchover using NSEs or the voice signaling protocol stack, there is not a switchover call flow as diagrammed for fax and modem relay. Cisco text relay packets are simply generated whenever a Baudot character is detected in the voice stream. Figure 5-21 illustrates Baudot characters being handled by Cisco text relay while voice packets pass concurrently along the same connection.

Figure 5-21 *Transport of Text Characters Using Cisco Text Relay*

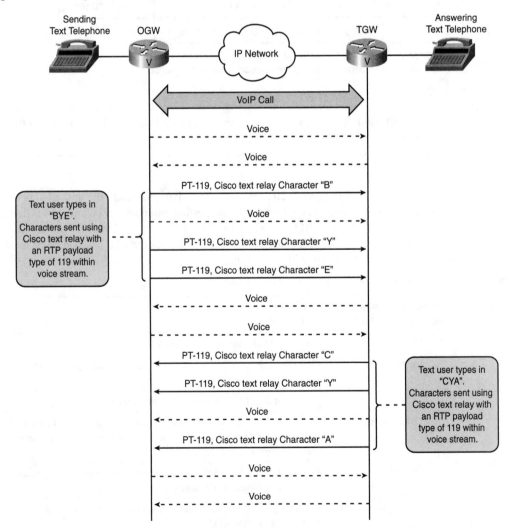

A Future Look at ITU-T T.38, V.150.1, and V.151

The three most promising standards for fax, modem, and text relay are T.38, V.150.1, and V.151, respectively. Although V.150.1 and V.151 have yet to be widely adopted compared to T.38, all of these standards offer a glimpse into the future of transporting modulated data over an IP network.

T.38 has been increasingly deployed in recent years as the de facto fax relay solution. With this increased deployment, T.38 has continued to evolve and offer new features and functionality.

Two of the more notable features adopted by later versions of the T.38 specification are SG3 and RTP support. Although Cisco's current T.38 implementation only supports G3 faxing, SG3 support is the next step in greatly increasing the performance of T.38 fax relay. With full SG3 support, T.38 allows page transmissions up to 33.6 Kbps.

RTP support is also described in later versions of T.38. The current Cisco implementation only uses UDPTL. With T.38 enclosed within RTP, additional features such as secure faxing using SRTP (Secure Real Time Protocol) would become available.

V.150.1 defines a standards-based modem relay implementation. Built upon the SPRT packet format already used by Cisco modem relay, V.150.1 provides support for a number of different modulations while ensuring interoperability between different vendors. SSEs are defined in V.150.1 as an out-of-band switchover mechanism.

Standards-based text relay is detailed by the V.151 specification. V.151 provides the means for text phones in different countries to interoperate with one another. In addition, provisions are made to send the V.151 text relay characters with redundancy across the same connection as the IP voice packets, just like Cisco text relay. The V.151 standard closes the disparity gap with typical telephone users and delivers VoIP communication benefits to the speaking and hearing impaired.

Summary

The relay transport method exists for modem, fax, and text communications and is another option in place of passthrough for transporting these types of modulated data. Whereas passthrough uses PCM to sample modulated signals, relay demodulates the signal and then relays the binary information across the IP network via a relay protocol where it is remodulated on the other side.

On Cisco voice gateways, two forms of fax relay are available: T.38 and Cisco fax relay. T.38 is standards-based and uses NSEs or the call signaling protocol to switch from voice to T.38 fax relay mode. T.38 is also the predominant choice for most fax implementations today. Cisco fax relay is proprietary and uses predefined dynamic RTP payload types to transition to Cisco fax relay from voice mode.

Cisco modem relay is the most widely used type of modem relay on Cisco voice gateways. Although Cisco modem relay is proprietary, it shares the SPRT packet format with standards-based modem relay, ITU-T V.150.1. To signal the transition from voice mode to Cisco modem relay, NSE messages are used.

Cisco text relay is a proprietary solution for passing Baudot text phone characters across an IP network. There is not an explicit switchover mechanism for Cisco text relay, so Cisco text relay activates only when a Baudot text character is detected.

CHAPTER 6

T.37 Store-and-Forward Fax

The ITU-T Recommendation T.37 offers an additional means of transporting fax transmissions beyond the methods of passthrough and relay that have been discussed in the previous two chapters. Often referred to as "store-and-forward fax" the T.37 specification details a process for integrating e-mail with fax communications. T.37 ensures that faxes arrive to users as e-mail, and it also allows users to transmit faxes by simply sending an e-mail.

This chapter first gives a general overview of T.37 and the main protocols and specifications that it is based on. Following that is a look at how e-mail is forwarded using the Simple Mail Transfer Protocol (SMTP). This discussion includes an analysis of the basic operation of the SMTP protocol and two of its service extensions, delivery status notification (DSN) and message disposition notification (MDN). The DSN and MDN service extensions are used frequently in T.37 as delivery and disposition notification methods for e-mail messages. The final two sections examine onramp and offramp independently as the component parts of an end-to-end T.37 call.

Overview of T.37 Store-and-Forward Fax

Approved by the ITU-T in 1998, the T.37 specification is a conglomerate of standards that address different facets of the conversion process from fax to e-mail and vice versa. The major standards referenced in T.37 are detailed in Table 6-1.

Table 6-1   *T.37 Standards*

Standard	Description
ITU-T T.30 and T.4	G3 fax standards that T.37 gateways must implement to converse directly with traditional fax machines
RFC 821 and 1869	Covers SMTP and Extended SMTP (ESMTP) procedures for relaying mail between mail transfer agents
RFC 2045–2049	Defines MIME (Multipurpose Internet Mail Extensions) and how it works
RFC 2301–2305	Details Internet fax procedures based on Internet mail

Generally speaking, these standards define the basic communication procedures (T.30 and SMTP) between the voice gateway and both the public switched telephone network (PSTN) fax and mail server used in a T.37 call. In addition, they cover the formatting rules and encoding methods (MIME and TIFF) used in the fax/mail conversion process for T.37. You can find ITU-T Recommendations at http://www.itu.int/ITU-T/ and RFC specifications at http://www.ietf.org/rfc.html.

The T.30 specification defines the communication protocol between the T.37 voice gateway and the PSTN fax machine. The operation of this protocol and a review of its component messages were covered in detail in Chapter 2, "How Fax Works."

The communication between the T.37 voice gateway and the mail server occurs via SMTP. The SMTP protocol is the unanimous choice for Internet mail today and it uses TCP to enforce a reliable transaction. The SMTP protocol and its operation within T.37 is discussed in detail in the next section.

MIME supplements SMTP by removing many of the formatting restrictions imposed by RFC 822. This allows the encapsulation of more complex nontext file formats as part of a standard e-mail message. In the case of T.37, MIME provides attributes that describe how the fax images are encoded within the e-mail so that the destination device can easily decode them.

The Cisco implementation of store-and-forward fax supports only a small subset of the possible content types and encodings supported by MIME. For example, a Cisco T.37 gateway can only process e-mails with plain text or enriched text in the body of the e-mail. In addition, it only handles fax pages that are graphically encoded as TIFF (Tagged Image File Format) or even more specifically as TIFF Profile F (TIFF-F) as an attachment to the e-mail. TIFF-F is defined in RFC 2301 and includes support for Modified Huffman (MH), Modified READ (MR), and Modified Modified READ (MMR) fax encodings. These fax encoding types are discussed in detail in the section "Page Encoding" of Chapter 2.

T.37 operates in two different modes: onramp and offramp. The onramp function handles incoming faxes to the voice gateway and coverts them to an e-mail, whereas the offramp function turns an incoming e-mail into a fax call. Each of these T.37 modes of operation is configured independently on a Cisco voice gateway and is discussed in more detail later in this chapter.

To this point, only real-time fax transport methods such as fax passthrough and fax relay have been discussed. T.37 takes a drastically different approach to transporting fax traffic over an IP network. Figure 6-1 illustrates this by showing the vastly different network path taken by a T.37 onramp and offramp store-and-forward fax call compared to the network path taken by a standard fax passthrough or fax relay real-time fax call.

Figure 6-1   *Call Path Comparison for T.37 and Passthrough/Relay*

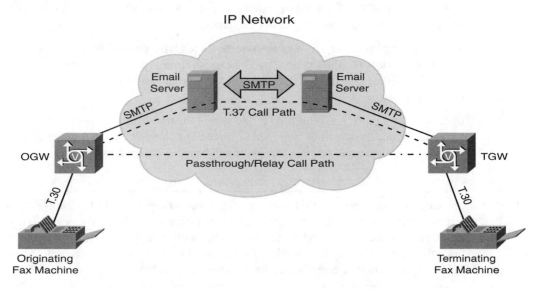

Both fax passthrough and fax relay assist with the transport of the fax while the fax is actually transmitting. On the other hand, T.37 has a data storage component to it so that it can handle the fax to e-mail or e-mail to fax conversion process. Consequently, depending on the mode of operation, the T.37 gateway either completely terminates or originates fax calls to handle the conversion to or from an e-mail. This is the reason for the "store" portion of the moniker often given to T.37: store-and-forward fax.

This storing mechanism used in T.37 clearly breaks the real-time aspect of fax communication that is seen for fax calls over the PSTN or through an IP network using fax relay or fax passthrough. Although this has the drawback that it decouples the real-time nature of fax communication, it does provide the user with the added convenience of sending and receiving faxes directly from a computer through e-mail.

SMTP Overview

As mentioned in the previous section and as illustrated in Figure 6-1, the T.37 gateway has the ability to communicate directly with G3 fax devices using the ITU-T T.30 fax protocol, which is covered in detail in Chapter 2. Similarly, the T.37 gateway also communicates natively with the mail server via the SMTP protocol.

SMTP is one of the fundamental elements necessary for understanding and effectively troubleshooting T.37. Therefore, this section discusses some SMTP basics before tackling the T.37 concepts of onramp and offramp.

Connecting through TCP port 25, SMTP is a relatively simple, text-based protocol. Widespread adoption of SMTP started back in the early 1980s, and today SMTP is the de facto standard for e-mail transmissions across the Internet.

SMTP is a "push" protocol, meaning that one device sends or "pushes" an e-mail to another device. SMTP does not allow one to "pull" messages from a server, so e-mail protocols such as Post Office Protocol (POP) or Internet Message Access Protocol (IMAP) must be used in this case.

Because of the "push" nature of SMTP, one side of the transaction is referred to as the SMTP client, and the other side is the SMTP server. The client side is the device that has a mail message to transmit, whereas the server will be receiving the message.

TIP   The term mail transfer agent (MTA) is commonly used to signify the SMTP endpoints or servers used to transfer mail from one system to another, whereas the term user agent (UA) is often used to indicate the end-user mail program or client that is used to interface with the mail server. Throughout this section, the term mail server is used interchangeably with MTA, and the term mail client is used interchangeably with UA.

This section covers the commands used in SMTP and basic operation of the protocol. The analysis of the protocol is through showing actual SMTP sessions between a mail server and a mail client. Then, a quick explanation of SMTP concepts relevant to T.37, such as DSN and MDN, is provided.

SMTP Commands and Sample Sessions

The easiest way to grasp how SMTP works is to look at a basic SMTP session. Example 6-1 details how a simple e-mail is transmitted between two mail devices using SMTP.

Example 6-1 *SMTP Session*

```
220 smtp-outbound.cisco.com ESMTP Sendmail 8.12.10/8.12.6 ; Fri, 20 Oct 2006
   16:01:02 -0400 (EDT)
HELO cisco.com
250 smtp-outbound.cisco.com Hello [192.168.1.1], pleased to meet you
MAIL FROM:<testuser@cisco.com>
250 2.1.0 testuser@cisco.com... Sender ok
RCPT TO:<myfriend@example.com>
250 2.1.5 myfriend@example.com... Recipient ok
DATA
354 Enter mail, end with "." on a line by itself
Subject: test message
From: testuser@cisco.com
To: myfriend@example.com
```

Example 6-1 *SMTP Session (Continued)*

```
Hello,
This is a test.
Goodbye.
.
250 2.0.0 k9k1234567890 Message accepted for delivery
QUIT
221 2.0.0 smtp-outbound.cisco.com closing connection
```

The SMTP session shown in Example 6-1 begins when the transmitting e-mail device or client initiates a TCP connection on port 25 to the receiving device, typically a mail server. The mail server answers the connection by identifying itself with a three-digit code followed by a greeting similar to the first line of Example 6-1. The three-digit codes preceding all the responses from the mail server are discussed later in this section. Notice that the e-mail client SMTP commands are shown in boldface type, whereas the e-mail server responses are shown in normal type.

The e-mail client responds to the server greeting with a **HELO** command and includes its domain name. The mail server then acknowledges the **HELO** command. Following that, the e-mail client submits the sending and receiving address to the mail server using the **MAIL FROM:** and **RCPT TO:** SMTP commands. To make a parallel to standard mail, these two pieces of information are known as the SMTP envelope. The sender's e-mail address and the recipient's e-mail address are the only information used by the SMTP server to deliver the message.

The SMTP content is the body of the message, which also includes header information, and it is transmitted after proper acknowledgment from the e-mail server to the client's **DATA** command. Upon completion of the e-mail transaction, the e-mail client gracefully ends the SMTP session with a **QUIT** command.

Example 6-1 illustrates a basic SMTP session using the SMTP command **HELO**. However, an improved version of SMTP known as Extended Simple Mail Transfer Protocol (ESMTP) is an alternative that has more features and a greater versatility through added service extensions. ESMTP uses the command **EHLO** rather than **HELO** as an identification command. An example of an **EHLO** command and response session is shown in Example 6-2.

Example 6-2 *EHLO Command and Response*

```
220 smtp.cisco.com Simple Mail Transfer Service Ready
EHLO cisco.com
250-smtp.cisco.com greets cisco.com
250-8BITMIME
250-SIZE
250-DSN
250 HELP
```

In Example 6-2, you can see how the **EHLO** command elicits a more detailed response from the SMTP server. The server now includes its supported ESMTP extensions in the response. These extensions let the client know the features and other capabilities for this SMTP server. From a T.37 perspective, either ESMTP or SMTP with their respective **EHLO** and **HELO** identification commands may be used.

In addition to the SMTP commands highlighted in Example 6-1 and Example 6-2, there are additional SMTP commands. Table 6-2 lists the common SMTP and ESMTP commands and provides a brief description of each.

Table 6-2   *Common SMTP/ESMTP Commands*

SMTP/ESMTP Command	Definition
HELO domain name	Hello: Identifies the SMTP client to the SMTP server
EHLO domain name	Extended Hello: Identifies the SMTP client to the SMTP server and requests a list of ESMTP extensions supported by the server
MAIL FROM: sender address	Mail From: Identifies the sender of the e-mail message
RCPT TO: recipient address	Recipient To: Specifies a single recipient for the e-mail transaction
DATA	Data: Indicates to the server that the client is ready to transmit the message content
RSET	Reset: Aborts the current mail transaction
VRFY user address	Verify: Requests that the server validate a mailbox address
EXPN mailing list	Expand: Requests that the server confirm the mailing list address and provide a list of users
HELP [SMTP command]	Help: Requests general help from the server or command specific help when a valid SMTP command is included
NOOP	No Operation: A null command that provides no function other than the reception of an OK reply from the server
QUIT	QUIT: Terminates the SMTP session

Notice in Example 6-1 and Example 6-2 that the SMTP server always precedes its response with a numeric, three-digit code. These codes are referred to as SMTP response codes, and their definitions are defined by RFC 821. Table 6-3 details the SMTP response codes and their definitions.

Table 6-3   *SMTP Response Codes*

SMTP Response Code	Definition
211	System status, or system help reply
214	Help message
220	<domain> service ready
221	<domain> service closing session
250	Requested mail action ok, completed
251	User not local; will forward to <forward-path>
252	Cannot VRFY user but message will be accepted and delivery attempted
354	Start mail input; end with <CRLF>.<CRLF>
421	<domain> service not available, ending session
450	Requested action not taken, mailbox unavailable (mailbox busy)
451	Requested action aborted; local error in processing
452	Requested action not taken; insufficient system storage
500	Syntax error, command unrecognized
501	Syntax error in parameters or arguments
502	Command not implemented
503	Bad sequence of commands
504	Command parameter not implemented
550	Requested action not taken; mailbox unavailable (mailbox not found, no access, rejected for policy reasons)
551	User not local; try <forward-path>
552	Requested action aborted; exceeded storage allocation
553	Requested action not taken; mailbox name not allowed (mailbox syntax incorrect)
554	Transaction failed

DSN and MDN

Some of the most commonly used services that are added to the basic functionality of SMTP relate to giving the sender of an e-mail message a notification about the status of the message. Two such notification methods are delivery status notification (DSN) and message disposition notification (MDN) messages. Both of these delivery and processing confirmation methods are frequently integrated with T.37 store-and-forward fax.

DSN messages provide a mechanism for the mail server to convey delivery status of an e-mail message back to the sender. Depending on the mail server configuration, a DSN message can provide positive/negative delivery status information. Negative DSN informs the sender that the message was unable to be delivered or has been delayed, whereas positive DSN updates the originator that the message was successfully delivered.

DSN messages can be requested only during an ESMTP session if the ESMTP mail server explicitly offers support for these messages. Example 6-2 shows an ESMTP mail server responding to an EHLO with DSN support as one of its service extensions. Furthermore, all mail servers in the message path must support DSN for these notifications to work correctly. This concept is important because many mail messages must be routed through more than one e-mail server.

An ESMTP mail server configured for DSN support will only generate DSNs under the conditions requested by the mail client. These conditions are signaled to the mail server by the client in the "RCPT TO:" SMTP envelope command. After the e-mail address, a **NOTIFY** attribute is used to request the type of delivery notification for a particular recipient required by the sender. Example 6-3 illustrates DSN notification requests during an ESMTP session.

Example 6-3 *ESMTP Session with DSN NOTIFY Parameters*

```
220 smtp.cisco.com Simple Mail Transfer Service Ready
EHLO cisco.com
250-smtp.cisco.com greets cisco.com
250-8BITMIME
250-SIZE
250-DSN
250 HELP
MAIL FROM:<originator@cisco.com> RET=HDRS ENVID=124567
250 <originator@cisco.com> sender ok
RCPT TO:<user1@cisco.com> NOTIFY=SUCCESS,DELAY ORCPT=rfc822;user1@cisco.com
250 <user1@cisco.com> recipient ok
RCPT TO:<user2@cisco.com> NOTIFY=FAILURE ORCPT=rfc822;user2@cisco.com
250 <user2@cisco.com> recipient ok
RCPT TO:<user3@cisco.com> NOTIFY=NEVER
R: 250 <user3@cisco.com> recipient ok
```

The receivers of the mail message (specified by "RCPT TO:") in Example 6-3 each have the **NOTIFY** parameter after their respective e-mail addresses. This **NOTIFY** parameter specifies the delivery conditions under which the DSNs are requested by the sender for that particular recipient. The possible settings for the DSN **NOTIFY** parameter are specified in Table 6-4.

Table 6-4   *DSN NOTIFY Parameter Settings*

DSN NOTIFY	Definition
SUCCESS	Requests a DSN when the mail message has been successfully delivered to the recipient's inbox. This DSN does not reflect that the message has been opened by the recipient.
FAILURE	Requests a DSN when the mail message cannot be delivered.
DELAY	Requests a DSN when the mail message delivery has been delayed.
NEVER	Requests that a DSN is never sent back to the sender.

Taking into account the DSN **NOTIFY** parameters defined in Table 6-4, let's analyze the DSN notification for user1 in Example 6-3. The "RCPT TO:" command for user1 requests DSNs for **SUCCESS** and **DELAY** as specified in the **NOTIFY** extension. This means that the sender of this mail message will receive DSN messages only when the mail message is successfully delivered to user1's inbox or if it is delayed in its path to user1's inbox.

Following the **NOTIFY** parameter and its values, there is another parameter in the "RCPT TO:" SMTP command for user1. This parameter is the **ORCPT** (Original Recipient Address), and it specifies an address corresponding to the actual recipient of the delivered message.

As part of the **ORCPT**, an "addr-type" is specified that defines the type of mail address appearing in the **ORCPT**. In the case of Example 6-3, the "addr-type" for the **ORCPT** parameters is shown to conform to the format specified in RFC 822.

The last DSN related parameters in Example 6-3 are **RET** (Return) and **ENVID** (Envelope ID). These parameters are part of the sender's mail address that is specified in the "MAIL FROM:" SMTP envelope command.

In Example 6-3, **RET=HDRS** informs the mail server that the client only wants to have the e-mail headers "returned" in any DSN corresponding to a failed message delivery. The other option is **RET=FULL**, and this parameter requests that the full e-mail be returned for a failed message delivery DSN.

The **ENVID** parameter allows the client to attach an identifier that will be transmitted along with the message. This **ENVID** is also included in any DSNs issued for any of the recipients in the SMTP transaction. The purpose of the **ENVID** is to allow the sender of a message to correlate the original message with any DSNs that are received for that particular message. For a detailed explanation of DSN as a service extension to the SMTP protocol and a definition of all its associated parameters (NOTIFY, ORCPT, RET, ENVID), refer to RFC 3461.

DSN messages are used within T.37 to indicate successful delivery of a fax mail. For instance, if a fax is converted to an e-mail by the onramp gateway and it is configured for DSN, the delivery status of the mail message containing the TIFF attachment of the fax is sent to the user specified in the gateway configuration.

Example 6-4 shows an actual DSN message indicating successful delivery of a fax-mail sent by the mail server to the user specified in the configuration of the onramp gateway. For more information on configuring DSNs on a Cisco onramp gateway, see the section "Dial-Peer Configuration for Onramp Fax" in Chapter 11, "Configuring T.37 Store-and-Forward Fax."

Example 6-4 *T.37 DSN Success Message*

```
From:          Administrator@faxmail.com
Subject:       Delivery Status Notification (Success)
Date:          May 22, 2007 7:24:42 PM EDT
To:            gsalguei@cisco.com


Your message

  To:     gsalguei
  Subject: Incoming Fax[DNIS=9913170][ANI=9194724118]
  Sent:   Tue, 22 May 2007 12:23:04 -0400

was delivered to the following recipient(s):

Gonzalo Salgueiro on Tue, 22 May 2007 19:24:42 -0400
    <RTP-ESC-T37.faxmail.com #2.0.0>

! Output omitted for brevity
```

Another notification to the sender that can prove useful is message disposition notification (MDN) messages. The difference between DSN and MDN is that DSN messages notify the sender of message delivery status by the mail server, whereas MDN messages notify the sender about how the already delivered message is processed by the recipient. For example, although a DSN will notify the sender that the mail message has been successfully deposited in a user's mailbox, it does not mean that the user has viewed the message. An MDN takes the process a step further and informs the sender when the recipient has actually opened the message.

An MDN is often referred to as a "read receipt" or a "return receipt" because it informs the sender that the mail message that was sent was opened by the recipient. A sender requests an MDN by including a "Disposition-Notification-To:" field in the header of the e-mail message. The address in the "Disposition-Notification-To:" field identifies where the disposition notification should be sent.

Example 6-5 illustrates the header for an e-mail that was delivered to the recipient **gsalguei@faxmail.com**. This header requests that an MDN be sent to the sender **gsalguei@cisco.com**. Note that the **Disposition-Notification-To:** field is found in the header information of the SMTP content portion of an SMTP message, unlike a DSN, which makes its notification request in the SMTP envelope.

Example 6-5 *E-mail Message Header with an MDN Request*

```
From:        gsalguei@cisco.com
Subject:     Incoming Fax[DNIS=9913170][ANI=9194724118]
Date:        May 22, 2007 2:05:26 PM EDT
To:          gsalguei@faxmail.com
Received:    from fax_2811 ([14.80.32.200]) by RTP-ESC-T37.faxmail.com with
Microsoft SMTPSVC(5.0.2172.1); Tue, 22 May 2007 21:06:43 -0400
Received:    (This is an incoming fax message from the PSTN) by fax_2811 for
  <gsalguei@faxmail.com> (with Cisco NetWorks); Tue, 22 May 2007 18:05:26 +0000
Message-Id:     <006A2007180526235@fax_2811>
X-Mailer:    Technical Support: http://www.cisco
Disposition-Notification-To:    gsalguei@cisco.com
Mime-Version:    1.0
Content-Type:    multipart/fax-message; boundary="yradnuoB=_00692007180523847.fax
  _2811"
X-Account-Id:    0
Return-Path:    gsalguei@cisco.com
X-Originalarrivaltime:    23 May 2007 01:07:04.0671 (UTC)
  FILETIME=[AD3C8EF0:01C79CD6]
```

Because an MDN reveals to the sender whether and when a recipient has opened the mail message, it is sometimes considered an invasion of privacy. Because of these privacy considerations, MDN support is not available in several mail clients. If it is supported, it is typically implemented in such a fashion that the recipient is explicitly asked whether to acquiesce to the MDN request by the sender.

For instance, when the recipient of the e-mail in Example 6-5 opened that mail message, his mail reader requested for him to accept or deny the sender's request for a read receipt to be sent back. The recipient agreed to the request, and the MDN shown in Example 6-6 was sent.

Example 6-6 *T.37 MDN Message*

```
From:        gsalguei@faxmail.com
Subject:     Read: Incoming Fax[DNIS=9913170][ANI=9194724118]
Date:        March 31, 2007 3:58:20 PM EDT
To:          gsalguei@cisco.com

! Output omitted for brevity

This is a receipt for the mail you sent to
"gsalguei" <gsalguei@faxmail.com> at 5/22/2007 1:05 PM

This receipt verifies that the message has been displayed on the recipient's
computer at 3/31/2007 2:58 PM
```

continues

Example 6-6 *T.37 MDN Message (Continued)*

```
<MIME Attachment Information Follows:>

Final-Recipient: rfc822;gsalguei@cisco.com
Original-Message-ID: <006A2007180526235@fax_2811>
Disposition: manual-action/MDN-sent-manually; displayed
```

Let's take a look at how the actual MDN message is actually formatted. Note that the MDN in Example 6-6 indicates in the Subject: that the recipient **Read:** the original message. Of course, there is no way of knowing whether the message was actually read or not, but the MDN does indicate in a human-readable explanation that the recipient did in fact open the message and even provides a timestamp for when it occurred.

The MDN also contains a MIME attachment with the information shown in Example 6-6. The **Original-Message-ID:** field is used to easily correlate the MDN receipt with the original e-mail. Note that the **Original-Message-ID:** field in the MDN in Example 6-6 matches up exactly with the Message-Id: field in the header of the original e-mail in Example 6-5.

The most important information in the MDN is found in the **Disposition:** field. The **Disposition:** field is a mandatory field for an MDN, and it is used to indicate what actions the recipient performed while processing the mail message.

Several attributes make up the information in the **Disposition:** field. The two most important parameters are the disposition-mode and the disposition-type. Table 6-5 defines the disposition-mode parameter settings.

Table 6-5 *Disposition-Mode Parameter Settings*

Disposition-Mode	Definition
manual-action	The message disposition described by the disposition-type parameter was an explicit instruction by the recipient.
automatic-action	The message disposition described by the disposition-type parameter was an automatic action not explicitly indicated by the recipient.
	Note: manual-action and automatic-action are mutually exclusive. One or the other must be specified.
MDN-sent-manually	The MDN was sent because the recipient explicitly gave permission.
MDN-sent-automatically	The MDN was sent because the mail client is configured to do it automatically.
	Note: MDN-sent-manually and MDN-sent-automatically are mutually exclusive. One or the other must be specified.

The MDN in Example 6-6 clearly specifies in the **Notification:** header that the "disposition-mode" is **manual-action/MDN-sent-manually**. This indicates to the sender that the recipient explicitly and manually acknowledged the request for an MDN to be sent. Table 6-6 defines all the disposition-type parameter settings.

Table 6-6   *Disposition-Type Parameter Settings*

Disposition-type	Definition
displayed	The e-mail message has been displayed by the mail client.
dispatched	The e-mail message has been dispatched somewhere (for example, forwarded, printed, faxed, and so on) without necessarily having been previously displayed.
processed	The e-mail message has been processed in some other way and has not been displayed by the mail client.
deleted	The e-mail message has been deleted.
denied	The recipient does not want to provide any information to the sender about how the e-mail message was processed.
failed	A failure prevented a proper MDN from being sent.

The **Notification:** field for the MDN shown in Example 6-6 has a "disposition-type" with a value of **displayed**. Referencing Table 6-6, this means that the recipient's mail client displayed the e-mail in Example 6-5. You can get further information on the operation of MDN and all its related parameters in RFC 2298.

T.37 Onramp

By integrating e-mail with standard G3 fax, T.37 store-and-forward fax allows an added dimension of flexibility and convenience that is not possible with fax relay or fax passthrough. Faxes can only be sent and received to and from standard fax devices in the case of fax relay and fax passthrough. In addition to that functionality, T.37 allows receiving faxes as e-mail and sending e-mail that can be delivered as faxes.

A T.37 call is naturally segmented into two completely independent parts: onramp and offramp. Cisco voice gateways can be configured as an onramp gateway, an offramp gateway, or a combination of both.

An onramp gateway is responsible for receiving a G3 PSTN fax call and then forwarding that fax call as an e-mail to a mail server. Figure 6-2 shows a high-level view of this process.

Figure 6-2 *T.37 Onramp*

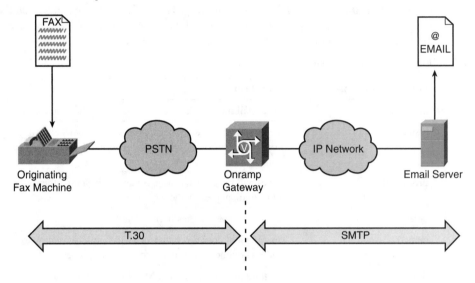

The onramp gateway in Figure 6-2 first communicates with the originating G3 fax device via the T.30 protocol. After the T.30 communication has been established and the fax page transmission attributes successfully negotiated, the originating G3 fax device sends the page data to the Cisco onramp gateway using the T.4 protocol. The T.4 protocol was covered in detail in the section "Page Encoding" of Chapter 2.

The onramp gateway then converts the received fax page data from the originating fax device into a TIFF file attachment. This conversion process on the T.37 onramp gateway uses an internal TIFF writer that encodes the images of the fax pages using the TIFF-F graphical encoding scheme. TIFF-F is the data format for compressed fax images used by standards-based T.37 gateways.

Following the TIFF conversion process, the onramp gateway constructs a standard MIME e-mail message. This e-mail contains the compressed images of the original fax pages as a TIFF attachment and is commonly referred to as a fax mail.

Finally, the onramp gateway forwards this fax mail to the appropriate mail server that is designated in its configuration. The onramp gateway and the mail server establish an SMTP communication on TCP port 25, and this fax mail is forwarded using the SMTP protocol as described in the previous section.

If necessary, this fax mail is forwarded between mail servers or MTAs until it arrives and is stored at the destination mail server. This fax mail can either be accessed as an e-mail by the recipient's mail client or UA or it can be forwarded via T.37 offramp to a standard G3 fax machine. The T.37 offramp function is covered in detail in the next section.

T.37 Offramp

Offramp functions in the exact reverse way that onramp does. An offramp gateway is responsible for accepting an e-mail and converting it to a standard fax format that is subsequently delivered to a standard G3 fax machine. Figure 6-3 traces through the process of an offramp fax call.

Figure 6-3 *T.37 Offramp*

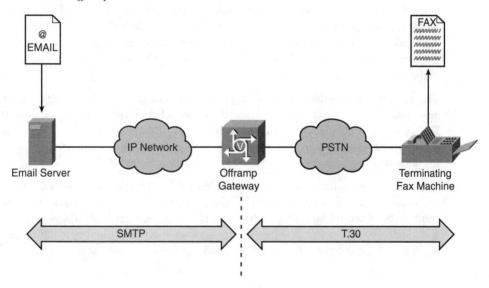

The offramp gateway communicates natively via the SMTP protocol with the mail server. The mail server or MTA forwards the e-mail over that SMTP connection as described in the "SMTP Commands and Sample Sessions" section earlier in this chapter. The e-mail is a MIME message that can have any combination of text and TIFF image content. Any portions of a multipart MIME message with other file or image formats such as JPG, Word, PDF, HTML are not supported and are discarded by the Cisco offramp gateway.

The format of the TIFF image of the fax document that is attached to the e-mail is often a point of confusion and consequently a common source of failure for T.37 offramp transactions. According to the standard RFC 2301, any implementation of T.37 must at least support the minimal black-and-white fax mode defined by TIFF Profile S (TIFF-S), which is based on the MH image encoding scheme used by default on most fax machines.

The Cisco implementation of T.37 supports the extended black-and-white fax mode defined by TIFF Profile F (TIFF-F). TIFF-F includes TIFF-S and encompasses all the possible G3 fax encoding methods (that is, MH, MR, and MMR). You can find a detailed discussion of the operation of MH, MR, and MMR in the section "Page Encoding" in Chapter 2.

NOTE   Even though Cisco T.37 gateways support TIFF-F, they do not support MMR encodings when communicating with G3 fax devices. The reason for this is because Cisco T.37 gateways do not support Error Correction Mode (ECM), and MMR is used only when the ECM feature is enabled for a fax transaction.

Once the fax mail is received by the offramp gateway and it verifies that the format of the contents is acceptable, it then converts the fax mail to a standard fax format. An internal TIFF reader processes the TIFF attachment and does the image conversion to T.4 page data. This process occurs as the offramp gateway receives the TIFF data so that no local storage of the TIFF image is necessary.

The text/TIFF content that was in the original e-mail is finally sent as standard fax data. The page data is sent via the T.4 protocol, and the fax negotiation and setup is done through the T.30 protocol. A detailed discussion of both T.30 and T.4 operation is found in Chapter 2. The terminating fax machine outputs the contents of the originating fax mail as a standard fax document.

The Cisco implementation of offramp provides a suite of features that allow the fax document that was generated from an e-mail to appear the same as if it was sent from another PSTN fax machine. One such feature is the optional capability to send a cover page with customizable content. Another feature allows the offramp gateway to define the information that populates the left, center, and right headers found at the top of a fax page.

Summary

The T.37 store-and-forward fax standard provides another option for fax communications over an IP network. Unlike other fax transport methods, T.37 allows for a direct integration of fax technology with e-mail. This chapter took an in-depth look at how T.37 performs this fax and e-mail integration.

In the first section, a general overview of T.37 was presented that included T.37's supporting standards. Also included in this first section was a discussion of how the transmission of fax information using a T.37 solution differs markedly from fax passthrough or relay solutions.

The next section discussed the SMTP protocol as it applies to T.37. Common SMTP commands and sessions were highlighted along with detailed examples about the DSN and MDN options. Both DSN and MDN are critical in providing a status about a fax mail within an SMTP network.

Last of all, the onramp and offramp functions of T.37 were discussed in the final two sections. The T.37 onramp function converts a normal G3 fax into an e-mail, whereas T.37 offramp conversely changes an e-mail to a standard fax document. The T.37 onramp and offramp functions can be enabled independently on a Cisco voice gateway or they can both be configured simultaneously.

CHAPTER 7

Design Guide for Fax, Modem, and Text

In the design and planning stage of many VoIP networks, accounting for modulated communications, such as faxes, modems, and text telephony devices is often omitted or forgotten. Unfortunately, because of some of the unique characteristics of transporting modulated communications over IP and certain gateway and protocol interoperability issues, this can lead to problems later during network implementation.

This chapter provides the design and planning information necessary to ensure that a proposed VoIP network solution will also properly handle the transportation of fax, modem, and text communications. Specifically, the following sections are covered:

- **General Passthrough and Relay Design Considerations**: Addresses basic design considerations that are applicable to the variety of transport methods based on passthrough and relay

- **Fax Design Considerations**: Covers design attributes that are only pertinent to transporting fax using Cisco voice gateways

- **Modem Design Considerations**: Discusses the design aspects of integrating modem communications over an IP network

- **Text Design Considerations**: Provides design details on how text telephone transmissions can be effectively transported using text over G.711 and Cisco text relay

The organization of this chapter is such that the first section, "General Passthrough and Relay Design Considerations," should be read first. Although it might be tempting to skip this first section as you head to specific design information contained later in the chapter, this first section contains foundational information on the passthrough and relay transport methods that is applicable to fax, modem, and text telephony. Therefore, understanding the first section of this chapter is critical in getting the most out of the rest of the chapter.

After the first section has been covered, you may skip directly to the fax, modem, or text design section. Each of these sections builds on the general concepts covered in the first section while providing additional information about the transport methods available for fax, modem, and text telephony.

General Passthrough and Relay Design Considerations

A number of design considerations must be looked at when designing VoIP networks that will successfully handle modulated communications such as fax, modem, and text. Not taking into account these design considerations from the beginning can cause problems later upon implementation.

This section focuses on passthrough and relay design considerations in a general sense, meaning that the information in this section applies equally to faxes, modems, and text devices. These considerations are summarized in Table 7-1. More specific design considerations directly applicable to fax, modem, and text communications are covered in subsequent sections of this chapter.

Table 7-1 *General Passthrough and Relay Design Considerations Summary*

Design Consideration	Explanation
Bandwidth	Utilizing much less bandwidth per call is one of the main benefits of relay. Passthrough relies on the G.711 voice codec for transport, and this uncompressed codec comparably consumes much more bandwidth.
Call control protocol	Not all call control protocols support all the various passthrough and relay transport methods. Therefore, it is important to know the limitations of each call control protocol from a fax, modem, and text transport perspective.
Quality of service (QoS)	The QoS requirements for modulated communications can be different from what is needed for a typical VoIP call. For example, fax traffic can handle a higher end-to-end delay than a standard VoIP call, but it typically cannot tolerate the same degree of packet loss.
Redundancy	Relay protocols typically offer built-in redundancy options, whereas the redundancy option with passthrough is less robust and not always supported.
Resource utilization	Certain passthrough and relay calls can be resource intensive to the voice gateway as certain thresholds are approached.
Secure Real-Time Transport Protocol (SRTP)	Fax and modem calls can use the secure RTP feature, but only for transport methods that make use of a full RTP header.
Timing and synchronization	Certain clocking dependencies exist that can affect fax, modem, and text calls. This is especially true when a form of the passthrough transport method is implemented as digital signal processor (DSP) playout buffers may eventually slip on calls of a significantly long duration.

Each design consideration in Table 7-1 is discussed in more detail in the following subsections. In addition, as you read each subsection, you will notice differences between passthrough and relay. Design considerations for one transport method are not always applicable to the other. If you are trying to decide whether passthrough or relay should be used for a particular network design, these subsections provide some valuable information.

Bandwidth

Bandwidth consumption of passthrough and relay calls is one of the most overlooked aspects of VoIP network design, and it can have a major impact on network capacity planning. Often, the VoIP network is designed with only traditional VoIP calls in mind. Modulated traffic such as faxes is often overlooked completely or the improper assumption is made that modulated communications and voice traffic can be accounted for in the same manner.

All passthrough and relay calls start out as voice calls using the user-defined codec. For this reason, it is important to know how much bandwidth a call is consuming before it switches over to passthrough or relay. Although bandwidth concerns might not be as critical in LAN environments, this is not usually the case in WANs.

Table 7-2 highlights the bandwidth consumed by some common voice codecs when being transported via the WAN protocol, Frame Relay. Even though Table 7-2 might not apply to your specific voice network, it is still essential to understand how much bandwidth your voice calls consume. If any of your voice calls transition to passthrough or relay, the bandwidth utilized per call can drastically change, which can impact bandwidth provisioning over a lower-speed link.

Table 7-2   *Bandwidth Consumption for a VoIP Call over Frame Relay*

Codec (bit rate)	Packetization Interval (ms)	Voice Payload (bytes)	Packets per Second	Bandwidth per Call (Kbps)
G.711 (64 Kbps)	20	160	50.0	82.8
G.711 (64 Kbps)	30	240	33.3	76.5
G.729 (8 Kbps)	20	20	50.0	26.8
G.729 (8 Kbps)	30	30	33.3	20.5
G.723 (6.3 Kbps)	30	24	33.3	18.9

The bandwidth calculations for each codec in Table 7-2 assume IP, UDP, and RTP header overhead to be 40 bytes and for the Frame Relay overhead to be 7 bytes (including a flag byte). However, assuming a constant header overhead, you can see how increasing the packetization interval includes more 10 ms DSP samples per packet and this in turn decreases the bandwidth used per call. For example, if G.711 uses the default 20 ms packetization interval, each call uses 82.8 Kbps of bandwidth. However, changing to a 30 ms packetization interval on the voice gateways lowers the bandwidth to 76.5 Kbps. Note that the initial sample value for each codec in Table 7-2 is the default on the Cisco voice gateways.

TIP

Cisco.com has a useful tool known as the Voice Codec Bandwidth Calculator that is available to registered Cisco.com users. This tool allows you to select from a number of different codecs, Layer 2 protocols, and other parameters, and it then calculates the amount of bandwidth consumed for the selected number of VoIP calls. You can find the Voice Codec Bandwidth Calculator at http://tools.cisco.com/Support/VBC/do/CodecCalc1.do.

Because passthrough always forces the use of the high-bandwidth G.711 codec, you can see how this can be a problem if only G.729 voice calls are planned across the WAN. A single fax passthrough call at 82.8 Kbps consumes more bandwidth than three G.729 calls at 26.8 Kbps each. If you plan on transporting fax, modem, or text telephony traffic using a passthrough transport mechanism such as modem passthrough, fax pass-through, or text over G.711, ensure that the proper amount of bandwidth is taken into account.

The calculations in Table 7-2 do not take into consideration the use of bandwidth reduction mechanisms such as Voice Activity Detection (VAD) and the Compressed Real-Time Transport Protocol (CRTP). VAD can dramatically reduce voice bandwidth by not transmitting voice packets when silence is occurring. Unfortunately, VAD causes problems during passthrough (because of signal clipping) and therefore it cannot be used when G.711 is transporting modulated data. In the cases of modem passthrough and fax pass-through, VAD is automatically disabled as part of the switchover.

If CRTP is used, the amount of bandwidth consumed per call can be reduced at the expense of CPU cycles on the voice gateway. For example, CRTP enabled for a standard G.711 call drops the bandwidth over Frame Relay from 82.8 Kbps to 67.6 Kbps. Although CRTP is effective at reducing bandwidth for voice, passthrough, and even Cisco fax relay calls, caution should be exercised if CRTP is to be enabled for large numbers of calls on a single voice gateway.

Although VAD and CRTP typically lower bandwidth requirements, redundancy is an option for some passthrough and relay transport methods and has the opposite effect. Redundancy increases the bandwidth consumed per call but provides the benefit of more reliable communications in networks where packet loss, jitter, and other impairments are present. The effect of redundancy on the amount of bandwidth consumed for passthrough and relay calls is covered in the section "Redundancy" later in this chapter.

Bandwidth calculations for passthrough-based calls are quite simple because passthrough always uses the G.711 codec. On the other hand, bandwidth calculations for relay calls can be a bit more complicated. Certain assumptions and worst-case scenarios have to be made to arrive at a bandwidth consumption value that will prevent oversubscription. However, despite this additional complication of calculating relay bandwidth consumption, a large reduction in the bandwidth consumed per call is gained when using a relay transport method compared to passthrough.

The consumption of less bandwidth is one of the major benefits of relay over passthrough, and it occurs because relay demodulates the incoming data. Therefore, only the necessary information is transported across IP, meaning that a 9600 bps fax call will only occupy 9600 bps plus the additional header overhead. Passthrough, on the other hand, does not make a discrimination of what is the actual modulated data, and it samples everything, consuming much larger amounts of bandwidth.

The reason that bandwidth calculations for relay are a bit more complicated has to do with the asymmetrical nature of most modulated communications to begin with. For example, during a fax call, a page is sent by the originating fax machine to the terminating fax machine. The bandwidth consumed during this page transmission will be at a maximum in one direction but zero in the other direction because a fax communication is half duplex. In addition, all the fax T.30 signaling messages occur at 300 bps, significantly slower than page transmission speeds. Therefore, bandwidth measurements for fax relay calls usually look at the maximum page transmission speed allowed for the call. However, you should realize that this peak bandwidth is not seen for the whole fax call, and when it does occur, it occurs in only one direction. Figure 7-1 highlights the varying and asymmetrical bandwidths for a T.38 fax relay call. Cisco fax relay is similar in nature.

The T.38 low-speed bandwidth of 8 Kbps and high-speed bandwidth of 25 Kbps as shown in Figure 7-1 are commonly used values in capacity planning for T.38 fax over Frame Relay or over Ethernet. In actuality, because the Frame Relay header is a few bytes smaller than Ethernet, using a Frame Relay encapsulation with T.38 saves a few additional kilobits of bandwidth. However, for the sake of making a network design estimate, the 25 Kbps value is widely used for both Ethernet and Frame Relay bandwidth calculations. This value assumes that the T.38 fax call has negotiated at its maximum speed of 14.4 Kbps.

As touched on previously, fax relay calls use less bandwidth if the fax endpoints negotiate a rate lower than 14400 bps. For example, a 7200 bps T.38 fax relay call consumes only about 18 Kbps of bandwidth compared to the 25 Kbps needed for a 14.4 Kbps fax call. However, unless you force all the fax calls to this lower rate using the **fax rate** command, you must budget for the maximum speed of 14.4 Kbps. More information on the **fax rate** command and how you can use it to restrict the page transfer speed and consequently the fax relay bandwidth can be found in Table 10-3 in Chapter 10, "Configuring Relay," as well as the section "Fax Relay Data Rate" in Chapter 12, "Troubleshooting Passthrough and Relay."

Figure 7-1 *Low- and High-Speed Bandwidths for a T.38 Fax Relay Call*

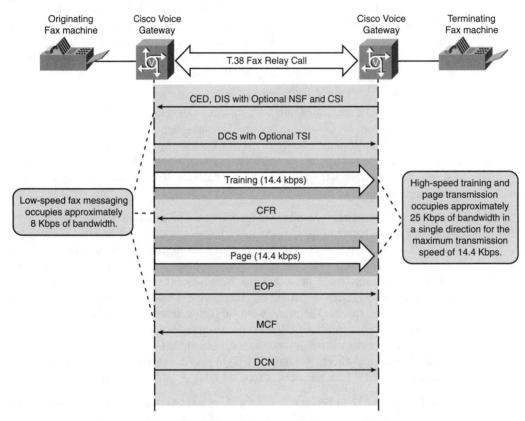

When planning for large numbers of fax relay calls, less bandwidth than the peak numbers discussed here will be seen for the aggregate number of calls. This occurs because all the faxes probably do not negotiate to the maximum 14.4 Kbps speed, and at any give moment not all the calls are consuming the maximum bandwidth with a page transmission. Recall that when pages are not being sent, a T.38 fax relay call needs only approximately 8 Kbps of bandwidth.

Although G3 fax calls are half duplex, modem calls are usually full duplex. However, modems rarely send and receive the maximum amount of data concurrently. For this reason, peak modem relay bandwidth is not used for planning bandwidth utilization by a modem. In fact, it is typically considered heavy modem usage when data is being sent and received more than 25 percent of the time. Therefore, an allotment of about 45 Kbps is generally allocated to each modem relay call. Table 7-3 highlights the peak bandwidth consumed by T.38 and Cisco fax relay and the average bandwidth for modem relay.

Table 7-3   *Fax and Modem Relay Bandwidth Consumption*

Relay Type	Bandwidth per Call (Approximate)
T.38 fax relay (fax speed of 14.4 Kbps over Frame Relay, T.38 redundancy disabled)	25 Kbps
Cisco fax relay (Fax Speed of 14.4 Kbps Over Frame Relay with default 20 byte payload)	48 Kbps
Cisco modem relay (V.34 modulation at a speed of 33.6 Kbps)	45 Kbps

In Table 7-3, the bandwidth for Cisco fax relay appears high because it uses a small 20 byte payload by default. However, the **fax rate** command has a **bytes** option that allows you to increase the payload size. Using the **fax rate** command to change the payload size from 20 to 40 bytes changes the Cisco fax relay bandwidth to a more manageable 32 Kbps per call.

TIP

The bandwidth consumed by Cisco text relay is negligible, so it has not been discussed in this section. Like fax and modem relay, the bandwidth consumed is asymmetric because only one person types at a time. Fast typists may add an additional 3 Kbps of bandwidth to an existing voice call in one direction when full redundancy is enabled. In reality, the bandwidth typically used is much less than that. If only text traffic will be passed over a connection, enabling VAD for the voice call should stop all voice packets. Then, only a couple kilobits of periodic text traffic in each direction will be all the bandwidth that is consumed.

To proactively manage call bandwidths within a VoIP network, various call admission control (CAC) methods can be used. By tracking the number of calls across a link or destined to a particular location or zone, CAC ensures that network paths do not become oversubscribed. Common CAC methods include Resource Reservation Protocol (RSVP), an H.323 gatekeeper, or Cisco Unified Communications Manager (Unified CM) location-based CAC. Consult a comprehensive VoIP resource for additional information about these CAC methods or search for them at Cisco.com.

In addition to CAC specifying bandwidth allocations for voice calls, fax and modem calls will usually have pre-assigned bandwidth allocation or adjustment values. With RSVP, a transition to T.38 fax relay causes an RSVP bandwidth adjustment to 80 Kbps, whereas transitions to modem passthrough, fax pass-through, or modem relay cause a bandwidth adjustment to 96 Kbps. If this bandwidth is unavailable, the call proceeds as best effort without RSVP.

An H.323 gatekeeper uses the same bandwidth adjustment values as RSVP. However, if bandwidth is unavailable, the transition does not occur, and the call proceeds using the original voice codec. Be aware that attempting to transport fax or modem calls using most voice codecs results in a call failure.

Unified CM can use a gatekeeper or locations-based CAC managing calls. However, Unified CM does not make any bandwidth adjustments after a voice call transitions to a fax or modem call. Whatever bandwidth has been allocated for the original voice codec from a CAC perspective will continue to be associated with the fax or modem call, too.

Implementing relay for fax, modem, or text will always save you bandwidth compared to a comparable passthrough call. In many network designs, especially those involving fax or modem traffic over a WAN, bandwidth is the overriding concern. If this is the case, a relay option will always be considered the best practice.

Call Control Protocol

The call control protocols used when transporting fax, modem, and text with Cisco voice gateways in IP networks are H.323, Session Initiation Protocol (SIP), Media Gateway Control Protocol (MGCP), and Skinny Client Control Protocol (SCCP). However, not all of these call control or voice signaling protocols support all the various passthrough and relay transport methods. Table 7-4 provides a quick overview of the transport methods supported by the H.323, SIP, MGCP, and SCCP voice signaling protocols for Cisco IOS voice gateways.

Table 7-4   *IOS Gateway Passthrough and Relay Support for H.323, SIP, MGCP, and SCCP Call Control Protocols*

Transport Method	H.323	SIP	MGCP	SCCP
Cisco Fax Relay	Yes[*]	Yes[*]	Yes[*]	Yes[*]
NSE-based T.38 Fax Relay	Yes	Yes	Yes	Yes
Protocol-based T.38 Fax Relay	Yes	Yes	Yes[**]	No
Fax pass-through	Yes	Yes	No	No
Modem passthrough	Yes	Yes	Yes	Yes
Cisco modem relay	Yes	Yes	Yes	Yes
Secure modem relay	No	No	Yes	Yes
Cisco text relay	Yes	Yes	Yes	Yes
Text over G.711	Yes	Yes	Yes	Yes

[*]   IOS platforms such as the 5350, 5400, and 5850 using the NextPort DSP cards do not support Cisco fax relay or the SCCP voice signaling protocol.

[**]   A call agent, such as Unified CM, must also support protocol-based T.38 fax relay.

The information in Table 7-4 shows that H.323 and SIP are the two call control protocols that provide you with the most options for transporting fax, modem, and text calls. The only exception to this is in the case of secure modem relay, which is supported only by MGCP and SCCP. However, secure modem relay is a niche application that is not widely implemented. You can find more information on secure modem relay in the section "Secure Modem Relay" later in this chapter.

The drawbacks of MGCP are the lack of support for fax pass-through and the requirement for a compatible call agent (CA) with protocol-based T.38 fax relay. Currently, only certain versions of Unified CM possess full interoperability with an IOS voice gateway configured for protocol-based T.38 and MGCP. See the section "Unified CM Integration" later in this chapter for more information about Unified CM support of T.38 fax relay.

The SCCP call control protocol lacks support for any transport method that uses a protocol-based switchover. Therefore, SCCP does not support fax pass-through or protocol-based T.38 fax relay. The transport methods in Table 7-4 that use alternative switchover methods, such as Named Signaling Events (NSE), are compatible with SCCP.

Of course, many other factors exist when choosing a call control protocol for a VoIP network, and fax, modem, and text support is typically not the major, deciding factor. However, if fax, modem, and text support is taken into consideration when selecting a voice signaling protocol, H.323 and SIP provide more options and flexibility as compared to MGCP or SCCP.

QoS

QoS is the measure of transmission quality and service availability for a network. A sufficient level of QoS must be ensured for the real-time traffic of fax, modem, and text; otherwise, these communications will not be reliable.

The transmission quality aspect of QoS is determined by the impairment factors of packet loss, delay, and jitter. Table 7-5 defines these factors while also commenting on how they impact fax, modem, and text traffic compared to VoIP.

As discussed in Table 7-5, a critical difference between fax, modem, and text traffic compared with VoIP traffic is its tolerance for packet loss. Packet loss causes sections of data to be lost in the fax, modem, or text communication. The bits that make up this lost data cannot be reconstructed by the voice gateway using VoIP mechanisms such as interpolation, prediction, or filling with silence.

This is the reason that extensive redundancy mechanisms are available for passthrough and relay. If fax, modem, and text traffic must reside on network paths with packet loss, it is imperative that a transport method using some form of redundancy or error correction be implemented. Data redundancy and error correction options for fax, modem, and text communications are discussed in more detail in the next section.

Table 7-5   *Fax, Modem, and Text Traffic Impairment Factors*

Factor	Definition	Comment
Packet Loss	A relative measure of the number of packets that were not received compared to the total number of packets transmitted	Although packet loss during a VoIP call is not recommended, it can be handled most of the time if it is less than 1 percent. Mechanisms exist within the voice gateways and the voice codecs themselves that can predict and interpolate a lost voice sample or the missing voice sample can be filled with silence. In addition, the human ear will generally not be able to detect a few missing voice samples during a conversation. However, for fax, modem, and text communications using either passthrough or relay for transport, packet loss can be devastating. Packet loss should not occur at all for fax, modem, and text calls; but if it is present, a transport method using redundancy should be implemented, as discussed in the next section.
Delay	The finite amount of time it takes a packet to reach the receiving endpoint after being transmitted from the sending endpoint	The recommendation for VoIP is to keep the one-way latency (mouth-to-ear) to less than 150 ms. For modem calls, this value is also especially applicable because high-speed modems are more sensitive to delay than fax or text devices. Delay should be minimized as much as possible for modem communications. In the case of fax and text calls using passthrough and relay, delay is not typically as much of an issue as it can be for voice and modems. Fax calls have been known to handle delays of 1 second or more, and the delay limit for text calls is usually defined by the user's patience in waiting for typed responses to appear. Generally, you will always be safe in the handling of delay for fax, modem, and text calls if you stick with the recommended VoIP value of no more than 150 ms.
Jitter	The delay variation between packets or the difference in the end-to-end delay between packets	Average one-way jitter of less than 30 ms is the recommendation to ensure VoIP QoS. This target value applies equally to fax, modem, and text communications, too, especially for passthrough, where the playout buffer is often fixed to a low value and will not dynamically adjust. With fax relay and its fixed 300 ms default playout buffers, keeping the jitter under 30 ms is not quite as critical.

In many networks, loss, delay, and jitter have already been addressed by a QoS solution for VoIP traffic. Fax, modem, and text communications are real-time traffic just like VoIP and are similarly affected by the factors of loss, delay, and jitter to varying degrees. Therefore, when designing QoS services specifically for fax, modem, and text telephony, it is natural to use the existing VoIP QoS mechanisms that are already in place.

Numerous VoIP QoS mechanisms and tools are currently available for ensuring the integrity of VoIP calls on Cisco voice gateways. For example, you can use Differentiated Services Code Point (DSCP) for the classification and marking of VoIP traffic, along with Low Latency Queuing (LLQ) for the scheduling and queuing of this traffic as it exits the voice gateway. Many other QoS tools are also available, which make the subject of QoS an involved topic that can easily consume another book within itself. Refer to a comprehensive resource on QoS, such as the *Enterprise QoS Solution Reference Network Design Guide*, which is linked off of the following Cisco web page to supplement the QoS information covered in this section:

http://www.cisco.com/go/srnd/

As mentioned previously, often fax, modem, and text implementations occur after a VoIP infrastructure and its appropriate QoS policies are already in place and functional. For these cases, just "piggybacking" on the existing VoIP QoS policy is the easiest and most efficient approach.

For example, this piggybacking concept can be easily applied to the classification and marking aspect of QoS for fax, modem, and text traffic. Whatever classification and marking method is currently applied to IP voice traffic in a network should be good enough for fax, modem, and text traffic, too. Having the same classification as a network's VoIP traffic ensures that the fax, modem, and text traffic will be processed in a prioritized manner by other QoS mechanisms such as LLQ.

Just like with VoIP, fax, modem, and text traffic have a call signaling component and a media component. Each of these must be classified appropriately as part of the QoS policy. As shown in Table 7-6, Cisco makes the following recommendations about marking VoIP call signaling and media packets. Assuming that a network adheres to these recommendations in Table 7-6 for its VoIP traffic, fax, modem, and text traffic should use this same classification scheme, too.

Table 7-6   *Cisco QoS Classification and Marking Recommendations for VoIP*

| Application | Layer 3 Classification | | Layer 2 Classification |
	IP Precedence (IPP)	Differentiated Services Code Point (DSCP)	Class of Service (CoS)
Call signaling	3	CS3/AF31	3
Voice media	5	EF	5

In Table 7-6, you see that Cisco recommends setting both the IPP and CoS bits to 3 and 5 for the call signaling and voice media, respectively. These settings provide a higher priority to the voice media than the signaling. This same classification scheme is carried on with DSCP, too, where voice media is given a higher priority of EF compared to the call signaling traffic with a value of AF31 or CS3.

The reason for two DSCP values being associated with call signaling has to do with the migration of call signaling from AF31 to CS3 on Cisco voice products. The AF31 setting will eventually be used only for locally defined mission-critical data applications, but in the interim both AF31 and CS3 are valid settings for call signaling traffic.

When viewing Table 7-6, you should understand that "voice media" is applicable to fax, modem, and text traffic and VoIP. You do not need to create a new classification for fax, modem, and text traffic. By marking your fax, modem, and text traffic the same as VoIP, you simplify your overall QoS policy while still providing the proper QoS for these traffic types.

In most cases, this piggybacking solution does not even require additional configuration on your voice gateways. For example, the marking of packets already occurs directly on a voice dial peer. Example 7-1 highlights the default classification for VoIP call signaling and media packets from the IOS command **show dial-peer voice**.

Example 7-1   *DSCP Values from **show dial-peer voice** IOS Command*

```
! Output omitted for brevity
        type = voip, session-target = `ipv4:192.168.10.10',
        technology prefix:
        settle-call = disabled
        ip media DSCP = ef, ip signaling DSCP = af31,
        ip video rsvp-none DSCP = af41,ip video rsvp-pass DSCP = af41
        ip video rsvp-fail DSCP = af41,
        UDP checksum = disabled,
! Output omitted for brevity
```

In Example 7-1, you see the highlighted settings of **ip media DSCP = ef** and **ip signaling DSCP = af31**. These DSCP values for the signaling and media traffic matching this dial peer are already correctly set by default. All the packets for VoIP calls matching this dial peer will have the DSCP values set accordingly. In addition, any packets from fax, modem, or text calls matching this dial peer will also be classified the same.

If you desire to change the classification of all traffic matching a particular dial peer, you can do so by using the **ip qos dscp** command. Example 7-2 highlights how this command changes the classification of call signaling packets from the default of AF31 to CS3.

Example 7-2 *QoS Dial Peer Configuration*

```
!
dial-peer voice 13 voip
 destination-pattern 13..
 session target ipv4:192.168.10.10
 codec g711ulaw
 fax rate 14400
 fax protocol t38 ls-redundancy 0 hs-redundancy 0 fallback cisco
 ip qos dscp cs3 signaling
 no vad
!
```

The dial peer in Example 7-2 uses the IOS command **ip qos dscp cs3 signaling** to set
the DSCP classification for all call signaling packets that match this dial peer to CS3. Also
notice that this VoIP dial peer is configured to handle voice calls using the G.711 codec, and
the command **fax protocol t38** instructs this same dial peer to use T.38 fax relay if V.21 fax
flags are detected at any point during the G.711 voice call. Example 7-2 typifies how a T.38
fax relay call can use the QoS classification already in place for a VoIP call.

In some instances, a separate QoS classification is desired for fax, modem, or text traffic.
Example 7-2 would not work in this situation, because both the voice and T.38 fax relay
traffic use the same dial peer and therefore inherit the same markings. Allowing separate
markings adds the complication of managing more QoS classifications, but it can allow
greater control and management of fax, modem, and text traffic.

The easiest solution for classifying fax, modem, and text traffic separately from your VoIP
traffic is to segment the traffic using specific dial peers. This works especially well if you
can isolate the fax, modem, and text traffic to unique dial peers by specific calling or called
numbers. When the fax, modem, and text traffic match their own unique dial peers, the
commands **ip qos dscp** [*value*] **signaling** and **ip qos dscp** [*value*] **media** can be configured
to classify the packets appropriately.

After the fax, modem, and text traffic has been effectively classified, other QoS tools such
as LLQ can act upon these classifications. LLQ can be easily configured to prioritize traffic
out an interface based on the DSCP value of the packet. Example 7-3 highlights a basic
LLQ configuration for prioritizing packets with a DSCP setting of EF.

Example 7-3 *Basic LLQ Configuration for Fax, Modem, and Text Traffic*

```
! Output omitted for brevity
!
class-map match-all fax_modem_text_traffic
 match ip dscp ef
class-map match-any call_signaling
 match ip dscp cs3
 match ip dscp af31
```

continues

Example 7-3 *Basic LLQ Configuration for Fax, Modem, and Text Traffic (Continued)*

```
!
policy-map WAN
 class fax_modem_text_traffic
  priority percent 33
 class call_signaling
  bandwidth percent 5
 class class-default
  fair-queue
!
! Output omitted for brevity
!
interface Multilink1
 description T1 to Branch Office
 ip address 1.1.1.1 255.255.255.252
 service-policy output WAN
 ppp multilink
 ppp multilink group 1
!
! Output omitted for brevity
```

In Example 7-3, two specific class maps are created to address the media and call signaling information for fax, modem, and text calls. The class map for the media is **fax_modem_text_traffic**, and the class map for the call control traffic is **call_signaling**.

The command **match ip dscp ef** defines the DSCP value that packets must have to be associated with the **fax_modem_text_traffic** map class. For packets to be associated with the **call_signaling** map class, a DSCP value of either **cs3** or **af31** must be present.

TIP	Be careful when implementing an LLQ configuration that does not take advantage of DSCP. For example, it is common for LLQ to be configured to simply prioritize all RTP traffic. This works fine for voice, passthrough, and Cisco fax relay traffic, but it does not work for T.38 fax relay or modem relay, which do not contain an RTP header. Marking traffic with appropriate DSCP values and then prioritizing the real-time DSCP traffic through a queuing strategy such as LLQ is the recommended method for handling QoS for faxes and modems.

The **policy-map WAN** is how LLQ prioritizes and allocates bandwidth for the specific traffic classes defined by the class map configuration. In the case of Example 7-3, the **fax_modem_text_traffic** class under **policy-map WAN** is configured for a priority percentage of 33 by the command **priority percent 33**. This means that up to 33 percent of the total bandwidth for the interface where this LLQ configuration is applied will always be available for traffic matching the **fax_modem_text_traffic** class map. In addition, this traffic is queued in a priority fashion, where traffic that is not part of the **fax_modem_text_ traffic** class may be held back to allow this prioritized traffic to be transmitted first.

For the **call_signaling** class under the **policy-map WAN** in Example 7-3, the command **bandwidth percent 5** is present. This command reserves 5 percent of the bandwidth for traffic that matches the **call_signaling** class in the event of interface congestion. With 5 percent of the bandwidth guaranteed for signaling traffic, the proper setup and teardown of fax, modem, and text calls is ensured, even during periods of contention for interface bandwidth.

Assigning an LLQ configuration to an interface is the last step when implementing LLQ. In Example 7-3, the command **service-policy output WAN** applies the LLQ configuration identified by the command **policy-map WAN** to the gateway's interface, **interface Multilink1**.

Although the DSCP classification and marking system along with LLQ queuing are two of the most common QoS tools, you should realize that many additional QoS tools are available, too. Ultimately, it does not matter exactly what QoS mechanisms you use as long as the factors of packet loss, delay, and jitter are controlled as discussed in Table 7-5. In many networks, these factors have already been addressed from a VoIP perspective, and in these cases it is perfectly acceptable to piggyback or use these same VoIP QoS settings for fax, modem, and text traffic, too.

Redundancy

In the context of passthrough and relay, redundancy is the concept of sending multiple copies of the same data segment. The reasoning behind the redundancy concept is that if a packet is lost or significantly delayed another packet carrying the same information will still arrive at the destination in a timely manner. This ensures that the integrity of the data connection remains intact even though packet loss or significant delay is occurring.

Passthrough calls are notorious for being very sensitive to packet loss, especially when carrying high-speed modem modulations such as V.34 and V.90. Lab testing shows that as little as 0.02 percent packet loss can cause passthrough calls to fail. If redundancy for passthrough is activated, calls can be sustained with up to 1 percent of random packet loss.

Relay transport methods may use improved redundancy or error correction mechanisms that allow them to handle substantially more packet loss than passthrough. In the case of T.38 fax relay and Cisco modem relay, calls can succeed with up to 10 percent random packet loss.

Multiple redundancy methods exist for passthrough and relay depending on the exact transport method selected. Table 7-7 summarizes these redundancy methods by the transport method used.

Table 7-7 *Passthrough and Relay Redundancy Methods*

Transport Method	Redundancy/Error Correction Support	Comments
Passthrough	One level of redundancy that allows a single repetition of packets based on RFC 2198.	This redundancy method is supported for both faxes and modems using NSE-based passthrough and configured with the **modem passthrough** configuration command. Redundancy is not supported for protocol-based fax pass-through configurations.
T.38 fax relay	Five levels of redundancy are supported for low-speed messages, and two levels are supported for high-speed messaging.	Multiple layers of redundancy are built in to the T.38 fax relay protocol, making T.38 fax relay the best choice for sending faxes over IP networks that contain high jitter and packet loss.
Cisco fax relay	None.	Cisco fax relay should be used only in VoIP networks free of packet loss.
Cisco modem relay	Error correction.	Instead of redundancy, Cisco modem relay uses an error correction mechanism that efficiently handles packet loss in most situations.
Cisco text relay	3 levels of redundancy.	Redundancy cannot be disabled. At least 1 level of redundancy is always enabled, and the default setting is 2 levels.
Text over G.711	None.	Unable to turn on redundancy for a G.711 voice call.

If you are planning on implementing fax, modem, or text communications over an IP network with impairments and other problems, you should choose a passthrough or relay transport method in Table 7-7 where redundancy is an option. For example, T.38 with its various levels of redundancy should be chosen over Cisco fax relay.

TIP   The Cisco implementation of T.38 fax relay transmits the low-speed T.30 messages a single byte at a time, as discussed previously in the section "T.38 Fax Relay" in Chapter 5, "Relay." Therefore, because of the greater number of packets that must be sent with just a single byte of data compared with bundling multiple bytes per T.38 packet, a greater opportunity exists for packet loss to affect the transmission of low-speed T.30 data. Always configuring at least one level of T.38 fax relay low-speed redundancy on Cisco voice gateways is highly recommended.

When implementing a passthrough redundancy solution, first make sure that the Cisco products being used all have redundancy support. Products such as the VG248 and ATA do not support modem passthrough redundancy and should not be used with other Cisco products that have this option enabled.

A major consideration to take into account when any sort of redundancy is enabled for a passthrough or call relay is bandwidth consumption. If you recall, the bandwidth consumption values displayed previously in Tables 7-2 and 7-3 did not take into account redundancy being enabled.

When redundancy is enabled, the bandwidth can increase significantly. In the case of passthrough, it will more than double because of the extra overhead necessary to identify the redundant data from the primary data within the packet payload. Table 7-8 shows the effects of redundancy on bandwidth for some passthrough and relay transport methods.

Table 7-8   *Bandwidth Consumptions over Frame Relay for Various Redundancy Levels*

Passthrough/Relay Transport Method	Bandwidth per Call (Approximate)
Passthrough G.711 with no redundancy	83 Kbps
Passthrough G.711 with 2198 single-layer redundancy	170 Kbps
T.38 Fax Relay with high-speed redundancy set to 0	25 Kbps
T.38 Fax Relay with high-speed redundancy set to 1	41 Kbps
T.38 Fax Relay with high-speed redundancy set to 2	57 Kbps

In Table 7-8, you can see that the bandwidth for passthrough more than doubles when redundancy is enabled to a value of 170 Kbps per call. As mentioned previously, this extra bandwidth for redundancy does raise passthrough tolerance to random packet loss to around 1 percent. However, compared to T.38 fax relay or modem relay with its much lower bandwidth consumption and higher tolerance for packet loss, modem passthrough with redundancy appears very inefficient.

The redundancy bandwidth values for Cisco text relay are not included in Table 7-8. The main reason for this is that the bandwidth consumed for Cisco text relay is negligible no matter what the redundancy level is set for. The main determination of bandwidth consumption with Cisco text relay is how fast the person types. Even with redundancy set to its highest value of 3, Cisco text relay should never reach a peak bandwidth greater than 3 Kbps.

The main design consideration for dealing with redundancy is that a tradeoff exists between it and the amount of bandwidth consumed. If an IP network is free of packet loss and high jitter, it is not necessary to enable redundancy when transporting fax, modem, or text communications. However, if packet loss does exist and you want to guarantee a successful call, you must decide how much extra bandwidth needs to be made available for handling redundant data.

Resource Utilization

Fax, modem, and text calls and their different transport methods may impact the resources of a voice gateway differently. In some cases, this can lead to a need for more DSP resources, and in other cases this can lead to a need for more bandwidth on an interface. Understanding how fax, modem, and text calls can impact the resources on a Cisco voice gateway is an important design concept. Properly planning the resource use of a voice gateway in the beginning can prevent problems later when traffic loads are heavy and resource availability is limited.

Specific design considerations can address the impact that fax, modem, and text calls have on voice gateway resources. Table 7-9 highlights the primary resource utilization design considerations for certain fax, modem, and text transport methods.

Table 7-9   *Fax and Modem Resource Utilization Considerations*

Transport Method	Resource Affected	Comment
Fax Relay and T.37 store-and-forward fax	DSP	Fax relay and T.37 calls are considered "medium complexity" from a DSP resource perspective, and situations can arise with C5510 DSPs in flex mode where the DSP can become oversubscribed.
Modem relay	DSP	Modem relay calls are considered "high complexity" from a DSP resource perspective, and situations can arise with C5510 DSPs in flex mode where the DSP can become oversubscribed.
Fax relay and T.37 store-and-forward fax	CPU utilization and memory	The processing of fax relay and T.37 calls consume more gateway resources than a voice or passthrough call.

As mentioned in Table 7-9, fax relay, T.37, and modem relay can affect the C5510 DSP when it is in flex mode or flex complexity. The C5510 DSP, the predominant DSP found on Cisco voice gateways today, allows for the oversubscription of DSP resources in flex mode, and this can cause issues without the proper preparation. Table 7-10 shows the primary codecs supported by the C5510, their associated complexity of flex, medium, and high, and the maximum number of calls supported on a DSP for particular complexity mode settings.

As Table 7-10 illustrates, codecs are broken into the codec complexity categories of low, medium, and high. These codec complexity categories group codecs by their DSP resource intensiveness. For example, the low-complexity codecs of G.711, passthrough, and clear channel codec require the least amount of DSP resources.

Table 7-10 *C5510 DSP Utilization for Various Codecs*

Codec	Codec Complexity	Maximum Calls Supported on DSP		
		High-Complexity Mode	Medium-Complexity Mode	Flex-Complexity Mode
G.711, passthrough, and clear-channel codec	Low complexity	6	8	16
Fax relay, T.37, G.726, G.729A, and G.729AB	Medium complexity	6	8	8
Modem relay, G.729, G.729B, G.728, G.723, and iLBC	High complexity	6	Not supported	6

The C5510 DSP can also be configured for a complexity mode, which is somewhat different from the codec complexity. The complexity mode defines how the DSP resources are partitioned into channels for handling calls. Each DSP channel can handle a single voice call. For example, if the DSP is configured for a complexity mode of medium, it can only handle calls of medium or low complexity. Table 7-10 illustrates how a C5510 DSP configured for medium-complexity mode can handle up to eight calls of either medium or low codec complexity.

In high-complexity mode, the DSP can handle calls with any codec complexity at the expense of only being able to handle six total calls compared with the eight calls that the DSP can deal with in medium-complexity mode. Configuring medium or high complexity on a C5510 DSP boils down to whether a high-complexity codec is mandatory. For example, if modem relay is to be supported, high-complexity mode must be used; if only medium-complexity or low-complexity codecs are used, however, medium-complexity mode yields more channels per DSP.

NOTE Before the C5510 DSP became the primary DSP used by Cisco voice gateways, the C549 DSP and the NextPort DSP were also widely implemented. The C549 DSP lacks the channel density and flex-complexity mode that is found on the C5510. Subsequently, the C549 has only a medium-complexity mode where four total calls are supported and a high-complexity mode where only two total calls are supported.

The NextPort DSPs were found exclusively on the 5350, 5400, and 5850 voice gateways. Unlike the C549 and C5510, there are not different complexity modes for the NextPort DSP. Instead, six channels are always available without any codec restrictions. With the introduction of the Cisco High Density Packet Voice/Fax Feature Card (part number AS5X-FC) using the 5510 DSP for the recent 5350XM and 5450XM models, most of the NextPort DSP products are no longer available.

An alternative to hard-coding a medium- or high-complexity mode on a C5510 DSP is to use the flex-complexity mode. Flex-complexity mode offers the ability to dynamically handle all the different codec complexities on the same DSP at the same time while only allocating just the resources necessary.

In most situations, flex-complexity mode is the best choice on the C5510 DSP because it offers dynamic complexity selection and increased call densities per DSP. However, it is possible to oversubscribe the C5510 in flex mode, and this results in a blocking design compared to the nonblocking nature of the medium-and high-complexity modes and their fixed DSP channel allocation.

For example, take the scenario of just a single C5510 DSP configured for flex complexity on a gateway. According to Table 7-10, the voice gateway can handle 16 simultaneous G.711 or low-complexity codec calls with this single DSP. However, if two fax relay calls are initiated, only 12 total calls can now be handled by the DSP rather than the original 16. The reason for this is because a medium-complexity codec, such as fax relay, is twice as resource intensive for the DSP in flex mode as a low-complexity codec. If a gateway is engineered to handle a certain call load based on low-complexity codecs on C5510 in flex mode, fax relay calls on this DSP, quickly lowering the supported call load. Calls in excess of what the DSP can support will fail. This is an example of the oversubscription issue for C5510 DSPs in flex mode.

This problem is even more serious with modem relay because it is a high-complexity codec and requires even more DSP resources than a medium complexity codec. Although the calculation of C5510 DSP resources in flex mode can be manually calculated, it is much easier to use the codec calculator tool at Cicso.com. Here you can enter the maximum number of fax and modem relay calls that a gateway will handle; a recommendation reflecting the number of DSPs necessary will be generated. Note that this tool is available only to registered users:

http://www.cisco.com/pcgi-bin/Support/DSP/cisco_prodsel.pl

TIP	Unlike fax and modem relay, text relay is not a factor when it comes to DSP resource allocation. Because text relay is not resource intensive and it works within any codec's media stream, text relay's impact on DSP resources is negligible. For example, if text relay is configured for a G.729A call, this call is still treated as a call using a medium-complexity voice codec, and no additional DSP resource allocation is necessary for text relay. DSP resource allocation for this G.729A call is the same no matter if text relay is present or not.

As shown in Table 7-9, in addition to affecting DSP resources, fax relay and T.37 store-and-forward fax also have a major impact on a voice gateway's CPU utilization and memory. Compared to a regular voice call, fax relay and T.37 use more of the voice gateway's CPU and in the case of T.37, memory resources, too. In fact, the impact on CPU utilization in some cases is often twice that of a normal VoIP call.

The fax relay and T.37 impact on different hardware platforms varies because a number of factors come into play, including the number of pages in the faxes, call per second rate, if any image conversion occurs on the gateway, and so on. The current Cisco voice gateways can handle at least half the total call capacity for the platform as fax relay and T.37 calls. Also, you should be aware that fax relay and T.37 onramp calls have a greater impact on the CPU than T.37 offramp.

In addition to affecting the CPU utilization, T.37 calls to a lesser extent also impact the system memory of the gateway. Compared to normal voice calls, only about an extra 10 MB is needed on the voice gateway per 100 T.37 calls. Unless memory is already running low, this additional memory requirement should not be much of an issue, especially on the newer platforms with larger memory capacities.

Whenever fax relay or T.37 store-and-forward fax is configured on a voice gateway, monitor the CPU utilization and memory statistics of the voice gateway as you approach the point when these calls make up about half the total call capacity. High CPU levels and low amounts of free memory can negatively impact many important functions and processes, so be cautious about adding large numbers of fax relay and T.37 calls to a voice gateway.

Secure RTP

Defined in IETF RFC 3711, Secure Real-Time Transport Protocol (SRTP) provides for encryption of the RTP protocol used by VoIP. Without SRTP, VoIP conversations can be easily captured and listened to with a simple packet-capture device or software program. SRTP encrypts the VoIP conversations so that they are protected from unauthorized eavesdropping.

One of the main benefits of the SRTP encryption scheme is that only the RTP payload is encrypted. Therefore, secure tunnels for the media do not have to be created, and the voice traffic can be routed normally. In addition, QoS settings in the IP header are not affected, and CRTP can still be used for bandwidth reduction over WANs.

With the increasing usage of SRTP for VoIP, the logical next step is securing modulated data communications that use passthrough and relay over the IP network, too. Much of the emphasis in securing modulated communications over IP has to do with fax traffic. With the appropriate software, extracting fax pages from a packet capture is just as easy as listening to a VoIP conversation.

Unfortunately, some of the transport methods for passthrough and relay do not use an RTP header, which is an obvious requirement for SRTP. Table 7-11 highlights the various passthrough and relay transport methods and their compatibility with SRTP.

Table 7-11 *Passthrough and Relay SRTP Support*

Passthrough/Relay Transport Method	SRTP Support
Passthrough (including NSE-based modem passthrough and protocol-based fax pass-through)	Supported. (The G.711 codec is used for all forms of passthrough, and it includes an RTP header.)
T.38 fax relay	Not supported. (The T.38 fax relay protocol in Cisco voice gateways uses a UDPTL header. More recent versions of the T.38 specification provide for an RTP header rather than UDP transport layer [UDPTL], but this has yet to be implemented on Cisco voice gateways.)
Cisco fax relay	Supported.
Cisco modem relay	Not supported. (Instead of an RTP header, a Simple Packet Relay Transport [SPRT] header is used.)
Cisco text relay	Supported.

All the supported transport methods in Table 7-11 include an RTP header. Therefore, if securing a fax call with SRTP is your objective, T.38 fax relay is not an option on a Cisco voice gateway. You must use either passthrough or Cisco fax relay. Of course, SRTP is not the only option for securing passthrough and relay traffic. Other options involving secure virtual private network (VPN) tunnels are available if SRTP does not meet your needs.

If you decide to implement SRTP for a passthrough or relay call, take into consideration that a small amount of additional bandwidth is needed for the extra 4 bytes of the SRTP authentication tag. For passthrough calls, this extra bandwidth is negligible, typically an additional 2 percent of overhead. For Cisco fax relay, budget an additional 6 percent of bandwidth per call when SRTP is used.

Timing and Synchronization

Timing and synchronization on the voice gateway are more critical for fax, modem, and text communications than for voice. Even seemingly minor timing problems can cause fax, modem, and text calls to fail.

The clocking on a voice gateway's digital interfaces and the lack of clock synchronization between DSPs on the originating and terminating gateways are two areas that can present timing and synchronization problems. Of the two, achieving error-free clocking on the voice gateway's digital interfaces is the more critical issue and it is also more prevalent.

Cisco voice gateways have a number of clocking configurations for digital interfaces such as T1 and E1. These clocking configurations allow the Cisco voice gateway to send or receive timing on the digital circuit. In the case of the Integrated Service Routers (ISR) and other select platforms, you can even pass the timing from a digital interface to the gateway's backplane for other modules and components to use. No matter how the timing is configured on a voice gateway, it is critical that the digital link is free of any errors, especially slips.

Slips and other errors on a gateway's digital interface are devastating to modulated communications such as fax, modem, and text. However, the effects of these same types of errors on voice traffic may be undetectable. Therefore, it is imperative that any digital interface that will handle modulated communications traffic be checked to ascertain whether any sort of errors are present. You can find more extensive clocking information for Cisco voice gateways and how to verify and troubleshoot timing errors in the section "Telephony Troubleshooting" in Chapter 12.

The second area where timing and synchronization problems can occur involves the DSPs on peer gateways. When using the passthrough transport method for long fax and modem calls, there can be issues because of the lack of clock synchronization between the DSPs on the originating and terminating voice gateways. Each of these gateways is typically timed from a local time-division multiplexed (TDM) source, a service provider, or the gateway's internal oscillator. For this reason, a clocking discrepancy, ever so slight in some cases, will always exist between the rates that each DSP processes voice packets. The only time that this discrepancy will not occur is if the DSPs in each gateway are pulling their timing from the same clock source. Figure 7-2 shows how the slight clocking discrepancy that exists between gateway DSPs can cause playout buffer problems.

In Figure 7-2, the DSP in the voice gateway on the left is being clocked at a marginally faster rate than the DSP in the voice gateway on the right. This in turn leads to playout buffer overruns for the gateway on the right as G.711 samples fill the playout buffer faster than it can be drained. The opposite occurs for the gateway on the left as it plays out the G.711 samples faster than the playout buffer fill rate and buffer underruns occur.

Figure 7-2 *Possible DSP Playout Buffer Problem for Long Passthrough Calls*

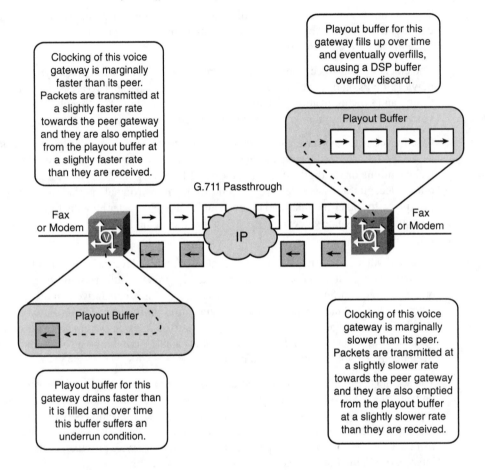

Playout buffer for this gateway fills up over time and eventually overfills, causing a DSP buffer overflow discard.

Clocking of this voice gateway is marginally faster than its peer. Packets are transmitted at a slightly faster rate towards the peer gateway and they are also emptied from the playout buffer at a slightly faster rate than they are received.

Playout Buffer

G.711 Passthrough

Fax or Modem

IP

Fax or Modem

Playout Buffer

Clocking of this voice gateway is marginally slower than its peer. Packets are transmitted at a slightly slower rate towards the peer gateway and they are also emptied from the playout buffer at a slightly slower rate than they are received.

Playout buffer for this gateway drains faster than it is filled and over time this buffer suffers an underrun condition.

TIP   This problem is rarely seen on IOS gateways that use the Telogy DSP firmware. A patented resync feature in the DSP firmware handles this asynchronous clocking problem in most cases, except for large timing discrepancies. Telogy DSP firmware is found on all platforms and models that use the C549 and C5510 DSP chips. Cisco products such as the AS5350, 5400, and 5850 using the NextPort DSP firmware, the 6608, the VG248, and the ATA do not use Telogy DSP firmware and are therefore more susceptible to this problem.

The amount of time it takes for this DSP asynchronous problem to appear can vary greatly because it is fully dependent on how far off the timing is between the DSPs. In most cases, you will not see this problem manifest itself unless large faxes consuming dozens of pages are sent or modem calls are left connected for hours.

Only the passthrough transport method suffers from this problem because of the way G.711 packets are constantly streamed between the two voice gateways. The relay transport method passes data only when necessary, and playout buffers are given multiple opportunities to reset during a typical call. In addition, in the case of fax relay, the playout buffer is statically set to 300 ms, a much larger value than what is typically seen for a passthrough call. Therefore, for long fax and modem calls over an IP network, passthrough is not recommended. Instead, fax relay or modem relay should be used as the transport method.

Fax Design Considerations

So far, this chapter has dealt with design criteria that is broadly applicable to both passthrough and relay for fax, modem, and text communications. However, in this section, the focus narrows to fax-specific design information. All the material in this section pertains only to design considerations for transporting fax data over passthrough and relay.

Gateway Interoperability Considerations

Because of the various methods for transporting fax calls over IP, the interoperability of different voice gateways must be considered when creating a network design. Table 7-12 provides a quick summary of the different fax transport methods that are available for fax. The technical details of these methods have already been discussed in Chapters 4 and 5.

From a design perspective, these different transport methods for fax highlighted in Table 7-12 require due diligence in verifying that a voice gateway supports a chosen transport method. Even between Cisco voice gateways, some well-known caveats concerning fax passthrough and relay support exist:

- The Cisco ATA does not support fax relay and only supports NSE-based passthrough.

- Platforms using the NextPort DSP hardware, including the AS5350, AS5400, and AS5850, support only T.38 fax relay. Cisco fax relay is not supported.

- Voice gateways (including the VG248) that use the SCCP or "skinny" voice signaling protocol do not support protocol-based T.38 or pass-through. NSEs must be used for a passthrough or T.38 fax relay switchover.

- The 6608 and 6624 voice gateways support only Cisco fax relay and NSE-based passthrough.

- Protocol-based pass-through is not currently supported by Cisco voice gateways for MGCP. Just like the SCCP voice signaling protocol, the MGCP protocol on Cisco voice gateways supports passthrough only if an NSE-based switchover is used.

Table 7-12 *Passthrough and Relay Transport Methods for Fax*

Transport Method	Protocol/Switchover	Explanation
Passthrough	G.711 (NSE-based modem passthrough)	This G.711 passthrough method implements a switchover that is handled by Cisco proprietary NSEs. This transport method is often referred to as modem passthrough because this is the IOS command used to configure it.
	G.711 (protocol-based fax pass-through)	This G.711 passthrough method handles the switchover within the H.323 or SIP signaling protocol. The SCCP and MGCP signaling protocols do not support protocol-based pass-through. This transport method is often referred to as pass-through because this keyword is used by the **fax protocol** command during configuration.
Relay	T.38 Fax relay (NSE-based switchover)	This is the standards-based version of fax relay that works only between Cisco voice gateways, because of the proprietary NSE switchover.
	T.38 fax relay (protocol-based switchover)	This is the standards-based version of fax relay that uses a switchover in the protocol stack of the voice signaling protocol. This ensures interoperability with third-party voice gateways.
	Cisco fax relay (RTP switchover)	This is the Cisco prestandard fax relay implementation that is supported only by Cisco voice gateways.

The Cisco voice gateways with the most flexibility are the IOS-based voice gateways running the Telogy DSP firmware on the C549 and C5510 hardware. These gateways typically support all the fax passthrough and relay transport options in Table 7-12, unless they must run the SCCP or MGCP voice signaling protocols. As noted previously, SCCP gateways support only NSE-based switchovers for passthrough and T.38 fax relay, whereas MGCP supports only NSE-based passthrough, too.

If third-party voice gateways are also included in a network design involving fax over IP, your choices of fax transport methods are restricted to protocol-based pass-through and protocol-based T.38. The other transport methods involve Cisco proprietary switchovers or protocols, which third-party voice gateways would not support.

Protocol-based pass-through interoperates with many third-party voice gateways, but it is not a standard. This transport method works because it uses procedures within the H.323 or SIP signaling protocol to convert the call to passthrough. The proposed standard for passthrough is V.152, but this specification has not been implemented on Cisco voice gateways. You can find more information about ITU-T V.152 in the section "A Future Look at ITU-T V.152" in Chapter 4, "Passthrough."

The only true standards-based solution for transporting fax over IP is protocol-based T.38 fax relay. In most circumstances, this is going to be your best method for achieving success-ful fax transmissions between Cisco voice gateways and other vendors. Nonetheless, for T.38 fax relay and even protocol-based pass-through it is recommended to consult the other voice gateway's vendor to confirm support of either of these IP fax transport options.

Error Correction Mode

The Error Correction Mode (ECM) feature provides a means for fax machines to ensure error-free page transmissions. This feature is optional, and not all fax devices support ECM. Even on fax machines that do support ECM, it can usually be disabled.

The ECM feature can be of critical importance for faxed information, especially contracts and legal documents. Without the ECM feature enabled, a small percentage of scan-line errors can occur without causing a complete call failure. This in turn may cause some parts of the received page to contain viewable errors or slight corruption.

All the technical details concerning ECM have already been covered in the section "Under-standing Error Correction Mode (ECM)" in Chapter 2, "How Fax Works." This section explores the ECM feature from a network design perspective, covering the advantages and disadvantages of the feature and some best practices for its implementation.

The main advantage of ECM is that you are ensured that an exact copy of the original document will arrive at the destination fax machine. As mentioned previously, this can be critical for many types of documents. In addition, ECM can eliminate the need to refax documents because the quality of the received document was poor.

Because of the ECM feature's tenacious behavior in ensuring an error-free transmission, ECM fax calls will fail before an errored fax page is allowed to go through. Although the majority of the time the sending fax machine will redial and try again at a later time, some consider this a disadvantage of ECM. They would prefer that the fax go through with minor errors rather than not go through at all.

Subsequently, ECM is not very tolerant of packet loss. In lab testing, ECM fax calls start to fail much sooner as the amount of packet loss is increased compared to non-ECM fax calls, which handle much higher levels of packet loss before failing. Furthermore, even if an ECM fax call does not fail because of packet loss, numerous retransmissions of errored scan lines can cause fax transmissions to last a long time. This is inefficient for customers that handle a large amount of fax traffic.

The need for non-ECM fax calls occurs in situations where the call must traverse an IP network that is not under your direct control, such as a service provider's network or the Internet. In these types of scenarios, you cannot control the amount of packet loss and jitter. Therefore, getting non-ECM faxes to go through with minor errors is still better than ECM faxes not going through at all. Naturally, in IP networks where packet loss is low, the advantages of ECM will outweigh any disadvantages.

The ECM feature is activated during the negotiation phase of the fax call between the originating and terminating fax devices. When using passthrough for the fax call, this negotiation is passed seamlessly between the fax machines using the G.711 codec. However, with fax relay, Cisco voice gateways offer the user the ability to disable the ECM feature by manipulating bit 27 of the DIS message. Bit 27 in the DIS message is used by the terminating fax device to signal its support of ECM. Remember that with fax relay calls, the voice gateway demodulates the fax T.30 messages. This allows the gateway to manipulate certain bits in the fax negotiation messages that control features such as ECM.

Both the T.38 and Cisco fax relay transport methods can flip bit 27 to signal that ECM is not supported even though the terminating fax device may have set the bit to signal that ECM is supported. When the originating fax device receives the DIS message, it sees that bit 27 indicates the lack of ECM support on the terminating fax device and then proceeds with a non-ECM fax call. Figure 7-3 shows this process.

Figure 7-3 *Disabling of the ECM Feature by a Cisco Voice Gateway*

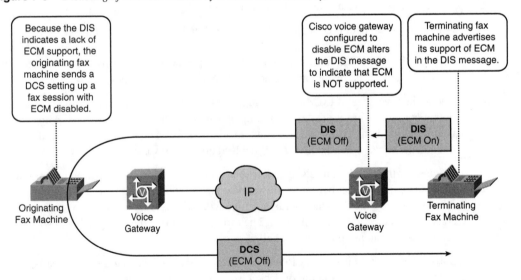

By default, fax relay configurations on Cisco voice gateways do not disable ECM in the manner shown in Figure 7-3, except for the 6608 Catalyst blade. However, if you decide that ECM should be disabled for fax calls on IOS voice gateways, you can use the IOS configuration command **fax-relay ecm disable** under the VoIP dial peer, or in the case of MGCP use the command **no mgcp fax t38 ecm**. You can find more information about these configuration commands in Chapter 10.

When ECM is disabled on a Cisco IOS voice gateway as diagrammed in Figure 7-3, a feature known as fax relay packet loss concealment is enabled. This feature further enhances the robustness of non-ECM fax calls by replacing corrupted scan lines with the previous scan line. For a few corrupted scan lines on a page, this feature is hardly noticeable, and it keeps error-free scan lines from arriving at the terminating fax device. However, when many scan lines are corrupted, this feature makes text "bleed" down the page. Basically, the packet loss concealment feature handles minor packet loss really well, but it does not compensate for high percentages of packet loss.

In most cases, the decision to use the ECM feature when implementing fax relay is best left up to the individual fax machines. Subsequently, if ECM is successfully negotiated by the fax endpoints, the voice gateway does not alter that decision. However, if the need exists for forcing ECM to be disabled for a fax relay call, this can be accomplished by Cisco voice gateways.

Super G3

Super G3 (SG3) or V.34 faxing uses different modulations and signaling than a normal G3 fax call. Rarely is this a problem, however, because SG3 is backward compatible with the ubiquitous G3 fax standard. If either the originating or terminating fax device does not support SG3, the fax transmission falls back to a normal G3 fax call. For more information about the technical details of SG3, see the section "Super G3 Faxing" in Chapter 2.

Cisco voice gateways do not support SG3 fax transmissions when either T.38 or Cisco fax relay is configured. Furthermore, unlike a G3 fax call, an SG3 call does not contain the V.21 flags necessary for the Cisco voice gateway to identify the call as a fax call. Therefore, T.38 and Cisco fax relay and protocol-based fax pass-through will not activate, leaving the fax call stuck with the configured voice codec. The only true support of SG3 on Cisco voice gateways is accomplished using NSE-based modem passthrough.

Occasionally, a situation can arise where SG3 fax machines never fall back to G3 mode when trying to use fax relay as the transport method. Without a fallback to a G3 negotiation, fax relay is never initiated by the Cisco voice gateways. The SG3 fax machines can potentially keep trying to negotiate over a highly compressed voice codec such as G.729 without success. The fax call eventually fails.

Although this situation and other SG3-to-G3 interoperability issues involving fax relay through a Cisco voice gateway are somewhat uncommon, they still pose problems that are easily fixed. The following solutions are how SG3 fax transmissions should be handled for Cisco voice gateways configured for fax relay:

- **Manually disable the SG3 feature on the fax machine itself**: Many fax devices tout this feature with some sort of marking to the effect of "High-Speed Faxing," "Super G3," or "V.34 Fax." Disabling SG3 at the fax machine itself ensures that this specific fax device will negotiate only standard G3 fax calls. Unfortunately, this solution does not scale for large numbers of fax machines spread across different locations.

TIP   The Super G3 feature requires ECM to be enabled. If ECM is not enabled, Super G3 will not work. On certain fax devices where a specific configuration option to disable SG3 does not exist, but an ECM disable option is available, disabling ECM will disable SG3.

- **Enable modem passthrough as the transport method**: Modem passthrough is the only transport option that handles SG3 calls at their native speeds. However, because of its NSE-based switchover mechanism, it does not interoperate with third-party equipment and can be implemented only between Cisco voice gateways. In many cases, fax relay is configured to handle G3 fax calls on a Cisco voice gateway in combination with modem passthrough to handle any SG3 fax calls. This scenario is covered for the MGCP voice signaling protocol in a sample configuration in the section "T.38 Fax Relay and Modem Passthrough Configuration for MGCP" in Chapter 10. Of course, this same sort of solution can be applied to the H.323, SIP, and SCCP protocols, too.

- **Enable the feature Fax Relay Support for SG3 Fax Machines at G3 Speeds**: Available in IOS Release 12.4(4)T and later, this feature suppresses the initial SG3 signaling so that the fax machines believe that only a standard G3 fax call is possible. Because it uses the V.34 modulation, SG3 is dependent on the Calling Menu (CM) message for bringing up V.34. The V.34 modulation was discussed in detail in the section "Modem Call Analysis" in Chapter 1 "How Modems Work." By squelching this CM message, this feature prevents the setup of V.34 and, consequently, SG3. This feature is controlled by default the commands **fax relay sg3-to-g3** for H.323, SIP, and SCCP voice gateways and the command **mgcp fax-relay sg3-to-g3** for MGCP. You can find more information about these commands in Tables 10-7 and 10-11 in Chapter 10. In addition to a specific software requirement, only certain hardware supports this feature. See the online document "Fax Relay Support for SG3 Fax Machines at G3 Speeds" at Cisco.com for more detailed information about the specific hardware requirements.

The decision on how to handle SG3 when transporting faxes over IP networks is often overlooked. Potentially, this can cause unnecessary problems later upon implementation. Therefore, it is recommended to adopt one of the solutions above to eliminate any SG3-related issues and to ensure a high fax call success rate.

Hairpin Calls

A hairpin call occurs when a standard inbound telephony call is simply routed back out another telephony interface on the same voice gateway. A VoIP component is not present for this sort of call. This type of call is also commonly referred to as a POTS-to-POTS call, TDM switching, or a TDM hairpin call.

A scenario involving a hairpin call is illustrated in Figure 7-4. In this figure, a Cisco voice gateway is connected to the PSTN by a digital T1 or E1 circuit. Voice calls are routed via VoIP to Unified CM, whereas fax calls are "hairpinned" from the PSTN interface to another T1/E1 digital interface on the gateway, which connects directly to a fax server.

Figure 7-4   *Hairpin Call*

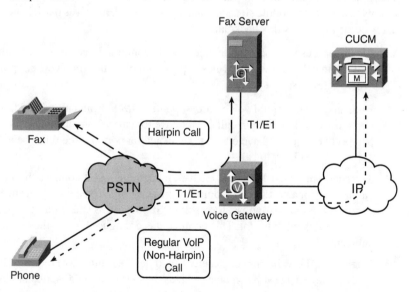

The most important aspect of any hairpin call on a Cisco voice gateway is whether the DSP can be dropped from the call after it is established. If the DSP can be dropped out of the call, a TDM connection through the voice gateway occurs, and this is the ideal scenario. All the bits transmitted between these ports are unaltered by the voice gateway. In Figure 7-4, a hairpin call with the DSP dropped is equivalent to the fax server being connected directly to the PSTN without the gateway present.

In some cases, because of hardware restrictions or user configuration, DSPs must remain involved for the call duration. With DSP involvement, the bits will always be altered to some extent as the DSP processes the call.

With fax calls, this DSP involvement can be plainly seen by running the command **debug fax relay t30 all-level-1**. You will see that by default T.38 fax relay occurs between the DSPs handling the hairpin call. This does not necessarily result in problems, but bypassing the DSP is the better option when it is possible. Naturally, when the DSP is bypassed, these debugs will not be present because the DSP has been removed from the call path.

A pure TDM hairpin call in its simplest form occurs within a single module slot of a voice gateway. This intraslot TDM hairpin can occur on digital or analog voice ports and is typically dependent on the module installed in the slot. For example, on ISR voice gateways such as the 2800 and 3800 series, a two-port FXS card (VIC2-2FXS) inserted into an HWIC slot on the motherboard module slot 0 will automatically perform TDM hairpins between the two FXS ports.

The other type of "DSP-less" TDM hairpin calls occur between module slots on a Cisco voice gateway. An interslot hairpin call requires that the voice gateway contain a TDM backplane to link the module slots and that the modules themselves participate in the timing that is occurring across this backplane.

Although numerous voice card and voice module combinations are possible when it comes to TDM hairpin calls, a few basic rules apply when planning for TDM hairpin calls on Cisco voice gateways:

- Both analog and digital voice ports support TDM hairpin calls. In addition, the two ports involved in a hairpin call do not have to match from an analog and digital perspective. You can have one port be an analog port and the other be a digital port during a TDM hairpin call.

- The command **local-bypass** is enabled by default, and it controls the TDM hairpin call feature for a particular module slot on a Cisco voice gateway. The negation of this command, **no local-bypass**, forces the DSP to be involved for all hairpinned calls involving this module slot. This command is configured under the **voice-card** submenu.

- Performing TDM hairpin calls across module slots (interslot) requires that the gateway have a TDM backplane, such as the 2800 and 3800 series of Cisco voice gateways. Other gateways without a TDM backplane are only capable of intraslot TDM hairpin calls. These gateways can pass calls between slots, but they will not be in a true TDM fashion, and the DSP will be involved.

- When performing interslot TDM hairpin calls, the DSP types must be the same. You cannot have C549 DSPs attached to one voice port and C5510 DSPs being used by the other voice port. For example, the NM-HDV module uses C549 DSPs and is capable of interslot TDM hairpin calls only with another NM-HDV module. Hairpin calls between an NM-HDV and an NM-HDV2 or other C5510-based module require that DSPs be involved.

- Both module slots in an interslot TDM hairpin call must be part of the gateway's TDM backplane clocking scheme. This is accomplished using the **network-clock-participate** command. If a module slot is not tied to the clocking used on the TDM backplane, the DSP must stay involved with the transmission, and it cannot drop out.

- Notable modules that do not support intraslot or interslot TDM hairpin calls are the older NM-1V, NM-2V, and NM-HDA.

You should always strive for TDM hairpin calls where the DSP is dropped from the call to ensure the best call success rate. However, for situations where a TDM hairpin call is not possible, a hairpin call with DSP involvement and T.38 fax relay between the DSPs should suffice.

Fallback

The fallback feature on Cisco IOS voice gateways provides a means for an alternate fax transport protocol to be used if the initial T.38 fax relay transport method fails to negotiate successfully. Fallback is only available with T.38 fax relay on H.323 and SIP voice gateways, and two different options are available. The fallback itself occurs seamlessly with either option, and in most cases the fax machines never realize that a fallback has even occurred.

The first fallback option occurs by default, without any additional configuration, whenever NSE-based T.38 fax relay is enabled for the H.323 and SIP protocols. The enabling of this type of fallback is accomplished by the IOS configuration command **fax protocol t38 nse**. This command, as defined by Table 10-5 in Chapter 10, instructs the voice gateway to implement T.38 fax relay using a switchover of Cisco proprietary NSEs. A detailed explanation of the NSE-based T.38 fax relay switchover was covered previously in the section "NSE-based Switchover for T.38" in Chapter 5.

However, in the event that this NSE-based T.38 switchover fails, the Cisco voice gateway immediately tries protocol-based T.38. The assumption here is that the voice gateway that does not support an NSE-based switchover may be a Cisco voice gateway incorrectly configured for protocol-based T.38 fax relay. Another possibility is that a third-party device that will support only a protocol-based T.38 switchover is on the other end of the call. Either way, if an NSE-based T.38 fax relay switchover fails, a protocol-based T.38 switchover is tried in the hopes of completing a successful fax call.

What this means from a network design perspective is that third-party voice gateways can be integrated into an architecture where NSE-based T.38 is the default configuration. A delay might occur in the switchover as the NSE negotiation fails, but a successful T.38 fax call using the voice signaling protocol stack should still be established. In addition, Cisco voice gateways that are configured for protocol-based T.38 can interoperate with NSE-based voice gateways. Just be aware that in rare situations the delay associated with falling back to another transport method can be too long for some fax devices, and the call might get disconnected early and fail.

The other fallback option is explicitly configurable via the CLI using the command **fax protocol t38 fallback** or **fax protocol t38 nse fallback** for H.323 and SIP voice gateways. These two commands allow for fallback to occur for both NSE-based T.38 and protocol-based T.38 fax relay.

The specific fallback options include the additional transport methods of **cisco** (Cisco fax relay), **pass-through**, and **none**. If for whatever reason T.38 fax relay is not supported or enabled, a completely different transport method can be specified. Figure 7-5 highlights a scenario where a fallback to pass-through occurs.

Figure 7-5   *T.38 Fax Relay Fallback to Pass-Through*

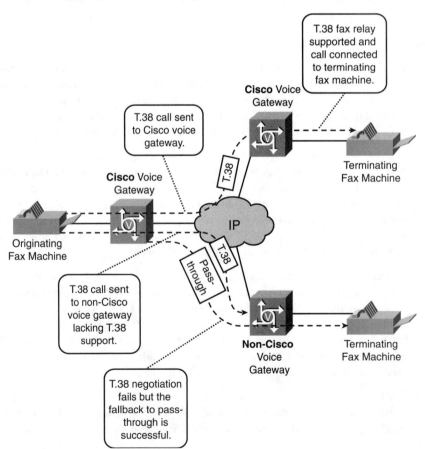

In Figure 7-5, using the IOS configuration command **fax protocol t38 fallback pass-through g711ulaw**, the originating Cisco voice gateway on the left side of the diagram successfully places a T.38 fax relay call to another Cisco voice gateway. A similar call to a third-party voice gateway lacking T.38 fax relay support fails to negotiate. However, instead of the fax call failing completely, a pass-through negotiation immediately follows. The pass-through transport method is supported by the non-Cisco voice gateway, and the fax call is successfully established with the terminating fax machine.

Although the two T.38 fax relay fallback options mentioned in this section are not always necessary, they do provide additional means of integrating different fax transport methods and switchovers. If the need exists to integrate third-party voice gateways lacking T.38 fax relay support into a network where T.38 fax relay is the primary transport method, the fallback option illustrated in Figure 7-5 is invaluable.

The most important design consideration concerning fallback is that in ideal network planning situations, this feature is not necessary. From a practical perspective, configuring all voice gateways to use the same T.38 fax relay transport method and switchover is the best recommendation. The fallback feature should be used only in situations where the same T.38 transport and switchover method cannot be implemented throughout the network.

T.37 Store-and-Forward Fax

As discussed in the previous chapter, T.37 store-and-forward fax provides a conversion between faxes and e-mail. This is a unique process for handling fax communications, and it allows T.37 to serve as an alternative transport method to fax passthrough and relay.

The ability to send and receive faxes directly from an e-mail client is the main allure of T.37. Without T.37, a typical fax scenario could be similar to the following:

1 Print a document.

2 Go retrieve it from a printer.

3 Walk the document over to an office fax machine.

4 Possibly wait for someone else to finish sending or receiving a fax.

5 Manually fax the document.

Compare this process to a T.37 scenario where you just e-mail the document and it automatically arrives at its final destination as a standard fax.

Receiving documents is also just as simple with T.37. Instead of walking over to the office fax and picking through the pile of received faxes, T.37 delivers the fax directly into your e-mail inbox. When it comes to efficiently sending and receiving fax documents, T.37 has a decided advantage over traditional faxing methods.

Because T.37 converts faxes to e-mail, the benefits of e-mail can be exploited and applied to faxes. For example, you can send a fax e-mail to a distribution list and fax a document to many people at once.

However, T.37 has its share of disadvantages, too. The one major disadvantage involves the fact that T.37 breaks the real-time nature of a traditional fax call. This makes it difficult to confirm that the fax ever reaches its final destination. In a traditional real-time scenario, the originating fax machine sends the document directly to the final destination. If the transaction is successful, the originating fax can instantly print a confirmation report. If the transaction is not successful, an error message is reported, and the fax failure is noted in transmission reports from the fax machine.

Receiving any sort of confirmation or status as to the delivery of a fax to its final destination with T.37 depends on DSN and MDN messages. Although these messages are potentially useful, they lack wide-ranging support from mail servers and e-mail clients. This, in turn, makes receiving status or delivery information for fax e-mail potentially unreliable.

Another disadvantage of the Cisco T.37 implementation is the lack of ECM support. Cisco voice gateways performing the T.37 onramp and offramp functions will not support the ECM option, and this leads to a couple of problems. In addition to potential image-quality problems in the TIFF file generated by an onramp gateway, certain errors in the scan lines can cause the TIFF to be incomplete and, even worse, the call may fail. Make sure that any digital interfaces used to receive onramp faxes are free of errors to mitigate the lack of ECM support with T.37.

TIP   A solution to consider that remedies T.37 disadvantages while still maintaining its advantages are fax servers. Fax servers can provide the e-mail "look and feel" of T.37, but they do not rely on DSN and MDN for status and confirmation. Instead, the fax servers send the fax using a real-time protocol such as T.38 fax relay and then can pass a true confirmation on to the user. More information about fax servers and how they can be integrated into Cisco voice networks is discussed in the next chapter.

A design consideration that is often overlooked when implementing T.37 store-and-forward fax on a Cisco IOS voice gateway is the greater amount of memory and CPU that is utilized by a T.37 call compared to a regular voice call. For more information about the impact of T.37 on a voice gateway's resources, refer back to the section "Resource Utilization," earlier in this chapter.

An interesting T.37 integration worth noting involves the Cisco Unity product. Although Cisco Unity is a well-known, feature-rich voice-mail product, it can also be integrated directly with T.37 onramp and offramp gateways. Designed for simple, small-scale, low-traffic fax needs, a T.37 and Unity integration allows for users to receive faxes in their Unity inboxes and to send faxes directly from e-mail.

Implementing this solution requires the Unity IP Fax Configuration wizard and properly configured onramp and offramp voice gateways. The Unity IP Fax Configuration wizard along with links for the onramp and offramp gateway configurations, a training video, and other documentation can be downloaded from the following site:

http://www.ciscounitytools.com/App_IPFaxConfigurationWizard.htm

Depending on the situation, T.37 store-and-forward fax is a viable alternative to real-time fax protocols such as fax relay and passthrough. This fax transport method is unique in that it takes advantage of the SMTP protocol for transferring fax data, and this allows for distinct solutions, such as a direct integration with Cisco Unity. However, you need to fully understand the advantages and disadvantages of T.37 and its design constraints before selecting it as your fax transport method.

Fax Detect Script

Cisco IOS gateways can run TCL scripts for handling a wide variety of both voice and fax features. Common TCL scripts for fax include the onramp and offramp scripts that are used when configuring T.37 store-and-forward fax. Another TCL script that is available from the Cisco website is the fax detect script. Registered users can download this script at http://www.cisco.com/cgi-bin/tablebuild.pl/tclware.

The fax detect TCL script allows for Cisco IOS voice gateways to provide a "single number reach" capability for voice and fax calls. One telephone number can be used as a voice line and fax line. The fax detect script makes the determination of whether the incoming call is a voice call or a fax call, and then routes the call appropriately. Voice calls are passed to an IP phone or another voice gateway, and fax calls are converted to an e-mail attachment using T.37 store-and-forward fax. Figure 7-6 provides a sample scenario of how the fax detect script can be implemented.

As shown in Figure 7-6, the fax detect script integrates easily into a T.37 onramp gateway. This allows incoming calls that are determined to be faxes to be converted into an e-mail attachment. This fax e-mail can then be accessed by an e-mail client for viewing.

The fax detect script identifies an incoming call as a fax call using one of two methods, a DTMF tone from the calling party or CNG tone detection. The voice gateway can play an optional audio prompt when the call is answered. This audio prompt can tell the user to press a certain DTMF number on their phone to indicate a fax call. The gateway then routes the call as a fax call, and the user presses Start on the fax machine to initiate the fax transmission.

Figure 7-6 *TCL Fax Detect Script*

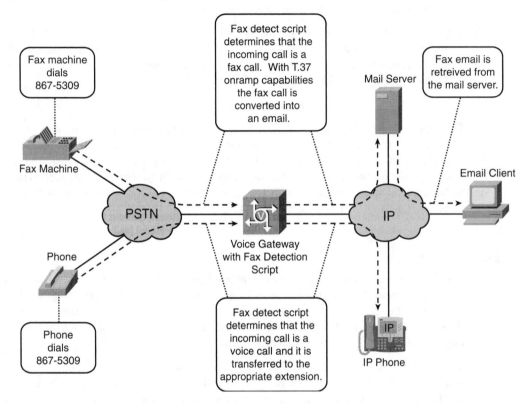

With CNG tone detection, the voice gateway listens for the 1100 Hz CNG tone. The calling fax devices play this tone, and the voice gateway listens for CNG even if an audio prompt is not present. The CNG tone is discussed in detail in the section "CNG Tone" in Chapter 2. The fax detect script requires the reception of three CNG tones before the call is classified as a fax call and routed as such. The CNG tone detection method is used frequently because most fax machines are automated and users do not manually place the calls and listen for audio prompts.

TIP   On the 5350, 5450, and 5850 voice gateways using the NextPort DSP modules and the fax detect script, calls are classified as fax calls after only two CNG tones. Also, there is a voicecap setting of v319=1 that can be configured on these platforms to lower this to one CNG tone. The caveat with this low of a setting, however, is that a normal voice conversation might trigger the fax detect script.

The voicecap feature on the 5350, 5450, and 5850 voice gateways using NextPort DSP modules can be configured using the **voicecap configure** and the **voicecap entry** commands. Refer to the document "Cisco IOS Voice Command Reference" for IOS Release 12.3T at Cisco.com for more information about configuring the voicecap feature.

Unfortunately, there can be some issues when depending on CNG tone detection for making the determination that an incoming call is a fax call. One problem is that many older fax machines (produced before 1995) do not send CNG tones. Another problem is that when some models of fax machines detect a person answering a call, they disable CNG. Therefore, when the audio prompt answers the incoming call on a voice gateway running a fax detection script, the fax machine hears the voice from the audio prompt and stops sending CNG. Without three CNG tones, the fax detect script's CNG detection function will never identify the incoming call as a fax call.

Many options exist for customizing the TCL fax detect script on IOS gateways. These options include different fax detection modes and the ability for users to create their own audio prompts. More information about these additional options and configuration examples and troubleshooting tips can be found online at Cisco.com in the document "Configuring Fax Detection."

For unique applications of the TCL fax detect script, Cisco offers assistance in creating a custom script for your voice gateway through the Cisco Developer Support Program. You can find more information about the Cisco Developer Support Program at http://www.cisco.com/go/developersupport/.

In addition to TCL, VoiceXML can be used to create a fax detect script. However, Cisco does not provide a VoiceXML fax detect script for download, so you must create your own. Assistance in creating a VoiceXML script can be obtained through the Cisco Developer Support Program. Additional information on VoiceXML and fax detection can be found online at Cisco.com in the document "Configuring Fax Detection for VoiceXML."

Unified CM Integration

The Unified CM product is the heart of most Cisco IP telephony deployments. Subsequently, its support of fax is a common design concern. After all, to fully migrate a legacy voice infrastructure over to IP, Unified CM must be able to handle both voice and fax communications.

In the past, fax support on Unified CM has lagged behind the fax capabilities of the Cisco voice gateways. This is one of the reasons for the implementation of Cisco proprietary NSE packets for handling the fax switchover. With NSE packets, voice gateways could bypass Unified CM whenever a fax switchover was necessary but not supported by Unified CM within the voice signaling protocol stack. Figure 7-7 illustrates an NSE-based T.38 fax switchover with Unified CM.

Figure 7-7 *NSE-Based T.38 Fax Relay Switchover with Unified CM*

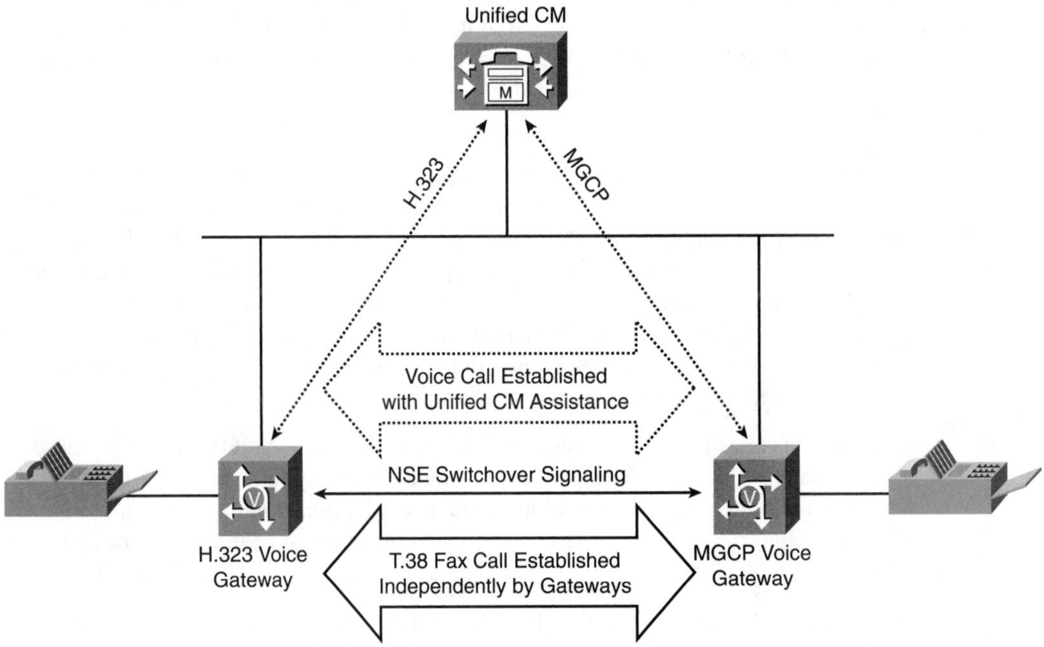

In Figure 7-7, Unified CM successfully establishes a voice call between an H.323 and an MGCP voice gateway. When V.21 fax flags are detected, the voice gateways need to switch over to T.38 fax relay so that the call can be properly handled as a fax call rather than a voice call. However, if Unified CM cannot support T.38 within the H.323 and MGCP protocol stack, the voice gateways can use an NSE switchover. This effectively bypasses the H.323 and MGCP voice signaling protocols and Unified CM, forcing the voice gateways to transition the initial voice call to T.38 fax relay on their own via the media stream.

TIP Support for NSE-based switchovers such as T.38 fax relay can be signaled ahead of time by the voice gateways using their respective voice signaling protocols. This proactively confirms that an NSE-based switchover can be handled by both voice gateways during the initial call setup. Within the H.323 call control protocol, the NSE switchover capability is indicated by a nonstandard capability setting in the H.245 Terminal Capability Set (TCS) message. For the SIP and MGCP call control protocols, the NSE switchover capability is indicated by the X-NSE attribute found in the SDP portion of certain SIP and MGCP messages. However, Unified CM drops optional capability attributes such as these because they are not recognized, and this causes the voice gateways to think that the peer gateway cannot handle an NSE switchover.

To remedy this scenario, IOS gateways include a **force** option in the **fax protocol t38 nse** command. The **nse force** option instructs the voice gateway to use an NSE-based switchover even if a confirmation of NSE support has not been obtained. In most Unified CM deployment models where NSE-based T.38 fax relay is being used, the **nse force** option will need to be implemented. You can find more information about the **fax protocol nse force** command in Table 10-5 of Chapter 10 as well as the section "Validating NSE Switchover Support" in Chapter 12.

More recent versions of Unified CM have added support for T.38 fax relay in the protocol stack of the voice signaling protocol. Assuming that the appropriate Unified CM version is being used, an NSE-based switchover between the Cisco voice gateways is no longer necessary, especially when H.323, SIP, and MGCP are the voice signaling protocols. Figure 7-8 illustrates Unified CM participation for a protocol-based T.38 fax relay switchover.

Figure 7-8   *Protocol-Based T.38 Fax Relay Switchover with Unified CM*

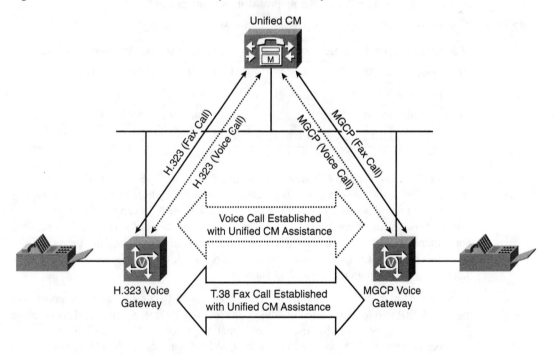

Although H.323 and MGCP voice gateways are illustrated in Figures 7-7 and 7-8, a SIP gateway could just as easily have been substituted for either gateway. The one major exception that occurs for the scenario modeled in Figure 7-8 is for voice gateways running SCCP. SCCP supports only NSE-based T.38 fax relay.

TIP	Cisco fax relay cannot directly integrate with Unified CM because it does not allow for the voice signaling protocol to handle the switchover. The switchover can occur only through RTP payload exchanges, as explained in the section "Cisco Fax Relay" in Chapter 5. Voice gateways can implement Cisco fax relay in Unified CM environments, but the voice gateways themselves will control the switchover in a manner similar to that shown in Figure 7-7.

With protocol-based T.38 support, Unified CM now understands T.38 communications and switches over to T.38 using standards-based methods. This now allows Unified CM to integrate directly with third-party H.323 and SIP gateways using T.38 and IP fax servers. Fax server integration with Unified CM is discussed in detail in the next chapter.

The critical piece of information necessary for deploying protocol-based T.38 with Unified CM is the software version where Unified CM picked up T.38 support for a particular voice signaling protocol. Table 7-13 highlights the Unified CM releases where T.38 support for the H.323, SIP, and MGCP signaling protocols was integrated.

Table 7-13 *Protocol-Based T.38 Fax Relay Support in Unified CM*

T.38 Signaling Protocol Support	Cisco Unified CM Software Release
H.323 support for T.38	4.1(1), 4.2(3), 5.0(1), and 6.0(1)
H.323 and MGCP support for T.38	4.2(3) and 6.0(1)
H.323 and SIP support for T.38	5.0(1) and 6.0(1)
H.323, SIP, and MGCP support for T.38	6.0(1)

You should realize that the software versions listed in Table 7-13 indicate the initial integration point for the support of the T.38 fax relay protocol. Subsequent releases following these initial release points will naturally also have the same T.38 support within a given major release. A major release is indicated by the first number of the Unified CM version. For example, the 5.0(1) release in Table 7-13 means that any 5.*x* release has the same T.38 support. The 4.2(3) release indicates that any 4.*x* release following this version, such as 4.3(1), will also contain the noted T.38 support.

As shown in Table 7-13, starting in Unified CM Release 6.0(1), full T.38 fax support over the H.323, SIP, and MGCP voice signaling protocols is available. Software releases before 6.0(1) contain support only for select voice signaling protocols. To achieve the greatest interoperability with T.38 fax relay in Unified CM deployments, the 6.0(1) release or later is recommended.

Comparing Fax Passthrough and Fax Relay

One of the most common design questions about transporting fax over IP has to do with selecting passthrough or relay as the transport method. The resounding question from a network design perspective is "which one is better?"

Unfortunately, the answer to this question is usually not simple and depends on a number of factors, most of which have already been discussed in this chapter. Therefore, the best way to decide between a fax passthrough or relay implementation is to consider the differences between these two transport methods before making a decision. Table 7-14 provides a quick summary of passthrough and relay differences, which can also be viewed as advantages and disadvantages of each.

The information in Table 7-14 should be used by matching up the fax transport requirements for a particular network design with the strengths and weaknesses of fax passthrough and relay. For example, if the main design requirements are that fax calls must be transported across IP in a secure manner at SG3 speeds, modem passthrough is the option that should be chosen. However, if the design requirements change and only SRTP is mandatory, fax pass-through and Cisco fax relay now also become viable options along with modem passthrough.

Years ago, Cisco fax relay and passthrough were the dominant solutions for transporting fax over IP. However, it is worth noting that recent trends show that more networks are implementing T.38 fax relay. This is occurring primarily because T.38 is standards based and offers flexibility in integrating third-party gateways and fax servers.

In addition, T.38 has a robust redundancy feature and recent updates to the standard have added RTP encapsulation and SG3 support. Although widespread adoption of these recent T.38 features has not yet occurred, selecting T.38 fax relay as a transport option now ensures an easy migration to updated versions in the future. If multiple fax transport options, including T.38 fax relay, are viable for a particular network design, T.38 fax relay is the recommended choice.

Table 7-14   *Differences Between Fax Passthrough and Fax Relay*

Attribute or Feature	Passthrough	Relay
Bandwidth	Utilizes full G.711 codec bandwidth. Modest reductions can be made with CRTP.	Consumes at least half the amount of bandwidth of a fax passthrough call.
Redundancy	Protocol-based fax pass-through does not support redundancy. NSE-based modem passthrough supports one level of redundancy via RFC 2198.	T.38 fax relay supports multiple layers of redundancy with separate settings for the low-speed and high-speed messages. Cisco fax relay does not support redundancy.

continues

Table 7-14   *Differences Between Fax Passthrough and Fax Relay (Continued)*

Attribute or Feature	Passthrough	Relay
Protocol support	Only NSE-based modem passthrough is supported by all the voice signaling protocols. MGCP and SCCP do not support protocol-based fax pass-through.	Both T.38 and Cisco fax relay are supported by all the voice signaling protocols. However, SCCP can use only T.38 with an NSE-based switchover.
Product support	Modem passthrough is supported by all Cisco IOS gateways and non-IOS gateways, including the ATA, 6608/ 6624, and VG248. Fax pass-through is supported only on H.323 and SIP IOS gateways.	Cisco fax relay is supported by all Cisco IOS gateways (except for NextPort DSP platforms), and it is supported by all non-IOS gateways, except for the ATA. T.38 fax relay is supported by all IOS gateways along with the VG248.
Third-party interoperability	Third-party devices do not support modem passthrough because of its proprietary NSE-based switchover. Protocol-based fax pass-through should interoperate with most third-party gateways.	T.38 fax relay using a protocol-based switchover is the de facto standard for fax transport over IP. T.38 fax relay using an NSE-based switchover and Cisco fax relay are supported only by Cisco voice gateways. Both NSE-based T.38 fax relay and Cisco fax relay use proprietary switchovers, and the Cisco fax relay protocol itself is also proprietary.
Unified CM support	Protocol-based fax pass-through is not supported by Unified CM. Modem passthrough uses NSEs so that the switchover happens without Unified CM involvement.	Protocol-based T.38 is fully supported for H.323, SIP, and MGCP in Unified CM 6.0(1). NSE-based T.38 and Cisco fax relay use a switchover mechanism that does not involve Unified CM.
SG3 support	When configured for NSE-based modem passthrough, SG3 fax calls can negotiate at their native speeds. Protocol-based fax pass-through does not support SG3.	Relay does not support SG3, and fax machines must be forced down to G3 speeds to work with either T.38 or Cisco fax relay.
ECM disable	Passthrough calls have no control over ECM, and this is entirely left up to the fax machines.	Relay offers the ability for Cisco voice gateways to disable ECM. See the section "Error Correction Mode" in this chapter.

Table 7-14   *Differences Between Fax Passthrough and Fax Relay (Continued)*

Attribute or Feature	Passthrough	Relay
Fallback support	Passthrough does not provide any fallback support to other transport options.	T.38 fax relay for H.323 and SIP provides multiple fallback options, including Cisco fax relay and protocol-based pass-through. Cisco fax relay does not support fallback.
SRTP and CRTP support	Passthrough can support CRTP for modest bandwidth savings and SRTP for secure faxing.	Because Cisco supports only T.38 with a UDPTL header, SRTP and CRTP are not possible with T.38 fax relay. Only Cisco fax relay can support CRTP and SRTP because it uses a standard RTP header.
DSP clock synchronization	In some instances where long faxes are occurring and significant DSP clock discrepancies exist, passthrough calls can experience problems. This issue is mitigated on the Telogy-based IOS gateways and was discussed previously in the section "Timing and Synchronization."	This issue does not affect fax relay.

Modem Design Considerations

Similar to fax, modem communications have the option of both passthrough and relay transport methods. The passthrough option for modems is simply named modem pass-through, and it shares this same syntax when it is configured on Cisco IOS gateways.

Modem passthrough is also applicable to fax calls and has already been discussed throughout the previous section, "Fax Design Considerations." The technical intricacies of modem passthrough and its NSE-based switchover are discussed in the section "Modem Passthrough with NSE" in Chapter 4.

Two relay options are available on Cisco IOS voice gateways: Cisco modem relay and secure modem relay. Cisco modem relay provides an alternative transport method to modem passthrough for V.34 and V.90 modulated calls. Secure modem relay is designed for transporting the V.32 or V.34 modulation of secure telephones. Because of the unique application for the secure modem relay transport method, it is discussed separately in its own subsection.

Comparing Modem Passthrough and Cisco Modem Relay

Of all the transport options available for fax and modem communications, modem passthrough enjoys the most widespread support among the Cisco voice gateways. All the Cisco IOS voice gateways support modem passthrough and all the non-IOS voice gateways. From a Cisco voice gateway interoperability standpoint, modem passthrough is always safe to use. However, when it comes to third-party voice gateway integration, the proprietary NSE-based switchover of modem passthrough is not supported by other vendors' products.

Cisco modem relay, on the other hand, is more restrictive. Because of the proprietary nature of the Cisco modem relay protocol and its NSE-based switchover, it is not supported by third-party gateways either. In addition, certain Cisco voice gateways, such as the 6608/6624, VG248, ATA, and any NextPort-based DSP gateway (5350, 5400, and 5850), also do not support Cisco modem relay. On Cisco voice gateways that do support modem relay, DSPs must use high complexity or flex mode. Compared to a modem passthrough call, a modem relay call consumes more DSP resources, as discussed previously in the section "Resource Utilization."

From a protocol interoperability perspective, both modem passthrough and Cisco modem relay work no matter what voice signaling protocol is used. As long as the voice gateway supports either feature, the voice signaling protocol does not matter. This is the main benefit of an NSE-based switchover, and it allows for modem passthrough and Cisco modem relay to be an effective transport method whether the voice signaling protocol is H.323, SIP, MGCP, or SCCP.

When deciding on whether to use modem passthrough or Cisco modem relay in a design situation, a number of factors concerning each of these transport methods should be studied. Table 7-15 summarizes some of the key differences between modem passthrough and Cisco modem relay.

If the design criteria for transporting modem traffic over IP has already been determined, Table 7-15 should assist in ascertaining the best choice. Both modem passthrough and Cisco modem relay have their advantages and disadvantages, but every network design is somewhat different.

In cases where both modem passthrough and Cisco modem relay are valid options, Cisco modem relay is the recommended transport option. Cisco modem relay is specifically engineered to transport modem communications over IP, whereas modem passthrough adapts a voice codec in an effort to accurately sample modulated data. Therefore, Cisco modem relay is more efficient and robust in maintaining successful modem over IP transmissions.

Table 7-15 *Differences Between Modem Passthrough and Cisco Modem Relay*

Attribute or Feature	Modem Passthrough	Cisco Modem Relay
Bandwidth	Uses full G.711 codec bandwidth. Modest reductions can be made with CRTP.	Consumes less bandwidth than a modem passthrough call.
Redundancy	Supports 1 level of redundancy via RFC 2198.	Instead of redundancy, Cisco modem relay uses an error correction mechanism.
Modulation support	Works with any common modem modulation.	Only V.34 supported. V.90 calls will also work, but they are forced down to V.34 speeds.
Protocol support	Works with any voice signaling protocol because of NSE-based switchover.	Works with any voice signaling protocol because of NSE-based switchover.
Product support	Supported by all Cisco IOS and non-IOS voice gateways.	Only supported by Cisco IOS gateways, except for platforms using the NextPort DSP. In addition, more DSP resources are consumed compared to a modem passthrough call.
Third-party interoperability	Proprietary NSE switchover prevents third-party interoperability.	Proprietary transport protocol and NSE switchover prevent third-party interoperability.
Unified CM support	Not applicable because switchover occurs without Unified CM involvement.	Not applicable because switchover occurs without Unified CM involvement.
SRTP and CRTP support	Both SRTP and CRTP are supported.	Neither SRTP nor CRTP is supported, because of the usage of the SPRT protocol header.
DSP clock synchronization	A potential problem for extended modem calls, mainly on gateways not using Telogy-based DSPs. See the section "Timing and Synchronization."	This issue does not affect modem relay.

Secure Modem Relay

Secure modem relay may also be referred to as "secure communication between STE endpoints." This transport method is different from Cisco modem relay, and it is specifically designed for transporting the specific V.32 or V.34 modulations used by secure telephone devices. These devices pass encrypted voice using these modulations in an effort to prevent eavesdropping.

NOTE   This section provides only a general overview of secure modem relay because of the unique, focused market segment that possesses a need for a feature such as this. For more detailed information about this transport method and its configuration and troubleshooting, refer to the online document "Secure Communication Between IP-STE Endpoint and Line-Side STE Endpoint" at Cisco.com.

The types of telephony devices that are supported by secure modem relay are known as secure terminal equipment (STE) endpoints. Line-side STE endpoints use a standard telephony connection such as an FXS or BRI port, whereas trunk-side STE endpoints support T1 and E1 interfaces. When an STE is connected directly to an IP network, it is known as an IP-STE endpoint. Third parties manufacture IP-STE endpoints compatible with Cisco modem relay, and they use a small SCCP stack and an abbreviated IP stack to connect to Unified CM.

TIP   Another common type of secure endpoint is known as a secure telephone unit (STU). Using older technology, the STU is no longer produced and is being replaced by the STE. STU endpoints are not supported by secure modem relay, so any communications involving STUs must use modem passthrough as the transport method.

Secure modem relay requires Unified CM and is compatible only with the following voice gateways: 2800s, 3800s, and the VG224. These voice gateways must also be running the Cisco IOS Advanced Enterprise Services image (cXXXX-adventerprisek9-mz).

Secure modem relay voice gateways support only the MGCP and SCCP voice signaling protocols for interacting with Unified CM. When configured for MGCP, the voice gateway has a T1 connection to the PSTN and is referred to as a trunk-side gateway. Analog FXS and BRI connections use voice gateways with an SCCP connection back to Unified CM and are called line-side gateways. Figure 7-9 shows the components of a secure modem relay deployment and how they interoperate.

Figure 7-9   *Secure Modem Relay Network Topology*

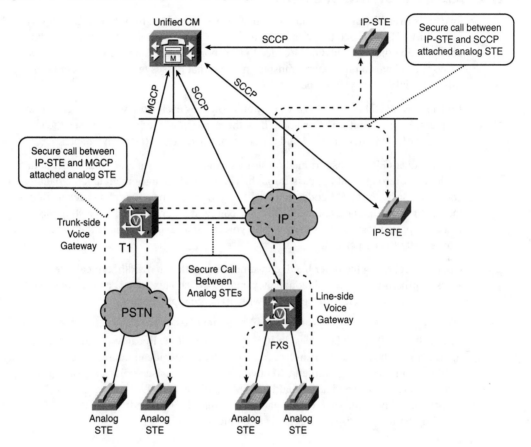

You can see in Figure 7-9 how the different STE devices interconnect with one another and Unified CM. No matter whether the endpoint is an IP-STE, an STE connected via a trunk-side voice gateway, or an STE connected via a line-side voice gateway, communication using secure modem relay is possible.

Secure modem relay is a feature that addresses a very specialized market segment where encrypted communications are necessary over an IP infrastructure. Although modem passthrough might work as an alternative to secure modem relay, it is not the best choice. If STE endpoints need to interoperate in a secure fashion over IP, secure modem relay is the recommended solution.

Text Design Considerations

Text calls over IP can be transported in one of two ways by Cisco IOS voice gateways: text over G.711 or Cisco text relay. The text over G.711 method is a manual passthrough configuration that uses the G.711 codec to transport the text tones across the IP network. Cisco text relay is a proprietary transport method that passes text characters out of band using special RTP payload types.

Both text over G.711 and Cisco text relay and how they each work were covered in previous chapters. For more information about how these transport methods work, see the section "Text over G.711" in Chapter 4 and the section "Cisco Text Relay" in Chapter 5.

The text over G.711 transport method suffers from the disadvantages that affect both modem passthrough and fax pass-through. These disadvantages include large bandwidth consumption by the G.711 codec and sensitivity to packet loss. Referring back to Table 7-2, the G.711 codec uses more than 80 Kbps of bandwidth per call, and lab testing has shown that once packet loss exceeds 0.1 percent, you can start experiencing text character loss rates greater than 1 percent.

Cisco text relay, on the other hand, consumes very little bandwidth, typically less than 3 Kbps. Furthermore, with full redundancy enabled, Cisco text relay can transport 99.95 percent of text characters successfully, with 10 percent packet loss.

Cisco text relay was introduced on select Cisco IOS voice gateways using C5510 DSPs, such as the 2800 and 3800 series, in IOS Version 12.4(6)T. Because Cisco text relay does not use a switchover mechanism like fax or modem relay, it can interoperate easily in any VoIP network, including Unified CM environments. The Cisco voice gateways just pass a text character out of band as it would a DTMF digit using DTMF relay. If a VoIP call can be established between Cisco voice gateways using the H.323, SIP, MGCP, or SCCP voice signaling protocols, Cisco text relay is a seamless addition.

TIP   Although a number of different text phone protocols are in use around the world, Cisco text relay currently supports only the text protocols of Baudot 45.45 bps and Baudot 50 bps.

The disadvantage of Cisco text relay is that the only Cisco products supporting this feature are certain IOS voice gateways. Therefore, one of these Cisco IOS voice gateways must originate and terminate a Cisco text relay session. For all other text connections over IP, text over G.711 must be used. Figure 7-10 illustrates a network where text over G.711 and Cisco text relay are implemented concurrently to support a variety of text over IP communications.

Figure 7-10 *Transporting Text Using Text over G.711 and Cisco Text Relay*

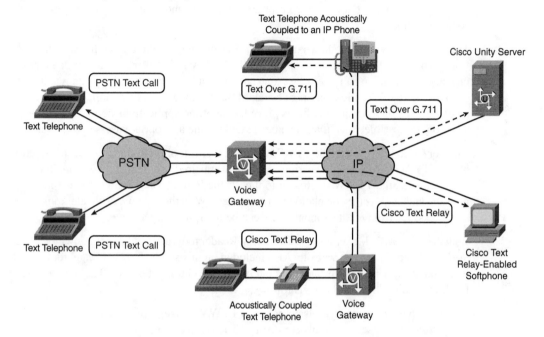

On the left side of Figure 7-10, text telephones are connected via the PSTN to a Cisco voice gateway. This Cisco voice gateway interconnects the PSTN text telephones to text devices on the IP network using either text over G.711 or Cisco text relay.

Specific dial peers on the voice gateway determine whether text over G.711 or Cisco text relay should be used. For connections to text telephones acoustically coupled to IP phones or connections to a Cisco Unity server, configure text over G.711 under the corresponding dial peer. For text connections to other Cisco voice gateways or supported third-party softphones, configure Cisco text relay under the dial peer as the transport method.

TIP Third-party softphones, such as the VTGO Advanced by IP blue, feature built-in Cisco text relay support. Because this tty device has a full integration of the Cisco text relay protocol, it can communicate directly to Cisco voice gateways without the need for using the less-efficient text over G.711 transport method.

In Figure 7-10, notice an example of a text telephone being acoustically coupled to a standard telephone and an IP phone. Although this might be the only option in many cases, you should ideally strive to have direct connections to the PSTN or IP network. Creating an acoustically coupled connection that is free of external, ambient noise can sometimes be difficult. This ambient noise can corrupt text characters and contribute to unreliable text communications.

The Cisco Unity server as shown in Figure 7-10 can integrate directly with text over G.711 from a voice-mail perspective. Using the Unity TTY WAV Maker tool, a user can type a message and then have this message translated into a WAV file that Unity can play to text telephones. The WAV file consists of standard Baudot tones, and these appear as characters on the text telephone when the file is played. One of the applications here is that text-telephone-accessible voice mails can be created for the appropriate users to retrieve.

Another Cisco Unity tool is the TTY WAV Reader. This tool performs the opposite function of the TTY WAV Maker. If a hearing- or speech-impaired user leaves a voice mail using a text telephone, the TTY WAV Reader tool pulls the Baudot tones from the voice-mail message and outputs the correlating text characters. With the TTY WAV Reader tool, voice-mail messages from text telephone users can be interpreted by anyone.

Both the TTY WAV Maker and the TTY WAV Reader tools are available for download from the CiscoUnityTools.com website. Also included on this site is the TTY Angel tool, which is similar to the TTY WAV Maker tool but includes additional features. The specific URLs for downloading these tools are as follows:

http://www.ciscounitytools.com/App_TTYWAVMaker.htm
http://www.ciscounitytools.com/App_TTYWAVReader.htm
http://www.ciscounitytools.com/App_TTYAngel.htm

Implementing any of these Unity TTY tools or providing connections to text phones that are acoustically coupled to IP phones requires that text over G.711 be implemented. Although this is not the most efficient or reliable choice, it is the only choice when planning for these devices. Otherwise, from a best practices standpoint, Cisco text relay should be used whenever possible for transporting text communications over IP.

Summary and Best Practices

Although design information for basic VoIP networks is not hard to find, applying VoIP-specific design information to modulated communications rarely works. Planning for modulated communications such as fax, modem, and text communications in IP networks requires focused design information tailored to these technologies.

This chapter provided the necessary design information required for implementing fax, modem, and text communications over IP. Organized into four distinct sections, a number of best practices were presented in each of these sections.

The first section discussed some general design considerations for passthrough and relay that are applicable whether faxes, modems, or text communications are being transported. The best practices covered in this first section include the following:

- Relay utilizes less bandwidth than passthrough. If bandwidth is a concern, always choose a relay transport method if possible.

- The H.323 and SIP call control protocols provide more options and flexibility for fax, modem, and text traffic compared to SCCP and MGCP.

- Packet loss is more harmful to a fax, modem, or text call than a voice call, so QoS is necessary. If you have already implemented a good QoS policy that prioritizes voice throughout the network, this is almost always adequate for fax, modem, and text communications, too.

- If any packet loss exists for fax, modem, or text traffic in your network, redundancy should be enabled.

- The C5510 DSP can be oversubscribed in flex-complexity mode. This can pose potential problems if fax relay, T.37, and modem relay are not properly planned for.

- Maintaining a correct clocking relationship that is free of errors on a voice gateway's digital interfaces is critical. In rare circumstances, timing disparities between DSPs can cause passthrough calls of a long duration to fail. Plan on using a relay transport method if fax or modem calls will need to be connected for long periods of time.

The next section discussed fax design considerations. Numerous transport methods are available when dealing with fax communications, so some of the best practices from this section are relevant only to a particular transport method. The best practices from this section are as follows:

- Cisco IOS voice gateways based on the Telogy DSP platform, such as C5510, offer the most versatility in transporting fax communications and should be selected when possible.

- T.38 fax relay is usually the best transport method for fax communications, especially when interoperability with third-party fax devices is necessary.

- Cisco voice gateways can disable ECM. The ECM option negotiated by the fax endpoints should not be disabled by the Cisco voice gateway unless you are willing to trade a higher call success rate for image quality.

- You should have a plan for dealing with SG3 fax transmissions. The two most popular methods are using modem passthrough or the IOS feature Fax Relay Support for SG3 Fax Machines at G3 Speeds.

- In situations where it is necessary for a fax hairpin call, you should aim for a TDM hairpin, where the DSP drops out of the call for best results.

- If T.38 fax relay is selected as your fax transport protocol, an NSE-based switchover or a protocol-based switchover for T.38 should be selected and implemented throughout the network. However, in cases where this is not possible, T.38 fallback can provide interoperability assistance between NSE-based T.38, protocol-based T.38, Cisco fax relay, and pass-through.

- T.37 store-and-forward fax is a transport option that uses a fax to/from e-mail conversion process rather than a real-time transport method such as passthrough or relay. In some situations, T.37 may be preferred over fax passthrough or relay.

- For the best T.38 fax relay integration with Unified CM, software Release 6.0(1) or later is recommended.

Modem design considerations were discussed next in this chapter. This section highlighted the modem transport methods of modem passthrough, Cisco modem relay, and secure modem relay. The best practices transporting modem traffic over IP consist of the following:

- Implement Cisco modem relay over modem passthrough if possible because of its improved efficiency and reliability.

- Secure modem relay is the best option for transporting secure communications based on STE endpoints.

The last section of this chapter covered text design considerations and its transport methods of text over G.711 and Cisco text relay. The best practices to take away from this section include the following:

- Implement Cisco text relay whenever possible even though it is a proprietary implementation that works only between select Cisco IOS gateways and select third-party softphones.

- If various text endpoints require a mixture of text over G.711 and Cisco text relay communications, use separate dial peers on the Cisco voice gateway to route calls with the necessary transport method to the appropriate text device.

The best practices and design information presented in this chapter provide you with the knowledge to properly plan for the integration of fax, modem, and text devices into an IP environment. Prudent application of the design principles in this chapter is essential to prevent problems and redesigns down the road.

CHAPTER 8

Fax Servers

Traditionally, fax servers were computers equipped with one or more fax modems connected to the public switched telephone network (PSTN). The function of the fax server was to accept incoming faxes and pass them on to users electronically or to store the fax documents locally. Conversely, the fax server also received documents from users, converted them into faxes, and transmitted them to other fax machines.

Because fax servers provide secure, automated, and efficient handling of fax documents, they have been widely deployed by companies needing dedicated fax solutions. For example, in a retail or manufacturing scenario, fax server functions include transmitting and receiving purchase orders, invoices, and order confirmations.

Certain government regulations such as the Health Insurance Portability and Accountability Act (HIPAA) and the Sarbanes-Oxley Act of 2002 have further heightened the demand and usefulness of fax server solutions. These types of regulations impose tighter controls over certain classifications of fax documents, and fax servers provide the secure, automated delivery and storage required by these regulations.

In today's world of IP communications, fax servers have evolved and now they can integrate into IP networks. Their original functionality of fax document handling has been retained and in many cases expanded to interoperate with other IP networked enterprise applications. In addition, IP-enabled fax servers are no longer tied to dedicated PSTN lines because they can now communicate with multiple voice gateways for PSTN access in different locations.

Fax servers can be integrated directly with Cisco products such as voice gateways and even Cisco Unified Communications Manager (Unified CM) as long as open standards and protocols are used. For example, T.38 fax relay is the standards-based fax relay protocol that is implemented between fax servers and Cisco equipment, while protocols such as H.323 and Session Initiation Protocol (SIP) provide the call control signaling for the call setup and teardown.

This chapter focuses on the design aspects of integrating fax servers with Cisco products. Because of the number of different players in the fax server industry that claim Cisco product compatibility, it is not possible to cover each of their products and solutions. Instead, general information applicable to the majority of fax server integrations is provided.

NOTE	Cisco currently resells a standalone fax server product. Known as the Cisco Fax Server, this product is actually the Captaris RightFax solution. All the information contained in this chapter is applicable to the Cisco Fax Server. More detailed information about the Cisco Fax Server is available at Cisco.com by searching for "Cisco Fax Server."

The three major sections making up this chapter are as follows:

- **Fax Server Basics**: Covers fundamental concepts that are necessary for understanding the function of fax servers and their importance in an IP networked environment.

- **Fax Server Solutions**: Covers the common integrations solutions between Cisco products and fax servers. When appropriate, specific configuration and troubleshooting information applicable to these fax server solutions is also provided.

- **Fax Server Redundancy and Failover**: Covers fault-tolerant solutions and recommendations for your fax server deployment.

Fax Server Basics

Fax servers can be broken down into three basic parts: the server hardware itself, the fax engine, and the application. The fax server hardware is usually selected by the user and not bundled with the fax server software. Vendors of fax server software provide minimum server hardware requirements related to CPU, memory, and hard drive space to ensure satisfactory performance.

The fax engine component of a fax server is one of two types: hardware based or software based. Hardware-based fax servers contain an additional piece of hardware to handle the processing of the fax call or to provide a telephony interface. This piece of hardware is a card inserted into the computer running the fax server software, known as a fax board. Subsequently, you may also see software-based fax servers referred to as "boardless," because they do not require this fax board hardware.

NOTE	Acquisitions and mergers have condensed the fax board marketplace down to one major player, Dialogic. The majority of all fax boards in use or being sold today will more than likely be a brand that is owned by this vendor. Current Dialogic Brooktrout fax boards should interoperate with practically all fax server software products, but it is still recommended that you always confirm fax board compatibility directly with the fax server software provider.

Depending on whether the fax engine is hardware or software based, fax servers can provide different interfaces for the sending and receiving of fax documents. Interfacing into the traditional PSTN world can be accomplished only through the installation of a fax board. Common fax board telephony interfaces include analog or digital connections such as FXO loop start or T1/E1 CAS and PRI circuits. Figure 8-1 shows an example of a hardware-based fax board manufactured by Dialogic.

Figure 8-1   *Dialogic Brooktrout TR1034 Fax Board*

Software-based fax engines that must send and receive fax documents over an IP network require that the fax server have an interface that provides IP network access such as an Ethernet port. With this sort of interface, the fax server can use the T.38 fax relay protocol to communicate with other IP fax devices such as Cisco voice gateways. When multiple Cisco voice gateways are accessible to the fax server through T.38, their telephony interfaces also become accessible to the fax server. This, in turn, can provide the fax server with multiple points from which to access the PSTN for the sending and receiving of faxes.

Certain advantages and disadvantages are associated with hardware- and software-based fax engines. Hardware-based solutions can offload the handling of fax calls from the host processor so that it can handle other CPU-intensive tasks. A hardware-based solution in some cases also allows for an easy migration from a PSTN-connected fax server to an IP-enabled fax server (because the fax board may be capable of both of these functionalities).

A software-based fax engine offers easier installation, less maintenance, and more flexibility compared to a hardware-based solution. Because software-based fax engines are designed for IP-based deployments, they cannot connect directly to the PSTN because this type of interface is found only on a fax board. However, this is not a drawback for integrations into an IP network, and software-based fax engines are usually the recommended choice.

The last component part of a fax server after the server hardware and the fax engine is the application. The fax server application is the piece of software that provides the interface through which the fax server is configured. The application also typically handles the sending and receiving of fax documents from the user perspective.

Regardless of whether a PSTN or an IP network interface is used for sending and receiving faxes, the fax server application typically provides users with several choices for accessing fax documents from a fax server. Figure 8-2 highlights the common methods by which users can access a fax server to send and receive documents.

Figure 8-2   *Fax Server User Access Methods*

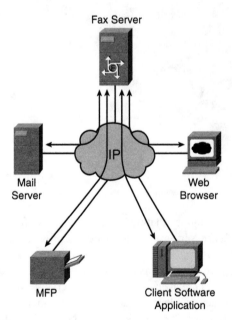

As shown in Figure 8-2, users typically access a fax server through an e-mail client, a Multi Function Printer/Product/Peripheral (MFP), a custom software application, or a web browser. Using an e-mail client enables a user to send faxes in the same manner as sending an e-mail. Receiving fax documents is just as easy with the fax pages presented to the user as an e-mail attachment. Most e-mail systems can be integrated with a fax server solution, but the level of integration and compatibility varies based on the mail server software and the fax server solution used.

Also referred to as a Multi Function Device (MFD), MFPs communicating with fax servers is a growing trend. Many users can use a single MFP for copying, printing, scanning, and faxing. Faxing with an MFP is as simple as using a standard fax machine in most cases, but instead of going directly to the PSTN, the MFP passes the fax to the fax server. In addition to transmitting the fax, this allows the fax server to integrate the fax directly into a document management and archiving system if necessary. Incoming faxes can be routed directly to a specific MFP by the fax server for instant printing, or users can just print faxes on the MFP from their fax mailbox when desired.

Often, the fax server software includes a client load that the fax server users can install. These custom software applications present the user an interface that allows for the sending and receiving of faxes directly from the user's computer. Generally, these custom applications also contain advanced features, such as user-customized cover sheets, and a GUI that is specifically geared toward handling faxes.

With a web browser, users can also communicate with a fax server. The simplicity of a web browser interface that often incorporates the same features as a custom software application make this a popular access method for fax servers. In addition, custom software does not have to be loaded on every computer, which allows for easier maintenance and updating, and fax server access is now computing platform independent. Any computer that has a web browser can access the fax server.

TIP   Most fax servers can also be accessed via an application programming interface (API). This API allows other applications and systems to access the fax server for automated and batch process jobs. Be aware, however, that APIs vary between different brands of fax server software, so it is recommended that you confirm with the fax server software vendor the ability of their API to interoperate with your specific applications and systems.

The fax server concept has expanded in recent years to encompass more than just fax transmissions. The ability to integrate with other enterprise systems has propelled the fax server into a critical business application for many companies. Table 8-1 briefly highlights a few of the more significant fax server capabilities.

Table 8-1 *Key Fax Server Capabilities*

Fax Server Capability	Explanation
E-mail integration	Users can send faxes from their desktop computers and receive fax documents as e-mail attachments. This is more efficient than printing a document and then manually faxing it. Also, individual fax mailboxes can be created that allow each person to have a personal fax number.
Accountability	All fax images that are sent and received can be easily stored electronically using a variety of business storage systems and archiving schemes. This provides an accounting of all fax transactions and prevents the problems of faxes being lost or misplaced at walkup fax machines due to negligence or the fax machine being out of paper or toner.
Archiving	All the fax transactions for a business can be easily archived and even indexed. This is difficult to accomplish with paper fax machines and can consume a large amount of storage space compared to the quick-access and low-storage space requirements that go along with electronic fax documents. Most important, archiving allows compliance with industry mandates such as the Sarbanes-Oxley Act of 2002 and HIPAA.
Workflow integration	If a business has standardized on a process management procedure or specific workflow application, fax servers can assist in automating the workflow. One example is automatically having faxed documents from certain employees forwarded to a supervisor for approval before being transmitted.
Security	Because of the e-mail integration feature, sensitive information does not have the chance of being unintentionally exposed at the office fax machine. Furthermore, incoming sensitive documents can be directly routed to the appropriate person or storage system that offers limited access.
MFP integration	MFPs incorporate multiple functions such as printing, scanning, copying, and faxing into one device. MFP integration with fax servers does not require a dedicated fax line for the MFP, and users can realize all the benefits of a fax server, such as document management and archiving.

To efficiently access the highlighted fax server capabilities in Table 8-1, it is important that fax servers integrate with Cisco IP network infrastructure equipment such as voice gateways and even Unified CM. Fax server integration with Cisco voice products can be accomplished in different ways. The fax server solutions discussed in the next section provide the most common integration options.

Fax Server Integration Solutions

Fax servers may be integrated with Cisco voice gateways and Unified CM in a number of different ways. However, practically all fax server integrations fall under one of the three integration methods or solutions discussed in this section.

The first fax server solution covered is the direct connection model where the fax server communicates directly with the PSTN through a telephony interface, such as a T1 or E1 digital circuit. A Cisco voice gateway is not technically required for this solution, but when one is used, the voice gateway's hairpin call or time-division multiplexing (TDM) cross-connect feature is used. These features allow the Cisco voice gateway to transfer certain TDM channels from a T1 or E1 circuit to a fax server. For all intents and purposes, the fax server has a direct PSTN connection.

The next fax server integration solution that is discussed involves a fax server communicating with a Cisco voice gateway using the T.38 fax relay protocol. This solution allows the fax server to access the benefits of IP networking by having the option to talk to multiple gateways that are connected to the PSTN. This solution also allows for the Cisco voice gateway to be shared with Unified CM for VoIP calls.

The last solution integrates the fax server and Unified CM directly. The fax server no longer talks directly to voice gateways from a call control perspective but instead relies on Unified CM to route the T.38 fax calls between the fax server and the appropriate gateway. This solution provides an additional benefit of allowing the fax server to communicate with other voice gateways that may have been previously inaccessible when communicated with directly because of differences in the voice signaling protocol. For example, fax servers cannot talk directly to voice gateways that are MGCP controlled by Unified CM. However, this is no longer a restriction when the fax server integrates directly with Unified CM and Unified CM handles the setup of the T.38 fax relay call to the MGCP endpoint.

You should realize that not all these integration methods apply to all fax server brands. In addition, even the Cisco voice gateways and Unified CM will most probably need certain levels of software to interoperate with fax servers in some of the deployment solutions that are covered. The prerequisites for each deployment solution are mentioned. You need to ensure that both the fax server software and the Cisco products support the listed prerequisites.

Fax Server TDM Integration with a Cisco Voice Gateway

In the older, traditional fax server deployment model, fax servers were connected directly to PSTN circuits or conventional PBX devices. To maintain this same sort of connectivity in modern VoIP networks, many voice gateways can pass TDM timeslots from a digital PSTN connection to a fax server using either the TDM hairpin call or the "drop-and-insert" feature, as shown in Figure 8-3.

Figure 8-3 *Fax Server TDM Integration with a Cisco Voice Gateway*

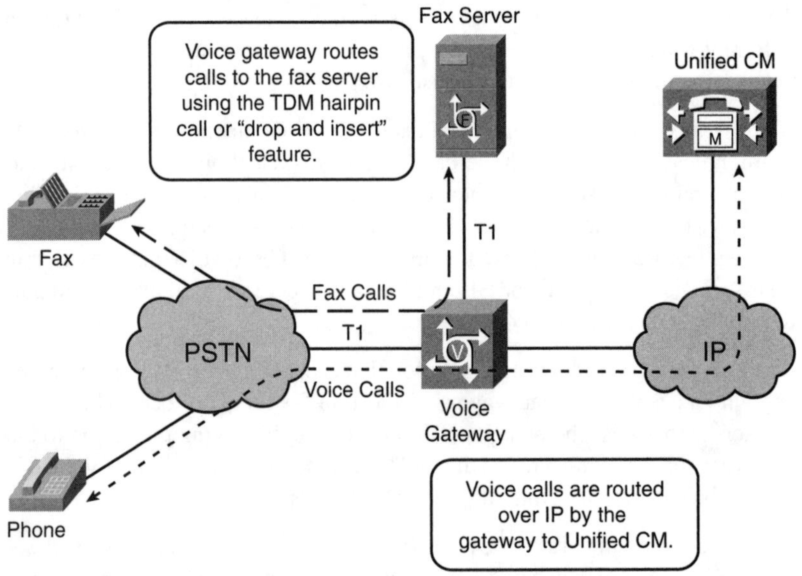

The ability of a Cisco voice gateway to take certain timeslots on a T1/E1 PSTN connection and cross-connect these to another T1/E1 connection to a fax server is known as drop and insert. For example, in Figure 8-3, assume that the T1 coming into the voice gateway from the PSTN has channels 13–24 provisioned as dedicated fax lines with their own Direct Inward Dial (DID) phone numbers. The rest of the PSTN T1 channels are dedicated voice lines that are terminated by the voice gateway and converted to VoIP for integration with Unified CM. Using the drop-and-insert feature a Cisco voice gateway takes the PSTN T1 channels of 13–24 that are dedicated to fax calls and cross-connects them to another T1 that connects directly to the fax server. This cross-connect within the Cisco voice gateway patches T1 timeslots from the fax server to the PSTN and essentially provides a direct PSTN connection for the fax server.

TIP   You can find information about the drop-and-insert feature by just searching at Cisco.com using terms such as "T1 drop and insert." Documents on Cisco voice gateway products that support drop and insert are available, as are configuration examples.

The hairpin call feature was discussed in Chapter 7, "Design Guide for Fax, Modem, and Text," in the section "Hairpin Calls." Assuming that a true TDM hairpin call occurs through the voice gateway, this fax server connection method is functionally equivalent to the drop-and-insert feature. However, the TDM hairpin call connections through the gateway are dynamically allocated when necessary. This allows increased flexibility because unlike the drop-and-insert feature, blocks of channels on the T1 or E1 circuit do not have to be statically allocated for voice and fax calls.

At first glance, the fax server solution diagrammed in Figure 8-3 might seem less optimal compared to directly integrating the fax server directly into the IP network with T.38 fax relay. In most cases, this is probably true; however, there are certain reasons for deploying fax servers in this manner.

Often, a fax server is connected as shown in Figure 8-3 as a temporary measure as a network evolves from a traditional PBX and fax server environment to one that is IP based. The addition of T.38 to some legacy fax servers may require a software upgrade and possibly a hardware upgrade. Before making these changes, connecting the fax server directly to a voice gateway via a T1 or E1 is a practical solution until a migration to T.38 fax relay can be implemented.

Another reason for deploying a fax server as shown in Figure 8-3 is to retain the high speeds of Super G3 faxing. Super G3 fax capability is also known as V.34 faxing and provides a top fax speed of 33.6 Kbps, which is significantly higher than the normal G3 speed of 14.4 Kbps. Even though support of Super G3 over T.38 fax relay has been standardized, Cisco products and some fax server vendors have yet to implement it as of the publication of this book.

Connecting a fax server by cross-connecting TDM timeslots with the drop-and-insert feature on a voice gateway has the following prerequisites:

- Cisco voice gateway supports the drop-and-insert feature using a TDM backplane or the appropriate voice WAN interface card (VWIC), such as the VWIC2-2MFT-T1/E1.

- The channels passed between the PSTN T1 and the fax server T1 must use Channel Associated Signaling (CAS) and not Primary Rate Interface (PRI) signaling.

- Fax server with a fax board supporting T1/E1 circuits and the appropriate software.

Specific prerequisites also exist for implementing the TDM hairpin call feature. As mentioned earlier, this information is provided in the section "Hairpin Calls" in Chapter 7. In most cases, the more flexible method of TDM hairpin calls is the recommended solution for the sort of deployment shown in Figure 8-3, but drop and insert is also a viable alternative.

Troubleshooting the fax server solution in Figure 8-3 hinges mainly around clocking. Ensuring that the TDM clocks are synchronized between the PSTN and the fax server is imperative as the T1 is cross-connected through the voice gateway with both the TDM hairpin call and drop-and-insert solutions. Voice gateways with a TDM backplane have quite a few clocking configurations, so make sure that the voice gateway's clocking scheme results in error-free operation of both T1 circuits. You can find additional information about clocking and physical layer troubleshooting in the section "Telephony Troubleshooting" in Chapter 12, "Troubleshooting Passthrough and Relay. "

Fax Server T.38 Integration with a Cisco Voice Gateway

The current trend with fax server deployments is to use the T.38 fax relay protocol for integrating the fax server directly into IP networks. Two primary integration models are possible when connecting a T.38-enabled fax server with Cisco equipment. The first model involves the fax server communicating directly with Cisco voice gateways, and the other model involves the addition of Unified CM to handle the call control signaling between the fax server and the voice gateways. In this section, integrating a T.38 fax server solution with just Cisco voice gateways is covered. The next section discusses how T.38 fax servers can be connected to Unified CM.

T.38 fax servers can communicate with multiple voice gateways directly. This capability allows a single centralized T.38 fax server to handle the faxing tasks for any location with a voice gateway providing PSTN access. A single fax server can now offer the benefit of economies of scale while providing least-cost routing via the different points of presence offered by each voice gateway. Figure 8-4 shows a fax server solution where T.38 is used for communication with voice gateways in different geographical locations.

Figure 8-4 *Fax Server T.38 Integration with a Cisco Voice Gateway*

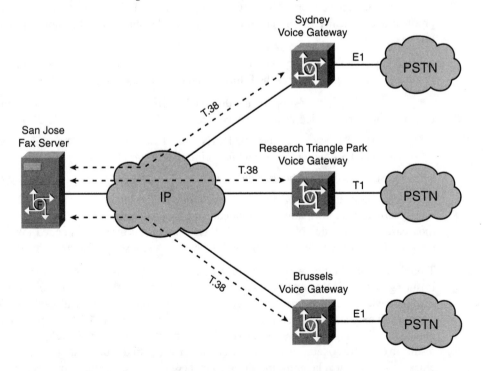

In Figure 8-4, a fax server in San Jose can, with T.38 fax relay, send and receive fax documents in the locations of Sydney, Research Triangle Park, and Brussels. As long as a voice gateway in a certain location has IP connectivity to a fax server, a T.38 fax server can handle the faxing requirements for that location.

In many cases, Unified CM is added to the topology in Figure 8-4. The voice gateway is then configured to send fax calls to the fax server and then VoIP calls to Unified CM. In this instance, a single PSTN connection can be shared between the fax server and Unified CM. Based on the incoming DID number, the voice gateway can discriminate between voice and fax calls and route the incoming calls accordingly. Figure 8-5 demonstrates the concept of a fax server and Unified CM both using the same voice gateway independently of one another.

Figure 8-5   *Voice Gateway Integrated Jointly with a Fax Server and Unified CM*

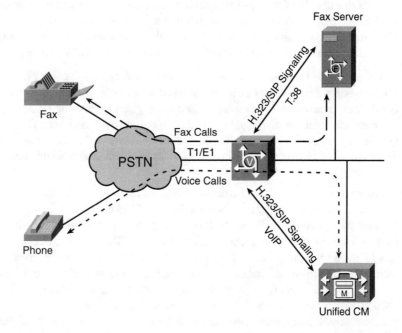

Even though Unified CM is involved from a voice gateway perspective in Figure 8-5, this type of solution still has the fax server directly communicating to a voice gateway. Conceptually, the deployment model in Figure 8-5 is exactly the same as Figure 8-4 from the fax server perspective. Neither the fax server nor Unified CM is aware of one another. The fax server never interacts directly with Unified CM.

If a voice gateway is Media Gateway Control Protocol (MGCP) controlled, adding fax server support requires the addition of another PSTN interface. Unlike the H.323 and SIP voice signaling protocols, which can share a PSTN interface between the fax server and Unified CM as shown in Figure 8-5, ports allocated to Unified CM via MGCP are dedicated resources. Therefore, if a voice gateway has a PSTN T1 connection that is MGCP controlled by Unified CM, another T1 interface will have to be provided for the fax server to access via H.323 or SIP.

As depicted in Figure 8-5, communication between a fax server and a Cisco voice gateway via T.38 fax relay must use the H.323 or SIP call control protocol. This choice of whether to use H.323 or SIP is somewhat of an arbitrary selection because Cisco voice gateways fully support both and so do most fax servers. If an existing H.323 or SIP infrastructure is already present or you are more comfortable with one protocol versus the other, this might make the selection process a bit easier.

Regardless of whether the SIP or H.323 protocol is chosen, the Cisco voice gateway always requires that the T.38 fax relay call start out as a standard VoIP call using a voice codec. Typically, the G.711 codec is used during this stage of the fax call setup between the fax server and the Cisco voice gateway. Although the Cisco voice gateway can support a wide array of voice codecs, fax servers typically support only the G.711 voice codec.

The fax server or the Cisco voice gateway can each signal a switchover to T.38 fax relay from the negotiated voice codec at any point after the initial VoIP call has been established. For the best interoperability between Cisco voice gateways and the fax servers, it is recommended that the terminating T.38 device initiate the switchover. Obviously, the terminating fax device can be either the fax server or the Cisco voice gateway depending on the direction of the call. Cisco voice gateways by default exhibit this behavior.

TIP   Cisco voice gateways can handle the switchover to T.38 fax relay in two different manners: by using the call control protocol itself or through the use of Named Signaling Event (NSE) packets. Because of the proprietary nature of Cisco NSE packets, Cisco voice gateways should always be configured to use a protocol-based T.38 switchover when interoperating with fax servers. You can find more information about how both protocol-based and NSE-based T.38 switchovers work in the sections "Protocol-Based Switchover for T.38" and "NSE-Based Switchover for T.38" in Chapter 5, "Relay." For Cisco voice gateway configuration assistance with protocol-based T.38 fax relay, see the section "IOS Gateway Fax Relay Configuration for H.323, SIP, and SCCP" in Chapter 10, "Configuring Relay."

The requirements for integrating a T.38 fax server with a Cisco voice gateway include the following:

- A Cisco IOS gateway with a voice port that is connected to the PSTN. Typically, this voice port is a digital connection such as a T1 or E1.
- A recent Cisco IOS version (12.3 or later) loaded on the voice gateway that supports H.323 and SIP.
- A fax server that offers T.38 support over the H.323 or SIP call control protocol.

In some respects, the requirements listed are generic because of the numerous fax server vendors and Cisco IOS voice gateways available. This leads to a large combination of potential integration possibilities, but the adherence of both the fax server and the Cisco voice gateway to the T.38 specification should mitigate any interoperability problems.

The configuration necessary for a Cisco voice gateway to interoperate with a fax server using T.38 fax relay is pretty basic in most cases. Although some caveats might apply for certain fax server vendors, implementing the following dial-peer configurations for H.323 and SIP should ensure a successful T.38 communication between the voice gateway and the fax server. Only the VoIP dial-peers configurations are shown in the following examples because the rest of the gateway configuration is what you use for a standard VoIP call. The VoIP dial-peer is where the main commands affecting fax server interoperability are configured.

Cisco voice gateways support H.323 Version 4 (starting in IOS Release 12.3(11)T) and the 1998 version of the ITU-T Recommendation T.38 using UDP transport layer (UDPTL) encapsulation. The T.38 configuration for a Cisco voice gateway is usually applied directly to the VoIP dial-peer. Example 8-1 highlights a Cisco voice gateway configuration for interoperating with a T.38 fax server using the H.323 signaling protocol.

Example 8-1 *H.323 IOS Dial-Peer Configuration for Communicating with a T.38 Fax Server*

```
!
dial-peer voice 6 voip
 incoming called-number .
 !
 ! Inbound fax calls to the voice gateway should match a T.38 enabled dial-peer. This
 ! can be accomplished by specifying a digit pattern or a "." that will match all
   calls
 !
 destination-pattern 14..
 codec g711ulaw
 !
 ! Most fax servers support only the G.711 voice codec
 !
 session target ipv4:1.1.1.1
 fax protocol t38 ls-redundancy 0 hs-redundancy 0 fallback none
 !
 ! Enable protocol-based T.38 for this dial-peer
 !
```

In Example 8-1, the H.323 VoIP dial-peer is configured for a typical G.711 voice call with the addition of the **fax protocol t38** command. This command in Example 8-1 enables protocol-based T.38 for the dial-peer. You can tell that protocol-based T.38 is being enabled because of the absence of the **nse** keyword in the command line.

The **fax protocol t38** command in Example 8-1 also specifies low-speed and high-speed redundancy values of 0. Check with your fax server vendor to confirm support and interoperability at higher settings.

In the past, the **fallback** setting in the **fax protocol t38** command line has not been applicable to fax server integrations and it was typically set to **none**, as shown in Example 8-1. Be aware, however, that recently some fax servers have started supporting a fallback to G.711 if the T.38 call fails. Therefore, it is recommended to check with your fax server vendor concerning the support of T.38 fallback to the G.711 codec. If your fax server supports this feature, a **fallback** setting of **pass-through** should be used on the Cisco voice gateway. In the event of a T.38 negotiation failure, an alternative transport method is now available to handle the fax call.

Configuring protocol-based T.38 for an SIP dial-peer is identical to the H.323 configuration in Example 8-1 with the exception of the addition of the command **session protocol sipv2**. By default, all VoIP dial-peers use the H.323 signaling protocol, and the **session protocol sipv2** is necessary to change the dial-peer signaling protocol to SIP.

TIP   Be aware that the **fax protocol t38** command used in Example 8-1 can also be configured globally under **voice service voip** rather than under the VoIP dial-peer. For more information about **voice service voip**, see the section "IOS Gateway Passthrough Configuration" in Chapter 9, "Configuring Passthrough."

Although issues such as misconfigurations, packet loss, jitter, and slips on digital circuits are problems that can affect fax server and voice gateway solutions, another common problem is T.38 fax relay interoperability. Because different vendors can interpret the T.38 specification differently, interoperability problems may arise between T.38 fax relay devices.

Troubleshooting for T.38 fax relay is covered in Chapter 12 of this book. You can use the **show** and **debug** commands covered in that chapter on the Cisco voice gateway to help narrow down any issues. However, if T.38 interoperability problems are encountered, the most helpful troubleshooting aid is a packet capture. Using packet captures to troubleshoot T.38 fax relay is covered in the sections "IP Troubleshooting Using Packet Captures" and "Analyzing T.38 Fax Relay Packet Captures" in Chapter 12.

Fax Server T.38 Integration with Unified CM

The main disadvantage to sharing voice gateway resources between a fax server and Unified CM as discussed in the previous section is that separate fax and VoIP networks are being used. Although this is the easiest and quickest way to integrate a fax server into a

Unified CM network, it is not always the most efficient from a management perspective. For example, separate dial plans must be maintained for the fax server network and the VoIP network. Although this sort of deployment model might be desired in some cases, a full integration directly with Unified CM is the best solution in most circumstances.

When a fax server is integrated directly with Unified CM, the setup of both inbound and outbound fax calls is handled by Unified CM. Therefore, the dial or route plan maintained by Unified CM is now responsible for routing T.38 fax relay calls involving the fax server and the voice gateways. Only upon the switchover and initiation of a T.38 fax relay media stream does Unified CM disengage, leaving the fax server and the voice gateway in direct communication with one another. Figure 8-6 graphically demonstrates a fax server integration with Unified CM involving the H.323 and SIP voice signaling protocols.

Figure 8-6   *Fax Server T.38 Integration with Unified CM*

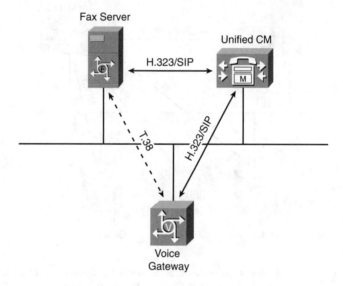

The fax server in Figure 8-6 integrates with Unified CM using either H.323 or SIP as the signaling protocol. The Cisco voice gateway in the figure also communicates with Unified CM using the H.323 or SIP call control protocols, too. Unified CM support for T.38 fax relay using the H.323 call control protocol starts in Version 4.1(1), and both H.323 and SIP support starts in Version 5.0(1).

Until Unified CM Release 5.0(1), the connection between the fax server and Unified CM had to use H.323 signaling, and the voice gateways would also typically use H.323 signaling. However, Release 5.0(1) introduced SIP support for T.38 fax relay. This allowed for a fax server to be connected to Unified CM by the SIP or H.323 signaling protocols, and the same for the gateways.

In Figure 8-6, note that the signaling protocol of the fax server and the voice gateway does not have to match. For example, the fax server could be connected to Unified CM running Version 5.0(1) using H.323, and the voice gateway could be connected using SIP. T.38 fax calls would still work in this scenario because Unified CM would translate the signaling between the fax server and the voice gateway during call setup.

Taking Figure 8-6 a step further, Unified CM offers T.38 fax relay support for the H.323, SIP, and MGCP signaling protocols starting in Release 6.0(1). With this release of software for Unified CM, the fax server can talk to H.323, SIP, and MGCP voice gateways, as shown in Figure 8-7.

Figure 8-7   *Fax Server T.38 Integration with Unified CM Using Multiple Call Control Protocols*

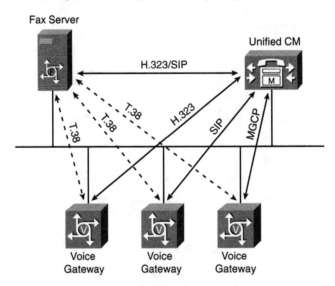

If MGCP voice gateways are present, a fax server integration with Unified CM Release 6.0(1) is practically a necessity. As shown in Figure 8-7, the fax server communicates with Unified CM using the H.323 or SIP signaling protocol. However, because Unified CM can handle the signaling translation between a fax server using the H.323 or SIP protocols and a voice gateway using the MGCP protocol, T.38 fax relay works between these two devices when each implements a different signaling protocol.

TIP   If you need only T.38 fax relay support for the H.323 and MGCP signaling protocols and not SIP, Unified CM Release 4.2(3) is a viable alternative to Release 6.0(1). For more information about the T.38 fax relay support among different Unified CM releases, see Table 7-13 in Chapter 7.

To implement a fax server as part of a Unified CM integration solution, the most important item to pay attention to is that the Cisco products and fax server software are running the correct software loads. The following prerequisites will help you better understand the hardware and software needed:

- Unified CM must be running a software version that supports T.38 fax relay for the signaling protocol used to communicate with the fax server and the voice gateways. For example, if the fax server will communicate with Unified CM via H.323 and the voice gateways are all MGCP, Unified CM Releases 4.2(3) and 6.0(1) will work. As mentioned previously, see Table 7-13 in Chapter 7 for more information about T.38 fax relay support in Unified CM.

- Cisco voice gateways must support T.38 fax relay. Make sure that an appropriate IOS image supporting T.38 fax relay and the necessary call control protocols is installed. Any version of IOS that is 12.3, 12.4, or later should work fine for the support of T.38 fax relay within the H.323 and SIP signaling protocols. For T.38 support using the MGCP protocol, 12.4(9)T1 or later is recommended for the IOS version.

- The fax server needs to be capable of handling T.38 over the H.323 or SIP signaling protocols. In addition, Unified CM is not always as flexible in its support of certain H.323 or SIP features as the Cisco voice gateways. Therefore, even if a fax server offers support for H.323 and SIP and interoperates with Cisco voice gateways, it does not necessarily mean that it will integrate with Unified CM. The best recommendation is to confirm with the fax server vendor whether interoperability with Unified CM has been tested and whether it is supported.

After these requirements have been met, configuring the Cisco products for a fax server integration with Unified CM is relatively straightforward. For the Cisco voice gateways, the required H.323 and SIP configuration commands have already been covered in the previous section. The configuration in Example 8-1 is valid for the voice gateways when they communicate directly with the fax server for the call setup or when they communicate with Unified CM. You just need to make sure that the session target IP address points to Unified CM when it is involved; otherwise, you should use the IP address of the fax server when Unified CM is not present.

For the voice gateways that are connected to Unified CM via the MGCP signaling protocol, ensure that the voice gateway is configured for protocol-based T.38. Note that protocol-based T.38 for MGCP is also known as call agent (CA)-controlled T.38. This type of configuration requires the MGCP commands **mgcp default-package fxr-package** and **mgcp package-capability fxr-package**. For the application of these commands and more information about properly configuring MGCP CA-controlled T.38 fax relay, see the section "IOS Gateway Fax Relay Configuration for MGCP" in Chapter 10.

TIP	When adding the commands **mgcp default-package fxr-package** and **mgcp package-capability fxr-package** to an existing configuration, you need to restart the MGCP process on the voice gateway before these commands take effect. This is typically accomplished by issuing the command **no mgcp** and then **mgcp** while in configuration mode.

When configuring Unified CM to connect to a fax server, no special configuration settings are necessary. For a T.38 fax server connected with the H.323 signaling protocol, you just add the fax server as an H.323 gateway to Unified CM. For a SIP-connected fax server, a standard SIP trunk is configured on Unified CM that points to the fax server. For more specific configuration steps on adding an H.323 gateway or a SIP trunk to Unified CM, refer to the Administration Guide for the Unified CM release that is being used.

Troubleshooting a fax server integration solution with Unified CM is more complex than a solution where the fax server communicates directly with the voice gateway. Not only can there be issues with the T.38 communication between the fax server and the voice gateway, there can also be problems with the H.323, SIP, and MGCP signaling protocols between Unified CM and the fax server and Unified CM and the voice gateways.

If there are H.323, SIP, or MGCP protocol issues, the T.38 fax call will typically never get set up. Therefore, if this scenario occurs, do not use any T.38 troubleshooting methods until after you have looked at the signaling protocols.

Most of the signaling protocol issues that are seen involve communication between the fax server and Unified CM. Because Unified CM and the voice gateways are both Cisco products, a high degree of interoperability exists from internal testing.

As mentioned previously, Unified CM does not offer the flexibility found on the Cisco IOS voice gateways when it comes to support of the H.323 and SIP call control protocols. This in turn has led to interoperability issues with fax servers in the past.

For example, when it comes to H.323 negotiations, Unified CM may require a media termination point (MTP) with H.323 fast start, and the H.245 tunneling feature is not supported. These settings might conflict with the H.323 stacks of certain fax servers, and such conflicts cause T.38 fax relay calls using the H.323 signaling protocol to fail between the fax server and Unified CM.

For the SIP signaling protocol, be aware that Unified CM uses deferred media in its SIP INVITE messages. Consequently, the SDP information related to the RTP media stream is not included in the SIP INVITE message, and this has caused issues with the SIP implementations of some fax server vendors.

If the fax server and Unified CM cannot communicate because of H.323 or SIP interoperability issues (such as the ones just mentioned), it is recommended to consult with Cisco and the fax server software vendor for additional diagnostic assistance. Often, these sorts of interoperability problems are known issues, and patches are available. Otherwise, the recommendation is for the fax server to bypass Unified CM and use H.323 or SIP to communicate with the voice gateway directly.

If the fax call is getting set up correctly but call failure occurs at some point during the T.38 session between the fax server and the voice gateway, you can troubleshoot this problem as you would a typical T.38 problem. As mentioned in the previous section, most of the problems that occur between a fax server and a voice gateway result from misconfigurations, IP network problems, errors on a digital telephony interface, or a T.38 interoperability problem. See Chapter 12 for additional information about troubleshooting T.38 fax relay.

Fax Server Redundancy and Failover

To provide a truly fault-tolerant fax server solution, multiple fax servers can be deployed in a redundant manner. This then allows network elements such as voice gateways, Unified CM, or even gatekeepers to fail over to a backup fax server when the primary fax server is no longer available. With a fault-tolerant solution, a fax server going down or losing connectivity to the IP network does not result in a total loss of an organization's fax processing ability.

Providing redundancy and failover for a fax server solution can be accomplished using one of the following methods:

- Dial-peers on a Cisco voice gateway
- Unified CM route group
- H.323 gatekeeper

Each of these methods provides a means for the Cisco gateway, Unified CM, or gatekeeper to reroute a fax call to an alternate fax server if a failover scenario occurs.

When dealing with a deployment model in which the fax servers communicate directly with Cisco voice gateways and Unified CM is not involved (as in Figure 8-4), a voice gateway's dial-peers offer a compelling solution for failover scenarios. When multiple dial-peers are configured for the same digit pattern, the voice gateway can hunt among these dial-peers until an available fax server is found.

A number of different conditions can trigger the voice gateway to hunt among its dial-peers for an alternate fax server. One condition is if a setup message to the primary fax server times out. The other conditions that can trigger the Cisco voice gateway to fail over to an alternate fax server typically involve the receiving of a disconnect cause code from the fax server, such as user busy.

If a more proactive failover solution is desired on the Cisco voice gateway, use the dial-peer-level command **monitor probe icmp-ping** command. As part of the IOS call fallback feature, this command configures the voice gateway to repeatedly send Internet Control

Message Protocol (ICMP) ping packets to the primary fax server to confirm its availability. If the pings start failing, this dial-peer is taken out of service automatically by the voice gateway, and alternate dial-peers can be instructed to route the fax call to a backup fax server. When the pings start succeeding again to the primary fax server, the gateway automatically does a "failback" by bringing this dial-peer back in service so that fax calls resume to the primary fax server.

In environments where the fax server communicates with Unified CM for the call control signaling instead of a Cisco voice gateway (as shown in Figure 8-6), Unified CM handles the failover scenario when a primary fax server becomes unreachable. This is typically accomplished by adding two or more fax servers to a route group within Unified CM. Within this fax server route group, you can then specify a distribution algorithm that specifies how Unified CM routes calls to the route group members when a failover occurs.

The "top-down" distribution algorithm option within a route group of fax servers is usually chosen for failover scenarios. With the top-down option, the first or "top" fax server is the primary, and Unified CM always routes calls to this primary fax server as long as it is available. If the primary fax server becomes unavailable, Unified CM tries the next fax server on the list.

Unfortunately, Unified CM does not have a proactive probing mechanism such as ICMP pings (which voice gateways have) to determine ahead of time the status of the primary fax server. Therefore, Unified CM always tries the "top" or primary fax server first for each call and hunts for alternate fax servers only upon call setup timeouts or certain disconnect cause codes.

The last option for handling redundant fax servers in failover scenarios involves the use of an H.323 gatekeeper. An H.323 gatekeeper offers lots of flexibility and options while always knowing the availability of each fax server through a registration procedure and an ongoing keepalive mechanism. In addition, an H.323 gatekeeper can work with both gateway and Unified CM deployments, as shown in Figures 8-4 and 8-6.

The most common method of handling fax server failover with a Cisco gatekeeper is to use the **zone prefix** command to assign priorities between two or more fax servers. The zone prefix with the highest priority points to the primary fax server. If the primary fax server becomes unregistered, the zone prefix with the next highest priority routes the call to an alternate fax server.

An important caveat to be aware of is that the fax server must register as a "gateway" with the gatekeeper and not as a terminal endpoint. H.323 terminal endpoints register a specific number, and they do not work with zone prefixes. Confirm that your fax server software is capable of registering the fax server as a gateway before trying to implement a fault-tolerant solution using a Cisco gatekeeper.

Summary

Fax servers have always been an option for businesses looking at a fax solution. However, the traditional fax server has evolved in much the same way as legacy TDM voice systems using key systems and PBXs have transitioned to VoIP solutions. The fax server evolution capitalizes on the T.38 fax relay protocol, which allows a direct integration of fax servers into IP networks.

This chapter introduced the fax server concept, and then looked at how common fax server solutions can be applied to Cisco products, such as voice gateways and Unified CM. The first section of the chapter covered some basic information about fax servers and provided a base of knowledge to better understand the fax server solutions that are covered in the next section. In addition, this section highlighted some of the capabilities that fax servers provide.

The next section of this chapter looked at some common fax server integration solutions. One solution that was discussed was a TDM fax server connection to the PSTN via a hairpin call or digital cross-connect in the Cisco voice gateway. Another solution explored how a fax server can integrate with Cisco voice gateways using T.38 fax relay. The last solution talked about how fax servers can integrate directly with Cisco Unified CM. Within each of these solutions, information about the implementation requirements, configuration assistance, and troubleshooting tips was also provided.

Although each of the fax server solutions discussed in this chapter has its own advantages and disadvantages, the solution where the fax server is integrated with Unified CM is the most comprehensive. This option is the only one that folds the fax server into the overall VoIP solution, providing centralized dial plan management for voice and fax and the best access to the VoIP network for the fax server.

The last section in this chapter discussed the different methods for ensuring a fault-tolerant fax server deployment. Various redundancy and failover options were discussed involving voice gateways, Unified CM, and Cisco gatekeepers. Each of these devices can communicate with multiple fax servers, a capability that enables them to handle failover situations with minimal impact on an organization's fax server traffic.

Configuration

CHAPTER 9

Configuring Passthrough

A passthrough call is handled in much the same manner as a regular VoIP call from a voice gateway perspective. There are a few events and minor changes that a Cisco voice gateway undergoes in preparation for a passthrough call.

The terminating gateway always uses tone detection to go into passthrough mode. After that, the terminating Cisco voice gateway can use three ways to signal the switchover to passthrough to the originating gateway. These methods are as follows:

- Named Telephony Events (NTE) messages in the Real-Time Protocol (RTP) stream
- Named Signaling Events (NSE) messages in the RTP stream
- Messages within the configured voice signaling protocol

The first method is the old legacy method implemented only by non-IOS gateways that run older versions of software. This method is deprecated, and you will rarely ever see it. The only reason this is still in existence on non-IOS gateways is for reasons of backward compatibility.

The second and third methods are the newer and most commonly implemented ones. NSE-based passthrough is supported on all Cisco voice gateways. Protocol-based pass-through is only supported on IOS gateways. The technical implementations of both of these methods are discussed in detail in Chapter 4, "Passthrough."

This chapter begins with a complete look at the passthrough configuration for fax, modem, and text on IOS gateways. This serves as an in-depth configuration guide for both the NSE and protocol-based passthrough methods implemented in IOS. In addition, this chapter covers the fax and modem passthrough configuration on non-IOS gateways such as the 6608, VG248, and the Analog Telephone Adaptor (ATA).

You should be aware that reading this chapter and the other configuration chapters in this section of the book is not necessary for understanding the troubleshooting chapters that follow. You might find that these configuration chapters are more useful as a reference that is simply turned to for understanding a particular command or completing a configuration task.

IOS Gateway Passthrough Configuration

Passthrough configurations for fax, modem, and text are available on IOS gateways. This section covers the necessary commands and configuration steps to properly implement each of them.

NOTE	The commands covered in this section are based on what is available in Cisco IOS Software Release 12.4(9)T1. Although some commands might have a different syntax or be unavailable in other IOS versions, the majority of the commands are applicable to any IOS version. In addition, be aware that the default settings for commands can change across different IOS releases. Default settings for the commands listed in this chapter might not necessarily be the default settings for the same command in an earlier or later IOS release.

One notion of IOS passthrough configuration that is applicable to both the NSE and protocol-based configurations is the concept of global configuration versus dial-peer configuration. A passthrough configuration can be applied system-wide under the **voice service voip** global configuration mode. Alternatively, a passthrough configuration can be applied on a per-call basis under the dial-peer configuration mode.

Hierarchically, the dial-peer configuration always takes precedence over the global configuration. For example, if both global and dial-peer passthrough configurations exist, the dial-peer configuration is used by the gateway for the call that matched the specific dial-peer.

The global passthrough configuration is used if the dial-peer passthrough configuration specifies for it to be used. This is done through the use of the **system** keyword on the end of the dial-peer passthrough configuration command. The default dial-peer passthrough configuration is to use the global configuration (that is, **modem passthrough system** for Session Initiation Protocol [SIP] and H.323 NSE-based passthrough and **fax protocol system** for protocol-based pass-through).

For example, if the command **modem passthrough system** is configured under the dial-peer, that instructs the gateway to use the modem passthrough configuration found under the global **voice service voip** configuration for the call that matched that dial-peer. Therefore, if no passthrough configuration exists on a dial-peer (default behavior), it will use the global passthrough configuration under **voice service voip**.

TIP   It could be a painstaking task to individually add fax/modem passthrough functionality to the dial-peers of an existing voice gateway used exclusively for voice, especially if that gateway has a complicated dial plan with lots of dial-peers. You can avoid this by configuring all the dial-peers at once by placing the passthrough configuration under **voice service voip** configuration mode. Just be aware that this will apply this passthrough configuration to all dial-peers and hence all calls unless it is explicitly overwritten at the dial-peer level.

NOTE   This configuration hierarchy used for passthrough is also the same for relay. You will see the same rules apply to the global **voice service voip** configuration in Chapter 10, "Configuring Relay."

As previously mentioned, passthrough can be negotiated in the RTP stream through the use of NSEs or it can be done through protocol messages of the call control signaling protocol (for example, H.323 or SIP). IOS gateways support both types. The configuration for each of these passthrough methods is completely different. This section presents the configuration commands for both passthrough varieties and discusses how they are implemented.

IOS Gateway NSE-Based Passthrough Configuration

The IOS configuration commands for NSE-based passthrough are identical for H.323, SIP, and Skinny Client Control Protocol (SCCP). Regardless of which of these voice signaling protocols are used, the configuration syntax will be pretty much the same. For this reason, they are discussed together.

The commands for configuring NSE-based passthrough for Media Gateway Control Protocol (MGCP) are totally distinctive. Both the syntax of the commands and the way they are implemented are completely different. Therefore, they are discussed in a separate section.

IOS Gateway NSE-Based Passthrough Configuration for H.323, SIP, and SCCP

For H.323, SIP, and SCCP, only a single configuration command is used to enable both fax and modem NSE-based passthrough. This configuration command is **modem passthrough nse**. Table 9-1 shows the syntax of the command and summarizes the various arguments of this command and the function of each of one.

Table 9-1   *modem passthrough IOS Configuration Command*

Command	Argument	Function
modem passthrough {**system** | **nse** [**payload-type** *number*] **codec** *codec-type* [**redundancy**] [**maximum-sessions** *number*]}	**system**	Specifies that the passthrough configuration found globally under the **voice service voip** configuration mode is to be used. **Note:** This command option is only found in dial-peer configuration mode where it is the default setting. It is not valid on SCCP voice gateways.
	payload-type	Indicates the RTP payload type value to signal a passthrough call. Acceptable payload type values are 98 to 117. **Note:** This command argument is optional. If no payload type is explicitly specified, the default value of 100 will be used.
	codec	Specifies the codec that the gateway will upspeed to for the fax/modem call. The only allowed codecs are either G.711 µ-law or G.711 a-law. **Note:** The default is g711 µ-law.
	redundancy	Enables RFC 2198 compliant packet redundancy to protect against packet loss. **Note:** When this feature is enabled, it does only a single repetition of RTP packets. By default, redundancy is disabled.
	maximum-sessions	Defines the maximum number of simultaneous passthrough calls for the gateway. **Note:** This argument is found only under the global **voice service voip** configuration mode.

One caveat of using the SCCP signaling protocol on IOS voice gateways is that all fax and modem configurations must take place globally under **voice service voip**. Therefore, the **system** option for the **modem passthrough** command described in Table 9-1 is not applicable to SCCP voice gateways.

TIP

Be aware that enabling the packet redundancy feature while it is unconfigured or unsupported on the opposing gateway might cause passthrough calls to fail.

A terminating gateway with the **modem passthrough** command configured can handle both modem and fax passthrough calls. The stimuli tones that the terminating gateway (TGW) detects determine whether the gateway switches to fax passthrough or modem passthrough mode. Also, it determines which NSEs are sent to the originating gateway (OGW).

For example, in the case of a high-speed modem call, a 2100 Hz tone with phase reversals is detected by the TGW. This forces the TGW into modem passthrough mode. It also causes the TGW to send both NSE-192 and NSE-193 messages to the OGW to signal a switch over to passthrough mode and to disable echo cancellers. For more information on NSE-based passthrough and how it works, see the section "NSE-Based Passthrough" in Chapter 4.

TIP

Because all Cisco gateways support NSE-based passthrough, it is always safe to use this configuration when interfacing directly with another Cisco gateway. This cannot be used with third-party devices because NSEs are Cisco proprietary signaling messages.

As discussed in the section "Super G3" of Chapter 7, "Design Guide for Fax, Modem, and Text," it is a common design practice to use modem passthrough in conjunction with a relay configuration. For example, if T.38 or Cisco fax relay is enabled, either of these relay protocols will take precedence over the modem passthrough configuration and handle all fax calls. However, if a high-speed modem call or Super G3 fax call comes in, it will be handled by modem passthrough.

The reason this operates transparently is that modem passthrough keys in on the 2100 Hz stimuli tones for switchover and NSE transmission, whereas fax relay protocols key in on fax flags for activation. A sample configuration pairing NSE-based modem passthrough along with Cisco fax relay is shown in the section "Cisco Fax Relay and Modem Passthrough Configuration for H.323 and SIP" in Chapter 10.

IOS Gateway NSE-Based Passthrough Configuration for MGCP

NSE-based passthrough configuration for MGCP uses completely different commands than SIP and H.323. For MGCP, there is no dial-peer configuration. It is entirely done in global configuration mode.

Table 9-2 covers the available commands for an MGCP NSE-based passthrough configuration. These commands support both fax and modem passthrough. The same configuration should be on both the TGW and OGW.

Table 9-2   *Passthrough IOS Configuration Commands for MGCP*

Command	Argument	Function
mgcp package-capability rtp-package		Enables the availability of the MGCP package for RTP on the voice gateway.
mgcp modem passthrough voip [mode nse] [codec *{g711ulaw | g711alaw}]* [redundancy]	**mode nse**	Uses RTP NSEs to signal the switchover to passthrough mode between voice gateways.
	codec	Specifies the codec that the gateway will upspeed to for the fax/modem call. The only allowed codecs are either G.711 μ-law or G.711 a-law. **Note:** The default is g711ulaw.
	redundancy	Enables RFC 2198 compliant packet redundancy to protect against packet loss. **Note:** When this feature is enabled it does only a single repetition of RTP packets. By default, redundancy is disabled.
mgcp timer nse-response t38 *time*		Sets the timeout period for awaiting an NSE response from the remote gateway. The valid range is 100 to 3000 ms. **Note:** The default is 200 ms.
mgcp fax t38 inhibit		Disables T.38 on the voice gateway. **Note:** T.38 is enabled by default and takes precedence over modem passthrough for the transport of all G3 fax calls unless it is disabled.

Of all the commands detailed in Table 9-2, the most important command is **mgcp modem passthrough voip**. This command manipulates the specific parameters related to NSE-based modem passthrough while the other commands are optional or are correctly set by default.

Unlike most other features supported within MGCP, this command for NSE-based passthrough does not require the call agent to support NSEs. The NSE negotiation occurs in the media stream so the passthrough feature is transparent to the call agent.

IOS Gateway Protocol-Based Pass-Through Configuration

Protocol-based pass-through uses the actual messaging of the signaling protocol to signal a switchover from voice mode to pass-through mode. H.323 and SIP are the only voice signaling protocols that support protocol-based pass-through. MGCP used to support protocol-based pass-through in older versions of IOS, but it is no longer supported in more current versions.

NOTE	The support for pass-through using the MGCP protocol stack was dropped because of protocol conflicts and reliability concerns. To implement passthrough with the MGCP protocol, NSE-based passthrough must be configured using the **mgcp modem passthrough voip** command. This command and its attributes are discussed in more detail in the preceding section, "IOS Gateway NSE-Based Passthrough Configuration for MGCP."

As discussed in the section "Protocol-Based Pass-Through for Fax" in Chapter 4, there is a different naming convention for protocol-based and NSE-based voice-band data (VBD). The "pass-through" terminology used for protocol-based pass-through stems from the configuration command syntax used on IOS gateways. Protocol-based pass-through uses the **fax protocol pass-through** syntax, as opposed to NSE-based passthrough, which uses the **modem passthrough nse** syntax.

TIP	Although it is possible to configure both **modem passthrough nse** (NSE-based passthrough) and **fax protocol pass-through** (protocol-based pass-through) for a particular call on a Cisco IOS gateway, this is not a recommended configuration. If both of these are configured, fax pass-through always takes precedence and renders modem passthrough inoperable.

The command-line interface (CLI) options to configure protocol-based pass-through are covered in Table 9-3. Some of the options for the **fax protocol** command deal with relay, and these relay options are covered in detail in Table 10-4 of Chapter 10.

Table 9-3 *fax protocol IOS Configuration Command*

Command	Argument	Function
**fax protocol {cisco	none	pass-through {g711alaw	g711ulaw}	system	t38 [fallback {cisco	none	passthrough {g711alaw	g711ulaw}}	ls-redundancy** *value* **[hs-redundancy** *value*] **| nse [force]] }**	**cisco**	Specifies Cisco fax relay as the fax relay protocol. **Note:** See Table 10-4 in Chapter 10 for additional information on this option.
	none	Turns off fax relay and pass-through.
	pass-through	Enables faxing over either G.711 μ-law or G.711 a-law codecs using the H.323 or SIP protocol stacks to signal the switchover to passthrough mode.
	system	Tells the dial-peer to use the global **fax protocol** setting configured under **voice service voip**. **Note:** This argument is available only within the dial-peer configuration and it is the default setting.
	t38	Sets T.38 as the fax relay protocol. **Note:** See Table 10-4 and 10-5 in Chapter 10 for additional information on this argument and its options.

There is no protocol-based pass-through for modem communications. Only fax calls can use protocol signaling messages to force a switchover to pass-through mode. The reason for this is because NSE-based passthrough uses tone detection of a 2100 Hz tone to trigger a switchover to passthrough mode, whereas protocol-based pass-through can only be triggered by the detection of fax flags.

Because NSE-based passthrough signaling is a Cisco proprietary signaling method, it cannot be used with third-party voice gateways. The main reason for the existence of protocol-based pass-through signaling is for interoperability with non-Cisco gateways. For a more detailed discussion of how protocol-based pass-through signaling works, see the section "Protocol-Based Pass-Through for Fax" in Chapter 4.

IOS Gateway Text over G.711 Configuration

Before the release of the Cisco text relay feature, the only way to transport text over an IP network was over a traditional G.711 voice session. This "passthrough-like" transport method of carrying text packets over a high bit rate codec is referred to as text over G.711.

Note that text over G.711 is much more rudimentary than the other passthrough methods that were previously discussed. There is no tone detection, no NSE messaging, and no codec upspeeding that takes place. However, text over G.711 should work well for all text telephone protocols, including the Baudot protocol that was discussed in the section "Baudot Protocol" of Chapter 3, "How Text Telephony Works."

The configuration for text over G.711 is simply that of a G.711 voice call. The gateway has no way of distinguishing that the call is a text call, so it is not possible to have an upspeed of the codec as seen with a passthrough scenario. Therefore, for G.711 to be used for the entire call duration, it must be manually set on the dial-peer.

One key difference from a default G.711 voice call is that VAD should be disabled for text over G.711. The reason for this is to avoid clipping the text tones when VAD engages and disengages as the VAD threshold is crossed.

Example 9-1 shows a standard text over G.711 configuration for an IOS gateway. PSTN text endpoints will consequently transmit and receive text over the G.711 voice call that is placed.

Example 9-1   *Text over G.711 Sample Configuration for IOS Gateways*

```
!
dial-peer voice 100 voip
 incoming called-number .
 destination-pattern 3923266
 session target ipv4:1.1.1.1
 codec g711ulaw
 no vad
!
```

6608 Catalyst Blade Passthrough Configuration

The 6608 is a line card for the Catalyst 6*xxx* series chassis that functions as a voice gateway. It has eight digital ports that can be used as a Primary Rate Interface (PRI; T1 and E1) or channel-associated signaling (CAS; T1 only). These digital ports are all MGCP controlled by Unified Communications Manager (CM), because that is the only signaling protocol the 6608 supports.

TIP   An interesting point to note is that each port on the 6608 is viewed as a separate gateway by Unified CM. Therefore, as this section discusses the fax configuration for the 6608, bear in mind that it applies on a per-port basis because each individual port functions independently as its own standalone gateway.

The Catalyst has another voice blade, known as the 6624. It is a 24-port analog FXS gateway. Although configurations for the 6624 are not specifically covered in this section, the fax configuration for the 6624 is exactly like the 6608. The only difference is that all 24 ports are treated as a single gateway by Unified CM.

The 6608 supports NSE-based fax and modem passthrough. However, before tackling a fax/modem passthrough configuration, first ensure that the individual port you are configuring is properly registered with Unified CM. Second, make certain that the T1/E1 is up and that a normal voice call can successfully be placed. Then, you should proceed to configuring fax and modem passthrough.

On the 6608, the fax passthrough configuration is as simple as disabling fax relay. The default fax configuration for the 6608 is Cisco fax Relay. Therefore, to do fax passthrough, ensure that the Fax Relay Enable box in the Fax and Modem Parameters section of Unified CM's gateway configuration screen is not checked. This configuration, shown in Figure 9-1, allows the 6608 to use NSE-based passthrough for the handling of all fax calls.

Figure 9-1   *Fax Passthrough Configuration for a 6608 Gateway*

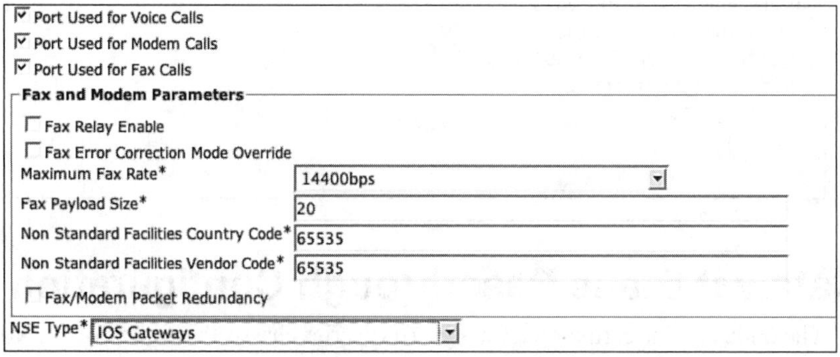

TIP   Much older versions of Unified CM had much fewer fax parameters to configure. Anything later than Version 3.2.2c SP-D should look approximately like the configuration screen seen in the figure used in this section, which is from a Unified CM running Version 5.0(4).

The configuration of modem passthrough on the 6608 is even easier than the fax passthrough configuration. Because NSE-based passthrough on the 6608 is enabled by default, no additional configuration is needed. However, to disable modem passthrough the box for Port Used for Modem Calls must be unchecked.

The only other configuration parameters that are important for fax and modem passthrough in the Fax and Modem Parameters section of the gateway configuration screen are NSE Type and Fax/Modem Packet Redundancy. The remaining other parameters in this section are used for fax relay configurations and are discussed in the next chapter. Table 9-4 summarizes all the pertinent configuration parameters for NSE-based fax and modem passthrough on the 6608.

Table 9-4   *Passthrough Configuration Parameters for the 6608*

Configuration Parameter	Options	Function
Fax Relay Enable	Enable/Disable	If box is not checked the 6608 uses NSE-based fax passthrough rather than Cisco fax relay. **Note**: Fax relay enabled is the default.
NSE Type	Non-IOS Gateways	Sets the 6608 to use the older legacy passthrough mode that uses NTE-based signaling. This would be the proper configuration only if connecting to another older non-IOS device. **Note**: This is the default signaling.
	IOS Gateways	Sets the 6608 to use the newer IOS method of NSE-based signaling for the passthrough switchover. In most scenarios, an IOS gateway or a recent non-IOS gateway is used as the remote, so the NSE-based configuration is needed. The 6608 supports both signaling types to maintain backward compatibility with older non-IOS devices.
Fax/Modem Packet Redundancy	Enable/Disable	If box is checked, it enables RFC 2198 packet redundancy. This option should typically not be needed for properly designed networks. It should be needed only for networks that have packet loss. Before enabling this feature, confirm that the peer gateway supports this feature, too; otherwise, calls might fail.

NOTE   When they were first released, non-IOS gateways (such as the 6608 and VG248) only supported NTE-based signaling for fax and modem passthrough. However, to be compatible with
IOS gateways that only implemented NSEs for the passthrough switchover, these non-IOS
gateways added support for NSEs. Today, all IOS and non-IOS gateways support NSEs, and
this is what all gateways should be configured for. In the event that communication with an
older, non-IOS gateway lacking NSE support is still necessary, legacy NTE settings are still
available on the non-IOS gateways for backward compatibility.

A complete passthrough configuration is defined by the parameters laid out in Table 9-4.
Based on those parameters, the configuration shown in Figure 9-1 has NSE-based
passthrough enabled for both faxes and modems and uses no packet redundancy. This
is considered the standard fax and modem passthrough configuration for a 6608.

VG248 Passthrough Configuration

The VG248 is a 48-port analog gateway that is controlled by Unified CM through the SCCP
signaling protocol. It is commonly used to provide analog lines to fax machines and
modems.

The VG248 is different from most other Cisco voice gateways. The hardware and software
architecture, supported features, and the user interface are unlike other platforms in the
Cisco family of gateways. For example, the VG248 configuration is accomplished through
an ASCII-like menu interface.

The VG248 supports modem and fax passthrough just like the 6608. All the modem and fax
passthrough parameters are configured using only two different menu configuration screens.
One sets the global passthrough parameters, the other sets the specific port parameters.

Starting from the main menu and making the following menu selections accesses the port
specific configuration screen:

`Configure > Telephony > Port Specific Parameters`

This leads you to the Port Selection screen. From this screen, select the specific port you
want to configure.

Similar to the 6608, the configuration on the VG248 for fax passthrough involves disabling
fax relay. This forces NSE-based fax passthrough to be used for all fax calls. Figure 9-2
illustrates configuring port 1 of a VG248 for fax passthrough by setting the Fax Relay
parameter to disabled.

Figure 9-2   *VG248 Port Specific Fax Relay Parameter Configuration*

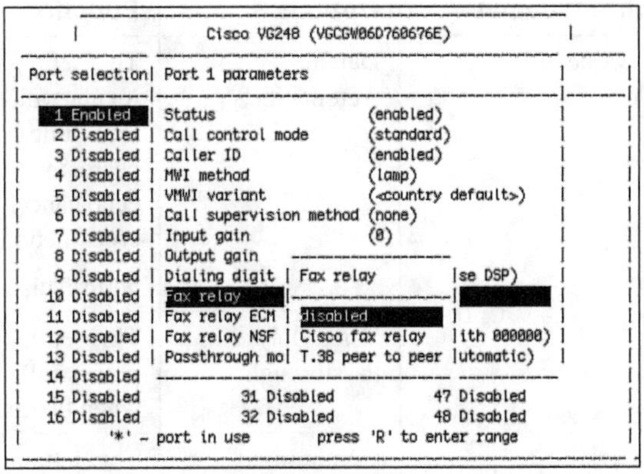

```
 ---------------------------------------------------------------
|              |            Cisco VG248 (VGCGW06D760676E)       |        |
|--------------|-------------------------------------------------|--------|
| Port selection| Port 1 parameters                             |        |
|--------------|                                                 |--------|
|  1 Enabled   | Status                    (enabled)            |        |
|  2 Disabled  | Call control mode         (standard)           |        |
|  3 Disabled  | Caller ID                 (enabled)            |        |
|  4 Disabled  | MWI method                (lamp)               |        |
|  5 Disabled  | VMWI variant              (<country default>)  |        |
|  6 Disabled  | Call supervision method  (none)               |        |
|  7 Disabled  | Input gain                (0)                  |        |
|  8 Disabled  | Output gain      -------------------           |        |
|  9 Disabled  | Dialing digit | Fax relay        |se DSP)      |        |
| 10 Disabled  | Fax relay     |-----------------|              |        |
| 11 Disabled  | Fax relay ECM | disabled        |              |        |
| 12 Disabled  | Fax relay NSF | Cisco fax relay  |ith 000000)   |        |
| 13 Disabled  | Passthrough mo| T.38 peer to peer |utomatic)     |        |
| 14 Disabled  |               -------------------              |        |
| 15 Disabled        31 Disabled            47 Disabled          |        |
| 16 Disabled        32 Disabled            48 Disabled          |        |
|       '*' - port in use        press 'R' to enter range        |        |
 ---------------------------------------------------------------
```

The only other port specific parameter pertinent for both a fax and modem passthrough configuration on the VG248 is passthrough mode. This parameter sets how the VG248 will behave when fax/modem tones are detected. Passthrough mode has four different options to specify which NSEs are used based on how it interprets the various stimuli tones. These options are discussed in more detail as part of Table 9-5.

The other port specific fax configuration parameters, such as Fax Relay ECM and Fax Relay NSF, are used only for a fax relay configuration. Consequently, they are discussed in the next chapter. Table 9-5 summarizes the function of all the pertinent port-specific passthrough configuration parameters and their options for the VG248.

Table 9-5   *VG248 Port-Specific Passthrough Configuration Parameters*

Configuration Parameter	Options	Function
Fax Relay	Disabled	If this option is selected, it forces the VG248 to use NSE-based fax passthrough.
	Cisco Fax Relay	Enables Cisco fax relay on the VG248. **Note:** This is the default setting, and it is discussed in the next chapter.
	T.38 Peer to Peer	Enables NSE-based T.38 fax relay on the VG248. **Note:** Discussed in the next chapter.

continues

Table 9-5   *VG248 Port-Specific Passthrough Configuration Parameters (Continued)*

Configuration Parameter	Options	Function
Passthrough Mode	Default: Automatic	This setting processes the call as a regular voice call if modem/fax tones are not heard. However, if tones are heard, the VG248 uses the appropriate echo canceller setting based on the type of stimuli tone. **Note**: This is the default setting.
	Voice Only: No Passthrough	This setting forces the VG248 to process all calls as voice calls even when fax/modem tones are detected.
	Passthrough Only: ECAN Disabled	This setting forces the VG248 to disable the echo cancellers (ECANs) anytime a 2100 Hz tone is detected. Most of the time, a 2100 Hz tone with phase reversals must be seen before ECANS are disabled. However, this setting forces the VG248 to always disable the ECANs when fax/modem tones are detected and the DSP enters passthrough mode.
Passthrough Mode *(Continued)*	Passthrough Only: ECAN Enabled	This setting forces the VG248 to always enable the ECANs whenever fax/modem tones are detected and the digital signal processor (DSP) enters passthrough mode. This means that the ECANs are enabled even if a 2100 Hz tone with phase reversals is detected.

Modem passthrough is enabled by default on the VG248. All the passthrough parameters discussed in this section are applicable to modem passthrough except for the disabling of fax relay to force fax passthrough. Regardless of the fax relay setting, modem passthrough will still function.

For both fax passthrough and modem passthrough to engage appropriately based on the detected stimuli tones, the passthrough mode should be set to automatic. Figure 9-3 shows port 1 of a VG248 being configured with this setting.

Figure 9-3   *VG248 Port Specific Passthrough Mode Parameter Configuration*

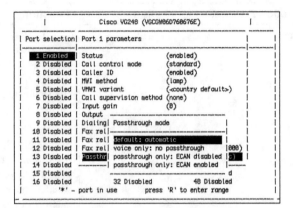

```
|            |          Cisco VG248 (VGCGW06D760676E)          |        |
|------------|-------------------------------------------------|--------|
| Port selection| Port 1 parameters                           |        |
|------------|-------------------------------------------------|--------|
|  1 Enabled |  Status                  (enabled)              |        |
|  2 Disabled | Call control mode       (standard)             |        |
|  3 Disabled | Caller ID               (enabled)              |        |
|  4 Disabled | MWI method              (lamp)                 |        |
|  5 Disabled | VMWI variant            (<country default>)    |        |
|  6 Disabled | Call supervision method (none)                 |        |
|  7 Disabled | Input gain              (0)                    |        |
|  8 Disabled | Output ----------------------------------------|        |
|  9 Disabled | Dialing| Passthrough mode              |        |        |
| 10 Disabled | Fax rel|-------------------------------|        |        |
| 11 Disabled | Fax rel| default: automatic           |        |        |
| 12 Disabled | Fax rel| voice only: no passthrough    |000)    |        |
| 13 Disabled | Passthr| passthrough only: ECAN disabled|5)     |        |
| 14 Disabled | -------| passthrough only: ECAN enabled |------ |        |
| 15 Disabled |                     ---------------------------- d       |
| 16 Disabled |         32 Disabled           48 Disabled      |        |
|        '*' - port in use        press 'R' to enter range     |        |
```

Setting the global passthrough parameters finishes the remainder of the passthrough configuration. Starting from the main menu and making the following menu selections accesses this global telephony configuration parameters screen:

```
Configure > Telephony > Advanced Settings
```

This Advance Settings screen has two configuration parameters of interest for a passthrough configuration. One is the Passthrough Signaling and the other is the Passthrough Codec. The other fax configuration parameter on this screen is Fax Relay Payload Size, but it is used only for fax relay, so it is discussed in the next chapter. Table 9-6 summarizes these pertinent global fax/modem passthrough configuration parameters.

The passthrough codec can be set to either G.711 μ-law or G.711 a-law. The default configuration setting for this parameter is G.711 μ-law. Figure 9-4 shows a VG248 configured to use a passthrough codec of G.711 μ-law.

The Passthrough Signaling parameter sets the passthrough signaling type used for fax/modem calls. The choices are Legacy and IOS Mode. Legacy mode uses the older NTE-based signaling. This setting is there to allow for backward compatibility with non-IOS gateways running older versions of software.

Table 9-6 *VG248 Global Passthrough Configuration Parameters*

Configuration Parameter	Options	Function
Passthrough Signaling	Legacy	Sets the VG248 to use the older legacy passthrough mode that uses NTE-based signaling. This would be the proper configuration only if connecting to another older non-IOS device.
	IOS Mode	Sets the VG248 to use the IOS method of NSE-based signaling for passthrough. This setting should almost always be used, regardless of whether the remote device is an IOS gateway or a non-IOS gateway. The VG248 supports both signaling types to handle those rare situations where backward compatibility needs to be maintained with older non-IOS devices.
Passthrough Codec	G.711 μ-law	Sets G.711 μ-law as the codec to be used for fax/modem passthrough calls. **Note:** This is the default setting.
	G.711 a-law	Sets G.711 a-law as the codec to be used for fax/modem passthrough calls.

Figure 9-4 *VG248 Global Passthrough Codec Parameter Configuration*

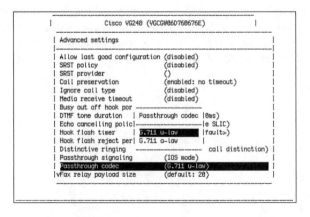

IOS mode forces the use of NSE signaling packets that are compatible with newer non-IOS software releases and all IOS devices. This is the setting that you should always use unless you are interfacing with a non-IOS gateway running an older version of software. Figure 9-5 shows a VG248 configured with IOS mode as its passthrough signaling method.

Figure 9-5   *VG248 Global Passthrough Signaling Parameter Configuration*

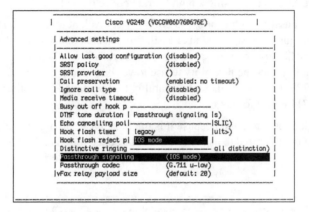

ATA Passthrough Configuration

The Cisco ATA (Analog Telephone Adaptor) only offers passthrough as a fax transport solution. Neither of the two ATA models have support for fax relay. There are no current or future plans to add such functionality. Although the ATA does not officially support modems when it is in passthrough mode, many customers have had success with modem calls over an ATA.

NOTE   The two currently available ATA models are the ATA 186 and the ATA 188. They are the same except for the fact that the ATA 186 has a single 10BASE-T Ethernet port, and the ATA 188 has two 10/100BASE-T Ethernet ports. Everything discussed in this section applies equally to both the ATA 186 and the ATA 188.

Within the scope of the passthrough configuration, the ATA can operate within two configuration modes: fax passthrough mode and fax mode.

These two modes of operation can be summarized as follows:

- **Fax mode**: Functionally equivalent to that of an IOS gateway statically configured to place or receive only G.711 voice calls. This mode is much like the text over G.711 configuration discussed earlier. In this mode, no codec switchover or upspeeding is done. The principal drawback of this configuration is that it limits all calls on the interface to only using a high bit rate codec (G.711).

- **Fax passthrough mode**: Functionally equivalent to that of an IOS gateway configured for standard fax passthrough. This includes tone detection and NSE signaling for codec upspeeding. Therefore, this configuration mode has the advantage that it allows the flexibility to use lower bandwidth codecs (for example, G.723 and G.729) for voice calls with the ability to dynamically negotiate the higher-bandwidth G.711 codec for fax calls.

Fax mode is covered first because it is the most basic. In this mode, the telephony (FXS) interface is configured to use only the G.711 codec for all calls. Also, in fax mode the ATA disables fax tone detection and VAD on the particular interface.

NOTE   Four different software images are available for the Cisco ATA based on the voice signaling protocol supported. Images for SCCP, SIP, MGCP and H.323 are available with each protocol load containing different features and functionality. The various configuration parameters and bits may vary from load to load.

The specific parameter used to set each port for fax mode is the AudioMode parameter. This parameter is a 32-bit value, where the lower 16 bits apply to the first line, and the upper 16 bits apply to the second line. These two ports can be configured independently. Table 9-7 defines the bits that make up the AudioMode parameter.

As discussed, the essential features that make up fax mode are that VAD is disabled, fax tone detection is disabled, and no low bit rate codecs are used. In addition, we'll negotiate out-of-band DTMF transmission and disable sending out-of-band hookflash (for H.323 only). Thus, based on Table 9-7, the correct value of the AudioMode parameter for G.711 fax mode configured on port 1 of on ATA would look like this (X = don't care): 0xXXXX0012. Figure 9-6 shows an actual Cisco ATA 188 running an SCCP load (Version 3.2(3)) that has ports 1 and 2 configured for fax mode.

Table 9-7   *ATA AudioMode Parameter Bit Definitions*

Bit Number	Definition
0 and 16	0/1: Disable/enable silence suppression for all audio codecs. Silence suppression is enabled by default. **Note**: These bits are obsolete for SCCP loads as of ATA Release 3.0
1 and 17	0: Enable selected low bit rate codec in addition to G.711. This setting is the default. 1: Enable G.711 only.
2 and 18	0/1: Disable/enable fax CED tone detection. This feature is enabled by default.
3 and 19	Reserved.
4–5 and 20–21	Dual-tone multi-frequency (DTMF) transmission method: •0: Always in-band •1: By negotiation •2: Always out-of-band •3: Reserved **Note**: These are unused/reserved bits for SCCP load.
6–7 and 22–23	Hookflash transmission method: •0: Disable sending OOB hookflash message •1: By negotiation (H.245 message). •2: Always out-of-band (H.245 message). •3: Use Q931 message to send user keypad information for DTMF or hookflash transmission **Note**: These are unused/reserved bits for SIP, MGCP, and SCCP loads.
8–15 and 23–31	Reserved.

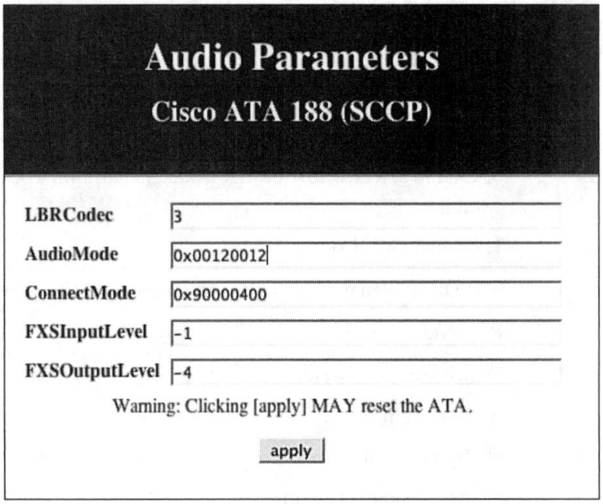

Figure 9-6 *Fax Mode Configuration for an ATA*

Audio Parameters

Cisco ATA 188 (SCCP)

LBRCodec	3
AudioMode	0x00120012
ConnectMode	0x90000400
FXSInputLevel	-1
FXSOutputLevel	-4

Warning: Clicking [apply] MAY reset the ATA.

apply

Typically, the fax mode configuration would be used only in an environment where the remote gateway does not support NSE-based passthrough. Consequently, the fax mode configuration is seen when the remote voice gateway is from a third-party vendor. Most Cisco voice gateways support NSE-based passthrough in recent versions of code. Therefore, if interfacing with a Cisco gateway, there would normally be no need for a fax mode configuration on the ATA.

TIP   In some scenarios, you must configure the ATA for fax mode even when interfacing with a Cisco voice gateway. An example of such a situation is if you are sending text from text telephony endpoint connected to the Cisco ATA. If you have a case like this, ensure that you disable both relay and passthrough on the remote Cisco gateway.

The second configuration available on the ATA is the fax passthrough mode. In this mode, the ATA can configure a port to use fax tone detection and NSE signaling in the RTP stream to trigger codec upspeed from a low bit rate codec to G.711. This operates the same way as NSE-based passthrough on other Cisco voice gateways.

NOTE   The Cisco ATA can only accept protocol-based signaling codec switch requests. It cannot send such requests. Therefore, to interoperate effectively with an ATA, other Cisco voice gateways should use an NSE-based passthrough configuration.

The fax passthrough mode configuration is a bit more complicated than the fax mode configuration that was just discussed. In addition to setting the AudioMode parameter, you must set the ConnectMode parameter.

In the fax passthrough mode configuration, the AudioMode parameter should have called terminal identification (CED) tone detection and VAD enabled and the ability to use a specified low bit rate codec for voice. Therefore, based on Table 9-7, the correct value of the AudioMode parameter for fax passthrough mode configured on port 2 of on ATA would look like this (X = don't care): 0x0015XXXX.

The ConnectMode parameter is another 32-bit value that must be set for fax passthrough mode. This parameter globally configures both ports simultaneously and affects many different things in the ATA configuration. This discussion is only concerned with the configuration settings that pertain only to fax passthrough (that is, bit 2 and bits 7 through 15). Table 9-8 defines these bits in the ConnectMode parameter.

Table 9-8   *ATA ConnectMode Parameter Bit Definitions*

Bit Number	Definition
2	0: Use the dynamic payload type 126/127 as the RTP payload type (fax passthrough mode) for G.711 μ-law/G.711 a-law. These legacy payload types were used in the past as a passthrough switchover mechanism before the transition to NSE-based switchovers.
	1: Use the standard payload type 0/8 as the RTP payload type (fax passthrough mode) for G.711 μ-law/G.711 a-law. These are the standards-based payload types used currently for NSE-based passthrough switchovers.
	Default: 0
7	0/1: Disable/enable fax passthrough redundancy.
	Default: 0
8–12	Specifies the fax passthrough NSE payload type. The value is the offset to the NSE payload base number of 96. The valid range is 0 through 23; the default is 4.
	For example, if the offset is 4, the NSE payload type is 100.
13	0: Use G.711 μ-law for fax passthrough codec.
	1: Use G.711 a-law for fax passthrough codec.
	Default: 0
14–15	0: Use fax passthrough.
	1: Use codec negotiation in sending fax.
	2: Reserved.
	3: Reserved.
	Default: 0

Figure 9-7 shows an example of a Cisco ATA 188 running an SCCP load (Version 3.2(3)) that has ports 1 and 2 configured for fax passthrough mode. The ConnectMode parameter in this example has a value of 0x90000400 in hexadecimal format. This corresponds to a binary format of 1001 0000 0000 0000 **0000 0100 0**000 0000. The bolded bits in this ConnectMode parameter are the important fax configuration bits defined in the preceding table.

Table 9-8 illustrates that the ConnectMode parameter in Figure 9-7 has fax configuration settings that indicate that fax passthrough is enabled, redundancy is disabled, payload type 100 is being used for NSEs, payload types 126/127 are being used for G.711 μ-law/G.711 a-law, and G.711 μ-law is the codec that will be used to transport faxes in-band. Also, using Table 9-7 it can be determined from the AudioMode parameter in Figure 9-7 that on ports 1 and 2 VAD is enabled, CED tone detection is enabled, and low bit rate codecs can be used for voice.

Figure 9-7   *Fax Passthrough Mode Configuration for an ATA*

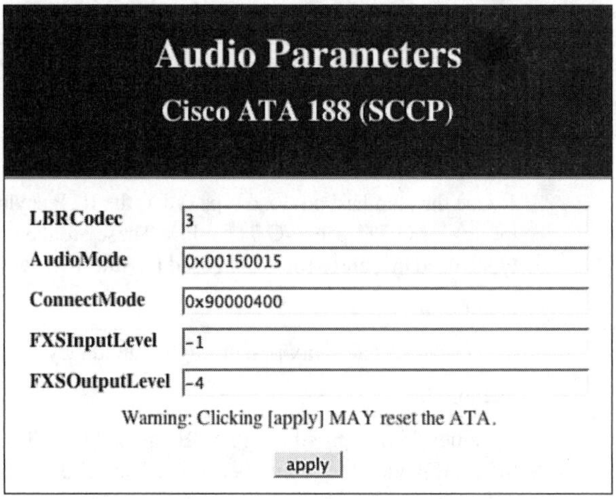

The fax passthrough mode on an ATA is the more frequently seen configuration of the two possible fax configurations. This is because so many ATAs interface with other Cisco voice gateways that also support NSE-based passthrough. This interoperability allows for minimal changes to the default ATA configuration.

Summary

Passthrough transparently transports fax, modem, and text modulated data directly over a G.711 codec across the IP network. NSE-based passthrough and protocol-based pass-through are the two primary forms of signaling a switchover to VBD mode. All Cisco voice gateways support NSE-based passthrough, whereas only IOS gateways configured for the H.323 or SIP call control protocols support protocol-based pass-through.

IOS gateways support the Cisco proprietary NSE-based passthrough signaling method for H.323, SIP, MGCP and SCCP protocols. NSE-based passthrough is configured identically for H.323, SIP, and SCCP using the **modem passthrough nse** command. The MGCP NSE-based passthrough configuration has its own command syntax, and its main configuration command is **mgcp modem passthrough voip.** Both fax and modem calls are supported by NSE-based passthrough because the switchover is triggered by the shared stimuli tone of 2100 Hz.

Protocol-based pass-through uses messages within the voice signaling protocol to signal a switchover to VBD mode. This method is used primarily to interoperate with non-Cisco voice gateways. Protocol-based pass-through is only supported for H.323 and SIP protocols and is configured with the **fax protocol pass-through** command. In addition, protocol-based pass-through can be used only for fax calls because it is triggered by detection of the V.21 fax preamble.

IOS gateways also support text over G.711. This is a basic configuration that configures the gateway for static G.711 voice calls. The reason for this basic configuration is that the gateway has no way of distinguishing a text call from a voice call, so no switchover signaling or codec upspeeding occurs.

The 6608 is a digital T1/E1 non-IOS gateway that supports passthrough for both fax and modem calls. Its passthrough configuration is done entirely from Unified CM gateway configuration screen. Older versions of code on the 6608 supported NTE signaled passthrough. More recent versions support NSE-based passthrough but maintain NTE support only for backward compatibility.

The VG248 is an analog non-IOS gateway that is configured through a menu CLI. The passthrough configuration is accomplished by setting both port-specific and global configuration parameters. The VG248 has the same NTE support as the 6608 and for the same reasons. NSE-based passthrough for both modem and fax calls is supported.

The ATA gateway is a non-IOS gateway that supports two passthrough modes of operation. The first passthrough mode is fax mode, which essentially configures the ATA only for static G.711 calls. This mode does not support NSE signaling nor codec upspeeding from high-compression voice codecs. The second passthrough mode is fax passthrough mode, which is the standard NSE-based passthrough with codec upspeeding. This mode operates like the NSE-based passthrough seen on IOS gateways.

The passthrough configuration on the ATA is very different from other voice gateways because it requires you to set the values of two different parameters based on certain bit value definitions. The ATA only officially supports fax calls.

CHAPTER 10

Configuring Relay

The configuration of modem, fax, and text relay is more involved than the passthrough configurations discussed in Chapter 9, "Configuring Passthrough." More configuration options and additional parameters can be modified. In the case of Cisco IOS gateways, this in turn leads to a larger number of command-line interface (CLI) commands to manage.

The relay configuration options for the voice signaling protocols of H.323, Session Initiation Protocol (SIP), Skinny Client Control Protocol (SCCP), and Media Gateway Control Protocol (MGCP) are discussed in this chapter. With few exceptions, H.323, SIP, and SCCP share the same command set, whereas MGCP uses a different command syntax. For this reason, MGCP configuration commands are discussed in separate sections.

This chapter first looks at how to configure fax, modem, and text relay on Cisco IOS gateways. Then, specific non-IOS voice gateways such as the 6608 and VG248 are discussed.

Just like the preceding chapter, this chapter may be most practical as a simple reference resource for commands and configuration tasks. In fact, having a specific configuration objective in mind increases the usefulness of this chapter. For example, if the objective is to configure T.38 fax relay for H.323 on an IOS gateway, this configuration information is easily found in the fax relay part of the "IOS Gateway Configuration" section. Chapter 7, "Design Guide for Fax, Modem, and Text," is the best resource for deciding on a configuration objective.

IOS Gateway Relay Configuration

The majority of Cisco voice gateways today use Cisco IOS Software. All of these IOS gateways share similar commands and configuration steps across a variety of different hardware platforms.

NOTE   The commands covered in this section are based on what is available in Cisco IOS Software Release 12.4(9)T1. Although some commands might have a different syntax or be unavailable in other IOS versions, the majority of the commands are applicable to any IOS version. In addition, be aware that the default settings for commands can change across different IOS releases. Default settings for the commands listed in this chapter might not necessarily be the default settings for the same command in an earlier or later IOS release.

The IOS configuration commands discussed in the first part of this chapter are grouped into three subsections: fax relay, modem relay, and text relay. Within each of these subsections, all the applicable commands along with relevant configuration tips are covered in detail.

Fax Relay

The configuration of fax relay on Cisco IOS gateways can be a little confusing at times. The main point of confusion is that practically all Cisco IOS gateways support two different types of fax relay that are incompatible with one another: Cisco fax relay and T.38 fax relay. In addition, many of the IOS fax relay commands are applicable to both fax relay types, whereas a couple may be specific to only one or the other.

To clarify the process of configuring fax relay on Cisco IOS gateways, the following, simplified steps can be used:

Step 1   Choose and configure a voice signaling protocol. H.323, SIP, MGCP, and SCCP are the most common voice signaling protocol options, and basic VoIP calls should work using one of these signaling protocols before configuring fax relay. Installed VoIP networks usually standardize on at least one voice signaling protocol, which can make the selection much easier. For networks with multiple voice signaling protocols or for those who are interested in comparisons of the different voice signaling protocols from a fax perspective, see the section "Call Control Protocol" in Chapter 7.

Step 2   Choose and configure Cisco fax relay or T.38 fax relay. Cisco fax relay is the default (except for platforms such as the 5350, 5400, and 5850 when they are using the NextPort digital signal processor [DSP] architecture). So, in many cases, additional configuration commands are not necessary. See the section "Default Fax Relay Configuration for H.323 and SIP" later in this chapter for an example of this sort of scenario. The notable exception to Cisco fax relay being the default occurs with MGCP. When MGCP is the voice signaling protocol, T.38 fax relay is the default.

Step 3   Configure any additional fax relay attributes. For example, with the
H.323 and SIP voice signaling protocols, the maximum fax speed can be
set using the **fax rate** command, or ECM (Error Correction Mode) can
be disabled with the command **fax-relay ecm disable**.

IOS Gateway Fax Relay Configuration for H.323, SIP, and SCCP

The IOS command set for fax relay with H.323, SIP, and SCCP is relatively the same.
Identical CLI command syntaxes can be used with each of these voice signaling protocols
to achieve the same configuration results.

The H.323 and SIP protocols take this same command set a step further, and the whole fax
relay configuration itself, from the command placement in the configuration to supported
relay features, is identical. In fact, it is even possible to switch between the H.323 and SIP
signaling protocols without altering the fax relay configuration.

The SCCP signaling protocol, on the other hand, has a few caveats and feature limitations that
prevent identical configurations to SIP and H.323, even though the same command syntax is
supported. These limitations and caveats for SCCP are discussed later in this section.

As for H.323 and SIP, all the fax relay commands are configured per call under the voice
dial-peers or globally under **voice service voip**. More information on understanding **voice
service voip** and its hierarchical relationship with voice dial-peers can be found in the
section "IOS Gateway Passthrough Configuration" in the preceding chapter.

In addition to H.323 and SIP sharing the same fax relay command set, the Cisco fax relay
and T.38 fax relay protocols themselves share the same commands. Unfortunately, this can
cause some confusion when configuring fax relay. In an effort to make fax relay configurations a bit clearer, Table 10-1 details the commands applicable for T.38 and Cisco fax relay
when H.323 and SIP are the voice signaling protocol.

Table 10-1   *Fax Relay Quick Reference Configuration Guide for H.323 and SIP*

Configuration Commands	Cisco Fax Relay	T.38 Fax Relay
Enable command	**fax protocol cisco** (Enabled by default)	**fax protocol t38**
Disable command	**fax rate disable** **fax protocol none** (*dial-peer*) **fax protocol none** (*voice service voip*)	**no fax protocol t38** **fax rate disable** **fax protocol none** (*dial-peer*) **fax protocol none** (*voice service voip*)

continues

Table 10-1   *Fax Relay Quick Reference Configuration Guide for H.323 and SIP (Continued)*

Configuration Commands	Cisco Fax Relay	T.38 Fax Relay
Additional commands	**fax rate**	**fax rate**
	fax nsf	**fax nsf**
	fax-relay ecm disable	**fax-relay ecm disable**
	fax-relay sg3-to-g3 (*dial-peer*)	**fax-relay sg3-to-g3** (*dial-peer*)
	fax-relay sg3-to-g3 (*voice service voip*)	**fax-relay sg3-to-g3** (*voice service voip*)

Table 10-1 shows columns for both Cisco fax relay and T.38 fax relay. If T.38 fax relay is the chosen configuration option, the commands for enabling, disabling, and configuring T.38 fax relay properties are shown in the T.38 fax relay column.

In the Cisco fax relay column, the appropriate configuration commands are also shown. As mentioned previously, notice that the additional commands are the same for both Cisco fax relay and T.38 fax relay. These commands pertain to whichever fax relay type is currently configured on the IOS voice gateway.

TIP   On the Cisco 5350, 5400, and 5850 series of voice gateways using the original NextPort DSP architecture, only T.38 fax relay is supported. However, with the newer AS5X-FC cards, both T.38 and Cisco fax relay are supported on these platforms.

The SCCP voice signaling protocol currently possesses a major fax relay feature limitation that H.323 and SIP does not. As shown earlier in Table 7-4 of Chapter 7, SCCP does not support protocol-based T.38 fax relay. Only Named Signaling Events (NSE)-based T.38, fax relay is supported for SCCP, and H.323 and SIP can support either switchover method for T.38. This changes things slightly from a configuration perspective for SCCP.

In addition, all the relay configuration for SCCP must occur under **voice service voip**. With H.323 and SIP, relay configurations can occur under both **voice service voip** and the dial-peer itself. Table 10-2 highlights the fax relay commands available for SCCP under **voice service voip**.

Table 10-2 *Fax Relay Quick Reference Configuration Guide for SCCP*

Configuration Commands	Cisco Fax Relay	T.38 Fax Relay
Enable command	**fax protocol cisco** (Enabled by default)	**fax protocol t38** **nse force**
Disable command	**fax protocol none**	**no fax protocol t38** **fax protocol none**
Additional commands	**fax-relay sg3-to-g3**	**fax-relay sg3-to-g3**

TIP   Cisco IOS gateway support for Cisco fax relay and NSE-based T.38 fax relay with the SCCP voice signaling protocol is introduced in Cisco IOS Releases 12.4(6)XE and 12.4(11)T.

Notice that because of the SCCP restriction of configuring the fax relay settings under **voice service voip**, additional configuration commands such as **fax rate** and **fax-relay ecm disable** are lost. These commands are present only under a dial-peer.

Tables 10-1 and 10-2 provide just a listing of the fax relay commands for H.323, SIP, and SCCP. To provide more detailed information, each of the commands from these tables and their arguments are now discussed.

The **fax rate** and **fax protocol** commands are probably the two most important fax relay commands. These two commands control the enabling/disabling of fax relay, the relay type, and the maximum speed that a fax relay call can transfer page data. Table 10-3 details the **fax rate** command, and Table 10-4 defines the **fax protocol** command.

Table 10-3 *fax rate IOS Configuration Command*

Command	Argument	Function
fax rate {12000 | 14400 | 2400 | 4800 | 7200 | 9600 | disable | voice} [bytes *rate*]	**12000** **14400** **2400** **4800** **7200** **9600**	Specifies the maximum allowable speed for the fax relay call. The Cisco gateway will alter the fax messaging to ensure that the selected speed is not exceeded. Faxes may negotiate to speeds lower than the configured fax rate.
	disable	Turns off fax relay completely for all calls matching the dial-peer.
	voice	Enforces a fax transmission speed that is less than the bandwidth used by the voice codec configured on the dial-peer. For example, the default dial-peer codec is G.729, an 8 Kbps codec. The command **fax rate voice** ensures that the fax will not negotiate above 8 Kbps or a fax transmission speed of 7200 bps. **Note:** This is the default setting for the **fax rate** command.
	bytes	Configures the number of bytes carried in each fax relay data packet for Cisco fax relay. For T.38 fax relay, this option is only supported on the NextPort DSP products, including the 5350, 5400, and 5850. For other voice gateways, the T.38 packetization rate is fixed at 40 ms and cannot be changed. Raising this value from the default of 20 ms will lower bandwidth consumption at the expense of increased delay.

Table 10-4   *fax protocol IOS Configuration Command*

Command	Argument	Function
fax protocol {cisco | none | pass-through | system | t38}	**cisco**	Specifies Cisco fax relay as the fax relay protocol. When the fax V.21 preamble is detected by the gateway's DSP, a transition to Cisco fax relay is initiated. **Note:** This is the default setting for the global configuration of this command under **voice service voip**.
	none	Turns off fax relay and pass-through.
	pass-through	Enables pass-through. See Table 9-3 in the section "IOS Gateway Protocol-Based Pass-Through Configuration" of Chapter 9 for additional information on this option.
	system	Tells the dial-peer to use the global **fax protocol** command setting configured under **voice service voip**. **Note:** This argument is available only within the dial-peer configuration, and it is the default setting.
	t38	Sets T.38 as the fax relay protocol. **Note:** The following settings are the default options for this command: fallback set to Cisco fax relay, low-speed and high-speed redundancy set to 0, and NSE-based transition disabled. See Table 10-5 for more detailed information on these settings.

If the **t38** option is chosen for the **fax protocol** command shown in Table 10-4, additional T.38 specific arguments are made available via the CLI. These arguments for the **fax protocol t38** command are detailed in Table 10-5.

Table 10-5 *fax protocol t38 IOS Configuration Command*

Command	Argument	Function
fax protocol t38 [**fallback** {**cisco** | **none** | **passthrough** {**g711alaw** | **g711ulaw**}} | **ls-redundancy** *value* [**hs-redundancy** *value*] | **nse** [**force**]]	**fallback**	The **fallback** option provides an alternative transmission method for completing the fax call if the transition to T.38 fax relay fails. The fallback choice can be set to **cisco** for Cisco fax relay, **none** to disable fallback, or **pass-through** for protocol-based pass-through using a G.711 codec. More information on the T.38 fax relay **fallback** option can be found in the section "Fallback" in Chapter 7.
	ls-redundancy **hs-redundancy**	Configures the redundancy settings for the T.38 fax protocol. Low-speed redundancy (**ls-redundancy**) is for the T.30 fax messaging, and high-speed redundancy (**hs_redundancy**) is for the page-transmission data. A value of 0 disables redundancy, a redundancy level of 5 is the maximum setting for low speed, and 2 is the maximum setting for high speed. **Note**: The default setting for both **ls_redundancy** and **hs_redundancy** is 0.
	nse [**force**]	This T.38 specific argument directs the gateway to use NSE packets for the T.38 switchover in what is termed NSE-based T.38 fax relay. If the other T.38 device does not indicate support for NSEs during the call setup, messages within the voice signaling protocol are used instead to signal the switchover to T.38 fax relay. However, the **force** option "forces" the gateway to use NSE packets for the transition regardless of whether NSE support has been indicated in the call setup.

Ancillary fax relay configuration commands include **fax nsf**, **fax-relay ecm disable**, and **fax-relay sg3-to-g3**. Table 10-6 and Table 10-7 discuss these commands and their functions.

Table 10-6   *fax nsf IOS Configuration Command*

Command	Argument	Function
fax nsf *word*		Configures the gateway to override the non-standard facilities (NSF) value sent by the terminating fax device. The NSF is composed of a two-digit country code followed by a four-digit vendor code. More information on the T.30 NSF message can be found in the "DIS, NSF, and CSI Messages" section of Chapter 2, "How Fax Works." Specific NSF values between certain pairs of fax machines can cause proprietary encodings. These encodings can break fax relay. This is an extremely rare occurrence, but setting the NSF to a value such as all 0s will fix and prevent this from happening. This command is not supported in gateways using NextPort-based DSPs (such as the AS5350, AS5400, and AS5850). These platforms will always overwrite the NSF with 0xff. You should be aware that before 12.4(6) and 12.4(6)T, this command did appear in the CLI for the NextPort-based DSP platforms, but it had no effect on the NSF values.

Table 10-7 *fax-relay IOS Configuration Command*

Command	Argument	Function
fax-relay {ecm {disable}l sg3-to-g3 [system]}	**ecm disable**	Enforces the ECM fax negotiation parameter to always be disabled. This should increase the success rate of completed faxes for IP networks with impairments such as packet loss and jitter, but the fax image quality may suffer. Configuring this command also enables the packet-loss concealment feature. This feature causes fax image scan lines that are missing or corrupted to be repeated or replaced with white space to keep the fax transaction from failing. The significance of the ECM feature in fax transactions is discussed in detail in the section "Error Correction Mode" in Chapter 7. **Note:** By default, this command is not configured, and ECM negotiations pass through the IOS voice gateway unaltered.
	sg3-to-g3 [system]	Enables the Super G3 (SG3) spoofing feature that convinces SG3 fax devices that only G3 fax transmissions are possible. SG3 is not currently supported over fax relay. Ideally, SG3 should fall back to G3 when fax relay is being used, but this is not always the case, and unreliable faxing becomes a problem. This command configures the gateway to force the SG3 device into a G3 fax transmission mode. More information on SG3 faxing and options for handling it in IP networks can be found in the section "Super G3" in Chapter 7. **Note:** This command is enabled by default under **voice service voip**. The **system** option, available only under the dial-peer, is also the default setting at the dial-peer configuration level. This means this feature is on by default for any fax relay call and would need to be explicitly disabled if that is the desired result.

IOS Gateway Fax Relay Configuration for MGCP

When MGCP is the voice signaling protocol, a new set of IOS CLI commands must be used for configuration. From a syntax perspective, you will notice that these commands share most of the keywords found in the H.323, SIP, and SCCP fax relay command set.

MGCP signaling makes use of the concepts of call agent (CA) controlled signaling and gateway-controlled signaling when it comes to transitioning to fax relay. Because Cisco fax relay can operate only in a gateway-controlled manner, these concepts are associated only with T.38 fax relay.

CA-controlled T.38 fax relay means that the transition to T.38 is handled by the CA using the MGCP protocol stack (a protocol-based switchover). On the other hand, the voice gateways themselves control the T.38 transition using NSE packets in gateway-controlled mode (an NSE-based switchover). More information on both of these concepts can be found in the sections "NSE-Based Switchover for T.38" and "Protocol-Based Switchover for T.38" in Chapter 5, "Relay."

When you are using the MGCP voice signaling protocol, both Cisco fax relay and T.38 gateway-controlled fax relay are enabled by default. However, because T.38 has precedence over Cisco fax relay, it will always be used when both Cisco and T.38 fax relay are both enabled. If T.38 fax relay is disabled using the command **mgcp fax t38 inhibit**, Cisco fax relay is used.

Table 10-8 shows the available MGCP fax relay commands in a quick reference format. The T.38 column is broken down into CA controlled and gateway controlled in certain areas to better highlight some command differences.

Table 10-8   *Fax Relay Quick Reference Configuration Guide for MGCP*

		T.38 Fax Relay	
Commands	**Cisco Fax Relay**	**CA Controlled** (Protocol-based switchover)	**Gateway Controlled** (NSE-based switchover)
Enable	Enabled by default (**ccm-manager fax protocol cisco**), but T.38 gateway-controlled fax relay is also enabled by default and has precedence.	**mgcp default-package fxr-package** **mgcp package-capability fxr-package** (Make sure that **no mgcp fax t38 inhibit** is also configured.)	Enabled by default (**no mgcp fax t38 inhibit**)

continues

Table 10-8 *Fax Relay Quick Reference Configuration Guide for MGCP (Continued)*

Commands	Cisco Fax Relay	T.38 Fax Relay	
		CA Controlled (Protocol-based switchover)	**Gateway Controlled** (NSE-based switchover)
Disable	**no ccm-manager fax protocol cisco**	**mgcp fax t38 inhibit** or remove the fxr packages necessary for enabling CA-controlled T.38 fax relay.	**mgcp fax t38 inhibit**
Additional commands	**mgcp fax t38 ecm** **mgcp fax t38 nsf** **mgcp fax rate** **mgcp fax-relay sg3-to-g3**	**mgcp fax t38 ecm** **mgcp fax t38 gateway force** **mgcp fax t38 hs_redundancy** **mgcp fax t38 ls_redundancy** **mgcp fax t38 nsf** **mgcp fax rate** **mgcp fax-relay sg3-to-g3**	

Notice in the Additional Commands section for Cisco fax relay that some commands use the starting syntax **mgcp fax t38**. Even though these commands use the **t38** keyword within the command itself, these commands are still applicable to Cisco fax relay.

When Cisco Unified Communications Manager or Unified CM is present, a feature known as **ccm-manager config** is available for automatically configuring the MGCP protocol for the portion of the gateway that is under the control of the call agent. From a fax relay perspective, whether the voice gateway is configured manually or through the **ccm-manager config** feature, the defaults and fax relay commands are the same.

The command **mgcp fax t38** encompasses the T.38 (and some Cisco fax relay) options that are available with MGCP. These options are functionally equivalent to what is available with the SIP and H.323 signaling protocols. Table 10-9 details the **mgcp fax t38** command and its arguments.

Table 10-9 *mgcp fax t38 IOS Configuration Command*

Command	Argument	Function
mgcp fax t38 {ecm | gateway force | hs_redundancy *value* **| inhibit | ls_redundancy** *value* **| nsf** *word*}	**ecm**	Allows ECM mode for fax relay transactions. When this command is enabled, the voice gateway allows the negotiation of ECM between the fax endpoints to occur unaltered. Negating this command, **no mgcp fax t38 ecm** causes the gateway to enforce the ECM fax parameter to always be disabled. **Note:** By default, this command is already enabled, and it is applicable to both T.38 and Cisco fax relay.
	gateway force	Specifies that the gateway will use NSE messages for the T.38 switchover even if the NSE capability was not confirmed during the MGCP call setup. This command is typically necessary in networks where T.38 must work between gateways using different call control protocols. **Note:** This command is disabled by default.
	hs_redundancy	Details the level of T.38 redundancy for high-speed data transmission (fax page information). **Note:** A redundancy level from 0 to 2 can be set, with the default value being 0.
	inhibit	Disables T.38 fax relay for the MGCP voice signaling protocol.
	ls_redundancy	Details the level of T.38 redundancy for low-speed data transmission (T.30 messaging). **Note:** A redundancy level from 0 to 5 is available, with 0 being the default value.
	nsf	Having a functional equivalence to the **fax nsf** command previously discussed in Table 10-6, this command allows for the overwriting of the received NSF value to prevent proprietary fax encodings from occurring. This command is applicable to both T.38 and Cisco fax relay.

Controlling the negotiation speeds of both Cisco and T.38 fax relay when the MGCP signaling protocol is used can be accomplished with the **mgcp fax rate** command. Table 10-10 discusses this command.

Table 10-10 *mgcp fax rate IOS Configuration Command*

Command	Argument	Function
mgcp fax rate {12000 | 14400 | 2400 | 4800 | 7200 | 9600 | voice}	**12000** **14400** **2400** **4800** **7200** **9600**	Specifies the maximum allowable speed for the fax relay call. The Cisco gateway will alter the fax messaging to ensure that the selected speed is not exceeded. Faxes may negotiate to speeds lower than this configured fax rate.
	voice	Enforces a fax transmission speed that is less than the bandwidth used by the voice codec configured on the dial-peer. For example, the default dial-peer codec is G.729, an 8 Kbps codec. The command **fax rate voice** ensures that the fax will not negotiate above 8 Kbps or a fax transmission speed of 7200 bps. **Note:** This command is enabled by default, with a setting of **voice**.

Table 10-11 discusses the MGCP command for controlling the Super G3 spoofing feature. This command is applicable to both T.38 and Cisco fax relay, and when it is enabled better interoperability with SG3 fax devices can be achieved.

Table 10-11 *mgcp fax-relay sg3-to-g3 IOS Configuration Command*

Command	Argument	Function
mgcp fax-relay sg3-to-g3		Enables the SG3 (Super G3) spoofing feature that convinces SG3 fax devices that only G3 fax transmissions are possible. SG3 is not currently supported over fax relay. Ideally, SG3 should fallback to G3 when fax relay is being used but this is not always the case and unreliable faxing becomes a problem. This command configures the gateway to force the SG3 device into a G3 fax transmission mode. **Note:** By default, this command is enabled.

The command that controls the enabling and disabling of the Cisco fax relay protocol for MGCP is the **ccm-manager fax protocol cisco** command. Table 10-12 details the configuration of this command.

Table 10-12 *ccm-manager fax protocol cisco IOS Configuration Command*

Command	Argument	Function
ccm-manager fax protocol cisco		Enabled by default, this command controls whether the Cisco fax relay protocol is on or off. Remember that gateway-controlled T.38 is also on by default and has precedence. So, even though **ccm-manager fax protocol cisco** is configured, Cisco fax relay is used only when T.38 fax relay has been disabled on the MGCP gateway.

When configuring CA-controlled T.38 fax relay where the transition to T.38 is handled by the MGCP protocol stack, there are two critical commands: **mgcp package-capability fxr-package** and **mgcp default-package fxr-package**. Both of these commands are necessary for ensuring that the CA is aware that the Cisco gateway can support a T.38 fax relay transition within the MGCP protocol. Table 10-13 discusses these configuration commands.

Table 10-13 *CA-Controlled T.38 Fax Relay IOS Configuration Commands for MGCP*

Command	Argument	Function
mgcp package-capability fxr-package **mgcp default-package fxr-package**		Together these two commands specify the use of the MGCP protocol stack for the transition to T.38 (CA-controlled T.38 fax relay). The command **mgcp package-capability fxr-package** is enabled by default and does not appear in the configuration, whereas the command **mgcp default-package fxr-package** is disabled by default. Therefore, in most cases, only the command **mgcp default-package fxr-package** needs to be configured. Resetting MGCP after these commands have been configured is also recommended. An MGCP Audit Endpoint (AUEP) message from the CA is needed for the gateway to communicate support for the fxr package. Additional information on MGCP CA-controlled T.38 can be found in the section "Protocol-Based Switchover for T.38" in Chapter 5.

Modem Relay

Two types of modem relay are available for Cisco gateways: Cisco modem relay and modem relay for secure communications between STE (Secure Terminal Equipment) endpoints, which is referred to as secure modem relay for the sake of brevity. Both of these modem relay types are Cisco proprietary implementations, although some aspects of secure modem relay are based on ITU-T Recommendation V.150.1.

Cisco modem relay is designed to carry V.34 modem traffic efficiently across IP. The voice signaling protocols supported by Cisco modem relay are H.323, SIP, MGCP, and SCCP. Slightly different configuration commands are used for configuring Cisco modem relay with MGCP, so this voice signaling protocol is discussed separately from H.323, SIP, and SCCP.

TIP	Gateway-controlled Cisco modem relay was introduced in Cisco IOS Release 12.4(4)T. The previous switchover method was referred to as signaling-assisted Cisco modem relay, and the voice signaling protocol (H.323, SIP, or MGCP) was used to confirm the Cisco modem relay capability. Signaling-assisted modem relay is no longer supported. The preferred switchover method is gateway-controlled Cisco modem relay, which uses only NSE packets for the capability notification (NSE-199) and switchover (NSE-203). For more information on gateway-controlled Cisco modem relay, see the section "Modem Relay" in Chapter 5.

Secure modem relay is available only for MGCP and SCCP gateways. This specialized type of modem relay allows for gateways to interconnect traditional STE and IP-based STE devices. Because of secure modem relay's limited deployment and specialized implementation, the discussion of secure modem relay within this book is confined to the section "Secure Modem Relay" in Chapter 7.

IOS Gateway Cisco Modem Relay Configuration for H.323, SIP, and SCCP

Cisco modem relay transports high-speed modem calls across IP networks using a Cisco proprietary relay protocol. The V.34 modulation along with V.42 error correction and V.42bis compression is officially supported. However, other high-speed modem modulations such as V.90 will work after they have been forced to train down by the Cisco modem relay feature.

TIP	Cisco modem relay should be used only between two Cisco gateways because the NSE transition and Cisco modem relay protocol itself are proprietary. For more information on Cisco modem relay and its transition using NSE packets, see the section "Modem Relay" in Chapter 5.

Cisco modem relay uses a single set of IOS configuration commands for gateways using H.323, SIP, and SCCP voice signaling protocols. These commands are configurable globally under **voice service voip** and locally under specific H.323 and SIP dial-peers.

The most important Cisco modem relay command is **modem relay nse**. This command enables the Cisco modem relay feature and represents the minimum configuration needed for Cisco modem relay to work. Table 10-14 details the **modem relay nse** configuration command and its options.

Table 10-14 *modem relay nse IOS Configuration Command*

Command	Argument	Function
modem relay nse [**payload-type** *number*] **codec** {**g711ulaw** | **g711alaw**} [**redundancy**] [**maximum sessions** *value*] **gw-controlled**	**payload-type**	Allows the setting of another RTP payload type to be used for the NSE switchover messages. **Note:** As is the case with all Cisco NSE packets, the RTP payload type defaults to a value of 100.
	codec	Before the transition to modem relay takes place, a codec upspeed must occur using the modem passthrough feature. This argument allows the user to indicate the **g711ulaw** or **g711alaw** codec for the codec upspeed that occurs right before the NSE switchover to modem relay. More information on the modem relay switchover including this codec upspeed can be found in the section "Modem Relay" in Chapter 5.
	redundancy	Enables RFC2198 redundancy for the G.711 packets that are sent during the passthrough phase of the modem relay call. When the NSE messages transition the call to modem relay, these redundant passthrough packets are no longer necessary. **Note:** This argument is disabled by default.
	maximum sessions	Defines the maximum number of redundant modem passthrough sessions that can be occurring at any one time. **Note:** This argument is available only when configured globally under **voice service voip**. The default value is 16.
	gw-controlled	Configures the modem relay transition to be completely controlled by the gateways themselves. An NSE-199 message is exchanged between the gateways as soon as modem ANSam tones are detected. In the older signaling-assisted method, the voice signaling protocol confirmed the Cisco modem relay support capability. **Note:** This argument has been enabled by default since it was introduced in Cisco IOS Release 12.4(4)T.

The other Cisco modem relay commands serve to manipulate certain user-configurable options. The command **modem relay gateway-xid** lets the user define certain V.42bis compression parameters that are set during the V.42 negotiation. This command is detailed in Table 10-15. The V.42 and V.42bis protocols were discussed previously in the sections "Error Control" and "Data Compression" in Chapter 1, "How Modems Work."

Table 10-15 *modem relay gateway-xid IOS Configuration Command*

Command	Argument	Function
**modem relay gateway-xid [compress { backward	both	forward	no}] [dictionary** *value*] **[string-length** *value*]	compress	Provides control of the V.42bis compression protocol operating between the modems. The compression options are as follows: • **backward** permits compression only in the backward direction, and compression is disabled in the forward direction. • **both** enables compression in both directions. This is the preferred setting. • **forward** allows compression to operate in the forward direction, whereas it is disabled in the backward direction. • **no** disables compression in both directions. **Note: both** is the default setting.
	dictionary	Allows for the size of the V.42bis compression dictionary to be set to a value between 512 and 2048. **Note:** The default value is 1024.
	string-length	Specifies the compression algorithm's string length to a value between 16 and 32. **Note:** The default setting is 32.

The commands **modem relay latency** and **modem relay sprt retries** allow further adjustment of the Cisco modem relay feature. Table 10-16 discusses each of these commands further.

Table 10-16 *modem relay latency and **modem relay sprt retries** IOS Configuration Commands*

Command	Function
modem relay latency *value*	Configures the estimated one-way delay for the modem relay path helping to optimize the data flow. The available range in milliseconds is 100 to 1000. **Note:** The default setting is 200 ms.
modem relay sprt retries *value*	Specifies the number of attempts that the Cisco modem relay Simple Packet Relay Transport (SPRT) protocol tries to send a packet before disconnecting. The configurable range is 6 to 30. **Note:** The default setting is 12.

When you are using the modem relay commands outlined in this section with an SCCP configuration, the commands are applicable globally only under **voice service voip**. With H.323 and SIP, you may configure these commands either globally under **voice service voip** or under a particular dial-peer.

IOS Gateway Cisco Modem Relay Configuration for MGCP

The configuration of Cisco modem relay for the MGCP voice signaling protocol is similar to that of H.323, SIP, and SCCP. The main difference is that with MGCP, the command syntaxes differ a little.

The main command that enables Cisco modem relay for MGCP is **mgcp modem relay voip mode nse**. Although this command still requires at least one additional argument, this core command enables Cisco modem relay and specifies a switchover using NSE packets. In conjunction with the **gw-controlled** argument, this command enables what is commonly referred to as gateway-controlled Cisco modem relay. Table 10-17 details the command **mgcp modem relay voip mode nse** and its arguments.

Additional Cisco modem relay options can be specified from the **mgcp modem relay voip** command. By using the **gateway-xid** argument, you can control the in-band xid parameter negotiation between the gateways. The full range of options for the command **mgcp modem relay voip gateway-xid** is shown in Table 10-18.

Table 10-17 *mgcp modem relay voip mode nse IOS Configuration Command*

Command	Argument	Function
mgcp modem relay voip mode nse { [codec {g711ulaw | g711alaw}] [redundancy] } gw-controlled	**codec {g711ulaw | g711alaw}**	Before the transition to modem relay takes place, an upspeed must occur using the modem passthrough feature. This argument allows the user to indicate the **g711ulaw** or **g711alaw** codec for the codec upspeed that occurs right before the NSE switchover to modem relay. More information on the modem relay switchover including this codec upspeed can be found in the section "Modem Relay" in Chapter 5.
	redundancy	Enables RFC2198 redundancy for the G.711 packets sent during the passthrough phase of the modem relay call. When the NSE messages transition the call to modem relay, these redundant passthrough packets are no longer necessary. **Note:** Redundancy is disabled by default.
	gw-controlled	Configures the modem relay transition to be completely controlled by the gateways themselves. An NSE-199 message is exchanged between the gateways as soon as modem ANSam tones are detected. In the older signaling-assisted method, the voice signaling protocol confirmed the Cisco modem relay support capability. This argument has been enabled by default since it was introduced in Cisco IOS Release 12.4(4)T.

Table 10-18 *mgcp modem relay voip gateway-xid IOS Configuration Command*

Command	Argument	Function
mgcp modem relay voip gateway-xid [**compress** {**backward**	**both**	**forward**	**no**}] [**dictionary** *value*] [**string-length** *value*]	compress	Provides control of the V.42bis compression protocol operating between the modems. The compression options are as follows: • **backward** permits compression only in the backward direction, and compression is disabled in the forward direction. • **both** enables compression in both directions, and this is the preferred setting. • **forward** allows compression to operate in the forward direction, whereas it is disabled in the backward direction. • **no** disables compression in both directions. **Note: both** is the default setting.
	dictionary	Allows for the size of the V.42bis compression dictionary to be set to a value between 512 and 2048. **Note:** The default value is 1024.
	string-length	Specifies the compression algorithm's string length to a value between 16 and 32. **Note:** The default setting is 32.

The commands **mgcp modem relay voip latency** and **mgcp modem relay voip sprt retries** are the last configurable options for Cisco modem relay with MGCP. Table 10-19 addresses the functions of these two commands.

Table 10-19 *mgcp modem relay voip latency and mgcp modem relay voip sprt retries IOS Configuration Commands*

Command	Function
mgcp modem relay voip latency *value*	Configures the estimated one-way delay for the modem relay path helping to optimize the data flow. The available range in milliseconds is 100 to 1000. **Note:** The default setting is 200 ms.
mgcp modem relay voip sprt retries *value*	Specifies the number of attempts that the Cisco modem relay SPRT protocol tries to send a packet before disconnecting. The configurable range is 6 to 30. **Note:** The default setting is 12.

Cisco Text Relay

Cisco text relay allows the modulated signals from text telephones to be transported reliably and efficiently over IP. These signals typically represent the alphanumeric characters making up a conversation between text telephone users.

NOTE	For additional information on text telephony, see Chapter 3, "How Text Telephony Works," and for more information on Cisco text relay and how it works, see the section "Cisco Text Relay" in Chapter 5.

The configuration of Cisco text relay is relatively simple because the same configuration commands are used for all the supported voice signaling protocols. The supported voice signaling protocols include H.323, SIP, MGCP, and SCCP.

All the voice signaling protocols use any text relay commands that are configured globally under **voice service voip**. However, just as with the other relay protocols, H.323 and SIP can also support text relay commands configured under the dial-peers, which take precedence over the global configuration.

The command to enable text relay is **text relay protocol**. While turning on the text relay feature, this command also sets the text relay protocol. At this time, only the Cisco proprietary version of text relay is supported. You can find additional information on the command **text relay protocol** in Table 10-20.

Table 10-20 *text relay protocol IOS Configuration Command*

Command	Argument	Function
text relay protocol [cisco | system]	**cisco | system**	Defines the text relay protocol. The option of **cisco** selects a proprietary text relay protocol known as Cisco text relay. The **system** option is available only when this command is configured under a voice dial-peer, and it points the dial-peer to **voice service voip** for the text relay protocol configuration information. Note that to use additional text relay configuration commands under the dial-peer itself, the command **text relay protocol cisco** must be configured under the dial-peer first. **Note:** The command **text relay protocol system** is enabled by default under every VoIP dial-peer. The command **no text relay protocol cisco** is the default option under **voice service voip**. This forces the Cisco text relay feature to be disabled for all voice signaling protocols by default.

After Cisco text relay has been enabled using the **text relay protocol** command, you can change certain attributes through the use of additional commands. One of these commands is **text relay rtp**, and it is defined in Table 10-21.

Table 10-21 *text relay rtp IOS Configuration Command*

Command	Argument	Function
text relay rtp {[**payload-type** {*value* | **default**}] [**redundancy** *level*]}	**payload-type**	Allows the user to specify a different RTP payload type to be used for the Cisco text relay packets. The valid range of options is from 98 to 117. **Note:** The default setting is an RTP payload type of 119.
	redundancy	Sets the amount of redundancy for the Baudot characters that are passed using the Cisco text relay protocol. **Note:** The options are a level from 1 to 3, and the default is a value of 2.

The other command that offers additional control of the Cisco text relay protocol is **text relay modulation**. This command controls the modulation options and the autobaud feature. Table 10-22 details the **text relay modulation** command and its settings.

Table 10-22 *text relay modulation IOS Configuration Command*

Command	Argument	Function
text relay modulation {**baudot45.45** | **baudot50**} {**autobaud-on** | **autobaud-off**}	**baudot45.45** | **baudot50**	Specifies the modulation rate. The option **baudot45.45** is commonly found in North America, and **baudot50** is used in countries such as Australia and New Zealand. When **autobaud-on** is set, this rate is only the initial modulation rate, and thereafter the most recently detected rate is used. When **autobaud-off** is enabled, the configured modulation rate (**baudot45.45** or **baudot50**) is always used. **Note**: The default is **baudot45.45**.
	autobaud-on | **autobaud-off**	Enables or disables the text relay autobaud feature. With **autobaud-on** configured, the gateway automatically detects the modulation rate being used (either 45.45 bps or 50 bps) and adjusts accordingly. When **autobaud-off** is configured, the gateway uses only the configured value of either **baudot45.45** or **baudot50**. **Note**: The default setting is **autobaud-on**.

IOS Example Configurations for Relay

Looking at configuration samples is a good way to grasp how the relay commands that have just been discussed form a proper fax, modem, or text relay configuration. In addition to relay examples, passthrough examples are mixed in, too, to illustrate how these two transport methods can be configured together to handle different types of modulated data.

The sample configurations in this section assume that the IOS gateway has already been properly configured with the selected voice signaling protocol. Regular voice calls should also work through the gateway using the voice signaling protocol before the fax, modem, and text configuration commands are inserted.

The following examples are illustrated in this section.

- Default fax relay configuration for H.323 and SIP
- Cisco fax relay and modem passthrough for H.323 and SIP
- T.38 Fax relay, Cisco modem relay, and Cisco text relay for H.323 and SIP
- T.38 fax relay and Cisco text relay for SCCP
- T.38 fax relay and modem passthrough for MGCP

Default Fax Relay Configuration for H.323 and SIP

Example 10-1 shows the default fax relay configuration for H.323 and SIP. At this point, no fax relay commands have been configured on the voice gateway. However, even though there are not any visible fax-specific commands in the configuration, default commands are present, and a fax call can be handled by the gateway.

Example 10-1 *Default Fax Relay Configuration for H.323 and SIP*

```
<snip>
! voice service voip is not present in the configuration when its options do not
! differ from the defaults. Default fax relay commands under voice service voip
! include the commands fax protocol cisco and fax-relay sg3-to-g3.
!
dial-peer voice 100 voip
 ! This H.323 dial-peer includes the default fax relay commands of fax rate voice,
 ! fax protocol system, and fax-relay sg3-to-g3 system
 destination-pattern 100
 session target ipv4:1.1.1.1
 incoming called-number .
 ! If a VoIP dial-peer will also be used as an inbound call leg, you must make sure
 ! that this peer is explicitly matched. The command incoming called number is
 ! commonly used for this purpose.
 !
dial-peer voice 200 voip
 ! This SIP dial-peer also includes the default fax relay commands of fax rate voice,
```

continues

Example 10-1   *Default Fax Relay Configuration for H.323 and SIP (Continued)*

```
! fax protocol system, and fax-relay sg3-to-g3 system
 destination-pattern 200
 session protocol sipv2
 session target ipv4:1.1.1.2
 !
 <snip>
```

So, you can see in Example 10-1 that although fax commands might not appear in the configuration file itself, fax relay and a few of its options are enabled by default. Basically, the default fax relay configuration for H.323 and SIP IOS voice gateways is as follows: Cisco fax relay is the fax relay protocol, the maximum fax speed is limited to the voice codec bit rate, and the SG3 message suppression feature is enabled. The only exception to this is for the 5300, 5400, and 5850 IOS gateways using the NextPort DSP architecture. These gateways do not support Cisco fax relay, so T.38 fax relay is the default instead.

An important concept that is often overlooked when configuring dial-peers for handling fax, modem, and text calls is that of an inbound VoIP dial-peer. If a fax call is coming inbound over IP to the voice gateway in Example 10-1, an explicitly configured VoIP dial containing the proper fax settings must be matched. Otherwise, the fax call will typically fail.

The most common method for matching an inbound VoIP dial-peer is to use the command **incoming called-number**. This command allows you to specify the called number of the incoming fax over IP call and associate that called number with a dial-peer.

In the case of Example 10-1, this command is configured under **dial-peer voice 100 voip**. If **dial-peer voice 200 voip** also needs to handle inbound fax calls from the IP side, it will also need a command such as **incoming called-number**. However, more specific patterns would need to be specified for the command **incoming called-number** rather than the wildcard "." pattern, which is a generic "catchall" for any incoming call on the IP side. More information on call legs and matching the correct inbound VoIP dial-peer can be found in the section "Call Legs in IOS Gateways" in Chapter 12, "Troubleshooting Passthrough and Relay."

The main point to take away from Example 10-1 is that some default fax relay configuration elements in the dial-peer configuration use the **system** keyword. This means that the dial-peer pulls the configuration parameter from the global **voice service voip** configuration.

Although the Cisco IOS voice gateways are configured by default to handle the transport of fax calls using Cisco fax relay, it is interesting to note that no such default transport mechanism is in place for handling modem calls. Therefore, modem passthrough or Cisco modem relay must be explicitly enabled if modem or SG3 fax calls need to be handled by the voice gateway.

Cisco Fax Relay and Modem Passthrough Configuration for H.323 and SIP

When fax and modem calls are occurring through the same gateway, it is possible to handle them using the same transport method or different methods/protocols may be used. For example, with the command **modem passthrough nse** for SIP and H.323 gateways, all fax and modem calls can be handled using voice-band data (VBD) and the G.711 codec.

However, fax and modem calls can also be handled through different means, too. Various passthrough and relay schemes can be used to handle fax and modem calls on the same gateway. Example 10-2 shows typical G3 fax calls being handled by the Cisco fax relay protocol while modem calls and SG3 fax calls are handled by NSE-based modem passthrough.

Example 10-2 *Cisco Fax Relay and Modem Passthrough Configuration for H.323 and SIP*

```
<snip>
!
!
voice service voip
 no fax-relay sg3-to-g3
! For modem passthrough to handle SG3 fax calls when either Cisco or T.38 fax
! relay is configured, the fax-relay sg3-to-g3 command must be disabled.
 modem passthrough nse codec g711ulaw
! Notice that modem passthrough is configured globally under voice service voip.
!
<snip>
!
dial-peer voice 100 voip
 destination-pattern 100
 session target ipv4:1.1.1.1
 incoming called-number .
! If a VoIP dial-peer will also be used as an inbound call leg, you must make sure
! that this peer is explicitly matched using a command such as incoming called
! number. More information on call legs and inbound VoIP dial peers can be found in
! the section "Call Legs in IOS Gateways" in Chapter 12.
!
! The H.323 dial-peer 100 above does not have specific fax or modem configuration
! lines defined so all fax and modem configuration information is default and
! pulled from voice service voip.
!
dial-peer voice 200 voip
 destination-pattern 200
 modem passthrough nse codec g711ulaw
 session protocol sipv2
 session target ipv4:1.1.1.2
 no fax-relay sg3-to-g3
 fax protocol cisco
!
! The SIP dial-peer 200 has specific fax and modem configuration lines that
! take precedence over anything that is globally configured under voice service
! voip. The configurations from a fax and modem perspective are identical for
! dial-peer 100 and 200 but they are configured in different ways.
<snip>
```

In Example 10-2, dial-peer 100 is set for H.323, and the fax and modem configuration is default. This means that all settings are pulled from **voice service voip**. As already demonstrated in Example 10-1, this means that Cisco fax relay is already enabled. In addition, the commands **modem passthrough nse** and **no fax-relay sg3-to-g3** have been configured globally under **voice service voip**. Therefore, fax calls will transition to Cisco fax relay whenever G3 fax flags are detected, whereas all other calls (modem and Super G3 fax calls) will use NSE-based modem passthrough.

TIP	By default, modem passthrough will not properly handle SG3 fax calls when it is configured at the same time as Cisco or T.38 fax relay. The reason for this is because the sg3 spoofing feature is also enabled by default and it blocks any SG3 negotiation whenever fax relay is enabled. If you would like for fax relay to handle your G3 fax traffic and for modem passthrough to handle your SG3 fax traffic at its native speeds, then you must explicitly disable the SG3 spoofing feature with the command **no fax-relay sg3-to-g3**.

As illustrated earlier in the book in Figure 5-15, modem passthrough will actually activate for the G3 fax call and the modem calls with the configuration in Example 10-2. The fax called terminal identification (CED) tone triggers modem passthrough before the V.21 fax flags are detected. Therefore, a normal G3 fax call will transition from voice mode to NSE-based modem passthrough to Cisco fax relay. This momentary transition to modem passthrough is not a problem. It is rarely noticed and occurs only because of the different triggers that these transport methods use.

For SIP dial-peer 200 in Example 10-2, Cisco fax relay and modem passthrough are also set, but they are configured explicitly under the dial-peer. In the real world, this would not be necessary because the same configuration is already defined globally, as discussed with dial-peer 100. However, for the sake of this example, dial-peer 200 demonstrates how the same configuration can also be set directly on the dial-peer using the commands **fax protocol cisco**, **modem passthrough nse codec g711ulaw**, and **no fax-relay sg3-to-g3**.

T.38 Fax Relay, Cisco Modem Relay, and Cisco Text Relay Configuration for H.323 and SIP

Different modulation types can each be configured with their own relay protocol. A fax modulation may use Cisco fax relay or T.38, modems can use Cisco modem relay or modem relay for secure communications, and text communications can use Cisco text relay. Each traffic type has its own unique relay transport methods.

Example 10-3 illustrates a configuration where fax, modem, and text traffic are each assigned an appropriate relay transport method. T.38 fax relay is chosen for the fax traffic, Cisco modem relay for modems, and Cisco text relay for text communication.

Example 10-3   *T.38 Fax Relay, Cisco Modem Relay, and Cisco Text Relay Configuration for H.323 and SIP*

```
<snip>
!
!
voice service voip
 text relay protocol cisco
! Cisco text relay has been enabled globally.
!
<snip>
!
dial-peer voice 100 voip
 destination-pattern 100
 modem relay nse codec g711ulaw gw-controlled
 session target ipv4:1.1.1.1
 incoming called-number .
! If a VoIP dial-peer will also be used as an inbound call leg, you must make sure
! that this peer is explicitly matched using a command such as incoming called
! number. More information on call legs and inbound VoIP dial peers can be found in
! the section "Call Legs in IOS Gateways" in Chapter 12.
 fax-relay ecm disable
 no fax-relay sg3-to-g3
 fax protocol t38 ls-redundancy 0 hs-redundancy 0 fallback cisco
!
! Dial-peer 100 is configured explicitly for Cisco modem relay and T.38 fax relay.
! Cisco text relay is picked up from voice service voip.
!
dial-peer voice 200 voip
 destination-pattern 200
 modem relay nse codec g711ulaw gw-controlled
 session protocol sipv2
 session target ipv4:1.1.1.2
 text relay protocol cisco
 text relay rtp redundancy 1
 no fax-relay sg3-to-g3
 fax protocol t38 ls-redundancy 0 hs-redundancy 0 fallback cisco
!
! Dial-peer 200 is configured explicitly for Cisco modem relay, T.38 fax relay, and
! Cisco text relay.
!
<snip>
```

In Example 10-3, H.323 fax calls matching dial-peer 100 will use the T.38 fax relay proto-col because of the command **fax protocol t38**. In addition, because this command line does not contain the **nse** keyword, the H.323 protocol stack will be used for the T.38 switchover rather than NSE packets. Whenever a switchover from voice mode to T.38 occurs using the voice signaling protocol itself, this is referred to as protocol-based T.38 fax relay.

Within this same T.38 command line, you see that both the low-speed (**ls-redundancy**) and high-speed (**hs-redundancy**) redundancy options for T.38 fax relay are set to zero. This effectively disables redundancy for T.38 fax relay.

The last option in the **fax protocol t38** command line under dial-peer 100 in Example 10-3 is **fallback**. This option allows the gateway to try an alternative transport method for the fax call should the switchover to T.38 fax relay fail. In this case, the **fallback** option is set to **cisco**, which means that a switchover to Cisco fax relay will be attempted by the voice gateway if the T.38 fax relay switchover is unsuccessful.

Another fax relay configuration command found under dial-peer 100 in Example 10-3 is **fax-relay ecm disable**. This is an optional fax relay configuration command that prevents fax machines from using the ECM feature. Optional fax relay commands such as this one are not required, but they allow the user to customize certain aspects of the fax relay configuration.

Dial-peer 100 in Example 10-3 also contains the command **modem relay nse codec g711ulaw gw-controlled**. This command activates gateway-controlled Cisco modem relay using an NSE-based switchover. Any V.34 modulated modem call should trigger cisco modem relay when this command is present.

Cisco text relay is not explicitly enabled under dial-peer 100. However, the combination of the default dial-peer setting of **text relay protocol system** and **text relay protocol cisco** under **voice service voip** enables Cisco text relay for this dial-peer.

Dial-peer 200 in Example 10-3 is a SIP dial-peer configured for T.38 fax relay and gateway-controlled Cisco modem relay like dial-peer 100. However, Cisco text relay is configured explicitly under dial-peer 200 even though Cisco text relay is already enabled globally under **voice service voip**.

The reason for the explicit configuration of Cisco text relay under dial-peer 200 is to access additional text relay options. In this case, the user wanted to configure **text relay rtp redundancy 1** for this SIP dial-peer. However, this optional text relay command cannot be accessed at the dial-peer level unless **text relay protocol cisco** is explicitly defined at the dial-peer level first.

T.38 Fax Relay and Cisco Text Relay Configuration for SCCP

As mentioned throughout this chapter, SCCP fax, modem, and text features are configured globally under **voice service voip**. Example 10-4 shows an SCCP configuration for T.38 fax relay and Cisco text relay.

In Example 10-4, the SCCP voice signaling protocol uses NSE-based T.38 fax relay, as shown by the keyword **nse** in the **fax protocol t38** command. The **force** keyword within this same command line ensures that NSEs are always used even if NSE support has not been verified on the remote device during the call setup.

Example 10-4 *T.38 Fax Relay and Cisco Text Relay Configuration for SCCP*

```
<snip>
!
!
voice service voip
 text relay protocol cisco
 fax protocol t38 nse force ls-redundancy 0 hs-redundancy 0 fallback cisco
!
! Fax modem and text configuration for SCCP takes place globally under voice service
! voip.
!`
<snip>
```

The **fax protocol t38** command here in Example 10-4 is configured the same as in Example 10-3 with regard to the redundancy and fallback settings. Both the low- and high-speed redundancy parameters are set to zero, which disables T.38 redundancy altogether. The **fallback** option in this command is set to **cisco**, which means that a Cisco fax relay switchover will be attempted if the switchover to T.38 fax relay fails.

The command **text relay protocol cisco** under **voice service voip** enables Cisco text relay for all SCCP ports. The optional text relay commands of **text relay rtp** and **text relay modulation** are also available here under **voice service voip** if needed.

T.38 Fax Relay and Modem Passthrough Configuration for MGCP

A common scenario for handling regular faxes along with modems or SG3 fax devices at the same time is to use a fax relay protocol for the fax traffic and modem passthrough for the modem or SG3 fax traffic. Although this scenario can be configured for the H.323, SIP, MGCP, or SCCP voice signaling protocols using T.38 or Cisco fax relay, Example 10-5 shows how this scenario is configured specifically for an MGCP voice gateway running NSE-based T.38 fax relay and modem passthrough.

Example 10-5 *T.38 Fax Relay and Modem Passthrough Configuration for MGCP*

```
<snip>
!
ccm-manager mgcp
no ccm-manager fax protocol cisco
ccm-manager music-on-hold
ccm-manager config server 14.80.32.199
ccm-manager config
!
! The command no ccm-manager fax protocol cisco disables Cisco fax relay.
!
mgcp
mgcp call-agent 14.80.32.199 2427 service-type mgcp version 0.1
```

Example 10-5   *T.38 Fax Relay and Modem Passthrough Configuration for MGCP (Continued)*

```
mgcp dtmf-relay voip codec all mode out-of-band
mgcp rtp unreachable timeout 1000 action notify
mgcp modem passthrough voip mode nse
mgcp package-capability rtp-package
no mgcp package-capability res-package
mgcp package-capability sst-package
no mgcp package-capability fxr-package
mgcp package-capability pre-package
no mgcp timer receive-rtcp
mgcp sdp simple
mgcp fax rate 14400
mgcp fax t38 nsf 000000
no mgcp fax-relay sg3-to-g3
mgcp rtp payload-type g726r16 static
!
! NSE-based T.38 fax relay is enabled by default as is NSE-based modem passthrough
! when the ccm-manager config option is used.
!
mgcp profile default
!
!
!
<snip>
```

By default, the command **no mgcp fax t38 inhibit** is configured for MGCP. Therefore, this command does not appear in the configuration shown in Example 10-5, but it still activates NSE-based T.38 by default for MGCP.

TIP   When the MGCP packages of **mgcp package-capability fxr-package** and **mgcp default-package fxr-package** are configured along with **no mgcp fax t38 inhibit**, protocol-based T.38 is enabled for MGCP. Along with a supported CA like Unified CM Version 4.2(3) or 6.0, the transition to T.38 is handled by the CA within the MGCP protocol stack.

The optional fax relay commands of **mgcp fax rate 14400** and **mgcp fax t38 nsf 000000** also appear in Example 10-5. These commands set the fax page transmission speed to 14.4 Kbps regardless of the voice codec and force the NSF to all 0s to guard against proprietary encodings between certain fax vendors.

The command **no ccm-manager fax protocol cisco** disables Cisco fax relay. By default, Cisco fax relay and T.38 fax relay are enabled for MGCP with T.38 having precedence. In the case of this configuration, Cisco fax relay is disabled because only T.38 fax relay is needed and it makes for a cleaner configuration.

As shown in Example 10-5, the command **mgcp modem passthrough voip mode nse** enables NSE-based passthrough for MGCP. By default, this command is not enabled, but when the **ccm-manager config** feature is used to download the gateway's MGCP configuration directly from Unified CM, modem passthrough is enabled. Whether **ccm-manager config** is used or not, make sure this command appears in the **mgcp** section of the configuration file if the modem passthrough feature is desired.

In addition, just as with modem passthrough and the H.323 and SIP call control protocols in Example 10-2, the SG3 spoofing feature must be disabled for modem passthrough when MGCP is the call control protocol. The command that accomplishes this for MGCP is **no mgcp fax-relay sg3-to-g3**.

6608 Catalyst Blade Fax Relay Configuration

The 6608 is a blade for the Catalyst 6000/6500 series of switches. This card is MGCP controlled by Unified CM and features eight T1 or E1 ports, each of which is treated as a separate gateway. The 6608 supports Cisco fax relay only, not modem relay or text relay.

The 6608 is configured via the Unified CM graphical user interface (GUI). Figure 10-1 illustrates the default fax settings for a 6608 port. This particular screenshot is from Cisco Unified Call Manager (CUCM) Version 5.0(4), but all Unified CM versions from the past few years have these same options.

Figure 10-1 *Cisco Fax Relay Configuration for a 6608 Gateway*

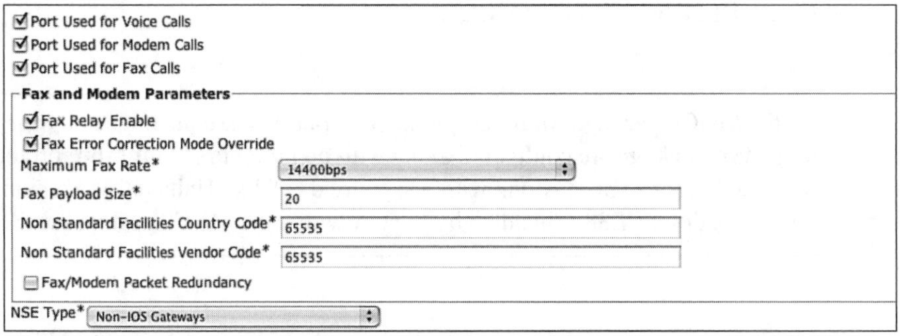

By default, the 6608 is configured for Cisco fax relay because the Fax Relay Enable box is checked, as shown in Figure 10-1. This setting also disables passthrough as the transport mechanism for fax calls. Table 10-23 details the additional Cisco fax relay GUI options for the 6608 in the Fax and Modem Parameters section.

Table 10-23 *Cisco Fax Relay Configuration Parameters for the 6608*

Configuration Parameter	Options	Function
Fax Relay Enable	Enable/Disable	When this box is checked, Cisco fax relay is enabled for the 6608. When this box is not checked, NSE-based passthrough is used to handle fax calls. **Note:** Cisco fax relay is enabled by default.
Fax Error Correction Mode Override	Enable/Disable	When this box is checked, the 6608 automatically disables ECM for all Cisco fax relay calls. **Note:** By default, this box is checked, and ECM is disabled.
Maximum Fax Rate	2400 4800 7200 9600 12000 14400	Sets the maximum speed at which faxes can negotiate. **Note:** The default setting is 14400 bps.
Fax Payload Size	20–48	Configures the number of payload bytes for each Cisco fax relay packet. **Note:** The default value is 20 bytes. Changing this value will alter the delay and bandwidth characteristics of the fax relay call.
Non Standard Facilities Country Code	0–65535	Overrides the country code portion of the T.30 NSF message to this configured value. **Note:** The default value is 65535.
Non Standard Facilities Vendor Code	0–65535	Overrides the vendor code portion of the T.30 NSF message to this configured value. **Note:** The default value is 65535.

The additional fax relay configuration parameters defined in Table 10-23 should look familiar because these same parameters are available in the IOS CLI. Although the 6608 and IOS gateways share the same behavior of having Cisco fax relay enabled by default, the maximum fax rate and ECM settings differ. The IOS gateways default to **fax rate voice** with ECM enabled, whereas the 6608 defaults to 14400 bps with ECM disabled. When integrating 6608 and IOS voice gateways, confirm that these settings are the same.

Another important field to pay attention to in the 6608 GUI configuration is Port Used for Fax Calls. If the box is not checked, Cisco fax relay will not function.

TIP The 6624 Catalyst blade contains 24 analog FXS ports. Like the 6608, this product is currently at an End of Life (EOL) status, but a large number of these cards are still being used. The configuration of the 6624 from a fax relay perspective should be the same as shown earlier for the 6608.

VG248 Fax Relay Configuration

The VG248 is an analog gateway consisting of 48 FXS ports controlled directly by Unified CM using the SCCP protocol. Since code version 1.3(1), the VG248 has supported both Cisco fax relay and NSE-based T.38 fax relay. Neither Cisco modem relay nor Cisco text relay is supported by the VG248.

There are only two main screens on the VG248 where the fax relay configuration parameters are set. One screen sets global attributes for fax relay, and the other screen is attached to each individual port on the gateway. This allows certain fax parameters to be configured on a port-by-port basis.

To access the screen where the global fax relay attributes are located, make the following selections from the main VG248 menu.

```
Configure > Telephony > Advanced Settings
```

Figure 10-2 shows the global fax relay configuration parameters from the VG248 Advanced Settings screen.

The last three settings on the screenshot in Figure 10-2 are the only ones relevant to configuring fax relay on the VG248. The first setting (highlighted) is Fax Relay Payload Size. With a default of 20 bytes, this setting permits a user to select specific payload byte sizes to be used with the fax relay protocol.

Figure 10-2 *VG248 Global Fax Relay Parameters Configuration*

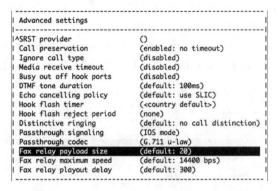

```
|--------------------------------------------------------|
| Advanced settings                                      |
|--------------------------------------------------------|
|ᴧSRST provider              ()                          |
| Call preservation         (enabled: no timeout)        |
| Ignore call type          (disabled)                   |
| Media receive timeout      (disabled)                  |
| Busy out off hook ports    (disabled)                  |
| DTMF tone duration        (default: 100ms)             |
| Echo cancelling policy     (default: use SLIC)         |
| Hook flash timer          (<country default>)          |
| Hook flash reject period   (none)                      |
| Distinctive ringing       (default: no call distinction)|
| Passthrough signaling      (IOS mode)                  |
| Passthrough codec         (G.711 u-law)                |
| Fax relay payload size     (default: 20)               |
| Fax relay maximum speed    (default: 14400 bps)        |
| Fax relay playout delay    (default: 300)              |
|--------------------------------------------------------|
```

The last two parameters are Fax Relay Maximum Speed and Fax Relay Playout Delay. The default setting for the Fax Relay Maximum Speed parameter is a modulation rate of 14400 bps, but with this parameter the VG248 can be configured to enforce lower modulation speeds to save bandwidth. The Fax Relay Playout Delay parameter allows you to tweak the playout buffer to handle varying amounts of jitter but overall end-to-end delay is directly affected. Only in rare circumstances should this value be changed from its default of 300 ms. These global fax relay parameters are summarized in Table 10-24.

Table 10-24 *VG248 Global Fax Relay Configuration Parameters*

Configuration Parameter	Options	Function
Fax Relay Payload Size	20–48	Configures the number of payload bytes for each fax relay packet.
		Note: The default value is 20 bytes. Changing this value will alter the delay and bandwidth characteristics of the fax relay call.
Fax Relay Maximum Speed	voice bandwidth 2400 4800 7200 9600 12000 14400	Sets the maximum speed at which faxes can negotiate. A specific speed can be set or the voice bandwidth setting can be used. Like the IOS command **fax rate voice**, the voice bandwidth setting will prevent faxes from negotiating at a speed greater than the amount of bandwidth used by the voice codec.
		Note: The default setting is 14400 bps.
Fax Relay Playout Delay	100–700	Specifies the playout buffer size for both Cisco and T.38 fax relay in milliseconds
		Note: The default setting is 300 ms.

The other fax relay configuration screen is associated with an individual voice port on the VG248 itself. This screen of port specific parameters can be accessed through the VG248 main menu as follows:

`Configure > Telephony > Port Specific Parameters > port`

Figure 10-3 shows a screenshot of the Port Specific Parameters for port 1.

Figure 10-3 *VG248 Port Specific Fax Relay Parameters Configuration*

```
--------------------------------------------------------------  --------
| Port selection | Port 1 parameters                        |          |
|----------------|------------------------------------------|----------|
|   1 Enabled    | Status                   (enabled)       |          |
|   2 Enabled    | Call control mode        (standard)      |          |
|   3 Disabled   | Caller ID                (enabled)       |          |
|   4 Disabled   | MWI method               (lamp)          |          |
|   5 Disabled   | VMWI variant             (<country default>) |      |
|   6 Disabled   | Call supervision method  (none)          |          |
|   7 Disabled   | Input gain               (0)             |          |
|   8 Disabled   | Output gain              (0)             |          |
|   9 Disabled   | Dialing digit detection  (default: use DSP) |       |
|  10 Disabled   | Fax relay                (T.38 peer to peer) |       |
|  11 Disabled   | Fax relay ECM            (enabled)       |          |
|  12 Disabled   | Fax relay NSF            (preserve value)  |         |
|  13 Disabled   | Passthrough mode         (default: automatic) |      |
|  14 Disabled   | ------------------------------------------ |         |
|  15 Disabled        31 Disabled           47 Disabled     |          |
|  16 Disabled        32 Disabled           48 Disabled     |          |
|          '*' - port in use      press 'R' to enter range  |          |
```

Only three parameters from the VG248 screenshot in Figure 10-3 are important for the configuration of fax relay. The first parameter is Fax Relay. This parameter is where fax relay on the VG248 is set to disabled, Cisco fax relay, or T.38 peer to peer.

When the Fax Relay parameter is set to disabled, fax passthrough can be used to handle fax calls. The Cisco fax relay setting and the T.38 peer to peer settings are only compatible with other Cisco gateways. Unlike Cisco fax relay, T.38 is not proprietary, but the NSE "peer-to-peer" switchover used on the VG248 works only with other Cisco gateways supporting NSE-based T.38 fax relay.

The second fax relay parameter is Fax Relay ECM. The only options here are enabled and disabled. When this parameter is enabled (default), the VG248 allows fax transactions using the ECM protocol to occur. When this parameter is disabled, the ECM feature is not permitted for fax relay calls.

The last fax relay parameter is Fax Relay NSF. This parameter has two options. The first option, preserve value, is the default and it keeps the NSF message exactly as the fax machine encoded it. The other option is override with 000000, and this option overwrites NSF values with all 0s.

Most of the fax relay parameters on this screen are exactly the same as what has been previously discussed with the IOS gateways and the 6608. Table 10-25 summarizes these parameters.

Table 10-25 *VG248 Port Specific Fax Relay Configuration Parameters*

Configuration Parameter	Options	Function
Fax Relay	Disabled	Disables fax relay, and NSE-based passthrough is used for fax calls.
	Cisco fax relay	Enables Cisco fax relay on the port. **Note:** This is the default setting.
	T.38 peer to peer	Enables NSE-based T.38 fax relay on the port.
Fax Relay ECM	Enabled/disabled	With ECM enabled, the VG248 allows fax machines to successfully negotiate the ECM feature. When ECM is set to disabled, the fax endpoints will not use ECM. **Note:** ECM is enabled by default for fax relay.
Fax Relay NSF	Preserve value	Allows the NSF to pass through the VG248 unaltered by the fax relay protocol. **Note:** This is the default setting.
	Override with 000000	Forces the NSF value to all 0s to prevent proprietary messaging between fax machines.

In most circumstances, configuring fax relay on the VG248 basically comes down to selecting the appropriate fax relay protocol, Cisco fax relay or T.38. The default setting of the other fax relay parameters are optimal for most situations.

Summary

This chapter covered the configuration of fax, modem, and text relay on both Cisco IOS and non-IOS gateways using the common voice signaling protocols of H.323, SIP, SCCP, and MGCP. Fax relay, modem relay, and text relay for IOS gateways were discussed first, and then specific non-IOS gateways were covered.

Two types of fax relay are supported by IOS gateways: Cisco fax relay and T.38 fax relay. Cisco fax relay is usually enabled by default except in the case where MGCP is the voice signaling protocol or when the IOS voice gateway uses the NextPort DSP architecture (5350, 5400, and 5850). In these cases, T.38 fax relay is the default fax transport method.

A significant amount of overlap is present in the commands used for configuring T.38 and Cisco fax relay on IOS voice gateways. You should be aware that in many instances the command syntax will be identical, especially for the configuration commands dealing with optional parameters such as ECM and NSF.

Cisco modem relay is configurable for the H.323, SIP, MGCP, and SCCP voice signaling protocols. With the exception of MGCP and its slightly different command syntax, the Cisco modem relay configuration commands are identical and not dependent on the defined voice signaling protocol. By default, Cisco modem relay is disabled on all IOS voice gateways.

The only form of text relay currently supported is Cisco text relay. Cisco text relay is not enabled by default and can be configured globally under **voice service voip** for all voice signaling protocols. For the voice signaling protocols of H.323 and SIP, text relay may also be configured at the dial-peer level.

Sample configurations for IOS gateways were also covered. These configurations reviewed common fax, modem, and text configurations while explaining the relevance of the commands themselves.

The 6608 is a non-IOS gateway configured through a graphical interface as part of Cisco CM. The configuration of Cisco fax relay was discussed for this gateway. T.38 fax relay, modem relay, and text relay are not supported.

The VG248 is another non-IOS gateway configured through a menu-driven CLI. The configurations of both Cisco fax relay and T.38 fax relay were discussed. However, like the 6608, modem relay and text relay are not supported.

CHAPTER 11

Configuring T.37 Store-and-Forward Fax

Recommendation T.37 store-and-forward fax allows for the transport of fax information using e-mail. This replaces the real-time nature of the fax transaction with the convenience of sending and receiving faxes directly from your favorite e-mail application.

Only Cisco IOS gateways support T.37. Non-IOS gateways such as the 6608, VG224, and ATA, which were discussed previously in the passthrough and relay configuration chapters, are not discussed here because of their lack of support for the T.37 specification.

When configuring T.37, onramp and offramp configurations are separate entities and therefore are discussed in separate sections. This does not preclude you from configuring onramp and offramp together on the same voice gateway, but you should address each one individually.

Within each onramp and offramp section, the configuration commands are further broken down into smaller subsections for easy reference. For example, the commands applicable to dial-peer-level configuration are grouped together, and the global configuration commands for configuring the mail transfer agent (MTA) parameters are also grouped together.

At the end of the onramp and offramp sections are sample configurations. These sample configurations provide you with a working example of the common commands necessary for creating a successful T.37 onramp or offramp configuration.

Enabling T.37 Store-and-Forward Fax

Whether you are configuring onramp, offramp, or both, T.37 first needs to be enabled globally on the voice gateway. This is accomplished using the configuration command **fax interface-type fax-mail**, as detailed in Table 11-1.

Table 11-1 *fax interface-type fax-mail IOS Configuration Command*

Command	Function
fax interface-type fax-mail	Enables T.37 functionality on the gateway and directs the gateway to use voice digital signal processors (DSPs) to process T.37 fax store-and-forward data.
	Note: Enabling or disabling this command requires a reload of the IOS voice gateway. By default, this command is disabled.

The most important item to remember about the command **fax interface-type fax-mail** is that the voice gateway must be reloaded upon enabling or disabling this command. This can make the configuration of T.37 onramp or offramp inconvenient for production voice gateways.

Even though some T.37 commands can be configured when **fax interface-type fax-mail** has not been enabled, other commands are unavailable because core T.37 functions are not yet operational. For example, all the debugs associated with T.37 are not available until this command has been configured and the gateway reloaded. In addition, the onramp fax script that is bundled with IOS for the Multimedia Mail over IP (MMoIP) dial-peer (**fax_on_vfc_onramp_app**) does not appear under **show call application voice summary** until this command has been configured and the gateway reloaded. Anytime T.37 onramp or offramp is being configured, this should always be the first command entered.

Loading the TCL Scripts

The IOS voice gateway requires a Tool Command Language (TCL) script to know how to handle an incoming onramp or offramp fax call. Unlike some scripts that are bundled with the IOS software itself, the onramp and offramp TCL fax scripts are typically downloaded from the Cisco website and placed on the voice gateway's flash memory. You can find the location of the latest TCL scripts for T.37 onramp and offramp faxing at the following website. Note that access to these scripts requires a valid cisco.com user account.

http://www.cisco.com/cgi-bin/tablebuild.pl/tclware

In the case of T.37 onramp faxing, the name of the onramp TCL script that needs to be downloaded is app-faxmail-onramp. As of the writing of this book the latest T.37 onramp TCL script is app-faxmail-onramp.2.0.1.3, and this is currently the recommended script to use. Offramp T.37 scripts are labeled app-faxmail-offramp. The latest recommended TCL script for T.37 offramp faxing is app-faxmail-offramp.2.0.1.1.

If you are configuring just onramp or just offramp, only the appropriate script needs to be downloaded. If you plan on configuring both T.37 onramp and offramp, make sure that the TCL script for each is downloaded.

After an onramp or offramp TCL script has been downloaded and unzipped, it is commonly loaded onto the voice gateway's flash memory using the same TFTP or FTP commands used for transferring IOS images. Alternatively, the TCL script can just remain on the TFTP server, and the voice gateway will load it directly from there.

NOTE   If you need more detailed information on downloading the onramp and offramp TCL scripts and making them accessible to the voice gateway, refer to the "How to Download the T.37 Store-and-Forward Fax Scripts" section in the "Configuring T.37 Store-and-Forward Fax" document located at http://www.cisco.com.

Even though an onramp/offramp TCL script is downloaded and accessible by the voice gateway, this script must be properly defined in the IOS configuration file to function correctly. This is accomplished through specifying the location of the script using the **service** command under the **application** section of the IOS configuration file. Table 11-2 describes both the **application** and **service** commands.

Table 11-2 *Global **application** and **service** IOS Configuration Commands*

Command	Function
application	A global configuration command used to enter application configuration mode. This mode is where voice applications and services are defined and configured.
service *service-name location*	Loads a TCL script and defines two critical parameters, a unique service name for the script and the script's location: • *service-name*—Name that identifies the onramp or offramp application. **Note:** This is a user-defined name and does not have to match the TCL script name. • *location*—Directory and filename of the onramp or offramp TCL script in URL format. For example, flash memory (flash:filename) or a TFTP server (tftp://../ filename) is a valid location. The **service** command is valid only when configured in application mode under the **application** command. This method was adopted in Cisco IOS Software Release 12.3(14)T and later and replaces the previous method of using the global command **call application voice** *application-name location*. Despite no longer being available within the context-sensitive help of the IOS command-line interface (CLI), the old deprecated **call application** command is still accepted for the time being. IOS handles this old command by automatically converting it to the new **service** command format. This conversion process is helpful in the event of an IOS upgrade or when an older T.37 configuration using the **call application voice** command is "cut and pasted" into a voice gateway running a newer version of IOS supporting the **service** command.

Without a **service** command defining the onramp or offramp script, T.37 will not function. The importance of these scripts will become more evident later in this chapter when you see how specific onramp and offramp dial-peers reference these TCL scripts.

Configuring T.37 Onramp Fax

Configuring T.37 onramp allows fax calls coming into the voice port of an IOS voice gateway to be converted to an e-mail attachment. The IOS gateway handles the conversion process, whereby the incoming, standard fax page is changed into a TIFF file and attached to an outgoing e-mail.

Dial-peers are still used to route the onramp call through the voice gateway, but there are some configuration differences compared to the dial-peer configuration used for a fax relay or fax passthrough call. First, the incoming plain old telephone service (POTS) dial-peer refers to an onramp TCL script for processing the call. Second, a MMoIP dial-peer is used for communicating with the e-mail server as opposed to a VoIP dial-peer. Last of all, this outgoing MMoIP dial-peer also calls a specific onramp service application for processing the e-mail portion of the onramp fax call.

Although configuring T.37 onramp on an IOS voice gateway might seem somewhat intimidating, the onramp configuration process can be greatly simplified by breaking the task into smaller parts. The onramp configuration process is broken down into a step-by-step quick reference guide in Table 11-3.

Table 11-3 *T.37 Onramp Fax Configuration Quick Reference Guide*

	T.37 Onramp Configuration Step Description	Covered in Section
Step 1	Enable T.37 onramp faxing by issuing the configuration command **fax interface-type fax-mail**. Reload the IOS voice gateway if necessary.	"Enabling T.37 Store-and-Forward Fax"
Step 2	Load and define the onramp TCL script on the voice gateway.	"Loading the TCL Scripts"
Step 3	Define and configure an incoming POTS dial-peer for onramp faxing. This includes applying the onramp TCL script defined in Step 2 to the POTS dial-peer configuration.	"Dial-Peer Configuration for Onramp Fax"
Step 4	Define and configure an MMoIP dial-peer. This includes referencing the IOS-bundled onramp application, **fax_on_vfc_onramp_app**, along with other T.37-specific MMoIP dial-peer commands.	
Step 5	Optionally configure the global onramp fax command **fax receive called-subscriber**.	"Fax Receive Configuration Command for Onramp Fax"
Step 6	Set up the e-mail portion of T.37 onramp using the appropriate Simple Mail Transfer Protocol (SMTP) and MTA commands.	"MTA Configuration Commands for Onramp Fax"

Table 11-3 breaks the configuration of T.37 onramp down into six clearly defined steps. Each of these steps is paired with a configuration subsection where you can find more detailed configuration assistance and command explanations. The step-by-step approach in Table 11-3 provides you with the best method for creating an onramp configuration in the simplest and most efficient manner possible.

TIP	Onramp faxing can be combined with authentication, authorization, and accounting (AAA) services using RADIUS or TACACS+ servers. This configuration option is not covered in this chapter. If you are interested in applying AAA services to a T.37 onramp configuration, refer to the section "Configuring Security and Accounting on the On-Ramp Gateway" in the "Configuring T.37 Store-and-Forward Fax" document located at http://www.cisco.com.

Dial-Peer Configuration for Onramp Fax

Just like a passthrough or relay call through a Cisco IOS gateway, T.37 onramp must also match an inbound and outbound dial-peer. In the case of T.37 onramp, the inbound dial-peer will always be a POTS peer, and the outbound dial-peer will be an MMoIP peer.

From a configuration perspective, the inbound onramp POTS dial-peer is configured the same as any other inbound POTS dial-peer for a VoIP call with the addition of the **service** command. Table 11-4 covers this command and its function.

Table 11-4   *service IOS Configuration Command for the POTS Dial-Peer*

Command	Function
service *service-name*	Identifies the T.37 onramp application that is to be called when a call matches this incoming POTS dial-peer.
	service-name is the name of the application that was defined in application configuration mode as the onramp store-and-forward fax application. For more detail about the script that this command is referencing, see "Loading the TCL Scripts."
	Note: This command was introduced in Cisco IOS Software Release 12.3(14)T. Before this version, the command was **application** *application-name*.

Because the **service** command defined in Table 11-4 references the TCL script specified by the **service** command under the application configuration mode, the user-defined service name for each must match. For example, if the command **service app_onramp flash:app_faxmail_onramp.2.0.1.3.tcl** is configured under the Application menu, **service app_onramp** must be configured under the onramp POTS dial-peer. The service name of **app_onramp** is the keyword that links the two service commands together.

The inclusion of the **service** command in Table 11-4 under the POTS dial-peer allows the gateway to properly process the incoming call as a T.37 onramp call. Therefore, it is critical that you make sure that incoming T.37 calls match this dial-peer. One common practice is to use the command **incoming called-number** *number* under the POTS dial-peer, where *number* represents the called party number or Dialed Number Identification Service (DNIS) as seen by the IOS gateway.

The T.37 onramp feature is designed for use with the command **direct-inward-dial** for correctly processing T.37 onramp calls on digital interfaces, such as T1 and E1. This command is commonly used on regular VoIP calls, too, and it instructs the gateway to make a routing decision based on incoming DNIS. The **direct-inward-dial** command does away with the need for the voice gateway to play dial tone and for the user to go through two-stage dialing. For an example of an onramp POTS dial-peer configuration using this command, see the section "Sample Onramp Configuration" in this chapter.

In addition to the inbound POTS dial-peer, T.37 onramp requires an outbound MMoIP dial-peer. This MMoIP dial-peer is responsible for routing the fax call to the mail server. Under the MMoIP dial-peer for onramp, there are a number of configuration commands, which are grouped and discussed in separate tables.

Table 11-5 defines the general configuration commands required for all onramp MMoIP dial-peers. If any of these configuration commands are not present for an onramp MMoIP dial-peer, onramp fax calls will fail.

Just like the onramp POTS dial-peer, the onramp MMoIP dial-peer needs an onramp specific script. However, this particular onramp script, **fax_on_vfc_onramp_app**, is bundled with IOS and does not need to be downloaded separately.

The presence of the **fax_on_vfc_onramp_app** script can be confirmed with the command **show call application voice summary**. If it is not shown in the list of applications in the output of **show call application voice summary**, it is likely that the command **fax interface-type fax-mail** has not been configured. Another possibility is that the **fax interface-type fax-mail** command has been configured but the gateway has not been reloaded after the command was added.

One command that is not T.37 specific but is just as critical as those highlighted in Table 11-5 is **destination-pattern**. This command is necessary for any outbound VoIP dial-peer, and it defines the digits that must be matched for this MMoIP dial-peer to handle the call.

Table 11-5   *Required MMoIP Dial-peer Configuration Commands for Onramp Fax*

Command	Function
service fax_on_vfc_onramp_app out-bound	Identifies the T.37 onramp application that is to be called when a call matches this MMoIP dial-peer. The **out-bound** keyword simply instructs the application that the calls it handles are outbound from the dial-peer. **Note:** This command was introduced in Cisco IOS Software Release 12.3(14)T. Before this release, the command was **application fax_on_vfc_onramp_app out-bound.**
information-type fax	Identifies the call information associated with this MMoIP dial-peer as being fax rather than voice. **Note:** The default configuration for this command is **information-type voice**.
session protocol smtp	Specifies that the session protocol for calls between the onramp gateway and the remote mail server is to be SMTP.
session target mailto:{*username* | **d** | **m** | **e**}[@*domain-name*]	Designates the e-mail address to which fax mail messages will be sent by the MMoIP dial-peer. • **mailto:** indicates that the argument that follows is an e-mail address. • *username* is a string that contains the username portion of an e-mail address. This can be a single user or a mailing list alias made up of multiple users. • **d** is a wildcard that is replaced by the called party number (DNIS). • @*domain-name* is a string that contains the domain name to be associated with the target address, preceded by the at sign (@). For example, @mycompany.com. **Note:** The other options of **m** and **e** are not applicable to T.37 onramp and are for use with the fax detection application. For more information, see the section "Fax Detect Script" in Chapter 7, "Design Guide for Fax, Modem, and Text."

Onramp commands that configure fax image related parameters are also available under the MMoIP dial-peer. As defined in Table 11-6, these commands configure fax image attributes such as image encoding, image quality check, and image resolution.

Table 11-6 *Optional MMoIP Dial-peer Configuration Commands for Onramp Fax*

Command	Function
image encoding {mh | mr | mmr | passthrough}	Sets the encoding method used for the fax mail TIFF images for calls that match the MMoIP dial-peer: • **mh**—Uses the Modified Huffman algorithm for image encoding. • **mr**—Uses the Modified READ algorithm for image encoding. • **mmr**—Uses the Modified Modified READ algorithm for image encoding. • **passthrough**—Image is not modified by the gateway with any image encoding method. Therefore, the image is encoded by whatever encoding method is used by the originating fax machine. For more detailed information on these three image-encoding schemes, see the section "Page Encoding" in Chapter 2 "How Fax Works." **Note:** The default configuration setting for this command is **image encoding passthrough**.
image quality check	This command enables/disables image quality checking. There is an image quality error rate threshold of 15 percent for the IOS gateway's built-in TIFF writer. If this command is enabled and the error rate threshold is exceeded, the fax image is not sent to the mail server. **Note:** The default behavior is for **image quality check** to be enabled. The default setting for this command should always be used unless problems are encountered.
image resolution {fine | standard | super-fine | passthrough}	Sets the resolution of the fax TIFF images that are forwarded by the specific MMoIP dial: • **fine**—Fax TIFF image resolution setting of 204 x 196 pixels per inch. • **standard**—Fax TIFF image resolution setting of 204 x 98 pixels per inch. • **super-fine**—Fax TIFF image resolution setting of 204 x 391 pixels per inch. • **passthrough**—Resolution of the Fax TIFF image is not to be altered by the gateway. **Note:** The default configuration setting for this command is **image resolution passthrough**.

The commands **image encoding** and **image resolution** provide a means for the onramp gateway to control how the TIFF image is created from the incoming fax call. Even though these same image encoding and resolution parameters also exist for regular T.30 fax calls, these commands applied to an onramp gateway function only with regard to the creation of the fax mail TIFF image.

The last group of configuration commands for the onramp MMoIP dial-peer includes the e-mail message notifications of delivery status notification (DSN) and message disposition notification (MDN). The DSN and MDN configuration commands provide for status messages about the fax e-mail to be relayed back to a user. Table 11-7 details the DSN and MDN configuration commands for an onramp MMoIP dial-peer.

Table 11-7   *DSN and MDN MMoIP Dial-Peer Configuration Commands for Onramp Fax*

Command	Function
dsn {**delayed** | **failure** | **success**}	This command requests in the header of the e-mail fax message that the next-hop mailer notify the sender of the e-mail status via a DSN. The following DSN types are supported: • **delayed** specifies that a DSN is sent when the fax e-mail experiences a delayed condition. The determination of whether the e-mail message is delayed is made independently by each mailer along the path and cannot be controlled by the sender. • **failure** requests that a DSN be sent if the fax e-mail has a delivery failure. • **success** specifies that a DSN message be sent when the fax e-mail has been successfully delivered. **Note:** DSN must be supported by the remote mail server to acquiesce to the notification request. **Note:** The **delayed**, **failure**, and **success** options for the **dsn** command are not mutually exclusive, and each one can be enabled individually. By default, all DSN commands are disabled.
mdn	This command requests in the e-mail fax message header forwarded by the matching MMoIP dial-peer that the remote mail server send an MDN to the sender when the recipient has opened the e-mail message with the TIFF fax attachment. **Note:** This command is disabled by default.

For the **dsn** command and each of its three options in Table 11-7, the DSN message generated by a remote mail server is sent to the e-mail address specified in the command **mta send mail-from**. This command is covered in detail in Table 11-9 in the section "MTA Configuration Commands For Onramp Fax."

As mentioned for the **dsn** command in Table 11-7, mail servers used in the transport and delivery of the fax mail message may not offer support for DSNs. This can cause DSN messages to not be sent even though they were requested with the appropriate **dsn** command under the MMoIP dial-peer. In the case of the command **dsn failure**, nonsupport of DSNs by remote mail servers might not be as big of a problem because a mail delivery failure always generates a nondeliverable or undeliverable message called a bounce.

Whereas DSN messages depend on mail servers to support the DSN extension, the MDN is handled by the receiving mail user agent. However, the mail user agent or client may not support MDNs, just like some mail servers may not support DSNs. When MDNs are sent by the mail client, the message is transmitted to the address defined in the **mta send return-receipt-to** command. For more information on the **mta send return-receipt-to** command, see the section "MTA Configuration Commands for Onramp Fax." If you need to review DSNs and MDNs, see the section "DSN and MDN" in Chapter 6, "T.37 Store-and-Forward Fax."

Fax Receive Configuration Command for Onramp Fax

The **fax receive called-subscriber** command is the only command used in configuring the fax receive parameters for T.37 onramp. Table 11-8 covers this command and its function.

Table 11-8   *fax receive called-subscriber IOS Configuration Command*

Command	Function
fax receive called-subscriber {**d** | *string*}	Configured under the POTS dial-peer, this command defines the called subscriber number that is sent to the originating fax machine via the T.30 called subscriber identification (CSI) message. For more information on the CSI message, see the section "DIS, NSF, and CSI Messages" in Chapter 2. • **d** is a wildcard that takes the DNIS number from the incoming call and inserts it into the CSI message. • *string* is a string that explicitly defines the called subscriber number to be sent to the sending fax machine. **Note:** This command is optional.

As shown in Table 11-8, because the onramp gateway is terminating the T.30 fax signaling, it has the optional ability to send CSI messages with different values. The purpose of these T.30 CSI messages is to inform the originating fax machine of the phone number associated with the receiving fax machine. This CSI information from the terminating fax machine is then typically shown on the originating fax machine's display.

MTA Configuration Commands for Onramp Fax

To send fax images over e-mail, an onramp gateway must be able to interact via SMTP with the MTA. Therefore, MTA-specific configuration commands are necessary for defining the different SMTP headers and other parameters associated with an e-mail. Table 11-9 lists the MTA commands for onramp and describes their function.

Table 11-9 *MTA Configuration Commands for Onramp Fax*

Command	Function
mta send filename [*string*] [**date**]	This command specifies a particular filename for the TIFF file in an e-mail attachment: • *string* specifies the filename of the e-mail attachment. • **date**, which is optional, adds today's date in the format yyyymmdd to the filename of the TIFF attachment. **Note:** If this command is not configured, the default name of Cisco_fax.tif is used. If the filename text string is configured but does not contain a filename extension, .tif is automatically added to the configured filename. **Note:** This command is optional.
mta send mail-from {**hostname** *string* | **username** *string* | **username s**}	The username and hostname specified by these two commands fully define the sender (that is, username@hostname) in the From: field of the onramp e-mail with the fax TIFF attachment: • **hostname** *string* specifies the hostname or IP address of the SMTP server to be used in the From: field. If specifying an IP address, it must be enclosed in brackets as follows: [XXX.XXX.XXX.XXX] • **username** *string* specifies the username of the sender in the From: field of the e-mail. • **username s** is a wildcard that specifies that the sender username in the From: field is derived from the calling party number or Automatic Number Identification (ANI). **Note:** These commands are optional unless the **mta send postmaster** command is not present. Also, as you can logically assume, the **mta send mail-from username** command is mandatory if the **mta send mail-from hostname** command is present.
mta send origin-prefix *string*	This optional command adds a user comment to the e-mail prefix header for additional identifying information.

continues

Table 11-9 *MTA Configuration Commands for Onramp Fax (Continued)*

Command	Function
mta send postmaster *e-mail-address*	Identifies the e-mail address where an e-mail should be sent if it is deemed undeliverable (that is, the postmaster account for the SMTP sever). This postmaster address is also used if the hostname and username information from the **mta send mail-from** command is either invalid or not configured. **Note:** This command is optional if the **mta send mail-from username** and the **mta send mail-from hostname** are present.
mta send return-receipt-to {**hostname** *string* | **username** *string* | **username s**}	Specifies the address to which message disposition notifications (MDNs) are sent: • **hostname** *string* specifies the hostname or IP address of the SMTP server to which MDNs are sent. If specifying an IP address, it must be enclosed in brackets as follows: [XXX.XXX.XXX.XXX] • **username** *string* specifies the username to which MDNs are sent. • **username s** is a wildcard that specifies that the username is derived from the calling party number (that is, ANI). The information configured for this optional command forms the whole address that return receipts will be sent to in the form of: disposition-notification-to:username@hostname.
mta send server {*hostname* | *ip-address* [**port** *port-number*]}	Specifies a destination e-mail server. This command is also used to identify a backup destination mail server in the event the primary is down. This command can be repeated to define up to 10 destination mail servers for backup purposes. The onramp gateway will try and contact the first destination mail server specified in the configuration. If that fails, the onramp gateway proceeds down the list of configured destination mail servers.

Table 11-9 *MTA Configuration Commands for Onramp Fax (Continued)*

Command	Function
	Domain Name System (DNS) mail exchange (MX) records are not used to look up the hostnames provided to this command: • *hostname* specifies the name of the destination e-mail server. • *ip-address* specifies the IP address of the destination e-mail server. • **port** *port-number*, which is optional, designates a particular port to use for the e-mail server. The default port is 25. **Note:** When using the *hostname* option of this command, configure the gateway to perform name lookups using the **ip name-server** command.
mta send subject *string*	This optional command specifies the text string to be used in the Subject: field of the onramp e-mail.
mta send success-fax-only	A fax call that disconnects abnormally after a successful initial T.30 negotiation may generate an e-mail with an empty TIFF attachment that cannot be opened. This can become a nuisance if a fax machine is configured to retry automatically when a line error is encountered. This optional command adds the functionality to drop the e-mail if a fax call disconnects abnormally.
mta send with-subject {d | s | both}	This optional command adds the capability of the onramp gateway to append the DNIS (called party number), ANI (calling party number), or both into the Subject: line of the e-mail that is sent: • **d**—Called party number is attached to the Subject: field. • **s**—Calling party number is attached to the Subject: field. • **both**—Both the called party number and calling party number are attached to the Subject: field.

All the onramp MTA commands in Table 11-9 provide a large amount of flexibility in customizing how the onramp gateway interacts with the MTA or mail server. To better illustrate how the MTA onramp commands configure the SMTP mail headers, it is best to look at a quick example. Example 11-1 takes the commands listed in Table 11-9 and shows some of them configured on an onramp gateway.

Example 11-1   *T.37 Onramp Gateway MTA Configuration*

```
! output omitted for brevity

fax interface-type fax-mail
mta send server 172.18.109.100 port 25
mta send subject Incoming Fax
mta send with-subject both
mta send filename pstn_fax
mta send origin-prefix This is an incoming fax message from the PSTN
mta send postmaster postmaster@pstngateway.com
mta send mail-from hostname zalo.com
mta send mail-from username $s$
mta send success-fax-only

!output omitted for brevity
```

A fax call is placed through the onramp gateway that contains the configuration snippet shown in Example 11-1. The full e-mail headers can now be analyzed to see how the MTA onramp commands control the SMTP header fields. You need to make sure that your e-mail client is capable of and is set up to display the full headers of an e-mail to see all the detailed SMTP header information. Example 11-2 shows the full headers of an e-mail that was sent from an onramp gateway using the MTA command configuration in Example 11-1.

Example 11-2   *Full Message Header from a Cisco T.37 Onramp Gateway*

```
From:            FAX=9194724118@zalo.com
Subject:           Incoming Fax[DNIS=9913170][ANI=9194724118]
Date:        May 22, 2007 11:13:31 AM EDT
To:          gsalguei@faxmail.com
Received:        from fax_2811 ([14.80.32.200]) by RTP-ESC-T37.faxmail.com with
   Microsoft SMTPSVC(5.0.2172.1); Tue, 22 May 2007 18:14:48 -0400
Received:        (This is an incoming fax message from the PSTN) by fax_2811 for
   <gsalguei@faxmail.com> (with Cisco NetWorks); Tue, 22 May 2007 15:13:31 +0000
Message-Id:       <003D2007151331124@fax_2811>
X-Mailer:      Technical Support: http://www.cisco
Mime-Version:      1.0
Content-Type:       multipart/fax-message; boundary="yradnuoB=_
   003C2007151328908.fax_2811"
X-Account-Id:       0
Return-Path:       FAX=9194724118@zalo.com
X-Originalarrivaltime:       22 May 2007 22:15:12.0734 (UTC)
   FILETIME=[AAD7D7E0:01C79CBE]
```

Looking at the different header fields for the e-mail in Example 11-2, you can see where the MTA commands in Example 11-1 are found. In the From: field of the e-mail headers, you see **FAX=9194724118@zalo.com**. This value was built from the MTA configuration commands of **mta send mail-from hostname zalo.com** and **mta send mail-from username s.**

In the Subject: field of Example 11-2, you see Incoming **Fax[DNIS=9913170] [ANI=9194724118]**. The configuration commands of **mta send subject Incoming Fax** and **mta send with-subject both** are responsible for the content in this field.

In the Received: field of the e-mail headers, you will see that the onramp gateway has included itself as the mail server that originated this message. Specifically, the onramp gateway's hostname appears as **fax_2811** with an IP address of **14.80.32.200**. In addition, the information configured by the command **mta send origin-prefix This is an incoming fax message from the PSTN** from Example 11-1 also appears as **(This is an incoming fax message from the PSTN)** in the second Received: field header line.

Sample Onramp Configuration

Example 11-3 combines many of the T.37 onramp commands discussed in the previous sections into a cohesive, working configuration. Comments are made for some of the commands to aid in understanding certain configuration sections, but for more detailed explanations refer back to the tables containing these commands.

Example 11-3   *T.37 Onramp Gateway Configuration*

```
! Output omitted for brevity
!
hostname fax_2811
!
! Output omitted for brevity
!
! Define the value to be used in the CSI message sent to the originating fax machine.
fax receive called-subscriber $d$
!
! Enable T.37 store-and-forward faxing.
fax interface-type fax-mail
!
! Specify the destination e-mail server that will receive onramp fax e-mails.
mta send server 172.18.109.100 port 25
! Specify text that will appear in the Subject: field of the e-mail header.
mta send subject Incoming PSTN Fax
! Indicate the filename that will be used for the fax image attached to the e-mail.
mta send filename pstn_fax
! Insert a user comment to the e-mail prefix header for additional identifying
! information.
mta send origin-prefix This is an incoming fax message from the PSTN
! Define the postmaster mail account for the onramp gateway.
mta send postmaster Administrator@faxmail.com
! Specifies the hostname and username for the originator (From: field of e-mail
! header.
mta send mail-from hostname cisco.com
mta send mail-from username FAXES
! Specify the hostname and username for where MDNs should be sent.
mta send return-receipt-to hostname cisco.com
mta send return-receipt-to username gsalguei
```

continues

Example 11-3 *T.37 Onramp Gateway Configuration (Continued)*

```
!
!
! Define the onramp script to be used by the POTS dial-peer.
application
 service app_onramp flash:app_faxmail_onramp.2.0.1.3.tcl
!
controller T1 0/1/0
 framing esf
 clock source line primary
 linecode b8zs
 pri-group timeslots 1-24
!
! Output omitted for brevity
!
voice-port 0/1/0:23
!
dial-peer voice 2 pots
! Link the onramp POTS dial-peer to the script defined in the application submenu.
 service app_onramp
! Ensure that this onramp POTS dial-peer matches the correct incoming number
 incoming called-number 9913170
 direct-inward-dial
 port 0/1/0:23
!
dial-peer voice 99 mmoip
! Define the IOS-bundled onramp script for the MMoIP dial-peer.
 service fax_on_vfc_onramp_app out-bound
 destination-pattern 9913170
! Specify that this MMoIP dial-peer handles fax
 information-type fax
! Indicate the e-mail address of where the fax e-mail should be sent (To: field)
 session target mailto:gsalguei@faxmail.com
! Request that an MDN message be sent back when the destination mail client has
! opened the fax message.
 mdn
! Request that DSN messages be sent.
 dsn delayed
 dsn success
 dsn failure
!
! Output omitted for brevity
```

In Example 11-3, the originating fax machine dials 991-3170 to reach the onramp gateway. The call arrives on voice port 0/1/0:23 and matches the inbound POTS dial-peer 2, which is configured with the appropriate onramp TCL script. On the outbound side, the MMoIP dial-peer 99 is matched, which directs the gateway to send the fax transmission as an e-mail.

This working onramp configuration contains all the required T.37 onramp commands and some of the optional ones that are commonly seen. Be aware that this onramp configuration can be combined with an offramp configuration to create a single gateway that supports both onramp and offramp functionality.

Configuring T.37 Offramp Fax

T.37 offramp faxing provides for the conversion of e-mails to G3 fax calls, the reverse of what is accomplished by the T.37 onramp function. Just as with onramp, a mixture of global configuration commands and dial-peer specific commands are necessary for generating a working T.37 offramp configuration. Table 11-10 simplifies the configuration of T.37 offramp to a few steps. Each step in the table references a section of this chapter where more information may be obtained for that configuration step.

Table 11-10 *T.37 Offramp Fax Configuration Quick Reference Guide*

	T.37 Offramp Configuration Step Description	Covered in Section
Step 1	Enable T.37 offramp faxing by issuing the configuration command **fax interface-type fax-mail**. Reload the IOS voice gateway if necessary.	"Enabling T.37 Store-and-Forward Fax"
Step 2	Load and define the offramp TCL script on the voice gateway.	"Loading the TCL Scripts"
Step 3	Define and configure an incoming MMoIP dial-peer for offramp faxing. This includes applying the offramp TCL script defined in Step 2 to the MMoIP dial-peer configuration.	"Dial-peer Configuration for Offramp Fax"
Step 4	Define and configure an outbound POTS dial-peer.	
Step 5	Configure the optional, global offramp fax commands.	"Fax Send Configuration Commands for Offramp Fax"
Step 6	Set up the e-mail portion of T.37 offramp using the appropriate SMTP and MTA commands.	"MTA Configuration Commands for Offramp Fax"

Comparing the configuration steps for offramp in Table 11-10 with the steps for onramp in Table 11-3, you will notice many similarities. Both offramp and onramp require a TCL script to be downloaded and made accessible to the voice gateway. They also both have global and dial-peer-level configuration commands applicable to each. This in turn makes the configuration of offramp a bit easier if onramp has been previously configured and vice versa.

Dial-Peer Configuration for Offramp Fax

As with any other standard VoIP call going through a Cisco voice gateway, T.37 offramp requires an inbound and outbound dial-peer. On the inbound side for the connection to the mail server, an MMoIP dial-peer is configured. On the outbound leg, a POTS dial-peer is needed. Unlike T.37 onramp, which requires T.37-specific commands on both dial-peers, T.37 offramp has only T.37-specific commands for the inbound MMoIP dial-peer. The offramp POTS dial-peer is just configured normally to route the offramp call out a particular telephony interface.

Table 11-11 defines the applicable configuration commands for the offramp MMoIP dial-peer. These commands are identical to the commands that are also used on onramp MMoIP dial-peers. Therefore, the commands are mentioned here in Table 11-11 as a quick reference to the supported offramp MMoIP dial-peer commands; but for more detailed information on these commands, refer back to Tables 11-5 and 11-6, where these commands were initially introduced.

Table 11-11 *MMoIP Dial-Peer Configuration Commands for Offramp Fax*

Command	Function
service *service-name*	Identifies the T.37 offramp application that is to be called when a call matches this incoming MMoIP dial-peer.
	The *service-name* parameter defines the name of the application that was defined in application configuration mode as the offramp store-and-forward fax application. For more detail about the script that this command is referencing, see "Loading the TCL Scripts."
	Note: This command was introduced in Cisco IOS Software Release 12.3(14)T. Before this release, the command was **application** *application-name*.
information-type fax	This command was introduced in the section "Dial-Peer Configuration for Onramp Fax" earlier in this chapter, and it has the same behavior regardless of whether offramp or onramp is configured. For more detail on this configuration command, see Table 11-5.
image encoding {**mh** | **mr** | **mmr** | **passthrough**}	These commands were introduced in the section "Dial-Peer Configuration for Onramp Fax" earlier in this chapter. Their function and behavior is the same except for two major caveats:
image resolution {**fine** | **standard** | **super-fine** | **passthrough**}	• Unlike onramp where these commands applied to the TIFF creation used in the fax e-mail, with offramp these commands apply to the image transmitted by the outbound fax call over the telephony voice port.
	• The command **image encoding mmr** is not supported for offramp because Error Correction Mode (ECM) is not supported for T.37. As explained in the section "Modified Modified READ" in Chapter 2, MMR can be used only on fax calls with the ECM feature enabled.
	For more detail on these configuration commands, see Table 11-6.

Fax Send Configuration Commands for Offramp Fax

A number of T.37 offramp commands are available that enable you to alter the fax send configuration parameters. These commands are not configured under a dial-peer but are global in nature.

Many of these fax send parameters deal with the formatting and information displayed on the fax image page and the cover page. Other commands enable you to adjust the fax transmission speed and the information contained in the T.30 transmitting subscriber identification (TSI) message. For easier presentation, similar commands are grouped together and discussed in the same table. Table 11-12 highlights the T.37 offramp commands that configure the fax headers that will appear on each fax page transmitted.

Table 11-12 *Fax Header Configuration Commands*

Command	Function
fax send center-header {**a** | **d** | **p** | **s** | **t** | *string*}	Specifies the header information to be displayed in the center position: • **a**—Date • **d**—Destination address • **p**—Page count • **s**—Sender address • **t**—Transmission time • *string*—Combination of text and $$ tokens
fax send right-header {**a** | **d** | **p** | **s** | **t** | *string*}	Specifies the header information to be displayed on the right: • **a**—Date • **d**—Destination address • **p**—Page count • **s**—Sender address • **t**—Transmission time • *string*—Combination of text and $$ tokens
fax send left-header {**a** | **d** | **p** | **s** | **t** | *string*}	Specifies the header information to be displayed on the left: • **a**—Date • **d**—Destination address • **p**—Page count • **s**—Sender address • **t**—Transmission time • *string*—Combination of text and $$ tokens

The optional fax header commands in Table 11-12 provide the ability to customize the appearance of the fax header line that will appear at the top of each fax transmitted by the offramp gateway. Three fields encompassing the left, right, and center header positions can be configured to show a variety of different parameters, including the date and page number.

The ability to automatically include a fax cover page is also configurable on the T.37 offramp gateway. Table 11-13 covers the commands for creating a fax cover page on the offramp gateway.

Table 11-13 *Fax Cover Page Configuration Commands*

Command	Function
fax send coverpage comment *string*	Defines customized text in the title field of a fax cover sheet generated by the offramp gateway. • *string*—ASCII character text string
fax send coverpage email-controllable	Allows the cover parameter in the fax e-mail address (that is, the To: field in the e-mail header) to determine whether a cover sheet is to be generated by the offramp gateway on a per-recipient basis. This cover parameter is enabled with **/cover=yes** following the telephone number in the To: field and disabled with **/cover=no**. Note: If the **fax send coverpage email-controllable** command is configured, the setting of the cover parameter in the To: field of the e-mail header will always override the setting of the **fax send coverpage enable** configuration command.
fax send coverpage enable	Enables the offramp gateway to generate fax cover sheets for faxes that originate from e-mail messages. Note: By default, the sending of fax cover pages is disabled.
fax send coverpage show-detail	Prints all the e-mail header information as part of the text on fax cover sheets generated by the offramp gateway.

The command in Table 11-13 that seems to cause the most confusion is **fax send coverpage email-controllable**. To better understand this configuration command, the following example is helpful. Suppose an e-mail address of a fax e-mail message uses the following To: field

FAX=+1-312-555-0119/cover=no@fax.com

This indicates that an offramp gateway configured with the command **fax send coverpage email-controllable** will ensure a fax is to be sent to the phone number 1-312-555-0119 with no cover sheet. A cover page will not be sent regardless of whether **fax send coverpage enable** is configured. Conversely, if this same example had **/cover=yes**, a cover page would be included even if the command **no fax send coverpage enable** were configured.

The last fax send configuration commands used in T.37 offramp faxing are **fax send max-speed** and **fax send transmitting subscriber**. Table 11-14 covers these commands in further detail.

Table 11-14 *fax send IOS Configuration Command*

Command	Function
fax send max-speed { **12000** | **14400** | **2400** | **4800** | **7200** | **9600** }	Specifies the maximum speed of the outbound fax transmission: • **12000**—Transmission speed of 12000 bps • **14400**—Transmission speed of 14400 bps • **2400**—Transmission speed of 2400 bps • **4800**—Transmission speed of 4800 bps • **7200**—Transmission speed of 7200 bps • **9600**—Transmission speed of 9600 bps **Note:** This command is optional, and the default speed of 14400 is used if the command is not explicitly configured.
fax send transmitting-subscriber { **s** | *string* }	This command defines the TSI that is sent to the terminating fax machine via the T.30 TSI message. For more information on the TSI message, see the section "DCS and TSI Messages" in Chapter 2. • **s** is a wildcard that indicates a substitution of the sender information defined in the username portion of the From: field of the RFC 822 header is to be used as the transmitting subscriber number • *string* is a string that explicitly defines the transmitting subscriber information to be sent to the receiving fax machine. **Note:** This command is optional.

The command **fax send transmitting subscriber s** in Table 11-14 may require some additional clarification. In the From: field of an e-mail, you will typically find the address shown in the following form:

Joe Smith <jsmith@mycompany.com>

The actual e-mail address of jsmith@mycompany.com is shown within the brackets, whereas Joe Smith is the display name. When the command **fax send transmitting subscriber s** is configured, the display name is inserted into the T.30 TSI message. Many fax machines will then show this TSI information on an external display.

MTA Configuration Commands for Offramp Fax

The MTA T.37 offramp commands configure the connection between the offramp gateway and the mail server. Table 11-15 defines these commands and their functions.

Table 11-15 *MTA Configuration Commands for Offramp Fax*

Command	Function
mta receive aliases *string*	Specifies a hostname to be used as an SMTP alias for the offramp gateway. Up to 10 different aliases can be configured. The gateway will accept an incoming e-mail as long as it matches one of the configured aliases. **Note:** If this command is not configured, the default alias is the offramp gateway's hostname.
mta receive disable-dsn	This command provides the ability to disable delivery status notifications (DSNs) from being generated by the offramp gateway. By default, the offramp gateway responds to all DSN requests that are received. When this command is configured, the offramp gateway will not send DSN notifications irrespective of whether the DSN notification was requested in the rcpt to: header of the e-mail message received by the offramp gateway. **Note:** This command is optional and was first introduced in Cisco IOS Software Release 12.4(13). Typically, it should not be configured unless the sender's inbox is being overloaded by DSNs because of an overzealous SMTP client that tries resending faxes nonstop over an extended period of time.
mta receive generate [mdn | permanent-error]	This optional command defines the type of fax delivery response message the offramp gateway should return: • **mdn** specifies that the offramp gateway process response MDNs from an SMTP server. • **permanent-error** directs the T.37 offramp fax gateway to classify all fax delivery errors as permanent so that they are forwarded in SMTP DSN messages with descriptive error codes to an MTA. The descriptive error codes allow the MTA to control fax operations directly because the MTA can examine the error codes and make decisions about how to proceed with each fax (whether to retry or cancel, for example).

Table 11-15 *MTA Configuration Commands for Offramp Fax (Continued)*

Command	Function
	The **default mdn** setting ensures that standard SMTP status messages are returned to the SMTP client with error classifications of permanent or transient.
	Note: The **mta receive generate** command replaced the **mta receive generate-mdn** command in Cisco IOS Software Release 12.3(7)T.
	Note: The command **mta send server** discussed in Table 11-6 must also be configured for the offramp gateway to know where to send the MDN messages.
mta receive maximum-recipients *number*	Sets the maximum number of simultaneous SMTP recipients handled by this gateway. This allows you to decide on how many resources to allocate for faxing at any given time.
	The range for this command is 0 to 1024.
	Note: The default value for this command is 0. This implies that no incoming mail messages are accepted; therefore, no faxes are sent by the offramp gateway.

The two critical MTA offramp commands in Table 11-15 are **mta receive aliases** and **mta receive maximum-recipients**. If these commands are not configured or configured incorrectly, offramp fax failures usually result.

Sample Offramp Configuration

The configuration of T.37 offramp on Cisco IOS voice gateways is not a difficult task, especially if you follow the quick reference configuration steps in Table 11-10. Following those steps can assist you in creating a working T.37 offramp configuration like the one shown in Example 11-4.

Example 11-4 *T.37 Offramp Gateway Configuration*

```
! Output omitted for brevity
!
hostname fax_2851
!
! Output omitted for brevity
!
! Define the TSI value to be sent by the offramp gateway to the terminating fax
! machine.
fax send transmitting-subscriber $s$
!
```

continues

Example 11-4 *T.37 Offramp Gateway Configuration (Continued)*

```
! Specify the left fax header to display the sender's address, the center header to
! display the transmission time and the right header to display the page number.
fax send left-header $s$
fax send center-header $t$
fax send right-header $p$
! Specify that a fax cover page be included with offramp fax transmissions.
fax send coverpage enable
! Include e-mail header information on the fax cover sheet.
fax send coverpage show-detail
! Specify a comment to be included on fax cover pages.
fax send coverpage comment OffRamp Fax From Cisco 2851
!
! Enable T.37 faxing on the voice gateway.
fax interface-type fax-mail
!
! Specify the mail server where MDN messages are sent.
mta send server 172.18.109.100 port 25
! Define additional hostnames to be used as an alias for this offramp gateway.
mta receive aliases 14.80.32.201
mta receive aliases fax_2851.faxmail.com
! Specify the number of simultaneous SMTP connections for the offramp gateway.
mta receive maximum-recipients 100
! Enable MDN response on the offramp gateway.
mta receive generate mdn
!
! Specify the location of the offramp TCL script. This script is referenced by the
! offramp MMoIP dial-peer.
application
service app_offramp flash:app_faxmail_offramp.2.0.1.1.tcl
!
! Output Omitted for Brevity
!
voice-port 1/0:23
!
! Configure the offramp outbound POTS dial-peer.
dial-peer voice 2 pots
destination-pattern 9194724118
port 1/0:23
forward-digits all
!
! Configure the inbound offramp MMoIP dial-peer.
dial-peer voice 99 mmoip
! Link this MMoIP dial-peer to the TCL offramp script defined under the application
! submenu
service app_offramp
! Specify that this MMoIP dial-peer handles fax
information-type fax
incoming called-number 9194724118
```

Example 11-4   *T.37 Offramp Gateway Configuration (Continued)*

```
! Specify the optional use of MH image encoding.
image encoding MH
! Specify the optional image resolution of super fine.
image resolution super-fine
!
! Output omitted for brevity
```

As mentioned previously in this chapter, offramp and onramp can be configured together on the same voice gateway. In this case, the offramp sample configuration in Example 11-4 would just be combined with the onramp sample configuration discussed earlier in Example 11-3.

Summary

The configuration of T.37 store-and-forward faxing can be easily divided into the two configuration subsections of onramp and offramp faxing. You configure onramp faxing to handle the conversion of normal G3 fax calls to e-mails, whereas offramp faxing reverses the onramp process and converts fax e-mails into normal telephony fax calls.

Even though they differ in functionality and commands, the configuration process for onramp and offramp faxing is still similar. In both cases, T.37 needs to be enabled on the gateway, and certain TCL scripts need to be downloaded and made available to both onramp and offramp gateways. Then, for each, you must configure the appropriate dial-peer level and global T.37 configuration commands followed by onramp- or offramp-specific MTA commands.

Tables are shown throughout this chapter to help in looking up detailed information on any T.37 onramp or offramp configuration command. Furthermore, at the end of both the onramp and offramp sections, a working sample configuration is shown with comments explaining the function of the important T.37 commands.

Troubleshooting

CHAPTER 12

Troubleshooting Passthrough and Relay

Troubleshooting fax, modem, and text problems in IP networks can become quite complex, and it requires a solid base of knowledge in several key areas. The previous chapters in this book covering how faxes, modems, and text devices work, their transport over IP, network design, and configuration provide the solid knowledge base required for understanding and using the information contained in this troubleshooting chapter.

Many aspects and methods of troubleshooting passthrough and relay overlap. Therefore, to eliminate redundancy, the content at the beginning of this chapter looks at these two transport mechanisms together along with their troubleshooting commonalities. Later in the chapter, troubleshooting tips and strategies that address passthrough and relay individually are discussed.

The organization of this chapter is built upon a troubleshooting methodology that has been successful in efficiently resolving fax, modem, and text problems. This methodology is outlined and explained in the first section of this chapter. Subsequent sections of this chapter are then expanded discussions of this troubleshooting methodology's component parts. Understanding this troubleshooting methodology and gaining experience applying it will greatly increase the usefulness of this chapter.

This chapter is composed of the following sections:

- **Attacking the Problem**: Introduces a systematic troubleshooting methodology for resolving fax, modem, and text problems

- **Fundamental Troubleshooting**: Covers quick, basic concepts that need to be addressed before going deeper into the troubleshooting process

- **Telephony and IP Troubleshooting**: Discusses and shows examples of troubleshooting techniques for the telephony and IP legs of a call

- **Troubleshooting the Switchover Signaling**: Includes diagnostic commands and sample debugs to assist in identifying problems as the voice call transitions to a fax/modem call

- **Passthrough and Relay Troubleshooting**: Covers debugs and other advanced tools associated with troubleshooting different passthrough and relay protocols

By the end of this chapter, you should have a practical arsenal of troubleshooting techniques along with the knowledge of how to properly apply those techniques. This should make the resolution of the simplest to the most complex fax, modem, and text problems much easier to achieve in the shortest amount of time.

Attacking the Problem

Fax, modem, and text problems in VoIP networks can range from simple issues to complex issues that may require a substantial amount of troubleshooting. However, with the appropriate troubleshooting methodology, you can attain more expedient resolutions.

People do not always troubleshoot problems in the same exact way. Different strategies, points of view, and levels of experience are just some of the factors that determine a person's troubleshooting methodology.

When it comes to troubleshooting fax, modem, and text problems, years of troubleshooting experience by a few Cisco TAC (Technical Assistance Center) engineers has led to the development of a specific troubleshooting methodology. This methodology provides a systematic and efficient troubleshooting approach that can assist you in achieving rapid fax, modem, and text problem resolutions.

Based on a "divide and conquer" notion of being able to narrow the problem down to a well-defined part of the fax, modem, or text call, this methodology offers a simple means to quickly hone in on the root cause of the problem. Figure 12-1 illustrates the recommended methodology for efficiently resolving fax, modem, and text issues.

Figure 12-1 shows two fax machines connected over an IP network via two voice gateways, but modems or text telephony devices could replace the fax machines in this illustration, too. The main concept demonstrated here is the systematic breakdown to the troubleshooting of fax, modem, and text problems.

As you look at Figure 12-1 from top to bottom, you will see a step-by-step troubleshooting methodology numbered one through five. While you are tackling fax, modem, and text problems, this model intuitively leads you to a resolution in a logical, orderly manner. After a troubleshooting step or section has been completed, its components can be eliminated, narrowing the scope of the problem.

When using the methodology illustrated in Figure 12-1, the first place to start is with fundamental troubleshooting. Fundamental troubleshooting encompasses a number of quick checks and tests that if performed early can curtail a lot of frustration later on. Some of these checks are global in scope and include testing voice calls in place of fax calls, testing calls over the public switched telephone network (PSTN), and reviewing the configuration of the gateways. Foundational items such as these are discussed in detail in the next section, "Fundamental Troubleshooting."

Figure 12-1 *Recommended Troubleshooting Methodology for Fax, Modem, and Text Problems*

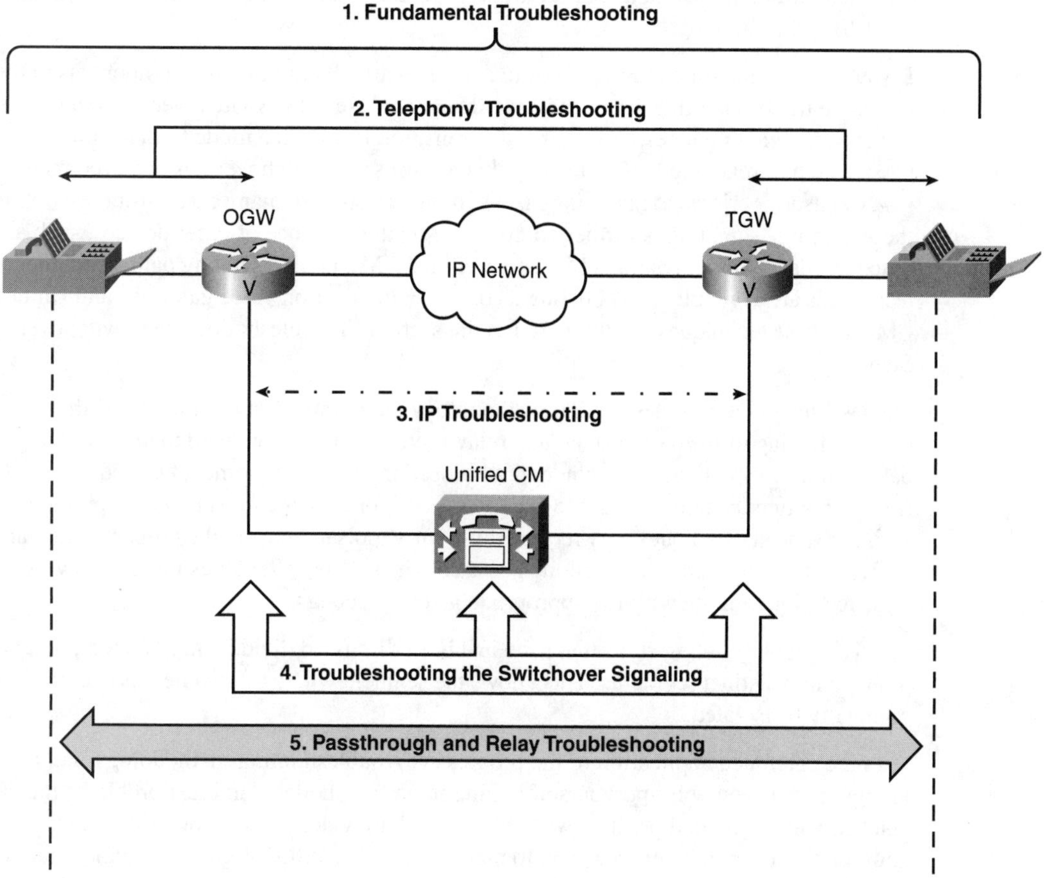

The next area to examine after fundamental troubleshooting is telephony troubleshooting. The telephony portion of a problem involves the analog or digital POTS (plain old telephone service) connection between the voice gateway and the fax/modem/text device. Issues or impairments on the telephony side can be a source of call degradation and failures. Troubleshooting the telephony portion of a fax/modem/text call can be found in the "Telephony and IP Troubleshooting" section of this chapter.

IP troubleshooting is the next step in the fax, modem, and text troubleshooting methodology identified in Figure 12-1. The IP portion of a call lies between the voice gateways, and this is an environment not inherently designed for modulated communications. Therefore, effective problem resolution within the IP network from a fax/modem/text perspective is important. More information about IP troubleshooting is covered in the section "Telephony and IP Troubleshooting."

If you have not identified the cause of the problem after examining the components in the first three troubleshooting areas, the next area to analyze is the switchover signaling. The switchover signaling is responsible for the transition from voice mode to the appropriate passthrough or relay mode. Confirming that a successful switchover has occurred on the gateway itself is critical to resolving fax and modem issues. In many cases, troubleshooting the switchover signaling is further complicated by the presence of other devices, such as Cisco Unified Communications Manager (Unified CM), in the signaling path. A number of techniques are available for validating a correct switchover on voice gateways and Unified CM and these techniques are discussed in the section "Troubleshooting the Switchover Signaling."

The last step in the troubleshooting methodology diagrammed in Figure 12-1 is the troubleshooting of the passthrough and relay protocols themselves and their underlying data. Quite a few debugs are included in this section, as well as some advanced troubleshooting techniques that are usually needed for only the most complex problems. These advanced techniques may require third-party tools to assist in the proper capture and analysis of the problem. The section "Passthrough and Relay Troubleshooting" covers these techniques along with the appropriate gateway debugs.

The five troubleshooting steps that have just been discussed divide a fax, modem, or text problem into distinct segments. This allows the segment where the problem is occurring to eventually be isolated.

With the continued application of the progressive troubleshooting methodology outlined in Figure 12-1, you will find yourself honing in on fax, modem, and text problems much quicker. Familiarity and practice with this methodology develops a troubleshooting intuition that eventually enables you to manipulate this methodology in a manner that is appropriate for your experience level.

For example, a fax problem may be presented in a manner where you are comfortable that the call connects fine but you feel that there is a problem in the transition to T.38. At this point, skipping to the section "Troubleshooting the Switchover Signaling" may make sense. Just be aware that jumping around too much defeats the purpose of this methodology, which is built upon a systematic elimination of problem areas.

Fundamental Troubleshooting

Before tackling what might appear to be a tough passthrough or relay problem, it is wise to always take a moment and check some call fundamentals. Spending a few extra minutes in the beginning confirming some basic information can save time and prevent unnecessary troubleshooting steps later.

Some of the basics that need to be addressed before engaging in a full troubleshooting session are real-world, commonsense items. These items are often taken for granted because they might seem simplistic and obvious at first. On quite a few occasions, however, performing these checks would have led to an expedited resolution.

Additional troubleshooting fundamentals involve looking at the problem from the perspective of a regular voice call and even removing the IP network from the picture. Finally, you will be provided with some best practices for enabling debugs in Cisco voice gateways. The completion of the fundamental tasks in this section ensures the efficacy of the later troubleshooting sections.

Checking the Condition of Originating and Terminating Devices

A variety of issues can occur on the fax, modem, or text devices themselves and cause failures. These issues range from fax machines not having any paper to modems having been accidentally unplugged. Although these issues are not always common, catching them early can save you some frustration and even embarrassment down the road. Table 12-1 highlights some common conditions and tests for determining the status of fax, modem, and text endpoints.

Table 12-1   *Checking the Condition of Fax, Modem, and Text Devices*

Condition	Description
Power	Is the device plugged in and powered on? This can usually be easily confirmed by the presence of lights on the device in question.
Connection to network	Is the device connected to the correct jack for network access? Follow the cable from the end device to the appropriate jack. If multiple jacks are present, confirm that the device is plugged in to the correct jack.
Error messages	Check the device for any error messages on the display. Sometimes fax, modems, and text devices display an error message or error code when there is a problem.
Fax machine paper and toner	Fax endpoints may have issues terminating a fax call when the paper or toner is empty. Even though the fax may be stored in memory, some users might mistakenly think a failure has occurred because the fax did not print immediately. Eventually, the memory will become full, too, and true failures will then occur.
Proper device configuration	Check the device to make sure that it is properly configured. For example, is the terminating modem set to AA (Auto Answer)? Also, some fax machines can be configured to not automatically answer an incoming call.

Testing with Voice Calls

After performing the checks in Table 12-1, the next step in checking basic functionality is to place a normal voice call over the fax, modem, or text connection. With many fax and text devices, placing this voice call is quite simple because a handset is built in to the device itself. When dealing with modems or fax/text devices without built-in handsets, you can use a regular analog phone.

Figure 12-2 illustrates a modem over IP topology where the modems have been disconnected and regular analog phones have been inserted in place of the modems. Naturally, fax machines or text telephony devices could just as easily replace the modems in this diagram.

Figure 12-2 *Testing the Connection by Placing a Voice Call*

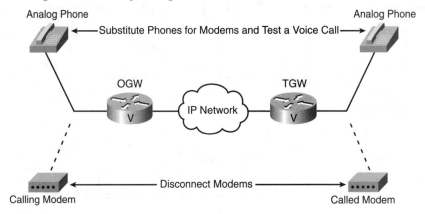

When an analog phone must be used for placing the voice call, make sure that the phone is plugged directly into the same jack or port that was being used by the device in question. The goal for this test call is to confirm the integrity of the call path that is used by the fax, modem, or text device that is having a problem. If possible, place the call from the same location as the fax, modem, or text device and refrain from shortening the connection by testing from patch panels or wiring closets.

Placing this voice call allows you to test for a number of different potential problems at one time. Table 12-2 highlights some of the important information you can gain by placing a regular voice call over the fax, modem, or text connection.

After voice calls have been reliably placed over the fax, modem, or text connection, it is usually safe to assume that the transport through the VoIP network is satisfactory from a voice protocol signaling and RTP audio path perspective. Voice calls that fail or have problems through the connection indicate that the problem at hand is a VoIP problem and not a problem attributable specifically to fax, modem, or text. Therefore, you should troubleshoot such an issue in the same way you troubleshoot a basic VoIP call failure.

Table 12-2   *Potential Problems Uncovered by Testing the Connection with a Voice Call*

Potential Problem Area	Description
Call routing	Does the originating side connect to the terminating side when the appropriate number is dialed? If not, there might be a call routing or dial plan issue.
Underlying voice signaling protocol	If the calls connect properly, this typically ensures that the underlying voice signaling protocol has done its job properly and certifies that the call setup procedure and capabilities exchange occurred successfully.
Establishment of audio path	After the call is connected, an audio path should be established, and the users on each end should be able to hear each other. If not, there might be a DSP/IOS problem or the RTP packets of the audio stream are getting blocked, discarded, or corrupted in the network.
Circuit quality	With the voice call established, you should hold a conversation with someone on the other end of the connection. During this conversation, both you and the other person should listen for voice quality issues such as choppy voice, robotic voice, echo, and clipping. The audio quality should be clean without impairments. If voice quality problems are detected, look for network problems such as queuing, policing, packet drops, and improper signal levels.

TIP   The main reasoning for placing a normal voice call over the fax, modem, and text connection is based on the premise that you should not expect fax, modem, or text calls to work over a connection where voice calls are not successful. After you have concluded that the problem at hand is not specific to fax, modem, or text calls, the problem should be troubleshot as you would any VoIP call issue. This book assumes you have familiarity with basic VoIP troubleshooting. If you do not, consult a good voice troubleshooting reference such as *Troubleshooting Cisco IP Telephony* (ISBN: 1-58705-075-7).

Testing with PSTN Calls

Faxes, modems, and text devices were originally designed to function in a standard PSTN environment. Their migration to VoIP networks poses additional challenges such as delay, jitter, and packet drops that may negatively impact their success. Therefore, it is critical to ensure that a problematic fax, modem, or text device works over the PSTN first before expecting it to work over an IP network.

Figure 12-3 illustrates a fax machine being moved from its VoIP network connection to a PSTN connection for testing. Be aware that a modem or text device could also be substituted for the fax machine in this diagram.

Figure 12-3 *Testing the Connection over the PSTN*

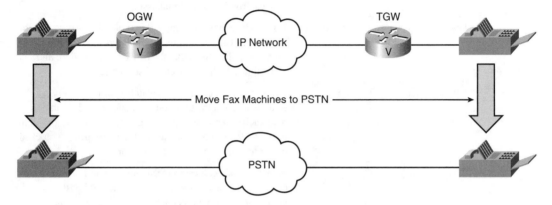

A straight PSTN connection between the two modulated end devices eliminates any adverse effects from the VoIP network. If the devices work fine over the PSTN but fail when connected over the VoIP network, you have confirmation that the issue is VoIP related. However, if the devices fail to work over the PSTN, there is a good chance that you are dealing with a problem that is not VoIP related at all.

Occasionally, fax, modem, and text devices develop problems even though everything has been working fine for years. Other times, users might unknowingly change a setting or configuration on the end device that can cause failures, too. Taking the time to test problematic devices over the PSTN is the best way to confirm that these end devices are operating correctly.

Confirming the Configuration

For fax, modem, and text calls to work successfully, the gateways on either side and Unified CM, if present, must be properly configured. However, for a variety of reasons, the gateway or Unified CM can be misconfigured or its configuration can inadvertently get changed.

Often, configuration changes are made for the installation of new equipment or to address another VoIP-related problem. Later on, these changes, especially when they involve dial-peers, are found to have unintentionally affected the handling of fax, modem, or text calls.

Another scenario involves the creation of a working configuration file to handle fax, modem, and text calls. However, this file is not written to NVRAM, and after a loss of power or IOS upgrade, the working configuration file is lost and fax, modem, or text problems can start to occur.

Therefore, it is prudent to take a few minutes and confirm the configurations of the gateways and Unified CM involved in a fax/modem/text problem. Not checking these configurations can result in a simple configuration error, causing you to unnecessarily spend time performing troubleshooting tasks.

The following list highlights a few of the most common configuration errors:

- For fax and modem calls, confirm that either passthrough or relay is being used and make sure that the passthrough or relay types match. For example, if NSE-based T.38 is configured on one side, NSE-based T.38 should also be configured on the other voice gateway to handle fax calls.

- If one of the gateways is a third-party device, make sure that the protocol stack is used for the passthrough or relay switchover and not Named Signaling Events (NSE). For example, protocol-based pass-through and protocol-based T.38 must be configured on the Cisco gateways for fax calls to interoperate with third-party gateways.

- Some gateways might have problems when the passthrough redundancy option is enabled on one side but not on the other. Make sure that the passthrough redundancy configuration is the same on both gateways.

Fax, modem, and text configurations can involve layered call handling strategies, multiple settings, and other options. For additional passthrough configuration information, see Chapter 9, "Configuring Passthrough;" and for more information about configuring relay, see Chapter 10, "Configuring Relay."

Debugging Best Practices

As you delve deeper into troubleshooting fax, modem, and text problems, you will eventually need to enable debug commands on the Cisco gateways and Unified CM, if it is present, to view certain pieces of information. However, enabling debugs in an incorrect manner can cause instability in those devices and impact their performance in a negative way. Therefore, it is highly recommended that you follow the best practices and tips in this section whenever it is necessary to enable debugs.

NOTE   Even in Unified CM environments, the majority of the debugging for fax, modem, and text issues is done on the voice gateways. The reason for this is that Unified CM is involved only in the switchover portion of the call, and it does not handle the actual fax, modem, or text media stream. Furthermore, the only types of switchovers that Unified CM is involved in are those that occur within the voice signaling or call control protocol. Alternative switchover methods such as NSE-based switchovers or payload type switching are all done in the media stream and occur exclusively between gateways without the knowledge of Unified CM. For this reason, the debugging best practices presented in this section focus on the Cisco voice gateways.

The first concept that you must understand when running a debug command on a Cisco voice gateway is that the debug output can be displayed to you through various methods. These methods include the console port, a vty session (such as Telnet or SSH), a syslog server, and an internal buffer on the voice gateway itself.

The most critical of these various debug display methods is the console port. This interface displays debug output by default at an output rate of 9600 bps, which is too slow to handle detailed debug information. In addition, the console port is interrupt driven. So, large amounts of debug information piped out of the console port may greatly impact the CPU and the processes currently running on the voice gateway. Therefore, it is highly recommended that you disable the logging of debug messages to the console port with the command **no logging console** whenever any debugging is to be enabled, especially on production gateways.

Performing debug commands over a Telnet or SSH vty session is a common method of viewing debug output, and it offers increased performance over the console port. However, you can still overwhelm the gateway by enabling too many verbose debugs, and this can cause debug messages to be throttled and lost.

The configuration command **logging monitor** controls the output of debug information over a vty session. This command is enabled by default and consequently does not appear in the configuration file. Only when debug logging is disabled for a vty session with the command **no logging monitor** will you see a change in the configuration file. Therefore, you should confirm that the command **no logging monitor** is not present in the configuration; if it is, configure the command **logging monitor** to enable debug output to be received over vty sessions.

In addition, each individual vty session controls the appearance of debug information with the enable-level commands **terminal monitor** and **terminal no monitor**. By default, an individual vty session is not able to view debug output. The user has to explicitly enable this function using the **terminal monitor** command. If the user wants to stop viewing debug output without disabling the debug commands that are currently running, the command **terminal no monitor** should be used.

The best place to capture debug output is the router's internal buffer. Writing to the internal buffer or DRAM of the voice gateway offers the best performance when collecting debug output.

By default, the gateway does not log to its internal buffer, so the command **logging buffered** must configured. Along with this command, you can specify a buffer size that is carved from the available processor memory on the voice gateway. Exercise caution when configuring this buffer size and make sure that enough processor memory is available. Using the command **show memory summary**, as shown in Example 12-1, you can view the available processor memory on the voice gateway.

Example 12-1   *show memory summary Command Output*

```
fax_2811# show memory summary
               Head    Total(b)   Used(b)    Free(b)    Lowest(b)  Largest(b)
Processor    44E76664   39360924   23113004   16247920   15858596   15740496
      I/O    37400000   12582912    6677876    5905036    5785696    5687900

! Output omitted for brevity
```

In Example 12-1, the value of **15740496** bytes in the output of the **show memory summary**
command is highlighted. This value represents the largest free block of processor memory
that is available and the upper limit on the size of the buffer log that can be configured. For
example, if the command **logging buffered 512000 debugging** is used to create a buffer
log that is 512 KB in size on the gateway from Example 12-1, plenty of space is available.
A buffer log of 512 KB or 512000 bytes is well under the **15740496** bytes that indicate the
upper limit of a buffer log for this gateway.

To view the log of the debug output that you created with the **logging buffered** command,
you must use the command **show log**. In addition to showing you the logging buffer, this
command summarizes the current logging configuration and statistics for the gateway.
Example 12-2 shows output from a **show logging** command.

Example 12-2   *show logging Command Output*

```
fax_2811# show logging
Syslog logging: enabled (11 messages dropped, 17 messages rate-limited,
                0 flushes, 0 overruns, xml disabled, filtering disabled)
    Console logging: level debugging, 6538 messages logged, xml disabled,
                     filtering disabled
    Monitor logging: level debugging, 6362 messages logged, xml disabled,
                     filtering disabled
        Logging to: vty514(6362)
    Buffer logging: level debugging, 2141 messages logged, xml disabled,
                    filtering disabled
    Logging Exception size (4096 bytes)
    Count and timestamp logging messages: disabled
    Trap logging: level informational, 93 message lines logged

Log Buffer (512000 bytes):

! Output omitted for brevity
```

The output from the command **show logging** in Example 12-2 lists the different methods
for logging debug output: **Syslog logging**, **Console logging**, **Monitor logging**, and **Buffer
logging**. Information such as the logging level and message logging statistics are then
shown for each method that is listed. One nifty piece of information that is displayed is that

of the vty session that is viewing debug output in the **Monitor logging** section. In the case of Example 12-2, the line **Logging to: vty514(6362)** provides you with the exact vty session where debug output is being displayed.

After the different logging methods have been displayed, the line **Log Buffer (512000 bytes)** is present in Example 12-2. This line indicates that the configured size of the internal logging buffer is 512000 bytes and that the contents of that log buffer are going to be displayed next.

No matter whether the debug output is being logged to a console port, a vty session, or an internal buffer, it is highly recommended to always configure a high level of detail on the timestamps associated with each debug message. The configuration commands **service timestamp debug datetime msec** and **service timestamp log datetime msec** activate a millisecond-level of timestamp granularity for the gateway's debug and log messages, respectively. Having this level of granularity is helpful in troubleshooting scenarios that occur in a short time span and are timing sensitive.

In addition to setting debug message timestamps to a granular level, another best practice is to configure the global command **service sequence-numbers**. This command assigns a sequence number to each logged message, which is helpful in spotting whether any syslog messages were dropped and unambiguously differentiating between log messages that share the same timestamp. Example 12-3 shows output from a simple **debug ip packet** with the command **service sequence-numbers** configured.

Example 12-3 *Debug Output with the Command **service sequence-numbers** Configured*

```
004221: *Apr  2 12:01:39.519: IP: tableid=0, s=172.18.251.73 (local),
   d=172.18.251.57 (FastEthernet0/0), routed via FIB
004222: *Apr  2 12:01:39.519: IP: tableid=0, s=172.18.251.73 (local),
   d=172.18.251.57 (FastEthernet0/0), routed via FIB
004223: *Apr  2 12:01:39.619: IP: tableid=0, s=172.18.251.73 (local),
   d=172.18.251.57 (FastEthernet0/0), routed via FIB
004224: *Apr  2 12:01:39.619: IP: tableid=0, s=172.18.251.73 (local),
   d=172.18.251.57 (FastEthernet0/0), routed via FIB
004225: *Apr  2 12:01:39.767: IP: tableid=0, s=172.18.251.73 (local),
   d=172.18.251.57 (FastEthernet0/0), routed via FIB
```

For each line of debug output in Example 12-3, notice that a sequence number is inserted before each message timestamp. These sequence numbers of **004221**, **004222**, **004223**, **004224**, and **004225** steadily increment without any missing values. This confirms that no debug messages in this debug snippet were lost.

Also notice in Example 12-3 that on two occasions the timestamps are identical for debug messages. The first occurrence is at **12:01:39.519**, and the second occurrence is at **12:01:39.619**. With the **service sequence-numbers** command activated, messages that contain the same timestamp are more easily differentiated and placed in the proper order.

A few other fundamental concepts and tips for handling debugs on Cisco gateways include the following:

- Before enabling any debugs, always remember to correctly configure your logging as just explained.

- Debug commands are turned on from the gateway's command line while in enable mode by issuing the command **debug** followed by specific arguments. These arguments vary depending on the type of information you want to view. For example, the command **debug fax relay t30 all-level-1** turns on debug output that shows T.30 messages during a fax relay call.

- You can run multiple debugs concurrently by issuing different debug commands. Previous debug commands are not disabled when new debugs are turned on. Enabling too many debugs can tax the gateway's resources and make the output very confusing to interpret. You should enable only the debug commands that you need at that moment; other debugs that are not needed should be disabled.

- Viewing all the debugs that are currently enabled for a gateway can be accomplished with the command **show debug**. Any debug listed in the **show debug** command output can be easily disabled just by inserting a **no** in front of the listed debug command.

- To disable all the debugs on a gateway simultaneously, you can use the command **no debug all** or **undebug all**. This command is useful when many debug commands are enabled and they all need to be turned off. You can even abbreviate this command to **un all** when debugs need to be disabled quickly.

Telephony and IP Troubleshooting

Ensuring the integrity of both the telephony and IP segments of a fax, modem, or text call is critical. Problems or errors in these areas can have more of a negative impact on fax, modem, and text calls than they would on a regular voice call.

Because fax, modem, and text calls actually contain specific data that cannot be altered during its transport, these calls are more susceptible to telephony and IP problems. Voice calls may experience some degradation from certain network impairments, and the parties involved on the call might not even realize the degradation is occurring. In addition, there are mechanisms in place for most compressed audio codecs, such as predictive algorithms and packet loss concealment techniques, that can assist in masking many network problems. But these techniques do not protect fax, modem, and text transmissions because they cannot tolerate or compensate for degradation and still successfully deliver the data they are entrusted to transport.

To properly troubleshoot the IP and telephony parts of a fax, modem, or text call, a familiarity with how an IOS voice gateway processes these calls is critical. For this reason, this section covers concepts such as dial-peers and call legs.

When starting any sort of telephony or IP troubleshooting, analyzing call leg information should be your first task. Viewing the call leg information about Cisco IOS gateways provides a wealth of information that can be quickly examined as you narrow down a problem.

In addition, some useful IOS **show** commands that are commonly used to troubleshoot IP and telephony issues for fax, modem, and text calls are also covered in this section. These concepts and commands are usually associated with regular voice calls, but they are equally important for fax, modem, and text calls, too.

TIP   This section of the chapter covers some general VoIP information and troubleshooting techniques in the context of fax, modem, and text calls. You can find more information in this area in a good Cisco-specific VoIP troubleshooting reference. One recommendation is the book *Troubleshooting Cisco IP Telephony* (ISBN: 1-58705-075-7).

In Figure 12-1, telephony troubleshooting and IP troubleshooting are identified as Step 2 and Step 3, respectively. However, because of the way a Cisco IOS voice gateway ties telephony and IP call legs together, there is a large amount of overlap when troubleshooting the call legs themselves.

Therefore, the beginning of this section discusses this overlapping material first; then, the focus shifts at the end of this section to telephony- and IP-specific troubleshooting techniques for both IOS and non-IOS gateways. Even though telephony troubleshooting and IP troubleshooting are being covered together at the beginning of this section, you should still look at them separately from a troubleshooting perspective.

Call Legs in IOS Gateways

One of the most fundamental concepts in routing a call through an IOS voice gateway is that of a call leg. The notion of a call leg is inexorably tied to that of a dial-peer.

In the case of a VoIP call, two types of dial-peers are used: POTS dial-peers and VoIP dial-peers. A POTS dial-peer configures the characteristics of its corresponding telephony interface and ties a dial string to a specific voice port on the local gateway. Correspondingly, a VoIP dial-peer sets the attributes of the IP connection and ties a dial string to a remote IP device.

In the case of IOS gateways, a VoIP call is logically broken into discrete segments known as call legs. A particular dial-peer is associated with each call leg. A call leg is a logical connection that has local significance only to the voice gateway where the dial-peer is matched.

All VoIP calls must match both an inbound dial-peer and an outbound dial-peer. The inbound dial-peer match corresponds to an inbound call leg. Similarly, an outbound dial-peer match corresponds to an outbound call leg. Both the call direction and the type of dial-peer that is matched completely define the call leg. Figure 12-4 illustrates this gateway-centric concept of a call leg and how it is used in the framework of a VoIP call.

Figure 12-4 *Call Legs on an IOS Voice Gateway*

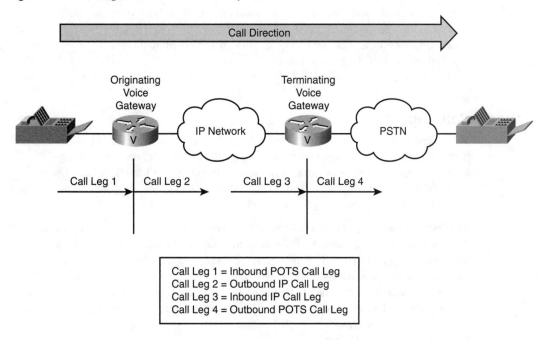

Figure 12-4 shows that a call leg can be either an inbound call leg or an outbound call leg depending on the direction of the call. For example, call leg 1 is an inbound POTS call leg, whereas call leg 2 is an outbound IP call leg on the originating voice gateway. If the call direction is reversed, so are the inbound and outbound call leg directions.

As a result of the dial-peers that are matched, outbound call legs are used for call routing and setting outbound call attributes, whereas inbound call legs set the call attributes in the reverse direction for that same gateway. When troubleshooting IOS gateways, it is important to always note the call legs and their equivalent dial-peers.

TIP	A common cause of fax/modem problems in IOS gateways is the omission of an inbound IP dial-peer that is properly configured for relay or passthrough. As a best practice, the terminating voice gateway should always have an inbound IP dial-peer that is configured similarly to the outbound IP dial-peer on the originating voice gateway. You should then confirm that after this inbound dial-peer is properly configured on the terminating voice gateway that it is matched by the incoming fax/modem call rather than another dial-peer or the system default, dial-peer 0. For additional information about voice dial-peers and understanding their inbound and outbound matching characteristics, refer to the document titled "Understanding Inbound and Outbound Dial Peers Matching on IOS Platforms" (Document ID: 14074) at Cisco.com.

Viewing Call Legs

With a fax, modem, or text call through a Cisco IOS gateway matching both inbound and outbound peers and subsequently generating a call leg for each, it is important to understand how to view and extract critical information about these call legs. The most basic IOS commands for viewing both telephony and IP call legs are **show call active voice brief** and **show call active fax brief**.

The **show call active voice brief** command displays both the telephony and IP leg of a call. A lot of information is output by this command, but this section looks at only the information relevant to fax, modem, and text calls. The fax, modem, and text call transport methods that are covered in detail in this section with regard to the output from the **show call active voice brief** command include modem passthrough, fax pass-through, fax relay, Cisco modem relay, and Cisco text relay. The **show call active fax brief** command is also covered, but it is used less frequently because it provides only telephony dial-peer information for fax relay calls.

Modem Passthrough Call Legs

Modem passthrough uses an NSE-based switchover mechanism to transport both fax and modem calls. When transporting fax calls, this transport method is often referred to as fax passthrough. The **show call active voice brief** command offers an easy and efficient means of viewing the call legs before and after a modem passthrough switchover while providing confirmation that the switchover occurred properly.

TIP	Although the **show call active voice brief** command proves helpful in confirming that an appropriate switchover has occurred, better techniques are available for viewing the actual switchover and diagnosing any switchover problems. These techniques are discussed in the next section, "Troubleshooting the Switchover Signaling."

Even before the call is connected the **show call active voice brief** can provide important information. Example 12-4 is an example of the **show call active voice brief** command for a modem passthrough call that has been placed through the gateway but has not yet connected.

Example 12-4   *show call active voice brief Command Output for a Modem Passthrough Call That Is Connecting*

```
11F1 : 9 2920260ms.1 +-1 pid:2 Answer 100 connected
 dur 00:00:00 tx:230/6392 rx:115/2233
 Tele 0/0/0 (9) [0/0/0] tx:6870/1940/0ms g729r8 noise:-74 acom:66  i/0:-79/-12 dBm

11F1 : 10 2924510ms.1 +-1 pid:1 Originate 200 connecting
 dur 00:00:00 tx:0/0 rx:230/4552
 IP 1.1.1.2:17932 SRTP: off rtt:0ms pl:2290/0ms lost:0/0/0 delay:70/70/70ms g729r8
  TextRelay: off

media inactive detected:n media contrl rcvd:n/a timestamp:n/a
 long duration call detected:n long duration call duration:n/a timestamp:n/a
```

Example 12-4 shows two call legs sharing the same call identifier of **11F1**. The first call leg is the POTS call leg because it is associated with telephony port **Tele 0/0/0** on the voice gateway. The second call leg is the VoIP call leg because it is associated with an IP address and UDP port number of **1.1.1.2:17932**.

The states of the call legs in this example are important to note. The POTS call leg is showing **connected**, and the VoIP call leg is displaying **connecting**. The **connected** state indicates that the POTS leg has completed the initial call setup, and the **connecting** state means that the VoIP leg is still in the process of connecting but has not yet received answer supervision. In this case, the far-end device connected over the VoIP leg is simply ringing.

When the far-end device answers the call, both call legs move into an **active** state. The exception to this is for IP call legs set up by the Media Gateway Control Protocol (MGCP) call control protocol. The MGCP IP call legs always remain in the **connecting** state and never switch to **active**. Example 12-5 illustrates a modem passthrough call that has **active** call legs but the switchover has still not occurred. The gateways have yet to detect the 2100 Hz stimuli tone necessary for initiating a transition to modem passthrough mode, so the call at this point is still in voice mode.

Example 12-5   *show call active voice brief Command Output for a Modem Passthrough Call Before Switchover*

```
11F1 : 9 2920260ms.1 +14780 pid:2 Answer 100 active
 dur 00:00:07 tx:253/7017 rx:238/4587
 Tele 0/0/0 (9) [0/0/0] tx:16090/4630/0ms g729r8 noise:-73 acom:6  i/0:-77/-79 dBm

11F1 : 10 2924510ms.1 +10530 pid:1 Originate 200 active
 dur 00:00:07 tx:99/1903 rx:253/4993
```

continues

Example 12-5 *show call active voice brief Command Output for a Modem Passthrough Call Before Switchover (Continued)*

```
 IP 1.1.1.2:17932 SRTP: off rtt:0ms pl:4810/0ms lost:0/0/0 delay:60/60/70ms g729r8
  TextRelay: off

  media inactive detected:n media contrl rcvd:n/a timestamp:n/a
 long duration call detected:n long duration call duration:n/a timestamp:n/a
```

The key parameter that informs you that the call in Example 12-5 is still a normal VoIP call is the presence of the **g729r8** codec. This codec is known for ensuring good voice quality while highly compressing the voice stream. However, the compression scheme this codec uses is optimized for human speech, and it adversely affects fax and modem signals. Consequently, a low compression codec such as G.711 is needed, and this is one of the benefits that modem passthrough provides. Modem passthrough upspeeds any codec that uses compression to G.711. Example 12-6 demonstrates how the call in Example 12-5 appears after the switchover occurs and the modem passthrough feature is now activated.

Example 12-6 *show call active voice brief Command Output for a Modem Passthrough Call*

```
11F1 : 9 2920260ms.1 +14780 pid:2 Answer 100 active
 dur 00:00:22 tx:1040/137129 rx:1016/128131
 Tele 0/0/0 (9) [0/0/0] tx:14270/14270/0ms g711ulaw noise:-66 acom:21  i/0:-69/-48
dBm

11F1 : 10 2924510ms.1 +10530 pid:1 Originate 200 active
 dur 00:00:22 tx:877/125447 rx:1040/128809
 IP 1.1.1.2:17932 SRTP: off rtt:1ms pl:40/0ms lost:0/0/0 delay:60/60/60ms g711ulaw
  TextRelay: off

 media inactive detected:n media contrl rcvd:n/a timesamp:n/a
 long duration call detected:n long duration call duration:n/a timestamp:n/a
   MODEMPASS
  nse buf:0/0 loss 0% 0/0  last 1359s dur:0/0s
```

In addition to the codec upspeed from **g729r8** to **g711ulaw** in Example 12-6, the IP call leg is now flagged with **MODEMPASS**. The presence of this parameter informs you immediately that a successful transition has occurred and a modem passthrough call is now in progress.

After a call has transitioned to modem passthrough, you can repeatedly use the **show call active voice brief** command to monitor the call progress. In addition to basic call information such as packets transmitted and received and call duration, other fields are of particular interest when troubleshooting fax and modem calls. Table 12-3 defines the highlighted items in Example 12-6 and explains their importance.

Table 12-3 *Important Parameters in the **show call active voice brief** Command Output for Modem Passthrough*

Field	Value	Description
ID	**11F1**	Defines a unique call identifier (ID) for POTS and IP call leg pairs.
pid	**pid:2** **pid:1**	Specifies a dial-peer ID (pid) that identifies the matched dial-peer in the configuration file for a particular call leg. In the case of Example 12-6, the POTS call leg is associated with dial-peer 2, and the VoIP call leg with dial-peer 1.
dir	**Answer/Originate**	Indicates the direction (dir) of the call leg. **Originate** defines a call leg that is sent from the gateway outbound, and **Answer** identifies an inbound call leg to the gateway.
addr	**100/200**	Indicates the address (addr) of the call leg. On the **Originate** call leg, this value defines the called number (**200**), and this value on the **Answer** call leg usually is the calling number (**100**). Be aware that the gateway dial-peer configuration or other devices in the call path may manipulate these values.
state	**active**	Defines the state of the call leg. The **active** state indicates that the call leg is in an established state, with media flowing in both directions.
Tele interface	**Tele 0/0/0**	Identifies the physical port on the gateway used by the POTS call leg.
codec	**g711ulaw**	Defines the codec algorithm in use by the call leg.
IP ip:udp	**IP 1.1.1.2:17932**	Identifies the remote IP address and UDP port for the IP call leg.
lost:lost/early/late	**lost:0/0/0**	Details lost, early, and late packet counts for the DSP playout buffer. Incrementing values in these counters indicate IP network problems that are negatively impacting the call.
MODEMPASS method	**MODEMPASS nse**	Indicates that modem passthrough has been successfully negotiated and established.

continues

Table 12-3 *Important Parameters in the **show call active voice brief** Command Output for Modem Passthrough (Continued)*

Field	Value	Description
buf:fills/drains	**buf:0/0**	Shows the number of buffer fill and drain events. Fill events occur when packets are being received faster than they are being played out, and drain events happen when packets are being played out faster than they are being received. If these counters are incrementing, this indicates that significant jitter is occurring in the IP network and it may be negatively impacting the call.
loss overall% multipkt/ corrected	**loss 0% 0/0**	Details packet loss percentage, number of consecutive packet loss events (multipkt), and the number of packets corrected by the RFC 2198 redundancy algorithm. If these counters are incrementing, IP network problems are negatively impacting the call.

TIP

Whereas Table 12-3 provides additional insight into counters and parameters for a **show call active voice brief** command during a modem passthrough call, almost all the parameters defined here are also relevant for fax relay and modem relay calls. The only exceptions are the parameters in the table taken specifically from the **MODEMPASS** line of the IP call leg. These counters are specific to modem passthrough only.

If you are currently proceeding with telephony troubleshooting, you should analyze the POTS call leg for additional information. The codec in use on this call leg is identified as **g711ulaw**, and the dial-peer that is matched for this call leg is shown as **pid:2**. The **Answer** parameter indicates that this POTS call leg "answered" or received the call and that this is the inbound call leg from the gateway's perspective.

When performing IP troubleshooting, you must analyze the IP call leg in Example 12-6. In addition to static call parameters such as the call ID and peer ID, a number of dynamic parameters in the IP leg are important to note. These dynamic items are the ones that should be monitored during a call while troubleshooting.

For example, there is a counter for lost packets in the IP call leg that in the case of Example 12-6 is set to **lost:0/0/0**. More precisely, the three counters here refer to lost, early, and late packets. If IP network issues are occurring, they are reflected in this counter. Incrementing values here can indicate jitter or packet loss in the IP network that is adversely affecting modem passthrough.

The dial-peer associated with the IP call leg usually contains most of the configuration information for a fax, modem, or text call. So, it is important to do a quick check of the configuration after the **show call active voice brief** command confirms the exact peer ID that is matched. For the modem passthrough call in Example 12-6, the pid for the IP call leg is 1 (**pid:1**), and this dial-peer configuration along with the POTS peer configuration is referenced in Example 12-7.

Example 12-7   *Dial-Peer Configuration for Modem Passthrough*

```
!
dial-peer voice 1 voip
 destination-pattern 200
 modem passthrough nse codec g711ulaw
 session target ipv4:1.1.1.2
 incoming called-number .
 fax protocol none
!
dial-peer voice 2 pots
 destination-pattern 100
 port 0/0/0
!
```

In Example 12-7, the configuration command **modem passthrough nse codec g711ulaw** is present under the VoIP dial-peer, **dial-peer voice 1 voip**. This configuration command is responsible for the gateway transitioning the call to passthrough and the output of the **show call active voice brief** in Example 12-6.

Fax Pass-Through Call Legs

Unlike modem passthrough that depends on NSE packets for the switchover, fax pass-through uses the VoIP signaling protocol to make the transition to passthrough mode. This results in a different appearance for the call when the **show call active voice brief** command is issued.

With modem passthrough, a successful switchover is marked by **MODEMPASS** in the IP call leg portion of the **show call active voice brief** command output. However, because fax pass-through uses the voice signaling protocol to handle the switchover, only the codec change can be observed. Example 12-8 shows a fax pass-through call before the switchover occurs. Notice that the codec is **g729r8**.

After the V.21 fax flags are detected and the call switches over to fax pass-through, the codec changes to **g711ulaw** to properly handle the transport of the fax messages. Example 12-9 shows a fax pass-through call after the switchover has occurred.

Example 12-8   *show call active voice brief Command Output for a Fax Pass-Through Call Before Switchover*

```
126C : 57 11407050ms.1 +14760 pid:2 Answer 100 active
 dur 00:00:08 tx:307/8548 rx:304/5927
 Tele 0/0/0 (57) [0/0/0] tx:19140/5990/0ms g729r8 noise:-74 acom:66  i/0:-79/-12 dBm

126C : 58 11411290ms.1 +10520 pid:1 Originate 200 active
 dur 00:00:08 tx:112/2154 rx:307/6092
 IP 1.1.1.2:17620 SRTP: off rtt:1ms pl:5930/0ms lost:0/0/0 delay:60/60/70ms g729r8
  TextRelay: off

  media inactive detected:n media contrl rcvd:n/a timestamp:n/a
 long duration call detected:n long duration call duration:n/a timestamp:n/a
```

Example 12-9   *show call active voice brief Command Output for a Fax Pass-Through Call*

```
126C : 57 11407050ms.1 +14760 pid:2 Answer 100 active
 dur 00:00:41 tx:1953/273736 rx:1869/256327
 Tele 0/0/0 (57) [0/0/0] tx:31300/31300/0ms g711ulaw noise:-17 acom:14  i/0:-14/-
61 dBm

126C : 58 11411290ms.1 +10520 pid:1 Originate 200 active
 dur 00:00:41 tx:1677/252554 rx:1953/258112
 IP 1.1.1.2:17620 SRTP: off rtt:4ms pl:40/0ms lost:1/0/0 delay:60/60/60ms g711ulaw
  TextRelay: off

  media inactive detected:n media contrl rcvd:n/a timestamp:n/a
 long duration call detected:n long duration call duration:n/a timestamp:n/a
```

With fax pass-through, you must keep watch for the codec change to confirm a successful transition. Because the switchover happens within the voice signaling protocol, fax pass-through appears like a regular VoIP call to the gateway when using the **show call active voice brief** command. For more information about fax pass-through and how it transitions using the voice signaling protocol, see the section "Protocol-Based Pass-Through for Fax" in Chapter 4, "Passthrough."

Fax Relay Call Legs

Cisco voice gateways support two types of fax relay: T.38 fax relay and Cisco fax relay. Both of these fax relay types appear almost exactly the same when looking at the call legs using the command **show call active voice brief**.

A notable caveat applies when viewing call legs for T.38 or Cisco fax relay calls. After the call has made the transition to fax relay, the POTS or telephony call leg is no longer shown using the **show call active voice brief** command. Instead, the command **show call active fax brief** must be used. The IP call leg, on the other hand, always remains viewable with the **show call active voice brief** command.

The switchover to T.38 fax relay can occur with NSEs or within the VoIP signaling protocol. However, from the **show call active voice brief** command perspective, the switchover mechanism is irrelevant. NSE-based or protocol-based switchovers appear the same. Example 12-10 highlights the **show call active voice brief** command for a T.38 fax relay call.

Example 12-10 *show call active voice brief Command Output for a T.38 Fax Relay Call*

```
11E2 : 4 2956390ms.1 +10500 pid:1 Originate 200 active
 dur 00:00:46 tx:707/13770 rx:914/12339
 IP 1.1.1.2:18496 SRTP: off rtt:3ms pl:4800/0ms lost:0/0/0 delay:60/60/70ms t38
  TextRelay: off

  media inactive detected:n media contrl rcvd:n/a timestamp:n/a
 long duration call detected:n long duration call duration:n/a timestamp:n/a
```

In Example 12-10, you can instantly tell that the transition to T.38 has been successful because **t38** appears as the codec in the IP call leg. Until the T.38 switchover occurs, this field is populated with the voice codec used for the initial VoIP call.

Cisco fax relay appears practically identical to T.38 fax relay in a **show call active voice brief**. The only distinguishing characteristic is the presence of the keyword **cisco** rather than **t38** as the codec for the IP leg. Example 12-11 illustrates a **show call active voice brief** for a Cisco fax relay call.

Example 12-11 *show call active voice brief Command Output for a Cisco Fax Relay Call*

```
121C : 26 1027355900ms.1 +10510 pid:1 Originate 200 active
 dur 00:00:45 tx:1113/22164 rx:1001/19972
 IP 1.1.1.2:18274 SRTP: off rtt:2ms pl:0/0ms lost:0/0/0 delay:0/0/0ms cisco
  TextRelay: off

  media inactive detected:n media contrl rcvd:n/a timestamp:n/a
 long duration call detected:n long duration call duration:n/a timestamp:n/a
```

Similar to T.38 fax relay, the presence of **cisco** as the codec in the IP call leg indicates that the switchover to Cisco fax relay was successful. In addition, as mentioned previously, the POTS call leg is no longer present under the command **show call active voice brief** for either T.38 or Cisco fax relay. Example 12-12 demonstrates how the fax relay POTS call leg is now viewable with the command **show call active fax brief**.

Example 12-12 *show call active fax brief Command Output for a Fax Relay Call*

```
11E2 : 3 2952150ms.1 +14740 pid:2 Answer 100 active
 dur 00:00:45 tx:890/19303 rx:311/6019
 Tele 0/0/0 (3) [0/0/0] tx:21420/8080/0ms 7200 noise:-74 acom:20  i/0:-14/-11 dBm
```

The POTS or telephony call leg displayed in **Example 12-12** could be for either a T.38 or Cisco fax relay call. Nothing in the POTS call leg distinguishes whether the call is T.38 or Cisco fax relay, so the POTS call leg for any fax relay call always appears in a similar fashion. When it might be necessary to confirm whether the POTS call leg shown in a **show call active fax brief** command is T.38 or Cisco fax relay, you can note the call identifier (**11E2** in the case of Example 12-12) and find the associated IP call leg with the same identifier with the command **show call active voice brief**. As previously shown in Examples 12-10 and 12-11, the IP call legs designate whether the call is T.38 or Cisco fax relay.

A notable parameter in the fax relay POTS call leg is the speed at which the fax call negotiates. In the case of Example 12-12, this speed is **7200** bps.

Cisco Modem Relay Call Legs

Cisco modem relay is unique in that the switchover uses a two-stage transition process. The initial voice call does not transition directly to Cisco modem relay but instead proceeds to modem passthrough first before finally transitioning to Cisco modem relay. Therefore, Cisco modem relay calls momentarily appear as modem passthrough calls. Example 12-13 shows a call in modem passthrough mode before it ultimately transitions to Cisco modem relay.

Example 12-13 *show call active voice brief Command Output for a Cisco Modem Relay Call Transitioning Through Modem Passthrough*

```
11FD : 15 643750ms.1 +5410 pid:2 Answer 100 active
 dur 00:00:02 tx:168/8311 rx:87/5217
 Tele 0/0/0 (15) [0/0/0] tx:520/520/0ms g711ulaw noise:-78 acom:57  i/0:-71/-13 dBm

 11FD : 16 646070ms.1 +3090 pid:1 Originate 200 active
 dur 00:00:02 tx:52/4565 rx:168/6967
 IP 1.1.1.2:17614 SRTP: off rtt:0ms pl:1770/0ms lost:0/0/0 delay:70/70/70ms g711ulaw
  TextRelay: off

  media inactive detected:n media contrl rcvd:n/a timestamp:n/a
 long duration call detected:n long duration call duration:n/a timestamp:n/a
  MODEMPASS
 nse buf:0/0 loss 0% 0/0  last 0s dur:0/0s
```

For the IP call leg in Example 12-13, **MODEMPASS** and the **g711ulaw** codec are displayed. These parameters indicate that the call is currently in modem passthrough mode. The call may remain as a modem passthrough call if the switchover to Cisco modem relay fails.

The trigger that initiates the final switchover from modem passthrough to Cisco modem relay is contained in the calling menu/joint menu (CM/JM) V.8 message exchange. For more information about CM/JM and V.8, see the section "Phase I: Network Interaction" in Chapter 1, "How Modems Work."

Parameters within the CM/JM messages detail information such as the modulation type and even whether the call is a high-speed modem call or a Super G3 fax call. For a call to successfully transition to Cisco modem relay, the CM/JM exchange should ideally indicate a V.34 high-speed modem call. The V.90 modulation should work, too, but it will be forced down to V.34 speeds.

Assuming that V.34 is successfully negotiated between the modems and the gateways, the call ultimately transitions from modem passthrough to Cisco modem relay. Example 12-14 highlights how a Cisco modem relay call appears when the **show call active voice brief** command is issued after the switchover to Cisco modem relay is complete.

Example 12-14   *show call active voice brief Command Output for a Cisco Modem Relay Call*

```
11FD : 15 643750ms.1 +5410 pid:2 Answer 100 active
 dur 00:32:07 tx:18604/347313 rx:125/10361
 Tele 0/0/0 (15) [0/0/0] tx:520/520/0ms modem-relay noise:-78 acom:57  i/0:-71/-13
   dBm
 MODEMRELAY info:0/464/0 xid:1/1 total:0/942/0
   speeds(bps): local 28800/31200 remote 28800/31200 phy/ec v34/v42 gateway-
     controlled

11FD : 16 646070ms.1 +3090 pid:1 Originate 200 active
 dur 00:32:07 tx:18752/124381 rx:18604/198481
 IP 1.1.1.2:17614 SRTP: off rtt:0ms pl:1770/0ms lost:0/0/0 delay:70/70/70ms
   modem-relay
   TextRelay: off

  media inactive detected:n media contrl rcvd:n/a timestamp:n/a
 long duration call detected:n long duration call duration:n/a timestamp:n/a
   MODEMPASS
   nse buf:0/0 loss 0% 0/0  last 0s dur:0/0s
```

In Example 12-14, notice the presence of the **modem-relay** keyword as the codec in both the POTS and IP call legs. This informs you that this call has completed a successful negotiation and transition to Cisco modem relay.

Also notice additional Cisco modem relay–specific statistics in the POTS call leg that were not present before. These statistics provide important information about the Cisco modem relay call itself and should be checked when troubleshooting Cisco modem relay calls. Table 12-4 details the Cisco modem relay statistics found in a **show call active voice brief**.

Table 12-4 *Important Parameters in the **show call active voice brief** Command Output for Cisco Modem Relay*

Field	Value	Description
info:rcvd/sent/resent	**info:0/464/0**	Specifies the number of received, sent, and re-sent information frames. Information or I-frames are responsible for transporting data over a V.42 connection. V.42 was discussed previously in the section "Error Control" in Chapter 1.
xid:rcvd/sent	**xid:1/1**	Details the number of received and sent exchange identification (XID) frames sent and received during the V.42 capability negotiation. XID frames were previously covered in the section "Error Control" in Chapter 1.
total:rcvd/sent/drops	**total:0/942/0**	Shows the total number of bytes received and sent between the modems and the number of Simple Packet Relay Transport (SPRT) packet drops. More information about SPRT and its format can be found in the section "Modem Relay" in Chapter 5, "Relay."
speeds(bps): local rx/tx **remote** rx/tx **phy/ec** physical/ error-correction mode	**speeds(bps): local 28800/ 31200 remote 28800/ 31200 phy/ec v34/v42 gateway-controlled**	Specifies the negotiated receive and transmit speeds for the local and remote connections and defines the physical layer and error correction layer protocols. Also, defines the method used for the switchover to modem relay.

Text Telephony Call Legs

Text telephony can be transported across VoIP networks using Text over G.711 or Cisco text relay. With Text over G.711, the **show call active voice brief** command looks like a normal G.711 voice call. However, for a Cisco text relay call, the **show call active voice brief** command appears differently, as illustrated in Example 12-15.

Example 12-15 *show call active voice brief Command Output for a Cisco Text Relay Call*

```
11F3 : 11 420984780ms.1 +11920 pid:1 Answer 100 active
 dur 00:31:02 tx:702/13164 rx:5537/109060
 IP 1.1.1.1:18286 SRTP: off rtt:0ms pl:108980/0ms lost:0/1/0 delay:60/60/70ms g729r8
  TextRelay: on

  media inactive detected:n media contrl rcvd:n/a timestamp:n/a
 long duration call detected:n long duration call duration:n/a timestamp:n/a
```

Example 12-15 *show call active voice brief Command Output for a Cisco Text Relay Call (Continued)*

```
11F3 : 12 420984780ms.2 +11920 pid:2 Originate 200 active
 dur 00:31:02 tx:5537/153356 rx:702/13164
 Tele 0/0/0 (12) [0/0/0] tx:1874750/12550/0ms g729r8 noise:-74 acom:29  i/0:-74/-
  45 dBm
```

The first thing that you will probably notice in Example 12-15 is that the codec is **g729r8**. Although **g729r8** works well for voice, it is not recommended for modulated communications. However, Cisco text relay does not use the voice codec for relaying the text telephony information, so any codec type can be used for a Cisco text relay call. The codec type is not important because Cisco text relay uses its own packets with a different RTP payload type. For more information about Cisco text relay and how it works, see the section "Cisco Text Relay" in Chapter 5.

What matters in Example 12-15 is the parameter **TextRelay: on**. This parameter informs you that Cisco text relay is enabled and that any text telephony character will be handled by the Cisco text relay protocol. Because Cisco text relay does not have any sort of switchover, the call leg will never transition to Cisco text relay mode. The Cisco text relay feature is either considered **on** or **off** for each IP call leg based on whether the Cisco text relay feature has been enabled in the configuration.

Call Leg Troubleshooting Techniques

There are a couple of helpful troubleshooting techniques when working with call legs. These techniques can prove quite useful when you need to analyze completed calls or you have to deal with large numbers of calls on production gateways.

The **show call history voice brief** and **show call history fax brief** commands are useful for analyzing calls that previously occurred on the IOS gateway. These commands provide a means for looking back at fax, modem, or text calls that might have had problems but are no longer active on the gateway. Example 12-16 highlights a **show call history voice brief** command for a past T.38 fax relay call.

Example 12-16 *show call history voice brief Command Output for a T.38 Fax Relay Call*

```
1209 : 19 137792170ms.18 +10520 +70420 pid:1 Originate 200
 dur 00:00:59 tx:1148/37504 rx:758/11683 10  (normal call clearing (16))
 IP 1.1.1.2:16746 SRTP: off rtt:1ms pl:4710/0ms lost:0/0/0 delay:60/60/70ms t38
  TextRelay: off

 media inactive detected:n media contrl rcvd:n/a timestamp:n/a
 long duration call detected:n long dur callduration :n/a timestamp:n/a FAXRELAY
  jitter:0 ms/0 mod:0 pages:0
```

The **show call history voice brief** command displayed in Example 12-16 provides some additional information that is not included with a **show call active voice brief** command. For example, because the call has been completed, the gateway can record the disconnect reason for the call. Therefore, in Example 12-16, you can see that the call was disconnected by **normal call clearing**, which is represented with a clearing cause code of **16**. This type of information can be critical when trying to figure out why calls are disconnecting prematurely. The call disconnect information displayed in the IP leg of Example 12-16 is also shown when looking at the completed POTS call leg using the command **show call history fax brief**.

In addition to the **t38** parameter that is found in the output of the command **show call active voice brief**, the **show call history voice brief** command displays a **FAXRELAY** parameter for the T.38 fax relay call in Example 12-16. This **FAXRELAY** parameter is just another indication that the call switched over successfully to T.38 or Cisco fax relay.

TIP

The call history buffer used by the **show call history voice brief** and **show call history fax brief** commands is set by default to retain only up to 50 call leg entries for a duration of 15 minutes. However, you can change these settings with the IOS commands **dial-control-mib retain-timer** and **dial-control-mib max-size**. Adjusting the call history buffer size and duration may be helpful when troubleshooting intermittent problems or problems when the gateway is experiencing a high call volume.

The ability to quickly parse through large numbers of calls in the output of a **show call active voice brief** or a **show call history voice brief** is critical when troubleshooting a problem when a heavy call volume is present. The following technique along with the CLI parsing features available in IOS provide a means for quickly isolating the call that you are interested in troubleshooting.

For example, suppose you are trying to troubleshoot a T.38 fax relay problem on a gateway that has more than 50 simultaneous calls. Manually looking through all 100+ call legs would take too much time. However, if you know a distinguishing characteristic about that T.38 call, such as a unique calling or called number, you can look for the call based on this information. Example 12-17 illustrates how a single call can be isolated from many others within a **show call active voice brief**.

In Example 12-17, the called number, **100**, is unique to the call that is being troubleshot. So, the command **show call active voice brief called-number 100** is used to search for lines in the output of **show call active voice brief** that contain this number. Only one call leg is returned, and the first line of this call leg provides the call ID for our call, **121B**. Now you can parse for this call ID of **121B** and get all the information for both call legs, as shown in Example 12-18.

Example 12-17 *Isolating a Single Call Using the Command* **show call active voice brief called number**

```
CAE-DH-3845-1# show call active voice brief called-number 100
121B : 26 26182740ms.1 +10490 pid:100 Originate 100 active
 dur 00:00:27 tx:1389/221304 rx:944/147843
 IP 172.18.122.74:17996 SRTP: off rtt:1ms pl:7845/40ms lost:0/0/0 delay:65/60/65ms
g711ulaw TextRelay: off

 media inactive detected:n media contrl rcvd:n/a timestamp:n/a
 long duration call detected:n long duration call duration:n/a timestamp:n/a
MODEMPASS nse buf:0/0 loss 0% 0/0  last 1588s dur:0/0s
```

Example 12-18 *Isolating a Single Call Using the Command* **show call active voice brief id**

```
CAE-DH-3845-1# show call active voice brief id 121b

121B : 25 26180600ms.1 +12630 pid:0 Answer  active
 dur 00:00:43 tx:1734/288115 rx:2701/431224
 Tele 0/1/0 (25) [0/1/0] tx:23870/23870/0ms g711ulaw noise:-11 acom:6  i/0:-14/-31
   dBm

121B : 26 26182740ms.1 +10490 pid:100 Originate 100 active
 dur 00:00:43 tx:2178/347544 rx:1734/274243
 IP 172.18.122.74:17996 SRTP: off rtt:2ms pl:21980/40ms lost:0/0/0 delay:65/60/65ms
   g711ulaw TextRelay: off

 media inactive detected:n media contrl rcvd:n/a timestamp:n/a
 long duration call detected:n long duration call duration:n/a timestamp:n/a
   MODEMPASS nse buf:0/0 loss 0% 0/0  last 4415s dur:0/0s
```

The command **show call active voice brief id 121b** parses through the output of the **show call active voice brief** command and displays the call legs with a call leg ID of **121B**. This enables you to clearly see both the POTS and IP call legs for troubleshooting purposes. Repeating this command allows you to monitor this call, including its statistics for its duration without being distracted by the other active calls occurring on the voice gateway.

This same parsing strategy is also applicable to the command **show call history voice brief** as long as there is a unique call leg component available within the same line as the call ID. Whereas the calling or called number is the most common parameter used for the initial parsing, the dial-peer ID may also be a good choice.

Telephony Troubleshooting

Although checking the POTS call leg using the **show call active voice brief** command and its variants is important in telephony troubleshooting, other commands exist that provide additional information. The most important of these IOS commands is **show controllers [t1|e1]**.

Voice gateways have a variety of analog and digital telephony interfaces that are used to connect to the PSTN or directly to fax, modem, and text devices. However, digital interfaces are responsible for more problems with fax and modem communications than analog interfaces.

With analog interfaces, common problems such as echo, static, and incorrect signal levels can often be heard during a voice call, so it is difficult for these problems to go unnoticed. Digital interfaces, on the other hand, can have issues that are negligible or even undetectable by voice users while causing modem and fax calls to fail.

The physical layer statistics of digital T1/E1 interfaces on IOS voice gateways are shown in the output of the command **show controllers [t1|e1]**. This output is displayed in Example 12-19.

Example 12-19 *Displaying the Physical Layer Statistics on an IOS Gateway Using the Command* *show controllers t1*

```
Router# show controllers t1 1/0
T1 1/0 is up.
  Applique type is Channelized T1
  Cablelength is long gain36 0db
  No alarms detected.
  alarm-trigger is not set
  Soaking time: 3, Clearance time: 10
  AIS State:Clear  LOS State:Clear  LOF State:Clear
  Version info Firmware: 20040802, FPGA: 255, spm_count = 0
  Framing is ESF, Line Code is B8ZS, Clock Source is Internal.
  Current port master clock:local osc on this network module
  Data in current interval (225 seconds elapsed):
     0 Line Code Violations, 0 Path Code Violations
     11 Slip Secs, 0 Fr Loss Secs, 0 Line Err Secs, 0 Degraded Mins
     11 Errored Secs, 0 Bursty Err Secs, 0 Severely Err Secs, 0 Unavail Secs
```

The output of **show controller t1** has a wealth of information that is vital for troubleshooting the physical layer. At a glance, you can see in Example 12-19 that **T1 1/0 is up** and is showing **No alarms detected**. Also, the configuration settings of the **Framing**, **Line Code**, and **Clock Source** on the T1 are clearly displayed.

There are additional T1/E1 counters found in the IOS **show controller [t1/e1]** and other commands and tools used for viewing this same information in the 6608, a non-IOS gateway. Table 12-5 defines the major T1/E1 impairments and error counters displayed on IOS gateways and the 6608.

In the majority of cases, network impairments and physical layer problems have a greater effect on fax, modem, and text calls than on regular voice calls. A perfect example of this is clock slips. A slight bit of clock slippage will likely have a negligible effect on voice quality but will wreak havoc on a fax/modem call. This happens because faxes and modems are extremely sensitive to line errors.

Table 12-5   *T1 and E1 Physical Layer Error Counters on Cisco Voice Gateways*

Error Counter	Definition
Line Code Violation (LCV)	An occurrence of either a bipolar violation (BPV) or an excessive 0s error event.
Path Code Violation (PCV)	A frame synchronization bit error in the T1-D4 and E1-no cyclic redundancy check (CRC) formats, or a CRC error in the Extended Super Frame (ESF) and E1-CRC formats.
Controlled Slip Seconds (CSS)	A 1-second interval containing 1 or more controlled slips.
Frame Loss Seconds	The number of seconds an out-of-frame error is detected.
Line Errored Seconds (LES)	A second in which 1 or more LCV error events were detected.
Degraded Minutes	A degraded minute is one in which the estimated error rate exceeds 1E-6 but does not exceed 1E-3.
Errored Seconds (ES)	Includes 1 or more PCVs, out-of-frame defects, controlled slip events, or a detected AIS defect within 1 second.
Bursty Errored Seconds (BES)	A second with fewer than 320 and more than 1 PCV error event, no Severely Errored Frame defects, and no detected incoming AIS defects. Controlled slips are not included in this parameter.
Severely Errored Seconds (SES)	For ESF signals, a second with 320 or more PCVs or 1 or more out-of-frame defects or a detected AIS defect.
	For E1-CRC signals, a second with 832 or more PCVs or 1 or more out-of-frame defects.
	For E1-no CRC signals, a second with 2048 LCVs or more.
	For D4 signals, a count of 1-second intervals with Framing Error events, or an out-of-frame defect, or 1544 LCVs or more.
Severely Errored Framing Second (SEFS)	A second with either 1 or more out-of-frame defects or a detected AIS defect.
Unavailable Seconds (UAS) or Failed Seconds (FS)	The number of seconds that the interface is unavailable.

Clock slips on a digital T1/E1 are the physical layer error that is most notorious for being a common source of fax/modem failures. The counter **11 Slip Secs** in Example 12-19 shows a scenario where T1 1/0 is experiencing clock slips. Slips typically result because of a disagreement on a unique clocking source to be used between the gateway and the device to which it is connected.

TIP

The problem of clock slips on digital circuits and their detrimental effect on fax and modem calls cannot be emphasized enough. Checking for digital circuit errors such as slips is a task that needs to be done for just about every fax and modem issue.

Slips on digital circuits usually occur because clocking of the span is incorrectly configured. Ensure that only one side is providing clock and the other is deriving its clock from it. Cisco gateways have various clocking schemes depending on the gateway architecture, the presence of additional network modules, and the clocking configurations of the devices that connect to the Cisco gateway. For additional information about correctly configuring the clocking on a Cisco voice gateway, the following documents are a good place to start. You can access them by searching for their titles at Cisco.com:

"Clocking Configurations On Voice-Capable IOS-Based Platforms" (Document ID: 48567)

"Clock Synchronization for AS5xxx Network Access Servers" (Document ID: 14169)

"Voice System Clocking"

Not only is it necessary to ensure that the voice gateway is free of slips and other errors on its digital interfaces, but any telephony digital span along the path must also be free of errors. Sometimes, the spans connecting directly to the voice gateway will be error free but faxes and modems will have problems because of slips on a different digital circuit that lies in the fax/modem call path.

If you have visibility into all the digital spans within the telephony call path, it is quite easy to confirm that they are error free. However, if the telephony call path uses digital spans in a service provider's network, checking for errors is usually more complicated. For an example of how impairments on a digital span, such as slips, may appear when using the command **debug fax relay t30 all-level-1**, see Example 12-68 later in this chapter.

The only non-IOS voice gateway covered in this book that has a digital connection is the Catalyst WS-X6608 blade. Because the 6608 resides in a Catalyst switch, there are a few methods for accessing information about its digital connections. You can query the card directly via HTML, use a special software utility known as Dick Tracy to pull information directly from the card, or interface to the card through the CLI on the Catalyst switch.

The best way to gather detailed information about T1/E1 errors is through the use of the Dick Tracy utility. This troubleshooting utility is also known as the 66XXTracy tool, and it is simply a program that runs on a PC and provides a user interface for direct communication with the 6608. Dick Tracy's primary function is to provide more detailed information about the 6608 than what is available using Unified CM or the Catalyst switch CLI. You can find more information about the Dick Tracy tool in the document "6608 Gateway Trace Collection using the 66xxTracy Tool" (Document ID: 63621) at Cisco.com.

The Dick Tracy tool supports different tasks that cover the various hardware and software components of the 6608. However, for fax/modem problems, the tasks that are used the most for troubleshooting are **4** and **6**. Task **4** is the SPAN (Framer) Task and covers the T1/E1 physical layer. Task **6** is the DSP Task and provides visibility into DSP-related functions.

To take a quick glimpse at the physical layer and D channel status on a specific port, you can use the Dick Tracy command **4 show status**. Example 12-20 shows the output of the Dick Tracy command **4 show status**.

Example 12-20 *Displaying the Physical Layer Overview on a 6608 Gateway Using the Dick Tracy Command*
4 show status

```
18:08:06.160 SPAN: Show Span Summary Status
    T1 4/8 is up
      No alarms detected.
    Alarm MIB Statistics
      Yellow Alarms -------> 0
      Blue Alarms --------> 0
      Frame Sync Losses ---> 2
      Carrier Loss Count --> 0
      Frame Slip Count ----> 0
      D-chan Tx Frame Count ----> 19
      D-chan Tx Frames Queued --> 0
      D-chan Tx Errors --------> 0
      D-chan Rx Frame Count ----> 16
      D-chan Rx Errors --------> 0
```

Example 12-20 tells you a number of critical items about this T1 port on the 6608. Most important, **T1 4/8 is up** with **No alarms detected**. This tells you immediately that this digital circuit is not currently having any major problems or alarms.

However, the problems that may affect fax without necessarily impacting voice calls are found in the counters a bit further down in Example 12-20. The **Frame Sync Losses** counter has actually incremented slightly, and this indicates a physical layer framing problem. The **Frame Slip Count** is the counter that tracks slips, the most well-known physical layer error that is responsible for fax and modem problems.

For chronic physical layer errors on a 6608 port, more granular statistics are available through another Dick Tracy command that is more or less identical to the **show controllers [t1|e1]** command in IOS gateways. This command is **4 show fdlintervals** *interval*, where *interval* defines the number of 15-minute interval blocks to be displayed. Having the ability to track error statistics in interval blocks over a 24-hour period is especially necessary for intermittent issues. Example 12-21 highlights the Dick Tracy command **4 show fdlintervals 3**.

Example 12-21   *Displaying the Physical Layer Statistics on a 6608 Gateway Using the Dick Tracy Command*
4 show intervals 3

```
18:59:07.690 SPAN: CLI Request --> Dump local FDL 15-min interval history
  3 Complete intervals stored.
  Data in current interval (544 seconds elapsed):
    0 Line Code Violations, 0 Path Code Violations
    0 Slip Secs, 0 Fr Loss Secs, 0 Line Err Secs
    0 Errored Secs, 0 Bursty Err Secs, 0 Severely Err Secs, 0 Unavail Secs
  Data in interval 1:
    0 Line Code Violations, 0 Path Code Violations
    0 Slip Secs, 0 Fr Loss Secs, 0 Line Err Secs
    0 Errored Secs, 0 Bursty Err Secs, 0 Severely Err Secs, 0 Unavail Secs
  Data in interval 2:
    0 Line Code Violations, 0 Path Code Violations
    0 Slip Secs, 0 Fr Loss Secs, 0 Line Err Secs
    0 Errored Secs, 0 Bursty Err Secs, 0 Severely Err Secs, 0 Unavail Secs
  Data in interval 3:
    2 Line Code Violations, 1 Path Code Violations
    1 Slip Secs, 2 Fr Loss Secs, 1 Line Err Secs
    2 Errored Secs, 0 Bursty Err Secs, 2 Severely Err Secs, 0 Unavail Secs
  24-Hr Totals:
    2 Line Code Violations, 1 Path Code Violations
    1 Slip Secs, 2 Fr Loss Secs, 1 Line Err Secs
    2 Errored Secs, 0 Bursty Err Secs, 2 Severely Err Secs, 0 Unavail Secs
```

In Example 12-21, FDL (Facilities Data Link) **interval 3** is showing minor problems. FDL
is available on T1 spans with ESF framing and provides a 4 Kbps channel between endpoints
for maintenance communications such as the querying of performance statistics. Depending
on when these errors occurred during a fax/modem call, the small number of these errors is
probably not enough to cause a complete call failure. However, errors such as **Line Code
Violations**, **Path Code Violations**, **Slip Secs**, **Fr Loss Secs**, and **Line Err Secs** should
ideally be showing a value of 0 and never incrementing during fax/modem calls.

Although not as detailed and granular as the Dick Tracy command **4 show fdlintervals**,
physical layer statistics can also be gathered through an HTTP session directly to the IP
address of a port on the 6608 card. The HTTP session is easily generated by entering the IP
address of the appropriate 6608 port into a web browser and clicking **Facility Data Link**
in the leftmost column of the menu that is initially displayed. Figure 12-5 shows local FDL
statistics for a 6608 port.

The Page Help link from the screen capture in Figure 12-5 provides detailed definitions of
the counters listed. You can also refer to Table 12-5 in this section. Some of the more helpful
counters in Figure 12-5 from a fax/modem troubleshooting perspective are **LCV**, **PCV**, and
probably most importantly **CSS**.

Figure 12-5 *Viewing FDL Statistics for a 6608 Port Using HTTP*

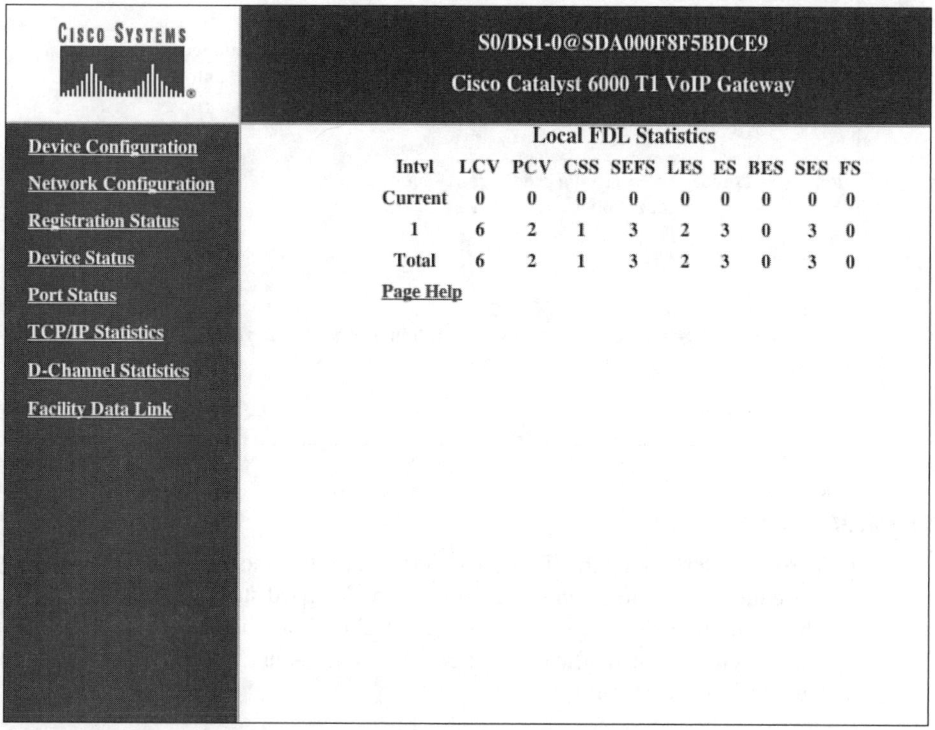

The last method for gathering physical layer information for the telephony port on a 6608 card is through the Catalyst host switch itself. The command **show port voice fdl** provides physical layer statistics, but they are not as comprehensive as the other methods previously discussed. Most important, a counter specifically for slips, which are notorious for causing fax and modem call failures, is not shown. Example 12-22 details the **show port voice fdl** Catalyst CLI command.

Although the **show port voice fdl** lacks the level of detail of previously discussed methods of troubleshooting the physical layer, the important parameters of **ErrorEvents**, **ErroredSecond**, **SeverelyErroredSecond**, **LES**, **BES**, and **LCV** are covered. Also, the added flexibility of being able to issue this command directly from the Catalyst CLI increases its usefulness.

Example 12-22 *Viewing 6608 Physical Layer Overview Using the Catalyst Command* ***show port voice fdl***

```
6500-2> (enable) show port voice fdl 4/8
Port  ErrorEvents        ErroredSecond       SeverlyErroredSecond
      Last 15' Last 24h Last 15' Last 24h Last 15' Last 24h
..... ........ ........ ........ ........ ........ ...........
4/8   1016     1016     2        2        2        2

Port  FailedSignalState FailedSignalSecond
      Last 15' Last 24h Last 15' Last 24h
..... ........ ........ ........ .........
4/8   0        0        0        0

Port         LES                 BES                 LCV
      Last 15' Last 24h Last 15' Last 24h Last 15' Last 24h
..... ........ ........ ........ ........ ........ ........
4/8   1        1        0        0        4        4
6500-2> (enable)
```

IP Troubleshooting

Properly troubleshooting the IP call leg is critical for fax, modem, and text telephony calls. Because these modulated communications were designed strictly for the PSTN, transporting them over IP adds additional challenges. Making sure the IP portion of the call path is operating as reliably and efficiently as possible is necessary for ensuring that fax, modem, and text calls are successful.

Although the previously discussed **show call active voice brief** command is helpful for detecting problems on the IP call leg for IOS gateways, additional tools are available for more detailed troubleshooting. On the Cisco voice gateways, additional commands provide statistical views of the IP packets received from the DSP perspective and packet captures with third-party tools provide the ultimate look at the IP call leg.

Cisco voice gateways provide views of the incoming IP media stream from the digital signal processor (DSP) perspective. This IP media stream carries the packetized fax or modem information. The DSP on the voice gateway can track information about the media stream that enables you to determine whether network problems are having a detrimental effect on the fax/modem/text call.

Within the DSP, a playout or jitter buffer is responsible for handling the individual packets that make up the incoming media stream. This playout buffer defines a fixed amount of delay for passthrough and relay calls to compensate for IP network impairments such as delay, jitter, and out-of-sequence packets. Figure 12-6 illustrates the concept of a playout buffer and how it handles the incoming IP packets.

Figure 12-6 *DSP Playout Buffer on an IOS Gateway for a T.38 Fax Relay Call*

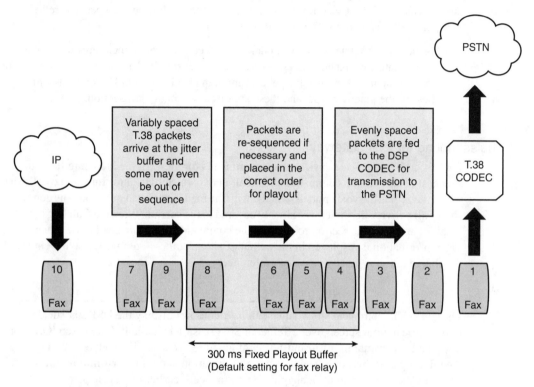

In Figure 12-6, you can see a media stream of T.38 fax relay packets entering the playout buffer from the IP network. For fax relay, the playout buffer is set to a fixed value of 300 ms in Cisco gateways. Sequence numbers carried by the T.38 UDPTL encapsulation are used to resequence the packets and line them up in the correct order for playout by the DSP codec to the PSTN. In the case of passthrough and Cisco fax relay, RTP sequence numbers are used rather than T.38 UDPTL.

For passthrough, the playout buffer is also set to a fixed value, but this value may vary. In IOS gateways, the fixed playout buffer size for modem passthrough and fax pass-through calls is actually derived from the last playout buffer setting in use by the voice call before the switchover occurs. Unlike the fixed buffer sizes for modem and fax calls, voice calls use an adaptive playout buffer, and a wide range of values are possible. When the call transitions to passthrough, the current adaptive voice playout buffer setting is converted into a fixed buffer size.

When dealing with long modem or fax passthrough calls, be cognizant of the lack of DSP clock synchronization that may cause these longer calls to fail. This issue was discussed in detail in the section "Timing and Synchronization" in Chapter 7, "Design Guide for Fax,

Modem, and Text." If you run into this issue, it is recommended that a relay transport method, such as T.38, Cisco fax relay, or Cisco modem relay, be used because relay transport methods do not suffer from this problem.

Troubleshooting the IP leg of a fax, modem, or text call can vary depending on whether you have an IOS gateway or a non-IOS gateway. For this reason, IOS and non-IOS gateways are addressed in separate sections. Packet captures can also be used in IP troubleshooting regardless of the gateway type, and these are discussed in the last section.

IP Troubleshooting for IOS Gateways

For Cisco IOS voice gateways, the best commands for viewing the incoming IP media stream statistics are the commands **show call active voice brief** and **show voice call** *port*, where the *port* is the voice port associated with the media stream in question. The command **show call active voice brief** was already covered in the section "Viewing Call Legs" earlier in this chapter, so this section focuses on the command **show voice call** *port*. Much of the same information is displayed in the output of either of these commands, so the choice of which one to use is mostly personal preference.

TIP	The Cisco IOS command **show voice call** *port* does not display the DSP statistical information to your screen over a Telnet or SSH session by default. Like Cisco IOS debug commands, **terminal monitor** must be configured for your session on the gateway to view the full output of this command. For more information about the **terminal monitor** command, see the section "Debugging Best Practices" earlier in this chapter.
	In addition, when you are using this command to view a particular timeslot of a digital T1/E1 circuit, you must format the user-defined *port* value in a specific manner for the command to be understood. The trick for formatting this *port* value correctly is to use the same designation for the port as seen with the command **show voice call summary**.

The output from the **show voice call** *port* command for a passthrough call appears just like it would for a normal VoIP call. Because passthrough uses a G.711 voice codec to transport the fax/modem/text information, this makes sense. Example 12-23 displays a **show voice call** *port* command for a modem passthrough call.

Example 12-23 *show voice call port Command Output for a Modem Passthrough Call*

```
fax_2851# show voice call 0/0/0

vtsp level 0 state = S_WAIT_RELEASEvpm level 1 state = FXSLS_CPC
vpm level 0 state = S_UP
```

Example 12-23 *show voice call port Command Output for a Modem Passthrough Call (Continued)*

```
          ***DSP VOICE TX STATISTICS***
Tx Vox/Fax Pkts: 1842, Tx Sig Pkts: 0, Tx Comfort Pkts: 0
Tx Dur(ms): 36850, Tx Vox Dur(ms): 36850, Tx Fax Dur(ms): 0
          ***DSP VOICE RX STATISTICS***
Rx Vox/Fax Pkts: 1810, Rx Signal Pkts: 0, Rx Comfort Pkts: 0
Rx Dur(ms): 36850, Rx Vox Dur(ms): 0, Rx Fax Dur(ms): 0
Rx Non-seq Pkts: 0, Rx Bad Hdr Pkts: 0
Rx Early Pkts: 0, Rx Late Pkts: 0
          ***DSP VOICE VP_DELAY STATISTICS***
Clk Offset(ms): -33920, Rx Delay Est(ms): 70
Rx Delay Lo Water Mark(ms): 60, Rx Delay Hi Water Mark(ms): 70
          ***DSP VOICE VP_ERROR STATISTICS***
Predict Conceal(ms): 30, Interpolate Conceal(ms): 0
Silence Conceal(ms): 10, Retroact Mem Update(ms): 0
Buf Overflow Discard(ms): 0, Talkspurt Endpoint Detect Err: 1
          ***DSP LEVELS***
TDM Bus Levels(dBm0): Rx -76.3 from PBX/Phone, Tx -76.3 to PBX/Phone
TDM ACOM Levels(dBm0): +6.0, TDM ERL Level(dBm0): +6.0
TDM Bgd Levels(dBm0): -71.9, with activity being silence
          ***DSP VOICE ERROR STATISTICS***
Rx Pkt Drops(Invalid Header): 0, Tx Pkt Drops(HPI SAM Overflow): 0
```

A number of important counters are highlighted in Example 12-23; these tell you a lot about the incoming media stream. These highlighted counters found in the output from a **show voice call** *port* command are defined in Table 12-6.

Table 12-6 *Important Parameters in the **show voice call** port Command for a Modem Passthrough Call*

DSP Counter	Definition
Rx Non-seq Pkts	Number of out-of-order packets received.
Rx Bad Hdr Pkts	Number of packets received with a bad header.
Rx Early Pkts	Number of packets received earlier than expected based on either sequence numbers or timestamps. This event causes the DSP to recalculate the minimum delay value and to set the playout-delay in the buffer. This can indicate that there was a congestion problem within the network and now the playout buffer is returning to a smaller size.
Rx Late Pkts	Number of packets received later than expected based on sequence numbers or timestamps. If this counter is incrementing, you know that packets are experiencing a source of delay or congestion within the network.
Rx Delay Est(ms)	The current delay value associated with the local voice playout buffer.

continues

Table 12-6 *Important Parameters in the **show voice call** port Command for a Modem Passthrough Call (Continued)*

DSP Counter	Definition
Rx Delay Lo Water Mark(ms)	The lowest playout buffer setting (Rx Delay Est) used for the current call.
Rx Delay Hi Water Mark(ms)	The highest playout buffer setting (Rx Delay Est) used for the current call.
Buf Overflow Discard(ms)	The amount of speech received by the DSP but discarded because of playout/jitter buffer overrun or dynamic adjustments made to the playout/jitter buffer by the DSP in attempting to lower the playout delay. Be aware that at the beginning of calls this counter may increment initially, but it should no longer increment after a couple of seconds.
Rx Pkt Drops(Invalid Header)	Number of dropped packets due to an invalid header.
Tx Pkt Drops(HPI SAM Overflow)	Number of drops involving the host processor interface (HPI) shared-access memory (SAM). This is typically an overrun of the interface responsible for DSP-to-HPI communications.

TIP

For modem passthrough and Cisco modem relay calls, you can view additional counters for troubleshooting the IP media stream with the **show call active voice brief** command. See the last two rows of Table 12-3 for additional modem passthrough counters and Table 12-4 for modem relay specific counters.

You should also be aware that the command **show voice call** *port* does not produce statistics for a Cisco modem relay call. Therefore, when statistics concerning the IP media stream are needed for Cisco modem relay, the **show call active voice brief** command as detailed earlier in Example 12-14 is your only option.

When a call transitions to either Cisco or T.38 fax relay, the output of **show voice call** *port* changes to display fax relay–specific statistics and counters. Example 12-24 displays the IOS **show voice call** *port* command for a T.38 fax relay call.

Example 12-24 *show voice call port Command Output for a T.38 Fax Relay Call*

```
fax_2851# show voice call 0/0/1
      vtsp level 0 state = S_CONNECTvpm level 1 state = FXSLS_CONNECT
vpm level 0 state = S_UP
calling number , calling name unavailable, calling time 10/26 19:02
fax_2811#       ***DSP FAX RELAY STATISTICS***
Max Jit Depth: 11, Max Nwk RxQ Depth 1, Jitter Overflow Pkt Drops: 0
```

Example 12-24   *show voice call port Command Output for a T.38 Fax Relay Call (Continued)*

```
Nwk RxQ Overflow: 0, Tx Pkts: 832, Tx Pkts Drops(Nwk Busy): 0
Rx Pkts: 257, Rx Pkts Loss: 0, Rx Invalid Pkts: 0, Rx Pkts Out Of Seq: 0
Recent Hi-Speed Modulation: V.17/long/14400TX Pages: 1
Max SendInQ Depth 2, Max RecvOutQ Depth 0
Max Hi-Speed Buf Usage 7, SendInQ Overflow 0, RecvOutQ Overflow 0
```

TIP   The **Nwk RxQ Overflow** and **Tx Pkts Drops(Nwk Busy)** counters in the **show voice call** *port* command are not correct in many IOS versions. Therefore, you should disregard the **Nwk RxQ Overflow** and **Tx Pkts Drops(Nwk Busy)** counters if they are not making sense for your specific troubleshooting situation.

The new counters found in the **show voice call** *port* command for a fax relay call differ from those displayed for a passthrough call. These fax relay–specific statistics are defined in Table 12-7.

Table 12-7   *Important Parameters in the **show voice call** port Command for a Fax Relay Call*

DSP Counter	Definition
Jitter Overflow Pkt Drops	Number of packet drops due to the expanding and shrinking of the playout buffer
Nwk RxQ Overflow	Number of network received queue overflows
Tx Pkts Drops(Nwk Busy)	Number of fax packets that are dropped because of a busy network
Rx Pkts Loss	Number of packets that were never received and considered lost in the IP network
Rx Invalid Pkts	Number of packets discarded because of invalid packet headers
Rx Pkts Out of Seq	Number of out-of-order packets received

The output from a **show voice call** *port* command for either a fax relay call or a passthrough call should be checked whenever the integrity of the IP call leg needs to be confirmed. All error counters should be zero. Errors counters that are not zero can be a problem, and any incrementing error counters are almost certainly a problem that needs to be remedied.

IP Troubleshooting for Non-IOS Gateways

The 6608, VG248, and ATA also have statistics and counters pertaining to the incoming RTP media stream. Although this information might not be quite as easy to access as it is on the IOS gateways, the information itself is almost identical.

The best way to look at the DSP counters on the 6608 is by using the Dick Tracy utility. You can find a reference to a document on Cisco.com providing more information about Dick Tracy in the section "Telephony Troubleshooting" earlier in this chapter. The Dick Tracy command **6 show call** *port* provides many lines of DSP-related counters and other information. The critical counters for troubleshooting fax and modem problems are highlighted for this command in Example 12-25.

Example 12-25 *The Dick Tracy Command **6 show call** for a Cisco Fax Relay Call*

```
22:24:08.300 (DSP) RX -> Port<0>
        Voice/Fax Pkts<424>
        Comfort Noise Pkts<0>
        Out-of-Sequence<0>
        Bad Protocol Hdr<0>
        Late Pkts<0>
        Early Pkts<0>
22:24:08.300 (DSP) LEVELS -> Port<0>
        Tx Power<-17>
        Tx Mean<0>
        Rx Power<-44>
        Rx Mean<0>
        Current Bkgnd Noise<-74>
        Current ACOM Level<45>
        Current ERL Level<45>
        Current Activity<4>
        Remote Noise Level<-67>
         ref1_loc <5>
        ref2_loc<0>
        max_ref_loc<5>
        ex_ecan_Stat1<100>
        tex_ecan_Stat2<4097>
         ex_ecan_version<37218>
22:24:08.300 (DSP) MODEM -> Port<0>
        Fill Events<0>
        Drain Events<0>
        Over All Loss<0>
        Consecutive Loss Events<0>
        RFC 2198 Loss Events<0>
        Last Drain Fill Time<0>
        Maximum Duration between Events<0>
        Minimum Duration between Events<0>
22:24:08.300 (DSP) TX -> Port<0>
        Voice/Fax Pkts<1085>
        Comfort Noise Pkts<0>
        Tx Duration<10850>
        Voice Tx Duration<17450>
        Fax Tx Duration<54880>
22:24:08.300 (DSP) ERROR -> Port<0>
        Dropped Rx Pkts : Bad Hdr<0>
        Dropped Tx Pkts : HPI SAM Overflow<0>
        Rx Control Pkts<1961>
        Tx Control Pkts<2205>
```

Example 12-25   *The Dick Tracy Command **6 show call** for a Cisco Fax Relay Call (Continued)*

```
        Dropped Rx Control Pkts<0>
        Dropped Tx Control Pkts<0>
22:24:08.310 (DSP) VPOE -> Port<0>
        Predictive Concealment<0>
        Interpolative Concealment<0>
        Silence Concealment<0>
        Retroactive Memory Update<0>
        Buffer Overflow Discard<0>
        Talkspurt Errors<0>
```

Table 12-8 defines the highlighted counters in Example 12-25. Notice that many of the counters documented here are the same or similar to the counters found in IOS gateways.

Table 12-8   *Important Parameters in the 6608 Dick Tracy Command **6 show call***

DSP Counter	Definition
Out-of-Sequence	Number of out-of-order packets received.
Bad Protocol Hdr	Number of packets received with a bad header.
Early Pkts	Number of packets received earlier than expected based on either sequence numbers or timestamps. This event causes the DSP to recalculate the minimum delay value and to set the playout delay in the buffer. This can indicate that there was a congestion problem within the network and now the playout buffer is returning to a smaller size.
Late Pkts	Number of packets received later than expected based on sequence numbers or timestamps. If this counter is incrementing, you know that packets are experiencing a source of delay or congestion within the network.
Fill Events	Number of events where the playout buffer is being filled. This occurs when we are receiving packets faster than our derived clock.
Drain Events	Number of events where the playout buffer is being drained. This occurs when we are receiving packets slower than our derived clock.
Over All Loss	Details packet loss on a percentage basis. Incrementing values in these counters indicate IP network problems that are negatively impacting the call.
Consecutive Loss Events	Number of consecutive packet loss events.

continues

Table 12-8 *Important Parameters in the 6608 Dick Tracy Command **6 show call** (Continued)*

DSP Counter	Definition
RFC 2198 Loss Events	Number of packets lost or errored but corrected by the RFC 2198 redundancy algorithm.
Dropped Rx Pkts : Bad Hdr	Number of packets dropped because of a bad header.
Dropped Tx Pkts : HPI SAM Overflow	Number of drops involving the HPI SAM. This is typically an overrun of the interface responsible for DSP-to-HPI communications.
Buffer Overflow Discard	The amount of speech received by the DSP but discarded because of playout/jitter buffer overrun or dynamic adjustments made to the playout/jitter buffer by the DSP in attempting to lower the playout delay.

Although minor errors may occasionally be tolerated by fax and modem calls, ideally the counters involving packet drops should not increment. Incrementing packet drop counters are indicative of the media stream encountering IP network problems.

TIP

For those interested in viewing repeated DSP stats such as the ones above for a call on the 6608, you can use the Dick Tracy command **6 set mask 8**. However, the counter fields with this command are abbreviated, so they are not as easy to read as they are with the command **6 show call**.

The VG248 non-IOS gateway also provides limited statistical information about the incoming IP media stream. To view this information, however, the DSP trace on the VG248 event log must be enabled. Instead of the default setting, the DSP logging level needs to be configured for the maximum (**Errors + warnings + info + trace**). Example 12-26 shows two lines of counters from the VG248 event log when the DSP trace is enabled.

Example 12-26 *DSP Counters from the VG248 Event Log*

```
17 17:02:44 5001   T DSP   24 Tx:348 Rx:348,Seq:0,Hdr:0,Late:0,Early:0
18 17:02:44    2   T DSP   23 Tx:846 Rx:846,Seq:0,Hdr:0,Late:0,Early:0
```

You can immediately see that the VG248 DSP counters for the incoming media stream are not as detailed as what is available for IOS gateways and the 6608. Nonetheless, you do receive a few counters that can be helpful. The **Seq** counter tracks out-of-sequence packets. The **Hdr** counter increments for packets with bad headers. The **Late** and **Early** counters track packets that are arriving early or late with regard to the rate that the packets in the buffer are being played out by the DSP.

The other important parameter in Example 12-26 is the port number. In this case, you can see DSP counters for ports **23** and **24**. Knowing the port number allows you to match up any counters with incrementing errors with the call that is being impacted.

The ATA non-IOS gateway also provides counters that analyze the incoming RTP media. These counters can be seen by accessing the following URL:

   http://*IP_address*/rtps

The *IP_address* is the address or DNS name of the ATA device itself. This URL for the IP media counters or RTP statistics is valid for all ATA loads including H.323, SIP, MGCP, and SCCP. Figure 12-7 displays the RTP statistics for an ATA with an SCCP load during a fax passthrough call.

Figure 12-7 *RTP Statistics for an ATA with an SCCP Load*

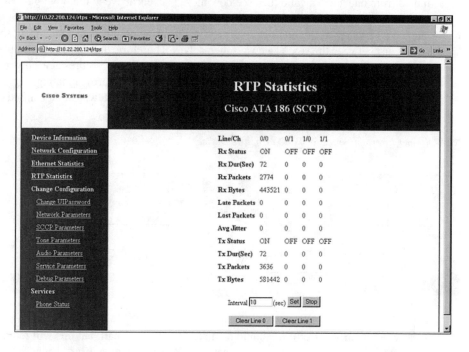

From an IP troubleshooting perspective, the RTP statistics shown by the ATA in Figure 12-7 provide three counters that should be monitored: **Late Packets**, **Lost Packets**, and **Avg Jitter**. Packets that are lost and late indicate IP network problems, and the average jitter should ideally remain below 150 ms for reliable fax performance on the ATA.

IP Troubleshooting Using Packet Captures

The best way to troubleshoot the IP portion of a fax/modem/text call is with a packet capture. Packet captures provide an unbiased, third-party view of what is occurring on the IP network. In addition, you can observe not only the incoming media stream, but also the outgoing one to ensure that the gateway is properly transmitting packets as it should.

NOTE	Although there is an abundance of packet-capturing software available, the easiest to acquire and use is probably Wireshark. The Wireshark software is used for the examples in this book and is available as a free download from http://www.wireshark.org/.

When troubleshooting the IP network with packet captures, it is best to grab a capture at each of the gateways. With captures on both sides, you can view the packets being transmitted from one gateway and then see how those packets arrive at the other gateway and vice versa. Be aware that in Unified CM environments, obtaining a packet capture at the Unified CM server itself shows only the call control signaling because the media stream occurs just between the voice gateways themselves. Therefore, unless you are troubleshooting just a call control signaling issue, it is best to obtain packet captures at each voice gateway because the media stream can be captured and the call control signaling. Figure 12-8 illustrates the placement of packet capture devices for voice gateways in a Unified CM environment.

Figure 12-8 *Proper Insertion Points for Packet Capture Devices*

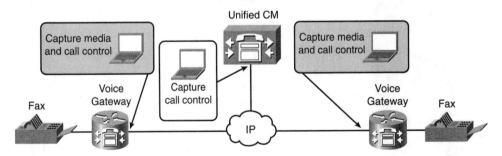

Ideally, simultaneous captures should be made for the same call, but this will require two capture devices, one at each voice gateway. You should also insert the packet capture devices as close as possible to the voice gateway's interface that is used for the origination and termination of the IP connection. In addition, it is sometimes helpful to gather DSP statistics for this call, too, to confirm that the voice gateway's counters are matching up with the trace from the packet capture software.

For modem and fax calls whose media stream uses an RTP encapsulation, Wireshark offers an RTP stream analysis feature for quickly analyzing the bidirectional RTP streams. The fax and modem transport methods that use RTP for encapsulation include modem passthrough, fax pass-through, and Cisco fax relay. Because modem relay uses SPRT and T.38 fax relay uses UDPTL rather than RTP, these transport methods usually have to be analyzed manually. Figure 12-9 highlights the RTP analysis feature in Wireshark for a modem passthrough call.

Figure 12-9 *Wireshark RTP Stream Analysis Feature for a Modem Passthrough Call*

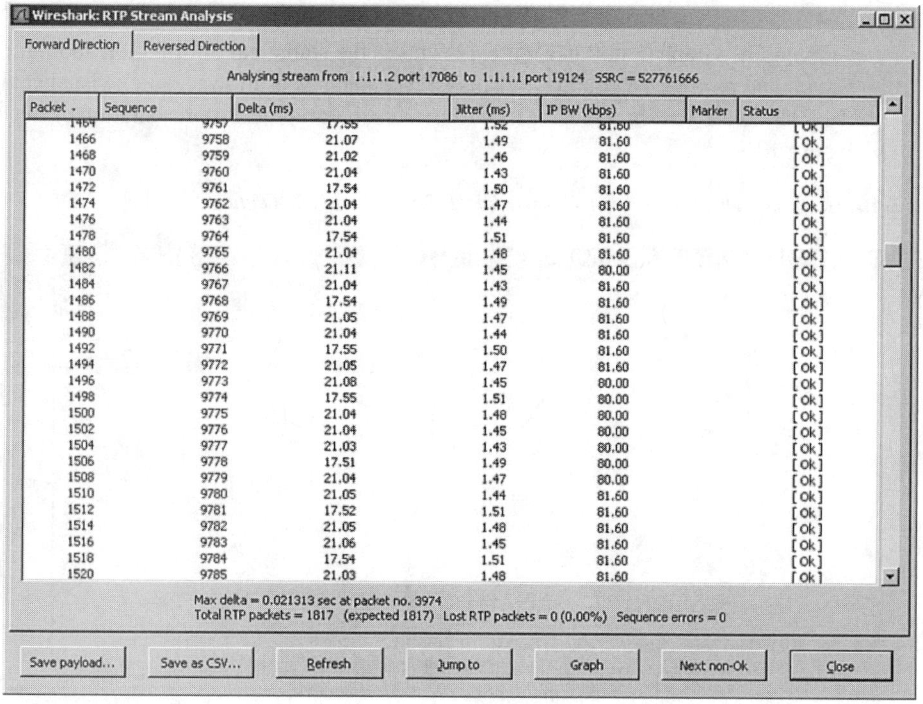

The RTP stream analysis feature in Wireshark can be activated by first highlighting a single RTP packet from the media stream that you are interested in viewing. Then, under the Statistics menu at the top, select RTP, and then Stream Analysis.

From the RTP analysis screen shot in Figure 12-9, you will notice how you can quickly check items such as jitter, lost packets, and out-of-sequence packets. The Jitter (ms) column displays the jitter between each packet, and the Delta (ms) column provides the exact amount of time between packets. By default, Cisco IOS voice gateways send G.711 passthrough packets every 20 ms, and you can see how this value is reasonably close to the delta times in Figure 12-9.

A Sequence column displays the RTP sequence number. This allows you to confirm that there are not any missing or out-of-order packets.

At the top of the screen capture, the direction of the stream, including the originating and terminating IP addresses and UDP port numbers, is provided. At the bottom of the window, the maximum delta (Max delta) is shown along with totals for lost RTP packets and sequence errors.

There is a tab for Reversed Direction in the upper-left corner of the window. This allows you to quickly view the RTP media stream and its statistical information for the opposite direction.

Clicking the Graph button in Figure 12-9 takes the statistical information about the RTP stream and produces a graphical display of the data. This allows a quick visual analysis of the RTP media stream. Figure 12-10 illustrates the graphical representation of the data in Figure 12-9.

Figure 12-10 *Graphical Display from the Wireshark RTP Stream Analysis Feature*

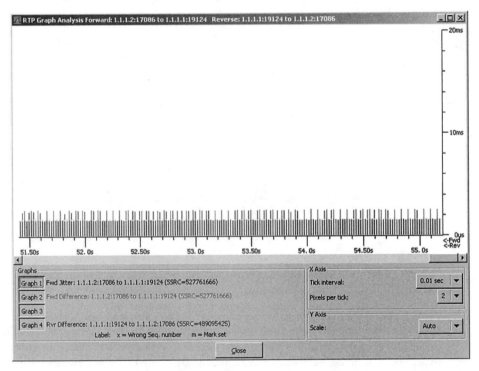

As expected, the graph in Figure 12-10 does not show any problems, but it shows you how the RTP media stream can be broken down graphically. Options such as the axis intervals and stream selection are even present to customize certain aspects of the graph.

However, for transport methods such as T.38 fax relay and modem relay that do not rely on an RTP encapsulation, the RTP stream analysis feature does not work. Instead, an approach that involves more manual work must be used. Figure 12-11 shows a T.38 fax relay call in Wireshark.

TIP

Modem passthrough with the redundancy option enabled tends to cause corrupted statistics when viewed with Wireshark's RTP stream analysis feature. Therefore, it is recommended that you disable redundancy on modem passthrough if you are trying to analyze the RTP media stream with Wireshark.

Figure 12-11 *Wireshark Packet Capture of a T.38 Fax Relay*

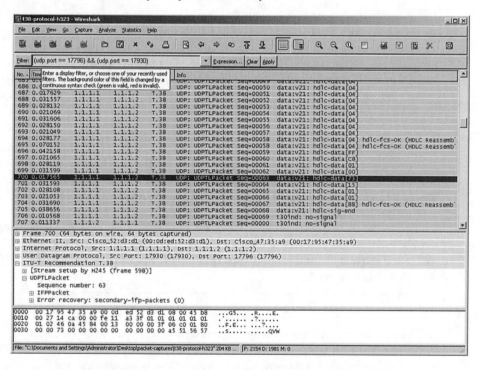

In Figure 12-11, the UDPTL sequence numbers are easily visible. However, you must manually look through the capture to find missing or out-of-order packets. This same manual searching procedure applies for detecting jitter, too. When searching for excessive jitter, make sure the Time Display Format is set to Seconds Since Previous Packet under the View menu.

Manually parsing through a long packet capture can be quite tedious. Hopefully, you will have some idea of where in the call the problem begins from a time perspective. If so, you can narrow down the portion of the packet capture with the problem. When looking at the capture, remember that you need to confirm that packets are arriving at evenly spaced time intervals and in sequence without any missing sequence numbers.

Troubleshooting the Switchover Signaling

When troubleshooting fax and modem issues, it is important to confirm that the switchover from voice mode to fax/modem relay or passthrough mode occurs in the proper manner. Recall that fax and modem calls on Cisco voice gateways always start off as a voice call initially and only after certain tones or flags are detected will a switchover happen. When this switchover does not happen, fax or modem calls almost always fail.

Referring back to Figure 12-1, troubleshooting the switchover signaling is the next logical step after telephony and IP troubleshooting, which was just covered in the previous section. At this point, through analyzing commands such as **show call active voice brief**, you should know whether the call is properly transitioning from voice to the appropriate fax/modem mode. In case the call is not making this switchover or you suspect problems in the switchover mechanism itself, this section details how you troubleshoot these problems on Cisco voice gateways.

TIP   Unlike fax and modem calls, text telephony calls over IP do not have switchover mechanisms. For Text over G.711, there is not a switchover because the text information is simply transported over the G.711 codec. With Cisco text relay, RTP packets with a payload type of 119 are sent whenever text tones are detected, but there is not a negotiated switchover for the text relay session. Therefore, only the various switchover methods for fax and modem calls are discussed in this section. For more information about Text over G.711 and text relay, see the section "Text over G.711" in Chapter 4 and the section "Cisco Text Relay" in Chapter 5.

The switchover mechanisms used by Cisco voice gateways can be divided into three different types: NSE based, protocol based, and RTP payload type. The troubleshooting of these different switchover types might be different, so it is important to determine the exact switchover type that you are using and to then troubleshoot accordingly. Figure 12-12 illustrates how these three different switchover methods can transition a call from voice mode to different fax/modem transport modes.

Figure 12-12 *Cisco Voice Gateway Fax and Modem Switchover Mechanisms*

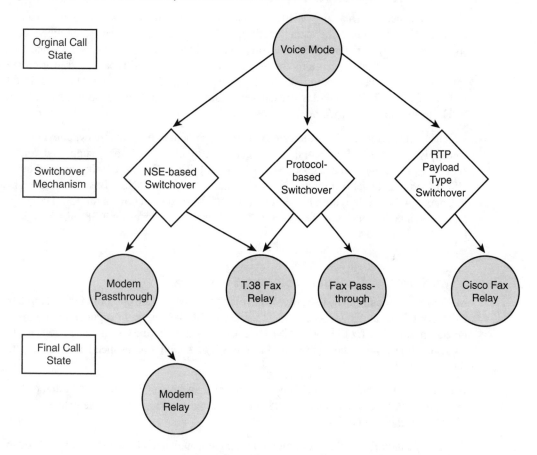

Figure 12-12 diagrams the different ways a call that is originally a voice call can be transformed into a fax/modem call. NSE-based switchovers are Cisco proprietary, but they are the only option for modem passthrough and modem relay. Although T.38 fax relay can use an NSE-based switchover, it can also use a protocol-based switchover mechanism.

Fax pass-through is capable of a protocol-based switchover only, and Cisco fax relay must use a switchover mechanism based on changing RTP payload types. Cisco fax relay is the only fax/modem transport mode that has its own unique switchover mechanism.

The following subsections are broken down by the various switchover mechanisms. The NSE-based switchover mechanism is discussed first, followed by protocol-based switchovers. The unique RTP payload type switchover used by Cisco fax relay is discussed at the end.

Troubleshooting NSE-Based Switchovers

Cisco voice gateways may use NSE-based switchovers for modem passthrough, modem relay, and T.38 fax relay. The main benefit of an NSE-based switchover is that the voice signaling protocol is not involved in the actual switchover itself. As long as the voice signaling protocol establishes a bidirectional media stream, the NSE packets transition the call from voice to fax/modem mode. If a bidirectional media stream cannot be established by the voice signaling protocol, voice calls are failing, and you need to resolve this problem before troubleshooting fax/modem issues.

Because of the passive role of the voice signaling protocol in NSE-based switchovers, you can apply the same NSE troubleshooting technique to all the commonly supported voice signaling protocols, such as H.323, SIP, MGCP, and SCCP. For more information about NSE-based switchovers for modem passthrough, see the section "NSE-Based Passthrough" in Chapter 4. For additional information about NSE-based switchovers for T.38 fax relay and Cisco modem relay, see the sections "NSE-Based Switchover for T.38" and "Modem Relay" in Chapter 5.

NSE-Based Switchover for Modem Passthrough

Modem passthrough can be used by Cisco voice gateways to transport both fax and modem calls. For G3 fax and low-speed modem calls, an NSE-192 message is generated by the detection of a 2100 Hz tone. This NSE-192 packet is used by the Cisco voice gateways to signal the transition of the call to passthrough, which includes an upspeed, if necessary, to the G.711 codec.

For Super G3 fax calls and high-speed modem calls, an ANSam tone triggers both the NSE-192 and an NSE-193 message. The NSE-193 message instructs the remote gateway to disable its echo cancellers.

The best method for troubleshooting modem passthrough and all NSE-based passthrough switchovers on IOS gateways is with the command **debug voip rtp session named-event**. Example 12-27 shows a capture of the **debug voip rtp session named-event** command for a high-speed modem call on a Cisco IOS voice gateway with the modem passthrough feature enabled.

Example 12-27 *debug voip rtp session named-event Command Output for a High-Speed Modem Call Using Modem Passthrough*

```
Jan 10 22:01:58.463:          s=DSP d=VoIP payload 0x64 ssrc 0x1EF2 sequence 0x1FBB
  timestamp 0x20631C26
Jan 10 22:01:58.463:          Pt:100   Evt:192    Pkt:00 00 00   <Snd>>>
Jan 10 22:01:58.471:          s=DSP d=VoIP payload 0x64 ssrc 0x1EF2 sequence 0x1FBD
  timestamp 0x20631C26
Jan 10 22:01:58.471:          Pt:100   Evt:192    Pkt:00 00 00   <Snd>>>
Jan 10 22:01:58.483:          s=VoIP d=DSP payload 0x64 ssrc 0x9A20101 sequence
  0x18C2 timestamp 0xADA80F0A
Jan 10 22:01:58.483: <<<Rcv> Pt:100   Evt:192    Pkt:00 00 00
```

Example 12-27 *debug voip rtp session named-event Command Output for a High-Speed Modem Call Using Modem Passthrough (Continued)*

```
Jan 10 22:01:58.491:        s=DSP d=VoIP payload 0x64 ssrc 0x1EF2 sequence 0x1FBF
  timestamp 0x20631C26
Jan 10 22:01:58.491:        Pt:100    Evt:192    Pkt:00 00 00   <Snd>>>
Jan 10 22:01:58.495:        s=VoIP d=DSP payload 0x64 ssrc 0x9A20101 sequence
  0x18C3 timestamp 0xADA80F0A
Jan 10 22:01:58.495:  <<<Rcv> Pt:100    Evt:192    Pkt:00 00 00
Jan 10 22:01:58.515:        s=VoIP d=DSP payload 0x64 ssrc 0x9A20101 sequence
  0x18C4 timestamp 0xADA80F0A
Jan 10 22:01:58.515:  <<<Rcv> Pt:100    Evt:192    Pkt:00 00 00
Jan 10 22:01:59.599:        s=DSP d=VoIP payload 0x64 ssrc 0x6 sequence 0x1FFA
  timestamp 0x20633FC6
Jan 10 22:01:59.599:        Pt:100    Evt:193    Pkt:00 00 00   <Snd>>>
Jan 10 22:01:59.611:        s=DSP d=VoIP payload 0x64 ssrc 0x6 sequence 0x1FFB
  timestamp 0x20633FC6
Jan 10 22:01:59.611:        Pt:100    Evt:193    Pkt:00 00 00   <Snd>>>
Jan 10 22:01:59.615:        s=VoIP d=DSP payload 0x64 ssrc 0x9A20101 sequence
  0x18FB timestamp 0xADA8325A
Jan 10 22:01:59.615:  <<<Rcv> Pt:100    Evt:193    Pkt:00 00 00
Jan 10 22:01:59.623:        s=VoIP d=DSP payload 0x64 ssrc 0x9A20101 sequence
  0x18FD timestamp 0xADA8325A
Jan 10 22:01:59.623:  <<<Rcv> Pt:100    Evt:193    Pkt:00 00 00
Jan 10 22:01:59.631:        s=DSP d=VoIP payload 0x64 ssrc 0x6 sequence 0x1FFD
  timestamp 0x20633FC6
Jan 10 22:01:59.631:        Pt:100    Evt:193    Pkt:00 00 00   <Snd>>>
Jan 10 22:01:59.647:        s=VoIP d=DSP payload 0x64 ssrc 0x9A20101 sequence
  0x18FF timestamp 0xADA8325A
Jan 10 22:01:59.647:  <<<Rcv> Pt:100    Evt:193    Pkt:00 00 00
```

In Example 12-27, NSE packets with the default RTP PT (payload type) of 100 are seen. Included within the NSE message is an Event type numbered either 192 (**Evt:192**) or 193 (**Evt:193**). The direction of the NSE event is notated by **<Snd>>>** for NSE packets transmitted by the gateway and **<<<Rcv>** for packets received by the gateway. You can tell that this is the terminating gateway because the first NSE-192 messages are sent from this gateway to initiate the switchover.

In this example, you can also tell that a Super G3 fax or a high-speed modem communication is occurring because of the presence of both an NSE-192 and an NSE-193. For typical G3 fax transactions and low-speed modem calls, only an NSE-192 would be present.

The 6608, VG248, and ATA non-IOS gateways also support modem passthrough and its NSE-based switchover. For the 6608, the DSP trace of **6 set mask 0x323** can be used to see incoming NSE messages. Example 12-28 displays incoming NSE messages using the Dick Tracy DSP trace **6 set mask 0x323**.

Example 12-28 *6608 Dick Tracy DSP Trace **6 set mask 0x323** for a Modem Passthrough Call*

```
17:39:40.550 (DSP) MDCX -> Port<0>
                         Enabling Digit Detection
                         Stopping Tones
                         Mode : SENDRECV
17:39:40.550 (DSP) RTP TxOpen -> Port<0> Remote IP<10.22.200.129> UDP Port<0x4022
(16418)> Handle<5>
17:39:40.550 (DSP) RTCP TxOpen -> Port<0> Remote IP<10.22.200.129> UDP Port<0x4023
(16419)> Handle<6>
17:39:42.760 (DSP) Report P2P Msg -> Port<0> Event<192> Duration<0> Volume<0>
17:39:43.360 (DSP) Report P2P Msg -> Port<0> Event<193> Duration<0> Volume<0>
```

After the connection is established with the MGCP **MDCX** message in Example 12-28, the modem passthrough switchover occurs upon the detection of the appropriate stimuli tones. In the case of a high-speed modem call, this stimuli tone is an ANSam. The 6608 only displays NSE messages that it receives using **Report P2P Msg**. Within this debug line, the NSE-192 and NSE-193 are flagged as **Event<192>** and **Event<193>**, respectively.

The VG248 shows modem passthrough NSE messages through its event log DSP trace. The NSE messages are not broken down by NSE-192 and NSE-193 events, but instead unique trace messages are used. These messages are a bit different for the originating and the terminating gateway, so the messages for each of these cases are looked at separately. Example 12-29 shows the how the modem passthrough switchover is displayed when the VG248 is the terminating gateway.

Example 12-29 *Terminating VG248 DSP Trace for a Modem Passthrough Call*

```
 76 17:39:08    0  T DSP    24 Tx:49 Rx:49,Seq:0,Hdr:0,Late:0,Early:0
 77 17:39:09  285  T DSP    24 Modem answer tone detected
 78 17:39:09    0  I DSP    24 Entering passthrough mode. Codec = G.711 mu law
 79 17:39:09    1  T DSP    24 Passthrough codec type = 1
 80 17:39:09    0  T SLIC   24 echo canceller enabled
 81 17:39:09    1  T SLIC   24 modem detection enabled
 82 17:39:09   10  T DSP    24 rx:00C1,0005,0001,0000

! Output omitted for brevity

106 17:39:09  220  T DSP    24 Phase reversed modem answer tone detected
107 17:39:09    0  I DSP    24 Disabling echo canceller
108 17:39:09    0  T SLIC   24 echo canceller disabled
```

Although the VG248 does not show the exact NSE events, the switchover messages themselves are more user friendly. The message **Modem answer tone detected** informs you that a 2100 Hz stimuli tone has been detected. At this point, the terminating VG248 sends an NSE-192 to the originating gateway while transitioning its own codec to G.711.

The sending of the NSE-192 is not displayed, but you can see the codec transition with the message **Entering passthrough mode** followed by **Codec = G.711 mu law**.

Also notice that the echo cancellers are still active by the message **echo canceller enabled**. The message **Phase reversed modem answer tone detected** tells you that a high-speed modem has been detected. This results in the VG248 sending an NSE-193 and a disabling of the VG248's own echo cancellers, which is confirmed by the message **echo canceller disabled**.

When the VG248 acts as the originating gateway, the modem passthrough switchover messages are different. Example 12-30 highlights the modem passthrough switchover messages for an originating VG248.

Example 12-30 *Originating VG248 DSP Trace for a Modem Passthrough Call*

```
 90 17:39:09   53  T DSP     23 Received NSE modem answer indication
 91 17:39:09    0  I DSP     23 Entering passthrough mode. Codec = G.711 mu law
 92 17:39:09    1  T DSP     23 Passthrough codec type = 1
 93 17:39:09    0  T SLIC    23 echo canceller enabled
 94 17:39:09    1  T SLIC    23 modem detection enabled
 95 17:39:09   10  T DSP     23 rx:00CF,C01E,ED80,0064
 96 17:39:09    1  T DSP     23 tx:0044

! Output omitted for brevity

113 17:39:09   24  T DSP     23 Received NSE echo canceller disablement
114 17:39:09    0  I DSP     23 Disabling echo canceller
115 17:39:09    1  T SLIC    23 echo canceller disabled
```

In Example 12-30, a VG248 acting as the originating gateway flags the reception of an NSE-192 with the line **Received NSE modem answer indication**. The VG248 then changes over to the G.711 codec. A short time later, the message **Received NSE echo canceller disablement** signifies the reception of an NSE-193 telling this gateway to disable its echo cancellers for this call.

Even though the ATA uses NSE-based modem passthrough for its switchover mechanism, it officially supports only normal G3 fax calls in passthrough mode. To view this switchover, a software utility known as prserv is required. The prserv utility runs on a PC and presents a real-time debug log and a log file of the ATA's call functions.

TIP

The prserv utility is bundled with an informative ATA fax document and the rtpcatch utility in a download titled ATAFaxPackage. Valid cisco.com users can download prserv from the following URL:

http://www.cisco.com/cgi-bin/tablebuild.pl/ata186

The prserv log for a fax passthrough call through an ATA clearly shows the NSE messages being sent and received and the codec upspeed. Example 12-31 highlights these messages from an ATA prserv log file.

Example 12-31 *Fax Passthrough Switchover Messages from an ATA prserv Log*

```
[0]Tx MPT PT=100 NSE pkt c0000000
[0]codec: 4 => 0
[0]Rx MPT PT=100 NSE pkt c0000000
```

The NSE-192 switchover packets in Example 12-31 are shown by the message **NSE pkt c0000000**, where the value **c0** is the hexadecimal representation of the NSE event ID value of 192. NSE messages sent by the ATA include **Tx** for transmit, and NSE messages that are received by the ATA contain **Rx**. The **codec** upspeed is notated by **4 => 0**, where the value **4** signifies the G.723.1 codec and **0** represents G.711.

NSE-Based Switchover for Cisco Modem Relay

Cisco modem relay requires that a switchover to modem passthrough be completed before a switchover to Cisco modem relay occurs. Therefore, the output from the command **debug voip rtp session named-event** for a Cisco modem relay call always begins with the display of the NSE-192 and NSE-193 messages seen with a modem passthrough call.

In addition to seeing the modem passthrough–specific NSE messages, Cisco modem relay uses NSE-199 and NSE-203 messages. The NSE-199 message is used by the Cisco voice gateways to confirm support of Cisco modem relay, whereas NSE-203 is responsible for initiating the actual switchover. Example 12-32 highlights the output from the **debug voip rtp session named-event** command for a Cisco modem relay call.

Example 12-32 *debug voip rtp session named-event Command Output for a Cisco Modem Relay Call*

```
3825#
*Mar 29 02:50:56.052: %ISDN-6-CONNECT: Interface Serial1/0/0:22 is now connected to
  9194724114 N/A
*Mar 29 02:50:57.724:           s=VoIP d=DSP payload 0x64 ssrc 0x1CDE1F6B sequence
  0x1FFA timestamp 0xFE1CC715
*Mar 29 02:50:57.724:  <<<Rcv> Pt:100    Evt:192    Pkt:00 00 00
*Mar 29 02:50:57.736:           s=VoIP d=DSP payload 0x64 ssrc 0x1CDE1F6B sequence
  0x1FFB timestamp 0xFE1CC715
*Mar 29 02:50:57.736:  <<<Rcv> Pt:100    Evt:192    Pkt:00 00 00
*Mar 29 02:50:57.736:           s=DSP d=VoIP payload 0x64 ssrc 0x1E84 sequence 0x1B15
  timestamp 0xDDF2C2C3
*Mar 29 02:50:57.736:           Pt:100    Evt:192    Pkt:00 00 00  <Snd>>>
*Mar 29 02:50:57.744:           s=DSP d=VoIP payload 0x64 ssrc 0x1E84 sequence 0x1B16
  timestamp 0xDDF2C2C3
*Mar 29 02:50:57.744:           Pt:100    Evt:192    Pkt:00 00 00  <Snd>>>
*Mar 29 02:50:57.756:           s=VoIP d=DSP payload 0x64 ssrc 0x1CDE1F6B sequence
  0x1FFD timestamp 0xFE1CC715
*Mar 29 02:50:57.756:  <<<Rcv> Pt:100    Evt:192    Pkt:00 00 00
```

Example 12-32 *debug voip rtp session named-event Command Output for a Cisco Modem Relay Call (Continued)*

```
*Mar 29 02:50:57.764:          s=VoIP d=DSP payload 0x64 ssrc 0x1CDE1F6B sequence
  0x1FFF timestamp 0xFE1CC855
*Mar 29 02:50:57.764:  <<<Rcv> Pt:100    Evt:199     Pkt:00 00 00
*Mar 29 02:50:57.764:          s=DSP d=VoIP payload 0x64 ssrc 0x1E84 sequence 0x1B18
  timestamp 0xDDF2C2C3
*Mar 29 02:50:57.764:          Pt:100    Evt:192     Pkt:00 00 00 <Snd>>>
*Mar 29 02:50:57.776:          s=VoIP d=DSP payload 0x64 ssrc 0x1CDE1F6B sequence
  0x2000 timestamp 0xFE1CC855
*Mar 29 02:50:57.776:  <<<Rcv> Pt:100    Evt:199     Pkt:00 00 00
*Mar 29 02:50:57.776:          s=DSP d=VoIP payload 0x64 ssrc 0x1E84 sequence 0x1B1A
  timestamp 0xDDF2C403
*Mar 29 02:50:57.776:          Pt:100    Evt:199     Pkt:00 00 00 <Snd>>>
*Mar 29 02:50:57.784:          s=DSP d=VoIP payload 0x64 ssrc 0x1E84 sequence 0x1B1B
  timestamp 0xDDF2C403
*Mar 29 02:50:57.784:          Pt:100    Evt:199     Pkt:00 00 00 <Snd>>>
*Mar 29 02:50:57.796:          s=VoIP d=DSP payload 0x64 ssrc 0x1CDE1F6B sequence
  0x2002 timestamp 0xFE1CC855
*Mar 29 02:50:57.796:  <<<Rcv> Pt:100    Evt:199     Pkt:00 00 00
*Mar 29 02:50:57.804:          s=DSP d=VoIP payload 0x64 ssrc 0x1E84 sequence 0x1B1D
  timestamp 0xDDF2C403
*Mar 29 02:50:57.804:          Pt:100    Evt:199     Pkt:00 00 00 <Snd>>>
*Mar 29 02:50:58.404:          s=VoIP d=DSP payload 0x64 ssrc 0x1CDE1F6B sequence
  0x2025 timestamp 0xFE1CDC55
*Mar 29 02:50:58.404:  <<<Rcv> Pt:100    Evt:193     Pkt:00 00 00
*Mar 29 02:50:58.416:          s=VoIP d=DSP payload 0x64 ssrc 0x1CDE1F6B sequence
  0x2026 timestamp 0xFE1CDC55
*Mar 29 02:50:58.416:  <<<Rcv> Pt:100    Evt:193     Pkt:00 00 00
*Mar 29 02:50:58.416:          s=DSP d=VoIP payload 0x64 ssrc 0x14 sequence 0x1B3D
  timestamp 0xDDF2D803
*Mar 29 02:50:58.416:          Pt:100    Evt:193     Pkt:00 00 00 <Snd>>>
*Mar 29 02:50:58.424:          s=DSP d=VoIP payload 0x64 ssrc 0x14 sequence 0x1B3E
  timestamp 0xDDF2D803
*Mar 29 02:50:58.424:          Pt:100    Evt:193     Pkt:00 00 00 <Snd>>>
*Mar 29 02:50:58.436:          s=VoIP d=DSP payload 0x64 ssrc 0x1CDE1F6B sequence
  0x2028 timestamp 0xFE1CDC55
*Mar 29 02:50:58.436:  <<<Rcv> Pt:100    Evt:193     Pkt:00 00 00
*Mar 29 02:50:58.444:          s=DSP d=VoIP payload 0x64 ssrc 0x14 sequence 0x1B40
  timestamp 0xDDF2D803
*Mar 29 02:50:58.444:          Pt:100    Evt:193     Pkt:00 00 00 <Snd>>>
*Mar 29 02:50:59.004:          s=DSP d=VoIP payload 0x64 ssrc 0x14 sequence 0x1B5D
  timestamp 0xDDF2EA73
*Mar 29 02:50:59.004:          Pt:100    Evt:203     Pkt:00 00 00 <Snd>>>
*Mar 29 02:50:59.016:          s=DSP d=VoIP payload 0x64 ssrc 0x14 sequence 0x1B5F
  timestamp 0xDDF2EA73
*Mar 29 02:50:59.016:          Pt:100    Evt:203     Pkt:00 00 00 <Snd>>>
*Mar 29 02:50:59.024:          s=VoIP d=DSP payload 0x64 ssrc 0x1CDE1F6B sequence
  0x2047 timestamp 0xFE1CEFB5
*Mar 29 02:50:59.024:  <<<Rcv> Pt:100    Evt:203     Pkt:00 00 00
*Mar 29 02:50:59.036:          s=VoIP d=DSP payload 0x64 ssrc 0x1CDE1F6B sequence
  0x2048 timestamp 0xFE1CEFB5
*Mar 29 02:50:59.036:  <<<Rcv> Pt:100    Evt:203     Pkt:00 00 00
*Mar 29 02:50:59.036:          s=DSP d=VoIP payload 0x64 ssrc 0x14 sequence 0x1B61
  timestamp 0xDDF2EA73
```

continues

Example 12-32 *debug voip rtp session named-event Command Output for a Cisco Modem Relay Call (Continued)*

```
*Mar 29 02:50:59.036:           Pt:100    Evt:203    Pkt:00 00 00   <Snd>>>
*Mar 29 02:50:59.056:           s=VoIP d=DSP payload 0x64 ssrc 0x1CDE1F6B sequence
  0x204A timestamp 0xFE1CEFB5
*Mar 29 02:50:59.056:  <<<Rcv> Pt:100    Evt:203    Pkt:00 00 00
3825#
```

The Cisco modem relay NSE-199 (**Evt:199**) and NSE-203 (**Evt:203**) messages are high-lighted in Example 12-32. You can see that the first NSE-199 packet is received by this gateway, because it is tagged with **<<<Rcv>;** and the first NSE-203 message is transmitted from this gateway, because it is showing **<Snd>>>**. For more information about Cisco modem relay and its NSE-based switchover, see the section "Modem Relay" in Chapter 5.

NSE-Based Switchover for T.38 Fax Relay

Even though T.38 is a standards-based protocol for fax relay, it can use proprietary NSE messages for the switchover. The NSE-200 message signifies a T.38 switchover request. The NSE-201 message represents a T.38 switchover ACK (acknowledgment), and the NSE-202 message is a NACK (negative acknowledgment) and means that the T.38 switchover request has been declined. The most common reason for a gateway to send an NSE-202 NACK is when the gateway is not properly configured for NSE-based T.38 fax relay. Example 12-33 shows the output from the **debug voip rtp session named-event** for a T.38 fax relay call.

Example 12-33 *debug voip rtp session named-event Command Output for a T.38 Fax Relay Call*

```
Jan 10 15:26:35.199:           s=VoIP d=DSP payload 0x64 ssrc 0x265F0102 sequence
  0x436 timestamp 0xC3D66FDD
Jan 10 15:26:35.199:  <<<Rcv> Pt:100    Evt:200    Pkt:00 00 00
Jan 10 15:26:35.211:           s=VoIP d=DSP payload 0x64 ssrc 0x265F0102 sequence
  0x437 timestamp 0xC3D66FDD
Jan 10 15:26:35.211:  <<<Rcv> Pt:100    Evt:200    Pkt:00 00 00
Jan 10 15:26:35.215:           s=DSP d=VoIP payload 0x64 ssrc 0x1EF0 sequence 0x1D70
  timestamp 0x206417B6
Jan 10 15:26:35.215:           Pt:100    Evt:201    Pkt:00 00 00   <Snd>>>
Jan 10 15:26:35.227:           s=DSP d=VoIP payload 0x64 ssrc 0x1EF0 sequence 0x1D72
  timestamp 0x206417B6
Jan 10 15:26:35.227:           Pt:100    Evt:201    Pkt:00 00 00   <Snd>>>
Jan 10 15:26:35.247:           s=DSP d=VoIP payload 0x64 ssrc 0x1EF0 sequence 0x1D74
  timestamp 0x206417B6
Jan 10 15:26:35.247:           Pt:100    Evt:201    Pkt:00 00 00   <Snd>>>
```

The terminating voice gateway initiates the T.38 fax relay switchover request with an NSE-200 (**Evt:200**) message when the V.21 fax flags are detected. Because the debug in Example 12-33 shows the NSE-200 messages being received (**<<<Rcv>**), you know that the gateway in this example is the originating gateway. You can also see that this originating gateway accepts the T.38 fax relay switchover request because it sends (**<Snd>>>**) NSE-201 (**Evt:201**) messages as its response. For more information about NSE-based T.38 switchover, see the section "NSE-Based Switchover for T.38" in Chapter 5.

TIP   T.38 fax relay on Cisco IOS voice gateways can also use a protocol-based switchover. When you are interoperating with third-party devices using T.38 fax relay, the protocol-based T.38 switchover should always be used. You can find more information about protocol-based T.38 switchovers for the voice signaling protocols of H.323, SIP, and MGCP in the next section, "Troubleshooting Protocol-Based Switchovers."

The only non-IOS gateway that supports T.38 fax relay is the VG248. Unfortunately, the NSE message detail on a per-packet basis that is provided on the IOS voice gateways is not seen on the VG248. Instead, the VG248 uses user-friendly phrases in its trace file to notify you of how the T.38 fax relay NSE-based switchover is progressing.

To view the NSE-based T.38 fax relay switchover on the VG248, the DSP trace function must be enabled in the event log. Example 12-34 highlights the important T.38 fax relay switchover messages from an event log DSP trace.

Example 12-34   *Originating VG248 DSP Event Log Trace for a T.38 Fax Relay Call*

```
437 17:41:22 3305  I POTS    24 Call 1 connected
438 17:41:23 1707  T DSP     24 Tx:557 Rx:546,Seq:3,Hdr:0,Late:0,Early:1
439 17:41:28 4989  T DSP     24 Tx:807 Rx:795,Seq:4,Hdr:0,Late:0,Early:1
440 17:41:33 4522  T DSP     24 Accepting NSE T.38 mode request
441 17:41:33    2  T DSP     24 rx:00CF,C800,0000,0064
442 17:41:33    1  T DSP     24 tx:0067,C900,0000
443 17:41:33    1  I DSP     24 Entering T.38 fax relay mode
```

Example 12-34 shows a DSP event log trace for a T.38 fax relay switchover when the VG248 is acting as the originating gateway. The debug message **Accepting NSE T.38 mode request** indicates that two NSE switchover transactions have occurred. The first transaction is that the VG248 has received an NSE-200 packet from the terminating gateway requesting a switchover to T.38 fax relay from voice mode. The second transaction is that this NSE switchover request to T.38 fax relay has been acknowledged with the transmission of an NSE-201 packet.

The message **Entering T.38 fax relay mode** confirms that the transition from a voice codec to T.38 fax relay is being completed. After this message has been displayed, the VG248 is expecting only T.38 packets in the media stream.

For a VG248 acting as the terminating gateway, the trace messages of **V.21 fax tones detected**, **Sending T.38 initiation NSE**, and **Received T.38 ACK NSE** will be observed. Example 12-35 highlights the important T.38 fax relay switchover messages for the VG248 when it is acting as the terminating gateway.

Example 12-35 *Terminating VG248 DSP Event Log Trace for a T.38 Fax Relay Call*

```
89 15:09:24   78  T DSP    24 V.21 fax tones detected
90 15:09:24    2  T DSP    24 Sending T.38 initiation NSE
91 15:09:24    2  T DSP    24 rx:00C1,0000,0001,0000
92 15:09:24    1  T DSP    24 tx:0067,C800,0000
93 15:09:24   27  T DSP    24 Received T.38 ACK NSE
94 15:09:24    2  I DSP    24 Entering T.38 fax relay mode
```

In Example 12-35, the message **V.21 fax tones detected** notifies you that fax preamble flags have been detected by the VG248. An NSE-200 is then sent to the originating voice gateway requesting a switchover to T.38 fax relay, as shown by the message **Sending T.38 initiation NSE**. When an NSE-201 acknowledgment to the T.38 fax relay switchover request is received, the message **Received T.38 ACK NSE** displays. After the NSE messages have been successfully exchanged for the T.38 fax relay switchover, the VG248 enters T.38 fax relay mode and displays the message **Entering T.38 fax relay mode**.

Validating NSE Switchover Support

If the output from the command **debug voip rtp session named-event** shows no NSE switchover messages or messages in only one direction, the most common reason for this problem is that the NSE switchover ability was not confirmed first within the voice signaling protocol. Although the voice signaling or call control protocol does not handle the actual switchover, in some cases it does confirm ahead of time that each voice gateway supports an NSE-based switchover. By the gateways validating NSE support for each other at the beginning of the call, the chances for a successful NSE-based switchover later in the call is greatly increased. When this NSE switchover capability within the call control protocol is not exchanged between the gateways, NSE messages may not be sent.

The two methods used for viewing the NSE switchover capability information within the call control protocol during the initial call setup are packet captures and debugs of the messages within the call protocol itself. Naturally, depending on the call control protocol being used, the NSE switchover capability information is displayed somewhat differently.

For NSE-based T.38 fax relay and the H.323 protocol, the NSE switchover capability information occurs within a nonstandard capability parameter in the H.245 terminal capability set (TCS) message. This parameter is encoded in an American Standard Code for Information Interchange (ASCII) format, and the NSE switchover confirmation information for T.38 fax relay can be seen if the ASCII values are decoded. Of course, a protocol analyzer such as Wireshark makes this decoding a bit easier, as shown in Figure 12-13.

Figure 12-13 *NSE Switchover Capability Parameter for an H.323 T.38 Fax Relay Call*

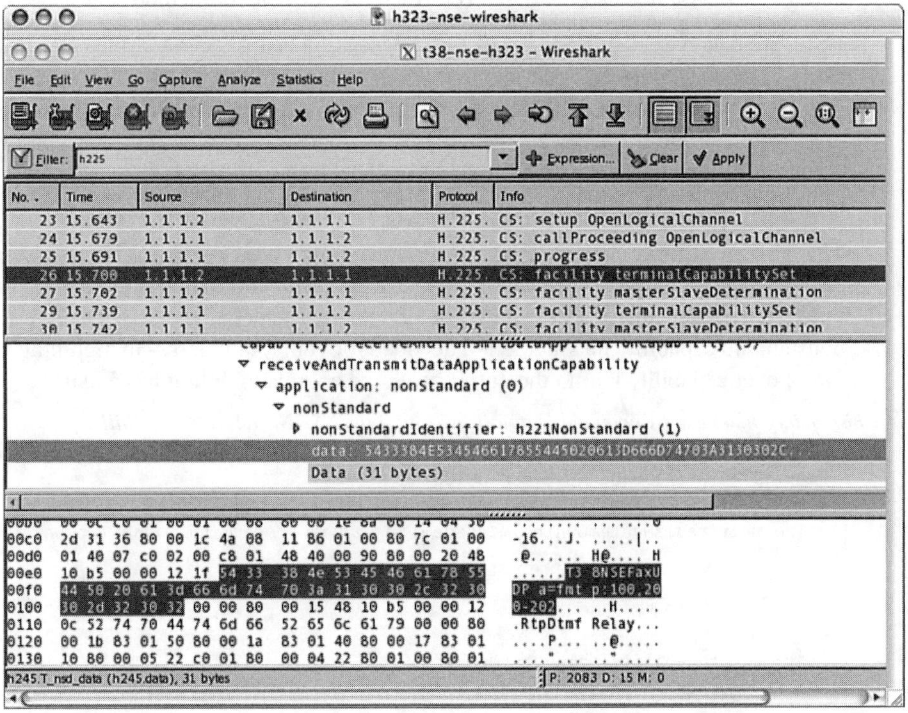

In Figure 12-13, you can see the highlighted data from the nonstandard capability message in the bottom third of the figure. Within this section, the raw hexadecimal data for the entire TCS message is displayed on the left side. On the right is an ASCII decode of that same raw data. In the case of Figure 12-13, the shaded portion of the raw data and its respective ASCII decode identifies the TCS nonstandard capability for NSE-based T.38 fax relay switchover support.

The ASCII decode of the NSE switchover capability in Figure 12-13 is shown as **T38NSEFaxUDP a=fmtp:100,200-202**. This information notifies the gateway that receives it that the sender of this TCS message can handle T.38 fax relay using NSE switchover messages with payload types of 100 and event IDs of 200-202.

If this message is not seen by the terminating gateway during the call setup, when fax tones are detected by the terminating gateway, it will not send NSE messages requesting a switchover to T.38 fax relay even if the terminating gateway has NSE-based T.38 configured. NSE-based T.38 switchovers do not occur for H.323 unless the capability of the gateways to handle such a switchover is validated by the method illustrated in Figure 12-13. Therefore, when troubleshooting NSE switchover problems for T.38 fax relay where NSE messages are not being sent by a voice gateway, you should always check that the voice gateways are confirming their support of the NSE switchover method first.

Be aware that even if an NSE-based T.38 negotiation is unsuccessful, the call is not necessarily going to be unsuccessful. As mentioned previously in the section "Fallback" in Chapter 7, in the event that an NSE-based switchover fails and does not occur, the terminating voice gateway automatically attempts a T.38 switchover using the call control protocol. In cases where the voice gateways and additional devices such as Unified CM support a T.38 protocol-based T.38 switchover, the call should succeed.

The NSE switchover capability information for T.38 within the H.323 TCS message can also be checked on IOS voice gateways using the command **debug h245 asn1**. However, unlike the packet capture trace in Figure 12-13, the hexadecimal ASCII data within the nonstandard capability message is not decoded for you. Example 12-36 highlights the NSE switchover capability within the output from the command **debug h245 asn1**.

Example 12-36 *debug h245 asn1 Command Output Illustrating the NSE Switchover Capability*

```
*Apr 19 02:01:23.840: H245 MSC OUTGOING PDU ::=

value MultimediaSystemControlMessage ::= request : terminalCapabilitySet :

<snip>

{
          capabilityTableEntryNumber 33
          capability receiveAndTransmitDataApplicationCapability :
          {
            application nonStandard :
            {
              nonStandardIdentifier h221NonStandard :
              {
                t35CountryCode 181
                t35Extension 0
                manufacturerCode 18
              }
              data '5433384E534546617855445020613D666D74703A...'H
            }
            maxBitRate 0
          }
        },
<snip>
```

In Example 12-36, the nonstandard capability within an H.323 TCS (**terminalCapabilitySet**) message for a T.38 NSE switchover is shown as highlighted by the line beginning with **data**. Decoding this ASCII **data** will provide you with the same information as displayed in the Wireshark trace in Figure 12-13.

TIP   Modem and fax passthrough also use an NSE-based switchover. However, with the H.323 protocol, the NSE capability for this switchover method is not communicated within the H.323 call control protocol. Instead, if modem passthrough is configured on H.323 voice gateways, passthrough NSE messages will always be sent and received when appropriate.

Similar NSE switchover capability notifications are also found within the Session Description Protocol (SDP) portion of certain SIP and MGCP messages. Just like H.323, an NSE switchover will not be initiated between SIP voice gateways for NSE-based T.38 fax relay unless the NSE switchover support has been declared earlier in the call. Example 12-37 details the NSE switchover capability for a SIP INVITE message in the output of the command **debug ccsip messages**.

Example 12-37   *debug ccsip messages Command Output Showing the NSE Switchover Capability*

```
*Apr 19 21:30:33.527: //-1/xxxxxxxxxxxx/SIP/Msg/ccsipDisplayMsg:
Sent:
INVITE sip:100@172.18.122.68:5060 SIP/2.0
Via: SIP/2.0/UDP 172.18.122.75:5060;branch=z9hG4bK19189B
From: <sip:172.18.122.75>;tag=AA696C4-1BCC
To: <sip:100@172.18.122.68>
Date: Sat, 19 Apr 2008 21:30:33 GMT
Call-ID: AD5125E9-D8E11DD-810DBA37-9A1C26F7@172.18.122.75
Supported: 100rel,timer,resource-priority,replaces
Min-SE:  1800
Cisco-Guid: 2886416544-227414493-2164832823-2585536247
User-Agent: Cisco-SIPGateway/IOS-12.x
Allow: INVITE, OPTIONS, BYE, CANCEL, ACK, PRACK, UPDATE, REFER, SUBSCRIBE, NOTIFY,
INFO, REGISTER
CSeq: 101 INVITE
Max-Forwards: 70
Timestamp: 1208640633
Contact: <sip:172.18.122.75:5060>
Expires: 180
Allow-Events: telephone-event
Content-Type: application/sdp
Content-Disposition: session;handling=required
Content-Length: 393

v=0
o=CiscoSystemsSIP-GW-UserAgent 9103 1012 IN IP4 172.18.122.75
s=SIP Call
c=IN IP4 172.18.122.75
t=0 0
m=audio 16982 RTP/AVP 0 100
c=IN IP4 172.18.122.75
```

continues

Example 12-37 *debug ccsip messages Command Output Showing the NSE Switchover Capability (Continued)*

```
a=rtpmap:0 PCMU/8000
a=rtpmap:100 X-NSE/8000
a=fmtp:100 192-194,200-202
a=ptime:20
a=X-sqn:0
a=X-cap: 1 audio RTP/AVP 100
a=X-cpar: a=rtpmap:100 X-NSE/8000
a=X-cpar: a=fmtp:100 192-194,200-202
a=X-cap: 2 image udptl t38
```

In Example 12-37, you see an **INVITE** message being sent out (as shown by **Sent**) by the IOS voice gateway to set up a call. Along with the standard message and codec parameters in the SDP portion of the message, optional attribute parameters are also seen relating to NSE capabilities. The line **a=X-cpar: a=rtpmap:100 X-NSE/8000** details the X-NSE attribute for using RTP payload type 100. The next attribute line, **a=X-cpar: a=fmtp:100 192-194,200-202**, indicates the NSE event IDs that are supported by the gateway. In this case, you see that modem passthrough (**192-194**) and NSE-based T.38 fax relay (**200-202**) are listed.

TIP   Unlike H.323, SIP voice gateways confirm modem passthrough support with the peer gateway before sending or responding to passthrough NSE messages. Not seeing modem passthrough support validated through SDP attribute parameters is the main cause of SIP voice gateways not generating or responding to NSE passthrough messages. In scenarios where SIP IOS voice gateways are communicating directly with one another, this passthrough NSE confirmation procedure is rarely a problem. However, in those scenarios where Unified CM or some other proxy device strip out the NSE passthrough capabilities attribute from the SIP messages, modem passthrough will more than likely fail.

The syntax for the NSE switchover capability within the SDP of the MGCP call control protocol varies slightly from that of SIP. Example 12-38 shows how the NSE switchover capability appears in output from the command **debug mgcp packets**.

Example 12-38 *debug mgcp packets Command Output Detailing the NSE Switchover Capability*

```
Sep 13 15:29:16.436: MGCP Packet sent to 14.80.32.199:2427--->
200 173 OK
I: C

v=0
c=IN IP4 14.80.32.200
m=audio 18576 RTP/AVP 99
```

Example 12-38 *debug mgcp packets Command Output Detailing the NSE Switchover Capability (Continued)*

```
a=rtpmap:99 G.729b/8000
a=X-sqn:0
a=X-cap: 1 audio RTP/AVP 100
a=X-cpar: a=rtpmap:100 X-NSE/8000
a=X-cpar: a=fmtp:100 192-194,200-202
a=X-cap: 2 image udptl t38
<---
```

In Example 12-38, you again see the declaration of the **X-NSE** parameter in one line, followed by **a=fmtp:100 192-194,200-202** in the subsequent line. This optional information informs the gateway that the sender supports NSE-based switchovers for events 192-194, which is passthrough, and events 200-202, which are the event IDs for T.38 fax relay.

The MGCP protocol tends to send NSE switchover messages quite freely, regardless of whether NSE capabilities support has been confirmed for the peer endpoint. In the cases of both modem passthrough and NSE-based T.38, MGCP voice gateways just about always send and respond to NSE switchover messages when configured. Therefore, validating NSE switchover support on MGCP voice gateways is not as critical as for H.323 and SIP gateways. Subsequently, NSE switchover problems with MGCP are typically configuration errors where modem passthrough or NSE-based T.38 are not configured correctly on the MGCP voice gateway or the MGCP process has not been restarted after a configuration change.

TIP   Cisco modem relay also uses an NSE-based switchover, but confirmation within the call control protocol is not required for sending and responding to Cisco modem relay NSE messages. Therefore, if Cisco modem relay NSE messages are not being sent by a voice gateway, this is typically a configuration problem. See the section "Modem Relay" in Chapter 10.

In some situations, especially those involving gateways using different call control protocols while connected through Unified CM, the T.38 NSE switchover capability does not get passed between the gateway endpoints. This can lead to the T.38 NSE switchover not occurring, because each gateway believes that the other lacks support for the NSE switchover mechanism. Figure 12-14 illustrates a scenario where the T.38 NSE switchover capability does not get passed between the gateways.

Figure 12-14 *NSE Switchover Capability Exchange Failure Scenario*

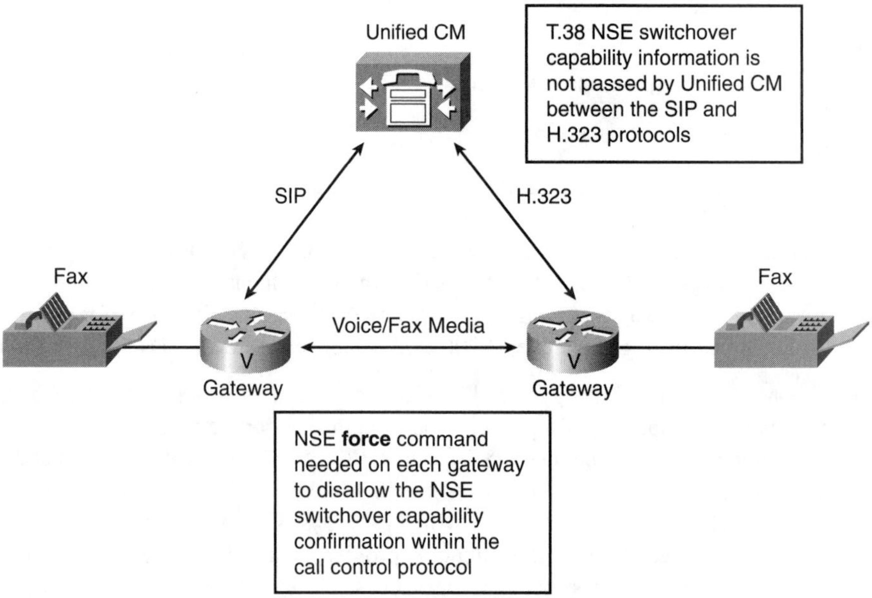

In Figure 12-14, an H.323 and SIP voice gateway are connected to Unified CM. If an NSE-based T.38 fax relay call is attempted in this scenario, the T.38 NSE switchover will never occur because Unified CM does not pass the T.38 NSE switchover capability information from one protocol to the other. So, both gateways end up believing that the other does not support NSE-based T.38. Fortunately, as discussed earlier in this section, the gateways will automatically attempt a protocol-based T.38 switchover in the event that the NSE-based T.38 switchover capability is not successfully negotiated. However, in Unified CM environments, a protocol-based T.38 switchover is contingent on Unified CM also supporting T.38 in the call control protocol, which can vary between Unified CM software versions. In addition, a call control protocol such as SCCP does not support protocol-based T.38 fax relay, so a fallback to this option when the NSE-based T.38 capability fails to negotiate is not possible.

The fix for this type of scenario portrayed in Figure 12-14 is the **force** keyword. For example, the command **fax protocol t38 nse** tells the gateway to confirm the other gateway's NSE switchover capability before executing an NSE switchover. On the other hand, the command **fax protocol t38 nse force** instructs the gateway to execute an NSE switchover upon detection of the necessary stimuli tone regardless of whether NSE support has been verified. For more information about configuring this **force** option for T.38 fax relay with the H.323, SIP, and SCCP protocols, see Table 10-6 in Chapter 10. For assistance with the MGCP protocol, see Table 10-9.

TIP   As a best practice, it is recommended to always enable the **force** option when you need NSE-based T.38 fax relay to work between gateways using different call control protocols in Unified CM environments.

Unfortunately, NSE-based passthrough does not have an equivalent **force** option like NSE-based T.38 fax relay. This can pose problems for scenarios such as Figure 12-14, especially for the SIP call control protocol. Unlike H.323 and MGCP, the SIP protocol on IOS voice gateways tends to be strict about needing to have the passthrough NSE switchover capability validated during the initial SIP call setup messages.

TIP   Devices such as media termination points (MTP), transcoders, and firewalls can also prevent NSE switchover messages from being exchanged. If you see NSE messages leaving one gateway but never making it to the other, this is something to consider. For NSE-based switchovers to be successful, the media streams should originate and terminate on the gateway endpoints themselves, and other devices should not be involved from a termination or filtering perspective.

Troubleshooting Protocol-Based Switchovers

Whereas NSE-based switchovers are Cisco proprietary, protocol-based switchovers make use of standards-based voice signaling protocols when a transition from voice to fax mode occurs. The main advantage of protocol-based switchovers is that Cisco voice gateways can interoperate with third-party devices for fax calls. Currently, a protocol-based switchover is not available for handling modem calls on Cisco voice gateways.

Troubleshooting protocol-based switchovers involves looking at the voice signaling protocol itself, because this is where the switchover is occurring. A familiarity with voice signaling protocols such as H.323, SIP, and MGCP is recommended when having to troubleshoot switchovers that occur within them.

TIP   The SCCP voice signaling protocol does not currently support any switchovers within the SCCP protocol itself and, therefore, is not discussed in this section. Only NSE-based switchovers are supported for SCCP.

Protocol-Based Fax Pass-Through and T.38 Switchovers for H.323

The H.323 voice signaling protocol can handle both fax pass-through and T.38 fax relay within its protocol stack. Both of these fax transport methods are triggered by the detection of V.21 fax flags on the terminating gateway, and both use the H.245 Request Mode message for initializing the switchover.

The H.245 Request Mode message specifies the new media stream parameters for the fax call. This in turn leads to the opening of logical channels for the new fax media stream and the closing of the logical channels that was handling the initial voice call. For taking a quick glance at the Request Mode and the opening and closing of the logical channels for both fax pass-through and T.38 fax relay, use the command **debug h245 events**. Example 12-39 shows the output of the **debug h245 events** command for a fax pass-through call.

Example 12-39 *debug h245 events Command Output for a Fax Pass-Through Call*

```
Jan 10 16:46:34.258: h323chan_chn_process_read_socket: fd=2 of type CONNECTED has
   data

Jan 10 16:46:34.262: h245_decode_remote_message: received Request PDU
Jan 10 16:46:34.262: h245_decode_remote_request: received Request Mode message
Jan 10 16:46:34.262: h245_encode_requestModeAck_response
Jan 10 16:46:34.262: h245_encode_closeLogicalChannel_request
Jan 10 16:46:34.262: h245_encode_openLogicalChannel_request
Jan 10 16:46:34.266: h323chan_chn_process_read_socket: fd=2 of type CONNECTED has
   data

Jan 10 16:46:34.266: h245_decode_remote_message: received Request PDU
Jan 10 16:46:34.266: h245_decode_remote_request: received Close Logical Channel
   message
Jan 10 16:46:34.266: h245_encode_closeLogicalChannelAck_response
Jan 10 16:46:34.270: h323chan_chn_process_read_socket: fd=2 of type CONNECTED has
   data

Jan 10 16:46:34.270: h245_decode_remote_message: received Request PDU
Jan 10 16:46:34.270: h245_decode_remote_request: received Open Logical Channel
   message
Jan 10 16:46:34.270: h245_encode_openLogicalChannelAck_response
Jan 10 16:46:34.274: h323chan_chn_process_read_socket: fd=2 of type CONNECTED has
   data

Jan 10 16:46:34.274: h245_decode_remote_message: received Response PDU
Jan 10 16:46:34.274: h245_decode_remote_response: received Close Logical Channel
   Ack message
Jan 10 16:46:34.274: h323chan_chn_process_read_socket: fd=2 of type CONNECTED has
   data

Jan 10 16:46:34.274: h245_decode_remote_message: received Response PDU
Jan 10 16:46:34.274: h245_decode_remote_response: received Open Logical Channel Ack
   message
Jan 10 16:46:35.814: h323chan_chn_process_read_socket: fd=2 of type CONNECTED has
   data
```

Example 12-39 shows an H.323 fax pass-through switchover, but an H.323 T.38 fax relay call looks exactly the same. The command **debug h245 events** is equally effective in analyzing an H.323 T.38 fax relay switchover because a Request Mode message is also used to create the new media streams. In fact, it is impossible to determine from the debug output alone if the call in Example 12-39 is a fax pass-through or a T.38 fax relay call.

Examining Example 12-39 in more detail, you can clearly see the incoming Request Mode message notated by **received Request Mode message**. Then, you can see the **closeLogicalChannel** and **openLogicalChannel** messages being sent from the voice gateway along with the messages of **closeLogicalChannelAck** and **openLogicalChannelAck**. Received from the other gateway are equivalent **Close Logical Channel** and **Open Logical Channel** messages and acknowledgment messages of **Close Logical Channel Ack** and **Open Logical Channel Ack**. These messages should line up with the same messages outlined in Figure 4-9 in the section "Fax Pass-Through with H.323 Signaling" in Chapter 4 and also Figure 5-11 in the section "Protocol-Based Switchover for T.38" in Chapter 5.

For a detailed look at the H.245 Request Modem message that is responsible for initiating the fax pass-through switchover in H.323, use the command **debug h245 asn1**. This debug gives the full asn1 decode of all H.245 messages, but the Request Mode and its acknowledgment are the ones that you are interested in from a fax pass-through and T.38 fax relay switchover perspective. Example 12-40 highlights the H.245 Request Mode message and the ACK as it appears in the output of **debug h245 asn1** for a fax pass-through call.

Example 12-40 *debug h245 asn1 Command Output for a Fax Pass-Through Call Showing Request Mode and Acknowledgment*

```
Jan 10 16:57:17.286: H245 MSC INCOMING PDU ::=

value MultimediaSystemControlMessage ::= request : requestMode :
    {
       sequenceNumber 1
       requestedModes
       {

        {

          {
            type audioMode : g711Ulaw64k : NULL
          }
        }
      }
    }
value MultimediaSystemControlMessage ::= response : requestModeAck :
    {
       sequenceNumber 1
       response willTransmitMostPreferredMode : NULL
    }
```

Example 12-40 shows a detailed view of both the H.245 Request Mode (**requestMode**) and the Request Mode ACK (**requestModeAck**) messages. The important parameter contained in this Request Mode message is the **audioMode** change to the G.711 μ-law codec, which is displayed as **g711Ulaw64k**.

The H.245 Request Mode message found in a T.38 fax relay switchover is markedly different from the one seen in Example 12-40 for fax pass-through. A number of T.38 protocol parameters are contained in the H.245 Request Mode message. These parameters are shown in the output of **debug h245 asn1** in Example 12-41.

Example 12-41 *debug h245 asn1 Command Output for a T.38 Fax Relay Call Detailing a Request Mode and Acknowledgment*

```
Jan 10 17:23:37.638: H245 MSC INCOMING PDU ::=

value MultimediaSystemControlMessage ::= request : requestMode :
    {
      sequenceNumber 1
      requestedModes
      {

        {

          {
            type dataMode :
            {
              application t38fax :
              {
                t38FaxProtocol udp : NULL
                t38FaxProfile
                {
                  fillBitRemoval FALSE
                  transcodingJBIG FALSE
                  transcodingMMR FALSE
                  version 0
                  t38FaxRateManagement transferredTCF : NULL
                  t38FaxUdpOptions
                  {
                    t38FaxMaxBuffer 200
                    t38FaxMaxDatagram 72
                    t38FaxUdpEC t38UDPRedundancy : NULL
                  }
                }
              }
              bitRate 144
            }
          }
        }
      }
    }
```

Example 12-41   *debug h245 asn1 Command Output for a T.38 Fax Relay Call Detailing a Request Mode and Acknowledgment (Continued)*

```
Jan 10 17:23:37.642: H245 MSC OUTGOING PDU ::=

value MultimediaSystemControlMessage ::= response : requestModeAck :
    {
      sequenceNumber 1
      response willTransmitMostPreferredMode : NULL
    }
```

The H.245 Request Mode and Request Mode ACK messages are shown, respectively, as **requestMode** and **requestModeAck** in Example 12-41. Whereas the **requestModeAck** looks practically identical to what was observed with a fax pass-through call, the **request-Mode** message contains an array of T.38 fax relay parameters. These parameters as displayed in Example 12-41 are the default for Cisco voice gateways and are defined in Table 12-9. The equivalent SIP T.38 parameter names are also included in this table because they are functionally the same and are referenced in the next section.

Table 12-9   *T.38 Fax Relay Parameters Found in H.245 Request Mode Messages and SIP SDP*

H.323/SIP Parameter	Description
t38FaxProtocol	Specifies the T.38 encapsulation of TCP, UDP, or even RTP in later versions of the T.38 standard. Cisco voice gateways support only UDP.
fillBitRemoval (H.323) **T38FaxFillBitRemoval** (SIP)	Indicates the capability to remove and insert fill bits in Phase C, non-ECM data to reduce bandwidth in the packet network.
transcodingJBIG (H.323) **T38FaxTranscodingJBIG** (SIP)	Indicates the ability to convert to/from Joint Bi-level Image Expert Group (JBIG) encoding to reduce bandwidth.
transcodingMMR (H.323) **T38FaxTranscodingMMR** (SIP)	Indicates the ability to convert to/from Modified Modified Read (MMR) from/to the current line format for increasing the compression of the data and reducing the bandwidth in the packet network.
version (H.323) **T38FaxVersion** (SIP)	Details the version number of Recommendation T.38. New versions should be compatible with previous versions. Cisco voice gateways support only version 0.
t38FaxRateManagement (H.323) **T38FaxRateManagement** (SIP)	Specifies the data rate management method. Method 1 implements local generation of the Training Check Frame (TCF) and is required for use with TCP. Method 2 is transfer of TCF and is required for use with UDP (UDPTL or RTP). Method 2 is not recommended for use with TCP. Cisco gateways support only method 2 (**transferredTCF**).

continues

Table 12-9 *T.38 Fax Relay Parameters Found in H.245 Request Mode Messages and SIP SDP (Continued)*

H.323/SIP Parameter	Description
t38FaxMaxBuffer (H.323) **T38FaxMaxBuffer** (SIP)	Indicates the maximum number of octets that can be stored before an overflow condition occurs for UDP encapsulation.
t38FaxMaxDatagram (H.323) **T38FaxMaxDatagram** (SIP)	Details the maximum size of a UDPTL packet that can be accepted.
t38FaxUdpEC (H.323) **T38FaxUdpEC** (SIP)	Specifies the type of error correction. Cisco gateways do not support forward error correction (FEC) and use only redundancy (**t38UDPRedundancy**).
bitRate (H.323) **T38MaxBitRate** (SIP)	Specifies the maximum page-transmission speed supported by the gateway.

Occasionally, the H.323 terminating voice gateway will not send the H.245 Request Mode message when it detects the fax V.21 flags. The most common cause of this issue is that the T.38 capability was not declared in the H.245 TCS message received from the originating voice gateway. You should confirm that the T.38 capability is declared in the TCS, as shown in Example 12-42, using the command **debug h245 asn1**.

Example 12-42 *debug h245 asn1 Command Output Illustrating T.38 Fax Relay Capability*

```
<snip>
{
        capabilityTableEntryNumber 29
        capability receiveAndTransmitDataApplicationCapability :
        {
          application t38fax :
          {
            t38FaxProtocol udp : NULL
            t38FaxProfile
            {
              fillBitRemoval FALSE
              transcodingJBIG FALSE
              transcodingMMR FALSE
              version 0
              t38FaxRateManagement transferredTCF : NULL
              t38FaxUdpOptions
              {
                t38FaxMaxBuffer 200
                t38FaxMaxDatagram 72
                t38FaxUdpEC t38UDPRedundancy : NULL
              }
            }
          }
        }
```

Example 12-42   *debug h245 asn1 Command Output Illustrating T.38 Fax Relay Capability (Continued)*

```
            maxBitRate 144
        }
      },
<snip>
```

In Example 12-42, the **application t38fax** capability is highlighted from a TCS message sent from the originating voice gateway. Included in this capability are additional T.38 parameters that were just defined previously in Table 12-9. When protocol-based T.38 switchovers are not working, always check for the **application t38fax** capability in the originating device's TCS. Otherwise, the H.245 Request Mode message later in the call may not be sent when the fax flags are detected by the terminating voice gateway.

Protocol-Based Fax Pass-Through and T.38 Switchovers for SIP

Like H.323, the SIP voice signaling protocol can also support both fax pass-through and T.38 fax relay switchovers. The SIP equivalent to the H.245 Request Mode message is known as a re-INVITE. The SIP re-INVITE message is responsible for transitioning the voice call to either fax pass-through or T.38 fax relay.

Within the SIP re-INVITE message are SDP parameters that define the new media stream for the fax call. These SDP parameters and the re-INVITE message itself are best viewed with the command **debug ccsip messages**. All SIP messages are displayed with this command, but it is important to find the re-INVITE when you want to confirm that a proper switchover has occurred. Example 12-43 shows a re-INVITE message pulled from a **debug ccsip messages** trace for a fax pass-through call.

Example 12-43   *debug ccsip messages Command Output Showing a Fax Pass-Through SIP Re-INVITE Message*

```
Apr  2 20:23:15.039: //-1/xxxxxxxxxxxx/SIP/Msg/ccsipDisplayMsg:
Sent:
INVITE sip:100@1.1.1.1:5060 SIP/2.0
Via: SIP/2.0/UDP 1.1.1.2:5060;branch=z9hG4bK2D30
From: <sip:200@1.1.1.2>;tag=108A9C-124F
To: <sip:100@1.1.1.1>;tag=10B180-57B
Date: Mon, 02 Apr 2007 20:23:15 GMT
Call-ID: 780921AE-E05111DB-8017B658-496D56BF@1.1.1.1
Supported: 100rel,timer,resource-priority,replaces
Min-SE:  1800
Cisco-Guid: 1971344507-3763409371-2148709976-1231902399
User-Agent: Cisco-SIPGateway/IOS-12.x
Allow: INVITE, OPTIONS, BYE, CANCEL, ACK, PRACK, UPDATE, REFER, SUBSCRIBE, NOTIFY,
INFO, REGISTER
```

continues

Example 12-43 *debug ccsip messages Command Output Showing a Fax Pass-Through SIP Re-INVITE Message (Continued)*

```
CSeq: 101 INVITE
Max-Forwards: 70
Timestamp: 1175545395
Contact: <sip:200@1.1.1.2:5060>
Expires: 180
Allow-Events: telephone-event
Content-Type: application/sdp
Content-Length: 173

v=0
o=CiscoSystemsSIP-GW-UserAgent 1413 1958 IN IP4 1.1.1.2
s=SIP Call
c=IN IP4 1.1.1.2
t=0 0
m=audio 18282 RTP/AVP 0
a=rtpmap:0 PCMU/8000
a=silenceSupp:off - - - -
```

Example 12-43 shows a SIP re-INVITE message being sent (as indicated by **Sent**) by the IOS voice gateway. This SIP re-INVITE is actually just another **INVITE** message that occurs later in the SIP call after the voice call has been fully set up. The SDP parameter **audio 18282 RTP/AVP 0** defines the UDP port number of **18282** that this gateway will use for the new media stream and an **RTP** payload type of **0**, which represents the G.711 μ-law codec. In addition, silence suppression or VAD (Voice Activity Detection) is disabled for this fax pass-through call as evidenced by the SDP parameter **silenceSupp:off**.

The re-INVITE message in Example 12-43 initiates the fax pass-through switchover, but the switchover is not complete until the other side accepts the SDP parameters within this re-INVITE with a SIP 200 OK message. Example 12-44 shows the SIP 200 OK response to the SIP re-INVITE message. This completes the SIP fax pass-through switchover.

The SIP **200 OK** message received (as indicated by **Received**) by the voice gateway in Example 12-44 accepts the fax pass-through re-INVITE switchover message shown in Example 12-43. The SDP parameters are the same with the exception of the connection information, which now reflects the IP address and UDP port number for the other gateway. In the **audio 18826 RTP/AVP 0** parameter line, the **RTP** payload type of **0** is confirmed, but the local UDP port number of **18826** for the other voice gateway is now displayed. The parameter **silenceSupp:off** is also confirmed in the SIP 200 OK message. For more information about SIP fax pass-through and its switchover, see the section "Fax Pass-Through with SIP Signaling" in Chapter 4.

Example 12-44   *debug ccsip messages Command Output Detailing a Fax Pass-Through SIP 200 OK Message*

```
Apr  2 20:23:15.051: //-1/xxxxxxxxxxxx/SIP/Msg/ccsipDisplayMsg:
Received:
SIP/2.0 200 OK
Via: SIP/2.0/UDP 1.1.1.2:5060;branch=z9hG4bK2D30
From: <sip:200@1.1.1.2>;tag=108A9C-124F
To: <sip:100@1.1.1.1>;tag=10B180-57B
Date: Mon, 02 Apr 2007 13:04:25 GMT
Call-ID: 780921AE-E05111DB-8017B658-496D56BF@1.1.1.1
Server: Cisco-SIPGateway/IOS-12.x
CSeq: 101 INVITE
Allow: INVITE, OPTIONS, BYE, CANCEL, ACK, PRACK, UPDATE, REFER, SUBSCRIBE, NOTIFY,
INFO, REGISTER
Allow-Events: telephone-event
Remote-Party-ID: <sip:100@1.1.1.1>;party=called;screen=no;privacy=off
Contact: <sip:100@1.1.1.1:5060>
Content-Type: application/sdp
Content-Length: 191

v=0
o=CiscoSystemsSIP-GW-UserAgent 9297 3656 IN IP4 1.1.1.1
s=SIP Call
c=IN IP4 1.1.1.1
t=0 0
m=audio 18826 RTP/AVP 0
c=IN IP4 1.1.1.1
a=rtpmap:0 PCMU/8000
a=silenceSupp:off - - - -
```

The SIP re-INVITE message for a T.38 fax relay call is similar to the re-INVITE message for fax pass-through. The difference is that the SDP parameters for the new media stream are T.38 specific rather than pass-through specific. Example 12-45 highlights a T.38 SIP re-INVITE message pulled from the output of **debug ccsip messages**.

Example 12-45   *debug ccsip messages Command Output Showing a T.38 Fax Relay SIP re-INVITE Message*

```
*Jan 10 20:27:27.439: //-1/xxxxxxxxxxxx/SIP/Msg/ccsipDisplayMsg:
Received:
INVITE sip:100@1.1.1.1:5060 SIP/2.0
Via: SIP/2.0/UDP 1.1.1.2:5060;branch=z9hG4bK82125
From: <sip:200@1.1.1.2>;tag=AFA28-21D8
To: <sip:100@1.1.1.1>;tag=AF87C-1E64
Date: Thu, 11 Jan 2007 03:42:02 GMT
Call-ID: C5A778EE-A01F11DB-8013B108-BD0EB9AE@1.1.1.1
Supported: 100rel,timer,resource-priority,replaces
```

continues

Example 12-45   *debug ccsip messages Command Output Showing a T.38 Fax Relay SIP re-INVITE Message (Continued)*

```
Min-SE:  1800
Cisco-Guid: 3273647268-2686390747-2148446472-3171858862
User-Agent: Cisco-SIPGateway/IOS-12.x
Allow: INVITE, OPTIONS, BYE, CANCEL, ACK, PRACK, UPDATE, REFER, SUBSCRIBE, NOTIFY,
INFO, REGISTER
CSeq: 101 INVITE
Max-Forwards: 70
Timestamp: 1168486922
Contact: <sip:200@1.1.1.2:5060>
Expires: 180
Allow-Events: telephone-event
Content-Type: application/sdp
Content-Length: 379

v=0
o=CiscoSystemsSIP-GW-UserAgent 2596 550 IN IP4 1.1.1.2
s=SIP Call
c=IN IP4 1.1.1.2
t=0 0
m=image 18238 udptl t38
c=IN IP4 1.1.1.2
a=T38FaxVersion:0
a=T38MaxBitRate:7200
a=T38FaxFillBitRemoval:0
a=T38FaxTranscodingMMR:0
a=T38FaxTranscodingJBIG:0
a=T38FaxRateManagement:transferredTCF
a=T38FaxMaxBuffer:200
a=T38FaxMaxDatagram:72
a=T38FaxUdpEC:t38UDPRedundancy
```

The T.38 parameters contained in the SDP portion of the SIP **INVITE** or re-INVITE in Example 12-45 are similar to the T.38 parameters found in the H.245 Request Mode message used with the H.323 voice signaling protocol. In fact, the highlighted SIP T.38 parameters in Example 12-45 are defined in Table 12-9 alongside the T.38 parameters used in H.323.

Because the re-INVITE message in Example 12-45 was received by the gateway (as shown by **Received**), you can determine that this is the originating gateway. If the SIP T.38 parameters are then agreeable with this gateway, a SIP 200 OK message will be returned to the terminating gateway, completing the T.38 fax relay switchover. For more details on the protocol-based T.38 switchover for SIP, see the section "Protocol-Based Switchover for T.38" in Chapter 5.

Protocol-Based T.38 Switchover for MGCP

The MGCP voice signaling protocol supports T.38 fax relay, but unlike H.323 and SIP does not support fax pass-through on Cisco voice gateways. Therefore, only the protocol-based T.38 fax relay switchover can be troubleshot for MGCP.

The FXR package on Cisco voice gateways is the MGCP package necessary for T.38 fax relay support. This package name is sent to the CA (call agent) in the response to the MGCP AUEP (Audit Endpoint) message. If the FXR package is not sent to the call agent in the AUEP response message, the T.38 switchover will not occur. You can view the AUEP transaction with the command **debug mgcp packets**. Example 12-46 displays the AUEP transaction captured using the **debug mgcp packets** command.

Example 12-46 *debug mgcp packets Command Output Showing an MGCP AUEP Message and Response*

```
*Jan 11 05:34:54.051: MGCP Packet received from 14.80.32.199:2427--->
AUEP 448 AALN/S0/SU0/0@fax_2851 MGCP 0.1
F: X, A, I
<---


*Jan 11 05:34:54.051: MGCP Packet sent to 14.80.32.199:2427--->
200 448
I:
X: 2
L: p:10-20, a:PCMU;PCMA;G.nX64, b:64, e:on, gc:1, s:on, t:10, r:g, nt:IN;ATM,
v:FXR;G;D;T;L;H;R;ATM;SST;PRE
L: p:10-220, a:G.729;G.729a;G.729b, b:8, e:on, gc:1, s:on, t:10, r:g, nt:IN;ATM,
v:FXR;G;D;T;L;H;R;ATM;SST;PRE
L: p:10-110, a:G.726-16;G.728, b:16, e:on, gc:1, s:on, t:10, r:g, nt:IN;ATM,
v:FXR;G;D;T;L;H;R;ATM;SST;PRE
L: p:10-70, a:G.726-24, b:24, e:on, gc:1, s:on, t:10, r:g, nt:IN;ATM,
v:FXR;G;D;T;L;H;R;ATM;SST;PRE
L: p:10-50, a:G.726-32, b:32, e:on, gc:1, s:on, t:10, r:g, nt:IN;ATM,
v:FXR;G;D;T;L;H;R;ATM;SST;PRE
L: p:30-270, a:G.723.1-H;G.723;G.723.1a-H, b:6, e:on, gc:1, s:on, t:10, r:g,
nt:IN;ATM, v:FXR;G;D;T;L;H;R;ATM;SST;PRE
L: p:30-330, a:G.723.1-L;G.723.1a-L, b:5, e:on, gc:1, s:on, t:10, r:g, nt:IN;ATM,
v:FXR;G;D;T;L;H;R;ATM;SST;PRE
L: p:20-120, a:G.GSM-F, b:13, e:on, gc:1, s:on, t:10, r:g, nt:IN;ATM,
v:FXR;G;D;T;L;H;R;ATM;SST;PRE
M: sendonly, recvonly, sendrecv, inactive, loopback, conttest, data, netwloop,
netwtest
<---
```

The first message in Example 12-46 shows the reception of an AUEP message from the CA as indicated by **MGCP Packet received**. The gateway's response (shown by **MGCP Packet sent**) notifies the call agent of the gateway's support of the FXR package. The CA is now aware that this MGCP endpoint supports a T.38 switchover within the MGCP protocol stack.

TIP   AUEP messages are typically seen when a gateway first registers with a CA or upon a restart. Confirming the presence of the FXR package in the AUEP response often involves restarting the MGCP process in IOS with the global configuration commands **no mgcp**, and then **mgcp**. If the **debug mgcp packets** command is running when this restart occurs, you should now see the AUEP message and its response containing the FXR package. If you do not see the FXR package in the AUEP response, see the section "IOS Gateway Fax Relay Configuration for MGCP" in Chapter 10 to make sure that the gateway is properly configured for MGCP CA-controlled T.38.

Further confirmation of the support of protocol-based T.38 with MGCP can be found in a CRCX (Create Connection) or MDCX (Modify Connection) message from the CA including the parameter **fxr/fx:t38** in the Local Connection Options (**L:**) line. This message occurs during the establishment of the voice call and informs the gateway that fax calls will be handled by protocol-based T.38. Example 12-47 shows an **MDCX** message being **received** with the **fxr/fx:t38** parameter and the gateway's response.

Example 12-47   *debug mgcp packets Command Output Illustrating an MGCP MDCX Message and Response*

```
*Jan 11 06:29:24.371: MGCP Packet received from 14.80.32.199:2427--->
MDCX 520 AALN/S0/SU0/0@fax_2851 MGCP 0.1
C: A000000001000076000000F5
I: 2
X: 4
L: p:20, a:G.729b, s:off, t:b8, fxr/fx:t38
M: recvonly
R: L/hu
Q: process,loop
<---

*Jan 11 06:29:24.375: MGCP Packet sent to 14.80.32.199:2427--->
200 520 OK

v=0
c=IN IP4 14.80.32.201
m=audio 17824 RTP/AVP 105
a=rtpmap:105 G.729b/8000
a=X-sqn:0
a=X-cap: 1 audio RTP/AVP 100
a=X-cpar: a=rtpmap:100 X-NSE/8000
a=X-cpar: a=fmtp:100 192-194,200-202
a=X-cap: 2 image udptl t38
<---
```

The gateway's **200 520 OK** response in Example 12-47 to the **MDCX** message with the **fxr/fx:t38** parameter is sent to the CA. This message includes the SDP line **a=X-cap: 2 image udptl t38**. This is an attribute line that serves as an acknowledgment by the gateway of support for T.38 using UDPTL as the encapsulation.

When the terminating MGCP endpoint or gateway in this case detects fax flags, it must notify the CA. The CA is then responsible for handling the T.38 fax relay switchover. Example 12-48 shows the MGCP **NTFY** (Notify) message that is **sent** from the gateway to the CA.

Example 12-48 *debug mgcp packets Command Output Detailing an MGCP NTFY Message*

```
*Jan 11 06:29:47.555: MGCP Packet sent to 14.80.32.199:2427--->
NTFY 271112584 aaln/S0/SU0/0@fax_2851 MGCP 0.1
N: ca@14.80.32.199:2427
X: 5
O: FXR/t38(start)
<---
```

The critical parameter in the **NTFY** message in Example 12-48 is **O: FXR/t38(start)**. The **O:** indicates an MGCP observed event, and **FXR/t38(start)** is the event itself. This event means that V.21 fax flags have been detected by the voice gateway. The terminating gateway/endpoint will send this sort of NTFY message only when it needs to signal to the CA that a G3 fax transmission is starting.

This **FXR/t38(start)** parameter in the NTFY message is the trigger that the call agent must see to start the change to a T.38 media stream. If this message is not sent or is not received by the CA, the T.38 switchover will not occur.

When the **NTFY** message in Example 12-48 is received by the CA, the CA sends MDCX messages to both the originating and terminating endpoints, changing the call to T.38. Example 12-49 highlights the **MDCX** message **received** from the CA at the originating endpoint that switches the call to T.38.

Example 12-49 *debug mgcp packets Command Output Showing an MGCP MDCX Switchover Message for T.38 Fax Relay*

```
*Jan 10 23:15:13.143: MGCP Packet received from 14.80.32.199:2427--->
MDCX 523 AALN/S0/SU0/1@fax_2811 MGCP 0.1
C: A000000001000075000000F5
I: 4
X: 18
L: a:image/t38
M: sendrecv
```

continues

Example 12-49 *debug mgcp packets Command Output Showing an MGCP MDCX Switchover Message for T.38 Fax Relay (Continued)*

```
R: L/hu, L/hf, D/[0-9ABCD*#], FXR/t38
S:
Q: process,loop

v=0
o=- 4 0 IN EPN AALN/S0/SU0/1@fax_2811
s=Cisco SDP 0
t=0 0
m=image 17824 udptl t38
c=IN IP4 14.80.32.201
a=X-sqn:0
a=X-cap:1 image udptl t38
<---

*Jan 10 23:15:13.151: MGCP Packet sent to 14.80.32.199:2427--->
200 523 OK

v=0
c=IN IP4 14.80.32.200
m=image 18330 udptl t38
a=X-sqn:0
a=X-cap: 1 audio RTP/AVP 100
a=X-cpar: a=rtpmap:100 X-NSE/8000
a=X-cpar: a=fmtp:100 192-194,200-202
a=X-cap: 2 image udptl t38
<---
```

The **MDCX** message in Example 12-49 shows the CA changing the call to T.38 fax relay using the SDP parameter **m=image 17824 udptl t38**. This media description parameter defines the media name and transport information for the new media session. In this case, the media parameter invokes **udptl t38** and notifies this originating gateway that the remote UDP port is **17824**.

The originating endpoint in Example 12-49 then confirms this switchover in the **200 523 OK** message that is **sent** back to the CA. Within this message, the same media parameter line, **m=image 18330 udptl t38**, is repeated with the exception of the port number. The port number **18330** represents the UDP port that this endpoint will use for the T.38 connection. This port information is then relayed by the CA to the terminating endpoint.

The T.38 fax relay communication ends upon the CA receiving a specific NTFY message from either endpoint. This **NTFY** message is shown in Example 12-50 and informs the CA that the fax transaction is no longer occurring.

Example 12-50 *debug mgcp packets Command Output Illustrating an MGCP NTFY Message Signifying the End of the Fax Call*

```
*Jan 11 06:30:20.735: MGCP Packet sent to 14.80.32.199:2427--->
NTFY 271112587 aaln/S0/SU0/0@fax_2851 MGCP 0.1
N: ca@14.80.32.199:2427
X: 7
O: FXR/t38(stop)
<---
```

In Example 12-50, the line **O: FXR/t38(stop)** within the **NTFY** message that is **sent** to the CA represents the end of the T.38 fax relay call. At this point, the call will need to be torn down because there is no provision at this time to return this call to voice mode as is possible with H.323 and SIP. Ideally, an **FXR/t38(stop)** observed event should be seen at the end of a successful T.38 fax transaction. If this message appears before the fax is completed, additional troubleshooting is necessary.

Troubleshooting a protocol-based T.38 switchover with MGCP is more involved than H.323 and SIP. However, methodically parsing through the output of **debug mgcp packets** for the messages mentioned in this section will confirm whether a proper switchover is occurring.

Protocol-Based Switchovers and Unified CM

As mentioned in the section "Unified CM Integrations" in Chapter 7, when Unified CM is involved in the call routing for a voice network, it plays an active role in protocol-based switchovers. Whereas NSE-based and PT-based switchovers occur without the knowledge of Unified CM, protocol-based switchovers depend on Unified CM to participate in relaying the switchover messages and transitioning the media stream from voice to fax. Because of Unified CM's direct involvement in protocol-based switchovers, Unified CM itself is an important component for troubleshooting and analyzing switchover signaling problems.

TIP   Unified CM does not support the protocol-based switchover of fax pass-through, where a compressed voice codec such as G.729 is changed to G.711. It supports only protocol-based switchovers that specify a media change from the current voice codec to the T.38 fax relay application.

Starting in Unified CM version 5.x and later, the Cisco Real Time Monitoring Tool (RTMT) is the tool used to retrieve traces from the Unified CM server. After the necessary traces have been enabled on the Cisco Unified Communications Manager Serviceability page, the event log viewer within Cisco RTMT displays the trace information. Refer to the document "Set Up Cisco CallManager Traces for Cisco Technical Support" (Document ID: 10124) at Cisco.com for assistance on enabling traces for all versions of Unified CM.

In many cases, troubleshooting protocol-based switchovers from Unified CM is critical because Unified CM is interconnecting gateways using different call control protocols. This means that Unified CM must successfully transfer switchover messages from one call control protocol to another and vice versa. Figure 12-15 shows a capture from the Cisco RTMT event log viewer where a T.38 fax relay switchover message is received via MGCP and translated to H.323.

Figure 12-15 *Cisco RTMT Screen Shot*

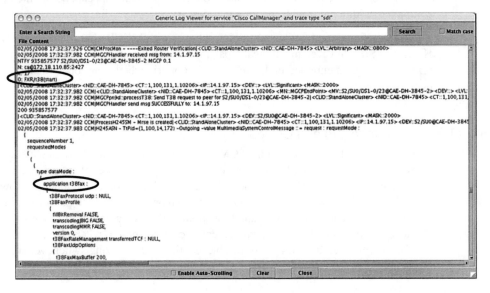

In Figure 12-15, an MGCP NTFY message containing the **FXR/t38(start)** parameter (circled) is received from a voice gateway. This message notifies Unified CM that fax flags have been detected and that the gateway is ready to transition to T.38 fax relay. Unified CM then communicates this information to an H.323 gateway using an H.245 Request Mode message that contains the parameter **application t38fax** (circled).

If you run into a situation where the terminating gateway sends the proper switchover message to Unified CM but this information is not passed to the originating gateway, viewing the Unified CM traces is the next logical step. Often, Unified CM is misconfigured and the call is not routed properly. Another common problem is that the Unified CM version does not support a protocol-based T.38 switchover for the configured call control protocol. Refer back to Table 7-13 to help you understand T.38 fax relay support in various Unified CM versions.

Troubleshooting the Cisco Fax Relay Switchover

Cisco fax relay uses a unique switchover method composed of RTP payload types. Like NSE-based switchovers, the Cisco fax relay switchover uses the existing RTP media stream and bypasses the voice signaling protocol. So, it does not matter whether the voice signaling protocol is H.323, SIP, MGCP, or SCCP when it comes to a Cisco fax relay switchover.

For IOS gateways, the debug command for viewing NSE switchovers is also the command to use for Cisco fax relay switchovers: **debug voip rtp session named-event**. Example 12-51 highlights a Cisco fax relay switchover using the command **debug voip rtp session named-event**.

Example 12-51 *debug voip rtp session named-event Command Output for a Cisco Fax Relay Call*

```
Jan 10 16:03:32.838:              s=VoIP d=DSP payload 0x60 ssrc 0x0 sequence 0x0
    timestamp 0x0
Jan 10 16:03:32.838:  <<<Rcv> Pt:96     Evt:0      Pkt:03 00 02
Jan 10 16:03:32.838:              s=DSP d=VoIP payload 0x61 ssrc 0xFFEB sequence 0x0
    timestamp 0x0
Jan 10 16:03:32.838:              Pt:97     Evt:0      Pkt:07 00 02   <Snd>>>
Jan 10 16:03:32.842:              s=DSP d=VoIP payload 0x60 ssrc 0xFFE2 sequence 0x0
    timestamp 0x0
Jan 10 16:03:32.842:              Pt:96     Evt:0      Pkt:07 00 02   <Snd>>>
Jan 10 16:03:32.842:              s=VoIP d=DSP payload 0x61 ssrc 0x0 sequence 0x0
    timestamp 0x0
Jan 10 16:03:32.842:  <<<Rcv> Pt:97     Evt:1      Pkt:B8 01 E0
Jan 10 16:03:32.866:              s=VoIP d=DSP payload 0x7A ssrc 0x189F0102 sequence
    0x818A timestamp 0x7CA0DBAF
Jan 10 16:03:32.866:  <<<Rcv> Pt:122    Evt:0      Pkt:CA 76 00
Jan 10 16:03:32.866:              s=VoIP d=DSP payload 0x7A ssrc 0x189F0102 sequence
    0x818A timestamp 0x7CA0DBAF
Jan 10 16:03:32.866:  <<<Rcv> Pt:122    Evt:0      Pkt:CA 76 00
Jan 10 16:03:32.866:              s=VoIP d=DSP payload 0x7A ssrc 0x189F0102 sequence
    0x818A timestamp 0x7CA0DBAF
Jan 10 16:03:32.866:  <<<Rcv> Pt:122    Evt:0      Pkt:CA 76 00
Jan 10 16:03:32.870:              s=DSP d=VoIP payload 0x7A ssrc 0x1 sequence 0x818A
    timestamp 0x2F1CA37E
Jan 10 16:03:32.870:              Pt:122    Evt:0      Pkt:46 07 00   <Snd>>>
```

In Example 12-51, you can see that the Cisco fax relay payload type (PT) 96 switchover message (**Pt:96**) is first received (**<<<Rcv>**) by the voice gateway. The voice gateway then ACKS the **Pt:96** message with a **Pt:97** message. This process is then reversed between the two voice gateways to complete the Cisco fax relay switchover.

Interestingly, you can also see some of the Cisco fax relay data packets in Example 12-51. These packets are sent and received with an RTP PT of 122 (**Pt:122**), which falls into the RTP dynamic payload type range covered by this debug command. You can find more information about Cisco fax relay and its switchover mechanism in the section "Cisco Fax Relay" in Chapter 5.

The Catalyst 6608 and VG248 non-IOS voice gateways also support Cisco fax relay and its RTP payload type switchover mechanism. For the 6608 card, you can use the Dick Tracy utility to view the Cisco fax relay switchover. More information about Dick Tracy is provided in the section "Telephony Troubleshooting."

The best traces to enable within Dick Tracy for viewing the Cisco fax relay switchover is **6 set mask 0x323**. Other masks are available, but this mask has been found to produce the best information about troubleshooting fax/modem issues. Example 12-52 highlights the portion of the Dick Tracy **6 set mask 0x323** trace containing the Cisco fax relay switchover.

Example 12-52 *6608 Dick Tracy DSP Trace **6 set mask 0x323** for a Cisco Fax Relay Call*

```
22:06:25.000 (DSP) MDCX -> Port<0>
                         Enabling Digit Detection
                         Stopping Tones
                         Mode : SENDRECV
22:06:25.000 (DSP) RTP TxOpen -> Port<0> Remote IP<10.22.200.129> UDP Port<0x4196
  (16790)> Handle<5>
22:06:25.000 (DSP) RTCP TxOpen -> Port<0> Remote IP<10.22.200.129> UDP Port<0x4197
  (16791)> Handle<6>
22:06:32.880 (DSP) Report P2P Msg -> Port<0> Event<192> Duration<0> Volume<0>
22:06:35.780 (DSP) RTP->Port<0> Received IOS_IND<PT96>
             Current State <NONE> New State <RECV_IND1>
22:06:35.780 (DSP) RTP->Port<0> Sending IOS_ACK<PT97>
             Current State <RECV_IND1> New State <SEND_ACK1>
22:06:35.790 (DSP) RTP->Port<0> Sending IOS_IND<PT96>
             Current State <SEND_ACK1> New State <SEND_IND2>
22:06:35.790 (DSP) RTP->Port<0> Received IOS_ACK<PT97>
             Current State <SEND_IND2> New State <RECV_ACK2>
```

Example 12-52 shows the MGCP **MDCX** message setting up the initial voice media stream and the remote IP address and UDP ports are shown. The Cisco fax relay switchover follows a short time later using the same RTP payload type 96 (**PT96**) and 97 (**PT97**) messages as just discussed for Cisco IOS gateways.

You will also notice the NSE-192 switchover message (**Event<192>**) for modem passthrough that was triggered by the fax called terminal identification (CED) tone. The fax CED tone occurs right before the fax flags that kick off the Cisco fax relay switchover. When modem passthrough and fax relay are both configured, modem passthrough begins its switchover first because its stimuli tone occurs first. However, fax relay ultimately controls any G3 fax call if it is configured.

Viewing the Cisco fax relay switchover on a VG248 requires enabling the DSP trace function for the event log. Example 12-53 details the Cisco fax relay switchover on the VG248.

Example 12-53 *VG248 DSP Trace for a Cisco Fax Relay Call*

```
44 17:02:48  320  T DSP     24 V.21 fax tones detected
  45 17:02:48   11  T DSP     24 rx:00C1,0000,0001,0000
  46 17:02:48    1  T DSP     24 tx:0067,C000,0000
  47 17:02:48    0  T DSP     24 Received fax relay indication
  48 17:02:48    0  I DSP     24 Entering Cisco fax relay mode
  49 17:02:48   11  T DSP     24 tx:0044
  50 17:02:48    1  T DSP     24 tx:0045,0006,0014,0001,0000,0000,0000,0000,0002,
     0000,0000
  51 17:02:48   17  I FaxRelay24 2089816241 fr-entered (10 ms)
  52 17:02:48    1  T DSP     24 rx:0081,7C90,10B1,0000,0C04,0000,0001,0000,0001,
     0000,000A,0000,0000
  53 17:02:48  178  T DSP     24 rx:0081,7C90,1165,0000,0C04,0000,0083,0000,0001,
     0000,0003,0000,0000
```

In Example 12-53, you can see that the VG248 DSP trace does not show the Cisco fax relay switchover in as much detail as the IOS gateways or the 6608. However, the critical information is available.

The VG248 trace message **V.21 fax tones detected** tells you that the VG248 has seen the HDLC flags from the terminating fax machine. This message also indicates that the VG248 is initiating the Cisco fax relay switchover by sending an RTP packet with a payload type of 96.

When the far-end device answers the RTP payload type 96 packet with a packet containing an RTP payload type of 97, the message **Received fax relay indication** is displayed by the VG248. Now the VG248 completes its switchover to Cisco fax relay and outputs the trace message **Entering Cisco fax relay mode**.

Example 12-53 shows the Cisco fax relay switchover on a VG248 when the VG248 terminates the fax call. When the VG248 is the originating gateway, an additional trace message is displayed for a Cisco fax relay switchover. This message is "Received fax mode indication," and it tells you that a VG248 in voice mode has just received a request to switchover to Cisco fax relay via an RTP packet with a payload type of 96.

Passthrough and Relay Troubleshooting

In this chapter's first section, "Attacking the Problem," a troubleshooting methodology for fax, modem, and text problems was presented. Figure 12-1 graphically demonstrates this methodology and breaks it down into its components. With all the other components being addressed in previous sections, the last one in this troubleshooting methodology, passthrough and relay troubleshooting, is discussed in this section.

Some of the techniques covered in this section are advanced, primarily because the more basic troubleshooting techniques have already been discussed in previous sections. The basic troubleshooting techniques previously discussed should have resolved the majority of fax, modem, and text problems that you will encounter. However, when the problems persist, the content here will prove beneficial.

The first topic covered is a more in-depth look at the DSP and some of its functions. Specifically, this includes DSP communication through the HPI (host port interface) and controlling the audio levels. Viewing DSP HPI messages is the best way to confirm DSP configuration parameters, switchovers, and other events; and ensuring proper audio levels for fax, modem, and text calls is necessary for reliable communication.

Next, troubleshooting sections for passthrough, fax relay, modem relay, and text relay discuss more advanced troubleshooting techniques for each of these transport methods. These techniques include specific configuration settings for certain problem scenarios and diverse debugging strategies that provide resolutions to more complicated fax, modem, and text issues.

The last section is PCM captures. This troubleshooting technique is mainly used by DE (development engineering) for analysis of complex fax and modem problems. However, the basics of PCM captures, including how to obtain them and analyze them, are covered because of the important information that they can provide.

Troubleshooting DSP Functions

In all Cisco gateways, the DSP is the critical component for bridging the PSTN with IP networks. Analog and digital voice communications from the telephony world depend on the processing capabilities of the DSP to properly encode the received signal for transport over IP and vice versa. Whether the call contains voice, fax, modem, or text information, the DSP is vital to the success of the call.

From a fax, modem, and text troubleshooting perspective, the DSP areas that need the most attention are the HPI communications and the audio signal levels. HPI communications occur between the DSP and the host, where the host would be the IOS software for most of Cisco's voice gateways. Decoding the HPI messages that are sent and received during a modem, fax, or, text call may provide additional insight into complex problems.

Incorrect signal levels can cause communication problems between fax, modem, or text devices and a voice gateway. For example, tone detection and other fundamental aspects of a normal fax, modem, or text call can be disrupted and cause a voice gateway to ignore or misinterpret key stimuli tones and other messages when the signal levels are not within the appropriate volume range. When this scenario occurs and signal levels are incorrect, you can configure the DSP on the voice gateway to alter and correct these signal levels so that they are more easily understood.

DSP HPI Troubleshooting

The interaction between a DSP involved in a fax, modem, or text call and the operating system software of the Cisco voice gateway can be quite complex. In the case of IOS gateways, the software architecture is such that there are multiple call processing and control layers present just between the voice signaling protocol and the DSP itself. Each of these layers within IOS has specific functions that are integral to ensuring proper call handling. Figure 12-16 provides a high-level overview of the call control layers within an IOS voice gateway that interface with a DSP.

Figure 12-16 highlights the multiple call control layers found in an IOS gateway. Each layer handles specific functions and can provide helpful information about the state of a fax, modem, or text call. All the layers are explained briefly, but this section concentrates on the HPI layer, which is the most important in confirming the proper programming and signaling between IOS and the DSP.

NOTE   Figure 12-16 applies only to Cisco voice gateways running IOS communicating with Telogy DSP resources. Gateways such as the AS5350, AS5400, and the AS5800/5850 can use older NextPort DSP resources, so the preceding diagram will differ slightly in that case. Non-IOS gateways will also use a different software architectural model. However, because Telogy-based Cisco IOS gateways make up the majority of the Cisco voice gateways sold, these are the focus in this section.

The Call Control Application Programming Interface (CCAPI) interconnects multiple service provider interfaces (SPI) with the session application layer. The session application layer includes voice signaling protocols such as MGCP and SCCP.

Figure 12-16 *IOS Software VoIP Call Control Layers*

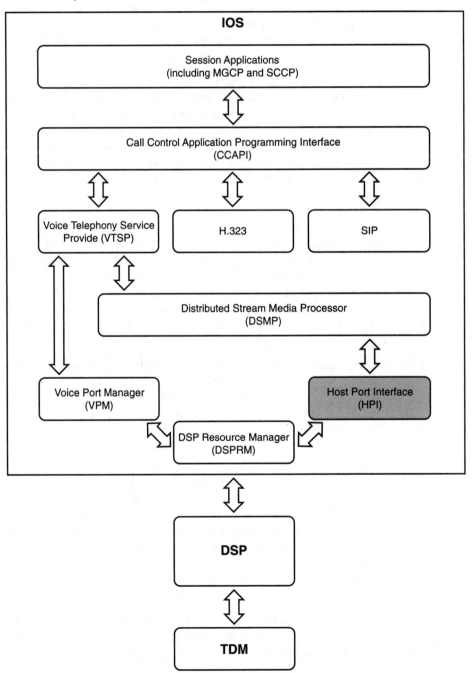

Multiple SPIs are bridged together by CCAPI. On the telephony side, there is the voice telephony service provider (VTSP) SPI, and on the IP side an SPI exists for voice signaling protocols such as H.323 and SIP.

The CCAPI process establishes, bridges, and terminates call legs. Using the command **debug voip ccapi**, you can view messaging within the CCAPI layer. These messages are helpful in tracking call routing decisions and determining which dial-peers are matched for a call.

The VTSP SPI ensures properly formatted messaging between CCAPI and the voice port manager (VPM) and the distributed stream media processor (DSMP). The VTSP messages can be viewed with the command **debug voip vtsp**. These messages contain call signaling information and all relevant messages that need to be passed between CCAPI and the DSP.

The DSMP layer facilitates the creation, modification, and destruction of streams by call legs, where a stream is simply a logical representation of a media flow. Communications within DSMP can be viewed with the command **debug voip dsmp**.

The VPM and HPI layers handle different portions of the messaging between IOS and the DSP. VPM contains all telephony signaling events, such as offhook and onhook transitions. Signaling messages within the VPM layer are seen with the debug command **debug vpm all**. This layer is useful when you need to troubleshoot the behavior of telephony events and how they can affect basic VoIP call setup problems.

However, for viewing fax-, modem-, and text-specific information, the most important layer is HPI. The HPI layer enables you to view critical fax, modem, and text messages from IOS that program the DSP and any incoming DSP messages that pertain to the call. In addition, this layer is close to the DSP, which means that the raw DSP messages are not processed by additional layers or interpreters.

Although the other layers in Figure 12-16 may contain fax, modem, and text troubleshooting information, this information is also presented in HPI, in a more effective and accurate format. These other layers tend to be more useful in troubleshooting more general VoIP problems, such as call setup and teardown.

The command **debug voip hpi all** combined with the command **no debug voip hpi stats** is the best way to look at HPI messages. Without the activation of the **no debug voip hpi stats** command, large amounts of DSP statistical information is regularly output and that makes finding the important fax, modem, and text messages more difficult.

CAUTION   Even with the HPI statistics disabled using the command **no debug voip hpi stats**, large amounts of information is generated with the **debug voip hpi all** command. If multiple calls are running on an IOS voice gateway, it is recommended to log the output of this HPI debug to a syslog server or the gateway's internal logging buffer while also disabling the console logging. See the section "Debugging Best Practices" earlier in this chapter for more information and tips on safely enabling debugs on Cisco IOS gateways.

All HPI messages include a specific packet ID and possibly a function code, too. These parameters define the HPI message type and its function and provide a unique string to search on when analyzing an HPI trace. However, be aware that occasionally some messages, such as the modemrelay_mode message, do not have their packet ID and function code displayed in the HPI debug. Table 12-10 summarizes the important HPI messages and their packet IDs for fax relay, Cisco modem relay, and passthrough.

Table 12-10 *Packet IDs and Functions of Important Fax and Modem HPI Messages*

HPI Message	Packet ID	Function
fax_mode	69	IOS message that programs the DSP with the fax relay parameters for the session.
voice_mode	73	IOS message that configures the DSP to handle a voice or passthrough call.
gen_peer_to_peer	103	IOS message that instructs the DSP to generate an NSE message.
modemrelay_mode	123 (Function Code 1)	IOS message that programs the DSP with the modem relay parameters for the session. **Note:** The modemrelay_mode packet ID and function code are not shown in the HPI debug message.
modem_relay_connected	123 (Function Code 128)	DSP message that indicates the establishment of a successful end-to-end modem relay connection while confirming the parameters that were negotiated.
modem_relay_terminated	123 (Function Code 129)	DSP message that specifies that the modem relay session is finished because of the included disconnect cause code.
tone_detect	193	DSP message that details a specific tone that was detected by the DSP.
FAX cleardown notification	194	DSP message indicating the detection of the end of the fax call.
report_peer_to_peer	207	DSP message notifying IOS that an NSE message was received.

In the following subsections, the HPI messages and their corresponding packet IDs that are summarized in Table 12-10 are analyzed in more detail. At this point, the other trouble-shooting steps covered in this chapter should have already been applied to your problem, so the focus here is on these HPI messages that are critical for confirming the proper programming and behavior of the DSP.

HPI Debugs for Fax Relay

Viewing the HPI messages for a Cisco or T.38 fax relay call allows you firsthand access to what is being seen by the DSP and the communications between the DSP and IOS during a call. If the DSP is not detecting V.21 fax flags or being programmed correctly, problems may result. Example 12-54 shows the DSP notifying IOS that a fax tone has been detected. This is a message that is typically seen on the terminating voice gateway, which can then trigger an NSE-based, RTP PT-based, or protocol-based switchover to either passthrough or fax relay.

Example 12-54   *tone_detect HPI Message from DSP to Host*

```
Apr 19 04:40:53.255: //4/81D367EB8007/HPI/[0/1:1]/hpi_receive_message:
    Packet details:
        Packet Id=193
Apr 19 04:40:53.255: //4/81D367EB8007/HPI/[0/1:1]/hpi_receive_message:
    V21 FAX tone detected
```

Example 12-54 shows the reception of a message from the DSP to the host (IOS), which is notated by **hpi_receive_message**. Included in this message line will be the port and channel of the call, **0/1:1**. This message is coded with a **Packet Id=193**, which indicates a tone_detect DSP event. The phrase **V21 FAX tone detected** specifies the precise tone that was seen by the tone_detect event. If this message is never detected by the DSP, the voice gateway will never know that a fax call is taking place, and a switchover will not occur.

In this example, the gateways are configured for NSE-based T.38 fax relay. Therefore, the gateways exchange NSE messages to signal the transition of the call from voice mode to T.38 fax relay mode. As discussed in the section "Troubleshooting the Switchover Signaling," the simplest way to view NSE messages is with the IOS command **debug voip rtp session named-event**. However, the NSE messages are also shown within HPI. Example 12-55 highlights T.38 NSE messages being sent and received on the T.38 terminating gateway after the detection of the V.21 fax tone in Example 12-54.

These are two separate NSE message events in Example 12-55. The first event is the terminating gateway sending an NSE-200 message changing the call to T.38 fax relay. This message from HPI to the DSP is known as a **gen_peer_to_peer** message with a **Packet Id=103**. You can tell that this is an NSE-200 by the **Event=200** field. The RTP payload type of **100** used by the NSE message is also specified.

Example 12-55 *gen_peer_to_peer and report_peer_to_peer HPI Messages*

```
Apr 19 04:40:53.259: //4/81D367EB8007/HPI/[0/1:1]/hpi_gen_peer_to_peer:
    RTP packet
    Packet details:
      Packet Length=24, Channel Id=1, Packet Id=103
      Event=200, Volume=-0(dBm0), Duration=0
      Disable redundancy=0, Redundancy interval=20(ms)
      SSRC: HI=0 LO=0, PayloadType=100
      gen_nte_lan=0

Apr 19 04:40:53.287: //4/81D367EB8007/HPI/[0/1:1]/hpi_receive_message:
    Packet details:
      Packet Id=207
Apr 19 04:40:53.287: //4/81D367EB8007/HPI/[0/1:1]/hpi_receive_message:
    Received Peer-to-Peer message
    Payload: C9 00 00 00
```

The second NSE message event is the notification by the DSP to the host that a T.38 acknowledgment NSE message has been received. This message is coded as a **Packet Id=207** (report_peer_to_peer) and means that a peer-to-peer message has been received. You can tell that this is an NSE T.38 acknowledgment message (NSE-201) by the **Payload** field containing a **C9** in the first byte position. A value of **C9** in hex is 201 in decimal.

In the case of fax relay, the programming of the DSP by IOS occurs with a fax_mode message, which is identified by a **Packet Id=69**. This is probably the most important message provided by the **debug voip hpi** command because it enables you to see how IOS programs the DSP based on what you have configured through the CLI. Example 12-56 displays an HPI **fax_mode** message from the host to the DSP for a T.38 fax relay call.

Example 12-56 *fax_mode HPI Message From Host to DSP*

```
Apr 19 04:40:53.291: //4/81D367EB8007/HPI/[0/1:1]/hpi_fax_mode:
    Fax Rate=0x00000003, Codec=0x00008000, Info Size=20(bytes)
Apr 19 04:40:53.291: //4/81D367EB8007/HPI/[0/1:1]/hpi_fax_mode:
    Fax Relay ECM Disable not set
Apr 19 04:40:53.291: //4/81D367EB8007/HPI/[0/1:1]/hpi_fax_mode:
    Packet details:
      Packet Length=28, Channel Id=1, Packet Id=69
      Max Transfer rate=3, Info Size=20(bytes), Fax ProtocolType=3,
      HS DataLength=40(ms), LS Data Redundancy=0, HS Data Redundancy=0,
      Fax Relay Control=0x00000000, NSF Country=0xAD
      NSF MFG=0x51, FAX TCF=2
```

You can see the large number of fax relay parameters passed down to the DSP from IOS in Example 12-56. Most of these parameters are not intuitively understood and must be decoded. Use Table 12-11 as a reference in decoding any **fax_mode** messages that you see when running the **debug voip hpi** command.

Table 12-11 *fax_mode HPI Message Parameters*

Parameter	Value	Description
Max Transfer rate or **Fax Rate**	1 (2400 bps)	Configures the maximum transmission rate to be used for the fax relay session.
	2 (4800 bps)	
	3 (7200 bps)	
	4 (9600 bps)	
	5 (12000 bps)	
	6 (14400 bps)	
Info Size	20–48	Specifies the size of the fax relay packet size in bytes, with a value of 20 being the default.
Fax ProtocolType	1 (Cisco Fax Relay)	Details the fax relay protocol to be used for transporting fax communications.
	2 (Fax over Frame Relay using FRF.11 Annex D)	
	3 (T.38 Fax Relay)	
HS DataLength	10, 20, 30, 40	Indicates the size of the high-speed (HS) data type in milliseconds (ms) with a default value of 40 ms.
LS Data Redundancy	0–5	Details the amount of T.38 redundancy for low-speed (LS) data used for T.30-level signaling.
HS Data Redundancy	0–2	Details the amount of T.38 redundancy for high-speed (HS) data used in transmitting the fax page.
Fax Relay Control	bit 0 (ECM Disable)	If set to a value of 1, ECM will be overwritten and set to disabled in all the relayed T.30 messages.
	bit 1 (Level 1 Debugs)	If set to 1, the fax relay Level 1 debugs will be enabled.
	bit 2 (Level 2 Debugs)	If set to 1, the fax relay Level 2 debugs will be enabled. Level 1 debugs are automatically disabled with this setting.
	bit 3 (NSF Override)	If set to 1, the NSF value will be overwritten by a user configured value.
	bit 4–15 (reserved)	Must be set to 0.

continues

Table 12-11 *fax_mode HPI Message Parameters (Continued)*

Parameter	Value	Description
NSF Country	0–0xFF	Country code setting used in the overwrite of the T.30 NSF message.
NSF MFG	0–0xFF	Manufacturer code setting used in the overwrite of the T.30 NSF message.
FAX TCF	1 (Local TCF Generation)	Specifies that the TCF is regenerated locally instead of being carried in the fax relay protocol.
	2 (TCF Transmitted Across the Network)	TCF is transported using the configured fax relay protocol.

Using the information in Table 12-11, you can easily decode the fax_mode message in Example 12-56. Some of the more important parameter settings that you should note would be that the DSP is being programmed for a T.38 fax relay call with no redundancy, ECM enabled, and a maximum page speed of 7200 bps.

The last fax relay message that is commonly seen in a **debug voip hpi debug** is the fax cleardown message. Example 12-57 shows an HPI fax cleardown message.

Example 12-57 *FAX Cleardown Notification HPI Message from DSP to Host*

```
Apr 19 04:41:57.835: //4/81D367EB8007/HPI/[0/1:1]/hpi_receive_message:
   FAX Cleardown notification
   Packet details:
     Packet Length=8, Channel Id=1, Packet Id=194
```

Example 12-57 shows a **Packet Id=194** message from the DSP to the host. This message represents a **FAX Cleardown notification**. The conditions that cause the DSP to generate this message are the detection and successful retransmission of the T.30 DCN message or the detection of no fax activity for 10 seconds.

The previous HPI debug messages were captured for a T.38 fax relay call, but all of these messages appear for Cisco fax relay, too, with the exception of the NSE switchover. Cisco fax relay uses a different switchover method, but the fax_mode, V.21 fax tone_detect, and fax cleardown messages should be present for a working Cisco fax relay call.

HPI Debugs for Cisco Modem Relay

The command **debug voip hpi** provides good information about a Cisco modem relay call, too. Just like with a fax relay call, you can view the message from IOS that programs the DSP. Example 12-58 shows the **modemrelay_mode** message as seen with the command **debug voip hpi**.

Example 12-58 *modemrelay_mode HPI Message from Host to DSP*

```
Apr 19 04:56:30.895: //2/BA2B053F8002/HPI/[0/1:1]/hpi_modemrelay_mode:
    MR Role=Called leg, MR DebugState=0x00000000, Latency=200(ms), Retries=12,
    XID Negotiation Enabled, dict_size=1024, StringLength=32, Compress direction=3,
    V14 rx pb hold time=50, tx hold count=16, hold time=20, protocol= 1, ec_protocol
    = 1
```

The **modemrelay_mode** message shown in Example 12-58 programs the DSP based on the user's configuration entered via the CLI. This message causes the voice codec that was being used by the DSP to be replaced by the modem relay codec and its specified parameters. The important parameters included in the HPI **modemrelay_mode** message are defined in Table 12-12.

Table 12-12 *modemrelay_mode HPI Message Parameters*

Parameter	Value	Description
MR Role	0 (Called leg)	Defines the originating (calling leg) and terminating (called leg) ends of the modem relay call.
	1 (Calling leg)	
MR DebugState	bit 0 (physical layer)	Indicates the modem relay–specific debugs that are to be enabled for the modem relay call. A bit value of 1 means that the particular debug is enabled, and 0 means that the debug is disabled.
	bit 1 (HDLC)	
	bit 2 (V.42 layer)	
	bit 3 (SPRT layer)	
	bit 4 (UDP layer)	
	bit 5 (event level)	
	bit 6 (error event)	
	bit 7–15 (reserved; set to 0)	
Latency	100–1000	Details the worst-case value in milliseconds for one-way delay across the IP network. This value helps determine the timeout values for SPRT acknowledgments. The default value is 200 ms.
Retries	6–30	Specifies the number of SPRT retransmission attempts due to an acknowledgment timeout before disconnecting.
XID Negotiation	0 (Disabled)	Defines the setting for the end-to-end XID negotiation.
	1 (Enabled)	

continues

Table 12-12 *modemrelay_mode HPI Message Parameters (Continued)*

Parameter	Value	Description
dict_size or **Negotiated dict. size**	512–2048	Details the compression algorithm's dictionary size in bytes, with a default value of 1024.
StringLength	16–32	Defines the string length of the compression algorithm.
Compress direction or **Compression direction**	0 (Disabled)	Specifies the V.42bis compression setting for the modem relay call to a value of disabled, forward direction only, backward direction only, or both directions.
	1 (Forward)	
	2 (Backward)	
	3 (Both)	
protocol or **Physical Layer**	1 (V.34 Modulation)	Details the physical layer modulation protocol. Cisco modem relay supports only V.34.
ec_protocol or **EC**	1 (V.42 EC Layer)	Indicates the error correcting layer protocol. Cisco modem relay supports only V.42.

Because of the XID negotiation, the parameters sent to the DSP from IOS in Example 12-58 might not necessarily be used for the modem relay call. Upon the completion of the modem relay negotiation by the DSP, the call is connected, and the final settings are sent by the DSP to the host using a **Packet Id=123** message with **FunctionCode=128**. These packet ID and function code settings specify that this is a modem_relay_connected message, which indicates the establishment of a successful end-to-end modem relay connection. Example 12-59 shows an example of this message.

Example 12-59 *modem_relay_connected HPI Message from DSP to Host*

```
Apr 19 04:56:39.851: //2/BA2B053F8002/HPI/[0/1:1]/hpi_receive_message:
    Modem Relay message
    Packet details:
      Packet Length=34, Channel Id=1, Packet Id=123
      FunctionCode=128
Apr 19 04:56:39.851: //2/BA2B053F8002/HPI/[0/1:1]/hpi_receive_message:
    Connected
      Physical Layer=1, EC=1, Modem dict. size=1024(words), StringLength=32,
Compression direction=3
      Negotiated dict. size=1024(words), StringLength=32, Compression direction=3
      Local RX/TX speed=31200/31200, Remote RX/TX speed=28800/31200
```

Example 12-59 repeats many of the same parameters seen previously in Example 12-58. Table 12-12 can also be used again in defining these parameters. Two new parameters are **Local RX/TX speed** and **Remote RX/TX speed**. These specify the negotiated data transmit and receive speeds for the local and remote modems.

When a Cisco modem relay call has terminated, a unique disconnect cause code is generated within the HPI modem_relay_terminated message. This modem_relay_ terminated message is indicated by the presence of **Packet Id=123** in conjunction with a **FunctionCode=129**. Example 12-60 highlights this message and the termination cause code that it contains.

Example 12-60   *modem_relay_terminated HPI Message from DSP to Host*

```
Apr 18 21:37:47.095: //1/BA2B053F8002/HPI/[0/1:1]/hpi_receive_message:
    Modem Relay message
    Packet details:
      Packet Length=18, Channel Id=1, Packet Id=123
      FunctionCode=129
Apr 18 21:37:47.095: //1/BA2B053F8002/HPI/[0/1:1]/hpi_receive_message:
    Terminated
    Cause=0x7C, Modem dict. size=2048(words), StringLength=32, Compression
      direction=3
```

In Example 12-60, the term **Terminated** confirms that this is a modem_relay_terminated message that is being sent from the DSP to IOS. Because the message direction is from the DSP to IOS, this means that the disconnect was received on the telephony interface of this gateway and that a modem relay disconnect message will now be sent to the remote gateway. Within this **Terminated** message is a termination cause code that specifies the reason for the disconnect of the Cisco modem relay call. In the case of Example 12-60, the termination cause is shown as **Cause=0x7C**, where **0x7C** is the actual termination cause code. Table 12-13 provides a list of all the Cisco modem relay termination cause codes.

Table 12-13   *Cisco Modem Relay Termination Cause Codes*

Modem Relay Termination Cause Code	Description	Modem Relay Termination Cause Code	Description
0x65	SPRT—Channel 1 max retransmit count exceeded on DSP.	0x78	V42—NR sequence exception.
0x66	SPRT—Channel 1 invalid transport frame type in transmit queue.	0x79	V42—Invalid acknowledgment received.
0x67	SPRT—Channel 2 max retransmit count exceeded on DSP.	0x7A	V42—Exceeded N401 retransmit count.
0x68	SPRT—Channel 2 invalid transport frame type in transmit queue.	0x7B	SPRT—Requested to transmit info t_frame that exceeds max allowed size.

continues

Table 12-13 *Cisco Modem Relay Termination Cause Codes (Continued)*

Modem Relay Termination Cause Code	Description	Modem Relay Termination Cause Code	Description
0x69	SPRT—Channel 1 invalid base sequence number received by DSP from remote host.	0x7C	V42—Received V42 DISC packet from client modem.
0x6A	SPRT—Channel 2 invalid base sequence number received by DSP from remote host.	0x7D	V42—Received V42 FRMR packet from client modem.
0x6B	SPRT—Received RELEASE request from peer.	0x82	V42—Failed to add packet to V42 transmit queue.
0x6C	SPRT—Channel 1 invalid transmit sequence number.	0x8C	V42—Invalid "VA."
0x6D	SPRT—Channel 2 invalid transmit sequence number.	0x8D	PHYSICAL—Modem data pump terminated/failed.
0x6E	SPRT—Invalid transmit t_frame type.	0xC9	SPRT—Channel 1 max retransmit count exceeded on line card.
0x6F	SPRT—Requested to transmit null (zero length) info t_frame.	0xCA	SPRT—Channel 2 max retransmit count exceeded on line card.
0x71	V42—Unexpected SABME received.	0xCD	SPRT—Channel 1 invalid base sequence number received by line card from DSP.
0x72	V42—Client modem capability appears incompatible with V42bis capability on originating leg gateway.	0xCE	SPRT—Channel 2 invalid base sequence number received by line card from DSP.
0x73	V42—Client modem capability appears incompatible with V42bis capability on terminating leg gateway.	0xCF	SPRT—Channel 1 invalid base sequence number received by line card from remote host.

Table 12-13 *Cisco Modem Relay Termination Cause Codes (Continued)*

Modem Relay Termination Cause Code	Description	Modem Relay Termination Cause Code	Description
0x74	V42—Exceeded max XID retransmit count.	0xD0	SPRT—Channel 2 invalid base sequence number received by line card from remote host.
0x77	V42—Exceeded max SABME retransmit count.		

Referencing Table 12-13, you can see that the modem relay termination cause code of **0x7C** as seen in Example 12-60 decodes to "V42—Received V42 DISC packet from client modem." This is the expected termination cause code for Cisco modem relay calls that are terminated gracefully by the client modems connected to the voice gateways.

TIP   The Cisco modem relay disconnect cause code is also displayed in the **show call history voice** command output. In most cases, it might be easier to grab the Cisco modem relay disconnect cause code from this **show** command instead of running the **debug voip hpi** command.

HPI Debugs for Passthrough

The modem passthrough and fax pass-through equivalent to the fax relay fax_mode message and the Cisco modem relay modemrelay_mode message is the **voice_mode** message. This message details the activities associated with a passthrough switchover, including the codec upspeed if necessary and the disabling of Voice Activity Detection (VAD). Example 12-61 highlights a **voice_mode** message with a **Packet Id=73** for a modem passthrough call.

Example 12-61   *voice_mode HPI Message from Host to DSP*

```
Apr 19 04:56:29.543: //2/BA2B053F8002/HPI/[0/1:1]/hpi_voice_mode:
    Packet details:
      Packet Length=34, Channel Id=1, Packet Id=73
      CodingType=1, Voice field size=160(bytes), VAD Flag=0,
      Echo Length=64(ms), ComfortNoise=enable, Inband detect=0x000000C1,
      DigitRelay=0, AGC Flag=0, ECAN TestGroup=0,
      ECAN TestNumber=0, DynamicPayload=0
```

The **CodingType** parameter in Example 12-61 details the codec to be used. A value of 1 refers to G.711 μ-law, and a value of 2 equates to G.711 a-law. A value of 0 for the **VAD flag** parameter indicates that VAD is disabled. For either modem passthrough or fax passthrough calls, a G.711 codec with VAD set to disabled should always occur in a **voice_mode** message. Otherwise, the passthrough call may fail.

Loss Planning

The primary purpose of loss planning in a traditional telephony environment is to maintain the voice signal at an optimal level throughout the network. This ensures the best voice quality from a user perspective and mitigates other voice-impacting impairments such as echo.

Loss planning in voice networks can take on another layer of complexity with voice gateways being inserted into the path of traditional telephony links or being part of an IP PBX solution. This has led to the development of standards such as TIA-912 and TSB-122 from the Telecommunications Industry Association (TIA). These specifications should be consulted when developing a loss plan for VoIP networks, and you can order them directly from the TIA website at http://www.tiaonline.org/standards.

Generally, if a proper network loss plan for voice has already been implemented, faxes, modems, and text devices should work fine under this existing loss plan. However, modulated communications can be more sensitive to levels that are too high or too low than a normal voice user. This in turn can lead to problems with fax, modem, and text calls.

In some cases, with signal levels that are too low, the switchover from voice mode to passthrough or relay may not occur properly because incoming information might not be detected. When signal levels are too high, which is a much more common scenario, the data can be clipped and corrupted. In the cases of incoming fax calls with levels that are too hot (around –9 dB or more), the DSP on the Cisco voice gateway might not even be able to decode the T.30 fax messages. If you are having fax, modem, or text problems that have not been solved by the other troubleshooting recommendations contained in this chapter, checking the levels for a problem call should be your next step.

The generally accepted reference for loss between two speech endpoints is between 8 and 12 dB, with a target of 10 dB. This amount of loss should also be provided for a fax, modem, or text call, too.

The best way to confirm whether the loss plan is correct for a particular path is through the use of third-party devices from companies such as Sage and Agilent. These devices and other comparable test tools typically include an external tone generator and a decibel meter. The external tone generator provides a 1004 Hz frequency tone at a power level of 0 dBm, and a decibel meter allows the loudness of this tone to be accurately measured. A 1004 Hz tone at a level of 0 dBm is the standard tone from which loss level measurements are made. The dBm notation specifies a decibel signal level from a power perspective with the reference point being that 0 dBm equals 1 milliwatt when the load termination is 600 ohm.

The VoIP gateway must also be properly configured when making loss level measurements. Only the G.711 codec should be used for the test call that will carry the 1004 Hz tone. In addition, both VAD and echo cancellation should be disabled for the call. This can be accomplished in IOS gateways with the commands **no vad** under the VoIP dial-peer and **no echo-cancel enable** under the voice port.

Figure 12-17 displays a sample topology involving modems and the placement of third-party devices for loss level planning. Of course, faxes, text devices, or even phones are applicable in this scenario, too.

Figure 12-17 *Measuring Signal Loss in VoIP Networks*

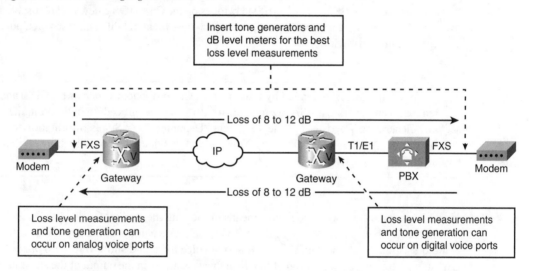

If you need the most accurate levels measurement for the modem connection in Figure 12-17, place third-party test tools at each modem location. Tones with a frequency of 1004 Hz and a power level of 0 dBm should be sent and measured for both directions. Ideally, both directions should have end-to-end attenuation ranging between 8 and 12 dB.

The impedance settings of the test tools should match what is set on the PBX and voice gateway as diagrammed in Figure 12-17. The impedance setting will almost always be 600 ohm, and the test tools should be terminating the connection because bridging may affect the results.

In addition to using third-party devices for loss level measurements, Figure 12-17 points out that Cisco voice gateways themselves can also be used. Although the external test tools are generally the preferred measurement method, Cisco voice gateways can perform adequately in such a role and are likely to be more readily available than such specialized third-party test tools.

Cisco IOS voice gateways can generate a continuous 1004 Hz tone through the use of the following IOS CLI commands in enable mode. These commands use the same syntax except for the parameter **local**, which generates the tone in the POTS direction or the parameter **network**, which sends the tone over the IP call leg. Note that these commands are not valid on Cisco IOS voice gateways using the NextPort DSPs as found on some 5350 and 5400 platforms.

```
test voice port port inject-tone local 1000
test voice port port inject-tone network 1000
```

Even though the CLI forces you to enter the tone as 1000 Hz, in reality this is a 1004 Hz tone that the IOS gateway generates. Furthermore, the tone is generated at 0 dBm, so proper loss measurements can be made. The 1004 Hz tones on the Cisco IOS gateways are disabled using the CLI command **test voice port** *port* **inject-tone local disable** and **test voice port** *port* **inject-tone network disable**.

TIP
Testing tones can also be generated by other means. Cisco IP phones such as the 7940 and 7960 models can generate a 1004 Hz tone at –15 dB using the procedure outlined in the section "Generating Test Tone" of the document "Using the 79xx Status Information for Troubleshooting" (Document ID: 7415). You can find this document by searching for it at Cisco.com.

Most Cisco voice gateways also have a means of viewing the decibel levels of tones and signals that are being processed by the DSP. On IOS voice gateways, the two most commonly used commands are **show call active voice brief** and **show voice call** *port*. Example 12-62 shows the location of the dBm measurements in the output of the **show call active voice brief** command.

Example 12-62 *show call active voice brief Command Output Showing Signal Levels*

```
1227 : 19 7099760ms.1 +2830 pid:1 Answer 100 active
 dur 00:00:21 tx:1199/191840 rx:1059/169440
 IP 1.1.1.1:18846 SRTP: off rtt:3ms pl:20550/0ms lost:0/1/0 delay:60/60/65ms
   g711ulaw TextRelay: off

 media inactive detected:n media contrl rcvd:n/a timestamp:n/a
 long duration call detected:n long duration call duration:n/a timestamp:n/a
1227 : 20 7099760ms.2 +2830 pid:2 Originate 200 active
 dur 00:00:21 tx:1059/177912 rx:1200/192000
 Tele 0/0/0 (20) [0/0/0] tx:23995/23995/0ms g711ulaw noise:-22 acom:25  i/0:
   -25/0 dBm
```

The input and output dBm levels for the **show call active voice brief** command in Example 12-62 are shown as **i/0:-25/0 dBm**. The incoming level on this voice port, **0/0/0**, is –25 dBm, and the output level is 0 dBm. The reason that the output level appears so hot is that a 1004 Hz tone at 0 dBm was generated from a remote gateway over the IP network and ultimately out of port **0/0/0** of this gateway. No loss occurs over an IP network, and any adjustment to the outbound signal level by the gateway itself is not reflected in these measurements. Therefore, the test tone is shown by the voice gateway as being transmitted out the voice port at 0 dBm. If output attenuation or gain is configured on this port, the true level coming out of this port will vary respectively.

Example 12-63 shows the specific line from the IOS command **show voice call** *port* that displays the input and output dBm levels. As discussed earlier in this chapter, to view the DSP statistical information associated with this command, **terminal monitor** must be enabled for your Telnet or SSH session.

Example 12-63   *show voice call port Command Output Showing Signal Levels*

```
! Output omitted for brevity

***DSP LEVELS***
TDM Bus Levels(dBm0): Rx -25.5 from PBX/Phone, Tx -0.5 to PBX/Phone
```

The **show voice call** *port* command displays a lot of DSP statistical information, but you should look for the section titled **DSP LEVELS,** as shown in Example 12-63. Within this section is a line titled **TDM Bus Levels**. This is where you can view the received (**Rx**) and transmitted (**Tx**) dBm levels for the signals currently being transported into and out of the physical voice port. In this scenario, a 1004 Hz tone has also been generated from the remote IP connected gateway. As mentioned previously, no loss across the an IP link, coupled with the fact that the output signal level is taken before any additional adjustments by the voice gateway, results in the outbound signal measurement in Example 12-63 reflecting a high value of **–0.5** dBm.

Viewing the signal levels on non-IOS gateways is possible only on the 6608. The VG248 and ATA do not provide a way for the user to look at inbound and outbound signal levels. Therefore, external devices must be used for any levels measurements that are needed with these platforms.

The 6608/6624 voice gateway displays the signal levels through the Dick Tracy command **6 show call**, as highlighted in Example 12-64. This same command is also used for IP troubleshooting, as earlier shown in Example 12-25.

The 6608/6624 parameters for signal levels that you should look at in Example 12-64 are named **Tx Power** and **Rx Power**. The **Tx Power** parameter displays the outbound signal level from the port, and **Rx Power** shows the signal strength coming in to the port.

Example 12-64   *6608 Dick Tracy **6 show call** Command Indicating Signal Levels*

```
! Output omitted for brevity

22:24:08.300 (DSP) LEVELS -> Port<0>
        Tx Power<-17>
        Tx Mean<0>
        Rx Power<-44>
        Rx Mean<0>
        Current Bkgnd Noise<-74>
        Current ACOM Level<45>
        Current ERL Level<45>

! Output omitted for brevity
```

After you have determined that a levels adjustment is necessary for a Cisco voice gateway, you can accomplish this in different ways depending on the type of voice gateway. For Cisco IOS gateways, CLI commands are issued under the voice port itself. The two commands that are used are **input gain** *dB* and **output attenuation** *dB*. Both commands allow the user to specify a range between –6 and 14 dB.

Using the **input gain** and **output attenuation** commands can be a little confusing if you do not pay close attention. Whereas a positive value for **input gain** increases the signal strength, a positive value for **output attenuation** decreases the signal strength. So, keep in mind that for **input gain**, a positive number signifies gain, whereas a negative number is loss. For **output attenuation**, a positive number signifies loss, whereas a negative number is actually a gain.

For the non-IOS gateways, there are dB settings available in port-specific configuration screens. The 6608/6624 allows input and output levels adjustments to be made on the **Port Configuration** page. A pull-down list of dB values is available for **Audio Signal Adjustment into IP Network** and **Audio Signal Adjustment from IP Network**. Just like with the IOS gateways, the range of configurable dB values on this screen are from –6 to 14 dB.

The VG248 non-IOS voice gateway also offers a port specific configuration page that contains level adjustments. This screen on the VG248 can be accessed as follows:

Configure > Telephony > Port Specific Parameters > *port*

The parameters **Input Gain** and **Output Gain** enable you to select dB adjustment values for a specific port in both the inbound and outbound direction. The range of values available for each of these parameters is –6 to 14 dB for the **Input Gain** and –14 to 0 dB for the **Output Gain**.

The ATA non-IOS voice gateway offers decibel level adjustments for its FXS ports on its **Audio Parameters** screen. As illustrated in Figure 9-6, the configuration parameters are titled **FXSInputLevel** and **FXSOutputLevel**. Both of these parameters handle a range of values from –9 to 2 dB.

Be aware that some Cisco voice gateway ports already have built-in levels adjustments. For example, IOS gateway FXS and FXO ports have 3 dB of output attenuation configured by default. On IOS gateways, you can check the default level settings with the command **show voice port** *port*. Example 12-65 highlights the default level settings for an IOS FXS (**Foreign Exchange Station**) interface on port **0/0/0** using the **show voice port** *port* command.

Example 12-65 *show voice port* port *Command Output Illustrating Default FXS Port Level Settings*

```
fax_2811# show voice port 0/0/0

Foreign Exchange Station 0/0/0 Slot is 0, Sub-unit is 0, Port is 0
 Type of VoicePort is FXS   VIC2-2FXS

! Output omitted for brevity

 In Gain is Set to 0 dB
 Out Attenuation is Set to 3 dB

! Output omitted for brevity
```

Example 12-65 displays how the **show voice port** *port* command uses the lines **In Gain is Set to 0 dB** and **Out Attenuation is Set to 3 dB** to reflect the current level settings for the voice port. In this case, no user-configured level setting commands have been executed, so you can see that 3 dB of output attenuation is set for this FXS voice port by default.

Something else to keep in mind is that any levels adjustment on the voice port is taken into account when the **test voice port** *port* **inject-tone** command is used. Therefore, in the case of the FXS port in Example 12-65, a 0 dBm 1004 Hz tone originated from this FXS port would actually measure –3 dBm coming out of it.

In Figure 12-18, level settings for each device and endpoint measurements are shown for a modem connection through a VoIP network. In the direction of Modem 1 to Modem 2, no attenuation or padding is configured, so levels are too high (or hot). In the direction from Modem 2 to Modem 1, there is too much attenuation and the levels are too low.

Figure 12-18 *Initial Level Settings for a Modem Connection*

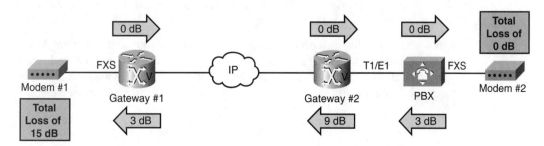

For the level settings in the direction of Modem 1 to Modem 2 in Figure 12-18, you can see that original signal from Modem 1 does not encounter any loss in its signal level as it heads through the network. This means that the signal level is probably too high for Modem 2, and connection problems are usually the result.

CAUTION   Changing loss levels to resolve one problem may introduce other problems, such as echo, especially if additional gain is introduced. Generally, making the minimal levels change necessary to resolve a problem on the voice ports closest to the problem device is the best practice. This ensures that the impact to other calls and devices will be as negligible as possible. Just be sure to thoroughly check other calls through a port where changes have been made to make sure that other calls have not been negatively impacted. Of course, if the port where the changes are being made is dedicated to fax or modem calls, this is not necessary.

The fix for modems that are receiving signals that are too high is to add attenuation in the network path. In this case, the proper setting according to TIA-912 is to configure the PBX for 9 dB of attenuation. Depending on the situation, however, you could also apply some attenuation on the FXS port of Gateway 1, resulting in less being needed on the PBX.

TIP   As mentioned earlier in this section, TIA-912 is one of the standards when it comes to signal-level loss planning in VoIP networks. This standard should be consulted for any serious level loss planning in your VoIP network. Because this loss planning section has a primary focus on just faxes, modems, and text devices, loss planning on a networkwide level is not discussed. Consult the specifications recommended in this section and other loss level planning references if major loss level adjustments are necessary.

For the direction of Modem 2 to Modem 1, the loss settings along the bottom of Figure 12-18 show too much loss in the network path. Remember that you want to see an 8 to 12 dB drop between the modem endpoints. In this case, you see that drops of 3 + 9 + 3 dB equal a 15 dB end-to-end loss.

The fix for too much loss in a network path is to increase the gain on the network devices. Once again, referring to TIA-912, the correct settings here are a 3 dB drop on the PBX, a 0 dB drop on Gateway 2, and a 9 dB loss on Gateway 1. Figure 12-19 shows the proper loss settings in both directions for the gateways and the PBX for the modem connection.

Figure 12-19 *Corrected Level Settings for a Modem Connection*

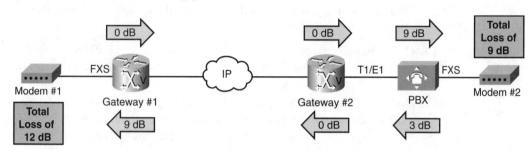

Making levels adjustments on digital ports is known as digital padding, and this should be avoided wherever possible. Because digital padding has the potential to increase quantization distortion, loss adjustments should be made on analog ports either before the encoding or after the decoding of the analog waveform. For example, the PBX in Figure 12-19 has a 9 dB drop in the direction of Modem 1 to Modem 2 and a drop of 3 dB in the direction of Modem 2 to Modem 1. The drops for both of these directions should occur on the analog FXS port and not on the T1/E1 connection going to Gateway 2.

Be aware that modems and faxes can be especially sensitive to levels that are set too high. In fact, most faxes and modems transmit their original signal as low as –13 dBm to ensure that the levels remain at a low value when they are received by the remote device. With proper loss planning, it is not uncommon for fax and modem signal levels to be around –20 dBm or possibly lower after traversing through the network.

Advanced Troubleshooting for Passthrough

Cisco voice gateways support two types of passthrough. The first type uses an NSE-based switchover for faxes and modems, and it is configured using the **modem passthrough** command in IOS voice gateways. The second type of passthrough uses a protocol-based switchover, and it is referred to as pass-through because it is configured by the IOS command **fax protocol pass-through**. In addition, pass-through is only for faxes because it is triggered only by the fax specific V.21 flags. From a troubleshooting perspective, both of these passthrough types are the same, except for their stimuli tones and switchover methods (which were covered in the previous section). Therefore, the troubleshooting information that follows applies to either passthrough type.

Troubleshooting passthrough is the same as troubleshooting a regular VoIP call in many respects, and only limited options are available for troubleshooting passthrough problems beyond what has already been discussed in this chapter. Therefore, it is important to review the fax/modem/text troubleshooting methodology introduced at the beginning of this chapter from a passthrough perspective and ensure that all the steps have been covered. These troubleshooting steps include the following:

- **Check the fundamentals**: This includes checking a variety of different items, including making sure that calls work over the PSTN and that the endpoint devices are in the proper working order.

- **Check the configuration**: Whether modem passthrough or fax pass-through is being used, one of these transport methods must be configured on both gateways. Make sure that both gateways are configured the same from a passthrough perspective.

- **Confirm that the correct dial-peers are matched**: Although both gateways may be configured the same from a passthrough perspective, the dial-peers with the passthrough configuration may not be used if there is a dial-peer matching problem. Check that the correct dial-peers are being matched using a command like **show call active voice brief**. This includes verifying that a correctly configured inbound VoIP dial-peer is being matched.

- **Verify if RFC 2198 redundancy is configured**: If one gateway is configured for redundancy and the other gateway is not configured for it or does not support it, passthrough calls may fail. This problem is most commonly seen on the VG248, which does not support RFC 2198 redundancy.

- **Confirm that the telephony leg is free of impairments**: Slips and other errors on a digital T1/E1 circuit are deadly for fax, modem, and text calls.

- **Check the IP network**: There should not be any packet loss, excessive jitter, or other IP network impairments affecting the packets of the call.

- **Confirm the switchover**: If the passthrough call does not complete a successful switchover, including upspeeding the codec to G.711 if necessary, calls will fail.

- **Check the audio levels**: Audio levels that are too low or too high can cause problems for fax and modem calls. Make sure that the levels for a call fall into an acceptable range.

Because fax and modem passthrough calls (and even Text over G.711 calls) use a voice codec for transportation of the modulated information, these calls are essentially voice calls. Thinking about fax and modem passthrough calls in this manner, along with the troubleshooting steps covered in this chapter, should provide the information necessary to resolve the majority of passthrough problems.

For more complex problems, which remain unresolved, the next step is to view the actual messaging that is being sent and received through the G.711 codec. This is accomplished through the use of Pulse Code Modulation (PCM) traces. PCM traces are simply an audio file of the tones and signals transmitted by fax, modem, and text devices.

In passthrough scenarios, PCM traces are the only way to really view what is happening between two endpoints that are sending modulated information. Unlike relay, passthrough calls are not demodulated by the Cisco voice gateways, so the voice gateways cannot provide any information into the actual communications between the modulated endpoints. For this reason, PCM traces are an indispensable tool for advanced passthrough troubleshooting. You can find more information about PCM traces, how they are obtained, and how to analyze them later in this chapter in the section "PCM Traces for Fax and Modem."

Advanced Troubleshooting for Fax Relay

Cisco voice gateways support two forms of fax relay: T.38 fax relay and the proprietary Cisco fax relay. The general operation of both of these fax relay types are similar despite having different switchover mechanisms and protocol encapsulations. For this reason, both fax relay types follow the same troubleshooting procedures except for a few minor differences.

Because of the Cisco voice gateway's demodulation of the incoming signals and active participation in the fax relay call, more troubleshooting options are available for fax relay than what exists for passthrough. However, before exploring these additional troubleshooting options, you should refer back to the passthrough troubleshooting steps in the previous section. Although these steps just serve as brief reminders of material discussed throughout this chapter, most of these steps are just as applicable to fax relay as they are to passthrough. After these steps have been confirmed and a fax relay problem still exists, use the following troubleshooting options and techniques.

Fax Relay Data Rate

One of the most common problems with fax relay is the complaint from users that it takes too long to send faxes. This problem stems from the fact that, by default, fax relay calls on Cisco IOS gateways will not exceed the bandwidth being used by the voice codec. Furthermore, the default codec for VoIP dial-peers on Cisco voice gateways is G.729, an 8000 bps codec. This results in Cisco voice gateways exhibiting the default behavior of not allowing fax relay calls to exceed 8000 bps. Under this scenario, all fax calls will use the fastest fax page-transmission speed that is under 8000 bps, which is 7200 bps. Faxes transmitting pages at 7200 bps will take almost twice the time to send the same information as a fax operating at the 14400 bps maximum speed.

The reason that this codec speed is enforced by default is to ensure that fax calls use no more bandwidth than a voice call. When sending combined voice and fax calls across WAN links where bandwidth is a premium, per-call bandwidth may be tightly controlled. Fax calls taking up more bandwidth than voice calls can cause quality of service (QoS) problems for all calls on that link.

As discussed in the section "Fax Relay" in Chapter 10, the IOS command **fax rate** for H.323, SIP, and SCCP, and **mgcp fax rate** for MGCP controls the maximum fax page transmission speed for fax relay. The default setting for these commands is **voice**, and this restricts the fax speed to being no greater than the codec bit rate that is configured for the dial-peer. When the codec is G.711, a 64 Kbps codec, this is not a problem; as pointed out previously, however, lower bit rate codecs such as the G.729 default voice codec can lead to slow fax transmissions.

The **fax rate** and **mgcp fax rate** commands enable you to override the **voice** setting with other values. Assuming that your network can handle higher speed faxes using more bandwidth, increasing the fax speed to the maximum value of 14400 bps with the **fax rate 14400** or **mgcp fax rate 14400** command is an easy solution.

Dealing with Packet Loss

In an ideal world, packet loss would not exist in VoIP networks. However, this is not the case in the real world, and packet loss is present. Fortunately, fax relay provides a couple of options to deal with it.

If possible, packet loss problems and other IP impairments should be resolved and not allowed to affect fax, modem, and text calls. Unfortunately, however, this is not always possible. In scenarios where communications must occur over the Internet or through a network where you have no control, resolving network impairments such as packet loss can be challenging.

So, when you find yourself in the position of narrowing down the cause of your fax problems to packet loss, what are your next steps? One option to try is the disabling of the Error Correction Mode (ECM) feature. ECM is a fax feature that ensures error-free page transmissions, which can be critical for many document types, such as contracts and other legal agreements.

When ECM is enabled, the receiving fax device requests any page segments that are received with errors to be re-sent until the complete page is received error free. Without the ECM feature, fax transmissions may contain errors that lead to degradation of the page information. However, a much higher percentage of fax transactions are completed, and often the errors are undetectable. ECM is discussed in more detail in the section "Understanding Error Correction Mode" in Chapter 2, "How Fax Works."

From a troubleshooting perspective, disabling ECM for both T.38 and Cisco fax relay can quickly increase the fax call completion rate. Because of ECM's persistence in securing an error-free document, even minor network errors can cause ECM fax transactions to fail or take a long time to complete. For example, as little as 2 percent packet loss will cause ECM faxes to fail. If users are willing to live with the possibility of occasional page imperfections to achieve a higher call completion rate, disabling the ECM feature is a valid solution. For more information about ECM pertaining to network design and whether it should be disabled on Cisco voice gateways, see the section "Error Correction Mode" in Chapter 7.

Most Cisco voice gateways by default do not change the ECM setting of the digital identification signal (DIS) message. The user must explicitly configure the voice gateway to disable ECM. On IOS gateways, the command is **fax-relay ecm disable** under the VoIP dial-peer for SIP and H.323 and **no mgcp fax t38 ecm** for the MGCP protocol. Be aware that these commands pertain to both T.38 and Cisco fax relay. More information about disabling ECM in IOS gateways can be found in the sections "IOS Gateway Fax Relay Configuration for H.323, SIP, and SCCP" and "IOS Gateway Fax Relay Configuration for MGCP" in Chapter 10.

For non-IOS gateways such as the 6608 and VG248, the ECM is disabled in a different manner. Unlike the other Cisco voice gateways, ECM is actually disabled by default on the 6608 for all fax calls, and the check box for **Fax Error Correction Mode Override** needs to be unchecked on Unified CM. The VG248 behaves like the IOS gateways and requires the user to explicitly set the **Fax relay ECM** parameter on the **Port specific parameters** screen to **disabled**. For more information about the ECM settings for the 6608 and VG248 gateways, see the sections "6608 Catalyst Blade Fax Relay Configuration" and "VG248 Fax Relay Configuration" in Chapter 10.

T.38 fax relay has another method for dealing with packet loss and other network impairments. Unlike Cisco fax relay, T.38 fax relay supports redundancy, and this is the recommended best practice for handling packet loss. The user can specify separate redundancy levels for both the low-speed T.30 level messaging and the high-speed messaging of the page data. If T.38 fax relay is already your fax relay protocol, implementing T.38 redundancy is a better option for dealing with packet loss than disabling ECM. The only drawback is that additional bandwidth will be consumed to handle the redundant packets. For more information about T.38 redundancy and its bandwidth requirements, see the section "Redundancy" in Chapter 7.

TIP   As shown previously in Figure 5-7, Cisco voice gateways break the T.30, low-speed information frames into many small packets. Therefore, because a greater opportunity exists for packet loss to affect this information, it is recommended to enable at least one level of low-speed redundancy for T.38 fax relay. Because redundancy is being added only to the low-speed T.38 packets, the increase in bandwidth is negligible.

T.38 fax relay along with the optional redundancy feature is configurable only on Cisco IOS voice gateways. The 6608 non-IOS gateway does not support T.38 fax relay, and although the VG248 does support T.38, it does not support redundancy.

The command for enabling T.38 fax relay redundancy on IOS voice gateways is **fax protocol t38 ls-redundancy** *value* **hs-redundancy** *value* for the H.323, SIP, and SCCP voice signaling protocols. This command is valid under the VoIP dial-peer (for H.323 and SIP only) or globally under **voice service voip**. For more information about this command, see the section "IOS Gateway Fax Relay Configuration for H.323, SIP, and SCCP" in Chapter 10.

For the MGCP voice signaling protocol on IOS voice gateways, the command for configuring T.38 fax relay redundancy is **mgcp fax t38 ls_redundancy** *value* **hs_redundancy** *value*. You can find more information about this configuration command in the section "IOS Gateway Fax Relay Configuration for MGCP" in Chapter 10.

SG3

Cisco voice gateways configured for either T.38 or Cisco fax relay can have problems with Super G3 (SG3) fax devices. SG3 fax devices implement a different negotiation procedure and modulation that is not supported by Cisco gateways using fax relay as the transport method.

Often, an SG3 problem will present itself as simply fax call failures between the SG3 fax machine and one or more other fax machines. Occasionally, the problem may even be intermittent. Although SG3 interoperability problems with fax relay on Cisco voice gateways are not exceedingly common, you should be prepared to troubleshoot them.

There are three different ways to handle Super G3 fax devices when fax relay is being used on Cisco voice gateways:

- Disable Super G3 on the fax machines.
- Use modem passthrough as the transport method for SG3 calls.
- Use the Cisco IOS voice gateway feature Fax Relay Support for SG3 Fax Machines at G3 Speeds, which is also commonly referred to as SG3 Spoofing. This is enabled by the IOS command **fax-relay sg3-to-g3** for H.323, SIP, and SCCP and **mgcp fax-relay sg3-to-g3** for MCCP.

All these SG3 solutions are discussed in more detail in the section "Super G3" in Chapter 7. The best way to address SG3 fax support is during the design stage. Discovering SG3 interoperability problems later on can limit some of your options.

If you suspect that SG3 is causing fax failures, the first step is to confirm that SG3 is even being attempted for fax calls. For the terminating fax machine, this is quite easy. Call the fax machine and listen to the first tone that is played. This tone will be either a CED tone from a normal G3 fax call or an ANSam, which indicates an SG3 fax machine. The CED tone is a flat 2100 Hz tone. Although the ANSam is also a 2100 Hz tone, it also has phase reversals present. These phase reversals in the 2100 Hz tone of an ANSam sound like rhythmic clicks or pops that occur about every half a second. If an ANSam is heard when you call a fax machine, you know that the fax machine is trying to negotiate an SG3 call.

The next step is to disable SG3 on both fax machines. If the fax calls continue to fail, you can rule out SG3 as the cause of the problem. If the calls start succeeding, you are more than likely running into an SG3 interoperability problem with fax relay. At this point, you must decide whether SG3 spoofing, modem passthrough, or manual disablement of the SG3 feature on individual fax machines is the best way to resolve your SG3 issue.

Since the release of Cisco IOS 12.4(4)T, which introduced the SG3 spoofing feature, SG3 is always forced to G3 speeds by the voice gateway itself. Whenever fax relay is enabled on an IOS voice gateway in IOS 12.4(4)T and later, the SG3 spoofing feature is also enabled by default. The calling menu (CM) message that is integral to the initial SG3 negotiation is squelched by the SG3 spoofing feature so that the only option is a fallback to normal G3 speeds that are compatible with fax relay.

NOTE   The SG3 spoofing feature is intelligent enough to block only an SG3 CM message and not block the CM messages used by high-speed modem calls. This allows for features such as modem passthrough and Cisco modem relay to be configured for high-speed modem calls while the SG3 spoofing feature is also enabled.

The only SG3 solution that allows for fax machines to communicate at their native SG3 speeds up to 33.6 Kbps is the NSE-based modem passthrough feature. You can enable the modem passthrough transport option to handle SG3 faxes in conjunction with fax relay for normal G3 faxes as demonstrated in Example 10-2 in Chapter 10. However, make sure that the SG3 spoofing feature has been disabled; otherwise, the SG3 CM will continue to be blocked, and the SG3 fax call will not be transported by modem passthrough.

Debugging T.30 Fax Messaging

The most frequently used tool for troubleshooting fax relay problems is the IOS command **debug fax relay t30 all-level-1**. This command displays the T.30 messaging that is passing through the Cisco voice gateway from the perspective of the gateway's DSP. Output that is equivalent to this IOS command can be found on Cisco non-IOS gateways using the procedures discussed at the end of this section.

Before using this command, you should have already determined that the Cisco voice gateways are properly switching over to either T.38 or Cisco fax relay. Otherwise, this debug command might not provide any output. The command **debug fax relay t30 all-level-1** should be used only for troubleshooting post-switchover T.38 and Cisco fax relay problems.

Before looking at the output from **debug fax relay t30 all-level-1**, it is important to understand the direction of the debug messages. Figure 12-20 illustrates how the T.30 debug messages are tagged from a directional perspective by the DSP.

Figure 12-20 *Directional Notation of T.30 Messages as Shown in **debug fax relay t30 all-level-1***

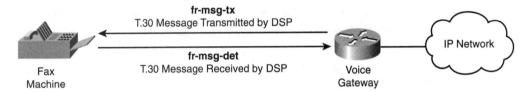

As diagrammed in Figure 12-20, all the messages that are output from **debug fax relay t30 all-level-1** are shown from the DSP's point of view as it faces the telephony leg or the gateway's physical voice port. A T.30 message preceded by **fr-msg-tx** signifies an outgoing message from the DSP, and an **fr-msg-det** means that a message has been detected by the DSP in the inbound direction.

Example 12-66 shows the output from the command **debug fax relay t30 all-level-1** for a two-page fax transaction. All of these T.30 message types were discussed earlier in the book, so see the pertinent sections in Chapter 2 for more information about a specific message listed in the debug output.

Example 12-66 *debug fax relay t30 all-level-1 Command Output for a Two Page Fax Transaction*

```
Apr 26 12:15:22.578: 0/0/0 (39)  653761544 fr-entered=10(ms)
    timestamp=653762364 fr-msg-det CSI
    timestamp=653763164 fr-msg-det NSF
    timestamp=653763964 fr-msg-det DIS
    timestamp=653766374 fr-msg-tx TSI
    timestamp=653767174 fr-msg-tx DCS
    timestamp=653772244 fr-msg-det CFR
    timestamp=653824474 fr-msg-tx MPS
    timestamp=653826014 fr-msg-det MCF
    timestamp=653851074 fr-msg-tx EOP
    timestamp=653852634 fr-msg-det MCF
    timestamp=653854804 fr-msg-tx DCN
Apr 26 12:16:56.170: 0/0/0 (39)  653855134 fr-end-dcn
```

The output from the command **debug fax relay t30 all-level-1** contains a lot of information in just a few lines. Immediately, you can tell the direction of the call. The **CSI**, **NSF**, and **DIS** messages are always sent by the terminating fax device. In the case of Example 12-66, these messages are marked **fr-msg-det**, which means that they are incoming into the telephony port of this gateway. Subsequently, you now know that this is the terminating gateway.

The debug output in Example 12-66 tells you that this was a non-ECM fax call. When the ECM feature is not enabled, **MPS** messages signal the end of pages and **EOP** signals that no additional pages remain to be sent. The output for an ECM fax call is shown next in Example 12-67.

In addition, you can see that following the **MPS** and **EOP** messages, **MCF** messages are returned. This indicates that pages were successfully exchanged between the two fax devices. At the end of the debug, there is a graceful disconnect ending with the **DCN** message. Basically, Example 12-66 epitomizes a typical, successful non-ECM fax call.

TIP

The output from the IOS command **debug fax relay t30 all-level-1** displays only the low-speed T.30 messages. High-speed messaging such as trainings and page transmissions are not shown. Therefore, if you see a CFR message in the debug output, you can deduce that the training was sent and came through without any problems despite not being able to see the high-speed TCF message. If you see an MCF message, you know that page information was successfully received.

When an ECM fax call takes place, the output from the command **debug fax relay t30 all-level-1** contains some minor changes. Because ECM breaks pages down into sections or partial pages, each section is followed by a Partial Page Sent (**PPS**) message. If **PPS** messages are seen in the output of **debug fax relay t30 all-level-1**, you know that an ECM call has occurred. Example 12-67 highlights the output from the command **debug fax relay t30 all-level-1** for a two-page ECM fax call.

Example 12-67   *debug fax relay t30 all-level-1 Command Output for a Two-Page ECM Fax Transaction*

```
Apr 26 12:11:31.930: 0/0/0 (37)  653530902 fr-entered=10(ms)
     timestamp=653531692 fr-msg-det CSI
     timestamp=653532492 fr-msg-det NSF
     timestamp=653533292 fr-msg-det DIS
     timestamp=653535722 fr-msg-tx TSI
     timestamp=653536522 fr-msg-tx DCS
     timestamp=653541592 fr-msg-det CFR
     timestamp=653585622 fr-msg-tx PPS
     timestamp=653587272 fr-msg-det MCF
     timestamp=653600032 fr-msg-tx PPS
     timestamp=653601692 fr-msg-det MCF
     timestamp=653614262 fr-msg-tx PPS
     timestamp=653615932 fr-msg-det MCF
     timestamp=653618102 fr-msg-tx DCN
Apr 26 12:12:59.474: 0/0/0 (37)  653618442 fr-end-dcn
```

The command **debug fax relay t30 all-level-1** is also useful in diagnosing a number of different fax problems. For example, Example 12-68 highlights a common fax problem involving repeated Failure to Train (**FTT**) messages.

Example 12-68 *debug fax relay t30 all-level-1 Command Output Illustrating Corrupted Training Sequences*

```
*Jul 17 08:07:34.397: 3/0 (342)  7397896 fr-entered=10(ms)
    timestamp=7405782 fr-msg-det NSF
    timestamp=7406932 fr-msg-det CSI
    timestamp=7407622 fr-msg-det DIS
    timestamp=7410702 fr-msg-tx TSI
    timestamp=7411842 fr-msg-tx DCS
    timestamp=7415832 fr-msg-det FTT
    timestamp=7419122 fr-msg-tx DCS
    timestamp=7423112 fr-msg-det FTT
    timestamp=7426382 fr-msg-tx DCS
    timestamp=7430362 fr-msg-det FTT
    timestamp=7433642 fr-msg-tx DCS
    timestamp=7437642 fr-msg-det FTT
*Jul 17 08:08:24.123: 3/0 (342)  7447632 fr-end   cause unknown 0x4
```

Example 12-68 shows a problem where the fax training is getting corrupted and then rejected by the terminating fax machine. The most common cause of a problem such as this is physical errors such as slips on one of the telephony legs of the call.

TIP   When using the command **debug fax relay t30 all-level-1** on voice gateways with many simultaneous fax relay calls occurring, the output can be confusing to read because all the fax messaging for all calls will be displayed together. In these situations, run the debug command for only the specific called or calling number that you are interested in with the commands **debug fax relay t30 called-number** or **debug fax relay t30 calling-number**.

Another example of the variety of problems that can be seen with the **debug fax relay t30 all-level-1** command is shown in Example 12-69. Here you can see that messages from the terminating fax machine are being repeated because there is never a response from the originating fax machine.

Example 12-69 *debug fax relay t30 all-level-1 Command Output Showing Messages Only from the Terminating Fax Machine*

```
*Apr 23 13:52:43.509: 0/1/1:23  211162261 fr-entered=10(ms)
    timestamp=211166931 fr-msg-tx CSI
    timestamp=211167561 fr-msg-tx DIS
    timestamp=211172031 fr-msg-tx CSI
    timestamp=211172651 fr-msg-tx DIS
    timestamp=211177121 fr-msg-tx CSI
```

Example 12-69 *debug fax relay t30 all-level-1 Command Output Showing Messages Only from the Terminating Fax Machine (Continued)*

```
          timestamp=211177751 fr-msg-tx DIS
          timestamp=211182211 fr-msg-tx CSI
          timestamp=211182841 fr-msg-tx DIS
          timestamp=211187311 fr-msg-tx CSI
          timestamp=211187931 fr-msg-tx DIS
          timestamp=211192341 fr-msg-tx CSI
          timestamp=211192971 fr-msg-tx DIS
          timestamp=211197371 fr-msg-tx CSI
          timestamp=211198001 fr-msg-tx DIS
         timestamp=211202401 fr-msg-tx DCN
```

In Example 12-69, the **CSI** and **DIS** messages from the terminating fax machine are being transmitted to the originating fax machine. However, there is never a response detected by this originating voice gateway from the originating fax machine.

In the case of the debug output shown in Example 12-69, the reason that this voice gateway is not detecting any messages from the originating fax machine is because of a levels problem. The incoming fax messages from the originating fax machine are too loud and are not understood by the originating voice gateway's DSP.

Although not all levels problems present themselves in this manner, too strong of a signal level can make fax messages unreadable by the voice gateway's DSP. In the case of Example 12-69, adding a decibel drop between the originating fax machine and the originating gateway resolved this issue. For more information about signal levels and loss planning for faxes and modems, refer back to the section "Loss Planning" in this chapter.

TIP   Additional fax problems can be diagnosed from the output of the **debug fax relay t30 all-level-1** command. One problem involves an NSF/NSS scenario where fax devices may try to engage in proprietary transactions that break fax relay. Example 12-72 highlights the debugs seen with this issue in the section "NSF/NSS" later in this chapter.

Another problem that can be diagnosed with the **debug fax relay t30 all-level-1** command is too much delay between the fax endpoints. See Example 12-73 in the section "Handling High Delay" later in this chapter to view sample debug output of this issue.

Non-IOS gateways such as the 6608 and VG248 are also able to display the same information as the IOS command **debug fax relay t30 all-level-1**. On the 6608 Catalyst blade, the Dick Tracy troubleshooting utility must be used to set the appropriate traces. For more information about the Dick Tracy utility, see the 6608 portion of the "Telephony Troubleshooting" section earlier in this chapter.

The following settings should be used in Dick Tracy for debugging Cisco fax relay calls: **6 set mask 0x323** and **6 set fr-debug 24 1**. These settings provide key DSP information and the T.30 messaging. The T.30 messaging shown with these commands is practically identical to the output from the **debug fax relay t30 all-level-1** command on IOS voice gateways. Example 12-70 highlights just the T.30 messages obtained from the **6 set mask 0x323** and **6 set fr-debug 24 1** settings using the Dick Tracy utility.

Example 12-70 *6608 Dick Tracy **6 set mask 0x323** and **6 set fr-debug 24 1** Command Output Showing T.30 Messages*

```
22:06:37.110 (FAX) DSP<0> Chan<2> ->    2135480 fr-msg-tx  NSF
22:06:38.090 (FAX) DSP<0> Chan<2> ->    2136460 fr-msg-tx  CSI
22:06:38.790 (FAX) DSP<0> Chan<2> ->    2137160 fr-msg-tx  DIS
22:06:41.920 (FAX) DSP<0> Chan<2> ->    2140290 fr-msg-det TSI
22:06:42.640 (FAX) DSP<0> Chan<2> ->    2141010 fr-msg-det DCS
22:06:47.160 (FAX) DSP<0> Chan<2> ->    2145530 fr-msg-tx  FTT
22:06:50.120 (FAX) DSP<0> Chan<2> ->    2148490 fr-msg-det TSI
22:06:50.840 (FAX) DSP<0> Chan<2> ->    2149210 fr-msg-det DCS
22:06:55.570 (FAX) DSP<0> Chan<2> ->    2153940 fr-msg-tx  CFR
22:06:58.570 (FAX) DSP<0> Chan<2> ->    2153940 fr-msg-det EOP
22:07:02.480 (FAX) DSP<0> Chan<2> ->    2184870 fr-msg-tx  MCF
22:07:05.450 (FAX) DSP<0> Chan<2> ->    2187840 fr-msg-det DCN
```

In Example 12-70, you can see that Dick Tracy uses the same directional notation for the directions of the T.30 messages as the IOS command **debug fax relay t30 all-level-1**. Messages coming into the DSP on the T1 or E1 port are coded as **fr-msg-det**, and outbound messages are shown as **fr-msg-tx**. In addition, the DSP number and channel number are shown as **DSP<0>** and **Chan<2>**, respectively. If a number of fax calls are occurring simultaneously, this extra information allows you to accurately follow the debug messages for a specific DSP and channel.

Example 12-70 also displays how Cisco voice gateways keep the bandwidth consumed by the fax call less than that of the voice codec that is used to initially establish the VoIP call. In this case, the voice codec is G.729, which consumes 8000 bps of bandwidth. Cisco voice gateways by default will then enforce a V.29 modulation, which includes both 9600 bps and 7200 bps speeds.

The originating fax device will always start with the fastest speed within a modulation type. So, a 9600 bps training is sent; but to force the originating fax machine to train down to the 7200 bps speed, the Cisco voice gateway corrupts the 9600 bps training sequence. This is the reason for the **FTT** in Example 12-70. The next training sequence is at 7200 bps, which the voice gateway allows to pass untouched, and it is confirmed with a **CFR**.

For the VG248 non-IOS gateway, you can view the T.30 fax messaging by setting the DSP logging level to **trace** mode. In addition to the T.30 messages, this DSP trace captures other information, too. For the sake of brevity, only the T.30 messages from the DSP trace are shown in Example 12-71.

Example 12-71 *VG248 DSP Trace Showing T.30 Messages*

```
11 23:09:25 14 I FaxRelay13 2591101559 fr-entered (10 ms)
21 23:09:26 13 I FaxRelay13 2591102420 fr-msg-det CSI
26 23:09:27 14 I FaxRelay13 2591103220 fr-msg-det DIS
45 23:09:29 13 I FaxRelay13 2591105850 fr-msg-tx TSI
54 23:09:30 14 I FaxRelay13 2591106650 fr-msg-tx DCS
101 23:09:35 14 I FaxRelay13 2591111730 fr-msg-det CFR
148 23:10:24 15 I FaxRelay13 2591160460 fr-msg-tx EOP
172 23:10:25 14 I FaxRelay13 2591162010 fr-msg-det MCF
194 23:10:28 15 I FaxRelay13 2591164580 fr-msg-tx DCN
205 23:10:28 14 I FaxRelay13 2591164920 fr-end 1
```

Example 12-71 shows how the VG248 provides the same output as the 6608 and the IOS
gateways with regard to viewing the T.30 messages. This uniformity between platforms
ensures that if you know how to read the T.30 messages on one platform you can understand
the messages on the other Cisco voice gateways, too.

Analyzing T.38 Fax Relay Packet Captures

Packet capture programs such as the freely available Wireshark program can decode T.38
fax relay and even graphically display the fax messaging that is being transported by T.38.
For more information about Wireshark and how to acquire this software program, refer
back to the section "IP Troubleshooting" in this chapter.

TIP

Sometimes the T.38 fax relay information in Wireshark is not displayed properly by default,
and this usually occurs when NSEs are used for the switchover. If the T.38 packets are
shown as RTP protocol packets and flagged in the "Info" field as "Unknown RTP version
0," you need to configure Wireshark to interpret the T.38 fax relay packets correctly.

The first step in configuring Wireshark to properly display T.38 fax relay packets is to save
the packets flagged as RTP into a separate file. In the "Filter" box toward the top of the
Wireshark window, enter "rtp" and then click "Apply." This will display only the RTP
packets. Save this RTP-filtered capture by selecting "Save As" from the "File" menu at the
top of the screen. Make sure that under the "Packet Range" of the "Save As" dialog box you
select "All Packets" and "Displayed." Now click "Save", and then open this newly saved
file in Wireshark.

After opening the RTP filtered capture, you will no longer see any signaling information
and the T.38 packets will probably still be flagged as RTP. To decode the RTP as T.38, you
need to do the following. Highlight one of the T.38 packets. Then, under the "Analyze"
menu at the top of the window, select "Decode As." In the new "Decode As" window that
is created, scroll down and select "T.38" from the list of protocols. Beside UDP, you can
also select "Both" so that the program will decode the UDP packets in both directions as

T.38 fax relay. Click "OK" in the "Decode As" window, and Wireshark will reprocess the capture file, displaying the T.38 packets correctly. The only drawback of this procedure is that the true RTP packets that occur before the T.38 switchover will now be incorrectly interpreted as T.38, too.

After loading a T.38 fax relay capture into Wireshark, select the "Statistics" menu from the top of the main window and click "VoIP Calls." A window will now display listing all the VoIP calls found in the packet capture. Select the call that contains the T.38 session, and then click "Graph" at the bottom of the screen. Figure 12-21 shows part of the graph from Wireshark for a T.38 fax relay call.

Figure 12-21 *Wireshark Graphical Display of a T.38 Fax Relay Call*

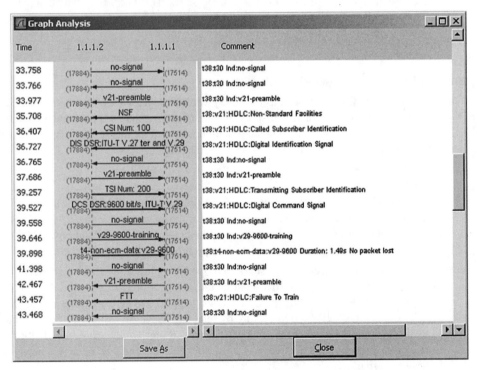

The graphical display of the T.38 fax relay call shown in Figure 12-21 is much easier to read than paging through hundreds if not thousands of lines of packets to see what is happening. The top of the display provides the IP addresses of the originating and terminating voice gateways. You can then see the T.38 encapsulated fax messaging flowing back and forth between the gateways.

The column on the left side provides the time of the fax message, in case you want to quickly find the packet containing that fax message in the capture file. The column on the right side of the graph provides additional information about each fax message and even keeps track of any packet loss during trainings and page transmissions.

TIP	At the bottom of the screen shot in Figure 12-21 is a "Save As" button. Clicking this button enables you to save an ASCII text file portraying this graphical T.38 call information. This feature is useful for e-mailing results to others or for just saving a quick copy of the T.38 transaction information for future reference.

If you need to quickly analyze T.38 packet captures, looking through the T.38 message transaction graphically saves you a lot of time. You can zero in quickly on problems and not spend lots of time looking at T.38 packets individually.

NSF/NSS

Both T.38 and Cisco fax relay can demodulate and effectively transport fax information because all G3 fax devices adhere to the same specifications. However, if the fax machines involved in a fax call decide to execute proprietary communications or encodings that fall outside of the G3 standards, fax relay can no longer transport the fax information. Fax relay on Cisco voice gateways supports only G3 compliant fax calls.

The means by which fax devices can signal the support of proprietary encodings is through the use of the Recommendation T.30 NSF message. As discussed in the section "DIS, NSF, and CSI Messages" in Chapter 2, an NSF message is composed of a separate country and vendor code. If this NSF country and vendor code from the terminating fax machine is recognized by the originating fax machine as being capable of proprietary communications, a nonstandard facilities setup (**NSS**) message is sent. At this point, proprietary encodings may be exchanged between the fax machines, which deviate from the G3 fax standards. If this call is taking place through Cisco voice gateways configured for fax relay, the call will more than likely fail. Example 12-72 shows how a proprietary fax transaction may appear when using the IOS command **debug fax relay t30 all-level-1**.

Example 12-72 *debug fax relay t30 all-level-1 Command Output Showing a Proprietary Fax Transaction*

```
*Apr  6 20:58:43.303: 1/1:15 (663)  3185794704 fr-entered (10ms)
   timestamp=3185798534 fr-msg-tx  NSF
   timestamp=3185799474 fr-msg-tx  DIS
   timestamp=3185800984 fr-msg-det NSS
   timestamp=3185801304 fr-msg-det DCS
```

The key message in the failed call in Example 12-72 is the presence of the **NSS**. Whenever this message is seen when fax calls are failing, it is reasonable to assume that proprietary communications are occurring that are incompatible with fax relay.

The fix in this situation is to override the value of the NSF sent from the terminating fax machine. By default, this value is overwritten by IOS gateways to a country code setting of US and a vendor code of Telogy. However, there have been rare cases where even this coding has run into problems. Setting the NSF value to all 0s is the safest approach to ensure that proprietary fax encodings do not occur.

On Cisco IOS gateways, you can use the dial-peer level command **fax nsf** for the H.323 and SIP voice signaling protocols and **mgcp fax t38 nsf** for MGCP. Despite the keyword **t38** in the **mgcp** command syntax, it is also valid for Cisco fax relay.

The only caveat for using these commands on the IOS gateways involves the 5350/5400/ 5850 platforms that use the NextPort DSP resources. Some IOS versions for these platforms no longer support the **fax nsf** command in the CLI. Other IOS versions contain the command, but it does not actually overwrite the NSF value with the user-configured values. Instead, these platforms always overwrite the NSF value with a string of 0xff characters, which is just as effective as overwriting the NSF with 0s.

On the 6608 non-IOS voice gateway, the NSF value is set through the gateway configuration screen GUI on Unified CM. You can enter a specific value for the country and vendor codes in the fields titled **Non Standard Facilities Country Code** and **Non Standard Facilities Vendor Code**. See the section "6608 Catalyst Blade Fax Relay Configuration" in Chapter 10 for any additional assistance in setting the NSF country and vendor code values.

The VG248 non-IOS gateway also provides the ability to alter the NSF value but with much more limited options. On the **Port specific parameters** screen, the **Fax relay NSF** parameter contains two options: **preserve value** or **override with 000000**. Configuring the **override with 000000** option should be used for resolving any issues where proprietary fax communications could be adversely affecting fax relay.

Handling High Delay

Fax machines, like most other modulated communication devices, were designed for PSTN environments where the delay time between when a message is sent and when it is received is minimal. Nonetheless, fax machines tend to have quite a high tolerance for delay. Even with the introduction of IP networks and their inherently much higher delay times compared to the PSTN, delay does not usually affect fax transmissions. Only certain high-delay scenarios, such as satellite hops or multiple VoIP networks, can introduce enough delay to cause fax failures.

Because measuring end-to-end delay through both VoIP and PSTN environments can be difficult, it is important to be able to recognize high-delay scenarios through other means. The best way to know that high delay is causing a fax problem is through analyzing the T.30

messages with the IOS command **debug fax relay t30 all-level-1**, as illustrated in Example 12-73. Viewing these same T.30 messages in non-IOS gateways has been discussed previously in this chapter in the section "Debugging T.30 Fax Messaging."

Example 12-73 *debug fax relay t30 all-level-1 Command Output Illustrating a Fax Failure Due to High Delay*

```
Jun 18 13:08:12.766 JST: 1/1:23 (210169)  490682740 fr-entered (10ms)
Jun 18 13:08:13.897 JST: 1/1:23 (210169)  490683878 fr-msg-det NSF
Jun 18 13:08:14.621 JST: 1/1:23 (210169)  490684598 fr-msg-det CSI
Jun 18 13:08:15.337 JST: 1/1:23 (210169)  490685318 fr-msg-det DIS
Jun 18 13:08:18.388 JST: 1/1:23 (210169)  490688368 fr-msg-tx  DCS
Jun 18 13:08:21.947 JST: 1/1:23 (210169)  490691918 fr-msg-det CSI
Jun 18 13:08:22.659 JST: 1/1:23 (210169)  490692638 fr-msg-det DIS
Jun 18 13:08:25.758 JST: 1/1:23 (210169)  490695738 fr-msg-tx  DCS
Jun 18 13:08:29.273 JST: 1/1:23 (210169)  490699248 fr-msg-det NSF
Jun 18 13:08:29.749 JST: 1/1:23 (210169)  490699728 fr-msg-det CSI
Jun 18 13:08:30.465 JST: 1/1:23 (210169)  490700448 fr-msg-det DIS
Jun 18 13:08:33.648 JST: 1/1:23 (210169)  490703628 fr-msg-tx  DCS
```

While Example 12-73 displays the typical T.30 messages, they start simply repeating themselves instead of proceeding with a training and confirmation. The critical messages to look at are the **DIS** and **DCS** messages because these are mandatory T.30 messages (whereas the others are optional).

The answering fax machine sends its **DIS** and the originating fax machine answers with a **DCS**, and then a training sequence. Recall that only low-speed T.30 messages appear in this debug, but a high-speed training always follows a DCS. Instead of a confirmation (CFR) to the training being sent by the answering fax machine, you see another **DIS**. The answering fax machine sends the **DIS** because it did not receive the **DCS** message in time. This behavior keeps repeating itself, and the two fax machines never synchronize their messaging and execute a successful negotiation before giving up and disconnecting the call.

The specific timer on the answering fax machine that is expiring before the DCS is received is known as the T4 timer. This timer should be set to a value of approximately 3 seconds, but some fax brands seem to have a "quicker" T4 timer than other brands. In Example 12-73, you can see that the timestamps between the DIS and DCS messages are showing slightly more than 3 seconds. Whenever message response times are around this T4 timer expiration value of 3 seconds, delay can be adversely affecting your fax calls. You can find more information about the T4 timer and its expiration in the section "Important G3 Timers" in Chapter 2.

One of the reasons that some T4 timers seem to expire quicker than others is because different fax brands may reset their timers based on different criteria. For example, some brands may reset their timer as soon as the fax flags of the DCS are detected, whereas others will ignore the fax flags and wait for the beginning of the actual message. This can cause a difference in how long the fax machine will wait for an expected message.

If the delay is too high, not much can be done from the voice gateway's perspective to resolve the problem. However, for delay problems where trimming back a half a second or less will make a difference, adjusting the playout or jitter buffers for the fax relay call can help.

CAUTION   Be aware that lowering the fax playout buffers can expose your fax calls to jitter problems. Most VoIP networks are designed for low jitter, so setting the fax playout buffers to 100 ms or possibly even less should not be a problem. If you are already familiar with the jitter characteristics of your network, you will already know the minimum playout value to set. Otherwise, you may want to monitor the adaptive playout buffer settings through the use of the **show call active voice brief** or **show voice call** *port* command for a few voice calls to determine a baseline of approximately how low you can safely set the fax relay playout buffer.

When a voice call transitions to fax relay on Cisco voice gateways, the playout buffer changes from a usually small, adaptive buffer to a larger, fixed buffer of 300 ms by default. This 300-ms playout buffer per gateway for fax relay calls adds an additional 600 ms of round-trip delay per call. By changing the fax playout buffer values, you can trim down this 600 ms of buffer delay, assuming that the jitter in your network does not exceed your newly configured value.

On IOS gateways, the fax playout buffer is changed with the following commands: **playout-delay fax** *value* for H.323 and SIP voice signaling protocols and **mgcp playout fax** *value* for MGCP. For the H.323 and SIP voice signaling protocols, you can configure this command under the voice port or under the VoIP dial-peer, which is the recommended way.

For the 6608 non-IOS voice gateway, the fax relay playout buffer is not adjustable and is fixed at 300 ms. The VG248 gateway has a configurable **Fax relay playout delay** parameter under the Advanced Settings menu. The range of values accepted for the **Fax relay playout delay** parameter is between 100 and 700 ms.

The playout buffer adjustments discussed in this section apply only to fax relay. Fax passthrough and modem passthrough do not use the same playout buffer scheme. However, because passthrough calls typically use a buffer setting based off of the voice playout buffer, the playout buffer for passthrough is almost always much lower than it is for fax relay. For this reason, large amounts of delay may negatively affect fax relay calls more than passthrough calls. If the amount of delay is large enough to affect passthrough calls, there is little you can do about the problem from a gateway perspective. As with large amounts of delay that cannot be mitigated by changing the fax playout buffers in fax relay, passthrough calls suffering from high delay must be rerouted to a path with lower end-to-end delay.

Advanced Troubleshooting for Modem Relay

Compared to fax relay, modem relay has limited troubleshooting resources on the IOS voice gateways themselves. Troubleshooting debug commands such as **debug modem relay** and its various options produce output that is useful only to developers familiar with the Cisco implementation of modem relay. This debug command output is not decodable by end users. Therefore, much of the troubleshooting for modem relay occurs on the modem endpoints themselves and through the viewing of statistical information about the call on the voice gateways.

Checking the Modem Endpoints

Modems are capable of a variety of configuration options, and some of these options can cause the modem calls to fail over a modem relay connection. For example, Cisco modem relay supports only the V.34 modulation. Any modem communication that is not capable of V.34 will fail to use Cisco modem relay as its transport through the VoIP network.

Assuming that the information in the rest of the chapter did not resolve your Cisco modem relay problem, you should look at the modem endpoints to ensure their configuration is compatible. Looking at a modem's configuration relies on establishing a connection with the modem's user interface. If you need more information about how to communicate with a modem using the user interface, see the section "User Interface" in Chapter 1.

Just about all modems have a default configuration that is typically pretty robust and is optimized to operate the best in commonly configured conditions and topologies. This default configuration is always a good place to start when troubleshooting modem communication problems over IP.

Often, a modem will be using a custom initialization (init) string that was configured to optimize performance. The problem is that this init string could unintentionally configure the modem for a parameter that is not supported by modem relay.

If you are having problems connecting over a Cisco modem relay connection, start by replacing the init string with the default factory configuration settings. On most modems, you can do this by just issuing the **AT&F** command. Other modems have more than one default, so in that case the command **AT&F1** is usually the right choice. To be absolutely sure, check your modem's manual.

The appropriate command for setting your modem back to its factory defaults should now be issued on both modem endpoints, and another modem relay call should be attempted. Sometimes, a simple change such as this can make the Cisco modem relay connection work.

If there are still issues with the modems working over Cisco modem relay, more in-depth modem configuration needs to take place. Because modem commands vary by model and manufacturer, this will involve consulting the manual for your modem brand to look up the correct configuration commands. Unfortunately, the factory defaults of some modem brands might not necessarily enable certain settings that are required for Cisco modem relay.

The two big requirements for Cisco modem relay are the V.34 modulation and V.42 error correction. If the modem is not configured for or is not capable of these settings, Cisco modem relay will not work. For more information about V.34 and a sample call breakdown, see the section "Modem Call Analysis" in Chapter 1. For more information about the V.42 error correction protocol, see the section "Error Control" in Chapter 1.

TIP   Be aware that Cisco modem relay can handle the V.90 modulation, too, but only by forcing it to negotiate down to V.34. However, to avoid unnecessary complications, it is recommended to hard code the modem endpoints to only attempt V.34 from the start.

In most cases, resetting the modem back to its factory defaults and then enabling V.34 and V.42 should make the modem compatible with Cisco modem relay. If problems are still experienced at this point, it is worth testing a pair of hardware-based modems for their added reliability and robustness, as discussed in the section "Hardware Versus Software Modems" in Chapter 1.

Hardware modems are generally much better at handling a variety of network conditions and impairments than software modems. For this reason, it is always a good test to confirm whether hardware modems work successfully over Cisco modem relay connections that can be subject to less favorable conditions than a pure PSTN connection. Remember to make sure that all hardware modems are also configured for V.34 and V.42.

TIP   In case your Cisco modem relay connection terminates on a gateway connected to the PSTN, Cisco has a dial-in lab in San Jose where test calls can be placed. This provides you another testing point when troubleshooting Cisco modem relay problems. Refer to the document "Customer Dial-In Lab (San Jose, USA)" (Document ID: 91756) at Cisco.com for a listing of the dial-in numbers. Your first choice should be the V.34 dial-in number, but the V.90 numbers should also work when using a Cisco modem relay connection.

When you are certain that the modem endpoints are set up correctly, it is a good idea to check out the local loop or the connection between the modem and Cisco voice gateway. Problems or impairments in the local loop are typically the biggest cause of modem relay issues. One test that can prove helpful is to try modem passthrough rather than modem relay. If modem passthrough also fails, a local loop problem is possibly affecting both of these transport methods. You can verify whether this is the case by trying a different local loop if possible.

Debugging Modem Relay

Because the modem relay debugs in IOS gateways are meant for developer-level decoding, the main troubleshooting command to use for modem relay problems is the **show modem relay statistics** command. This command contains a number of options, but the most useful are **phy**, which provides physical layer statistics, and **pkt**, which lets you view HDLC framing information.

The command **show modem relay statistics phy** provides a glimpse at the physical or modulation layer of the modem relay call. Example 12-74 illustrates the output from **show modem relay statistics phy**.

Example 12-74   *show modem relay statistics phy Command Output*

```
fax_2811# show modem relay statistics phy

ID:11DB

Physical Layer Statistics
        num_local_retrain=0 num_remote_retrain=0
        num_local_speed_shift=1 num_remote_speed_shift=1
        num_sync_loss=0

        Total Modem Relay Call Legs = 1
```

When a **retrain** or **speed shift** is detected, the appropriate counters are incremented for the **show modem relay statistics phy** command in Example 12-74. The retrains and speedshifts are tracked for both the local and remote sides. The local side in this case will be the gateway's DSP that is acting like a modem and communicating with the client modem or remote side across the telephony leg.

Retrains can dramatically affect modem performance and ideally should never increment. Speedshifts can quickly lower and raise the transmission speeds and are typically based on changes in line quality. They are not necessarily bad unless they are continuously occurring. For more information about retrains and speedshifts, see the section "Retrains and Speedshifts" in Chapter 1.

If retrains are a problem, the cause is almost always in the local loop connection between the endpoint modem and its locally connected voice gateway. Incorrect loss levels and poor or deteriorating line quality can cause error thresholds to be exceeded, which in turn leads to retrains.

To view low-level errors on the modem relay connection, you can use the command **show modem relay statistics pkt**. Recall that with V.42 error correction, HDLC frames are used to transport data across the connection in a synchronous fashion. As detailed in Example 12-75, the command **show modem relay statistics pkt** provides a view of low-level HDLC errors that can lead to speedshifts and retrains.

Example 12-75 *show modem relay statistics pkt Command Output*

```
fax_2811# show modem relay stat pkt

ID:11DB

Packetizer Statistics
        frames_inprogress=0 good_crc_frames=817
        bad_crc_frames=0 frame_aborts=0
        hdlc_sync_detects=2 hdlc_sync_loss_detects=1
        bad_frames=0

        Total Modem Relay Call Legs = 1
```

In Example 12-75, error counters such as **bad crc frames**, **frame aborts**, and **bad frames** indicate problems in the modem connection. Like retrains, these errors are almost always in the local loop connection on the telephony side of the voice gateway.

Advanced Troubleshooting for Cisco Text Relay

If you are already familiar with the general concepts of how a voice gateway feature such as Dual Tone Multi Frequency (DTMF) relay works, Cisco text relay is similar. In both cases, tones are taken from the incoming audio on the telephony side of the call and relayed across the IP network. On the other side, the tones are accurately replayed back into the audio stream out of the far end voice gateway's voice port. The main difference is that with DTMF relay these tones represent DTMF keys, whereas with Cisco text relay the tones are Baudot characters used by text telephones.

Assuming that all the basics have already been covered in the section "Fundamental Troubleshooting" at the beginning of this chapter, the first step in troubleshooting Cisco text relay problems is to confirm that Cisco text relay is enabled for the call. You can use the **show call active voice brief** command as discussed earlier in this chapter in the section "Text Telephony Call Legs" to verify the **TextRelay** status.

After you have confirmed that Cisco text relay has been enabled for a call, two IOS debug commands can help you troubleshoot: **debug voip hpi notification** and **debug voip rtp session text-relay**. As shown in Example 12-76, the best debug for viewing the transmitted and received text characters on an IOS gateway is the command **debug voip hpi notification**.

Example 12-76 *debug voip hpi notification* *Command Output Showing Text Characters*

```
! Output omitted for brevity

May  4 09:29:38.115: //17/C93D52148030/HPI/[0/1:1]/hpi_receive_message:
    Received TTY PKT report
    TEXTRELAY; Snd; 13; 0x4800;
May  4 09:29:38.683: //17/C93D52148030/HPI/[0/1:1]/hpi_receive_message:
    Received TTY PKT report
    TEXTRELAY; Snd; 14; 0x4500;
May  4 09:29:41.223: //17/C93D52148030/HPI/[0/1:1]/hpi_receive_message:
    Received TTY PKT report
    TEXTRELAY; Snd; 15; 0x4C00;

! Output omitted for brevity

May  4 09:29:51.711: //17/C93D52148030/HPI/[0/1:1]/hpi_receive_message:
    Received TTY PKT report
    TEXTRELAY; Rcv; 33; 0x4200;
May  4 09:29:52.763: //17/C93D52148030/HPI/[0/1:1]/hpi_receive_message:
    Received TTY PKT report
    TEXTRELAY; Rcv; 34; 0x5900;
May  4 09:29:53.675: //17/C93D52148030/HPI/[0/1:1]/hpi_receive_message:
    Received TTY PKT report
    TEXTRELAY; Rcv; 35; 0x4500;
```

The output from the command **debug voip hpi notification** in Example 12-76 displays the individual text characters starting with the keyword **TEXTRELAY**. For large captures, this easily allows you to pull all the characters by simply parsing for all lines that include **TEXTRELAY**.

Following **TEXTRELAY** is the direction of the text character that was captured. Messages showing **Snd** in this field reflect text characters that are being transmitted by the gateway. If **Rcv** is specified rather than **Snd**, the text character in this debug line was received by the voice gateway.

The next parameter after **Snd** or **Rcv** is the sequence number of the Cisco text relay packet. For the text characters that are being sent (**Snd**) in Example 12-76, the sequence numbers are **13**, **14**, and **15**. For the received text characters (**Rcv**), the sequence numbers are **33**, **34**, and **35**.

The last parameter in the **TEXTRELAY** debug line is the actual text character encoded in the ASCII hexadecimal format. Despite at least one level of redundancy always occurring with Cisco text relay, only the primary character is shown with this debug. You will not see any of the redundant characters. When there is not another primary character in the DSP buffer, idle padding of **00** is used for the next character.

Table 12-14 highlights the ASCII characters and their hex values that are supported by the text telephony Baudot character set. Refer to this table whenever you need to quickly convert the ASCII hexadecimal value obtained from the **debug voip hpi notification** to the equivalent Baudot text character.

Table 12-14 *ASCII Characters Supported by the Text Telephony Baudot Character Set*

ASCII Hexadecimal Value	Baudot Character	ASCII Hexadecimal Value	Baudot Character
7	BELL	3F	?
A	LF	41	A
D	CR	42	B
20	Space	43	C
21	!	44	D
22	"	45	E
23	#	46	F
24	$	47	G
26	&	48	H
27	'	49	I
28	(	4A	J
29	)	4B	K
2C	,	4C	L
2D	-	4D	M
2E	.	4E	N
2F	/	4F	O
30	0	50	P
31	1	51	Q
32	2	52	R
33	3	53	S
34	4	54	T
35	5	55	U
36	6	56	V
37	7	57	W
38	8	58	X
39	9	59	Y
3A	:	5A	Z
3B	;		

Applying Table 12-14 to Example 12-76, you can decode the transmitted (**Snd**) ASCII values of **0x48**, **0x45**, and **0x4C** to the Baudot text characters of H, E, and L. The received (**Rcv**) ASCII values of **0x42**, **0x59**, and **0x45** correlate to the Baudot text characters of B, Y, and E.

The Cisco text relay debug command **debug voip rtp session text-relay** is more of a developer-level debug because of the added complication of viewing Cisco text relay information displayed as an RTP packet in hexadecimal form. Nonetheless, you can still quickly obtain some pertinent information from this debug without having to manually decode every hexadecimal value. Example 12-77 displays output from the command **debug voip rtp session text-relay**.

Example 12-77 *debug voip rtp session text-relay Command Output Detailing Cisco Text Relay Packets*

```
May  4 16:50:08.287:            s=VoIP d=DSP payload 0x77 ssrc 0x16B00101 sequence
    0xFB timestamp 0x58A1D679
May  4 16:50:08.287: <<<Rcv> Pt:119     Evt:64    3     247   33    192    Cnt:F7 47
May  4 16:50:08.287: RTP:80 F7 00 FB 58 A1 D6 79 16 B0 01 01 F7 47 40 03 F7 21 C0
    00 77 00 00 48 00 01 45 37 EC C3

May  4 16:50:21.611:            s=DSP d=VoIP payload 0x77 ssrc 0x0 sequence 0x20FE
    timestamp 0xA872F249
May  4 16:50:21.611:            Pt:119     Evt:128   3     119   0     0      Cnt:F7
    25 <Snd>>>
May  4 16:50:21.611: RTP:80 77 20 FE A8 72 F2 49 00 00 00 00 F7 25 80 03 77 00 00
    42 C6 DE 78 C8 22 E1 7D FB 4F BD
```

Cisco text relay uses an RTP payload type of 119, and this is clearly shown in Example 12-77 as **Pt:119**. The direction of the packet is also shown by **<<<Rcv>** for received packets and **<Snd>>>** for packets that are sent.

Because the beginning of the hexadecimal output in Example 12-77 uses an RTP header, the first part of the Cisco text relay packet information is easily decoded. For example, in the first packet, a Synchronization Source (SSRC) value is declared as **ssrc 0x16B00101**, and then this same value is found in the hexadecimal string as **16 B0 01 01**. This also occurs with the RTP timestamp and sequence number being decoded as **timestamp 0x58A1D679** and **sequence 0xFB**. These same values appear in the hexadecimal string as **58 A1 D6 79** and **FB,** respectively. For additional information, take a look at the diagram of the RTP header in Figure 4-4.

Within the RTP payload are the Baudot text characters encoded in a format based on RFC 4351. Both primary and redundant characters can be seen. In the case of the first text relay packet in Example 12-77, the redundant character is **48**, and the primary character is **45**. This part of the hexadecimal trace can be difficult to decode based on the proprietary nature of Cisco text relay. For viewing the characters being sent and received in a text relay call, the command **debug voip hpi notification** is a better choice.

Just as IOS gateways can transmit test tones for loss level planning, they can also originate text telephony tones in the Baudot format. The command for initiating these tones is as follows:

```
test voice port port text-relay {local | network} {baudot45.45 | baudot50} ASCII_hex_
value number_sent
```

A call must be in progress before this command will work. The **local** option sends the tone out the telephony port, and the **network** option sends the tone over the IP leg. A Baudot transmission rate of either 45.45 bps (**baudot45.45**) or 50 bps (**baudot50**) must also be specified. Finally, the ASCII hexadecimal character for a supported Baudot character (*ASCII_hex_value*) along with the number of times this character should be sent (*number_sent*) is configured.

By being able to generate Baudot test tones directly on the gateway, you can test one of the most common causes of text telephony problems. This problem has to do with external noise leaking into the text phone conversation.

Many text telephones use acoustic couplers, and in noisy environments and other situations where the acoustic coupler does not make a good connection with the telephone handset, external noise can cause corrupted Baudot characters. However, by muting one side and using the voice gateway to generate text characters, it is easy to determine what part of the connection is causing problems with the Baudot characters. An environment with a questionable noise level can be removed, and then the voice gateway can generate text characters to see whether the problem is still present.

PCM Traces for Fax and Modem

PCM traces are audio captures of a fax/modem conversation. In the same manner that a VoIP conversation can be recorded, fax and modem calls can be recorded, too. These recordings or PCM traces are almost always required when resolving the most complex fax and modem problems.

Capturing and analyzing PCM traces is not for everyone because of the advanced nature of this troubleshooting technique. In many cases, only engineers with quite a bit of fax/modem knowledge and experience will use PCM traces. However, for those rare cases where they are needed, basic PCM trace knowledge is a good skill for everyone who troubleshoots fax/modems to possess. For this reason, PCM traces are discussed here in an introductory fashion, in case you ever run into a troubleshooting scenario where they are needed.

While fully interpreting PCM traces can be quite challenging, basic interpretation is easily attainable if you have grasped the fundamental fax and modem concepts from Chapters 1 and 2. Analyzing PCM traces can provide you information beyond what is available from packet captures and voice gateway debugs.

Before a PCM trace can be interpreted or analyzed, it must be captured. A few different methods are available for capturing PCM traces, and each has its own advantages and disadvantages. These different PCM capture methods are discussed in the next section, followed by a section discussing how to analyze them.

Capturing PCM Traces

You can obtain a PCM trace in multiple ways. Some ways will be better than others depending on the situation, tools available, and expertise of the person obtaining the capture. Table 12-15 highlights the most commonly used PCM capture methods and notes their specific advantages and disadvantages.

Table 12-15 *PCM Capture Methods*

Capture Method	Description	Advantages	Disadvantages
Cisco PCM capture tool	Uses the DSP within the Cisco IOS gateway itself and creates a proprietary logger file that must be decoded by a Cisco internal program.	• Built directly into the IOS voice gateway • Works for analog and digital voice ports • Provides PCM traces from three different reference points within the DSP • Allows for the capture of multiple calls at the same time	• Requires the logger file to be sent in to Cisco for the extraction of the PCM trace. • Not supported on non-IOS gateways or IOS gateways with NextPort DSP cards such as the AS5350/AS5400. • Does not officially support fax and modem relay calls.
Packet capture PCM extraction	Packet capture software programs such as Wireshark have a feature that extracts the PCM from G.711 calls.	• Makes PCM traces directly from a G.711 packet capture • Captures on the IP side of the voice gateway	• Only works for passthrough calls using the G.711 codec.

continues

Table 12-15 *PCM Capture Methods (Continued)*

Capture Method	Description	Advantages	Disadvantages
Third-party test gear	Third-party test tools such as those made by GL Communications can capture PCM traces from digital voice ports using special cards and software on a PC.	• Monitors the T1/E1 call signaling to intelligently capture calls from an entire T1/E1 span whenever they occur • Hard drive space to store large numbers of captures • Ability to capture and analyze on the same device	• Test gear with PCM capture functionality is expensive. • Gear must be shipped to the location with the problem.

For the capture methods displayed in Table 12-15, the easiest to use is a packet capture PCM extraction. The other methods involving the PCM capture tool and third-party test gear require you to follow a specific setup procedure. In addition, in the case of the Cisco PCM capture tool, a proprietary file has to be decoded by Cisco to obtain the PCM trace itself. However, the packet capture PCM extraction method does not enable you to view the raw fax/modem signals on the telephony side of the gateway, whereas the other methods do. Depending on the issue that you are troubleshooting, this could be a problem. Just be aware that each method listed in Table 12-15 can prove useful when you need to obtain a PCM trace.

Cisco PCM Capture Tool

The Cisco PCM capture tool requires you to enable a feature known as the HPI logger. The HPI logger will then stream the DSP trace information to a file. The steps for enabling the HPI logger on Cisco IOS gateways are as follows:

Step 1 Configure the HPI capture buffer size using the IOS configuration command **voice hpi capture buffer** *size*, where *size* refers to the capture buffer size. This capture buffer is used internally for the DSP messages, and a typical value is **1000000**.

Step 2 Configure the HPI capture destination with the configuration command **voice hpi capture destination** *location*. This command specifies the file location of the HPI logger file. If you want to store the file on the router's internal flash, you can use the configuration command **voice hpi capture**

destination flash:pcm.dat, where **pcm.dat** is the arbitrary name selected in this example for the HPI logger file itself. For storing the file on a TFTP server, the configuration command **voice hpi capture destination tftp://***ip_address***/pcm.dat** can be used, where *ip_address* is the IP address of the TFTP server. If a UNIX-based server is being used with the TFTP option, remember to touch the file on the server and do a chmod to give write permission. An FTP server is also a valid location by using the command **voice hpi capture destination ftp:// ***username***:***password***@***ip_address***/pcm.dat**. The *username* and *password* refer to the login credentials for the FTP server itself. If you are obtaining PCM captures for only one or just a few short calls, often the **flash:** location is the most convenient provided that there is enough space. For capturing many calls or for calls of a long duration, the TFTP and FTP options are preferred because they are less likely to run into file-size restrictions.

Step 3   Enable the PCM capture tool for a specific voice port using the command **test voice port** *port* **pcm-dump caplog** *bit_index* **duration** *time*. The *port* parameter defines the specific port or timeslot in the case of a digital interface for the PCM capture. The *bit_index* defines the bit values for the three locations in the DSP where the capture file is taken: Rin, Sin, and Sout. The Rin location is the incoming PCM information from the IP side before it is processed and played out the voice port by the DSP. Sin is the inbound PCM coming into the voice port before it is processed by the DSP. And, Sout is this same PCM stream after is has been processed by the DSP. The best approach is to grab all of these captures by setting *bit_ index* to a value of 7. The last parameter is the **duration**, with a *time* value in seconds. Setting *time* to a value of 0 keeps the PCM capture tool running indefinitely. To disable the PCM capture tool, use the command **test voice port** *port* **pcm-dump disable**.

TIP   The timeslot of a digital interface that are you wanting to enable a Cisco PCM capture for must be formatted using a particular syntax. The trick for providing the timeslot information in the proper format is to use the same designation for the port as seen with the command **show voice call summary**.

As mentioned in Table 12-15, the Cisco PCM capture tool does not officially support fax or modem relay calls. The most common problem with using the Cisco PCM capture tool with fax and modem relay calls is that not all the PCM traces from the various DSP locations (such as Rin, Sin, and Sout) are fully captured. Even though your mileage may vary when using the Cisco PCM capture tool for fax and modem relay calls, the tool works well for passthrough calls.

Although the Cisco PCM capture tool can extract PCM captures from single or multiple calls, realize that you need to know which voice port or timeslot the call will occur on ahead of time. Otherwise, by the time you see the call on a specific port or timeslot and enable the Cisco PCM capture tool, you will have missed the beginning of the call. Therefore, when dealing with digital interfaces and multiple timeslots, you might need to busy out timeslots on the digital interface to force the call to a particular timeslot for a successful PCM capture.

You can track the function of the PCM capture tool while it runs with the command **show voice hpi capture**. This command will let you know the status of the HPI capture buffer and the status of the file transfer to the specified capture destination.

After your capture file has been obtained at your capture destination, this file can be decoded only by a Cisco TAC engineer because of its proprietary nature and the special program needed to decode it.

Packet Capture PCM Extraction

Extracting PCM from a packet capture is easily accomplished through software programs such as Wireshark. The main criterion for extracting PCM from a packet capture is that the RTP packets contain the G.711 μ-law or G.711 a-law codec. In addition, passthrough redundancy for these codecs should be disabled before making the packet capture because the RFC 2198 packet format usually causes a poor PCM extraction.

The RTP analysis feature within Wireshark can be used to extract the PCM from a G.711 call. See Figure 12-9 and its surrounding text for more information about the RTP analysis feature. Figure 12-9 displays an RTP analysis screen shot, and on this screen is a Save Payload button. Clicking this button brings up another window that allows you to save the G.711 payload as a raw G.711 file or a regular audio file with a .au file extension. Most audio analysis programs play either format, but most of the time the raw G.711 format is preferable.

Third-Party Test Tools

Third-party tools are available that can capture the PCM directly from voice ports. One of the more commonly used tools is the T1/E1 Call Capture and Analysis Software that comes on test sets from GL Communications. You can find more information about this software at the GL Communications website, http://www.gl.com.

In most cases, the GL Communications unit is bridged into the T1/E1 link that is connected directly onto the voice gateway. PCM traces can be made automatically whenever a call is detected, and multiple PCM traces can be captured simultaneously. This ability can be helpful for intermittent problems or for cases where you are unable to determine ahead of time the timeslot that will be used for the fax/modem call that needs to be captured.

Any third-party test tools that are used for capturing PCM traces will have their own instructions and manuals for setting up the test tool correctly. Refer to these instructions and manuals when capturing the PCM trace to ensure that a quality capture file is obtained.

Analyzing PCM Traces

After a PCM trace file has been obtained from one of the three methods outlined in the previous section, the file must be processed so that it can be seen and heard. A number of available audio programs can accomplish this task. Some of the more popular programs are Adobe Audition (formerly CoolEdit), Audacity, and Goldwave. The examples in this section use the free, open source Audacity program, but any of the others work just fine, too. You can download Audacity from http://audacity.sourceforge.net/.

Most PCM trace files are of a raw G.711 format, including the PCM files from a GL Communications test set and those from a G.711 packet capture extraction using Wireshark. Within Audacity, these files are opened by clicking Import Raw Data under the Project menu at the top of the Audacity screen. This brings up a dialog box in which you can select the specific PCM trace file that you want to open. After you select a file, a window appears in which you can select the raw data parameters. For the case of a raw G.711 file, make the selections as shown in Figure 12-22.

Figure 12-22 *Importing G.711 PCM Trace Files into Audacity*

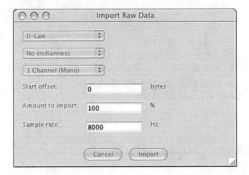

In Figure 12-22, you can see that **U-Law** was selected as the coding for the PCM trace. For cases where G.711 a-law is the codec rather than G.711 μ-law, change the coding in this dialog box to **A-Law**.

Another notable exception occurs when importing PCM trace files into Audacity if the PCM trace files were gathered using the Cisco PCM capture tool. These file types will use a coding of **Signed 16 Bit PCM** rather than **U-Law**, as shown in Figure 12-22.

There will always be two PCM capture files for each call, representing the audio in each direction. Remember to import both PCM trace files to analyze the fax/modem audio in both directions.

The ability to analyze PCM traces when the passthrough transport method is being used for the modem or fax call is important. Unlike fax and modem relay where debugs and statistics are available to let you see some of what is happening during the call, passthrough does not let you see anything about the modem or fax protocols that are being transported. PCM traces are the only way for you to gain insight into what is happening on a call from a fax/modem protocol perspective.

Fax Call PCM Trace Analysis

Analyzing a basic fax call with a PCM trace is not too difficult. After both the audio streams for both directions are opened in Audacity, you can figure out what is happening. Figure 12-23 illustrates bidirectional PCM traces for a successful one-page fax call.

Figure 12-23 *PCM Trace of a Successful Fax Call*

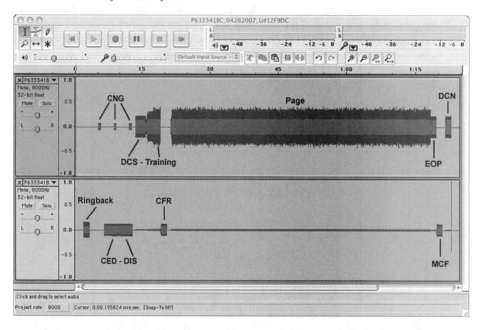

In Figure 12-23, you will see that there are two smaller windows with waveforms within the Audacity window. Each of these smaller windows displays a PCM trace file representing an audio direction from the call. In this case, the top PCM trace file is the audio sent by the originating fax machine, and the bottom window representing another PCM trace file is from the terminating fax device.

The audio signals in Figure 12-23 have already been labeled, but what will always let you know which side is originating is the presence of page information. This is pretty much always the longest signal in the trace, and when you play it in Audacity it sounds like white noise. In addition, the 1100 Hz CNG tones that are repeated every 3 seconds also let you know that the top window is the audio from the originating fax device. For more information about CNG and all the other messages seen in Figure 12-23, see the section "Analyzing a Basic Fax Call" in Chapter 2.

If the top window is the PCM trace for the originating fax call, the bottom trace is the audio from the terminating fax device. If you could listen to this trace, you would hear that the first signal is ringback, which confirms that this trace is coming from the terminating end.

The rest of the messages for both of the traces fall into place at this point. The mandatory CED-DIS is always sent by the terminating side before the page, whereas the DCS and training messages always occur before the page on the originating side. At the end of this one-page fax, there will be an EOP with the terminating side confirming the reception of the page data with an MCF. The originating side then responds with a DCN to end the call.

If you are first able to understand the PCM analysis of the successful fax call detailed in Figure 12-23, you will be better equipped to recognize abnormalities in PCM fax traces where there are problems. Figure 12-24 highlights a PCM trace from a problem fax call.

Figure 12-24 *PCM Trace of a Problem Fax Call*

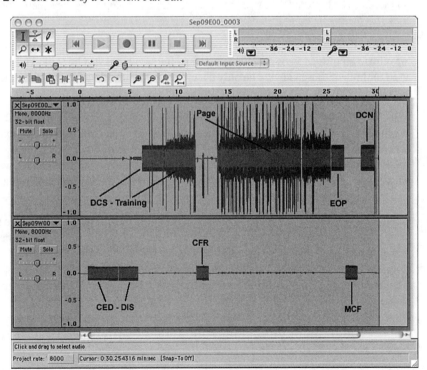

Compared to the good fax call in Figure 12-23, the fax call in Figure 12-24 has visible and audible problems. The vertical lines in the audio stream from the originating side (top window within Audacity) are blips of noise that negatively impact this fax call. The fax page itself is most affected by these blips of noise, which sound like pops of static when the audio is played.

The root cause of the extraneous noise in Figure 12-24 is due to PSTN-related impairments. These impairments were not quite enough to prevent the call from completing, but it was sufficient to cause corrupted scan lines in the final page, which made some of the text difficult to read.

Scan line corruption is one fax issue where PCM traces are practically a necessity. You are unable to see scan line corruption problems with Cisco voice gateway debugs. Only a PCM trace can confirm the presence of impairments that cause scan line corruption problems. In many cases, these impairments are enough to completely fail the call. Furthermore, they are not usually visible by looking at the T1/E1-level errors on the voice gateway because the errors are occurring before the digital link connected to the voice gateway.

In rare occasions, corruption of scan lines can occur and not be noticeable on a typical PCM trace that uses a view of the waveform amplitude. Figure 12-25 shows two PCM traces of the same page that contain corrupted scan lines, but different views are used. The top PCM trace shows the corrupted fax page in the waveform amplitude view just like Figures 12-23 and 12-24. The bottom PCM trace of the exact same fax page uses the spectral or frequency view.

In Figure 12-25 the same 30 or so seconds of a fax page transmission are shown in the waveform amplitude view and the spectral or frequency view. The same PCM trace file is used for both of these views. The only difference is how the data from these same trace files is being displayed.

When PCM trace files are loaded into most audio programs, including Audacity, the trace is brought up in a waveform view where amplitude is plotted on the vertical axis against time on the horizontal axis. However, there are a number of other ways to view the PCM trace, including a spectral view where frequency is plotted on the vertical axis versus time. This can clearly be seen on the bottom PCM trace where the vertical axis has a low value of 31 Hz and a high value of 4 kHz.

In the first PCM trace in Figure 12-25 containing the waveform view, there are not any noticeable problems as you saw previously in Figure 12-24. However, changing the waveform trace at the top to a spectral view gives you the PCM trace at the bottom. On this trace, you can see vertical lines that are faint noise blips. There are enough of these noise blips to cause scan line corruption on this fax page. Parts of this fax page range from difficult to almost impossible to read.

Figure 12-25 *PCM Trace Waveform and Spectral Views of a Fax Page with Corrupted Scan Lines*

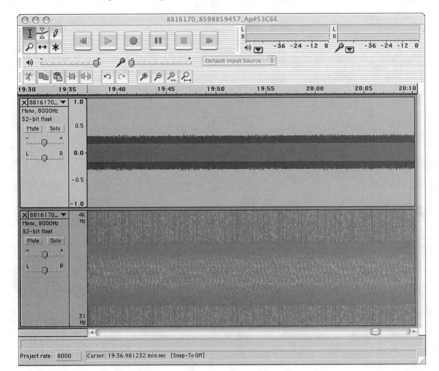

The scan line corruption problem shown in this trace was caused by T1-level errors on certain trunks running between central offices (CO) in a service provider's network. Of course, the T1 coming into the customer's voice gateway was clean; so, without PCM traces, it would have been difficult to determine the existence of corruption in the fax signal and where this corruption originated.

PCM traces can also help diagnose issues involving message collisions. Sometimes when there is too much delay in a fax call, message collisions result. Figure 12-26 is a screen shot of a PCM trace where message collisions occur for the fax call.

In Figure 12-26, you can see a message collision between the second DIS message and the first DCS and Training message. All G3 fax calls implement ITU-T Recommendation T.30, which implements a half-duplex message flow. Recommendation T.30 messages should never be communicated at the same time.

Figure 12-26 *PCM Capture of Fax Message Collisions*

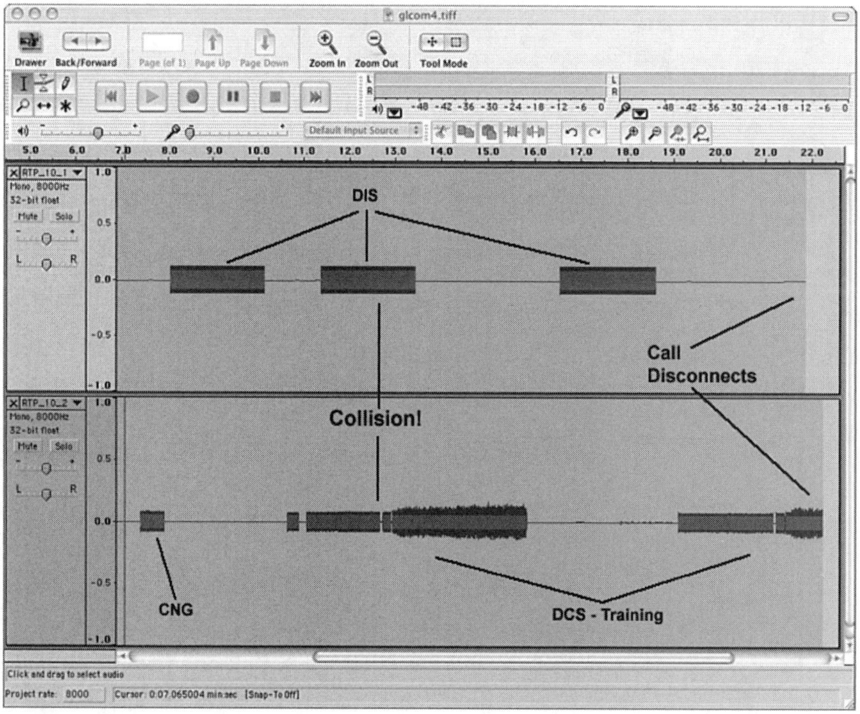

Message collisions such as the one illustrated in Figure 12-26 almost always result in fax failures. The main cause of message collisions is too much delay between the fax machines. For more information about handling high-delay scenarios with fax calls over IP, see the section "Handling High Delay" earlier in this chapter.

Modem Call PCM Trace Analysis

Analyzing PCM traces of modem calls is more difficult than fax calls. This difficulty has to do with the more complex negotiations and full duplex nature of most modem calls. However, some basic analysis can still take place to help you troubleshoot modem problems.

After a modem PCM trace has been loaded into an audio program such as Audacity, you will see the modem negotiation at the beginning of the call. Depending on the modulation and supported negotiation procedures, this negotiation can be quick or somewhat long. Figure 12-27 shows a V.34 negotiation procedure where the four phases of a V.34 negotiation are noted.

Figure 12-27 *PCM Trace of a V.34 Negotiation and Its Phases*

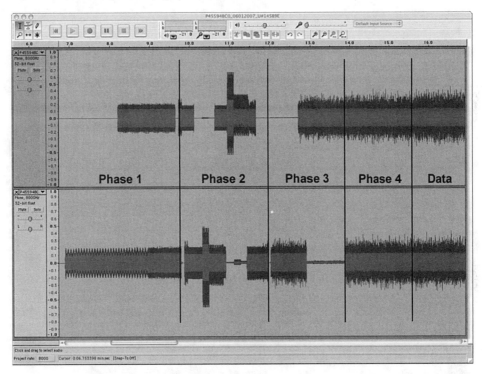

Experienced modem experts can listen to the trace in Figure 12-27 and hear whether there are problems in certain phases. They also will view the phases in the frequency spectrum for an even more detailed analysis. However, for our simplified purposes, knowing that the PCM trace in Figure 12-27 exemplifies a good V.34 negotiation allows for basic comparisons with other V.34 negotiations. Any V.34 PCM trace with a successful negotiation should bear a strong resemblance to Figure 12-27. For more information about the V.34 phases, see the section "Modem Call Analysis" in Chapter 1.

When problems occur in the V.34 negotiations, the phase where the problem is occurring will be longer than usual, taking up more time as messages and other signals are repeated. Sometimes, the best way to identify these problems is by listening to the trace, where repetitive signals are easier to detect.

In many cases, the modem call negotiates correctly, but problems occur later in the communication. One of the most troublesome issues for a modem connection is retrains. Retrains stop all data flow and interrupt the modem connection for as long as it takes for a complete new negotiation to take place. Figure 12-28 shows a V.34 retrain occurring. For more information about retrains, see the section "Retrains and Speedshifts" in Chapter 1.

Figure 12-28 *PCM Trace of a V.34 Retrain*

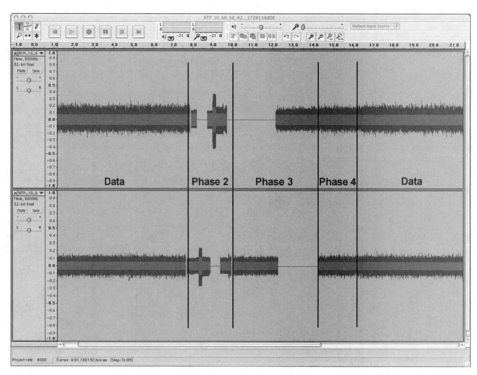

In Figure 12-28, you see a PCM trace of a retrain occurring during the data communication portion of a V.34 call. Notice that the call is already in data mode when the retrain occurs and that the call returns to data mode after the retrain is finished. While the retrain is occurring, all data communication between the modems is discontinued.

Unlike Figure 12-27, which contains Phase 1 of the V.34 negotiation, the retrain in Figure 12-28 does not have the first phase. All retrains begin at Phase 2, and only in the initial V.34 modem negotiation will you see the Phase 1 negotiation.

PCM traces for modems are truly necessary for only the most complex cases, but their usefulness in identifying problems is undoubtedly without equal. See the section "Advanced Troubleshooting for Modem Relay" earlier in this chapter for additional tips to resolve any problems found in a PCM trace. As emphasized previously, confirming proper line conditions and levels for the connection between the modem and the Cisco voice gateway should be one of the first troubleshooting steps.

Summary

Troubleshooting fax, modem, and text problems can be time-consuming and complex. However, the appropriate troubleshooting methodology can make the process easier.

The troubleshooting methodology discussed in this chapter is based on dividing any fax, modem, or text problem into smaller components (a "divide and conquer" strategy). There are a total of five components or areas detailed in this troubleshooting methodology, and each one was covered by its own section in this chapter.

The starting point for the troubleshooting methodology introduced at the beginning of this chapter was fundamental troubleshooting. This section discussed some simplistic but necessary troubleshooting steps. These steps included checking the configuration, performing voice calls over the same connection, and confirming that the fax/modem/text devices work over the PSTN.

The next area that was covered was telephony troubleshooting. Because many problems associated with faxes, modems, and text devices working over an IP network still originate from the telephony side, it is important to be able to troubleshoot the gateway's voice port. The main focus here was on digital voice ports such as T1 and E1 because errors on these interfaces are well-known culprits of fax, modem, and text failures.

IP troubleshooting followed telephony troubleshooting as the next area to look at in the methodology. Problems in the IP network can cause degradation or failure of the fax, modem, or text call. IP troubleshooting techniques included viewing the incoming media streams on the Cisco voice gateways to identify potential network impairments and using packet captures to confirm valid media streams in both directions.

After troubleshooting the telephony and IP segments, the next recommended step in resolving fax, modem, and text problems is troubleshooting the switchover signaling. The switchover signaling is responsible for transitioning the call from a voice call to a fax or modem call. Common gateway debug commands were discussed in this section, highlighting the best approaches for confirming on Cisco gateways that the switchover transition is successful.

The last step in the fax, modem, and text troubleshooting methodology introduced in this chapter was passthrough and relay troubleshooting. In this discussion, you learned a number of techniques for troubleshooting fax, modem, and text calls after a successful switchover has occurred. More advanced troubleshooting practices including detailed debugs and PCM traces were covered, and these provide the techniques necessary for handling the most complex fax, modem, and text problems.

CHAPTER 13

Troubleshooting T.37 Store-and-Forward Fax

Implementations of T.37 store-and-forward fax on Cisco IOS voice gateways require that the gateway handle both telephony and Simple Mail Transfer Protocol (SMTP) interface connections along with an image-conversion process. These additional tasks result in a higher degree of complexity for the voice gateway compared to handling and processing a standard fax passthrough or fax relay call.

This increased involvement by the Cisco voice gateway in T.37 store-and-forward fax calls results in much longer configurations and additional debug options. Subsequently, T.37-specific problems require a different troubleshooting methodology to deal with the increased complexity of this unique fax transport solution.

This chapter introduces a graphical troubleshooting methodology for T.37 onramp and offramp faxing. However, because T.37 onramp and offramp perform opposite functions, this methodology is applied to each of them in separate troubleshooting sections within this chapter. These troubleshooting sections are self-contained from the perspective that you do not need to read one to understand the other. If you need to troubleshoot an offramp problem, you can skip the "T.37 Onramp Troubleshooting" section altogether and go straight to "T.37 Offramp Troubleshooting."

The first major section of this chapter is titled "Checking the Basics," and it applies to troubleshooting both onramp and offramp problems. Following this section are "T.37 Onramp Troubleshooting" and "T.37 Offramp Troubleshooting," which feature in-depth troubleshooting techniques for each of these T.37 transport methods.

Checking the Basics

Before executing detailed onramp or offramp troubleshooting techniques, some basic troubleshooting items must be checked. Although confirming some of these items might seem obvious and somewhat simplistic, you can save a lot of frustration and time down the road if you pay due diligence to these possible issues in the beginning.

Table 13-1 highlights some basic items that you should check or validate before proceeding with more in-depth troubleshooting. Because Table 13-1 contains only T.37-specific items, it is probably worthwhile to also refer back to Table 12-1 for a list of more generic fax-related items to check, too.

Table 13-1 *Basic Items to Check Before Proceeding with More In-depth T.37 Troubleshooting*

Item to Check	Comments
Confirm that onramp and offramp TCL scripts are accessible by the voice gateway.	After the appropriate onramp or offramp TCL script has been downloaded, the voice gateway must be able to access this script either through internal flash storage or by using FTP or TFTP.
Confirm that the user-defined script names match.	A user-defined script name is attached to the downloaded onramp or offramp TCL script using the **service** command under the Application submenu. The dial-peer then uses the **service** command to reference this script using the same user-defined name. These names must match exactly.
Validate the SMTP connection between the gateway and the mail server.	In both onramp and offramp scenarios, there should not be any problems in establishing and maintaining the SMTP connection. The best way to check the SMTP connection is by initiating a Telnet session to the SMTP port of the mail server from the voice gateway for the case of onramp. When offramp is being implemented, the SMTP Telnet session should occur in the opposite direction. An example of an SMTP Telnet session is shown in Example 6-1 in Chapter 6, "T.37 Store-and-Forward Fax."
Check the configuration.	Certain configuration commands are mandatory for the proper operation of both onramp and offramp. Refer to Chapter 11, "Configuring T.37 Store-and-Forward Fax," for the required onramp and offramp configuration commands.
Confirm that any digital interfaces involved in T.37 faxing are clean.	Line errors, such as slips, on the telephony links of the onramp or offramp gateway are just as detrimental to T.37 faxing as they are to passthrough and relay. For more information about checking digital telephony links, see the section "Telephony Troubleshooting" in Chapter 12, "Troubleshooting Passthrough and Relay."

If after the simple checks in Table 13-1 have been completed and you are still experiencing an onramp or offramp problem, more advanced T.37 troubleshooting is necessary. These advanced troubleshooting techniques are covered in the next two sections. If you are encountering an onramp-specific problem, proceed to the next section, "T.37 Onramp Troubleshooting," or for an offramp problem, skip to the section "T.37 Offramp Troubleshooting."

CAUTION	The next two sections of this chapter involve the enabling of specific debug commands on the voice gateway to troubleshoot onramp and offramp problems. The debug commands always have the potential to negatively impact the performance and stability of the voice gateway. Therefore, exercise extreme caution and refer to the section "Debugging Best Practices" in Chapter 12 before enabling debugs on onramp or offramp gateways in production environments.

T.37 Onramp Troubleshooting

Because T.37 onramp converts incoming fax calls to e-mails, troubleshooting onramp requires a thorough understanding of both the ITU-T T.30 protocol and SMTP. The T.30 protocol and its messages are discussed in detail throughout Chapter 2, "How Fax Works," and SMTP is covered in the section "SMTP Overview" of Chapter 6.

To better visualize the T.37 onramp process that occurs in a Cisco voice gateway, consult Figure 13-1. This figure illustrates how an incoming fax call comes in through the gateway's telephony port, is converted into a Tagged Image File Format (TIFF) image, and then sent via e-mail to a mail server.

Figure 13-1 highlights the main IOS processes that are involved in an onramp fax call. These processes include T.30, fax media service provider (FMSP), document media service provider (DMSP), fax over IP (FOIP), mail service provider interface (MSPI), and mail transfer agent (MTA).

Included in Figure 13-1 is a table that details the primary purpose and function of each of these processes along with the corresponding debug command that provides the best visibility and troubleshooting information. This allows the appropriate debug command to be quickly referenced after a problem has been isolated to a certain process or processes within the onramp gateway itself.

In addition to illustrating the software components or processes of a Cisco onramp gateway, Figure 13-1 expresses a troubleshooting methodology. You can see how a normal fax call connects to the onramp gateway's voice port on the left side of the diagram, interfacing directly with the T.37 onramp FMSP process. The FMSP process handles the telephony fax call and passes the fax page information and any relevant signaling to DMSP. The DMSP process converts the fax page data into a TIFF image, which is passed to MSPI for transmission to the mail server. The FOIP process provides visibility into the onramp function as a whole, while the T.30 and MTA processes allow viewing of the T.30 and SMTP messages occurring between the onramp gateway and the fax machine and mail server, respectively.

Figure 13-1 *Graphical Illustration of T.37 Onramp for a Cisco Voice Gateway*

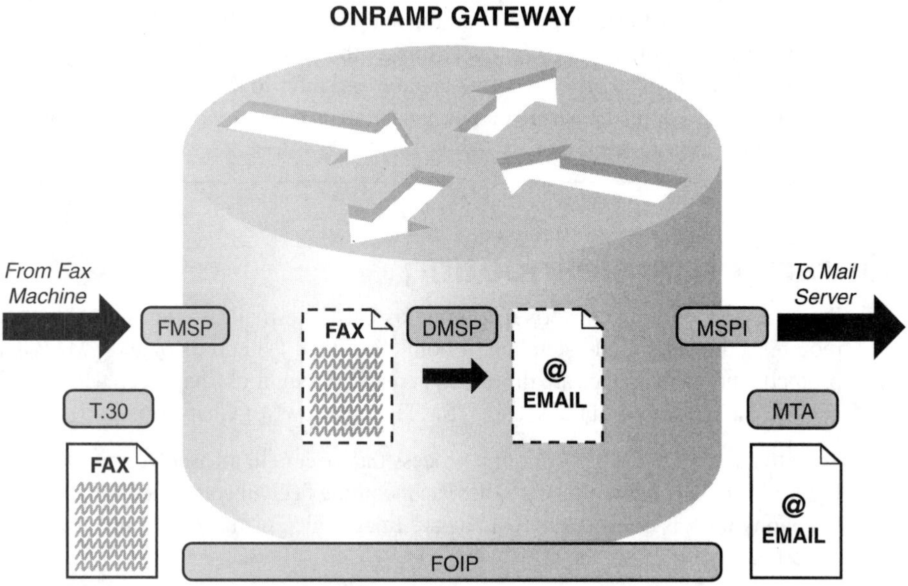

	Purpose:	Troubleshoot the T.30 messaging between the fax machine and the onramp gateway.
T.30 =	**Command:**	*debug fax relay t30 all-level-1*
FMSP =	**Purpose:**	Troubleshoot the interaction between the telephony interface and the onramp application.
	Command:	*debug fax fmsp, debug fax fmsp receive t30*
DMSP =	**Purpose:**	Troubleshoot the internal TIFF writer's conversion from T.4 fax data to TIFF image data.
	Command:	*debug fax dmsp*
FOIP =	**Purpose:**	Troubleshoot the state transitions between all of the T.37 applications.
	Command:	*debug fax foip detail*
MTA =	**Purpose:**	Troubleshoot the SMTP/ESMTP messaging for the session between the onramp gateway and the mail server.
	Command:	*debug fax mta detail*
MSPI =	**Purpose:**	Troubleshoot the mail service provider interface on the onramp gateway that is responsible for setting up and maintaining the SMTP/ESMTP connection between the gateway and the mail server.
	Command:	*debug fax mspi*

When looking at Figure 13-1 as a troubleshooting methodology, it is best to track the onramp call from left to right as it chronologically progresses through the gateway. For example, you want to ensure that the call first proceeds successfully from a T.30 and FMSP perspective before looking at the MSPI and MTA processes. The IOS debug commands are listed for each process in Figure 13-1 so that you can easily identify the appropriate debug command that needs to be enabled for troubleshooting a particular process.

TIP Before you start any detailed onramp troubleshooting, be aware that the T.37 onramp application has specific memory requirements. The onramp application requires at least 2 MB of input/output (IO) memory and 8 MB of processor memory to be free on the voice gateway before an onramp fax call will be accepted. If this free memory is not available, the onramp fax call fails, and the following error message is generated by the voice gateway: %LAPP_ON_MSGS-6-LAPP_ON_CAUSE_NO_MEMORY: No memory available. You need to either physically add more memory to the voice gateway or you can try adjusting the memory allocation on the voice gateway. You can use the command **show memory** to view the current IO and processor memory allocation, and then the configuration command **memory-size iomem** provides a means for adjusting the split between these two memory types. This allocation adjustment might resolve the issue if processor or IO memory has extra space that can be allocated to the other to meet the minimum memory requirements mentioned previously.

The FOIP process behaves as an umbrella because it provides visibility into the complete T.37 onramp application and all the component processes involved. In many cases, debugging the FOIP process is a good place to start when T.37 is failing and a culprit process has not been identified.

Although a number of options are available when issuing an FOIP debug command, the command that provides the best information is the command **debug fax foip detail**. Example 13-1 shows the output from the command **debug fax foip detail** for a successful one-page onramp fax call.

Example 13-1 *debug fax foip detail Output for a T.37 Onramp Call*

```
Jun  6 13:10:06.630: //77/1481B1528015/FOIP_ON/lapp_on_change_state:
   Old State=LAPP_ON_CS_HANDOFF(0),
   New State=LAPP_ON_CS_VTSP_FMSP_CONFERENCING(1)
Jun  6 13:10:06.630: //77/1481B1528015/FOIP_ON/lapp_on_conference_created:
   VTSP and FMSP Are Conferenced;
   Waiting for FMSP Call Detail Event
Jun  6 13:10:06.630: //77/1481B1528015/FOIP_ON/lapp_on_change_state:
   Old State=LAPP_ON_CS_VTSP_FMSP_CONFERENCING(1),
   New State=LAPP_ON_CS_FMSP_CALL_DETAIL(2)
```

continues

Example 13-1 *debug fax foip detail* Output for a T.37 Onramp Call (Continued)

```
Jun  6 13:10:13.482: //77/1481B1528015/FOIP_ON/lapp_on_setup_mspi:
   Envelope From=FAXES@cisco.com
Jun  6 13:10:13.482: //77/1481B1528015/FOIP_ON/lapp_on_setup_mspi:
   Envelope To=gsalguei@faxmail.com
Jun  6 13:10:13.482: //77/1481B1528015/FOIP_ON/lapp_on_setup_mspi:
   RFC822 To Comment=gsalguei
Jun  6 13:10:13.482: //77/1481B1528015/FOIP_ON/lapp_on_setup_mspi:
   Faxmail Subject=Incoming PSTN Fax
Jun  6 13:10:13.482: //77/1481B1528015/FOIP_ON/lapp_on_setup_mspi:
   Disposition Notification=gsalguei@cisco.com
Jun  6 13:10:13.482: //77/1481B1528015/FOIP_ON/lapp_on_setup_mspi:
   Originator TSI=RFC822 From Comment=9191231234

! Output omitted for brevity

Jun  6 13:10:13.486: //78/1481B1528015/FOIP_ON/lapp_on_conference_created:
   FMSP and DMSP Are Conferenced
Jun  6 13:10:13.486: //78/1481B1528015/FOIP_ON/lapp_on_conference_created:
   Sending RECEIVE ENABLE to FMSP
Jun  6 13:10:13.486: //77/1481B1528015/FOIP_ON/lapp_on_change_state:
   Old State=LAPP_ON_CS_FMSP_DMSP_CONFERENCING(3),
   New State=LAPP_ON_CS_FMSP_PAGE_ACCEPT_REQUESTED(4)
Jun  6 13:10:14.486: //79/1481B1528015/FOIP_ON/lapp_on_call_connected:
   MSPI call connected:
   Start Conferencing DMSP and MSPI
Jun  6 13:10:35.614: //77/1481B1528015/FOIP_ON/lapp_on_change_state:
   Old State=LAPP_ON_CS_FMSP_PAGE_ACCEPT_REQUESTED(4),
   New State=LAPP_ON_CS_FMSP_PAGE_ACCEPT_REQUESTED(4)

! Output omitted for brevity

Jun  6 13:10:40.130: //77/1481B1528015/FOIP_ON/lapp_on_conference_destroyed:
   VTSP/FMSP Conference Destroyed
Jun  6 13:10:40.130: //77/1481B1528015/FOIP_ON/lapp_on_conference_destroyed:
   FMSP/DMSP Conference Destroyed
Jun  6 13:10:40.130: //77/1481B1528015/FOIP_ON/lapp_on_conference_destroyed:
   DMSP/MSPI Conference Destroyed
Jun  6 13:10:40.130: //77/1481B1528015/FOIP_ON/lapp_on_change_state:
   Old State=LAPP_ON_CS_CONFERENCE_DESTROYING(7),
   New State=LAPP_ON_CS_DISCONNECTING(8)

! Output omitted for brevity
```

The debug output in Example 13-1 shows how a T.37 onramp call flows through the gateway. Using Figure 13-1 as a reference might prove helpful here to visualize the proper communication path between the onramp processes. The command **debug fax foip detail** displays the conferencing of the related processes and their teardowns at the end of the fax call.

Throughout Example 13-1, you can see that each debug message contains the parameter setting of **FOIP_ON**. This setting indicates that the current debug message is from a T.37 onramp call. As you will see later in the section "T.37 Offramp Troubleshooting," the **debug fax foip detail** command is also used to troubleshoot T.37 offramp problems.

The first conferencing of processes that occurs in the **debug fax foip detail** output is that **VTSP and FMSP Are Conferenced**. VTSP is a lower-level process that is used for all voice calls that connect through a telephony voice port on a Cisco IOS gateway. By conferencing VTSP with FMSP, the incoming fax transmission can now be handled as a T.37 onramp call. You can find more information about VTSP and a diagram of where it fits in with some other IOS processes responsible for VoIP call control in the section "DSP HPI Troubleshooting" in Chapter 12.

After VTSP and FMSP have been joined together for the incoming fax call, the call can now take on the T.37 onramp properties that are detailed in the configuration file. The command **debug fax foip detail** shows how T.37 configuration commands are applied to an onramp call. For example, **Envelope From=FAXES@cisco.com** in Example 13-1 results from the configuration commands **mta send mail-from hostname cisco.com** and **mta send mail-from username FAXES**, which were used in the onramp configuration that generated this debug output. Similarly, from the dial-peer level configuration command **session target mailto:gsalguei@faxmail.com**, you see **Envelope To=gsalguei@faxmail.com** in the debug output.

Additional e-mail header information that FOIP shows being generated from specific T.37 configuration commands includes the mail subject and the presence of the Message Disposition Notification (MDN) e-mail address. The mail subject appears in Example 13-1 as **Faxmail Subject=Incoming PSTN Fax**, and this correlates to the configuration command **mta send subject Incoming PSTN Fax**.

The MDN e-mail address is configured by the commands **mta send return-receipt-to hostname cisco.com** and **mta send return-receipt-to username gsalguei**. These two configuration commands are responsible for **Disposition Notification=gsalguei@cisco.com** appearing in the debug output. For more assistance on any of the configuration commands mentioned in the previous two paragraphs, refer back to Chapter 11.

Although all this debug information is e-mail header specific, you will see that the MSPI process has not yet become part of the T.37 onramp call. This information is just being collected and shown in the output of the command **debug fax foip detail**, and it will be passed on after MSPI is conferenced in as part of the onramp call.

After the e-mail header information has been collected, **FMSP and DMSP Are Conferenced**. This allows FMSP to pass the fax page information to DMSP, where the TIFF image is created.

The MSPI process now becomes involved and accomplishes the following tasks. A connection to the mail server is established and confirmed in the message **MSPI call connected** while the message **Start Conferencing DMSP and MSPI** informs you that

DMSP has bridged in MSPI. This is important because DMSP has created the TIFF image from the fax page data, and this TIFF image is handed over to MSPI for transport to the mail server.

When the T.37 onramp call is complete in Example 13-1, you can see that the conferences between the onramp processes are subsequently torn down. The conference teardown between processes is shown by the messages **VTSP/FMSP Conference Destroyed, FMSP/DMSP Conference Destroyed,** and **DMSP/MSPI Conference Destroyed**.

As mentioned earlier, the command **debug fax foip detail** is a good place to start when your troubleshooting focus has not been narrowed down to a specific onramp process. If for some reason the output from this debug command does not steer you toward the problem, checking the onramp telephony interface as discussed in the next section should be the next step.

Troubleshooting the Onramp Telephony Interface

The onramp telephony interface is composed of the physical voice port that connects to the fax machine along with the associated FMSP T.37 process. In addition, the raw T.30 fax messaging can be viewed on this telephony interface, too, if you want to troubleshoot the actual fax connection itself.

When a fax machine initiates a call to the onramp telephony interface, this interface acts exactly as a terminating fax machine. All the T.30 messaging is terminated by this interface, and it is not propagated further into the onramp gateway. However, the page data is extracted and passed to the next T.37 onramp process, DMSP.

TIP

T.37 onramp for analog FXS telephony interfaces is not supported by the current TCL scripts that are downloadable from Cisco.com. Although it is possible to gain FXS interface support with a custom TCL script, a digital T1 or E1 interface is generally recommended for T.37 onramp. For more information about onramp TCL scripts, see the section "Loading the TCL Scripts" in Chapter 11.

While visualizing the onramp telephony interface as the terminating fax machine, you can easily confirm the T.30 messaging between this interface and the originating fax machine using the command **debug fax relay t30 all-level-1**. This command is exactly the same as the command used to troubleshoot the T.30 messaging for T.38 and Cisco fax relay calls. In fact, internally the T.37 onramp gateway handles the T.30 fax messaging as a T.38 fax relay call. This is the main reason that the **debug fax relay t30 all-level-1** command is effective at looking at the raw T.30 messages on an onramp gateway.

Example 13-2 shows the command **debug fax relay t30 all-level-1** for a T.37 onramp call. Notice that the output from this command is identical to that seen when this command is used for a T.38 or Cisco fax relay call.

Example 13-2   *debug fax relay t30 all-level-1 Output for a T.37 Onramp Call*

```
Jun  6 08:42:51.727: 0/1/0:23  659277 fr-entered=10(ms)
    timestamp=662637 fr-msg-tx CSI
    timestamp=663127 fr-msg-tx DIS
    timestamp=665267 fr-msg-det TSI
    timestamp=665957 fr-msg-det DCS
    timestamp=669377 fr-msg-tx CFR
    timestamp=689147 fr-msg-det EOP
    timestamp=689537 fr-msg-tx MCF
    timestamp=692027 fr-msg-det DCN
```

Example 13-2 clearly shows the fax negotiation, including the digital identification signal (**DIS**) and digital command signal (**DCS**) mandatory messages between the originating fax machine and the onramp gateway. The training signal is then acknowledged with a confirmation or **CFR** by the onramp gateway. After a single page is received and followed by an End of Procedure (**EOP**) message, the onramp gateway confirms the page reception with a message confirmation or **MCF** message.

You should use the command **debug fax relay t30 all-level-1** to confirm that the fax negotiation is successful. If the fax negotiation fails, the gateway will never create the e-mail with the TIFF image and send it to the mail server. You can find common failure scenarios and how to troubleshoot them using this debug command in the section "Debugging T.30 Fax Messaging" in Chapter 12. In addition, you can find detailed information about each of the T.30 messages displayed by the **debug fax relay t30 all-level-1** command output in the section "Analyzing a Basic Fax Call" in Chapter 2.

The T.37 FMSP process bridges the telephony fax call into the T.37 onramp application. On the telephony side, FMSP handles the T.30 signaling with the originating fax machine, and on the T.37 onramp side FMSP passes through the fax image data and any other necessary control information. The best FMSP debug options to run for troubleshooting are **debug fax fmsp** and **debug fax fmsp receive t30**.

The debug command **debug fax fmsp** automatically enables the FMSP debug options of **debug fax fmsp error call, debug fax fmsp error software,** and **debug fax fmsp inout**. When troubleshooting the FMSP process, the **debug fax fmsp** command is the best place to start. Example 13-3 displays the output from this command.

Example 13-3   *debug fax fmsp Output for a T.37 Onramp Call*

```
Jun  6 09:14:17.851: //38/232D5851800B/FMSP/faxmsp_call_setup_request:
   session=0x45A68580, vdbPtr=0x4570871C,data dir=ONRAMP, conf dir=DEST
Jun  6 09:14:17.851: //38/232D5851800B/FMSP/faxmsp_bridge:
   confID=0x1C, srcCID=38, dstCID=37
Jun  6 09:14:17.851: //38/232D5851800B/FMSP/faxmsp_bridge:
   ramp data dir=ONRAMP, conf dir=DEST
Jun  6 09:14:17.851: //38/232D5851800B/FMSP/faxmsp_bridge:
   Explicit caps ind. done; Wait for registry cap ind
Jun  6 09:14:17.851: //38/232D5851800B/FMSP/faxmsp_caps_ind:
   peer_bridge_info=0x45A0A0EC, cap_ind_state=0x3
Jun  6 09:14:17.851: //38/232D5851800B/FMSP/faxmsp_caps_ack:
   direction=0, srcCID=37, dstCID=0
Jun  6 09:14:17.855: //38/232D5851800B/FMSP/faxmsp_codec_download_done:
   per_bridge_info=0x45A0A0EC, application_data=0x463CEAC0,
   state=0x2, direction=2
Jun  6 09:14:24.699: //38/232D5851800B/FMSP/faxMsp_session_info_ntf:
   Rsln0, Encode=1, Speed=42, MinScanLength=0

! Output omitted for brevity

Jun  6 09:14:54.059: //38/232D5851800B/FMSP/faxmsp_call_disconnect:
   per_bridge_info=0x45A0A0EC, state=0x31
Jun  6 09:14:54.059: //38/232D5851800B/FMSP/faxmsp_get_num_of_pages:
   session=0x45A68580, per_bridge_info=0x45A0A0EC,
   t30_context=0x45A68598, state=0x31, page#=1
Jun  6 09:14:54.059: //38/232D5851800B/FMSP/faxmsp_do_call_history:
   cause=normal call clearing (16): Normal connection (21)
```

In Example 13-3, a one-page fax is sent to the onramp gateway, and the **debug fax fmsp** command provides information to let you know how the call is progressing through the FMSP process. In the first line of the debug output, notice the function **faxmsp_call_ setup_request**, which indicates that the incoming fax call is being handled by the FMSP process.

The FMSP process is then involved in the capabilities exchange and the bridging of the call legs. These are functions that occur with every VoIP call, but in the case of T.37 onramp, the FMSP process is directly involved. Confirmation that FMSP is successfully running and handling the fax call is confirmed by the message **faxmsp_codec_download_done**.

At the completion of the onramp fax call, you see **faxmsp_call_disconnect** followed a bit later by **cause=normal call clearing (16)**. This notifies you that the onramp fax call has been torn down with a disconnect cause of 16, which reflects a normal disconnect procedure.

As shown in Example 13-3, the **debug fax fmsp** also provides a count of the number of fax pages received. Notice that the function **faxmsp_get_num_of_pages** returns a value of **page#=1**, which means that only a single page was received in this example.

If you are interested in seeing the detailed interaction between FMSP and the originating fax machine, use the command **debug fax fmsp receive t30**. This command displays the T.30 messaging for the fax call along with its phases. Example 13-4 highlights a small snippet of the output from the **debug fax fmsp receive t30** command for an onramp call.

Example 13-4   *debug fax fmsp receive t30 Output for a T.37 Onramp Call*

```
Jun  6 09:16:39.439: //42/75CAA36D800C/FMSP/fax2_phaseB_receive:
   CSI_PACKET(9913170)
   DIS_PACKET(speed=5, resolution=1, encoding=1)
Jun  6 09:16:39.439: //42/75CAA36D800C/FMSP/fax2_phaseB_receive:
   fax2_response_receive, PROCESSING
Jun  6 09:16:41.427: //42/75CAA36D800C/FMSP/fax2_phaseB_receive:

   fax2_response_receive, PROCESSING
Jun  6 09:16:42.407: //42/75CAA36D800C/FMSP/fax2_phaseB_receive:
   fax2_response_receive, PROCESSING
Jun  6 09:16:42.999: //42/75CAA36D800C/FMSP/fax2_response_receive:
   msg dump (size=23):
   FF C0 C2 AC AC 4C CC 4C 9C CC 9C 8C 9C 04 04 04 04 04 04 04
   04 04 04
Jun  6 09:16:42.999: //42/75CAA36D800C/FMSP/fax2_response_receive:
   received=TSI,  remote id string:=          9191231234
Jun  6 09:16:42.999: //42/75CAA36D800C/FMSP/fax2_phaseB_receive:
   fax2_response_receive, PROCESSING
```

The **debug fax fmsp receive t30** command indicates the phase of the fax call for FMSP quite regularly. The fax call phase is indicated throughout the debug output by a keyword, such as **phaseB**, in Example 13-4. Scanning for these different fax phases is a quick way to parse through the debug output and determine that the fax call is progressing correctly from an FMSP perspective. The phases of a fax call were discussed earlier in Chapter 2 in the section "Phases of a Fax Call."

Along with the fax call phases, specific T.30 messages are displayed in Example 13-4. These messages should line up with the messages found using the **debug fax relay t30 all-level-1** command that was discussed earlier in this section. However, the **debug fax fmsp receive t30** command provides a bit more detailed information about these messages, and you get to view these messages from the FMSP perspective.

The initial T.30 messages of CSI and DIS are indicated in Example 13-4 by **CSI_PACKET** and **DIS_PACKET**. Because FMSP is terminating the fax call in an onramp scenario, these messages are being sent from FMSP to the originating fax machine.

Compared to the command **debug fax relay t30 all-level-1**, the CSI and DIS messages in Example 13-4 are presented along with key decodes of the data that they contain. In the case of the debug message **CSI_PACKET**, you see that the fax number of the onramp gateway is displayed as **9913170**. This CSI value of **9913170** is simply the Dialed Number Identification Service (DNIS) information received by the gateway during the incoming onramp call setup. In the case of the **DIS_PACKET** message, the following parameters from the T.30 DIS message display: **speed=5**, **resolution=1**, and **encoding=1**.

To decode the parameters included with the **DIS_PACKET** message in Example 13-4, use Table 13-2. Be aware that this table also applies to **DCS_PACKET** messages that are found in the output of the command **debug fax fmsp receive t30**. In addition, note that both the **DIS_PACKET** and **DCS_PACKET** messages also display in the output of another FMSP debug command, **debug fax fmsp send t30**. The output of this debug command is discussed in the section "Troubleshooting the Offramp Telephony Interface."

Table 13-2   *DIS_PACKET and DCS_PACKET Message Parameter Values*

Parameter	Value	Explanation
Speed	0 (2400 bps)	This value represents the highest speed within a chosen modulation type for DIS messages. For DCS messages, this parameter reflects the negotiated speed at which the fax page data will be transmitted. Parameter numbers 6–9 are used when V.17 is the confirmed modulation.
	1 (4800 bps)	
	2 (7200 bps)	
	3 (9600 bps)	
	4 (12000 bps)	
	5 (14400 bps)	
	6 (7200bps)	
	7 (9600 bps)	
	8 (12000 bps)	
	9 (14400 bps)	
Resolution	0 (standard)	Based on a horizontal resolution of 203 pixels per inch, a fax image generally consists of three different vertical resolutions: • Standard (98 lines per inch) • Fine (196 lines per inch) • Super fine (391 lines per inch) The passthrough mode specifies that the T.37 gateway does not alter the fax/TIFF image resolution.
	1 (fine)	
	2 (super fine)	
	3 (pass through)	
Encoding	0 (Modified Huffman)	The algorithms used to encode fax pages and fax TIFF image are Modified Huffman (MH), Modified Read (MR), and Modified Modified Read (MMR). You can find more information about these encoding methods in the section "Page Encoding" in Chapter 2. The passthrough mode setting indicates that the T.37 gateway does not change the encoding method.
	1 (Modified READ)	
	2 (Modified Modified READ)	
	3 (pass through)	

Referring to Table 13-2, the **DIS_PACKET** in Example 13-4 with the parameters of **speed=5**, **resolution=1**, and **encoding=1** can now be easily decoded. This DIS message is offering a page transmission speed of 14400, a resolution of fine, and an encoding method of MR.

The originating fax machine responds to the CSI and DIS T.30 messages in Example 13-4 with a TSI and DCS. The TSI message is identified in the debug as **received=TSI**. In addition, the previous debug line shows a hexadecimal dump of the TSI message beginning with **FF C0 C2**, where **FF** is the HDLC address field, **C0** is the control field, and **C2** is the facsimile control field (FCF) value for the TSI message. Even though Example 13-4 highlights only a small debug snippet, be aware that all the received T.30 messages in the **debug fax fmsp receive t30** output show a full or partial hexadecimal trace. You can refer back to Chapter 3, "How Text Telephony Works," and the section "Analyzing a Basic Fax Call" for more detail about reading the hexadecimal output for each received T.30 message. For most FMSP troubleshooting tasks, it is not necessary to decode the hexadecimal trace of the T.30 messages, but this information is still provided for those who might be interested.

Troubleshooting the TIFF Image Creation

The process responsible for the conversion of the incoming fax page into a TIFF image is DMSP. Unfortunately, the debugs for DMSP do not provide a lot of visibility into what is actually occurring in the TIFF creation process. Most of the information presented by the **debug fax dmsp** command relates to the bridging of the DMSP process with FMSP and MSPI. Example 13-5 highlights the relevant messages from the **debug fax dmsp** command when DMSP bridges to its peer processes.

Example 13-5 *debug fax dmsp Output Showing DMSP Bridge Establishment for T.37 Onramp*

```
Jun  6 12:40:43.610: //76/F598F2C08014/DMSP/docmsp_call_setup_request:
   ramp data dir=ONRAMP, conf dir=DEST
Jun  6 12:40:43.610: //76/F598F2C08014/DMSP/docmsp_caps_ind:
   CallId=76, srcCallId=74
Jun  6 12:40:43.610: //76/F598F2C08014/DMSP/docmsp_bridge:
   conf id=0x38, srcCallId=76, dstCallId=74,
   ramp data dir=ONRAMP, conf dir=DEST, encode out=1
Jun  6 12:40:43.610: //76/F598F2C08014/DMSP/docmsp_bridge:
   Bridge done
Jun  6 12:40:44.610: //76/F598F2C08014/DMSP/docmsp_bridge:
   conf id=0x39, srcCallId=76, dstCallId=75,
   ramp data dir=ONRAMP, conf dir=SRC, encode out=1
Jun  6 12:40:44.610: //76/F598F2C08014/DMSP/docmsp_bridge:
   Bridge done
Jun  6 12:40:49.618: //76/F598F2C08014/DMSP/docmsp_xmit:
   srcCallId=74, dstCallId=76, direction=0
```

The function **docmsp_bridge** in Example 13-5 indicates that the DMSP process is getting connected or bridged to another T.37 onramp process. Looking at Figure 13-1, you can see that the DMSP process sits directly between FMSP and MSPI, so DMSP must be bridged to each of these T.37 onramp processes for the onramp call to be successful.

The first time that this function is found in the debug output, the DMSP and FMSP processes are being bridged together because DMSP is marked as the destination by **conf dir=DEST**. When the DMSP process is the destination, the FMSP process must be the bridge source in the case of T.37 onramp.

The next occurrence of the **docmsp_bridge** function confirms the connection between the DMSP and MSPI processes. In this case, **conf dir=SRC** indicates that the DMSP process is the source of the connection. When the setup of each bridge is completed, you will see the message **Bridge done**, indicating that communication is now established between the processes.

At the end of the onramp call, these same bridges must be torn down. Example 13-6 highlights the bridge disconnect messages from the command **debug fax dmsp**.

Example 13-6 *debug fax dmsp Output Showing DMSP Bridge Disconnect for T.37 Onramp*

```
Jun  6 12:41:06.978: //76/F598F2C08014/DMSP/docmsp_xmit:
   srcCallId=74, dstCallId=76, direction=0
Jun  6 12:41:10.330: //76/F598F2C08014/DMSP/docmsp_bdrop:
   confID=0x1, srcCallId=56, dstCallId=76, state=0x4A
Jun  6 12:41:10.330: //76/F598F2C08014/DMSP/docmsp_bdrop:
   Bridge drop done
Jun  6 12:41:10.330: //76/F598F2C08014/DMSP/docmsp_bdrop:
   confID=0x9, srcCallId=57, dstCallId=76, state=0x4B
Jun  6 12:41:10.330: //76/F598F2C08014/DMSP/docmsp_bdrop:
   Bridge drop done
Jun  6 12:41:10.330: //76/F598F2C08014/DMSP/docmsp_call_disconnect:
   Free msp data block
```

In the **debug fax dmsp** output in Example 13-6, the DMSP bridges to the FMSP and MSPI processes are torn down. These teardowns between the onramp processes are known as bridge drops and are indicated by the message **Bridge drop done**. After the bridge drops have been completed, the function **docmsp_call_disconnect** confirms the end of the onramp fax call from the DMSP perspective.

One of the most common problems with T.37 onramp concerns a bad TIFF file being received in the fax mail. For example, the mail user opens the TIFF attachment from the e-mail and finds a TIFF that is blank, incomplete, or corrupted. This sort of issue is rarely a DMSP problem, even though this process is the logical place to start troubleshooting. The most common causes of TIFF problems are listed in Table 13-3.

Table 13-3   *Common Causes of TIFF Problems with T.37 Onramp*

Possible Cause of Onramp TIFF Problem	Explanation and Solution
Errors such as slips on digital connections (T1/E1).	Just like with the passthrough and relay transport methods for fax calls, slips and other physical line errors can be detrimental to T.37 onramp calls, too. Make sure that all digital connections in the path between the originating fax machine and the onramp gateway are error free. If the problem is severe enough, the **debug fax relay t30 all-level-1** command may show failure to train (FTT) and retrain negative (RTN) messages. Otherwise, the best command to use to confirm the integrity of digital circuits connected to the onramp gateway is **show controller [t1/e1]**, as discussed in the section "Telephony Troubleshooting" in Chapter 12.
Interruptions on the SMTP connection.	If interruptions occur on the SMTP connection when the TIFF file is being transferred or the connection is excessively delayed, incomplete TIFFs can result. The command **debug fax mta detail** should make this sort of problem viewable. For more information about this debug command, see the next section, "Troubleshooting the Onramp SMTP Connection."
Originating fax machine is disconnected before the fax transaction is finished.	The simplest way an incomplete TIFF is produced is when the originating fax machine disconnects prematurely. Make sure that the originating fax machine is behaving correctly and that it stays connected until all the fax pages are received and a T.30 disconnect (DCN) message has been sent. The command **debug fax relay t30 all-level-1** is the best command for verifying that fax transaction completes properly.

The lack of Error Correction Mode (ECM) support by Cisco onramp voice gateways makes the reception of bad TIFF files more prevalent. If the ECM feature were supported, the onramp gateway would have the opportunity to ensure that the original fax image was received in an error-free state. However, without ECM support, errors present in the original fax image received by the onramp gateway can lead to TIFF problems within the e-mail attachment.

Perhaps the best place to start to identify which possible cause in Table 13-3 is responsible for onramp TIFF problems is to look at the output from the commands **debug fax t30 all-level-1, show controller [t1/e1]**, and **debug fax mta detail**. Typically one of these commands will lead you toward the source of any onramp TIFF problems.

TIP   The IOS command **mta send success-fax-only** provides a means for the onramp gateway to not forward incomplete TIFFs when the originating fax machine gets disconnected before the fax transaction has finished. When this command is enabled, the onramp gateway does not send the SMTP terminating dot to exit SMTP data mode until the T.30 fax transaction has been successfully completed. Because most fax machines try again upon a T.30 failure, this command prevents users from receiving multiple incomplete TIFF images in their mailbox when premature T.30 disconnects are a problem.

Troubleshooting the Onramp SMTP Connection

In Figure 13-1, the MSPI process is responsible for establishing and maintaining the SMTP connection to the mail server. In addition, after the TIFF is created by DMSP, it is passed to MSPI for transport as an e-mail attachment. From a troubleshooting standpoint, the MSPI process can be looked at directly with **debug fax mspi**. Also, you can look strictly at the SMTP commands that are exchanged during the session with **debug fax mta**.

Although a number of different options exist for the **debug fax mta** command, the most useful is **debug fax mta detail**. This command clearly shows all the messages that occur within the SMTP transaction, and it is the best debug to use for any SMTP communication problem between the onramp gateway and the mail server. Example 13-7 displays the output from **debug fax mta detail** for a successful one-page fax transaction.

Example 13-7   *debug fax mta detail Output for a T.37 Onramp Call*

```
Jun  6 15:47:44.942: //-1/15C6E7528020/SMTPC/esmtp_client_engine_getln:
   (C)R: 220 RTP-ESC-T37.faxmail.com Microsoft ESMTP MAIL Service, Version:
      5.0.2172.1 ready at  Wed, 6 Jun 2007 18:49:53 -0400
Jun  6 15:47:44.942: //-1/15C6E7528020/SMTPC/esmtp_client_engine_writeln:
   (C)S: EHLO fax_2811
Jun  6 15:47:45.422: //-1/15C6E7528020/SMTPC/esmtp_client_engine_getln:
   (C)R: 250-RTP-ESC-T37.faxmail.com Hello [14.80.32.200]
Jun  6 15:47:45.422: //-1/15C6E7528020/SMTPC/esmtp_client_engine_getln:
   (C)R: 250-TURN
Jun  6 15:47:45.422: //-1/15C6E7528020/SMTPC/esmtp_client_engine_getln:
   (C)R: 250-ATRN
Jun  6 15:47:45.422: //-1/15C6E7528020/SMTPC/esmtp_client_engine_getln:
   (C)R: 250-SIZE
Jun  6 15:47:45.422: //-1/15C6E7528020/SMTPC/esmtp_client_engine_getln:
   (C)R: 250-ETRN
Jun  6 15:47:45.422: //-1/15C6E7528020/SMTPC/esmtp_client_engine_getln:
   (C)R: 250-PIPELINING
Jun  6 15:47:45.422: //-1/15C6E7528020/SMTPC/esmtp_client_engine_getln:
   (C)R: 250-DSN

! Output omitted for brevity
```

Example 13-7 *debug fax mta detail Output for a T.37 Onramp Call (Continued)*

```
Jun  6 15:47:45.422: //-1/15C6E7528020/SMTPC/esmtp_client_engine_getln:
   (C)R: 250 OK
Jun  6 15:47:45.422: //-1/15C6E7528020/SMTPC/esmtp_client_engine_writeln:
   (C)S: MAIL FROM:<FAXES@cisco.com> RET=HDRS
Jun  6 15:47:45.966: //-1/15C6E7528020/SMTPC/esmtp_client_engine_getln:
   (C)R: 250 2.1.0 FAXES@cisco.com....Sender OK
Jun  6 15:47:45.966: //-1/15C6E7528020/SMTPC/esmtp_client_engine_writeln:
   (C)S: RCPT TO:<gsalguei@faxmail.com> NOTIFY=SUCCESS,FAILURE,DELAY
       ORCPT=rfc822;gsalguei@faxmail.com
Jun  6 15:47:46.514: //-1/15C6E7528020/SMTPC/esmtp_client_engine_getln:
   (C)R: 250 2.1.5 gsalguei@faxmail.com
Jun  6 15:47:47.062: //-1/15C6E7528020/SMTPC/esmtp_client_engine_getln:
   (C)R: 354 Start mail input; end with <CRLF>.<CRLF>
Jun  6 15:47:47.062: //-1/15C6E7528020/SMTPC/esmtp_client_engine_writeln:
   (C)S: Received: (This is an incoming fax message from the PSTN) by fax_2811 for
<gsalguei@faxmail.com> (with Cisco NetWorks); Wed, 06 Jun 2007 15:47:47 +0000
Jun  6 15:47:47.062: //-1/15C6E7528020/SMTPC/esmtp_client_engine_writeln:
   (C)S: To: "gsalguei" <gsalguei@faxmail.com>
Jun  6 15:47:47.062: //-1/15C6E7528020/SMTPC/esmtp_client_engine_writeln:
   (C)S: Message-ID: <005B2007154747062@fax_2811>
Jun  6 15:47:47.062: //-1/15C6E7528020/SMTPC/esmtp_client_engine_writeln:
   (C)S: Date: Wed, 06 Jun 2007 15:47:47 +0000
Jun  6 15:47:47.062: //-1/15C6E7528020/SMTPC/esmtp_client_engine_writeln:
   (C)S: Subject: Incoming PSTN Fax
Jun  6 15:47:47.062: //-1/15C6E7528020/SMTPC/esmtp_client_engine_writeln:
   (C)S: X-Mailer: Technical Support: http://www.cisco
Jun  6 15:47:47.062: //-1/15C6E7528020/SMTPC/esmtp_client_engine_writeln:
   (C)S: Disposition-Notification-To: gsalguei@cisco.com
Jun  6 15:47:47.062: //-1/15C6E7528020/SMTPC/esmtp_client_engine_writeln:
   (C)S: MIME-Version: 1.0
Jun  6 15:47:47.062: //-1/15C6E7528020/SMTPC/esmtp_client_engine_writeln:
   (C)S: Content-Type: multipart/fax-message;
Jun  6 15:47:47.062: //-1/15C6E7528020/SMTPC/esmtp_client_engine_writeln:
   (C)S:   boundary="yradnuoB=_005A2007154744534.fax_2811"
Jun  6 15:47:47.062: //-1/15C6E7528020/SMTPC/esmtp_client_engine_writeln:
   (C)S: From: "9191231234" <FAXES@cisco.com>

! Output omitted for brevity

Jun  6 15:48:08.066: //-1/15C6E7528020/SMTPC/esmtp_client_engine_writeln:
   (C)S: Content-Type: image/tiff; name="pstn_fax.tif"; application=faxbw
Content-Disposition: attachment
Jun  6 15:48:08.066: //-1/15C6E7528020/SMTPC/esmtp_client_engine_writeln:
   (C)S: Content-Transfer-Encoding: base64
Jun  6 15:48:08.094: //-1/15C6E7528020/SMTPC/esmtp_client_engine_writeln:
   (C)S: --yradnuoB=_005A2007154744534.fax_2811--
Jun  6 15:48:08.094: //-1/15C6E7528020/SMTPC/esmtp_client_engine_work_routine:
   Sending terminating dot ...(socket=0)
Jun  6 15:48:08.094: //-1/15C6E7528020/SMTPC/esmtp_client_engine_writeln:
   (C)S: .
```

continues

Example 13-7 *debug fax mta detail Output for a T.37 Onramp Call (Continued)*

```
Jun  6 15:48:08.358: //-1/15C6E7528020/SMTPC/esmtp_client_engine_getln:
  (C)R: 250 2.6.0  <005B2007154747062@fax_2811> Queued mail for delivery
Jun  6 15:48:08.358: //-1/15C6E7528020/SMTPC/esmtp_client_engine_writeln:
  (C)S: QUIT
Jun  6 15:48:08.826: //-1/15C6E7528020/SMTPC/esmtp_client_engine_getln:
  (C)R: 221 2.0.0 RTP-ESC-T37.faxmail.com Service closing transmission channel
```

The debug output in Example 13-7 matches up with an ESMTP mail transaction as was discussed in the section "SMTP Commands and Sample Sessions" in Chapter 6. Refer back to this section for any additional information about ESMTP transactions and the meanings of any messages.

When reading the debug output in Example 13-7, the direction of each of the SMTP messages is easily identified. For messages in the direction of the onramp gateway to the mail server, you will see a "Command Sent" or **C(S)** in the debug line. SMTP messages coming in the opposite direction from the mail server to the onramp gateway are noted by a "Command Received" or **C(R)**.

After the SMTP session is initiated by the onramp gateway in Example 13-7, you see that the mail server answers with a greeting. In response to this greeting, the onramp gateway sends an ESMTP greeting of **EHLO fax_2811**. A list of SMTP extensions or features supported by the mail server soon follows.

One notable item in this list of supported features by the mail server is the presence of **DSN** support. If you are planning to implement the Delivery Status Notification (DSN) feature within SMTP, you must make sure that the mail server supports DSN messages and that they are enabled as shown in Example 13-7. Be aware that the DSN extension is available only with ESMTP. For additional information about DSN messages and how they work, refer to the section "DSN and MDN" in Chapter 6.

The onramp gateway then transmits the envelope information for the fax mail message. The first line of the envelope information in Example 13-7 is **MAIL FROM:<FAXES@cisco.com> RET=HDRS**, where **FAXES@cisco.com** is the sender's e-mail address. The **RET=HDRS** parameter specifies that any DSN responses returned to the sender's e-mail address should contain only the e-mail headers and not the e-mail content. The other option is RET=FULL, which indicates that the full e-mail is returned to the sender.

The next item contained within the envelope in Example 13-7 is **RCPT TO: <gsalguei@faxmail.com> NOTIFY=SUCCESS,FAILURE,DELAY ORCPT=rfc822; gsalguei@faxmail.com**. This line details the recipient's e-mail address of **gsalguei@ faxmail.com**, and the conditions under which a DSN is being requested from the mail server. In this case, the onramp gateway requests that the mail server notify the sender with a DSN if the e-mail to the recipient is successful, delayed, or experiences a delivery failure (**NOTIFY=SUCCESS,FAILURE,DELAY**). For more information about DSN configuration, refer to Table 11-7 in Chapter 11.

After the envelope information in Example 13-7, the SMTP "DATA" including the fax TIFF is sent from the onramp gateway to the mail server. Within the "DATA" portion of the fax mail, additional header information is transmitted. This information includes items such as the e-mail subject (**Subject: Incoming PSTN Fax**) and the MDN request, which displays the destination e-mail address (**Disposition-Notification-To: gsalguei@cisco.com**) for the receipt.

Unlike the DSN information, which can be viewed only by analyzing the SMTP envelope information, the MDN request is part of the e-mail headers. However, you will more than likely have to enable the viewing of full e-mail headers on your e-mail client to view the MDN e-mail address. Refer back to Example 6-5 in Chapter 6 to see how the MDN request appears within the full headers of an e-mail.

Always view the full e-mail headers to be sure that the MDN request makes it to the e-mail client. If the MDN request exists in the full e-mail headers but an MDN is still not sent when the e-mail is opened, the problem is probably with the e-mail client.

Many e-mail clients do not support MDNs, or MDN message support must be explicitly enabled. E-mail clients such as Microsoft Outlook and Outlook Express offer MDN support by default. For more information about MDN messages and how they work, see the section "DSN and MDN" in Chapter 6. If you are interested in configuring the MDN feature on an onramp gateway, refer to Table 11-7 in Chapter 11.

After "DATA" mode transfers all the e-mail header and text information along with the optional TIFF image in Example 13-7, a **terminating dot** is sent to the mail server. This **terminating dot** is followed by the **QUIT** command to force a graceful disconnect of the SMTP session.

TIP

An easy way to troubleshoot the mail server in an onramp scenario is just to telnet to it on TCP port 25, which is the SMTP port, from the onramp gateway. From this point, you can manually complete the SMTP transaction and confirm that the mail server is working correctly. Example 6-1 in Chapter 6 provides an example of how a manual SMTP session would appear.

If you need to troubleshoot this same SMTP connection from the perspective of the T.37 process that is responsible for establishing and maintaining it, you need to use the command **debug fax mspi**. Unfortunately, you can glean only a small amount of information from this debug because the majority of the output relates to internal functions within the MSPI process. In addition, you lose the visibility into all the SMTP commands that are exchanged when you run the **debug fax mspi** command on its own. Therefore, it is recommended to run this command along with **debug fax mta detail**. However, for the sake of clarity,

Example 13-8 shows only the **debug fax mspi** output by itself for the initial call setup at the beginning of the debug.

Example 13-8 *debug fax mspi Output for a T.37 Onramp Initial Call Setup*

```
Jun  6 15:41:23.394: //119/329E716A801F/MSPI_ON/mspi_call_setup_request:
   Outgoing Peer Tag=99
   Envelope From=FAXES@cisco.com
   Envelope To=gsalguei@faxmail.com
   Mime Outer Type=2
Jun  6 15:41:24.394: //119/329E716A801F/MSPI_ON/mspi_check_connect:
   MMccb(Count=0)
Jun  6 15:41:24.394: //119/329E716A801F/MSPI_ON/mspi_check_connect:
   SMTP Connected To The Server !
Jun  6 15:41:24.394: //119/329E716A801F/MSPI/mspi_bridge:
   MMccb(State=CONNECTED, Type=Onramp), Destination Call Id=120
```

In Example 13-8, the first line from the **debug fax mspi command** output presents the envelope information and the outgoing MMoIP dial-peer identifier. The SMTP "MAIL FROM" information appears as **Envelope From=FAXES@cisco.com**, and the SMTP "RCPT TO" information shows as **Envelope To=gsalguei@faxmail.com**. The outbound MMoIP dial-peer that is matched for this onramp call is shown by the line **Outgoing Peer Tag=99**.

The next important line in Example 13-8 confirms the connection to the mail server with the line **SMTP Connected To The Server**. From this point on, MSPI is conferenced with DMSP, and any TIFF information is ready to be received.

The MSPI process also displays the call disconnect information when the call is terminated. Example 13-9 highlights some of the specific messages concerning the teardown of the call from the output of the **debug fax mspi** command.

Example 13-9 *debug fax mspi Output for a T.37 Onramp Call Disconnect*

```
Jun  6 15:41:49.970: //119/329E716A801F/MSPI/mspi_bridge_drop:
   MMccb(State=DESTROYING, Type=Onramp), Destination Call Id=120
Jun  6 15:41:49.970: //119/329E716A801F/MSPI/mspi_call_disconnect:
   Cause Value=normal call clearing (16),
   MMccb(State=DISCONNECTING, Type=Onramp)
Jun  6 15:41:49.970: //119/329E716A801F/MSPI_ON/mspi_onramp_call_history:
   MMccb(Disconnect Cause=normal call clearing (16) 16)
```

In Example 13-9 you see the **mspi_call_disconnect** function being displayed as the call is terminated. This function provides the disconnect cause value. In the case of Example 13-9, a normal disconnect occurs as indicated by **Cause Value=normal call clearing (16)**.

TIP	The command **debug mmoip send email** *address* enables you to generate a test e-mail from the onramp CLI. This is a good test command to use when trying to narrow down problems between the onramp gateway and the mail server. If this command is successful, it confirms that the SMTP connection maintained by MSPI is functioning correctly.

When troubleshooting the onramp SMTP interface, the **debug fax mta detail** is usually the most helpful, especially if you need to analyze the interaction between the onramp gateway and the mail server. If visibility into the MSPI process is needed, it is recommended to run the command **debug fax mspi** along with the command **debug fax mta detail**.

T.37 Offramp Troubleshooting

The T.37 offramp application converts e-mails containing text and TIFF attachments to fax calls. This conversion process depends on the offramp gateway successfully receiving the fax e-mail over an SMTP connection with the TIFF file in the proper format. Only then can a normal fax call be generated from the offramp gateway's voice port to the terminating fax device.

Figure 13-2 illustrates the IOS processes involved in a Cisco offramp gateway. Each of these processes have a dedicated function in the overall offramp application, and each can provide troubleshooting information through debugs specific to that process.

Chronologically following a call through the offramp application diagrammed in Figure 13-2 is the best way to understand how T.37 offramp works in a Cisco voice gateway. On the left side of Figure 13-2, you can see an incoming SMTP connection where the MSPI process receives the e-mail with the optional TIFF attachment. The MSPI process then passes any text and TIFF information to the DMSP process. The DMSP process then takes this text and TIFF information and formats it into a standard fax page. This standard fax page is then passed to the FMSP process from DMSP for transmission to the terminating fax device. Both the T.30 and MTA functions in Figure 13-2 are not T.37 offramp-specific processes, but they provide excellent visibility into the call as it enters and leaves the T.37 offramp gateway.

While Figure 13-2 illustrates the internal software processes that compose the T.37 offramp function, it also expresses a troubleshooting methodology just like the onramp diagram in Figure 13-1. For example, if the terminating fax machine never even receives an offramp call, it would not be logical to start troubleshooting T.30. In this instance, the problem is clearly located further back in the T.37 offramp application because T.30 is used only if a call successfully connects between the offramp gateway and the terminating fax machine.

Figure 13-2 *Graphical Illustration of T.37 Offramp for a Cisco Voice Gateway*

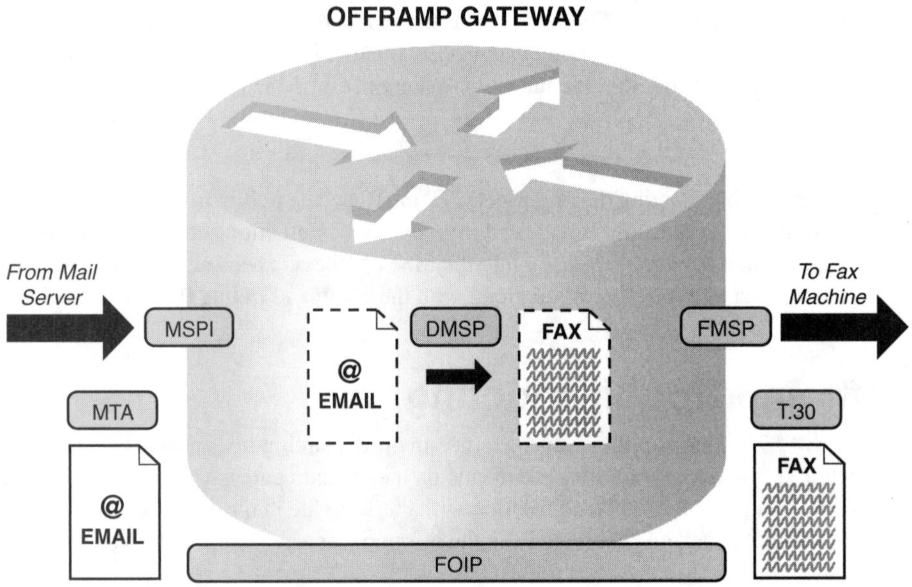

		Purpose:	Troubleshoot the SMTP/ESMTP messaging for the session between the mail server and the offramp gateway.
MTA	=	Command:	*debug fax mta*
MSPI	=	Purpose:	Troubleshoot the mail service provider interface on the offramp gateway that is responsible for setting up and maintaining the SMTP/ESMTP connection between the mail server and the gateway.
		Command:	*debug fax mspi*
DMSP	=	Purpose:	Troubleshoot the conversion from TIFF image data to T.4 fax data.
		Command:	*debug fax dmsp*
FOIP	=	Purpose:	Troubleshoot the state transitions between all of the T.37 applications.
		Command:	*debug fax foip detail*
FMSP	=	Purpose:	Troubleshoot the interaction between the offramp application and the telephony interface.
		Command:	*debug fax fmsp, debug fax fmsp send t30*
T.30	=	Purpose:	Troubleshoot the T.30 messaging between the offramp gateway and the terminating fax machine.
		Command:	*debug fax relay t30 all-level-1*

If you are not sure where to begin troubleshooting a T.37 offramp problem, a good place to start is with the FOIP process. The FOIP process has visibility into the other offramp processes, and it can provide information about them during a call.

The best command for viewing offramp FOIP messages is **debug fax foip detail**. This debug outputs helpful information about the call setup, the gateway-generated cover page, and the number of pages that are being created. Example 13-10 displays call setup information from the **debug fax foip detail** command.

Example 13-10 *debug fax foip detail Output for a T.37 Offramp Call Setup*

```
*Jun 26 22:22:48.847: //1318/9B019F1687A9/FOIP_OFF/loffSetupPeer:
  Peer(Tag=2, Encap Type=1, Matched Digits=7,
  Destination Pattern=4724118, Prefix=)
```

In Example 13-10, the value of **FOIP_OFF** tells you that the call is an offramp call. The next line provides useful troubleshooting information about outbound dial-peer matching. The matched dial-peer is shown in the debug output as **Tag=2**. This refers to **dial-peer voice 2 pots** in the gateway's configuration file, and the destination pattern that is matching this dial peer is highlighted as **Destination Pattern=4724118**.

After the call has been set up with the correct dial-peer matching, the offramp gateway can produce a cover page if configured. The **debug fax foip detail** command displays the creation of this fax cover page in Example 13-11.

Example 13-11 *debug fax foip detail Output Showing a T.37 Offramp Cover Page Creation*

```
*Jun 26 22:23:19.291: //-1/xxxxxxxxxxxx/FOIP_OFF/loff_edit_cover_page:
  from_personal_name: 17, [Gonzalo Salgueiro]
  loff_edit_cover_page: 21, ["Gonzalo Salgueiro", ]
*Jun 26 22:23:19.291: //-1/xxxxxxxxxxxx/FOIP_OFF/loff_edit_cover_page:
  [gsalguei@faxmail.com]
*Jun 26 22:23:19.291: //-1/xxxxxxxxxxxx/FOIP_OFF/loff_fill_cover_page:
*Jun 26 22:23:19.291: //-1/xxxxxxxxxxxx/FOIP_OFF/loff_fill_cover_page:
  ----------------------------------------------------------------
*Jun 26 22:23:19.291: //-1/xxxxxxxxxxxx/FOIP_OFF/loff_fill_cover_page:
  Title:       OffRamp Fax From Cisco 2851
*Jun 26 22:23:19.291: //-1/xxxxxxxxxxxx/FOIP_OFF/loff_fill_cover_page:
*Jun 26 22:23:19.291: //-1/xxxxxxxxxxxx/FOIP_OFF/loff_fill_cover_page:
  To:          4724118
*Jun 26 22:23:19.291: //-1/xxxxxxxxxxxx/FOIP_OFF/loff_fill_cover_page:
*Jun 26 22:23:19.295: //-1/xxxxxxxxxxxx/FOIP_OFF/loff_fill_cover_page:
  From:        "Gonzalo Salgueiro", gsalguei@faxmail.com
*Jun 26 22:23:19.295: //-1/xxxxxxxxxxxx/FOIP_OFF/loff_fill_cover_page:
*Jun 26 22:23:19.295: //-1/xxxxxxxxxxxx/FOIP_OFF/loff_fill_cover_page:
  Date:        Tue, 26 Jun 2007 18:03:03 -0400
*Jun 26 22:23:19.295: //-1/xxxxxxxxxxxx/FOIP_OFF/loff_fill_cover_page:
```

continues

Example 13-11 *debug fax foip detail Output Showing a T.37 Offramp Cover Page Creation (Continued)*

```
*Jun 26 22:23:19.295: //-1/xxxxxxxxxxxx/FOIP_OFF/loff_fill_cover_page:
  Subject:      Offramp Fax Testing
*Jun 26 22:23:19.295: //-1/xxxxxxxxxxxx/FOIP_OFF/loff_fill_cover_page:
*Jun 26 22:23:19.295: //-1/xxxxxxxxxxxx/FOIP_OFF/loff_fill_cover_page:
  Details:
*Jun 26 22:23:19.295: //-1/xxxxxxxxxxxx/FOIP_OFF/loff_fill_cover_page:
                 Received: from gsalgueiwxp ([172.18.109.74]) by RTP-ESC-
T37.faxmail.com with Microsoft SMTPSVC(5.0.2172.
*Jun 26 22:23:19.295: //-1/xxxxxxxxxxxx/FOIP_OFF/loff_fill_cover_page:
    ----------------------------------------------------------------------
```

The fax cover page being created in Example 13-11 includes the elements of **Title, To, From, Date, Subject,** and **Details**. The **Title** element is populated by the configuration command **fax send coverpage comment**. All the other elements are populated by the incoming e-mail headers or by the offramp gateway itself (**Date** and **Details**).

As shown in Example 13-12, the **debug fax foip detail** command also tracks the number of fax pages that are generated from an incoming fax e-mail. From a troubleshooting perspective, this can prove quite useful because the number of pages indicated in this debug output should match what is received by the terminating fax machine.

Example 13-12 *debug fax foip detail Output Showing a T.37 Offramp Page-Count Message*

```
*Jun 26 22:23:19.331: //1321/9B019F1687A9/FOIP_OFF/loffMapEvent:
  Page Number=0x1
*Jun 26 22:23:19.331: //1321/9B019F1687A9/FOIP_OFF/loffMapEvent:
  Page Number=0x2

! Output omitted for brevity

*Jun 26 22:26:19.095: //1321/9B019F1687A9/FOIP_OFF/loffMapEvent:
  Page Number=0x6
```

In Example 13-12, the fax pages being generated are shown by the counters (in hexadecimal format) **Page Number=0x1** and **Page Number=0x2**. These messages indicate the generation of the first and second page. In the case of this example, a total of six pages were generated, and the last page-count debug message appeared as **Page Number=0x6**.

For the troubleshooting scenarios where the FOIP debugs do not lead you toward the problem cause, confirming the proper progression of the call through the offramp gateway should be the next step. You do this by taking a systematic look at the T.37 processes, starting with the SMTP connection and the MSPI process, as covered in the next section.

Troubleshooting the Offramp SMTP Connection

The offramp T.37 application is activated with the reception of a fax e-mail by the MSPI process. Without a successful fax mail reception, T.37 offramp fails from the beginning. Therefore, it is important to effectively troubleshoot the offramp SMTP connection and its MSPI process before looking at other offramp processes.

If you just need to view SMTP and the messages exchanged between the mail server and the offramp gateway, use the **debug fax mta** command. Example 13-13 highlights the envelope information being received by the offramp gateway from the mail server using the command **debug fax mta**.

Example 13-13 *debug fax mta Output Showing the T.37 Offramp SMTP Envelope Information*

```
*Jun 26 21:23:51.403: //-1/xxxxxxxxxxxx/SMTPS/esmtp_server_engine_work_routine:
   Calling smtp verb: mail
*Jun 26 21:23:51.951: //-1/xxxxxxxxxxxx/SMTPS/esmtp_server_engine_work_routine:
   Calling smtp verb: rcpt
*Jun 26 21:23:51.951: //-1/xxxxxxxxxxxx/SMTPS/esmtp_server_engine_command_rcpt:
   context(0x4503FF1C)
*Jun 26 21:23:51.951: //-1/xxxxxxxxxxxx/SMTPS/esmtp_server_engine_command_rcpt:
   context(0x4503FF1C)
*Jun 26 21:23:52.499: //-1/xxxxxxxxxxxx/SMTPS/esmtp_server_engine_work_routine:
   Calling smtp verb: data
```

In Example 13-13, you can see the e-mail envelope information of "MAIL FROM" and "RCPT TO" being received by the offramp gateway. The word **mail** indicates that the "MAIL FROM" command was received, and **rcpt** shows that the command "RCPT TO" was received. These commands are followed by **data**, where any text or TIFF information is communicated to the offramp gateway. For additional information about SMTP and its messages, see the section "SMTP Overview" in Chapter 6.

Now that the **data** command has been received in Example 13-13, the mail server passes the e-mail header information to the offramp gateway. This e-mail header information is sent as plain text, and the offramp gateway uses some portions of this header information and includes it in the final fax. Example 13-14 highlights the e-mail header information communicated during data mode to the offramp gateway.

Example 13-14 *debug fax mta Output Showing the T.37 Offramp E-mail Header Information*

```
*Jun 26 21:23:53.043: //-1/xxxxxxxxxxxx/SMTPS/esmtp_server_engine_work_routine:
   (S)R: `Received: from gsalgueiwxp ([172.18.109.74]) by RTP-ESC-T37.faxmail.com
with Microsoft
SMTPSVC(5.0.2172.1);'
*Jun 26 21:23:53.043: //-1/xxxxxxxxxxxx/SMTPS/esmtp_server_engine_work_routine:
   (S)R: `        Tue, 26 Jun 2007 17:04:35 -0400'
*Jun 26 21:23:53.043: //-1/xxxxxxxxxxxx/SMTPS/esmtp_server_engine_work_routine:
   (S)R: `From: "Gonzalo Salgueiro" <gsalguei@faxmail.com>'
```

continues

Example 13-14 *debug fax mta Output Showing the T.37 Offramp E-mail Header Information (Continued)*

```
*Jun 26 21:23:53.043: //-1/xxxxxxxxxxxx/SMTPS/esmtp_server_engine_work_routine:
   (S)R: `To: <FAX=4724118@fax_2851.faxmail.com>'
*Jun 26 21:23:53.043: //-1/xxxxxxxxxxxx/SMTPS/esmtp_server_engine_work_routine:
   (S)R: `Subject: Offramp Fax Testing'
*Jun 26 21:23:53.047: //-1/xxxxxxxxxxxx/SMTPS/esmtp_server_engine_work_routine:
   (S)R: `Date: Tue, 26 Jun 2007 17:04:08 -0400'
*Jun 26 21:23:53.047: //-1/xxxxxxxxxxxx/SMTPS/esmtp_server_engine_work_routine:
   (S)R: `Message-ID: <001a01c7b835$89823da0$4a6d12ac@amer.cisco.com>'
```

In Example 13-14, a few of the e-mail headers that are received by the offramp gateway from the mail server during "DATA" mode are shown. The common headers that appear at the top of most e-mails can be seen. These include the **From:**, **To:**, and **Subject:** lines, which are shown in Example 13-14 with the values of **"Gonzalo Salgueiro" gsalguei@faxmail.com, FAX=4724118@fax_2851.faxmail.com**, and **Offramp Fax Testing**, respectively. Header lines such as these can be used by the offramp gateway for the cover page, as illustrated previously by the fax cover page creation in Example 13-11. The other header lines received by the offramp gateway that are not used are just discarded.

If an MDN request has been sent to the offramp gateway by the mail server, you will see a "Disposition-Notification-To:" message in the "DATA" mode e-mail headers of **debug fax mta**. Cisco offramp gateways support MDN requests and send a receipt after the fax pages have been transmitted out the voice port to the terminating fax device. Just remember that the configuration command **mta receive generate mdn** is required. For more information about this command, see Table 11-15 in Chapter 11; and for more information about MDNs and how they work, refer to the section "DSN and MDN" in Chapter 6.

In the case of DSNs, unfortunately their request in the "RCPT TO:" envelope header is not seen by **debug fax mta**. However, DSN requests are supported by the Cisco offramp gateway by default unless they are explicitly disabled by the command **mta receive disable-dsn**. For more information about DSNs, see the section "DSN and MDN" in Chapter 6. For configuration information, refer to Table 11-15 in Chapter 11.

Further down among the e-mail header information for an offramp SMTP session will be some lines discussing any TIFF attachments to the e-mail. Example 13-15 highlights the pertinent debug lines from **debug fax mta** that relate to the TIFF attachment.

In Example 13-15, the presence of a TIFF **attachment** named **Fax-tiff.tif** is confirmed. The offramp gateway takes this TIFF attachment and uses the DMSP process to convert the TIFF image into a standard fax page.

Example 13-15 *debug fax mta Output Showing the T.37 Offramp TIFF Attachment Information*

```
*Jun 26 21:23:53.067: //-1/5F833BAF8786/SMTPS/esmtp_server_engine_work_routine:
   (S)R: `Content-Type: image/tiff;'
*Jun 26 21:23:53.067: //-1/5F833BAF8786/SMTPS/esmtp_server_engine_work_routine:
   (S)R: `      name="Fax-tiff.tif"'
*Jun 26 21:23:53.067: //-1/5F833BAF8786/SMTPS/esmtp_server_engine_work_routine:
   (S)R: `Content-Transfer-Encoding: base64'
*Jun 26 21:23:53.067: //-1/5F833BAF8786/SMTPS/esmtp_server_engine_work_routine:
   (S)R: `Content-Disposition: attachment;'
*Jun 26 21:23:53.067: //-1/5F833BAF8786/SMTPS/esmtp_server_engine_work_routine:
   (S)R: `      filename="Fax-tiff.tif"'
*Jun 26 21:23:53.067: //-1/5F833BAF8786/SMTPS/esmtp_server_engine_work_routine:
   (S)R: `'
```

After the TIFF and text information have been received by the offramp gateway, the SMTP session is terminated. Example 13-16 shows the termination of the SMTP session using the command **debug fax mta**.

Example 13-16 *debug fax mta Output Showing a T.37 Offramp SMTP Session Termination*

```
*Jun 26 21:27:53.811: //-1/5F833BAF8786/SMTPS/esmtp_server_engine_work_routine:
   Calling smtp verb: quit
*Jun 26 21:27:53.811: //-1/5F833BAF8786/SMTPS/esmtp_server_engine_clear_state:
   context(0x4503FF1C)
```

The SMTP command **quit** and the function **esmtp_server_engine_clear_state** are found in Example 13-16. These debug messages signify the end of the SMTP connection between the mail server and the offramp gateway.

Whereas the command **debug fax mta** shows the actual SMTP dialogue between the mail server and the offramp gateway, the actual mail interface on the offramp gateway is set up and maintained by the MSPI process. Sometimes looking at the MSPI debug output can provide a quick synopsis of the more important parameters received from the mail server without having to parse through all the detailed message information provided by the **debug fax mta** command. Example 13-17 shows the relevant debug lines from the **debug fax mspi** command for a T.37 offramp call.

Example 13-17 *debug fax mspi Output for T.37 Offramp*

```
Incoming Dial-peer(Tag=99), Outgoing Dial-peer(Tag=2), Cover Page=TRUE
*Jun 26 22:04:50.203: //-1/xxxxxxxxxxxx/MSPI_OFF/mspi_offramp_new_rcpt:
   Envelope To=FAX=4724118@fax_2851.faxmail.com, Length=32,
   MMccb(Incoming Dial-peer=99, Outgoing Dial-peer=2,
   Telephone Number Dial=4724118, Sub Address=, Cover Page=TRUE
```

continues

Example 13-17 *debug fax mspi Output for T.37 Offramp (Continued)*

```
*Jun 26 22:04:51.299: //1310/18BEB0BB879F/MSPI_OFF/mspi_offramp_rfc822_header:
   Envelope From=gsalguei@faxmail.com, Size=21
   Subject=Offramp Fax Testing
   From Personal Name=Gonzalo Salgueiro
   From="Gonzalo Salgueiro" <gsalguei@faxmail.com>
   To=<FAX=4724118@fax_2851.faxmail.com>
    Notification Type=0
*Jun 26 22:04:51.299: //1310/18BEB0BB879F/MSPI_OFF/mspi_offramp_rfc822_header:
   MMccb(Called Number=4724118, Calling Number=, Incoming Dial-peer=99)

! Output omitted for brevity

*Jun 26 22:08:42.103: //1310/18BEB0BB879F/MSPI/mspi_call_disconnect:
   Cause Value=normal call clearing (16),
   MMccb(State=DISCONNECTING, Type=Offramp)
```

The **debug fax mspi** output in Example 13-17 highlights some of the key information received over the incoming SMTP connection. Whereas the previously discussed **debug fax mta** is detailed in this regard, the **debug fax mspi** is much more brief; it shows only the critical parameters that are used in routing the call and completing the cover page.

The "To:" information of **FAX=4724118@fax_2851.faxmail.com** is used by the offramp gateway to route the call appropriately. The DNIS of **4724118** is parsed from the destination e-mail address ("To:") and matched by the gateway with the correct dial-peers. In the case of Example 13-17, the appropriate inbound MMOIP dial-peer tag is 99, and the outbound POTS dial-peer tag is 2, as shown by the debug messages of **Incoming Dial-peer=99** and **Outgoing Dial-peer=2**, respectively.

The need for a fax cover page is indicated in Example 13-17 by the presence of the parameter **Cover Page=TRUE**. This parameter setting details that the information from the "To:," "From:," and "Subject:" headers of **FAX=4724118@fax_2851.faxmail.com, "Gonzalo Salgueiro" gsalguei@faxmail.com**, and **Offramp Fax Testing** will be used in the cover page creation by the DMSP process.

At the conclusion of the call, the **debug fax mspi** command also provides the relevant disconnect information. In the case of Example 13-17, the **mspi_call_disconnect** function returns a cause value of **normal call clearing**.

TIP   A common troubleshooting technique for confirming the function of MSPI and the SMTP connection of the offramp gateway is a manual replication of the SMTP session itself. You can do this just by telnetting to port 25 of the offramp gateway and providing the appropriate SMTP commands. For example, from a UNIX or Windows command line, you can issue the command **telnet** *ip-address* **25**, and then you just issue SMTP commands as illustrated in Example 6-1 of Chapter 6. This is a quick way to troubleshoot SMTP issues on offramp gateways, and it removes the mail server as a possible source of any problems. For more information about how SMTP sessions work and the applicable commands, see the section "SMTP Commands and Sample Sessions" in Chapter 6.

Troubleshooting the Creation of the Fax Page Image

After the offramp MSPI process has successfully received the e-mail information, this information is passed to the DMSP process to be rendered into standard fax pages. The DMSP process can render both text and TIFF information from the incoming e-mail.

Visibility into the DMSP process and its conversion of e-mail information to standard fax pages is quite limited. The debug that provides the best insight into DMSP is accessed via the command **debug fax dmsp**. This is the default DMSP debug setting, and this command enables the DMSP debug options of **debug fax dmsp inout, debug fax dmsp error call**, and **debug fax dmsp error software**. Example 13-18 shows the output from the **debug fax dmsp** command for a T.37 offramp call.

Example 13-18   *debug fax dmsp Output Showing DMSP Bridge Establishment for T.37 Offramp*

```
*Jun 26 23:28:46.907: //1365/C00449CF87E0/DMSP/docmsp_call_setup_request:
   ramp data dir=OFFRAMP, conf dir=SRC
*Jun 26 23:28:46.907: //1365/C00449CF87E0/DMSP/docmsp_caps_ind:
   CallId=1365, srcCallId=1364
*Jun 26 23:28:46.907: //1365/C00449CF87E0/DMSP/docmsp_bridge:
   conf id=0x59, srcCallId=1365, dstCallId=1364,
   ramp data dir=OFFRAMP, conf dir=SRC, encode out=0
*Jun 26 23:28:46.907: //1365/C00449CF87E0/DMSP/docmsp_bridge:
   Bridge done
*Jun 26 23:28:46.907: //1365/C00449CF87E0/DMSP/docmsp_bridge:
   conf id=0x5A, srcCallId=1365, dstCallId=1362,
   ramp data dir=OFFRAMP, conf dir=DEST, encode out=0
*Jun 26 23:28:46.907: //1365/C00449CF87E0/DMSP/docmsp_bridge:
   Bridge done
```

Example 13-18 highlights the bridge establishment occurring between the DMSP process and MSPI and FMSP. Referring back to Figure 13-2, you can see that DMSP must connect to both the MSPI and FMSP processes for the offramp call to succeed.

The first bridge that occurs is between DMSP and MSPI. This bridge is initiated by the **docmsp_call_setup_request** including the parameters of **ramp data dir=OFFRAMP, conf dir=SRC**, where the data direction is offramp, and the conference direction indicates that MSPI is the source of the bridge.

The other bridge that is connected is between the DMSP and FMSP processes. The parameters change to **ramp data dir=OFFRAMP, conf dir=DEST** when this bridge is being established.

After the establishment of each bridge, the debug line **Bridge done** is seen. Make sure that the DMSP process always successfully establishes these communication bridges with its peer processes. After this task is completed, the DMSP process is prepared to handle conversion of the e-mail information to fax pages.

The first page that must be generated by the DMSP process if it has been configured in the offramp gateway is the fax cover page. The DMSP process generates a debug line including the function **docmsp_generate_page** when the cover page is generated, as shown in Example 13-19.

Example 13-19   *debug fax dmsp* Output Showing T.37 Offramp Cover Page Generation

```
*Jun 26 23:28:46.907: //1365/C00449CF87E0/DMSP/docmsp_generate_page:
    application_data=0x46E3F60C, per_bridge_info=0x44FF4158
```

The rest of the **debug fax dmsp** command output is buffer-related messages that do not provide a lot of troubleshooting information. However, these messages do tell you the type of fax page that the DMSP process is currently rendering. So, when the DMSP process is converting text into a fax page, messages similar to the one in Example 13-20 are seen in **debug fax dmsp**.

Example 13-20   *debug fax dmsp* Output Showing T.37 Offramp E-mail Text Converted to a Fax Page

```
*Jun 26 23:28:46.915: //1365/C00449CF87E0/DMSP_OFF/docmsp_text2fax_put_buffer_
    callback: t2f_segment=0x46EB2864, buffer length=1482, fax_status=1
```

In Example 13-20, the DMSP process is currently processing e-mail text and converting this into a standard fax page. The function **docmsp_text2fax_put_buffer_callback** is the indicator that this is what is happening. In addition, the parameter **t2f_segment** is found in the next line, affirming that the text-to-fax conversion is taking place within the DMSP process.

When a TIFF image is being processed by DMSP, the debugs change compared to those seen previously in Example 13-20. Example 13-21 highlights the TIFF-to-fax message from the **debug fax dmsp** command.

Example 13-21 *debug fax dmsp Output Showing T.37 Offramp TIFF Image Converted to a Fax Page*

```
*Jun 26 23:29:46.443: //1365/C00449CF87E0/DMSP_OFF/docmsp_tiff_reader_get_buffer_
    callback: tiff_segment=0x46EC3A1C
```

In Example 13-21 you can see that a TIFF image is now being converted into a standard fax page. The function **docmsp_tiff_reader_get_buffer_callback** in conjunction with the **tiff_segment** parameter in the following line verifies the activation of the TIFF reader. Anytime fax pages are being generated by DMSP, messages similar to the ones in Example 13-20 and Example 13-21 are seen when **debug fax dmsp** is enabled.

When multiple page faxes are processed by an offramp gateway, it is possible to also see the completion of each fax page within the DMSP process. Example 13-22 highlights the message that is seen in the **debug fax dmsp** output whenever a fax page has been successfully rendered.

Example 13-22 *debug fax dmsp Output Showing T.37 Offramp Fax Page Completion*

```
*Jun 26 23:30:46.575: //1365/C00449CF87E0/DMSP_OFF/docmsp_tiff_reader_put_buffer_
    callback: END_OF_FAX_PAGE
```

In Example 13-22, the debug line **END_OF_FAX_PAGE** is shown. For each successfully rendered fax page, this message is output by the **debug fax dmsp** command. The number of occurrences of this **END_OF_FAX_PAGE** message within the output from the **debug fax dmsp** command should correlate exactly with the number of fax pages received on the standard fax machine that is terminating the offramp call.

One of the most frequent problems encountered with T.37 offramp is the creation of compatible TIFF files that will be accepted as e-mail attachments by the offramp gateway. Cisco offramp gateways support only the TIFF file format described in RFC 2301, *File Format for Internet Fax*, and RFC 2302, *Tag Image File Format (TIFF) - image/tiff MIME Sub-type Registration*, which is known as TIFF Profile F, or TIFF-F. The TIFF-F profile details TIFF encodings for the MR and MMR fax encoding algorithms. In addition, TIFF-F supports the MH encoding offered by the TIFF Profile S. Make sure that any TIFF attached to an e-mail that is destined to a Cisco offramp gateway adheres to the TIFF-F specification.

TIP	If you are having problems with the offramp gateway accepting TIFF images, first confirm that simple text e-mails work. Performing this step ensures that the offramp gateway is working correctly and further isolates the problem as a TIFF issue. In addition, if the format of your TIFF image is in question and you have T.37 onramp working, you can take the TIFF image generated by the Cisco onramp gateway and use it for your offramp gateway testing. The TIFF image created by a Cisco onramp gateway is correctly encoded for the conversion to a standard fax by Cisco offramp gateways.

Troubleshooting the Offramp Telephony Interface

The offramp telephony interface is responsible for taking the fax pages generated by the DMSP process and transmitting them out the gateway's voice port to the destination fax machine. The main process involved in the offramp telephony interface from the T.37 perspective is FMSP. The FMSP process communicates with the destination fax machine using the ITU-T T.30 protocol, which was covered in detail throughout Chapter 2.

The best technique for troubleshooting the T.30 messaging between the FMSP process and the terminating fax machine is the command **debug fax relay t30 all**. This command has previously been discussed in detail in the section "Debugging T.30 Fax Messaging" in Chapter 12. Refer to this section for any additional information about this debug command.

Although the **debug fax relay t30 all-level-1** command is more widely used for trouble-shooting fax relay problems, it is also pertinent to T.37 because of the way that the offramp application uses T.38 fax relay internally to handle the T.30 messaging. Example 13-23 displays the output of **debug fax relay t30 all-level-1** for a six-page T.37 offramp fax call.

Example 13-23   *debug fax relay t30 all-level-1 Output for a T.37 Offramp Call*

```
*Jun 27 03:12:57.187: 1/0:23 (10)  561073 fr-entered=10(ms)
    timestamp=573663 fr-msg-det NSF
    timestamp=574653 fr-msg-det CSI
    timestamp=575343 fr-msg-det DIS
    timestamp=575883 fr-msg-tx TSI
    timestamp=577143 fr-msg-tx DCS
    timestamp=582383 fr-msg-det CFR
    timestamp=592453 fr-msg-tx MPS
    timestamp=595013 fr-msg-det MCF
    timestamp=634193 fr-msg-tx MPS
    timestamp=636743 fr-msg-det MCF
    timestamp=651963 fr-msg-tx MPS
    timestamp=654283 fr-msg-det MCF
    timestamp=705183 fr-msg-tx MPS
    timestamp=707743 fr-msg-det MCF
```

Example 13-23 *debug fax relay t30 all-level-1 Output for a T.37 Offramp Call (Continued)*

```
        timestamp=758463 fr-msg-tx MPS
        timestamp=761023 fr-msg-det MCF
        timestamp=775073 fr-msg-tx EOP
        timestamp=777633 fr-msg-det MCF
        timestamp=778023 fr-msg-tx DCN
 *Jun 27 03:16:35.327: 1/0:23 (10)   779213 fr-end-dcn
```

The fax transmission in Example 13-23 begins with a typical message exchange between the terminating and originating fax devices. In this case, the originating fax device is the offramp gateway, and a standard fax machine is the terminating device. The terminating fax machine sends the first T.30 messages, including the **NSF**, **CSI**, and **DIS**. The offramp gateway answers with **TSI** and **DCS** messages followed by the training.

Upon receiving an error-free training signal, the terminating fax machine responds with a **CFR**. The fax page information is exchanged with each page followed by an **MPS**. Each page is acknowledged with an **MCF**. The last page is followed by an **EOP** rather than an **MPS** to indicate that this is the final page. Upon the acknowledgment of the **EOP** with an **MCF**, the offramp gateway disconnects the fax call with a **DCN**. All of these messages and their precise meaning are covered in detail in the section "Analyzing a Basic Fax Call" in Chapter 2.

If problems are ever experienced on the terminating fax machine such as missing or corrupted pages or an incomplete fax communication, check the output from the **debug fax relay t30 all-level-1** command. The T.30 fax transaction should be clean and absent of repeated FTT and RTN messages. The debug output should also display all the expected fax pages followed by a DCN. If problems are observed in the output of this debug, check the digital interfaces in the fax transmission path for any errors, such as slips.

The FMSP process controls the T.30 messaging and the transfer of the fax pages from the DMSP process to the terminating fax machine. Therefore, it is important to look at the debugs related to this process when troubleshooting problems related to communications between the offramp gateway and the terminating fax machine.

For more detailed T.30-level troubleshooting information, the **debug fax fmsp send t30** is an excellent debug. Example 13-24 highlights one of the messages from the output of the command **debug fax fmsp send t30**.

Example 13-24 *debug fax fmsp send t30 Output for a T.37 Offramp Call*

```
 *Jun 27 03:34:55.343: //19/22B973EB8016/FMSP/fax2_phaseB_transmit:
    send DCS_PACKET: BR=9, resolution=1, encoding=0, local_id_string=Gonzalo
      Salgueiro
    msg dump (size=6):
    FF C8 C1 00 46 1E
```

In Example 13-24, you can see that the **debug fax fmsp send t30** command provides more detail than the command **debug fax relay t30 all-level-1**. In addition to marking this particular T.30 message as a **DCS**, a hex dump of the first few bytes of the packet are included, **FF C8 C1 00 46 1E**. Within the hex information, **FF** is the HDLC address field, **C8** is the control, and **C1** is the FCF. Interestingly, the function name of **fax2_phaseB_ transmit** also provides helpful information by relaying the phase of the fax call from the T.30 perspective. For more information about the **DCS** message and how to decode it and any other T.30 messages found in **debug fax fmsp send t30**, see the section "Analyzing a Basic Fax Call" in Chapter 2. The phases of a fax call are also discussed in Chapter 2 in the section "Phases of a Fax Call."

Also notice in Example 13-24 that the **debug fax fmsp send t30** command decodes some of the more important fax negotiation parameters contained in the **DCS** message. Applying Table 13-2 to the **DCS** parameters of **BR=9, resolution=1, encoding=0** tells you that the offramp gateway has set the page transmission speed to 14400 bps with a resolution of fine using the MR encoding algorithm. These settings will be used during the T.30 fax session between the offramp gateway and the terminating fax device.

The main purpose of the **debug fax fmsp send t30** command is to provide a more in-depth look at the T.30 fax messaging from the FMSP process perspective. In most cases, the command **debug fax relay t30 all-level-1** is adequate, but the **debug fax fmsp send t30** command is available when more detailed troubleshooting is required.

For looking at the FMSP process from a function perspective, the command **debug fax fmsp** must be used. This is the default **debug** command for the FMSP process, and it actually enables the commands of **debug fax fmsp inout, debug fax fmsp error call,** and **debug fax fmsp error software**. Example 13-25 highlights the FMSP call setup from the command **debug fax fmsp**.

Example 13-25 *debug fax fmsp Output for a T.37 Offramp Call Setup*

```
*Jun 27 00:35:54.278: //1388/2CCCF9B487FE/FMSP/faxmsp_call_setup_request:
    session=0x4508A748, vdbPtr=0x464258A0,data dir=OFFRAMP, conf dir=SRC
```

In Example 13-25, the FMSP call setup is indicated by the function **faxmsp_call_setup_ request**. Within this call setup message, you can see that this call is an offramp call (**data dir=OFFRAMP**) and that the other process making this connection with FMSP is the source (**conf dir=SRC**). Referring back to Figure 13-2, this other process is obviously DMSP because this is an offramp fax call.

When the FMSP process has completed the call setup process and it is bridged with DMSP, the call to function **faxmsp_codec_download_done** displays in the debug output. Example 13-26 shows this function in the output of **debug fax fmsp**.

Example 13-26 *debug fax fmsp Output Showing a T.37 Offramp Codec Download*

```
*Jun 27 00:35:54.282: //1388/2CCCF9B487FE/FMSP/faxmsp_codec_download_done:
   per_bridge_info=0x46D48158, application_data=0x467660EC,
   state=0x2, direction=2
```

At the end of the **debug fax fmsp** command output, the number of pages transmitted over the fax connection is displayed. Example 13-27 highlights this fax page-count message in the output of **debug fax fmsp** command.

Example 13-27 *debug fax fmsp Output Showing T.37 Offramp Fax Page Count*

```
*Jun 27 00:39:32.878: //1388/2CCCF9B487FE/FMSP/faxmsp_get_num_of_pages:
   session=0x4508A748, per_bridge_info=0x46D48158,
   t30_context=0x4508A760, state=0x31, page#=6
```

In Example 13-27, the function **faxmsp_get_num_of_pages** provides information about the total number of pages transmitted over the T.30 fax connection. In this case, the number of fax pages sent is shown as six by the parameter **page#=6**.

TIP

A useful troubleshooting command for generating a test offramp fax call is **debug mmoip send fax** *number*. This command fully tests the FMSP process generating a true fax page and sending it to the number specified in the command itself. This command also validates the part of the offramp configuration that routes the fax call out the appropriate voice port. If T.37 offramp calls are failing, this command can assist in troubleshooting the problem.

Using the debug commands of **debug fax fmsp, debug fax fmsp send t30,** and **debug fax relay t30 all-level-1**, detailed troubleshooting of the last leg of the T.37 offramp application is possible. These debug commands should be implemented whenever problems are suspected within the FMSP process or between the offramp gateway and the terminating fax machine located out the gateway's telephony interface.

Summary

This chapter covered troubleshooting commands and techniques necessary for effectively resolving T.37 store-and-forward fax problems. First, some basic items were identified that should be checked before delving deeper into more advanced T.37 troubleshooting.

The chapter then examined T.37 onramp troubleshooting techniques. A diagram of the T.37 onramp application detailed the processes involved with onramp faxing while also serving as a troubleshooting methodology. Subsequently, this led to in-depth troubleshooting of the onramp processes of FMSP, DMSP, and MSPI and the key protocols of SMTP and T.30.

Offramp troubleshooting was discussed next, and like onramp a similar diagram was presented that outlined the offramp application and provided an offramp-specific troubleshooting methodology. The same processes and protocols that were discussed in onramp were also discussed in offramp, but from the offramp perspective.

The onramp and offramp sections of this chapter were designed to be independent of each other. Therefore, a reading of either the onramp or offramp section is not required to understand and grasp the troubleshooting information provided in the other.

INDEX

Symbols

"push" protocols, 192

Numerics

6 set mask0x323 command, 462–464
6 show call command (Dick Tracy), 419–423, 481
6608 line card configuring passthrough, 295–298

A

abbreviations (text telephone communication),
116–117
accessing fax servers, 267
acoustic coupling, 113
acronyms (text telephone communication),
116–117
adaptive Huffman encoding, 48
ADP (Answer Detection Pattern), 47
advanced troubleshooting
Cisco text relay, 506–510
fax relay, 487
high delay, 500, 502
NSF/NSS messages, 499–500
packet loss, 488, 490
Super G3, 490–491
T.30 fax messaging, 491–496
modem relay, 503–506
passthrough, 485–486
AFE (analog front end), 9
Americans with Disabilities Act, 107
TRS, 118–119
amplitude, 27
analog modem architecture, 8–9
analyzing
PCM traces, 510, 515
of fax calls, 516–519
of modem calls, 520–522
T.38 packet captures, 497–499
APIs, accessing fax servers, 267
application command, 353
ASK (Amplitude Shift Keying), 30
asynchronous framing, 19–20
AT interface, 21–25

B

bandwidth considerations for VoIP networks with
fax, modem and text capability, 209–214
basic troubleshooting checks, performing,
383–385

debugging best practices, 387–391
verifying configuration, 386–387
baud rate, 27
Baudot text protocol, 107, 121
character set, 121, 123
EIA-TIA-825-A specification, FSK, 123–124
shift synchronization, 123
Baudot, Emile, 121

C

C5510 DSP
complexity mode, 225
flex-complexity mode, 226
CAC (Call Admission Control), managing
bandwidth consumption on VoIP networks, 213
CA-controlled T.38 fax relay, 321
call analysis, 34
call setup, 35–42
data mode, 42, 45
call disconnect, 49
data compression, 48–49
error control, 45–48
ECM fax calls, 82–84
call analysis (fax)
CED tone, 67
CFR messages, 73
CNG tone, 66
CSI messages, 70
DCN messages, 76
DCS messages, 71–72
DIS messages, 68
EOM messages, 75
EOP messages, 75
FTT messages, 73
MCF messages, 76
MPS messages, 75
NSF messages, 69
RTN messages, 76
RTP messages, 76
TCF messages, 73
TSI messages, 71–72
call control protocol considerations for VoIP
networks with fax, modem and text capability,
214–215
call disconnect, 49
call legs, 392–393
Cisco modem relay call legs, viewing, 402–404
fax passthrough call legs, viewing, 399–400
fax relay call legs, viewing, 400–402